3—

Characters in 20th-CENTURY LITERATURE

Book II

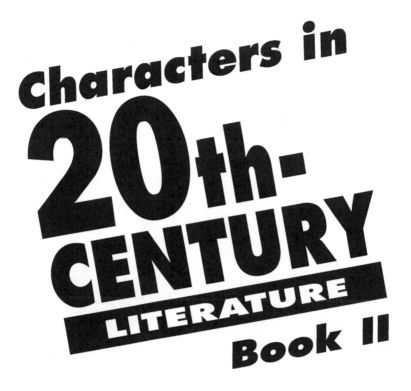

Characters in 20th-CENTURY LITERATURE

Book II

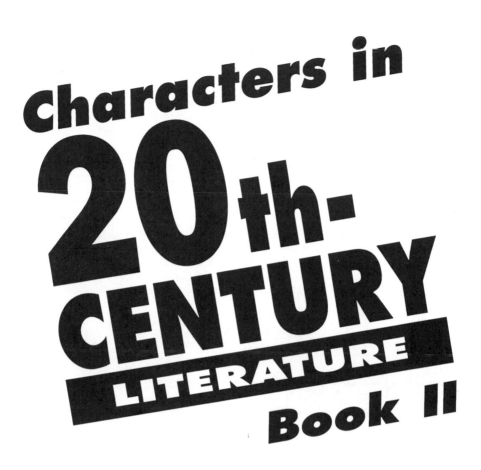

Kelly King Howes

Gale Research Inc.

An International Thomson Publishing Company

I(T)P

Changing the Way the World Learns

NEW YORK • LONDON • BONN • BOSTON • DETROIT • MADRID
MELBOURNE • MEXICO CITY • PARIS • SINGAPORE • TOKYO
TORONTO • WASHINGTON • ALBANY NY • BELMONT CA • CINCINNATI OH

Gale Research Inc. Staff

Lawrence W. Baker, *Senior Developmental Editor*
Kenneth Estell, *Developmental Editor*
Jolen M. Gedridge, *Associate Editor*
Jessica Proctor, *Assistant Editor*
Mary Beth Trimper, *Production Director*
Evi Seoud, *Assistant Production Manager*
Mary Kelley, *Production Assistant*
Cindy Baldwin, *Art Director*
Arthur Chartow, *Technical Design Services Manager*
Mary Krzewinski, *Graphic Designer*
Benita Spight, *Data Entry Services Manager*
Gwendolyn Tucker, *Data Entry Supervisor*
Arlene Ann Kevonian, *Data Entry Associate*

♾️™ This book is printed on acid-free paper that meets the minimum requirements of American National Standard for Information Sciences--Permanence Paper for Printed Library Materials, ANSI Z39.48-1984.

Library of Congress Cataloging-in-Publication Data

Howes, Kelly King.
  Characters in 20th-century literature II/Kelly King Howes.
    p. cm.
  Includes bibliographical references and index.
  ISBN 0-8103-9203-8 : $54.95
    1. Characters and characteristics in literature. 2. Literature,
Modern—20th century—History and criticism. I. Title. II. Title:
Characters in twentieth-century literature two.
PN56.4.H7   1995   94-2687
809'.927—dc20   CIP

Printed in the United States of America

I⟨T⟩P™ Gale Research Inc., an International Thomson Publishing Company.
         ITP logo is a trademark under license.

To my parents,
Robert Hamilton King and Kathryn Ann Cleary King

Contents

Preface   ix

Preface

The process by which authors transform mere words on a page into characters who seem as real as the people around us is one of literature's deepest mysteries. It may also be the aspect of writing that brings the most pure pleasure to readers, even as it helps to covey an author's intentions and ideas. Such characters as John Updike's Harry "Rabbit" Angstrom, Gabriel Garcia Marquez's Florentino Aziza, and Dorothy Parker's Hazel Morse are remembered in the same way that old friends or particularly interesting acquaintances are recalled long after they are no longer physically present. One of the purposes of *Characters in 20th-Century Literature* is to introduce readers to some of the most recent arrivals to the world of fictional characters, as well as to reacquaint them with some they may have previously overlooked.

The Scope of the Work

The essays in *Characters in 20th Century Literature, Book II* (CTCL) elucidate the function and significance of nearly 2,000 characters from more than 180 works of 150 major novelists, dramatists, and short story writers. This volume is the second edition of a work by the same title that was published by Gale Research in 1990 and that covered the most representative and widely discussed works by authors who were either still alive or had died since 1899. The current edition of *CTCL* continues where the first volume left off, providing entries that both supplement and expand this series' scope. For example, the second edition includes both an entry on John Updike, who was well covered in the first *CTCL* but whose important novel *Rabbit at Rest* was published in 1990, and E. Annie Proulx, a relatively unknown author whose 1993 novel *The Shipping News* was critically acclaimed.

A special effort has been made to cover the work of women writers and others from a wide spectrum of ethnic and cultural backgrounds. Thus *CTCL* focuses not only on such authors as Thomas Pynchon and Phillip Roth but on Ayi Kwei Armah of Ghana and Janet Frame of New Zealand.

The Organization of the Work

The book is arranged alphabetically by author. Each author entry begins with the author's name, birth and death dates, nationality, and principal genres. The author's works are chronologically arranged, and the title heading offers the full title (including the original-language title, where necessary), genre, and date of publication. The essay on each work begins with a brief plot synopsis followed by descriptions of characters and analysis of how they illustrate the author's central themes and aesthetics. Major characters are elucidated in some depth, while attention to minor characters is commensurate with their significance. *CTCL* is designed to help students and general readers understand authors' ethical or philosophical points of view and discover trends or patterns in his or her major works.

All characters' names are boldfaced when first mentioned in the character profiles. Essays vary in length, reflecting the magnitude, complexity, and importance of individual works. A list of critical essays and articles for further reading concludes each author entry. This section includes references to several literary series published by Gale Research, including *Contemporary Literary Criticism, Black Literature Criticism,* and *Dictionary of Literary Biography.* The book concludes with an index to characters and titles.

The final list of authors for *CTCL* was compiled with the invaluable assistance of an advisory board composed of respected librarians and teachers, whose professional perspectives and guidance ensured that this book would best serve its intended audience. Advisors included Sallie Brodie, Kathy Martin, Gerald Newman, Alan Nichter, and Brooke Workman. Editors from Gale Research's Literary Criticism Series who also helped shape the author list included Jeffrey Chapman, James P. Draper, Marie Lazzari, Sean Pollock, and David Segal.

Acknowledgements

I would like to thank Dedria Bryfonski and Amy Marcaccio for entrusting me with this project; my former developmental editors, Carol DeKane Nagel and Jane Hoehner, for their competence and encouragement; my current developmental editor, Kenneth Estell, for his support and professionalism; and Gale's extremely able research team, for assistance I couldn't have done without. Thanks also to Todd Chapman for computer back-up at a crucial time, and to my husband Rob Howes, who as usual not only kept me in good spirits but provided an interesting setting in which to do my work.

Kōbō Abe

1924–

Japanese novelist, dramatist, short story writer, and scriptwriter.

The Woman in the Dunes (*Suna no onna;* novel, 1962)

Plot: While out collecting insects, schoolteacher and amateur entomologist Niki Jumpei is captured by residents of a primitive seaside village. Along with a nameless woman whose name is never revealed, he is imprisoned in a house set in a deep pit in the dunes. The two must continually shovel the constantly encroaching sand to keep the house from being buried. Niki is also expected to father children with the woman. though he intends to escape, his one attempt to do so fails. By the end of the novel, Niki has lost interest in escaping and the woman is pregnant.

Characters: Abe is among the Japanese novelists familiar to American audiences, and *The Woman in the Dunes* is his most famous novel. The book gained notoriety following the success of the film based on it at the 1964 Cannes Film Festival. Like the rest of Abe's work, *The Woman in the Dunes* is not notably Japanese in tone and reflects instead the more Western themes of existentialism and isolation from society. Critics have praised Abe's effective use of a reportage narrative style that blends meticulous detail with dreamlike or fantastic elements. He is often compared to such writers as Franz Kafka and Samuel Beckett, whose works also feature surreal settings, grotesque images, symbolic and allegorical elements, and an overwhelming sense of alienation. *The Woman in the Dunes* presents a portrait of modern Japanese society that is both bizarre and frighteningly realistic.

Through the novel's protagonist, **Niki Jumpei**, Abe explores the loss of identity experienced in Japan after World War II. Abe confines the action with a simple plot structure in order to focus on Niki's inner reactions. His search for identity is portrayed symbolically, through his desire for escape. In the beginning Niki is a decent but ineffectual schoolteacher whose life is drab and mundane. Like the insects he collects, he is trapped, and he hides his insecurity behind his overly rational, scientific demeanor. Abe himself was trained as a physician and thus shares his character's scientific background.) Niki's imprisonment in a house on a dune and his need to keep the sand from engulfing it represent the quality of his effort to make his way through the shifting reality to the roots of his existence—a journey thwarted again and again by the relentless natural element surrounding him. As the novel progresses, Niki grows more savage, particularly in his treatment of the woman exiled with him. Some commentators believe that *The Woman in the Dunes* portrays the conflict between the two kinds of *kokyo* (homeland): the place where one is physically born, which bears no authentic relationship to one's true being, and the place in which one is *truly* at home. Niki's wish to return to his home is paradoxical, because his former life did not allow him to live fully, so he should have no desire to return to it. This paradox suggests that identity resides not in any specific place but in the continuous process of searching. Some

1

critics see the novel's ending as ambiguous and infused with futility, but others claim that Niki does achieve a measure of understanding and dignity. Abe's preoccupation with alienation is often linked to his childhood: raised in Manchuria, China, which was invaded by the Japanese in 1931, he was disgusted by the way the Japanese treated the Chinese. Through Niki and other alienated characters in his fiction, Abe portrays a modern Japanese society that is rapidly becoming more urbanized while it is losing its links with the past.

The only other significant character in *The Woman in the Dunes* is **the woman** of the novel's title. Abe does not describe her and never reveals her name; she is seen primarily through Niki's eyes. These factors make her an elusive, mysterious figure who adds to the story's atmosphere of ambiguity. Her behavior is inconsistent—she exhibits both pity and hard heartedness, she is both innocent and seductive—and thus resembles the shifting sand that engulfs the two prisoners. Critics consider the woman a kind of mirror in which Niki sees reflected the loneliness, alienation, and absurdity of his own life. Although she is intellectually superior, she serves mainly as a sexual vehicle to destroy Niki's overreliance on reason. His sexual relationship with the woman reveals his savage instincts as well as his occasional tenderness and compassion.

The Ark Sakura (novel, 1988)

Plot: The novel's central figure is an eccentric recluse named Pig who prefers, however, to be called Mole. Believing that a nuclear holocaust is imminent, he converts a huge underground quarry into an "ark" with enough space for 385 people. He stocks the ark with food, water, weapons, and booby traps designed to thwart any intruders. Then Mole goes to town to recruit his crew in an orderly fashion, but his plans are disrupted by a trio of con artists: a vendor named Komomo and his two accomplices, a young man and a girl, who help him cheat the unwary. Komomo sells Mole a *eupcaccia*—a legless insect that intrigues Mole because of its ability to survive by eating its own feces—and the three accompany Mole back to the ark. When Mole falls into the ark's gigantic, high suction toilet (through which he has been illegally dumping a variety of unsavory refuse), his leg becomes stuck. Komomo and the others hint that they may amputate his leg or flush him away. Mole's worries increase when he finds out that other outsiders have infiltrated the ark: his own father, Inototsu, has assembled a gang of elderly garbage disposers called the Broom Brigade who plan to overrun Mole's sanctuary. Komomo kills Mole's father and proclaims himself the gang's leader. Assorted street toughs from the outside also make their way into the ark, heightening the atmosphere of anarchy. Mole's solution to convince the invaders that nuclear war has begun is to set off some dynamite. He is eventually expelled from the ark and emerges into a world about to suffer nuclear destruction.

Characters: This labyrinthine, allegorical farce applies the biblical story of Noah and the flood to a modern world threatened with technological destruction in a humorous and apocalyptic manner. Often compared, like much of Abe's work, with the novels of Franz Kafka for its blend of realistic and surreal elements, *The Ark Sakura* exhibits the loss and alienation that are also hallmarks of Abe's fiction. The novel satirizes life in modern Japan, portraying a group of outcasts who pit themselves against the dominant order, conformity, and ambition of their society.

The novel's central character resembles other isolated protagonists in Abe's work. **Mole** is an eccentric, obese recluse who exemplifies his alienation from society by building an underground realm where he intends to rule supreme. Mole's personality defects are attributed in part to his childhood: the child of a rape, he ardently hates his sleazy father. At an early age he himself was falsely accused of rape and chained, as punishment, to some toilet pipes—an image that is repeated when he becomes entrapped in the ark's gigantic toilet. Mole's given name, Pig, therefore refers both to his appearance and his origins. The eupcaccia (the insect Mole buys from Komomo) is also an apt metaphor for the novel's protagonist. Able to feed on itself, the insect can thereby live self-sufficiently and apart from others. Mole even dreams of establishing his own country with a picture of the eupcaccia emblazoned on its flag. Essentially naive, Mole allows himself to be duped by the three conartists. His pathetic yearning for the girl and his failure to convince the others that nuclear war has begun further prove his naivete. Mole is not, however, embittered when he is thrown out of the ark into a world about to be destroyed, for he explains, "Most people get the death sentence." Mole is another comical yet compelling character in Abe's fiction whose attempts to escape the dangers and emptiness of modern life are unsuccessful.

The three disreputable characters who trick Mole to get into the ark and then take over are led by **Komomo**, an aging huckster who sells Mole the bizarre insect that eats its own feces. Once arrested for selling on the black market, Komomo has a passion for guns and belongs to the ominous "Self-Defense Forces." His two associates are **the shill**, a smarty trickster whose past crimes include working for loan sharks and defrauding credit card companies; and **the girl**, pretty and manipulative, who serves to provoke rivalry between the three men and who is finally expelled with Mole. Mole's father, **Inototsu,** is a filthy, violent drunk and murderer who raped Mole's mother; Mole, not surprisingly, despises him. Inototsu leads **the Broom Brigade**, the elderly streetsweepers who infiltrate the ark, and is eventually killed by Komomo.

Further Reading

Allen, Louis. "Piranesian Prospects." *Times Literary Supplement,* No. 4454 (August 12–18, 1988): 892.

Contemporary Literary Criticism. Vols. 8, 22, 53. Detroit: Gale Research.

Currie, William. "Abe Kōbō's Nightmare World of Sand." In *Approaches to the Modern Japanese Novel,* edited by Kinya Tsurutu and Thomas E. Swann. Tokyo: Sophia University, 1976.

Kakutani, Michiko. "Half Boys' Clubhouse and Half Survivalist Bunker." *New York Times,* (March, 23 1988): C24.

Kessler, Jascha. Review of *The Ark Sakura. Los Angeles Daily News,* (August 28, 1988): 22, 25.

Leithauser, Brad. "Severed Futures." *New Yorker,* (May 9, 1988): 122—26.

Miner, Earl. "Life Is a Sandpit." *Saturday Review* Vol., 47, no. 36 (September 5, 1964): 32.

Montgomery, Scott L. "Abe Kōbō and Oe Kenzaburo: The Problem of Selfhood in Contemporary Japan." *Book Forum* Vol., no. 1 (1984): 30–31.

Van Wert, William F. "Levels of Sexuality in the Novels of Kōbō Abe. *International Fiction Review* Vol. 6, no. 2 (summer 1979): 129–32.

White, Edmund. "Round and Round the Eupcaccia Goes." *New York Times Book Review* (April 10, 1988): 9.

Yamanouchi, Hisaaki. "In Search of Identity: Abe Kōbō and Oe Kenzaburo." In *The Search for Authenticity in Modern Japanese Literature,* Cambridge: University Press, 1978. 153–74.

Chinua Achebe

1930–

Nigerian novelist, short story writer, poet, and essayist.

Anthills of the Savannah (novel, 1988)

Plot: The novel takes place in the fictional West African country of Kangan, where a coup has toppled the former dictator. Three men, friends since childhood, have all attained positions of prominence in the new government. Sam is Kangan's president; Chris Oriko, a former journalist, is Commissioner for Information; and Ikem Osodi, a journalist and poet, is now editor of the *National Gazette* newspaper. Chris's lover is Beatrice Okoh, a highly educated civil servant; Ikem's girlfriend is the semiliterate shopgirl Ewele. When the novel begins, Chris and Ikem both realize that their old friend Sam is not the kind of president they had hoped he would be. Sam is insecure in his position and intoxicated with power, and he has grown increasingly imperious and paranoid. A recent referendum to make Sam "President for Life" failed when one region of the country, Abazon, refused to vote. To punish the people of Abazon, Sam has denied them access to water despite conditions of drought in their dry savannah land. An Abazonian delegation arrives in the capital to beg for mercy, but Sam suspects that they are actually planning an insurrection and that someone close to him is encouraging them. Chris, though keenly aware of Sam's shortcomings, also wants to keep his own position, because he feels he can serve his country well. The more radical Ikem has been publishing editorials critical of Sam's administration. Beatrice, meanwhile, more aware than the others of the complexities of the situation, feels that neither Chris—or Ikem is truly in touch with the people they claim to represent.

Sam eventually orders Chris to fire Ikem from his newspaper post on suspicion of organizing the Abazon protest, but Chris refuses. Ikem is nevertheless fired. While addressing a university rally, Ikem makes some passionate statements interpreted as direct threats against the president, and the next day he is shot dead by the police. Chris goes into hiding and eventually escapes from the capital on a bus bound for Abazon. The bus is stopped by a drunken mob celebrating the news that Sam has been ousted from power by another coup. While trying to prevent the rape of a young girl, Chris is killed, unaware that Sam has also been murdered. Later, Beatrice gathers some friends at her apartment to perform the traditional naming ceremony for Ikem and Ewele's baby daughter. In a ceremony symbolizing hope and unity, Beatrice names the baby Amaechina, or "May the Path Never Close."

Characters: Achebe's novels chronicling post—colonial Nigeria have made him one of the most acclaimed contemporary African writers. Produced after a writing hiatus of over twenty years (during which Achebe was active in his country's civic affairs), *Anthills of the Savannah* has been lauded as his most complex and accomplished work. The novel incorporates different narrative voices, thus underlining the theme that no one voice can speak for all Africans and that storytelling—while essential to a people's survival—is nevertheless a subjective art. In an interview Achebe explained that his purpose in *Anthills* was to "retell modern African history in fictional terms"; indeed, *Anthills* is richly woven with traditional African folklore and proverbs as well as Western political ideology and influences. In exploring how individual power may be misused to the detriment of all, Achebe suggests that Africans ought to take responsibility for what has happened in their countries and not attribute their troubles entirely to the colonialism or international capitalism. Through the dynamic characters in *Anthills,* Achebe also emphasizes the vital roles of women and the urban working class in guiding Africa toward its future.

Of the three friends who attended Lord Lugard College as boys, **Chris Oriko** has always placed himself in the "middle," between brilliant Ikem and athletic Sam. As an adult Chris also occupies a middle position as he maneuvers between Sam's paranoid excesses and Ikem's reforming passion. Prominent in the group that ousted the former dictator, Chris was also instrumental in Sam's appointment to president and is himself the new regime's Commissioner for Information. Increasingly aware that Sam is intoxicated with power and disillusioned by life within Sam's circle, Chris is still reluctant to surrender his own influence. A former journalist, Chris wants to believe in objective fact and tries to maintain a detached, clinical stance, but in fact he is burdened with suspicion, confusion, and doubt. Chris eventually realizes that he cannot remain in the "middle" forever. His refusal to fire Ikem is the definitive act that sets in motion a deadly chain of events: Ikem is assassinated, Chris is forced to flee the capital, and eventually both he and Sam are killed. But on the bus toward Abazon, he comes into close contact with "the people." A London-educated member of Kangan's elite class, Chris had only a theoretical identification before. He is in the process of developing a much deeper insight when he dies; Achebe acknowledged in an interview that the tragedy was that "he died just as he was beginning to see," but Chris's final words indicate his awareness: "The Last Green" which Emmanuel misheard as "The Last Grin") refers to a private joke that compared him and his two friends to three green bottles looking down pompously from a high shelf, but bound to topple eventually.

Ikem Osodi is the accomplished poet and journalist to whom Chris passes his post as editor of the *National Gazette* when he becomes Commissioner for Information. Although Ikem is a London-educated intellectual, he feels connected with and sympathetic for the poor majority of his country, even though he has little contact with them. Ikem's scathing editorials have incited his old schoolmate Sam, who suspects Ikem of treachery. Whereas Chris aspires to objectivity, Ikem asserts instead that "passion is our hope and strength." Ikem's extremist views differentiate him from both Sam and Chris, but like them he relishes his position of power. In his speech at the university after being dismissed from the newspaper, Ikem promotes the role of the storyteller, demonstrating in his riveting speech not only his passion and conviction but his own skill with language. Declaring that the writer must challenge those who usurp freedom, Ikem claims: "Writers don't give prescriptions. Writers give headaches." Yet his passion is also his downfall, for Ikem's statements are construed as treasonous and result in his death. Yet his legacy lives on, through his friends' memories as well as through his daughter. The baby's name—Amaechina, or "May the Path Never Close"—expresses the openness and continuity that Ikem championed.

The third of the boyhood friends who attain prominence in Kangan, **Sam**, is recommended by the others as a good candidate for president. Athletic, courteous, and self-consciously urbane in the manner of the classic English gentleman, Sam is, Chris and Ikem believe, somewhat slow-witted but basically decent. Trained at Sandhurst, an English military institution, Sam is not fit for political leadership, and he seems to know it. He also senses that his friends Chris and Sam regard him as intellectually inferior to themselves. Sam's insecurity causes him to shift between pomposity and paranoia, imperialism and nervous suspicion. At a conference on African unity, he meets an emperor and a President for Life and decides to imitate their regal style by attempting to get himself designated President for Life as well. Sam adopts the expression "Kabisa!" ("Finished!" or "That's all!"), proclaiming it whenever someone challenges or disagrees with him. Sam's insecurity eventually escalates into despotism. He suspects the Abazonian delegates of insurrection and his closest friends of disloyalty. Sam eventually causes the deaths of his friends, after which he is killed himself by a member of his royal entourage. Probably modeled after the six men who, at the time the novel was written, had served as heads of state in Nigeria since its 1960 independence, Sam illustrates how power concentrated in a single person may result in great harm to the majority.

Beatrice Okoh the most successfully developed female character in Achebe's fiction, is a seminal figure in *Anthills*, because she articulates many of the novel's strongest themes. At Beatrice's birth, her disappointed father—who had longed for a boy—named her Nwanyibuife, or "A Woman Is Also Something." Although Beatrice has always resented this designation for implying diminished value, she ultimately fulfills its prophecy. Beatrice holds an honors degree in English from the University of London and a high-level civil service position in Kangan government. Dynamic, intelligent, and independent, she pleases her lover, Chris, not only through her beauty but through her calm strength and sophistication. Beatrice is transformed as the novel progresses, connecting with her personal and cultural heritage through memory, myth, and proverb, and finally becoming a kind of priestess who blends her knowledge of the past with her vision of the future. In contrast to both Chris and Ikem, Beatrice cultivates a broad view of her country's troubles and strengths; she admonishes Chris that "this world belongs to the people of the world not to any little caucus, no matter how talented." Achebe has said that women will play an important role in Africa's future through their instinct for survival, and Beatrice exemplifies the archetype. The naming ceremony with which *Anthills* concludes is an important scene, because Beatrice declares that women should name babies. She adopts the traditionally masculine role herself, and she gives Ikem and Ewele's baby a masculine name, Amaechina. The scene is notably infused with hope. The ceremony juxtaposes the wisdom culled from the past, an awareness of the present, and the expectation of brighter days to come. Although Beatrice's question, "What must people do to appease an embittered history?" is tinged with despair, her life exemplifies the resilience that, Achebe suggests, can propel Africa toward the future.

Critics praise Achebe's skillful use of African proverbs and myths, drawn from the rich storehouse of his Ibo (or Igbo) heritage. Achebe demonstrates this resource in *Anthills* through the character of **the tribal elder from Abazon**, who speaks eloquently to Ikem and other listeners at a restaurant after arriving in the capital with the other delegates from Abazon to petition Sam for mercy. Expressing appreciation to Ikem for helping the people of Abazon through his writings, the old man celebrates storytelling as a means for recording memories and as a guide to the future. "It is only the story that can continue beyond the war and the warrior," he says. "The story is our escort; without it, we are blind." Critics regard this public activity, which appears in some way in each of Achebe's novels, as evidence of the author's faith in the strong communality of African culture, a quality that flourished before colonization and that can still strengthen African societies.

Whereas Chris, Ikem, Beatrice, and Sam occupy elite positions in Kangan society, Ikem's girlfriend, **Elewe,** is a semiliterate shopgirl more closely associated with her people's traditional ways. Beatrice marvels that despite her poor origins, Elewe is astoundingly resilient and self-confident. Elewe speaks the last line of the novel when, in response to Beatrice's contemplative tears, she asks: "What kind trouble you wan begin cause now? I beg-o. Hmmm!" That final "Hmmm!" many mean that the matters discussed in the novel are not yet resolved—that storytelling does indeed cause "trouble"—or that no pat answers exist for the questions asked here. The baby daughter of Elewe and Ikem, **Amaechina,** symbolizes hope for those gathered at her naming ceremony, and openness, continuing access between past and present. **Elewe's uncle** also symbolizes the country's poor but resilient majority; he condemns the egotism of the powerful, observing: "We have seen too much trouble in Kangan since the white man left because the people who make plans make plans for themselves only and their families."

Emmanuel Obote is a dedicated student leader who reveres Chris and who is with him when he is killed. Emmanuel reports to Beatrice and the others that Chris died with dignity and that his final words were "The Last Grin." Emmanuel thinks Chris was making a joke to comfort him, but Beatrice explains that Chris must have said "The Last Green," in reference to an old joke between them. Typifying the Kangan youth, who will lead their nation into the future, Emmanuel declares during Amaechina's naming ceremony that they must accept no restrictions on their minds, even if they are physically imprisoned.

Other characters in *Anthills* include **Major Johnson Ossai**, the brusque, sinister, brutal head of security for the military regime who uses a Samsonite paper stapler as a torture device; he makes himself invaluable to Sam by quelling Sam's insecurities. **Professor Reginald Okong**, one of the most threatening members of Sam's entourage, is a former political scientist; not realizing he was "fostering a freak baby," Chris initially recommended Okong for office. **General Ahmed Lango**, another member of Sam's inner circle, leads the coup that finally defeats and assassinates him.

Further Reading

Achebe, Chinua. Interview by Kay Bonetti. *Missouri Review* Vol. 12, no. 1 (1989): 61—83.

Ascherson, Neal. "Betrayal." *New York Review of Books* Vol. 35, no. 3 (March 3, 1988): 3—4, 6.

Black Literature Criticism. Vol. 1. Detroit: Gale Research.

Contemporary Literary Criticism. Vols. 1, 3, 5, 7, 11, 26, 51, 75. Detroit: Gale Research.

Gikandi, Simon. *Reading Chinua Achebe: Language and Ideology in Fiction.* London: James Currey, 1991.

Gordimer, Nadine. "A Tyranny of Clowns." *New York Times Book Review,* (February 21, 1988), 1, 26.

Ikegami, Robin. "Knowledge and Power: The Story and the Storyteller; Achebe's *Anthills of the Savannah.*" *Modern Fiction Studies* Vol. 37, no. 3 (Autumn 1991): 493–507.

Innes, C. L. *Chinua Achebe.* Cambridge: Cambridge University Press, 1990.

Killiam, G. D. *The Novels of Chinua Achebe.* New York: Africana Publishing, 1969.

Okoye, Emmanuel Meziemadu. *The Traditional Religion and Its Encounter with Christianity in Achebe's Novels.* Bern: Peter Lang, 1987.

Okri, Ben. "Vicious Circle." *Observer* (September 20, 1987): 28.

Owusu, Kofi. "The Politics of Interpretation: The Novels of Chinua Achebe." *Modern Fiction Studies* Vol. 37, no. 3 (Autumn 1991): 459—70.

Povey, John. Review of *Anthills of the Savannah. African Arts* Vol. 21, no. 4 (August 1988): 21—3.

Ravenscroft, A. "Recent Fiction from Africa: Chinua Achebe's *Anthills of the Savannah;* A Note." *Literary Criterion* Vol. 23, nos. 1—2 (1988): 172—75.

Siebers, Tobin. "Chinua Achebe and Proverbial Wisdom." In *Morals and Stories.* New York: Columbia University Press, 1992.

Udumukwu, Onyemaechi. "Achebe and the Negation of Independence." *Modern Fiction Studies* Vol. 37, no. 3 (Autumn 1991): 471—91.

Wren, Robert M. *Achebe's World: The Historical and Cultural Context of the Novels of Chinua Achebe.* Washington, DC: Three Continents Press, 1980.

Isabel Allende

1942–

Chilean novelist, journalist, dramatist, and juvenile fiction writer.

The House of the Spirits (*La Casa de los Espiritus*; novel, 1982)

Plot: Set in an unnamed South American country, the novel begins at the childhood home of Clara del Valle, whose recollections in a diary comprise the first part of the book. Clara's clairvoyant powers became evident early in life; even as a child she could accurately predict the future and move objects without touching them. Her greenhaired sister Rosa is a legendary beauty whose untimely death sends Clara into a nine-year silence not broken until she announces that she will marry Estaban Trueba, the willful, tyrannical, 35-year-old owner of a large country estate and Rosa's former fiance. An archconservative with a monumental temper, Estaban also contributes to the novel's narration with his often sorrowful remembrances of his own and his family's lives.

The couple moves into Estaban's huge house in town. Their home is soon filled with the spiritualists, artists, and charity cases the sensitive Clara gathers around her, the kindly spirits with whom she frequently communicates, and the Trueba's three children: practical Blanca and the twins, Jaime and Nicolás, the latter compassionate and reserved and the former a playboy. As the years progress, Blanca has a love affair with the son of the foreman at the family's country estate; when she becomes pregnant, her enraged father forces her to enter a loveless marriage with a French count. Jaime becomes a physician and dedicates himself to helping the poor, while Nicolás dabbles in Eastern mysticism. Estaban enters politics, rising to the rank of senator.

Blanca's daughter, Alba, who grows up nurtured and instructed by the other family members, chronicles the family's tragic collision with the turbulent forces of twentieth-century Latin America. A new, democratically elected socialist government comes to power, its president a close friend of Jaime. Ardently opposed to communism and convinced he is performing a patriotic duty, Estaban helps arrange a right-wing military coup. Meanwhile, Jaime and Alba (who has fallen in love with a student radical) assist the guerrilla resistance movement, and both are captured. Jaime is tortured and killed and Alba is interrogated, beaten, and raped by a policeman bent on revenge against the Truebas, for he is one of Estaban's illegitimate children. Alba survives her ordeal and reunites with her grandfather, who has been forced to recognize his grave errors. Convinced that her family's and her country's legacies must not be forgotten, Alba begins to write the story that will become this novel.

Characters: Isabel Allende, the novel's author, is the niece of Chilean president Salvador Allende, who was assassinated during the 1973 coup led by Augusto Pinochet. Allende drew on the history of her own family and country to create this richly detailed portrait of Chilean life. Often compared to Colombian novelist Gabriel Garciá Marquez, Allende is among those Latin American writers who employ the "magic realism" technique, highly evident in this novel. While *The House of the Spirits* is occasionally faulted as derivative, melodramatic, or overburdened with the author's socialist views, it is praised for its memorable characters and evocative language.

The novel's central female figure is **Clara del Valle Trueba**, whose diary chronicles the earliest period of Trueba family history. Like those of her daughter and granddaughter, Clara's name evokes images of purity and light. From childhood she is a radiant, highly sensitive person with a clairvoyant gift: she can predict the future, interpret dreams, move objects without touching them, and communicate freely with the spirits who inhabit her house and to whom she often appeals for help. Clara's contrasting strength and gentleness, reticence and gaiety make her somewhat enigmatic, and her stubbornness is evident not only in the nine-year silence she maintains after her sister's death but in her resistance to her husband's overwhelming passion for her. Clara enters into marriage with Estaban willingly but with no love, and she never accepts his domination or his desire to completely possess her. She provides a strong contrast to Estaban in her compassion (particularly for the poor and downtrodden), her moral sensibility, and her intuitive awareness. Allende based Clara on her own beloved maternal grandmother, and that esteem is manifested in Alba's reverence for the Trueba family's matriarch. After Clara has herself, through death, passed into the spirit world and her granddaughter has been captured and tortured, her ghost visits Alba in prison and exhorts her to survive. Clara embodies resistance to oppression as well as—through her own diary and through inspiring Alba to chronicle the Truebas' life—the writer's determination to observe and record what happens.

Modeled after Allende's conservative, violent, beloved maternal grandfather, **Estaban Trueba** is a wealthy landowner and senator whose ill temper and misguided ideas have tragic consequences for himself and his family. Willful, moody Estaban is greedy for power and money and generally indifferent to others' needs, for he neglects his mother, behaves insensitively toward his adored wife, estranges himself from his children, and tragically misjudges his country's political situation. Since his young manhood, Estaban has held little regard for the peasants of his country estate; indeed, he views them as irresponsible children who need his tyrannical direction to survive. This attitude is also manifested in his virulent anti-Communist position. The father of numerous illegitimate children with peasant women, he never anticipates that one of them (the child of an early rape) will take revenge for Estaban's neglect by brutalizing his beloved granddaughter. Neither does he realize that the leaders of the right-wing coup he has helped to put in power will eventually scorn him, kill one of his sons, and exile the other. Most critics contend that despite his cruelty and irascibility, Estaban wins the reader's sympathy through his sorrowful confessions of his poor judgment and the damage it has wrought. His overwhelming love for Clara and inability to reach her and his essential loneliness also make him a tragic figure. Estaban has been said to embody the legendary *macho* quality of the Latin American male—a violent, authoritarian force that not only hurts Estaban himself, but his country and the people he loves as well.

Allende has explained in interviews that *The House of the Spirits* evolved from a letter she wrote to her dying grandfather, promising never to forget him or their family history. Like the author who created her, **Alba Trueba** chronicles the past and the present. Her narrative voice dominates the latter part of the novel, documenting the violent effects of the period on the Trueba family. The story ends as Alba begins writing about the events that comprise the novel. Strong-spirited and rebellious but fiercely loyal to her family, Alba grows up nurtured by all of them. Her grandfather particularly adores her, despite the socialist views she develops as she reaches adulthood, which clash with Estaban's conservatism. Alba's compassion for her country's poor and mistreated leads her to join the resistance movement when the new socialist government is overturned. Although Alba's lover, the radical **Miguel**, is a member of a lower social class, the two share the same political ideals. Allende's account of Alba's imprisonment and torture has been praised for its journalistic description. Indeed, activist Alba and her grandmother, Clara, have been said to represent the indomitable spirit of the Latin American woman. When Alba is tortured to the point of despair, Clara's ghost appears in her prison cell and urges her to live. Inspired by her grandmother, Alba does survive, and she resolves to complete the narrative she began in prison. Also the instrument through which Estaban is purged of his character flaws, Alba rejoins her still beloved grandfather and shepherds him toward a peaceful death.

Several significant characters populate the novel's early pages, which chronicle Clara's childhood and marriage to Estaban. **Rosa del Valle**, often called **Rosa the Beautiful**, is Clara's adored sister; her death sends Clara into a nine-year silence. Rosa's green hair and ethereal quality exemplify the blending of fact and fantasy characterizing the technique of "magic realism" employed by Allende and other Latin American writers. Estaban's love for Rosa, to whom he is engaged shortly before her death, is transferred to Clara, whom he marries nine years later. Other notable characters from the novel's first section include **Uncle Marcos**, a mad inventor who builds and flies away on a mechanical bird, leaving his niece a set of books that help her develop her magical powers; **Férula Trueba**, Estaban's sister, who is devoted to Clara but curses Estaban; **Barrabás**, the gigantic dog sent to Clara by her absent Uncle Marcos; and the peasant woman **Pancha Garciá**, Estaban's first rape victim and the mother of his illegitimate son Estaban Garciá.

Although some critics consider Allende's portrayal of the three Trueba children rather insubstantial, others claim that these characters add interesting dimensions to the family saga. Practical, self-effacing **Blanca Trueba** is not as radiant a personality as her mother, but her passion and rebelliousness are manifest in her lifelong love for **Pedro Tercero Garciá**. Portrayed as a dynamic peasant hero, guitarist Garciá was reportedly modeled after Victor Jara, a Chilean folksinger murdered during Pinochet's coup. Garciá loses three fingers when Estaban, enraged to learn that Blanca has been having an affair with this young peasant, attacks him with an ax (Jara suffered a similar mutilation). Taciturn, compassionate **Jaime Trueba** becomes a doctor. His socialist political views lead him to assist the resistance movement after the coup; he and Alba even steal food from Estaban's stores to help the guerrilla fighters. Jaime is finally captured, cruelly tortured, and killed by the right-wing military forces. Pleasure-loving **Nicolás Trueba** is an aimless playboy who eventually associates himself with an Eastern religious group and denounces his father's greed. Having already killed one of his sons, the coup leaders further punish Estaban by banishing Nicolás from the country.

Colonel Estaban Garciá is one of the most significant of the many minor characters in *The House of the Spirits*. The child of Estaban Trueba's rape of one of the peasants at his country estate, Garciá suffers the humiliation of illegitimacy and resents his father for neglecting him. He becomes a policeman and eventually oversees the prisoners taken during the military coup. This gives Garciá an opportunity to vent his anger at the Trueba family by supervising Alba's interrogation and torture and even raping her himself. Thus he reinforces the theme of retribution and the linking of past and present, which are important aspects of the novel. Two other particularly notable characters in *The House of the Spirits* are **the President**, Jaime Trueba's close friend and the leader of the socialist government, who is assassinated by agents of the military coup (and who was reportedly modeled after Salvador Allende); and **the Poet**, an internationally acclaimed writer who resembles slain Chilean poet Pablo Neruda and who is also killed during the coup. **Count Jean de Satigny** is the effete French dandy whose diligent courtship of Blanca succeeds only after he alerts Estaban to his daughter's love affair with a peasant; the forced marriage of Jean and Blanca remains, by mutual consent, platonic.

Further Reading

Coleman, Alexander. "Reconciliation Among the Ruins." *New York Times Books Review*, (May 12, 1985): 22–3.

Contemporary Literary Criticism. Vols. 39, 57. Detroit: Gale Research.

Earle, Peter G. "Literature as Survival: Allende's 'The House of the Spirits.'" *Contemporary Literature* Vol. 28, no. 4 (winter 1987): 543–54.

García Pinto, Magdalena. Interview in *Women Writers of Latin America: Intimate Histories*, Austin: University of Texas Press, 1988, 23–42.

Gordon, Ambrose. "Isabel Allende on Love and Shadow." *Contemporary Literature* Vol. 28, no. 4 (winter 1987): 530–42.

Hart, Patricia. *Narrative Magic in the Fiction of Isabel Allende.* Rutherford, N.J.: Fairleigh Dickinson University Press, 1989.

Jones, D. A. N. "Magical Realism." *London Review of Books* (August 1, 1985): 26–7.

Lehmann-Haupt, Christopher. Review of *The House of the Spirits. New York Times*, (May 9, 1985): 23.

Riquelme Rojas, Sonia, and Edna Aguirre Rehbein. *Critical Approaches to Isabel Allende's Novels.* New York: P. Lang, 1991.

West, Paul. "Narrative Overdrive." *Nation* Vol. 241, no. 2 (July 20 and 27, 1985): 52–4.

Yardley, Jonathan. "Desire and Destiny in Latin America." *Washington Post Book World*, (May 12, 1985): 3–4.

Martin Amis
1949–

English novelist, critic, short story writer, editor, scriptwriter, and nonfiction writer.

Time's Arrow (novel, 1991)

Plot: The novel's title refers to its unusual structure, which reverses "time's arrow" to chronicle *in reverse* the life of the central character. The narrator is the protagonist's soul, who witnesses what happens in this peculiar "backward" world without understanding it. The novel opens on the deathbed of Tod T. Friendly, an elderly, retired physician. After several weeks in the hospital, he returns to his home, where he suffers a heart attack, then has a car crash, followed by several encounters with a woman named Irene who tells him she knows about his secret. Tod grows younger and goes to work at American Medical Services, and his increasing virility results in a number of affairs with various women he meets there. Once a year Tod receives a coded letter advising him that the weather in New York continues to be "temperate." Eventually Tod moves to New York, where he meets with a mysterious adviser who tells him that the Naturalization and Immigration Service may soon revoke his citizenship and that he should leave the city. Tod now acquires a different name, John Young, and works as an emergency room surgeon. The novel traces his life in backward motion to the year 1948, when he sets sail "for Europe, and for war." Under the name Hamilton de Souza, the protagonist spends some time in Portugal, then seeks refuge at the Vatican, and finally arrives in Germany. The reader now learns his original name and identity: Odilo Unverdorben, a Nazi doctor stationed at the Auschwitz concentration camp, where he conducts gruesome experiments on Jews and administers the poison gas used to kill them. *Time's Arrow* now relates Odilo's relationship with his wife and his student years, ending when he is a carefree child, soon to return to his mother's womb.

Characters: Marked by the wit and post-modern inventiveness found in Amis's previous novels, *Time's Arrow* is generally considered his most accomplished and morally compelling work. Amis was praised for his highly effective portrayal of a "backward" world in which garbage men distribute trash instead of collecting it, food is vomited instead of eaten, and people take candy away from children. Commentators agreed that the novel's unusual structure provides a particularly appropriate framework for focusing on the inversion of morality that brought about the Holocaust.

The novel is narrated by the soul of the protagonist, who is born **Odilo Unverdorben**, but assumes the aliases **Hamilton de Souza**, **John Young**, and **Tod T. Friendly**, during his life of flight from the dark secret in his past. The device of splitting the central character in two allows Amis to create a narrative perspective that is both involved in and detached from the story. When the novel begins, Tod T. Friendly is an old man on the edge of death. As he grows younger and healthier, we learn that he is harboring an unexplained fear and guilt. Through the course of the novel, Tod moves to less and less luxurious homes, has affairs with more and more women, and takes jobs of decreasing prestige. In New York, where he is known as John Young, he works as an emergency room surgeon, and his emotional coldness makes him seem "stronger" than the other doctors. As history moves backward through time, the protagonist sails for Europe, spending a short period of apparent refuge in Portugal, where he is known as Hamilton de Souza. At the Vatican, he begs a priest for protection and hints at the sins he has committed. Finally he arrives at Auschwitz and his original identity—that of Odilo Unverdorben, who performs unspeakable acts of experimentation on, and participates in the killing of, Jewish prisoners. We learn that his wife Herta disapproved of his work, and that the couple was devastated by the death of their baby. Their courtship is chronicled, as are Odilo's experiences in medical school, and he is an innocent child at the novel's conclusion.

Meanwhile, the novel's narrator, in his naivete and ignorance of history, asks, "Is it just me, or is this a weird way to carry on?" He witnesses Odilo's life and shares in his experiences and feelings but cannot comprehend what happens in this inverted world in which people are "always looking forward to going places they've just come back from, or regretting doing things they haven't yet done." The brilliant central irony of *Time's Arrow* allows only Auschwitz to make sense to the narrator, for there doctors—who otherwise wound and make sick healthy people—are bringing Jews to life and sending them back to their homes. The inversion of time transforms the Nazi's massive destruction of human life into a miracle of creation, thus underlining the true horror of that period of history. It also encourages the reader to consider the nature of good and evil and the concept that Odilo Unverdorben, "as a moral being, is absolutely unexceptional, liable to do what everybody else does, good or bad . . . once under the cover of numbers."

The novel's secondary characters are presented only through the narrator's confused, uncomprehending perspective. Thus Tod's mistress **Irene** seems to be a slovenly woman who always leaves his home in a disordered state, when actually she is obviously his housekeeper. Irene tells Tod that she knows about his secret because he has talked about it in his sleep. Tod's New York correspondent, **Nicholas Kreditor**, informs him that he is in danger of being deported and should acquire a new identity and leave town. In Italy, Odilo seeks refuge at the Vatican and tries to receive absolution from **Father Duryea**, an Irish priest. At Auschwitz, Odilo retrieves from a trash can letters from his wife **Herta** in which she questions the nature of the work he is performing. When she visits him at the camp, Herta tells him that he has become a stranger to her. The novel chronicles in reverse the story of the couple's courtship, the death of their baby, and the disintegration of their marriage.

Further Reading

Contemporary Literary Criticism Vols. 4, 9, 38, 62. Detroit: Gale Research.

Dictionary of Literary Biography Vol. 14. Detroit: Gale Research.

Dunford, Judith. Review of *Time's Arrow*. *Tikkun* (May-June 1992): 75.

Lehman, David. "From Death to Birth." *New York Times Book Review* (November 17, 1991): 15.

Saynor, James. "Only the Good Die Young." *Observer* (September 22, 1991): 59.

Wood, James. "Slouching Towards Auschwitz to Be Born Again." *Manchester Guardian Weekly* (October 6, 1991): 14.

Updike, John. Review of *Time's Arrow*. *New Yorker* (May 25, 1992): 85.

Ayi Kwei Armah
1939–

Ghanaian novelist, short story writer, poet, and scriptwriter.

The Beautyful Ones Are Not Yet Born (novel, 1968)

Plot: The novel takes place in Takoradi, Ghana, where the protagonist works as a railway clerk. Referred to only as "the man," he originally intended to get a university education, but instead he married at an early age due to the unexpected pregnancy of Oyo, his current wife. He makes barely enough money to support his family, while other Ghanaians have supplemented their incomes through the graft and corruption widely practiced since the 1957 revolution, which gained independence from England and installed Kwame Nkrumah as leader. The man refuses to accept the bribes he is frequently offered, despite his wife's yearning for material comforts; Oyo does not understand the man's desire to maintain his honesty and integrity. Meanwhile, Joseph Komsoon, the man's morally bankrupt and opportunistic old school friend, has become a prominent, wealthy government official. He lives ostentatiously in a grand old colonial mansion, owns a chauffeur-driven Mercedes Benz, and drinks imported liquor, while his avaricious wife, Estella, flaunts her European clothing and jewelry. Koomson is utterly unconcerned that his life-style contradicts the principles on which the socialist government was founded, and he is almost universally admired and envied.

Frustrated by the betrayal of hope that followed Ghana's independence and isolated by his principles, the man finds some solace in talking to his friend Teacher, who shares his views. Although just as disgusted with his country's corruption and moral decay as the man, Teacher has reacted by separating himself from society. He lives austerely and has never married or had a family; yet his life is also lonely and bereft of purpose. They discuss the lure of "the Gleam"—the term that describes the shiny, luxurious possessions that all of Ghana's citizens, no matter how lowly, will apparently do anything to acquire. Admitting to being tempted by the Gleam, the man suspects that his honesty is only a cover for weakness.

When Nkrumah's government is deposed, Koomson, who fears assassination, arrives at the man's house and pleads for help in escaping. Despite his disgust with Koomson, the man agrees to help his old friend. They leave the house by crawling through its latrine and make their way to the sea. Discarding his own principles, the man bribes a nightwatchman to give them a boat, and after they are safely launched, the man swims alone to shore. While walking home, he sees a bus on which is painted the slogan "The Beautyful Ones Are Not Yet Born." He watches the bus driver give a policeman a bribe; the man and the driver exchange a weary wave of camaraderie before going their separate ways.

Characters: Considered one of Africa's best English-language writers, Armah is lauded not only for his insightful portrayals of postcolonial Ghana but also for his explorations of the universal conditions of human alienation and social morality. *The Beautyful Ones Are Not Yet Born* is his first novel, which provides a compelling portrait of a corrupt society and one man's doubt-riddled struggle to resist it. Set in the years following Ghana's independence from England, the novel conveys the betrayal the Ghanaian people feel as their spirits are crushed by graft and decay, represented in the book by many powerful (and repulsive) images of human excrement. Most Ghanaians strive to acquire "the Gleam," luxurious trappings and possessions (epitomized in the glittering facade of the opulent Atlantic-Caprice Hotel) that signify power, prestige, and material comfort. The novel's protagonist is seen as a victim not only of contemporary events but of Ghana's long history of foreign dominance, capitulation, and cultural betrayal. While some critics have interpreted the book as a document of unrelenting despair, others maintain that Armah holds out a faint glimmer of hope at the end, suggesting that Ghana's redemption may be forged by the "beautyful ones" of the future.

Referred to only as **"the man,"** the novel's protagonist is both representative of other Ghanaians and a social outcast, isolated by his sense of morality. His job as a telegraph operator for a railroad is both dull and poorly paid, and his wife and children resent their pinched circumstances. The man is intelligent enough to have sought a college degree, but Oyo's pregnancy put an end to those plans. Although tortured by thoughts of what he might have accomplished if he had gone to college, the man also admits to himself that, at the time of his wedding, he was pleased to be marrying and beginning a family. The man is most distinguished by his moral focus: he resists the practice of bribery commonly used to obtain upward mobility (whereas his old schoolmate Koomson exemplifies what benefits can accrue to the corrupt). Yet the man's refusal to compromise his principles earns him the contempt of his family and coworkers, and only Teacher seems to share his views. Unlike Teacher, however, the man admits to feeling the lure of the Gleam, and he worries that his steadfast integrity is actually disguised weakness or even selfishness. The man's extreme fastidiousness and disgust with the excrement around him parallel his reaction to his society's corruption and decay. A few commentators have suggested that the man's repulsion is typical of the expatriate African, or "been-to" (an African who has spent time abroad and then returned); others, however, contend that many people forced to regularly endure such sickening sights and smells retain an aversion to them.

Despite the man's doubt and despair, he experiences occasional moments of clarity that seem to confirm his principles and provide some hope. Although he often feels like a criminal—as if his own principles are skewed rather than those of the corrupt people around him—he knows that he is actually guiltless. While Teacher's response to despair is withdrawal, the man remains engaged with life, thus investing his struggle with a measure of dignity. His journey literally through excrement (when he escapes through the latrine with Koomson) and his subsequent purifying plunge into the ocean help the man shed his former fastidiousness and with it his somewhat arrogant, superior stance. He will still not capitulate his standards, but he has a broader sense of moral complexity, evident in his weary but comradely exchange with the bribe-giving bus driver. The man's role does not appear to be to generate profound change or attain spectacular success but to help prepare the way for the "beautyful ones" who will follow him. A few commentators have felt that the novel's conclusion suggests defeat, but most have detected in it an enduring, if faint, note of optimism.

Whereas the man has resisted the Gleam and the dishonesty required to attain it, his old school friend **Joseph Koomson** has not. A former dockworker and labor organizer, after Ghana's 1957 revolution he became active in the ruling socialist party. He eventually received a coveted government appointment and now bears the overblown title of "His

Excellency Joseph Koomson, Minister Plenipotentiary, Member of the Presidential Commission, Hero of Socialist Labor.'' Koomson lives in one of the mansions abandoned by Europeans who fled after the country gained independence, and in fact he imitates Ghana's colonizers. Koomson speaks with a haughty, fake English accent, owns a chauffeured Mercedes Benz, and claims to drink only imported alcohol. He is greatly admired by those around him, including the family of his lowly friend, the man, whom he condescends to visit occasionally. Portrayed as greedy, materialistic, and without responsibility for the people he is supposed to serve, Koomson is the novel's strongest embodiment of moral betrayal. Instead of working for any common good, Koomson and his fellow officials strive only for opulent life-styles. When the man shakes Koomson's hand, he notices its softness, which seems inappropriate for a socialist revolutionary; the man compares Koomson to the African chiefs of past centuries who sold their own people into slavery for the ''trinkets of Europe.'' While the novel clearly condemns Koomson and his type, Armah stresses that greed, consumerism, and dishonesty are not confined to the ruling class but have infected all levels of society. At the end of the novel, the regime of Kwame Nkrumah is deposed, and Koomson, fearing for his life, begs his old friend for help. Despite his misgivings, the man does help Koomson escape, sending him off in a boat to safety in another country. Thus the man demonstrates the complexity of his own morality, which contrasts strongly with Koomson's.

Teacher is the only acquaintance in moral sympathy with the man. Through Teacher, Armah sheds light on the centuries of oppression in Ghana's history that conditioned the country's citizens to despair and disillusionment. As Teacher reminds the man during one of their discussions, he had once been an enthusiastic supporter of the independence movement led by Nkrumah. Now betrayed, he has no more interest in politics and considers it a futile pursuit. Like the man, Teacher resists the lure of the Gleam, but he does so by withdrawing from society; his life-style is austere, and he is isolated both socially and personally. He has chosen not to marry, which eliminates for him the kind of moral dilemmas the man faces but also leaves him with ''a half-life of loneliness.'' Although he seems serene, Teacher gradually reveals the same bewilderment as the man, suggesting that trying to separate oneself from a detestable situation may not necessarily be the proper course. Whereas the man may be said to represent Everyman, Teacher plays the artist, intellectual, or writer who has rejected society, which in turn has also deprived Teacher of outlets for creativity and of the opportunity for a meaningful life. While a few critics have suggested that Armah affirms Teacher's aloofness as the only possible response to his circumstances, most contend that the man's willingness to live and struggle within his society is favored.

The novel contains two significant female characters. **Oyo**, the man's wife, is initially impatient with her scrupulous husband, bewildered by his refusal to take bribes to acquire the kind of comforts she sees others enjoying. Expressing her desire to attain the opulence that Armah calls ''the Gleam,'' Oyo tells the man, ''Everybody is swimming toward what he wants. Who wants to remain on the beach asking the wind, 'How . . . How . . . How?''' By the end of the novel, however, Oyo respects her husband's honesty and she seems to share his viewpoint, a state that contributes to the faint note of hope on which the novel ends. In contrast to Oyo, **Estella Koomson** has benefited materially from her husband's moral laxity. She is an avaricious social climber who prefers anything European to locally made products, thus exemplifying the Eurocentrism that Armah portrays as a negative element of postindependence Ghanaian society. Oyo envies Estella's life of luxury, seeing in it a ''cleanliness''—which, for his part, the man describes as having ''more rottenness in it than the slime at the bottom of a garbage dump.''

Two of the novel's minor characters appear only in the recollections of the man and Teacher. **Rama Krishna** was a friend of the man who changed his Ghanaian name to an exotic one that reflected his new religious orientation. Retreating from the corrupt society, he adopted an extreme form of spirituality, even abstaining from sex to maintain his purity and strength. Ironically, Rama Krishna died of tuberculosis, and his heart had become a mass of knotted worms; thus the rot of the outside world had found its way inside him. Teacher's friend **Manaan** had been an early supporter of Nkrumah's administration, seeing in it a brighter future for Ghana. Profoundly disillusioned by the corrupt government, she retreats into madness and now wanders the streets, muttering incoherently.

Further Reading

Achebe, Chinua. "Africa and Her Writers." In *Morning Yet on Creation Day: Essays,* 29–45. New York: Anchor Press/Doubleday, 1975.

Ama Ata Aidoo, Christina. Introduction to *The Beautyful Ones Are Not Yet Born.* New York: Collier Books, 1969.

Black Literature Criticism. Vol. 1. Detroit: Gale Research.

Chakava, Henry. "Ayi Kwei Armah and a Commonwealth of Souls." In *Standpoints on African Literature.* Edited by C. Wanjala, 197-208. Nairobi, Kenya: East African Literature Bureau, 1973.

Contemporary Literary Criticism. Vols. 5, 33. Detroit: Gale Research.

Fraser, Robert. *The Novels of Ayi Kwei Armah: A Study in Polemical Fiction.* London: Heinemann, 1980.

Griffiths, Gareth. "Structure and Image in Kwei Armah's *The Beautyful Ones Are Not Yet Born.*" *Studies in Black Literature* Vol. 2, no. 2 (Summer 1971): 1–9.

Lazarus, Neil. "*The Beautyful Ones Are Not Yet Born*: Pessimism of the Intellect, Optimism of the Will." In *Resistance in Postcolonial African Fiction,* 46–79. New Haven, Conn. Yale University Press, 1990.

Miller, Charles. "The Arts of Venality." *Saturday Review* Vol. 51, no. 35 (August 31, 1968): 24–5.

Ogungbesan, Kolawole. "Symbol and Meaning in *The Beautyful Ones Are Not Yet Born.*" *African Literature Today* Vol. 7 (1975): 93–110.

Palmer, Eustace. "Ayi Kwei Armah: *The Beautyful Ones Are Not Yet Born.*" In *An Introduction to the African Novel.* London: Heinemann, 1972, 129–42.

Review of *The Beautyful Ones Are Not Yet Born,* by Ayi Kwei Armah. *Times Literary Supplement* No. 3500 (March 27, 1969): 333.

Sale, J. Kirk. "The Man in the Middle." *New York Times Book Review* (September 22, 1968): 34.

Wright, Derek. *Ayi Kwei Armah's Africa: The Sources of His Fiction.* London: Hans Zell Publishers, 1989.

————, ed. *Critical Perspectives on Ayi Kwei Armah.* Washington, D.C.: Three Continents Press, 1992.

Isaac Asimov
1920–1992

American novelist, short story writer, nonfiction writer, essayist, editor, and autobiographer.

The Foundation Trilogy (*Foundation*, 1951; *Foundation and Empire*, 1952; *Second Foundation*, 1953)

Plot: The trilogy takes place far in the future and covers a period of over 400 years, focusing on a huge, dying galactic empire. The first book, *Foundation*, comprises five sections. The opening section, "The Psychohistorians," introduces Hari Seldon, a prominent scientist on Trantor, the administrative planet. Seldon is the father of psychohistory, which applies a mathematical model to predict human behavior. Thus the scientist has predicted that the fast-approaching end of the empire will be followed by 30,000 years of anarchy. He believes, however, that this period can be reduced to 1,000 years by establishing—at opposite ends of the galaxy—two foundations, one devoted to physical science and one to psychology. The first of these foundations is established on the planet Terminus, and scientists are to document all human knowledge for posterity. *Foundation*'s remaining four sections ("The Encyclopedists," "The Mayors," "The Traders," and "The Merchant Princes") describe how the First Foundation establishes itself, fends off several threats from neighboring planets, and becomes a major power in the empire.

In "The General," the first section of *Foundation and Empire*, the foundation faces the threat posed by Bel Riose, an ambitious young general who imagines that he can conquer the empire. Eventually, the social and economic forces predicted by Seldon bring him down. By contrast, the title character in "The Mule" could never have been foreseen by Seldon: a genetic mutant, The Mule circumvents Seldon's Plan through his ability to alter people's emotions. By converting his enemies into allies, the Mule bloodlessly conquers of much of the empire and moves toward Terminus. The Second Foundation, supposedly located at "Star's End," is reintroduced in the second half of *Foundation and Empire*, and figures prominently in the trilogy's third volume. The Mule realizes he cannot succeed until he brings down the Second Foundation, whose psychologists control the minds of many people. Instead, they bring down the Mule by destroying his individuality and free will. In the book's second half, the First Foundation—which also resists the idea of being controlled by an outside force—seeks the Second Foundation. By the end of the book, the First Foundation is duped into thinking that the Second Foundation has been vanquished. This error fulfills Seldon's requirement that those whose behavior is being analyzed must be unaware of it, and thus Seldon's Plan can move forward.

Characters: Considered one of the most influential science-fiction writers of all time, Asimov is credited with creating critical status for the genre as well as attracting a wider audience. His fiction is renowned for scientific authenticity, readability, and intellectual sophistication. Originally published in the periodical

Astounding Science Fiction between 1942 and 1950, the *Foundation Trilogy* is Asimov's best-known work; in 1966, it won the Hugo Award for best all-time science-fiction series. A "future history" that is loosely modeled after Edward Gibbon's *Decline and Fall of the Roman Empire* (1776–88), the trilogy manifests Asimov's concern for the question of human survival in the face of advancing technology, overpopulation, and nuclear warfare. Also evident in the novel are investigations of necessity and free will and the idea of historical relativism. Some critics complain that the trilogy's characters lack dimension or are anachronistic, yet others find them colorful, effective players in a fascinating science-fiction epic.

The most significant character in *Foundation* is **Hari Seldon**, the initiator of the Seldon Plan. Seldon is long dead by the end of the first volume, but his projected image appears from the "Vault" to give advice during various crises. One of the empire's greatest scientists, Seldon formulates the science of psychohistory, which reduces human behavior to mathematical equations and thus claims that it can predict how people will act. For the plan to work, however, the human group being analyzed must be very large and must be unaware of the analysis. Seldon believes that a lengthy "Dark Age" is coming that will last 30,000 years, but he feels certain that it can be shortened to 1,000 if two foundations—one focused on the preservation of human knowledge and one on psychology—were to be established at opposite ends of the universe. Other prominent characters in *Foundation* include the intelligent, hardheaded **Salvor Hardin**, the first mayor and protector of the foundation, whose motto is "violence is the last refuge of the incompetent." Initially rather hot-tempered, Hardin eventually mellows into a wise, cautious leader who helps the foundation maintain its independence. The shrewd, forceful **Hober Mallow**, the first of the foundation's Merchant Princes, articulates the concept that its various crises will be resolved not by individual heroics but by economic and social forces.

Foundation and Empire is dominated by **the Mule**, considered one of Asimov's most memorable characters. The Mule diverts the Seldon Plan by changing people's emotions, which allows him to bloodlessly conquer much of the empire and to create out of the fragmented old empire a new, unified civilization. For much of this volume, the Mule disguises himself as a runaway jester, **Magnifico**, who gains sympathy through his misshapen appearance and timidity. The Mule's presence in Asimov's trilogy puts a positive light on individual freedom and motivation but the Mule is sterile, which suggests that he is only an aberration. Furthermore, the Second Foundation psychologists eliminate the qualities of independence and motivation from the Mule's mind, and he lives out his life in oblivious contentment.

Demonstrating the force of historical necessity, the young, ambitious **General Bel Riose** is highly capable and charismatic, loved by his soldiers and even his political opponents, and seems like someone who could conquer the empire. He insists he is not a "silly robot" on a predetermined course, but Bel Riose fails because his emperor, Cleon II, will not tolerate a strong general and Cleon recalls Bel Riose and executes him.

Other significant characters in the second volume include the trader. **Torin Darell** and his wife, **Batya**, who investigate rumors of the Mule's creeping conquest of the empire. Asimov has earned acclaim for his portrayal of Bawtya. Intelligent, courageous, and compassionate she has been called his most successful female character. She is kind to the Mule who, disguised as Magnifico, travels with her and Torin, and he repays her by not manipulating her emotions. **Lathan Devers** is a trader commissioned by the foundation's Merchant Princes to be captured by Bel Riose, then to report on the general's activities and, if possible, thwart his plans.

Another well-portrayed female character in the trilogy is **Arcadia Darell**, the fourteen-year old granddaughter of Batya who, in the third volume, helps to divert the First Foundation in its search for the Second Foundation. In fact, the precocious, highly romantic Arcadia has been psychologically controlled by the Second Foundation since birth. Another agent of the Second Foundation is **Pelleas Anthor**, who tricks the Terminus conspirators into believing that the Second Foundation has been destroyed. **Han Pritcher** defects from the First Foundation to become the Mule's general. He believes the Mule will fulfill of Seldon's prophesied unification and peace. When Pritcher is unable to locate the Second Foundation, the Mule enlists the aid of **Bail Channis**, whose mind he decides not to tamper with. An expansive personality who seems to thrive on war and adventure, Channis is eventually revealed to be another agent of the Second Foundation.

Other significant characters in *Second Foundation* include foundation scientist **Ebling Mis**; Mule's would-be predecessor **Lord Stettin**, and his seemingly vapid but actually powerful wife, **Lady Callia**, who turns out to be a Second Foundation agent; **Homir Munn**, librarian and expert on the Mule who at the bidding of the Terminus conspirators, searches the Mule's old palace for information that would divulge the whereabouts of the Second Foundation; and **Preem Palver**, master psychologist and first speaker of the Second Foundation, who disguises himself as a farmer (and speaks, as several critics have noted, with the accent of a Jewish merchant from New York's Lower East Side) and who eventually performs the restructuring of the Mule's memory so that he no longer seeks the Second Foundation.

Further Reading

Contemporary Literary Criticism. Vols. 1, 3, 9, 19, 26. Detroit: Gale Research.

Dictionary of Literary Biography. Vol. 8. Detroit: Gale Research.

Fiedler, Jean, and Jim Mele. *Isaac Asimov.* New York: Ungar, 1982.

Gunn, James. *Isaac Asimov: The Foundations of Science Fiction.* New York: Oxford University Press, 1982.

Moore, Maxine. "Asimov, Calvin, and Moses." In *Voices for the Future: Essays on Major Science Fiction Writers.* Edited by Thomas D. Clareson. Popular Press, 1976, pp. 88–103.

Olander, Joseph D., and Martin Harry Greenberg, eds. *Isaac Asimov.* New York: Taplinger, 1977.

Patrouch, Joseph F. *The Science Fiction of Isaac Asimov.* Garden City, NJ: Doubleday, 1974.

Patten, Brian. "Asimov's Laws." *Books and Bookmen* (July 1973): 104.

Toupence, William F. *Isaac Asimov.* Boston: Twayne, 1991.

Watt, Donald. "A Galaxy Full of People: Characterization in Asimov's Major Fiction." In *Isaac Asimov.* Edited by Joseph D. Olander and Martin Harry Greenberg. New York: Taplinger, 1974, pp. 135–73.

Margaret Atwood

1939–

Canadian novelist, short story writer, poet, and essayist.

Cat's Eye (novel, 1989)

Plot: For the first time in many years, painter Elaine Risley travels from Vancouver to her home town, Toronto, where a retrospective showing of her work is to take place. As she walks through the city streets, marveling at Toronto's transformation (on the surface, at least) from dull provincialism to cosmopolitan sophistication, Elaine recalls some significant scenes from her childhood and recounts her evolution to the fiftyish, successful artist she is now.

Elaine's now deceased father was a forest entomologist who, for the first eight years of her life, traveled through Canada's northern wilderness tracking insect infestations. The family's idyllic, unconventional existence changed dramatically when Mr. Risley accepted an academic position in Toronto and moved his wife, Elaine, and her brother, Stephen, to a middle-class suburb. Eager for acceptance into the unfamiliar social milieu, Elaine befriended two relatively ordinary girls, Carol Campbell and Grace Smeath, and an extraordinary one, Cordelia. For the next two years the magnetic, manipulative Cordelia led Carol and Grace in tormenting Elaine—continuously criticizing, mocking, and playing tricks on her. This behavior culminated in an incident in a deserted ravine, where Elaine was forced to retrieve her hat and fell into a half-frozen creek while the other girls abandoned her to her fate.

Eventually Elaine achieved independence from Cordelia; during their high school years she even treated Cordelia much as she had been treated. Reaching college age, Elaine decided to become an artist. She had an affair with her drawing instructor but became pregnant by her other lover, a fellow art student whom she married and—after the births of two daughters— later divorced. Increasingly recognized and praised for her feminist paintings, Elaine remarried and moved to Vancouver. During this period she has seen Cordelia only twice, the last time in a private psychiatric hospital Cordelia had been committed to. During Elaine's return to Toronto, she realizes that she is still haunted by Cordelia and by other images of the past, while at the same time she struggles with some aspects of the present. Although Elaine expects to see Cordelia at the retrospective or walking through Toronto, her old tormentor never appears. At the novel's end, when Elaine flies back to Vancouver, she has apparently forgiven Cordelia.

Characters: Considered one of Atwood's most accomplished novels, *Cat's Eye* is particularly praised for its insightful, meticulously detailed depiction of life in 1950s Toronto. Indeed, the parts of the novel that focus on Elaine's childhood have been called its most effective due to their powerful evocation of cruelty, loss, yearning, and eventual redemption.

The central figure in *Cat's Eye* is **Elaine Risley**, a successful painter of about fifty who has spent most of her adulthood in Vancouver. When she returns to her home town of Toronto for a retrospective of her work, Elaine confronts some of the traumas that shaped her early years and that still seem to influence her life. Thus the novel features two narrative voices: the punchy, staccato, often comic prose the grown-up Elaine uses to speak about the present, and the more descriptive passages in which she recounts the past. Elaine resembles other Atwood narrators in her isolation from most of the people around her and her critical stance toward mass culture—qualities that, in *Cat's Eye,* may be attributed not only to Elaine's artistic sensibility but to the emotional damage she has suffered. Elaine's first eight years of life were sheltered, unconventional, and idyllic, as she and her mother and brother followed her entomologist father through the forests of northern Canada. When the family moved to a middle-class Toronto suburb, the formerly happy, tomboyish Elaine found herself adrift in a strange world of female trappings with which her friends Grace and Carol were already comfortable. Elaine craved acceptance into this world, and her unconventional mother was ill-equipped to help her. Thus Elaine fell under the power of the cruel, manipulative Cordelia, who (Elaine later realizes) projected her own sense of inadequacy onto her new friend by methodically berating and tormenting her.

The abuse culminated in the incident in the ravine, where Elaine faced great danger and emerged stronger, no longer willing to submit to Cordelia's domination. Atwood has been particularly praised for her depiction of this scene, which represents an epiphany in Elaine's development. During their high school years Elaine and Cordelia reversed roles, with Elaine gaining power (and even using it unkindly) as Cordelia grew more passive and neurotic. Elaine's artistic talent played an important role in this change: at the age of eight she had looked into a "cat's eye" marble and seen her future as an artist, and her ability to express and define herself through art helped her to survive her childhood trauma. Yet Elaine's later life is also plagued with trouble. As an art student she becomes pregnant, she marries and eventually divorces her first husband, she attempts suicide, she experiences nagging worries about her two daughters, and her current marriage seems rather dull. Although her paintings—which challenge the traditional depictions of women in Western art, connecting them with oppressive political systems—are enthusiastically embraced by feminists, Elaine does not particularly identify with them and resents their attempts to define her. Some critics assert that this alienation, along with her continuing regret that she could not sustain a friendship with Cordelia, suggests that Elaine is unable to connect with other women. Elaine's reconciliation with her past (if that is, indeed, what she achieves) begins before her mother's death, when she rediscovers the cat's eye marble and sees her entire life reflected in it, and culminates in her return to the ravine. There she forgives the emotionally mutilated Cordelia and, finally, seems to recover from the injurious past.

In his review of *Cat's Eye* in *The New York Review of Books,* Robert Towers calls Cordelia an "expertly drawn little villainess—arrogant, manipulative, and inventive in her cruelty." The charismatic Cordelia wields power over not just meek, conventional Grace and Carol but the more sensitive Elaine, whom she targets as a special victim. Cordelia is the youngest of three daughters of wealthy parents; her mother is passive and absentminded, her father superficially charming but abusively misogynistic beneath the surface. Cordelia's personality too is duplicitous: she can act scrupulously polite and refined one moment and rebellious the next, drawing mustaches on catalogue models and talking about "dog poop." Atwood suggests that because Cordelia fails to conform to her society's expectations and is unable to win approval from her father, she projects onto Elaine the role of the "bad child" who needs instruction and punishment. Elaine later realizes that Cordelia was herself the bad child, craving love and acceptance but overcome with fear, loneliness, and an overpowering sense of inadequacy. When the girls become teenagers their roles are reversed, and Cordelia is dependent on Elaine's friendship. Whereas Elaine escapes the stifling confines of middle-class life through art, Cordelia sinks deeper into neurosis, until she is finally confined to a psychiatric institution. While the fact that Cordelia shares the same name as the tragic but innocent heroine in Shakespeare's *King Lear* can be viewed as ironic, Atwood's Cordelia may also be seen as an innocent victim, damaged by her father's—and, by extension, her society's—loathing for women.

Although Elaine's family provides her with a secure and happy early childhood, they do not protect her from Cordelia's cruelty. **Mr. Risley** is a forest entomologist, as Atwood's father was, and Atwood's descriptions of Mr. Risley's work reflect her own knowledge and appreciation of such pursuits. Kind, unworldly, absentminded Mr. Risley is detached from the everyday reality of his children's lives in Toronto. **Mrs. Risley**'s role in Elaine's traumatic experiences is notable for, as many critics have pointed out, she might have been expected to recognize what was happening to her daughter and rescue her. In fact, when Mrs. Risley discusses the ravine incident with the adult Elaine, she tells her daughter how worried she had been; she seems to crave forgiveness for her inaction, but Elaine is not yet ready to dispense it. Through Elaine's brilliant, intellectual brother, **Stephen**, Atwood introduces several contemporary theories of quantum physics (drawing from the work of such scientists as Carl Sagan and Stephen Hawking), including the expansion of the universe, string theory, and particularly the concept of time as having shape rather than as linear. Whereas Elaine responds to the family's move to the alien world of Toronto by trying to conform to its expectations, Stephen retreats into a private realm of thought, eventually becoming a successful physicist. Most critics deem his murder by terrorists improbable and awkward, an incident included merely to give the novel a topical flavor.

The two girls who provide Elaine with her first exposure to middle-class life and culture and who assist Cordelia in tormenting Elaine are **Carol Campbell** and **Grace Smeath**. The bland, relatively normal Carol responds to vulgarity with a feminine "Ew!" and the sanctimoniously proper Grace invites the other girls to her house to cut pictures of household appliances from catalogues. The two girls' parents—particularly the grotesquely fat **Mrs. Smeath**—are also significant characters in the novel. A grimly pious evangelical Christian, Mrs. Smeath not only is aware of the cruel treatment Elaine is receiving but seems to approve of it. Elaine later expresses her hatred for Mrs. Smeath, achieving a kind of vengeance when she portrays her in her paintings as a monstrous, reptilian figure. **Mrs. Campbell** conforms to the conventional wife and mother type through her passivity and dependence, her overriding concern with appearances, and her veneration of domestic objects; Elaine is fascinated with her "twin" sweater sets, which her own mother does not wear. Another repressive father figure, **Mr. Campbell** has been known to whip his daughter with the buckle end of a belt.

Atwood's portrayal of Cordelia's family helps explain her behavior. Childlike, relieved from worries about money, and expected to fulfill only a decorative function, **Cordelia's mother** spends her time painting pretty pictures and redecorating her house. Critics have identified Cordelia's misogynistic father as the embodiment of the hostile patriarch: charming and affable in public, he treats his wife and daughters with contempt and even rage in private. Echoing him, Cordelia repeats his command to "Wipe that smirk off your face" when she torments Elaine. Unlike Cordelia, her sisters Perdita and Miranda have adapted to conventional expectations. Intensely focused on their appearance, they joke that they look like "Haggis McBaggis," thus expressing a fear of rejection instilled by their father's cheerful but sinister complaint that he is "surrounded by hags." All four females in Cordelia's family behave in a markedly different way when the father is not at home, relaxing their usual rigid correctness.

Other characters in *Cat's Eye* include **Josef**, Elaine's highly romantic but essentially insincere art instructor with whom she has an affair; and **Jon**, her fellow art student, by whom she becomes pregnant and to whom she is married for a time. (Elaine stays in Jon's empty apartment when she returns to Toronto for the retrospective.) The fact that Elaine is involved with both men at once and that her marriage to Jon eventually fails signify her impaired ability to commit to and sustain relationships.

Further Reading

Banerjee, Chinmoy. "Hiding Art in Cat's Eye." *Modern Fiction Studies* Vol. 36, no. 4 (Winter 1990): 513–22.

Brookner, Anita. "Unable to Climb Out of the Abyss." *Spectator* Vol. 262, no. 8377 (January 28, 1989): 32–3.

Contemporary Literary Criticism. Vols. 2, 3, 4, 8, 13, 15, 25, 44. Detroit: Gale Research.

Dictionary of Literary Biography Vol. 53. Detroit: Gale Research.

Ingersoll, Earl G. "Margaret Atwood's 'Cat's Eye': Re-Viewing Women in a Postmodern World." *Ariel* Vol. 22, no. 4 (October 1991): 17–27.

Kanfer, Stefan. "Time Arrested." *Time,* Vol. 133, no. 6 (February 6, 1989): 70.

Lurie, Alison. "The Mean Years." *Ms.,* Vol. 17, no. 9 (March 1989): 38–41.

"Margaret Atwood: Author of *Cat's Eye*." *Bestsellers* Vol. 89, no. 2. Detroit: Gale Research.

McCombs, Judith. *Margaret Atwood: A Reference Guide.* Boston, MA: G. K. Hall, 1991.

McDermott, Alice. "What Little Girls Are Really Made Of." *New York Times Book Review,* (February 5, 1989): 1, 35.

Robinson, Lillian S. "Coming of Age in Toronto." *Nation* Vol. 248, no. 22 (June 5, 1989): 776–79.

Strehle, Susan. "Margaret Atwood: *Cat's Eye* and the Subjective Author." In *Fiction in the Quantum Universe.* Chapel Hill: University of North Carolina Press, 1992, 159–89.

Thurman, Judith. "When You Wish Upon a Star." *New Yorker* Vol. 65, no. 15 (May 29, 1989): 108–110.

Towers, Robert. "Mystery Women." *New York Review of Books* Vol. 36, no. 7 (April 27, 1989): 50–52.

Donald Barthelme
1931–1989

American short story writer, novelist, essayist, and author of books for children.

"Me and Miss Mandible" (short story, 1964)

Plot: The story is composed of twenty-seven diary entries chronicling the experiences of a thirty-five-year-old insurance claims adjuster who, due either to a bureaucratic error or as punishment for trying to help an old woman collect on a claim, has been made a fifth-grade student at Horace Greeley Elementary School. The narrator accepts his odd situation and even admits that he has long felt different from others and is in need of "reworking." He believes the teacher, Miss Mandible, wants her overgrown student sexually, but he is distracted by the attentions of a precocious female student named Sue Ann Brownley. The narrator records the activities, conflicts, and percolating emotions of his fellow fifth-graders, such as when Sue Ann viciously kicks his ankle to revenge a perceived grievance, or Bobby Vanderbilt manipulates Miss Mandible, or Frankie Randolph concentrates on the love affairs of Elizabeth Taylor, Eddie Fisher, and Debbie Reynolds. The narrator accommodates himself to his surroundings by learning to pack his own lunch and smoking only "in the boy's john, like everyone else"; in some ways he finds the classroom a welcome refuge from the demands of adult life. At the end of the story, Sue Ann Brownley discovers the narrator having sex with Miss Mandible in the cloakroom. The narrator fails to convince the school authorities that he is not a corruptible minor, and Miss Mandible is consequently "ruined but fulfilled."

Characters: Highly acclaimed for his unconventional, experimental fiction, Barthelme employs a "verbal collage" technique that some critics have termed an "anti-story." Barthelme's short fiction often seems to resist explication, for plot and character are much less important than inventive wordplay and irony. Barthelme's method juxtaposes fragments of information and conversation, with references to contemporary culture, technology, and mass media, as well as flashes of humor and sadness. Reviewers have identified in Barthelme's fiction such themes as the inability of language to effectively convey feelings, the complications and frailties of relationships between men and women, the relentless triviality of contemporary life, and the role of the artist in the modern world. A playful parody of precocious children, bureaucratic foolishness, and general hypocrisy, "Me and Miss Mandible" is probably the best known of Barthelme's earliest stories. Infused with the surrealism and irrationality, it led many commentators to compare Barthelme with Franz

Kafka and Jorge Luis Borges. Black humor and underlying morality also characterize Barthelme's writing.

The story's **narrator** is a thirty-five-year-old insurance claims adjuster acclimating himself to his new role as a fifth-grade student and making the best of a situation that no one else around him seems to recognize as irrational. Through his diary entries the narrator discloses that his adult life has consisted of a grim stint in the army, when he felt his identity slipping away from him, followed by a marriage and career that both ultimately failed. His current predicament is apparently a punishment for misinterpreting his employer's stated dedication to serving its customers: he helped an elderly widow collect a claim rightfully due her. The narrator admits that since his army days, when he frequently questioned the value of apparently pointless activities, he has felt isolated from others. He yearns to be "typical" and feels that he needs "reworking in some fundamental way." Thus he adjusts his habits to his new life—he gives up alcohol, smokes only in the boy's bathroom, and petitions for a larger desk. However, the demands of adult sexuality do not subside and find gratification in Miss Mandible. The narrator's musings on the unreliability of "signs" underscore the idea that life and society promise things that are often unattainable. For example, the narrator's company's motto—"Here to Help in Time of Need"—proves untrue; his wife, **Brenda** (whom Sue Ann Brownly resembles in some unpleasant ways), is unfaithful to him; the American flag no longer means the same thing to everyone. Lacking confidence, unstable, and anxious, the narrator possesses traits common to many of Barthelme's characters. Some critics consider the narrator a parody of such celebrated literary protagonists as Fyodor Dostoyevsky's Underground Man, James Joyce's Stephen Daedalus, and J. D. Salinger's Holden Caulfield. Through this simultaneously absurd and poignant narrator, Barthelme explores such matters as the blurred distinction between children and adults ("There are only individual egos, crazy for love"), the arbitrary nature of social conventions, conformity, and the brutal fact that "arrangements sometimes slip . . . errors are made . . . signs are misread."

Miss Mandible teachers the fifth grade class to which the narrator is assigned. He suspects that she wants him sexually and that she knows he does not belong there, even though she treats the adult-sized narrator as just another eleven-year-old child. She worries about the advanced quality of the narrator's essays and asks if someone is helping him write them. She also doesn't push the issue of the desk being far too small for him. The narrator views these incidents as proof that she fears he will be sent away. The narrator's sexual attraction to Miss Mandible and belief that she desires him too are constant reminders of life outside the classroom—although at the same time the narrator considers his teacher more childlike than the worldly Sue Ann, and he notes that the classroom is a veritable cauldron of titillation. Near the story's end Miss Mandible finally gives in to her passion. The narrator reports that even though the teacher's career is ruined by seducing a "minor," she achieves sexual fulfillment. Some critics have found this ending vaguely hopeful or at least indicating that the connections human beings make with each other are valuable.

The most notable of the students among whom the narrator finds himself is **Sue Ann Brownley,** a girl who, "although between eleven and eleven-and-a-half (she refuses to reveal her exact age) . . . is clearly a woman, with a woman's disguised aggression and a woman's peculiar contradictions." Sue Ann expresses dominance over the narrator by kicking his ankle, and this hostility reminds him of his wife, Brenda, who left him for another man. The narrator believes Sue Ann and Miss Mandible are competing for him. Sue Ann mistakenly thinks that making him limp is a victory, but it is the teacher who has sex with the narrator in the cloakroom. Sue Ann, who discovers the pair, vengefully reports this scandal to the principal. Like another female student, **Frankie Randolph** (an avid reader of *Movie-TV Secrets* magazine), Sue Ann passionately follows the escapades of various American celebrities. The narrator muses that Elizabeth Taylor, Eddie Fisher, and Debbie

Reynolds are exaggerated and shallow models of social behavior. Other students at Horace Greeley Elementary include **Bobby Vanderbilt,** a boy obsessed with sports cars, and **Harry Broan,** who is frequently teased because his wealthy father invented the Broan Bathroom Vent. He seems grateful that the narrator refuses to fight him.

"Views of My Father Weeping" (short story, 1970)

Plot: Through a series of paragraphs separated by bullet points, the story interweaves the narrator's attempts to learn how his father died with "views" of the father weeping and behaving incongruously (such as making thumbprints in a tray of cupcakes, shooting a water pistol, clumsily upsetting the furniture in a doll's house, and attending a class in good behavior). The sections of the story about the accident, in which his father was supposedly run over by a carriage, are pointedly realistic. Two witnesses, including a little girl, agree that the carriage's passenger appeared to be an aristocrat. Other observers provide conflicting accounts of the father's behavior at the time of the collision: one claims the old man was drunk and caused the accident himself, while another asserts that it was the driver's fault. Eventually the little girl reveals the coachman's name to be Lars Bang. He visits the narrator's home and informs him that he was indeed involved in the mishap and will explain the circumstances later. Subsequently the narrator is drinking wine with Lars Bang, two other men, and a beautiful young girl. The coachman explains that the narrator's drunken father set upon the passing coach and attacked the pair of horses, who ran over him as they fled in panic. Lars Bang concludes that the narrator is "now in possession of all of the facts," but the girl then claims that "Bang is an absolute bloody liar." The story ends with "Etc."

Characters: "Views of My Father Weeping" features the fragmented style that character-izes Barthelme's work. In place of a standard plot, disconnected episodes or narrative chunks are strung together to form a "verbal collage"; characters are only sketchily defined and serve primarily as vehicles for Barthelme's inventive wordplay. Although some critics have faulted Barthelme for failing to convey in his fiction any sense of morality or order, others have countered that—by decrying the creative vacuum of modern life in an innovative, insightful way—he does take a moral stance. In any case "Views of My Father Weeping" is considered one of Barthelme's most accomplished stories. It blends heavily realistic, nineteenth-century-style narrative passages with paragraphs relaying twentieth-century concerns, images, and motifs. Barthelme challenges the concept of traditional realism, because he believes it forces on the reader a false sense of order. Instead he prefers "dreck" (a term first used in his 1967 novel *Snow White*): an accumulation of seemingly irrelevant material that "can supply a kind of 'sense' of what is going on." A compelling if bewildering story, "Views of My Father Weeping" uses a highly unconventional narrative pattern to explore the difficulties of the father-son relationship.

Like other Barthelme protagonists, the unnamed **narrator** is—at least within the story's contemporary segments—bewildered, disoriented, and isolated in his struggle to gather and synthesize information about his father. In the segments narrated in the style of a nineteenth-century novel, the son adopts the cool, detached tone of a detective as he attempts to uncover the facts of his father's death. The "views" of the father weeping and performing other acts, however, give the reader a broader view of the son's strong but ambiguous, contradictory feelings of guilt, sorrow, resentment, hostility, and love. Critics have interpreted the story in various ways: some maintained that the realistic narrative about the carriage accident does not record an actual event—it is, rather, the narrator's wish or fantasy about his father's death or a reflection of his own fear of death. No clear vision of the father ever emerges from the story; different fragments portray him as clownish, childish, stern, and drunken. Reviews have noticed that, despite the narrator's attempts to learn the facts about his father, language can never adequately convey personality, relationships, and emotions. The word "Etc." at the story's end also underscores this inconclusiveness.

The segments of the story written in the style of nineteenth-century writers introduce only a few notable characters. **Lars Bang** is the coachman driving the carriage that killed the narrator's father, and he provides an orderly version of the incident. Described as helpful but vaguely malicious, Bang relates the details of the accident "as if he were telling a tavern story," characterizing the father as a brutal, irresponsible drunkard who caused his own death. Bang asserts that this account is the true one, but **the beautiful girl** who is listening with the narrator contradicts him and claims that "Bang is an absolute bloody liar." The narrator notes that the coachman's name is "not unlike my own name," which hints that Bang may be the narrator's double and that both are liars trying to hide their involvement in the father's death. In any case, the story offers no resolution or confirmation. Its final "Etc." implies that Bang's story may or may not be true and that these events and processes will continue indefinitely. The eleven- or twelve-year-old **little girl** who witnesses part of the accident later goes to the narrator's room to offer new information (the coachman's name) in exchange for some promised candy; it may or may not be significant that the narrator has previously claimed that he "could be out in the streets feeling up eleven-year-old girls in their soldier drag, there are thousands, as alike as pennies. . . ."

"The Indian Uprising" (short story, 1968)

Plot: The story is marginally structured as a report of a battle between troops led partly by the narrator and a band of "Comanches" and their ghetto-dwelling sympathizers. Between accounts of the fighting and of the torture of a captured Comanche are the narrator's disjointed observations, conversations with Sylvia (his most recent lover, apparently), yearning for an unidentified "you," and encounters with a plain, rather stern schoolteacher, Miss R. When he decides that he knows nothing, the narrator goes to Miss R for instruction, who says she reveres only the "hard, brown, nutlike word," Miss R alternates between berating the narrator and addressing him in fond endearments. Meanwhile Sylvia betrays the narrator by joining the Indians in their uprising. At the end of the story, the narrator and his friends Block and Kenneth are attacked by their enemies, with whom, the reader learns, Miss R is actually allied. She orders the narrator to remove his belt and shoelaces, suggesting that he may now be tortured by his captors.

Characters: "The Indian Uprising" is considered one of Barthelme's most intriguing and accomplished short stories. Although it is loosely structured as a kind of battle account, the story exemplifies its author's innovative, fragmented technique. Barthelme's style is a "collage" assembled from apparently unrelated observations and bits of information—the statement of the narrator in "The Indian Uprising" that "strings of language extend in every direction to bind the world into a rushing, ribald whole" is an apt description for Barthelme's philosophy. In his 1967 novel, *Snow White,* Barthelme suggests that the accumulated, ironically intoned details he terms "dreck" may reveal as much or more about life than more conventional, realistic narrative. surfeited with ironic humor and inhabited by characters who are only vaguely portrayed, "The Indian Uprising" parodies the mythology of American "Wild West" fiction and cinema. Commentators have interpreted the story— which first appeared during the turbulent protests against the Vietnam war—as commentary on how obsessed we are with war and how we romanticize it.

The story offers little background information about its **narrator,** who seems to be one of the leaders of the troops the "Comanches" and their sympathizers are attacking. He participates in the torture of the captured Comanche and describes various battle scenarios. These descriptions are interlaced with seemingly unrelated comments directed at various women in his life as well as his accounts of his visits with Miss R. His relationship with this teacher, which he initiates after deciding that he "knows nothing," seems ironic when Miss R turns out to be a member of the insurgency. Some critics have identified the narrator as a member of the well-educated, affluent urban class, too smug and self-deluded to recognize what is going on around him. His frequent comments about the table he is making from a door seemed to some critics to mean the narrator is preoccupied with trivial details even in the midst of a crisis. Others critics have focused on the narrator's relationships with women, including Sylvia—who seems to be his current lover—and a never-identified "you" who may be Sylvia or someone else. It is even possible that the uprising is a metaphor of the struggle to obtain fulfillment in love, a battle waged not against a band of savage-eyed Indians but against Sylvia. Another reviewer called the narrator an artist who destroyed himself by never internalizing social values, which left him open to the onslaught of life's "primitive" elements. At the end of "The Indian Uprising," the narrator is taken prisoner, stripped of the "bindings" of belt and shoelaces, and subjected to chaos and the unknown.

Most of the story's other characters—some critics have argued, that they are not characters at all but vehicles for Barthelme's verbal experimentation—are women, and images of love and war are closely intertwined. As the story opens, it appears that **Sylvia** is the narrator's main love interest, but she eventually abandons him, running off to join the Comanches and "uttering shrill cries." The story may be a metaphor for the narrator's break-up with Sylvia, whose angry words can then be viewed as the insurgent forces opposing him. The narrator also longs for an unidentified "you"; this woman is apparently a star of pornographic films and may even be Sylvia. **Miss R** is the teacher to whom the narrator's friends send him for further education. She is supposedly unorthodox but successful with difficult cases like himself. Her methods are bizarre—she alternately insults and cajoles the narrator, calling him "my darling, my thistle, my poppet." Miss R claims that truth lies in the "litany" and that she reveres only "the hard, brown, nutlike word." Some reviewers have felt that she parodies the traditional schoolteacher type or is an ironic reversal of this stereotype, since she turns out to be on the Indian side in the uprising. Also referred to in the story is **Jane**; the narrator has heard that she was "beaten up by a dwarf in a bar on Tenerife," and (despite his stated desire to remain "nonevaluative") he admonishes her for having an affair with a married man.

Other characters mentioned in "The Indian Uprising" include the **captured Comanche brave,** whose torture comprises a central motif in the story and who ultimately reveals his name to be Gustave Aschenbach, the name of the emotionally tortured protagonist in Thomas Mann's 1912 novel, *Death in Venice;* and the narrator's friends **Block** and **Kenneth,** who seem to be his co-defenders against the siege of the Indians.

Further Reading

Aldridge, John W. "Donald Barthelme and the Doggy Life." 1968. Reprinted in *The Devil in the Fire: Retrospective Essays on American Literature and Culture, 1951–1971.* 261–66. New York: Harper's Magazine Press, 1972.

Barth, John. "Thinking Man's Minimalist: Honoring Barthelme." *New York Times Book Review* (September 3, 1989): 9.

Contemporary Literary Criticism. Vols. 1, 2, 3, 5, 6, 8, 13, 23, 46, 59. Detroit: Gale Research.

Couturier, Maurice, and Régis Durand. *Donald Barthelme.* London: Methuen, 1982.

Critical Essays on Donald Barthelme. New York: G. K. Hall, 1992.

Gass, William H. "The Leading Edge of the Trash Phenomenon." In *Fiction and the Figures of Life,* 97–103. New York: Knopf, 1970.

Gordon, Lois. *Donald Barthelme.* Boston: Twayne, 1981.

Klinkowitz, Jerome. "Donald Barthelme." In *Literary Disruptions: The Making of a Post-Contemporary American Fiction.* 62–81. Champaign: University of Illinois Press, 1975.

Leitch, Thomas. "Donald Barthelme and the End of the End." *Modern Fiction Studies* Vol. 28, no. 1 (spring 1982): 129–43.

McCaffery, Larry. "Meaning and Non-Meaning in Barthelme's Fictions." *Journal of Aesthetic Education* Vol. 13, no. 1 (January 1979): 69–79.

Molesworth, Charles. *Donald Barthelme's Fiction: The Ironist Saved from Drowning.* Columbia: University of Missouri Press, 1982.

Review of Contemporary Fiction (special issue on Barthelme) Vol. 11 (summer 1991): 75–82.

Robison, James C. "1969–1980: Experiment and Tradition." In *The American Short Story, 1945–1980.* Edited by Gordon Weaver 77-110. Boston: Twayne, 1983, 77–110.

Roe, Barbara L. *Donald Barthelme: A Study of the Short Fiction.* New York: Twayne, 1992.

Romano, John. "Working Like a Stand-Up Comic." *New York Times Book Review* (October 4, 1981): 9, 23.

Short Story Criticism Vol. 2. Detroit: Gale Research.

Stengel, Wayne B. *The Shape of Art in the Short Stories of Donald Barthelme.* Baton Rouge: Louisiana State University Press, 1985.

Trachtenberg, Stanley. *Understanding Donald Barthelme.* Columbia: University of South Carolina Press, 1990.

Upton, Lee. "Failed Artists in Donald Barthelme's 'Sixty Stories.'" *Critique: Studies in Modern Fiction* Vol. 26, no. 1 (fall 1984): 11–17.

Ann Beattie

1947–

American short story writer, novelist, children's writer, and critic.

Chilly Scenes of Winter (novel, 1976)

Plot: The novel is set in the mid-1970s in a large American city, probably Washington, D.C. The central character is twenty-seven-year-old Charles, who obsesses over Laura. Though they had an affair, she has returned to her husband, Jim, and her stepdaughter, Rebecca. Charles and his best friend, Sam, were college students during the 1960s. As with some of their generation, they lack direction and purpose. Charles admires the more cynical Sam for his success with women, but Sam regards Charles as a foolish romantic for pining after Laura. Indeed, Charles idealizes her and spends his time imagining scenes that bear no relation to reality. Meanwhile, his own family and other friends make various emotional demands on him. Charles's mother, Clara, is a self-pitying hypochondriac who constantly demands attention and sympathy from Charles and his sister, Susan. She is eventually admitted to a psychiatric hospital. Clara's second husband, Pete, tries unsuccessfully to win his stepchildren's love; although Susan tolerates him, Charles considers Pete a loser who misapprehends his wife's true character or problems. When Sam loses his job, he moves in with Charles, further burdening his friend, and Charles's former lover, Pamela, also arrives, seeking help with her problems.

While on a date with Laura's close friend Betty—whom he pursues only to feel closer to Laura—Charles learns that Laura has left her husband. Although somewhat hurt that Laura has not informed him herself, Charles immediately contacts Laura and begs to see her. She suspects that Charles is more concerned about his own needs than hers, but Laura allows him to come to her apartment. Charles pronounces their reunion a "happy ending.".

Characters: *Chilly Scenes of Winter,* Beattie's first novel, was highly acclaimed by critics, who felt she captured the mood of the 1970s with the same skill and perception as J. D. Salinger captured the 1950s in his classic, *Catcher in the Rye.* Beattie is said to have based the novel's characters on her own friends and other members of her generation—educated idealists of the 1960s counterculture, they now experience doubt, indecisiveness, and ennui. Written in spare, dispassionate prose, the novel contains many references to American popular culture, including names of junk food restaurants and rock n' roll celebrities. While some commentators find the accumulated details in Beattie's work irritating and the milieu she chronicles shallow and limited, most lauded her perceptive portrayals of young adults struggling with frail relationships, self-identification, and alienation.

The central figure in *Chilly Scenes of Winter* is **Charles,** a bewildered dreamer. Nearly thirty, he seems suspended in extended adolescence. Despite his education and intelligence, he works in a boring bureaucratic job. Listening to Bob Dylan and Janis Joplin, reminiscing about the sixties with his friend Sam, and yearning for Laura are all that sustain him. Critics have praised Beattie's portrait of the disillusioned sixties idealist, a nostalgic, gentle male character. The protagonist shares traits with Jay Gatsby in F. Scott Fitzgerald's acclaimed 1925 novel, *The Great Gatsby.* Like Jay, Charles escapes his mundane life by inventing an ideal love. His obsession with Laura enables him to evade the emotional demands of others, such as his freeloading, unemployed friend Sam or his neurotic mother. Charles believes that Clara feigns mental illness in order to shirk responsibility, and he scorns his stepfather for failing to realize this. The irony is that Charles is unable to train his perceptive abilities on himself. His fantasies focus particularly on a dessert Laura prepared with oranges and cognac, which symbolizes his wish to have his life magically put in order. When he reunites with her at the end of the novel, she serves him the special dessert. A few reviewers have denounced the novel's "happy ending," as Charles describes it, as facile and unrealistic, but others have asserted that Beattie planted enough clues about Charles's character to leave the reader undeluded about his future.

Between Charles and his companion, **Sam,** exists a strong bond based on their shared past and mutual disillusionment with adult life. Despite a successful college career, Sam is too unmotivated to attend law school, so he clerks in a clothing store until he loses his job and moves in with Charles. Self-centered and much more cynical than his idealistic friend (personifying the quintessential 1970s youth), Sam leads an essentially aimless life. Yet Charles believes his friend possesses all the desirable qualities he lacks, particularly an ability to attract women. Sam does engage in a series of brief sexual liaisons, but he has no wish to commit himself to anyone, and Charles's obsession with Laura exasperates him. However, Sam's excessive grieving over his beloved dog's death parallels Charles's yearning for Laura and suggests that Sam harbors a similar need for love. Critics who have detected similarities between *Chilly Scenes of Winter* and *The Great Gatsby* have compared Sam to the cynical, aloof Nick Carroway.

Charles's family provides one of the novel's several disheartening views of love and marriage. His mother, **Clara,** is a hypochondriac with addictions to bathing, alcohol, laxatives, and movie magazines. Neurotic and prone to theatrics, she constantly complains to her children, accusing them of ignoring or minimizing her problems. Self-absorbed and blind to her children's needs, Clara resembles other parents in Beattie's fiction. Charles considers **Pete,** Clara's second husband, a loser who misapprehends his wife's mental condition. After she is committed to a psychiatric hospital, Pete enrolls her in dance lessons to help her forget about her troubles. Then he obsessively seeks his stepchildren's love. Charles's nineteen-year-old sister, **Susan,** is no sixties flower child. Wiser and more mature than her brother, she decries his obsession with Laura, telling Charles: "You deliberately make yourself suffer all the time because then you can be aware of *yourself.*" Susan understands their mother and stepfather better than her brother. She perceives Clara's ailments as essentially real if overdramatized, and she tolerates the annoying Pete for her mother's sake and out of pity.

Other characters in the novel include **Laura,** the idealized object of Charles's yearning. Charles considers her the epitome of domestic bliss and free of bourgeois constraints, but Laura is neither of these things. Her relationship with her husband, **Jim, or "Ox,"** is emotionally barren, but when the marriage breaks up, she regrets losing her stepdaughter, **Rebecca.** Reviewers who have found similarities between *Chilly Scenes of Winter* and *The Great Gatsby* have compared Laura to Daisy Buchanan. Charles's former lover, **Pamela,** brings some comic relief to the novel: described as "a compendium of 1970s cultural cliches" by critic Christina Murphy, she is a vegetarian who is considering becoming a lesbian. Susan is dating a pompous medical student, **Mark.** Charles considers Mark superficial, crass, and ambitious. Charles takes Laura's good friend **Betty** on a date just to feel closer to his true beloved; she supplies the news that Laura has left her husband.

"Janus" (short story, 1986)

Plot: Andrea is a real estate agent who owns a beautiful bowl that she places in homes she is trying to sell as a way to influence the buyers' impressions. Andrea thinks about the bowl often, analyzing its attractions and her own relationship to it. Her stockbroker husband calls the bowl "pretty" but is otherwise uninterested in it. Andrea becomes increasingly convinced that it brings her luck, and she grows even more deliberate in using it. When she forgets to retrieve the bowl after showing a house, she returns for it in panic. Andrea dreams about the bowl, though she is unable to discuss with her husband that it is responsible for her professional success. She feels her mysterious relationship with the bowl is almost a love affair for she is possessive and anxious about losing it. The bowl was a gift from a lover who bought it for her after they admired it a craft fair. Before they broke up, he complained that Andrea was "two-faced" because she refused to leave her husband for him. The story ends with Andrea's reflection about the bowl: "In its way, it was perfect: the world cut in half, deep and smoothly empty."

Characters: Some critics regard Beattie's short fiction as even more accomplished than her novels. Like the short stories of American writers J. D. Salinger, John Cheever, and John Updike—whose work also frequently appeared in the *New Yorker* magazine and to whom she is frequently compared—Beattie's stories concern characters who live relatively uneventful but regret-tinged lives. "Janus" is one of Beattie's most celebrated stories. It was published in the collection *Where You'll Find Me, and Other Stories,* in which reviewers detected a shift toward more lyrical, subjective writing than Beattie had previously employed. The beautiful, perpetually empty bowl serves as a central metaphor for the sense of loss that hovers over the story.

The protagonist of "Janus" is **Andrea,** a real estate agent who attributes her professional success to a bowl she describes as "both subtle and noticeable." She obsesses over it, analyzes her own and other people's reactions to it, and believes that she has some deep, mysterious connection with it. Given to her by a former lover, the bowl becomes a kind of lover itself—her feelings about it are like a guilty secret, for she feels possessive of it as well as anxious that it will be lost or damaged. Andrea attributes her success to the bowl and wishes she could thank it in some way. The anxiety she experiences when she forgets it in a house she has shown she believes is similar to stories of parents who discover they have driven off without their children. The bowl may also bear some association with her childlessness. Andrea's devotion to it may be a metaphor for a writer's devotion to her craft or of the protagonist's desire to remain, like the bowl, "still and safe, unilluminated." The latter possibility is supported by the lover's accusation that Andrea is "two-faced" because she refuses to choose between her husband and her lover.

The only other significant character in the story is Andrea's unnamed **husband,** a stockbroker with whom she seems to have a placid, fairly satisfactory marriage. He tells friends that he appreciates Andrea's combination of aesthetic sense and practicality. Andrea's husband calls the bowl "pretty" but does not share her fascination with it. The two are similar in personality: both are quiet, reflective, and slow to judge but very firm once they have made a decision. Andrea reflects that while she enjoys irony, her husband becomes "impatient or dismissive when matters become many-sided or unclear." This may explain why she feels hesitant to discuss with him her mysterious feelings about the bowl.

Picturing Will (novel, 1989)

Plot: The novel comprises three sections, and interspersed throughout them are the italicized musings of a voice not identified until the end of the novel. The central character of the first section, entitled "Mother," is Jody, a talented photographer who makes her living filming mundane events. Four years earlier, when her son, Will, was one year old, Jody's husband, Wayne, abandoned them. She has since struggled to support herself and her child. Her kind, nearly ideal lover, Mel, wants Jody to marry him and move to New York, where he believes her artistic gift is more likely to be appreciated. Near the end of this section Jody and her friends are driving to a party when they accidentally run over a deer; Jody photographs the scene and the participants' reactions.

The second section, entitled "Father," takes place two years later. Jody has married Mel, moved to New York, and achieved fame through the sponsorship of Lord Haverford, a gallery owner the other characters call "Haveabud." Jody's photographs of the deer accident propel her to prominence, for which she was featured in *Vogue* magazine. Now seven years old, Will travels with his stepfather, Haveabud, and the art promoter's young ward, Spencer, to visit Wayne, living with his third wife, Corky, in Florida. Wayne is as irresponsible and impervious to other people—including his own son—as usual. Will witnesses Haveabud seducing Spencer in a hotel room and sees his father being led away by police. Then he returns to his mother in New York.

Set about twenty years later, the final section, "Child," is narrated by Will, now an art historian. During a visit to his mother and stepfather, Will learns that Mel has long labored on a book about childraising. Mel presents the manuscript to Will as a source of advice for his own life. It turns out that the wise observations about parents and children that appear throughout the novel are Mel's, and that he has been the devoted guardian that Will did not have in Jody or Wayne.

Characters: This critically praised novel differs from Beattie's previous work because it does not focus on the concerns of angst-ridden survivors of the 1960s but on the various members of a contemporary family and their connections with each other. Commentators have identified as its central theme the vulnerability of children in the face of their parents' other interests and obsessions. Beattie suggested in interviews that she injected more of her own viewpoint into this novel than in her previous fiction.

The central character in the first section of *Picturing Will* is **Jody,** whose last name—along with most information about her background—is never disclosed. The only background supplied that she married Wayne against the advice of her friends and family and that she has struggled since Wayne's departure to support herself and Will. Her job as a clerk in a photography studio grew into a career as a photographer much in demand for shooting the social milestones of her small town. She brings a strong aesthetic sense to her work and is more talented than her job requires. (Jody's reflections on art and photography provide an informative window into the creative process.) At the beginning of the novel Jody appears to be a self-sacrificing single mother, but by the end of the "Mother" section her character is more complex. The speed with which she jumps from the car and begins photographing the horrified witnesses to the deer accident, for example, signifies a kind of ruthlessness that will be borne out in her later career. As the second section opens Jody has married Mel and achieved fame as a photographer. At the same time she has passed on much of the responsibility for her son's upbringing to Mel. Beattie suggests that Jody prefers the creation of art over the creation of a child's life: her well-developed aesthetic sense does not extend to accurately "picturing" Will and his needs. Beattie has openly discussed her own decision not to have children. Her portrait of a woman who devotes the best part of her time and energy to her work rather than to her son may reflect Beattie's interest in the costs such a choice imposes on both parent and child.

Although he is the title character, Jody's son, **Will,** is not particularly well developed. Five when the novel begins and in his mid-twenties when it closes, Beattie dramatizes through him a central concern: the vulnerability of a child when a parent fails "to rise to the occasion" of parenthood. Wayne epitomizes this failure—he abandons his son—but Jody also is indicted for her devotion to her career and lack of interest in Will. Will survives his childhood, and much of the credit is given to Mel, who nurtures Will in ways his biological parents cannot. By the end of the novel Will is a well-adjusted art historian. Mel gives him a manuscript, a caring legacy to pass on to his own children.

At the beginning of *Picturing Will,* Jody's supportive lover, **Mel,** seems bland and unexciting. As the novel progresses, however, his importance grows; he helps Jody to develop her career because he introduces her to Lord Haverford and he nurtures her son. Reversing the classic fairy-tale model, the stepparent turns out to be the *good* parent who will guide Will through childhood. The reader learns at the end of the novel that the italicized musings laced throughout the story—delivered in a voice that novelist and critic T. Coraghessan Boyle called "inspired, rhapsodic and true"—are from a journal Mel has been keeping over the years. He gives his wise, thoughtful observations about parents' responsibilities and children's needs and fears to Will as a legacy of love, for Will to pass along when the proper time comes. Through his writing Mel might have been, like Jody, an artist, but that he chose the role of committed parent instead provides a twist on the stereotypes of men's and women's roles in childraising.

Jody's first husband, **Wayne,** exemplifies the bad parent model. Handsome and glib, Wayne is a self-centered, self-pitying whiner who, Jody says, "had always been *about* to create a life for himself." Wayne proves consistently unreliable and insensitive. When seven-year-old Will arrives in Florida for a visit with his father, Wayne is too busy being unfaithful to his wife to attend to his son, and as Will leaves, Wayne is being arrested on a drug charge. The novel's final section reveals that Wayne has completely disappeared from Will's life and reportedly lives in Mexico City.

Other characters in *Picturing Will* include Wayne's third wife, **Corky.** One of Will's numerous surrogate parents, she hopes her kindness to the boy will spur Wayne's interest in having a child with her. **Mary Vickers** is Jody's unhappily married friend. **Wagoner, or "Wag,"** is Mary's appealing little boy and Will's playmate. **Lord Haverford,** or **"Haveabud,"** is the charming but pederastic art gallery owner who champions Jody's photography. **Spencer** is a dinosaur-loving little boy who, in a disturbing scene in a hotel room, is seduced by Lord Haverford, his supposed protector.

Further Reading

"Ann Beattie: Author of *Picturing Will.*" In *Bestsellers*, Detroit: Gale Research, 1990, 7–9.

Boyle, T. Coraghessan. "Who Is the Truest Parent?" *New York Times Book Review,* (January 7, 1990), 1, 33.

Contemporary Literary Criticism. Vols. 8, 13, 18, 40. Detroit: Gale Research.

Dictionary of Literary Biography: 1982 Yearbook. Detroit: Gale Research.

Edwards, Thomas R. "A Glazed Bowl of One's Own." *New York Times Book Review,* (October 12, 1986), 10.

Epstein, Joseph. "Ann Beattie and the Hippoisie." *Commentary* Vol. 75, no. 3 (March 1983), 54–8.

Friedrich, Otto. "Beattieland." *Time,* (New York). (January 22, 1990), 68.

Iyer, Pico. "Shadows of the 'Sixties." *London Magazine* (ns) Vol. 22, no. 12 (March 1983): 87–91.

Lyons, Gene. Review of *Picturing Will. Vogue,* (January 1990), 106, 108, 110.

McCaffery, Larry, and Sinda Gregory. "A Conversation with Ann Beattie." *Literary Review* (Fairleigh Dickinson University) Vol. 27, no. 2 (winter 1984): 165–77.

McKinstry, Susan Jaret. "The Speaking Silence of Ann Beattie's Voice." *Studies in Short Fiction* Vol. 24, no. 2 (spring 1987): 111–17.

Murphy, Christina. *Ann Beattie.* Boston: G. K. Hall, 1986.

O'Hara, J. D. Review of *Chilly Scenes of Winter. New York Times Book Review* (August 15, 1976), 14–18.

Porter, Carolyn. "Ann Beattie: The Art of the Missing." In *Contemporary American Women Writers: Narrative Strategies.* Edited by Catherine Rainwater and William J. Scheick, Lexington: University Press of Kentucky, 1985, 9–25.

Romano, John. "Ann Beattie & the '60s." *Commentary* (February 1977), 62–4.

Silk, Mark. "The Beattietudes." *Boston Review* Vol. 11, no. 6 (December 1986), 22–3.

Updike, John. Review of *Chilly Scenes of Winter. New Yorker* (November 29, 1976), 164–66.

Wyatt, David. "Ann Beattie." *Southern Review* Vol. 28, no. 1 (winter 1992), 145–59.

Thomas Bernhard
1931–1989

Austrian novelist, dramatist, poet, autobiographer, and journalist.

The Lime Works (*Das Kalkwerk;* novel, 1970)

Plot: The novel opens after an eccentric, reclusive scientist named Konrad has killed his crippled wife at their home, a barricaded, decaying lime works in Austria. The police discover him several days later, cowering beneath a manure pit, and he is taken to prison to await trial. The remainder of the book is narrated by an unnamed insurance salesman, who pieces the Konrads' story together from the sometimes contradictory accounts of various townspeople, including their estate managers, Fro and Wieser, and Hoeller, the manager of the lime works.

Living off his inheritance, Konrad and his wife traveled the world for many years, searching for a place conducive to writing. Here Konrad will write his intended masterpiece, a definitive scientific study to be entitled *The Sense of Hearing.* Though completely obsessed with this project, Konrad is unable to commit his ideas to paper. He finally decides that the abandoned lime works, which fascinated him since his childhood, will provide the seclusion and freedom from distraction he needs to begin his book. Forced to pay an outrageous price to the owner, his own nephew, Konrad sets about fortifying the place against intruders. Konrad's crippled wife hates the lime works and disdains her husband's grand project. Konrad uses his unwilling partner as the subject in a series of tortuous hearing experiments. She in turn torments him with frequent demands for attention and accusations that he is mad. Over the years Konrad produces nothing, claiming that interruptions keep him from working on his treatise. His anger and frustration grow, and he sinks deeper and deeper in debt. The death of Konrad's wife is either murder, committed by a man driven insane by his obsession, or the ironic result of a gun-cleaning accident.

Characters: Considered something of an *enfant terrible* in his native country for his uncompromisingly negative attitude toward Austria, Bernhard is a major writer and an original stylist. His book *The Lime Works* earned acclaim as one of the best German-language novels published after World War II. It features several characteristics typical of Bernhard's work as a whole. Its relentlessly pessimistic view of the human condition is permeated with images of death, sickness, and insanity. It is written in dense, repetitive, rhythmical prose, a style Bernhard is noted for. He uses a labyrinthine, deceptive structure to explore such themes as meaning, redemption, and the destructive nature of a marriage, which only moves its partners from the "purgatory of loneliness into the hell of togetherness." Bernhard also regarded creativity as futile in the face of inevitable annihilation.

The portrait of **Konrad,** the central character in *The Lime Works,* is drawn from the sometimes contradictory impressions and observations of various townspeople. By these accounts he may be a genius, a lunatic, or simply a deluded fool, although Konrad's estate managers say that he viewed himself as a brilliant scientist and philosopher. Much of the novel reflects Konrad's convoluted, compulsive thinking. Like other protagonists in Bernhard's fiction, Konrad is a misanthropic, isolated artist whose self-destruction Bernhard develops without pathos. Konrad's work, *The Sense of Hearing,* will be the definitive study of the auditory faculty. He claims the book exists in whole within his own mind and that he only distraction prevents him from committing it to paper. Critics note similarities between this grandiose project and the undertakings of other Bernhard characters—they evidence these characters' megalomania. Disapproving of society's excess and consumerism, Konrad withdraws himself and his wife from contact with the outside world.

Yet as time passes and he writes nothing, Konrad becomes more obsessed and infuriated that interruptions are all that hinder him. The reader learns that Konrad lacks far more than just peace and quiet; courage, decisiveness, boldness, and "fearlessness in the face of realization" are wanting as well. Not only does Konrad fail to write his book, but he also murders his wife. Whether this act is somehow a logical outcome of his failure, a response to his wife's nagging and taunting, an accident, or even a mercy killing, it seems in keeping with the author's reference system. Bernhard is said to have modeled Konrad and other protagonists after his eccentric grandfather, who raised him and heavily influenced his outlook.

Konrad's wife is identified only as "the Konrad woman" or **Mrs. Konrad;** her maiden name is Zryd. A tall, once beautiful woman, she is crippled in an accident and over the years become increasingly debilitated. Taking the wrong medication for many years aggravates Mrs. Konrad's condition. This element may derive from Bernhard's distrust of the medical establishment. Although Konrad's wife dreams of living in idyllic Toblach, her childhood home, and craves contact with other people, she suffers exile with him at the lime works. Their marriage is a pattern of mutual obedience and cruelty: Konrad experiments on his wife's hearing, and she torments him in return. Her methods include bribing their nephew not to sell Konrad the lime works, constantly demanding cider and other attentions, and ceaselessly knitting and unraveling mittens (which especially aggravates Konrad). She also proclaims Konrad's grand project a ludicrous delusion and calls him a "highly intelligent mental case." Some critics blame Mrs. Konrad for driving her husband crazy, thus bringing about her own death. Others view her as only one among many contributing factors in Konrad's frustration.

The novel's other characters are sketchy and exist to provide different perspectives on Konrad. **The narrator** is an anonymous insurance salesman who sells policies to people he finds in local taverns. While he constructs Konrad's story from gossip and supposition, he is notably untouched by it. **Fro and Weiser** are estate managers whose statements they claim are Konrad's own; **Höeller** is the lime works manager and handyman whose wood chopping and bizarre laughing distract Konrad from his work.

Further Reading

Birkerts, Sven. "Thomas Bernhard." In *An Artificial Wilderness: Essays on 20th-Century Literature, 77–84.* New York: William Morrow, 1987.

Bostick, Alan D. "Thomas Bernhard: An Appreciation on the Occasion of His Death." *Review of Contemporary Fiction* Vol. 10, no. 1 (spring 1980): 289–94.

Brokoph-Mauch, Gudrun. "Thomas Bernhard." In *Major Figures in Contemporary Austrian Literature.* Edited by Donald G. Daviau, 89–116. New York: Peter Lanf, 1987.

Contemporary Literary Criticism. Vols. 3, 32, 61. Detroit: Gale Research.

Craig, D. A. "The Novels of Thomas Bernhard; A Report." *German Life & Letters* Vol. 25, no. 4 (July 1972): 343–52.

Dictionary of Literary Biography. Vol. 85. Detroit: Gale Research.

Goodwin-Jones, Robert. "The Terrible Idyll: Thomas Bernhard's *Das Kalkwerk.*" *Germanic Notes* Vol. 13, nos. 3–4 (1984): 171–92.

Honegger, Gitta. "Thomas Bernhard." *Partisan Review* Vol. 58, no. 3 (summer 1991): 493–505.

Indiana, Gary. "Gloom with a View." *Village Voice,* (September 30, 1986): 56.

Kennedy, William. "Many Metaphors." *New Republic* (December 15, 1973): 28–30.

Malin, Irving. Review of *The Lime Works. Review of Contemporary Fiction* Vol. 7, no. 2 (summer 1987): 196–97.

Paul Bowles
1910–

American novelist, short story writer, translator, composer, poet, travel writer, autobiographer, and scriptwriter.

The Sheltering Sky (novel, 1949)

Plot: Port and Kit Moresby, an American couple of independent means, have traveled all over the world during the entire twelve years of their marriage. The novel begins shortly after World War II. The Moresbys have arrived in Oran, Morocco, with their friend Tunner, another American. The couple's marriage is obviously unstable, as Port spends a night with a prostitute. At their hotel the three meet an Australian travel writer and photographer, Mrs. Lyle, who is traveling with her heavyset and apparently homosexual son, Eric. The Lyles offer the Moresbys a ride to the inland town of Boussif, but Kit is repulsed by the Lyles and refuses to accompany them. Instead, she and Tunner take a train to Boussif, during which time Tunner successfully seduces Kit. After Kit rejoins Port in Boussif, Port decides to resolve his marital difficulties. Though he knows nothing of Kit and Tunner's infidelity, he considers Tunner an obstacle and sends him off with the Lyles. Later Port discovers his passport is missing and eventually finds out that Eric Lyle stole it. Kit and Port travel by bus to the town of El Ga'a, where Port becomes very ill. Because the town is besieged by an epidemic of meningitis, the Moresbys go to Sbâ. Port, now delirious from what turns out to be typhoid, is installed in a French fortress.

Feeling oppressed from caring for her sick husband, Kit leaves the fortress to meet Tunner, arriving by truck. Locked out of the fortress, she and Tunner spend the night in the desert. That night Port dies. With her husband dead, Kit feels a weight has been lifted from her. Wandering into the desert, she joins an Arab caravan and soon becomes sexually involved with two men, the younger of whom, Belqassim, she finds an especially pleasing lover. When the caravan arrives at its destination, Belqassim takes Kit into his home, but his jealous wives attack her. He marries her but gradually loses interest in her. Convinced she is being slowly poisoned, Kit leaves and through the local post office tries to reestablish contact with her friends. The authorities send the mentally unstable Kit on a three-day plane ride to Oran, where an American embassy employee, Miss Ferry, retrieves her and takes her to a hotel. Miss Ferry informs Kit that Tunner has been making inquiries about her and that she promised to inform him when Kit is found; Miss Ferry notes that while it is difficult to permanently lose people in the desert, they can disappear without a trace into the city. Miss Ferry leaves Kit in the car alone for a moment and returns to find her gone.

Characters: *The Sheltering Sky* established Bowles as an important postwar novelist. Infused with the nihilistic or existential sense that life and death are essentially meaningless and that consciousness is inherently limited, the novel has been likened to Albert Camus's *The Stranger* and Samuel Beckett's *Waiting for Godot,* both published within ten years of *The Sheltering Sky.* The dramatic North African setting draw on Bowles's many years of residence in Morocco; the Sahara Desert is an effective metaphor for the emptiness and isolation the main characters experience. One of Bowles's central concerns is to explore the loneliness and alienation of people adrift in places far from their origins. Like other protagonists in Bowles's fiction, the Moresbys are rootless travelers whose efforts to escape their own malaise lead only to greater confusion and even death. Their spiritual desolation may be partially attributed to the aftereffects of World War II, when many people felt their sense of security shaken, or it may be even more deeply rooted in the human psyche. In any case, they seem powerless to evade their dismal fates.

A thin man with a wry expression, **Port Moresby** is a disenchanted, wealthy American in his mid-thirties with no inclination to work. He has spent most of his adult life traveling outside the United States. With no intention of returning home or any plans to curb his wandering, Port is by Bowles's definition a *traveler* rather than a tourist. Despite his material affluence, Port is spiritually bankrupt and unable to commit himself to any thing, person, or idea. Although he perceives that his marriage is faltering and would like to rejuvenate it, he lacks the energy to make the effort such a commitment would entail. Port is alienated and desolate; his nihilism is expressed in his comment to Kit that "nothing" lies behind "the sheltering sky." His death is also meaningless, for he might have been inoculated against typhoid. Critics have commended Bowles for the scene in which Port lies languishing in the final throes of the disease, clinging desperately to the slender thread of consciousness that separates him from oblivion.

Port's wife, **Kit Moresby,** is small and blonde with an intense gaze. Although she traveled with her husband the entire twelve years of their marriage and shares to some extent his alienation, Kit's psyche is not as despairing as Port's. She recognizes and regrets the emptiness of their relationship. When Port contracts typhoid, Kit is forced to deal with its reality and eventually nurse him, a role she finds oppressive. When he dies, Kit experiences a variety of emotions, including fear and grief, but more than anything else she feels exhilaratingly free. In fact, when Port dies she is not even with him but out in the desert with Tunner, already her lover. Some critics perceive her coupling with the Arab men an affirmative act, whereas other reviewers judge it a step—either deliberate or passive— toward her undoing. Indeed, Kit further disintegrates with Belqassim, whom she serves as a mindlessly contented sexual slave. She seems fulfilled in this surrender of responsibility. With no common language to connect them, Kit eventually refuses to speak or even recognize her own name, signifying her desire to escape consciousness. Exactly what happens to Kit at the end of the novel is never specified, but it is strongly suggested that she disappears into the city and will never be seen again. Like her husband, Kit succumbs to forces her personality is too weak to grapple with.

Tunner, the American the Moresbys travel with to Morocco, is extremely handsome, slightly younger than the couple, and more solidly built. Not a particularly well-developed character, Tunner is agreeable and as purposeless as his friends, yet Kit finds him untrustworthy. While the Moresbys are travelers, Tunner is a tourist who will ultimately return to his New York home. Meanwhile, he is stimulated by the Moresbys and relishes the prospect of seducing Kit. Tunner's approach to life is more active than the Moresbys', for he succeeds in ravishing Kit and tries to locate her after she disappears.

Soon after they arrive in Morocco, the three Americans meet the unsavory Australian pair whose path will cross their own several times. **Mrs. Lyle** is a large, sallow-complexioned travel writer and photographer with brightly hennaed hair. Domineering and insensitive, she criticizes her son constantly as she does the Arab culture around her; indeed, she seems only to communicate through complaints and quarreling. Overweight and apparently homosexual, **Eric Lyle** lies obviously about his past and continually tries to borrow money from Port. Kit's suspicions about him are accurate, for he steals Port's passport, intending to sell it. The characters later learn that he is exchanging sexual favors with his mother in exchange for her financial support.

Other characters in *The Sheltering Sky* include **Belqassim,** the handsome Arab trader who becomes Kit's captor and lover and whose "perfect balance between gentleness and violence ... gave her particular delight"; **Marnhia,** the beautiful Arab prostitute Port consorts with during his first night in Morocco; **Daoud Zozeph,** the Jewish shopkeeper who provides milk for Kit's sick husband and later hides her in his house; **Captain Broussard** and **Lieutenant d'Armagnac,** members of Morocco's French colonial government; and **Miss Ferry,** the snobbish, prim employee of the American embassy who takes Kit back to the hotel in Oran.

Further Reading

Bertens, Hans. *The Fiction of Paul Bowles: The Soul Is the Weariest Part of the Body.* Atlantic Highlands, N.J.: Humanities, 1979.

Contemporary Literary Criticism. Vols. 1, 2, 19, 53. Detroit: Gale Research.

Dictionary of Literary Biography. Vols. 5, 6. Detroit: Gale Research.

McAuliffe, Jody. "The Church of the Desert: Reflections on *The Sheltering Sky.*" *South Atlantic Quarterly* 91 (spring 1992): 419–26.

O'Brien, Geoffrey. "White Light White Heat." *VLS,* no. 44 (April 1986): 10–13.

Olson, Steven E. "Alien Terrain: Paul Bowles's Filial Landscapes." *Twentieth Century Literature* 32, nos. 3 & 4 (fall & winter 1986): 334–39.

Sawyer-Lauçanno, Christopher. *An Invisible Spectator: A Biography of Paul Bowles.* New York: Weidenfeld Nicolson, 1989.

Voelker, Joseph. "Fish Traps and Purloined Letters: The Anthropology of Paul Bowles." *Critique: Studies in Modern Fiction* Vol. 27, no. 1 (fall 1985): 25–36.

Wagner, Linda W. "Paul Bowles and the Characterization of Women." *Critique: Studies in Modern Fiction* Vol. 27, no. 1 (fall 1985): 15–24.

Wolff, Tobias. "A Forgotten Master: Rescuing the Works of Paul Bowles." *Esquire,* (May 1985): 221–22.

T. Coraghessan Boyle

1948–

American short story writer, novelist, and editor.

"Greasy Lake" (short story, 1985)

Plot: The story's unnamed narrator and his friends Digby and Jeff are suburban nineteen-year-olds who consider themselves "bad characters." On summer vacation from college, they spend their time drinking, smoking marijuana, and driving out to stagnant Greasy Lake. One night the three find a 1957 Chevrolet and a big "chopper" motorcycle parked at opposite ends of the lake's parking lot. Digby claims the car belongs to another friend of theirs, who is no doubt inside having sex with a girl. They shine their lights on the Chevy, honk the horn, and even look inside the car's windows. Then they realize that the Chevy's occupant is not their friend at all but a real bad character—a "man of action" in steel-toed boots who, furious at the interruption, comes out kicking. The narrator and his friends fight off their attacker until the narrator hits him on the head with a tire iron and knocks him unconscious. Unsure if the Chevy driver (whose name, they later learn, is Bobby) is alive or dead, the three young men stand gaping at him until the girl emerges from the car. In a fever of primal brutality, they jump her and nearly rape her. When the arrival of another car interrupts them, they scatter into the "feculent undergrowth" along the lake's edge. Wading through the muck and weeds, the narrator first discovers a floating corpse, then hears the threatening voice of Bobby, which both relieves and terrorizes him. With the young men gone, Bobby goes to work battering the narrator's mother's station wagon, and the boys from the other car—fraternity brothers—join in the vandalism. When Bobby and the others leave, the narrator and his friends emerge from hiding and survey the car's damage. Finding it still drivable, they pile into the station wagon just as a Mustang pulls up. Inside are two young women high on drugs. One asks if they have seen her biker friend Al. The narrator answers no and, commenting that the three look like "some pretty bad characters," the young women invites them to "party" with her and her friend. The narrator and his friends refuse and drive away from Greasy Lake.

Characters: "Greasy Lake" is the title story of a collection praised for its wit, technical skill, and (according to reviewer Larry McCaffery) "lush, baroque language." The story exhibits Boyle's gift for social satire and the verbal energy that characterizes all of his fiction. With its title taken from a song by rock singer Bruce Springsteen, "Greasy Lake" features four male "spirits in the night" in search of excitement. However, Boyle underpins his playful, often slapstick portrayal of American life with a more sinister element.

The unnamed **narrator** tells the story as an older, maturer person looking back on his foolish youth. His inflated, often ironic rhetoric heightens the story's humor. Despite its many slapstick elements, the incident serves as a kind of initiation rite for the participants. After a series of stupid mistakes, the narrator comes close to actually being the "bad character" he only previously mimicked: he deals Bobby a nearly fatal blow, then attacks and nearly rapes Bobby's girlfriend. The narrator escapes into the murky lake, injured and shaken. Then, stumbling through the stagnant water, the narrator discovers the body of a drowned biker, an experience he describes as one of life's inescapable "nasty little epiphanies." His horrific discovery signifies that a seemingly innocent prank can dangerously backfire. Yet it also matures the narrator to some degree. When the young woman calls him and his friends "pretty bad characters"—praise they would previously have relished—he thinks he is going to cry.

The narrator and his fellow initiates believe they are acting cool; they roll their own marijuana cigarettes and are smooth dancers; they wear their sunglasses day and night, inside and out. They think of themselves as "bad characters" but clues indicate their immaturity. **Digby,** who flaunts his gold earring, says he "allows" his father to pay his college tuition, but the karate skills he brags about prove ineffective against Bobby's brawn. Digby also misidentifies the Chevy as a friend's car. **Jeff,** who is thinking about quitting school to become a "painter/musician/head-shop proprietor," meanwhile vomits out of the car window on their way to Greasy Lake. Like the narrator, Digby and Jeff are so chastened by the evening's events that they recognize the irony in the young woman's assessment of them as "bad characters." They turn down her invitation to take some drugs with her and her friend.

Bobby is the quintessential "bad character" in the story. He is a big, greasy thug who favors expletives. His shiftless brawn, mask-like face, and steel-toed boots make him a terrifying opponent. Called "the fox" by the narrator and his friends, **Bobby's girlfriend** is small and dressed only in underwear and a man's shirt. She calls the three teenagers "animals" and they act accordingly, jumping her in "purest primal badness" that shocks even them. **The two blonde fraternity boys,** who arrive at the lake in a sportscar, might otherwise avoid someone like Bobby, but when the girl accuses the narrator and his friends of trying to rape her, they threaten—in flat, midwestern accents—to kill her attackers. After battering the station wagon for a while, they suddenly stop and speed away, as if the possible consequences of their act have only just occurred to them. Other characters in the story include the dead bearded biker, **Al**, who the narrator speculates was either shot in a drug deal gone bad or was drunk and drowned in the lake; and **Al's two friends**, twenty-five- or twenty-six-year-old women in tight jeans and with "hair like frozen fur" who lurch across the parking lot and invite the narrator, Digby, and Jeff to join them in taking some drugs.

World's End (novel, 1987)

Plot: *World's End* tells the intertwined stories of three families living in and around the community of Peterskill in New York's Hudson River Valley. Accounts of the seventeenth- and twentieth-century representatives of each family comprise alternating chapters. The seventeenth-century chapters feature the Van Brunt, tenant farmers who are virtual indentured servants; the Van Warts, the wealthy, exploitative Dutch landlords who own the Van Brunt farm; and the Kitchawank Indians, the original inhabitants of the area, who have been cheated out of their land. The most prominent Van Brunt is Jeremias, a rebellious man whose sister Katrinchee bears a child, Jeremy, by the Kitchawank's leader, Mohonk. Jeremias's son, Wouter, is disillusioned when his father is finally cowed by the Van Warts, and he betrays his cousin Jeremy and friend Cadwallader Crane, who are unjustly hanged for their roles in an "uprising."

The central figure in the book's twentieth-century chapters is Walter Van Brunt, an alienated twenty-two-year-old who was raised by friends of his socialist parents after the disappearance of his father, Truman, and the death of his mother, Christina. Walter has been told that his father betrayed his family and friends during the Peterskill Riots of 1949. Truman allegedly helped a mob attack blacks, women, and communists at a concert that was to feature performer and black activist Paul Robeson. Walter's mother died of grief soon after her husband abandoned her and their young son.

Years later, while riding home one night on his motorcycle, Walter crashes into a historical marker and consequently loses his foot (later in the book he also loses the other foot in a similar mishap). The accident spurs Walter to investigate his family history. This leads to the unlikely alliance with Depeyster Van Wart, the wealthy heir to the Van Wart estate, who claims to have known Truman well. Meanwhile, Depeyster's wife, Joanna, is having an affair with the last of the Kitchawanks, Jeremy Mohonk, while his daughter Mardi seduces Walter, recently married to sweet Jessica Wing. Tom Crane, a nature-loving draft dodger and Walter's best friend, wins Jessica's heart after she leaves Walter. Walter eventually travels to Alaska to search for his father. There Truman lives in self-imposed exile for betraying his old friends; he claims that treachery runs deep in the Van Brunt blood and inevitably manifests itself. Walter returns to Peterskill bitter about the relationship between Tom and Jessica, and in a snowstorm betrays them by setting adrift the *Arcadia* (the ecology-education sloop on which Tom is a crew member). However, Walter freezes to death in that snowstorm. Tom then has to sell his beloved land to Depeyster Van Wart to pay for repairs to the *Arcadia*. Depeyster, meanwhile, revels in the birth of a son and deliberately overlooks the fact that the baby has Jeremy Mohonk's green eyes.

Characters: Winner of the Pen/Faulkner Award for fiction in 1988, *World's End* exhibits the satiric flair, black humor, and skillful blend of formal and colloquial language for which Boyle is noted. A native of Peekskill, New York (where anti-Communist riots occurred in 1949), Boyle has said that the novel represents an attempt to imagine his own family's past. He intentionally invokes the literary tradition of Washington Irving—the nineteenth-century author of such classic American stories as "The Legend of Sleepy Hollow" and "Rip Van Winkle"—through the novel's Hudson River Valley setting and several of the characters' names as well as some of the things that happen to them. In juxtaposing a sociologically detailed, often comic account of 1960s America with a fictionalized historical narrative, Boyle asserts the continuity of such essential human forces as betrayal, revenge, lust, and the thirst for power.

The surname of **Walter Van Brunt**, the central figure in the contemporary sections of *World's End,* is taken from the ''The Legend of the Sleepy Hollow,'' in which a scrawny, stuck-up Yankee schoolteacher is bested by Dutch farmer Abraham Van Brunt. But Walter actually bears more resemblance to Ichabod Crane, the protagonist of Irving's story; both are victims of mysterious midnight accidents. Walter is a tall, handsome, red-haired twenty-two-year-old who feels alienated and abandoned due to his father's disappearance in circumstances of shame and betrayal. Although he has a college degree, Walter works as a laborer at Depeyster Manufacturing and continues to live with his tolerant godparents, Hesh and Lola Solovay. After work, Walter usually drinks with his friends at a bar called the Throbbing Elbow. On his twenty-second birthday, Walter shuns a celebratory dinner with the Solovays and his girlfriend Jessica Wing in favor of a midnight swim in the river with wild, promiscuous Mardi Van Wart. The two climb onto an abandoned merchant ship, where Walter thinks he sees the ghosts of some of his dead or missing relatives. Walter's later run in with a historical marker, which results in the loss of his foot, is a literal collision with history and a symbolic event that pushes him to confront the mysteries of his past. He wants the truth about his father, hoping to find that he is not the lying traitor Hesh and Lola have described, and thus seeks out Depeyster Van Wart, who knew Truman at the time of the riots. Depeyster calls Truman a real patriot; he also takes a liking to Walter and becomes a kind of surrogate father to the young man. Meanwhile, only months after his marriage to Jessica, Walter has an affair with Mardi. He rationalizes his behavior by fashioning himself an existential hero. He identifies with Meursault, the nihilist protagonist of Albert Camus's 1942 novel *The Stranger;* Walter claims that he is ''a creature of his own destiny, soulless, hard, free from convention and the twin burdens of love and duty.''

Walter's interest in the conventional Depeyster Van Wart and LeClerc Outhouse bewilders his friends. He even wears a suit and wingtip shoes for the desk job that Depeyster gets him. Then Walter journeys to Alaska to confront his father, but the meeting only confirms his worst fears. Walter finds out that Truman was guilty of betraying his wife and friends and that treachery is in the Van Brunt blood. Walter is named for his double-crossing ancestor, Wouter Van Brunt, and he fulfills his genetic destiny when, just before his own death, he sets the *Arcadia* adrift during a snowstorm. Some critics regard the novel's ending, which seems to confirm the cyclical nature of history, as empty and despairing, though others find it in keeping with Boyle's usual black humor.

Among the other characters in the novel's contemporary sections is the likable **Tom Crane**, a more conventional hero than his longtime friend Walter. Tom and his grandfather **Peletiah Crane** (a former superintendent of Peterskill's schools) are the modern descendants of a long line of schoolteaching, tolerant Cranes. Like his ancestor Cadwallader, the ecology-minded Tom thinks of himself as a ''saint of the forest.'' He drops out of college, moves into a shack on land owned by his indulgent grandfather (and coveted by Depeyster Van Wart), and relishes his independent, slothful life, which consists of little else but reading, sleeping, and cooking tofu dishes for himself and the occasional visitor. One such guest is old friend Jessica Wing Van Brunt, with whom Tom becomes romantically involved when her marriage to Walter collapses. Just before Walter betrays his two old friends, Tom is remarkably pleased with his circumstances: Jessica has moved in with him, he has succeeded in dodging the Selective Service (because of extreme scrawniness), and he has landed a job on the crew of the counterculture *Arcadia,* a beautiful sailing sloop commissioned to educate the public about Hudson River ecology. But during a heavy snowstorm, Walter sets it adrift—with Tom and Jessica sleeping peacefully below decks. The sloop is severely damaged and Tom must sell his beloved land to Depeyster to pay for repairs. At the novel's end, Tom also loses his best friend but keeps Jessica's love as well as the house left him by his grandfather.

Depeyster Van Wart is the twelfth heir to the Van Wart manor and descendent of the patroons who once tyrannized the Van Brunt family. Fifty years old, tanned, athletic, and educated at Yale, he manages his anxieties and frustrations by chewing fine dirt taken from the walls of his cellar. Depeyster is desperate for a male heir, but his wife, Joanna, has only borne one child, their daughter Mardi, and Depeyster's overzealous attempts to produce a son have long since alienated Joanna. No more a friend to the working man than his ancestors, Depeyster played a key role in the 1949 riots, which disrupted the outdoor concert planned by the socialist Kitchawank Colony and permanently altered the life of Walter Van Brunt. With no son of his own, Depeyster happily adopts Walter as his protegee, offering him an office job and assuring him that his father was a noble patriot and not a scoundrel. Later Truman tells Walter that he and Depeyster first met when they were both serving overseas in World War II; back in Peterskill, Depeyster lured Truman away from the liberal ideals of his wife and friends. At the end of the novel, the Van Wart power is ironically undermined by the male infant born to Joanna and celebrated to be Depeyster's heir. The child is actually Jeremy Mohonk's, thus a descendent of a family long oppressed by the Van Warts. While Depeyster notices the baby's dark skin and genetically unexplainable green eyes, he deliberately and permanently dismisses his "unsettling thoughts" from his mind.

Jeremy Mohonk, the last of the Kitchawank Indians, shares with his forebears the trademark green eyes inherited from Katrinchee Van Brunt, who long ago coupled with the Indian leader Mohonk. Jeremy shares some of this history with **Sasha Freeman**; he meets the nature-loving Marxist intellectual when both are tramping through the woods, and she influences his ideas. Ever rebellious and defiant, Jeremy tries to stake his claim on land owned by **Rombout Van Wart**. A confrontation between the two ends with Jeremy attacking Rombout, for which Jeremy is sentenced to seventeen hellish but unrepentant years in Sing Sing prison. He is released in time to witness the 1949 riots and manages to bite a chunk out of Truman Van Brunt's traitorous ear. Like Depeyster Van Wart, Jeremy longs for a male heir, but his heavy, good-natured wife, **Alice One Bird**, never bears children. "Charity lady" Joanna has his child, however, allowing Jeremy to perpetuate his own line (in fact if not in name) at the same time as he exacts revenge—always a central force in the Mohonk family—on the Van Warts. Jeremy's white lover, **Joanna Van Wart**, the wife of wealthy industrialist Depeyster, became alienated from her husband long before she met Jeremy, due in part to Depeyster's exhaustive and unsuccessful attempts to impregnate her. Joanna's seeming interest in the cause of Indian relief results more from her sexual attraction to Jeremy than any humanitarianism. After Jeremy rejects her, Joanna convinces Depeyster that he is the father of her child.

Although he does not appear until nearly the end of the novel, **Truman Van Brunt** is a pivotal character in *World's End* because he is the focus of Walter's search for answers. Walter hopes to learn that his vanished father did not betray his friends' socialist ideals, but he is disappointed with the truth. As a young man, Truman was a good-looking, daring, athletic redhead who labored by day in a factory and studied history by night. Although he did join the communist party after marrying Christina Alving and professed to subscribe to her views, Truman was more in love with his wife than committed to socialism. It was not too difficult for the wily Depeyster Van Wart to persuade Truman that disrupting the concert his friends had planned was a patriotic act. Afterward, devastated by his own treachery, Truman fled Peterskill and eventually settled in Alaska, where he teaches school and drinks excessively. For over twenty years, Truman has been writing a manuscript entitled *Colonial Shame, Betrayal, and Death in Van Wartville: The First Revolt*. Truman maintains that Wouter Van Brunt's despicable behavior proves that the Van Brunt genes are tainted, and he tells his son that none of them can escape, because "it's in the blood, Walter. It's in the bones." Feeling he is doomed, Walter goes home to fulfill his fate.

Boyle seems to have borrowed the name of Walter's mother, **Christina Alving Van Brunt**, from the character Helen Alving, a central figure in *Ghosts* (1882), written by nineteenth-century Norwegian playwright Henrik Ibsen. Indeed, both Boyle's character and Ibsen's are betrayed by their mates, but while Helen Alving's husband was an adulterer, Christina's committed a different kind of treachery. Gentle and compassionate, Christina is so aggrieved by her husband's abandonment that she essentially starves herself to death. Twenty years later, Truman tells Walter that he did love his wife, but that her goodness seemed to provoke him to hurt her.

Christina leaves her son to **Hesh and Lola Solovay,** who are committed socialists and loyal friends with whom she and Walter were once inseparable. Lola is described as silver-haired, with a leathery tan and a "sinewy embrace"; she tells Walter the story of the 1949 riots. Big, plainspoken Hesh is still angry over Truman's betrayal and resents Walter's association with the treacherous, politically conservative Depeyster Van Wart.

Walter's tall, pale wife **Jessica Wing Van Brunt,** is a sweet-natured, serious microbiologist who aspires to graduate school but takes a mundane laboratory job to support her wayward husband. Like Walter's mother, his wife wants a calm home life and never reproaches him for his sloth, and like his father, who betrayed Christina's virtue, Walter reacts against Jessica's goodness. After she discovers Walter in bed with Mardi, Jessica leaves him and finds happiness with the congenial Tom Crane.

Some critics have accused Boyle of casting the novel's female characters as either virtuous wives or temptresses. A prime example of the latter is sensuous **Mardi Van Wart,** a small, wild-haired hippy clad in a revealing paper miniskirt the first time Walter meets her A daring, heedless drug user who regards her parents—particularly her industrialist father—with contempt, Mardi persuades Walter to swim out to the ghost ships with her at the beginning of the novel and later seduces him.

Other notable characters in the novel's contemporary chapters include **Piet Aukema,** a disreputable dwarf who encouraged Truman to betray his friends and, when he ends up in a hospital bed across from Walter's, tells him where to find his father; and **Herbert Pompey,** one of Walter's friends, a black hippy poet and musician apparently descended from the slaves of the original Van Wart patroons.

The first family of Van Brunts in America is headed by **Harmanus Van Brunt,** a humble farmer so eager to escape his bleak prospects in Holland that he virtually signs his life away to the patroon, who extracts yearly quotients of money, food, and livestock from his tenants in exchange for the use of the land. Harmanus finally acquires the mysterious eating disorder that afflicts several later Van Brunts—an overpowering, unquenchable hunger that seems to drive its victims insane. Although the malady doesn't kill him, Harmanus perishes after a series of mishaps resulting from his having to cut off his son's gangrenous foot. The family's bad luck continues when Harmanus's wife, **Agatha,** dies with their youngest child in a fire after daughter **Katrinchee** has run off with the Indian leader Mohonk. Believing that her family's deaths were a punishment for her own sinfulness, Katrinchee shaves her head in penance and lives alone in a bark hut with her son by Mohonk, Squagganeek (later called Jeremy).

The only surviving member of this initial Van Brunt family, **Jeremias,** like his twentieth-century relative, loses his foot in a freak accident (a snapping turtle bite leads to gangrene). Taken in by the Van der Meulen family, Jeremias grows up rebellious and resentful of the Van Warts. He is reunited with his sister and nephew and makes a home for them that is soon expanded by his comely wife, **Neeltje** (he defies her father, the patroon's deputy, to marry her), and their own children. Throughout the years, Jeremias refuses to witness the annual payment of money, butter, wheat, and poultry that comprise his "rent" to the patroon. Yet Jeremias is ultimately defeated when he refuses to participate in a roadbuilding project and is forced to beg forgiveness of the patroon. With a single blow, Jeremias's spirit is crushed, and he lives out his days a meek, defeated man, finally succumbing to the same pathological hunger that his father suffered.

Jeremias's son **Wouter Van Brunt** witnesses his father's defeat, which he regards as his father's weakness. As an adult, he too resents the Van Warts' exploitiveness. On "rent day," after learning that both he and Cadwallader Crane are to be pushed off their land, he instigates a small "revolt" and starts the patroon's barn afire. Later, however, in a betrayal that prefigures those perpetrated by Truman and Walter, Wouter implicates his cousin Jeremy and friend Cadwallader for the crime, for which they are executed. This is the "first revolt" recounted in Truman's voluminous manuscript.

Given a new name by his uncle Jeremias, **Jeremy Mohonk** (originally called **Squagganeek**) has the distinctive green eyes of his mother, Katrinchee, but the ungovernable spirit of his Indian father, Mohonk. The teenaged Jeremy escapes into the woods just as he and his cousin Wouter are about to be put into the stocks for defying the patroon. Jeremy returns for a while to Native American ways, becomes a husband and father, and loses his ability to speak. After returning to settle on the Van Brunts' farm, Jeremy is betrayed by Wouter and unjustly hung. The gawky naturalist **Cadwallader Crane**, who befriended Wouter after Jeremy's escape, also dies for his part in the "revolt." Crane's personality and fate both seem to be exaggerated versions of those of his twentieth-century counterpart, Tom Crane.

The novel's seventeenth-century characters also include **Joost Cats**, the patroon's schout (deputy), a "lean, ferrety little fellow" who rides slumped over in the saddle and who begrudgingly relinquishes his daughter to the rebellious Jeremias Van Brunt. Generous, hardworking **Staats** and **Meintje Van der Meulen** take Jeremias into their home after his family dies. The story's villains include the three successive Dutch patroons, **Oloffe Stephanusn Van Wart**, **Stephanus Oloffe Rombout Van Wart**, and **Rombout Van Wart (17th C)**, all of them domineering, exploitative, and arrogant. Voluptuous **Saskia Van Wart**, Rombout's daughter, is the seventeenth-century version of modern temptress Mardi Van Wart. **Jan Pieterse** owns the area's trading post; called "Composed of Mouth" by the Kitchawanks, he helps to swindle the Indians out of their land and encourages their dependence on the white man's goods and liquor. Pieterse hoodwinks **Sachoes**, the Kitchawank's chief, into relinquishing the land. Sachoes's wife, **Wahwahtaysee**, is a skilled medicine woman; his son Mohonk fathers a son with Katrinchee Van Brunt. **Wolf Nysen** is a legendary local figure said to have gone mad, murdered his family, and fled into the hills; when his body is found and buried on the Van Brunt farm, it seems to bring a curse upon the whole community.

Further Reading

Batchelor, John Calvin. "Hudson River Frolic." *Book World—The Washington Post* (November 1, 1987): 4.

Clute, John. "Van Warts and All." *Times Literary Supplement* No. 4456 (August 26–September 1, 1988): 927.

Contemporary Literary Criticism. Vols. 36, 55. Gale Research.

Cotts, Cynthia. Review of *World's End. VLS* No. 60 (November 1987): 3.

DeMott, Benjamin. "Ghost Ships in the Hudson." *New York Times Book Review* (September 27, 1987): 1, 52–3.

Dictionary of Literary Biography, 1986 Yearbook. Detroit: Gale Research.

Eder, Richard. "Kismet Comedy from New Holland to New York." *Los Angeles Times Book Review* (October 11, 1987): 3.

Kakutani, Michiko. Review of *World's End. New York Times* (September 23, 1987): C27.

McCaffery, Larry. "Lusty Dreamers in the Suburban Jungle." *New York Times Book Review* (June 9, 1985): 15–16.

Ray Bradbury

1920–

American novelist, short story writer, playwright, poet, children's author, and editor.

The Martian Chronicles (novel, 1950)

Plot: The book comprises twenty-six loosely connected stories or sketches about the exploration and the colonization of Mars by earthlings in the late twentieth century. The book contains in its short prologue a kind of paean to the rocket ship. In the story "Ylla," the title character, a Martian wife, dreams of the arrival of an attractive Earthman. Her jealous husband subsequently helps to kill one such visitor. In "The Earth Men," the Martians believe the members of a second expedition from earth are hallucinations and "cure" themselves by killing the men. The explorers in "The Third Expedition" are eliminated by a Martian trap that causes telepathic hallucinations of long-lost people from their own pasts. Spender, a member of the fourth expedition to Mars, is introduced in "—And the Moon Be Still as Bright." The Martians have by now all died of chicken pox. Spender develops a deep respect for the ancient Martian civilization and believes that his fellow Earthmen will exploit this new planet to its detriment; thus he plots to save his new home by killing new arrivals. One such exploiter is Sam Parkhill, an ambitious entrepreneur who hopes to strike it rich on Mars. "The Settlers" and "The Green Morning" continue the saga of colonization and exploitation of Mars; the latter story features a Johnny Appleseed-like ecologist figure. In "Night Meeting" Tomás Gomez has a strange, enlightening encounter on a deserted Martian road. The main character in "The Martian" tries to ingratiate himself with the Earthmen by turning into whomever they most wish to see. A group of African Americans fleeing racism on Earth emigrate to Mars in "Way in the Middle of the Air," and in "Usher II" a man named Stendahl devises a trap for those who censor imaginative literature. The final stories in *The Martian Chronicles* tell of a nuclear war on Earth and its effects on colonizers to Mars, many of whom return to their home planet. Sam Parkhill meets with disappointment in "The Off Season," while "The Silent Towns," "The Long Years," and "There Will Come Soft Rains" depict the loneliness of a nearly deserted Mars. The novel's last story is "The Million-Year Picnic," in which a father fleeing from nuclear war on Earth brings his family to Mars. He encourages his children to think of themselves as the new Martians.

Characters: When *The Martian Chronicles* was published, it marked an important step in the development of the genre. Bradbury's poetic, sophisticated prose and his emphasis on moral concerns rather than technical gadgetry attracted a wider range of critical attention than previous science fiction novels. Although it takes place in the future and involves space travel to another planet, *The Martian Chronicles* reflects the primary concerns of American society during the 1950s, including the fear of nuclear war, racism, censorship, and the possible dangers of technology. As many commentators have noted, Bradbury's Mars closely resembles the small, midwestern American town in which he grew up. Composed of six previously published stories and twenty additional sketches combined into a loose structure, the novel contains no characters who could be considered central—nor are they particularly well developed. Rather, Bradbury uses them to explore such themes as the role and value of the imagination, the transforming power of the environment on the settler, the importance of family love and cultural diversity, and the dangers of racism, greed, and misuse of natural resources. Some reviewers detected in *The Martian Chronicles* a Calvinistic sense of permanently lost innocence, but others find the novel essentially optimistic.

Spender, a crewman on the fourth expedition to Mars, is often considered to be Bradbury's mouthpiece. He is filled with awe for the ancient, now vanquished, Martian civilization, which was infused with a respect for the past and a dedication to the value of life itself. These are qualities that Bradbury—who is thought to have modeled the ancient Martians after the American Indians and Mexicans he encountered during his travels as a youth— affirms in all of his writings. Spender's enthusiasm for Martian philosophy and the Martian environment cause him to see himself as the last Martian; to preserve the essential Martian nature from the greedy and heedless Earthmen, he plots against them. Spender shares his views with **Captain Wilder**, the leader of the fourth expedition, who basically agrees with the young crewman but takes the more pragmatic position that changes on Mars are inevitable.

Sam Parkhill embodies the negative values that Spender decries. In the days before nuclear war breaks out on Earth, Parkhill is an entrepreneur who plans to establish a hot dog stand to feed the mine workers expected on Mars. His entire entrepreneurial vision consists of modeling life on Mars after its familiar patterns on Earth. His greed proves fatal when he misinterprets the intentions of visiting Martians, resulting in a murderous encounter. At the opposite end of the moral spectrum from Parkhill is **William Stendahl**, an eccentric millionaire who opposes the literary censorship put in place by the Mars colony's "moral climate" controllers. Stendahl builds a mechanical house modeled after the one in Edgar Allan Poe's acclaimed short story "The Fall of the House of Usher." There he traps the censors and, scorning their ignorance of Poe's work, kills them by methods described in that nineteenth-century author's works.

Another agent of moral stature in *The Martian Chronicles* is **William Thomas.** He brings his family to Mars to protect them from the nuclear war about to begin on Earth as well as to escape its oppression. Unlike Sam Parkhill and other settlers, Thomas has no desire to recreate American society on Mars. He proves this when he burns the financial documents that symbolize capitalistic greed. Thomas's warm, loving family—the children look at their reflections in a pool of water to see "the new Martians"—represent the best qualities of humanity and the possibility of regeneration. The fact that Bradbury made "The Million-Year Picnic," which tells the story of Thomas and his family, the final chapter in *The Martian Chronicles* suggests to many critics that he intended the novel's ultimate message to be one of hope for the future.

Other characters in *The Martian Chronicles* include **Tomás Gomez,** who enters a kind of time warp on a deserted road and learns about the essential similarity between himself and a Martian from either the past or the future; **Benjamin Driscoll,** a latter-day Johnny

Appleseed who seeds Mars with trees in order to increase its oxygen supply—he is one of several settlers representing various minority concerns; and **Ylla,** the Martian woman made from the same model as the unhappy American housewife, who dreams of a tall, attractive Earthman, leading her jealous husband to kill just such an alien visitor.

Further Reading

Concise Dictionary of American Literary Biography: Broadening Views, 1968–1988. Detroit: Gale Research, 1989.

Contemporary Literary Criticism. Vols. 1, 3, 10, 15, 42. Detroit: Gale Research.

Dictionary of Literary Biography. Vols. 2, 8. Detroit: Gale Research.

Greenberg, Martin H., and Joseph D. Olander, eds. *Ray Bradbury.* New York: Taplinger, 1980.

Johnson, Wayne L. *Ray Bradbury.* New York: Ungar, 1980.

Nolan, William F. *The Ray Bradbury Companion.* Detroit: Gale Research, 1975.

Slusser, George Edgar. *The Bradbury Chronicles.* San Bernardino, Calif.: Borgo Press, 1977.

Toupence, William F. *Ray Bradbury and the Poetics of Reverie: Fantasy, Science Fiction, and the Reader.* Ann Arbor, Mich.: UMI Research Press, 1984.

———.‘‘Some Aspects of Surrealism in the Works of Ray Bradbury.’’ *Extrapolation* 25 (fall 1984): 228–38.

Richard Brautigan
1935–1984
American novelist, poet, and short story writer.

Trout Fishing in America (novel, 1967)

Plot: Set in the early 1960s, the novel is a loose chronicle of the unnamed narrator's yearlong travels with his ‘‘woman’’ and their baby through the American West. The narrator, an ardent trout fisherman, yearns to locate the finest trout streams and most idyllic pastoral settings. The book's forty-seven chapters relate his fishing and camping experiences as well as childhood recollections, meetings with famous people, and his encounters with two mythical, noncorporeal presences called Trout Fishing in America and Trout Fishing in America Shorty. But the narrator never locates the pristine wilderness he seeks. When he discovers the ‘‘Cleveland Wrecking Yard,’’ where used trout streams are being sold by the yard, the narrator and his family finally move into a California cabin with some friends.

Characters: Brautigan is often aligned with the counterculture movement of the 1960s, for his gentle tone and surrealism greatly appealed to the ‘‘flower children’’ of that era. With lyrical prose, simple syntax, and a whimsical style, Brautigan explored serious subjects through a lighthearted, ironic voice. Widely recognized as Brautigan's most important work, *Trout Fishing in America* has been called a pastoral tragedy that chronicles the narrator's search for an American Eden. Many critics consider it within the tradition established by such authors as Mark Twain and Ernest Hemingway, whose protagonists also seek freedom from social constraints. One of the novel's central concerns is the tension between an ideal America and its reality—between its past and present, its wilderness and cities. *Trout Fishing in America* refers frequently to such historical figures as Lewis and Clark and Benjamin Franklin, and commentators note the novel's connections to such American classics as Thoreau's *Walden* and Hemingway's "Big Two-Hearted River." A few critics have detected underlying despair in the novel, but most consider its ultimate message one of optimism, resilience, and belief in the transforming power of imagination.

The narrator is considered to be Brautigan himself; in fact, the book's cover bears a photograph of the author accompanied by a woman. Like Brautigan, the narrator is a writer who passed his childhood unhappily in the home of an alcoholic father. Also like his creator, he was raised in Tacoma, Washington; Portland, Oregon; and Great Falls, Montana; locations featured or mentioned in various parts of the book. The narrator is a dropout and rambler on a loosely structured quest for utopia. He travels through the forests of northern California and Idaho and often enjoys trout fishing, but he notices that the American wilderness is aglow with the artificial light of Coleman lanterns, symbols indicating that the wide-open frontier—and its freedom and unlimited possibility—no longer exists.

One recollection from the narrator's boyhood is that he mistook a steep, white, wooden staircase for a waterfall. Near the end of the book, he learns that the Cleveland Wrecking Yark not only sells trout streams but also waterfalls, which are stacked up near a collection of used toilets. The reader may conclude that the narrator's utopia, like the waterfall that was really a staircase, is forever lost. However, it is possible that his visionary sense will continue to guide him. Some critics believe the novel is a kind of "portrait of the artist," in this case a trout fisherman, whose imagination and ability to transcend expands as the book progresses. When the narrator as a little boy discovered that a trout stream he was looking for did not exist, he ate his bait (a wadded-up lump of bread), thus "hooking" himself. Boy or man, he can only escape the distressing aspects of modern life through his fertile imagination. Commentators have compared Brautigan's narrator to other protagonists in American literature who seek meaning or escape through nature, notably Hemingway's Jake Barnes (from *The Sun Also Rises*) and Nick Adams ("Big Two-Hearted River" and other stories) and Twain's Huckleberry Finn.

Not a conventional character, **Trout Fishing in America** is a surreal-figure in the novel who can talk (often in a silly, whimsical voice) and write. He may personify the novel itself—or the *idea* of the novel—but he also serves as the narrator's muse, protector, and guide. At various points he takes the forms of a hotel, a wealthy gourmet, a place from which the narrator finally returns, and a witness to such historic events as the discovery of Montana's Great Falls by Lewis and Clark. Some commentators see him as representing the American ideal, and his counterpart, Trout Fishing in America Shorty, to be a type at the other end of the spectrum. One critic who compared the novel to the nineteenth-century American classic *Moby Dick,* called Trout Fishing in America, like Herman Melville's white whale, a fluid, mysterious, ultimately unknowable symbol.

The novel's other surrealistic figure is **Trout Fishing in America Shorty,** described as "a legless, screaming middle-aged wino . . . descended upon North Beach [a neighborhood in San Francisco] like a chapter from the Old Testament." Critics have found this character to depict the *real* America, whereas Trout Fishing in America represents the ideal. Critic David L. Vanderwerken called Trout Fishing in America Shorty an "emissary from the actual" more along the lines of the realistic or naturalistic author as Nelson Algren—to whom, in fact, the narrator wishes to send him.

Accompanying the narrator on his quest is his "**woman,**" said to be Ginny Adler, Brautigan's wife during the time he wrote the novel. After Brautigan's death, Adler recounted that Brautigan did indeed complete much of *Trout Fishing in America* during a long camping trip the couple took with their year-old daughter Ianthe (who appears as **the narrator's baby** in the novel). The narrator's woman appears in only seven chapters, and the reader learns little about her beyond her domestic, sexual, and child care roles. Unlike the predecessors to whom his work is often compared—most notably Mark Twain and Ernest Hemingway—Brautigan includes a woman and a child in his protagonist's search for freedom and meaning.

A notable character from the narrator's past is **the Kool-Aid Wino**, the sickly child of a family of German-born farm laborers who, due to an unexplained "rupture," is unable to join his parents and siblings in the fields. He has made an elaborate ritual of drinking diluted, sugarless grape Kool-Aid, and the narrator compares him to "the inspired priest of an exotic cult" who "created his own Kool-Aid reality and was able to illuminate himself by it." One critic claimed the Kool-Aid Wino to be a Christ figure who offers the narrator communion; he may also exemplify the use of imagination to escape bleak circumstances.

Further Reading

Abbott, Keith. "Shadows and Marble: Richard Brautigan." *Review of Contemporary Fiction* Vol. 8 (fall 1988): 117–25.

Clayton, John. "Richard Brautigan: The Politics of Woodstock." *New American Review,* no. 11 (1971): 56–68.

Contemporary Literary Criticism. Vols. 1, 3, 5, 9, 12, 34. Detroit: Gale Research.

Dictionary of Literary Biography: Yearbook. Vols. 2, 5. Detroit: Gale Research.

Foster, Edward Halsey. *Richard Brautigan.* Boston: Twayne, 1983.

Hayden, Brad. "Echoes of *Walden* in *Trout Fishing in America.*" *Thoreau Journal Quarterly* (July 1976): 21–6.

Hearon, Thomas. "Escape through Imagination in *Trout Fishing in America.*" *Critique: Studies in Modern Fiction* Vol. 26, no. 1 (1974): 25–31.

Malley, Terrence. *Richard Brautigan.* New York: Warner Paperback Library, 1972.

McGuane, Thomas. Review of *Trout Fishing in America. New York Times Book Review* (February 15, 1970): 49.

Schmitz, Neil. "Richard Brautigan and the Modern Pastoral." *Modern Fiction Studies* (spring 1973): 109–25.

Vanderwerken, David L. "*Trout Fishing in America* and the American Tradition." *Critique: Studies in Modern Fiction* Vol. 16, no. 1 (1974): 32–40.

Wright, Lawrence. "The Life and Death of Richard Brautigan." *Rolling Stone* Issue 445 (April 11, 1985): 29–61.

Anita Brookner

1928–

English novelist.

Hotel du Lac (novel, 1984)

Plot: As the novel opens, thirty-nine-year-old Edith Hope is ensconced at the Hotel du Lac. Her friends banished her to the Swiss resort after she jilted her fiance, Geoffrey Long, just before their wedding. Edith writes romance novels under the pen name Vanessa Wilde, and she plans to use her vacation to work on her latest book, *Beneath the Visiting Moon.* Although her friends consider her a mild-mannered spinster with a dull life, Edith has been carrying on a clandestine affair with a married auctioneer, David Simmonds. Edith becomes acquainted with some of the hotel's guests, including the extravagant Mrs. Pusey and her voluptuous daughter, Jennifer; slender, beautiful Monica and her dog Kiki, and deaf old Comtesse de Bonneuil. Another fellow sojourner is the cultured, cynical Philip Neville, who espouses the benefits of self-interest. During Edith's stay at the Hotel du Lac, Neville offers her a marriage of convenience that will provide her with a respectable position and relieve her of having to write romance novels. Edith accepts and writes David that their affair is over, but on her way to mail the letter she encounters Neville coming out of Jennifer's room. Edith destroys her letter and instead sends David a telegram, informing him that she is "returning."

Characters: Well known for her elegant, tightly controlled prose and well-constructed plots, Brookner won England's prestigious Booker-McConnell Prize for Fiction for *Hotel du Lac.* Characterized by critics as a contemporary comedy of manners, the novel resembles Brookner's other works in its melancholy tone and its heroine who yearns to experience an ideal love. *Hotel du Lac* explores the gap between the notion of romantic love and the reality of relations between men and women, reflecting Brookner's interest in the romantic novels of nineteenth-century French novelists Gustave Flaubert and Honoré de Balzac. Brookner has been praised for her ability to plumb emotional depths with unsentimental insight, narrative precision, and wit.

The novel is narrated primarily from the perspective of thirty-nine-year-old, unmarried **Edith Hope**, although the viewpoint occasionally shifts. Like other Brookner protagonists, Edith Hope is mild mannered, pleasant looking, and controlled; she is also intelligent and professionally accomplished but often lonely and dissatisfied. Many critics have noted that Edith also differs from other central characters in Brookner's fiction: she has more analytical capacity, more self-reliance, and more independence than the female characters usually express. The meek, complacent image Edith projects conceals from her friends her appealing, even sly inner nature. They consider her an old maid and disapprove of her breaking off her engagement and having an affair with a married man.

While at the hotel, Edith wears a long cardigan sweater in the style of acclaimed modernist writer Virginia Woolf, consciously emulating Woolf's romantic moodiness. Writing fiction under the "more thrusting" pen name of Vanessa Wilde, Edith focuses on the feminine yearning for the ideal, full-blown romance that never seems to occur in real life. She tells her agent that she writes for the "tortoises"—meek, mousy girls—who, in her books, triumph over the "hares"—or temptresses—who have beauty and audacity on their side. Although Edith knows that the hares always win and she tells Neville that she is a "domestic animal," not a romantic. Nevertheless she maintains her romantic ideals to the end. Edith claims that without love she feels "excluded from the living world. I become cold, fish-like, immobile. I implode." Yet the setting for her dilemma, forging a solitary life with integrity, is populated by characters who have failed that quest. Edith's final choice—to return to her married lover, an uncertain and lonely future at best–may be either consistent with her romantic ideals or purely pragmatic. Some commentators have found the novel's conclusion unsatisfying, and even Brookner admitted to having second thoughts about her heroine's choice. the author pointed out that her character was rooted in the nineteenth century, when fiction was dominated by the concept of longing for something unattainable.

The other guests at Hotel du Lac provide comic yet poignant foils to the main character as well as heighten the rift between romance and reality. The extravagantly dressed, flirtatious seventy-nine-year-old **Mrs. Iris Pusey** at first seems charming to Edith, then narcissistic, greedy, and annoying, repeating such tiresome platitudes as "a woman owes it to herself to have pretty things." Mrs. Pusey symbolizes the covetous, self-indulgent type of woman who is both utterly dependent on and contemptuous of men—character traits Edith saw in her own mother. Mrs. Pusey's thirty-nine-year-old daughter, **Jennifer**, is cut from the same cloth: both are primarily interested in eating, shopping, and attracting men. Describing the fleshy, nubile Jennifer, whose clothes all seem slightly too tight for her, as having a "bottom like a large Victoria plum," Edith seems both fascinated by Jennifer's overt sensuality, referring to her as an "odalisque" (a concubine), and envious of her lack of self-consciousness. To critics, Jennifer is the embodiment of the physicality not found in the more cerebral Edith.

When she first sees mysterious, beautiful **Monica**, Edith thinks she may be a dancer. She later learns that this tall, thin woman, who has married into a wealthy family, has been exiled due to infertility. Unable to produce an heir for her husband, Sir John, Monica will probably be divorced eventually. Edith foresees a lonely life ahead for her, an existence already endured by **Comtesse de Bonneuil**, a deaf old lady with a bulldog face and such vulgar habits as belching and sitting with her legs apart. The Comtesse spends her time in a "palpable" silence, waiting for her son to visit with his impatient, unfriendly wife, who has forced her out of the beautiful home she once enjoyed.

Several critics have noted that none of the novel's male characters are particularly admirable. Edith rejects her dull fiance **Geoffrey Long,** because of his "mouselike seemliness"—a description Edith's friends might apply to Edith as well. Edith resents Geoffrey's plan to dispose of her favorite wicker chair, in which she relaxed after gardening. She objects that his replacement, an iron bench, will be uncomfortable, which suggests either that she finds her life content or that she refuses to abandon her work to marry. Edith's lover, **David Simmonds,** is a boyish, redhaired auctioneer with a wife and family. Edith loves him despite knowing that he is "foxy," self-indulgent, will never leave his wife, and is oblivious that the affair causes her loneliness and inconvenience. Brookner uses Edith's letters to David to partially explicate the plot, an epistolary technique common in eightcenth-century novels. Some commentators have complained that the light, chatty tone in Edith's letters is out of keeping with her basic nature. Others have noted how Edith edits events as well as her reactions to them.

Philip Neville, a sophisticated apparently wealthy man proposes marriage to Edith—and she initially accepts. He claims that the loveless union he offers would free her to live a dignified, carefree life. Neville has been compared to Gilbert Osmond of Henry James's 1881 novel, *The Portrait of a Lady,* who viewed his wife as a kind of acquisition to his expensive art collection. Neville makes the case for self-interest in their discussion about the relationship between love and happiness, claiming that if one makes no major emotional commitment one can concentrate on pleasing oneself. Strongly attracted to him, Edith eventually rejects Neville when she discovers his sexual liaison with Jennifer.

Other characters in *Hotel du Lac* include Edith's interfering friend **Penelope**, who introduces Edith to Geoffrey. As Edith plans her wedding, Penelope talks her into choosing an oppressive bedroom decor. Edith finds oppressive Edith's agent, **Harold Webb,** suggests that she write books with "sex for the young woman executive," which leads to the important conversation about the tortoise and the hare. **Mrs. Dempster,** Edith's "dramatic and unpredictable" cleaning lady, believes Edith committed such an affront to decency when she jilted Geoffrey that Mrs. Dempster announces she can no longer work for Edith. **Terry,** the grocery clerk who helps Edith with her garden and loves it as much as she does, proves a more faithful friend. Edith's parents also make brief appearances in the book: **Mr. Hope** is someone who gave her the good advice not to make judgments too quickly; **Mrs. Hope,** a former beauty, is so disappointed with her life as she grows older that she has become slatternly and resentful.

Further Reading

Bayles, Martha. "Romance à la Mode." *New Republic,* (March 25, 1985), 37–8.

Contemporary Literary Criticism. Vols. 32, 34, 51. Detroit: Gale Research.

Dictionary of Literary Biography: 1987 Yearbook. Detroit: Gale Research.

Gross, John. Review of *Hotel du Lac. New York Times* (January 22, 1985), C17.

Jebb, Julian. "Unblinking." *Spectator* 253, no. 8150 (September 22, 1984): 26–7.

Lee, Hermione. "Cleopatra's Way." *Observer* (September 9, 1984), 22.

Mars-Jones, Adam. "Women Beware Women." *New York Review of Books* Vol. 32, no. 1 (January 31, 1985): 17–19.

Sadler, Lynn Veach. *Anita Brookner.* Boston: Twayne, 1990.

Skinner, John. *The Fiction of Anita Brookner: Illusions of Romance.* New York: St. Martin's Press, 1992.

Tyler, Anne. "A Solitary Life Is Still Worth Living." *New York Times Book Review,* (February 3, 1985): 1, 31.

Rita Mae Brown

1944–

American novelist, poet, essayist, and scriptwriter.

Rubyfruit Jungle (novel, 1973)

Plot: The novel centers on the childhood and early adulthood of feisty, determined Molly Bolt. Born in Pennsylvania, Molly moves with her adopted parents to Florida. She realizes at an early age that she is a lesbian, and her romantic interest in girls causes her no guilt or unease. Intelligent and ambitious, Molly plans to escape her impoverished existence through a scholarship to college, and she does well in high school while carrying on a number of love affairs. At the University of Florida, Molly and her lover are both expelled because of their lesbian relationship, and Molly transfers to New York University to pursue a degree in filmmaking. There she relishes the gritty realities of city life and develops several interesting relationships. Although Molly encounters discrimination in her male-dominated program, she earns respect with her final project, which is a documentary about her adoptive mother. Unable to procure a job in her chosen field, Molly becomes an editorial assistant but remains determined to make her mark in the world.

Characters: Although Brown resists the idea of literary categorization, she is often ranked as one of America's leading lesbian feminist writers. Her serial comic novels are conventionally structured but feature unconventional, often lesbian characters distinguished by good looks, wit, and ambition. First published by a small feminist press, *Rubyfruit Jungle* became an underground hit and was reissued by a larger publisher, eventually selling over a million copies. Identified by several critics as a female-centered picaresque (a chronicle of the life and adventures of a central character), this autobiographical novel features terse, energetic prose and an irreverent tone that nevertheless relays the protagonist's serious efforts to break down societal barriers.

The course of **Molly Bolt**'s early life closely resembles that of her creator, who was also born in Pennsylvania, moved with her adoptive parents to Fort Lauderdale, was expelled from the University of Florida, and went on to graduate from New York University. Molly shows signs of her irrepressibility at an early age, when she maintains her cheerfulness and self-esteem despite a harsh, unsupportive mother and impoverished circumstances. Bright, sassy, and resourceful, Molly is only seven when she devises a scheme to raise money by selling peeks at a friend's uncircumcised penis. Her lesbian orientation is evident by the time she is in the sixth grade, when she falls in love with the beautiful Leota. From this time on, Molly is never uncomfortable with her sexuality. Ever ambitious, she carefully calculates how she must handle high school in order to survive and go on to better things. As a result, she becomes a model student who outwardly fits into the social scene, even though she is indulging in sex with other girls. Determined to "go my own way and maybe find some love here and there," Molly begins a college career that eventually takes her to the gritty, thrilling streets of New York City. There she encounters for the first time the notion that lesbians must conform to either the "butch" or the "femme" stereotypes—an idea that Molly scornfully rejects. Her independence is manifested in other ways too, such as when she defies the ideas and expectations of her male-dominated film department to make a compelling documentary about her adoptive mother. The experience of recording her mother's reflections on her life seems to help Molly make peace with her past, thus girding her for the struggle that lies ahead. As the novel ends, Molly is isolated and alienated but fiercely determined to exercise her independence and achieve her goals. Her outsider status, unconventionality, and yearning for freedom have caused several critics to compare Molly to the title character of Mark Twain's *The Adventures of Huckleberry Finn*, while others liken her to one of Horatio Alger's protagonists, who overcome humble beginnings to pursue a distinctly American vision of success.

The young Molly's less than nurturing home life with her adoptive parents does not seem to have significantly lessened her self-esteem or her determination to make her own way in the world. During Molly's childhood, her adoptive mother **Carrie Bolt** is hateful and vindictive, continually asserting, for example, that her lesbianism is unnatural. Molly does reconcile with Carrie when she returns to Florida to make her documentary, which poignantly reveals Carrie's inability to alter her bleak circumstances. Carrie's newfound acceptance of Molly at this point strikes some commentators as implausible. Molly's adoptive father **Carl Bolt** is a more sympathetic character who expresses his pride in Molly's academic successes and relishes her independent spirit.

In love with the pretty **Leota B. Bisland**, Molly is shocked and disappointed to learn that girls are not allowed to marry each other. After graduating from college, Molly returns to her home town and visits the now-married Leota, whom she describes as looking twenty years older than she is, with "two brats hanging on her like possums." Molly firmly rejects Leota's prediction that she too will someday meet the right man and settle down. Molly has another early sexual experience with her friend **Leroy**, with whom she sleeps in order to dispel his fear that he is a homosexual. Although the rather slow Leroy is generally a sympathetic friend, he tells Molly that her sexual orientation is unnatural. Molly's high school classmates include **Connie**, an intelligent girl who shares Molly's interest in Latin but who drops Molly as a friend because she fears Molly will rape her; and **Carolyn Simpson**, the school's attractive head cheerleader, who hypocritically hides her lesbian relationship with Molly.

Molly's adjustment to New York city life is eased by her friend **Calvin**, who is black, streetwise, and gay. Her lovers there include **Holly**, a beautiful black woman from a wealthy family who chides Molly for overemphasizing her working-class origins, and **Polina Bellantoni**, an older, white medieval scholar who is initially shocked by Molly's sexual overtures but who eventually allows herself to be seduced. Polina's unpleasant sexual fantasy about being a man picked up by another man in a Times Square subway station restroom serves, assert some critics, to highlight the often repressive nature of heterosexuality. Molly also has an affair with Polina's daughter **Alice**, who, unlike her mother, is "all there with no hang-ups, no stories to tell, just herself." Alice eventually succumbs to Polina's insistence that she end the relationship.

Further Reading

Chew, Martha. "Rita Mae Brown: Feminist Theorist and Southern Novelist." *Southern Quarterly* Vol. 22, no. 1 (Fall 1983): 61–80.

Contemporary Literary Criticism Vols. 18, 43, 79. Detroit: Gale Research.

Fishbein, Leslie. "*Rubyfruit Jungle*: Lesbianism, Feminism, and Narcissism." *International Journal of Women's Studies* Vol. 7, no. 2 (March–April 1984): 155-59.

Fox, Terry Curtis. "Up from Cultdom—and Down Again." *Village Voice* Vol. 22. no. 37 (September 12, 1977): 41.

Harris, Bertha. Review of *Rubyfruit Jungle*. *Village Voice* Vol. 19, no. 14 (April 4, 1974): 33–7, 44.

Henze, Shelly Temchin. "Rita Mae Brown, All American." *New Boston Review* Vol. 5, no. 5 (April–May 1979): 17–18.

Mandrell, James. "Questions of Genre and Gender: Contemporary American Versions of the Feminine Picaresque." *Novel: A Forum on Fiction* Vol. 20, no. 2 (Winter 1987): 149–70.

A. S. Byatt
1936–
English novelist, critic, and editor.

Possession (novel, 1990)

Plot: The novel takes place in England in 1986. Roland Michell is a postdoctoral research assistant at the University of London. While looking through an old book that once belonged to Randolph Henry Ash, the Victorian poet on whom Roland's work is focused and whom he worships, he discovers what appears to be a love letter from the supposedly happily married Ash to an unidentified woman. Roland pockets the letter and, after further research, identifies its probable recipient as Christabel LaMotte, an obscure writer of poetry and fairy tales revered by lesbian feminist literary scholars. Roland shares his discovery with Maud Bailey, a lecturer at the University of Lincoln, a distant relative of Christabel, and an expert on her work. Despite an undercurrent of antagonism between the two, Roland and Maud intend to uncover the nature of the poets' relationship, which has the potential to alter scholars' views of their work.

Traveling to Lincolnshire, Maud and Roland visit Seal Court, the country estate on which Christabel spent the last thirty years of her life. There they discover another set of letters, but Seal Court's current owner, Sir George Bailey, claims the letters now belong to him, and he plans to sell them to alleviate his own financial problems. Meanwhile, other scholars have also become embroiled in the mystery, including Professor Blackadder, Roland's employer and an Ash scholar; Leonora Stern, an American professor convinced of Christabel's lesbianism; Mortimer Cropper, Ash's unscrupulous American biographer; and Beatrice Nest, who has for many years been editing the journals of Ash's wife, Ellen. As the story of the Victorian lovers gradually unfolds, Maud and Roland find themselves growing attracted to one another, though both resist such a Victorian notion as "falling in love."

The suspense peaks in a dramatic meeting of most of the characters in the graveyard in which Ash and his wife are buried, where Cropper intends to steal a mysterious black box from Ash's grave. Although Cropper is thwarted by his fellow researchers, the box is found to contain a letter revealing that the idyllic month Ash and Christabel spent in Yorkshire resulted in the birth of a child. Maud is discovered to be the direct descendant of both poets and therefore owner of their letters. Roland, whose employment prospects had previously looked bleak, receives four promising job offers, and he and Maud finally admit their love for each other. The novel ends with a fanciful postscript describing an encounter between Ash and his young daughter.

Characters: Winner of England's prestigious Booker Prize in 1990, this acclaimed and highly erudite novel combines elements of detective and mystery stories, academic satire, and the "romance" referred to in the title. *Possession* juxtaposes the restrained but passionate love affair of two nineteenth-century poets with that of two rather jaded, thoroughly modern scholars. The novel explores the differences in how love and sex have been approached in each period, the impact of the past on the present, and the possible implications of biographical research. Composed not only of standard narrative but of poetry, letters, and journal excerpts, *Possession* is a melange of styles and voices, and Byatt has been enthusiastically lauded for her skill in creating and blending these elements. The text relates a thrilling love story and mystery, but it is also densely woven with literary allusions and symbolism.

Twenty-nine-year-old **Roland Michell** is the novel's closest approximation of a hero. He is an impoverished postdoctoral researcher at the University of London, working part time with Professor James Blackadder on an edition of Randolph Henry Ash's poetry. Roland's life is dull, his relationship with his girlfriend Val uninspired, and his future employment prospects dismal. His languid outlook begins to change, however, when he discovers love letters written by his beloved poet and investigates the story behind them. Roland appeals to Maud Bailey for help because he knows she is an expert on Christabel LaMotte, though he is put off by the beautiful scholar's frigid demeanor and apparent snobbery. Painfully class-conscious, Roland feels both inferior to and resentful of the upper-middle-class Maud. Yet as they uncover more about the passion between Ash and LaMotte, Roland and Maud are drawn closer together. Though Roland suspects he is falling in love with Maud, due to his tendency to intellectualize his emotions, he resists believing that he has entered such a conventional "romantic" state. However, being immersed in the restrained yet emotionally resonant perspective of the Victorian age proves liberating for Roland. As the novel draws to a close, he abandons his former view of language as inherently limited and discovers that it now seems full of potential; it is suggested that he may even become a poet. Roland's material prospects have also improved by the end of the novel (contributing to what some critics have viewed as its rather implausible conclusion) and, like the heroes of all romances, he also wins the woman he loves.

Maud Bailey, a lecturer at the University of Lincoln, is a feminist scholar who has written a much-praised study on her distant relative Christabel LaMotte. Maud has a glacial beauty that she tries to dim by constantly wearing a scarf over her long blonde hair; due to her strong feminism and to having been emotionally damaged, Maud resents the effect her beauty seems to have on other people. Once disastrously involved with an arrogant, self-important, and colossally insensitive man named Fergus Wolff, Maud now distances herself from further hurt and degradation. Thus she appears to Roland as frigid and snobbish. Like him, Maud has absorbed a literary orthodoxy that Byatt skillfully satirizes in some of their exchanges. For instance, even though Maud is a psychoanalytical critic she claims she is interested in the *textual,* not the personal, and that a psychological analysis does not require delving into an author's life. The cerebral, antiromantic stance that both Roland and Maud represent is contrasted and eventually defeated by the highly emotional doubts, inhibitions, and passions of their Victorian counterparts. Despite their supposed sophistication, these two modern scholars have not yet found real fulfillment. When Maud finally admits her love for Roland and allows him to "possess" her, she achieves a satisfaction similar to what Christabel achieved with Ash. In a perhaps implausible but certainly romantic twist, Maud finds that she is a direct descendant of her beloved poet. Thus she plays an enhanced role in keeping Christabel's legacy alive.

Byatt has been particularly praised for her successful invention of two fictional poets who, most critics agree, are convincing representatives of their period and profession. **Randolph Henry Ash** is probably modeled after English Victorian poet Robert Browning; Ash's "Ask to Embla," is a dramatic monologue similar to Browning's work. Unlike the woman poet with whom he develops a relationship, Ash was well known and much respected in his own day and continues to be idolized and studied by modern scholars. His speculative, rather verbose letters reveal a forceful, broad intellect and an interest in typical nineteenth-century areas of inquiry, such as faith and doubt, amateur geology and biology, Darwinism, spiritualism, and world mythologies. His passion for Christabel, with whom he connects both intellectually and emotionally, obviously causes him great inner turmoil, for he feels a tender regard for his devoted wife and has a public reputation for integrity. Ash's final response to this struggle is to arrange for a month of solitary research in Yorkshire, where he is joined by Christabel. After this brief period of passionate happiness, the two part forever. The novel's postscript reveals that Ash knew of his daughter Maia's existence and actually visited her, relaying a message for her "aunt" that never reached Christabel, just as Ash apparently never read Christabel's letter describing Maia's birth and life.

Christabel LaMotte is the obscure poet and fairy tale writer who, because of her independent vision and close relationship with another woman artist, has been adopted as a heroine by lesbian feminist scholars, including Professor Leonora Stern. Thus the possibility that her life might have included an important heterosexual liaison is of major interest to Maud and others who know and love her work. LaMotte is reportedly based on nineteenth-century poets Christina Rosetti or Emily Dickinson, and her spare, intense verse with its eccentric punctuation does notably resemble Dickinson's. Maud and Roland discover that her most celebrated work, an epic poem called "The Fairy Melusina" that focuses on a French water-spirit, contains many details gleaned from her stay in Yorkshire with Ash. Long before she met Ash, LaMotte made a pact to live a withdrawn, independent life with Blanche Glover. The two promised to support each other in their artistic work, a promise that Blanche, at least, considered broken when Christabel departed for Yorkshire. Modern feminist scholars believe that the two women shared a lesbian relationship, a question never completely resolved in the novel. The letter recovered from Ash's grave reveals Christabel's unhappiness during the last thirty years of her life, when she watched her daughter grow apart from her. Maia loves neither her ''aunt'' nor poetry, and only Christabel's many-times-great granddaughter Maud recognizes her value.

The highly entertaining academic characters in *Possession* enable Byatt to work out the progress of the mystery and lampoon a variety of literary theories, attitudes, and pretensions. Confined to a small basement room in the British Library, sarcastic, dour **Professor James Blackadder** has been working since 1951 on an edition of Ash's poetry, and he has been disillusioned by this Dickensian task. Although he makes an unpleasant impression on the reader at first, Blackadder shows another side when he warmly recommends Roland to potential employers inquiring about him, and he offers Roland a full-time research assistantship. **Professor Beatrice Nest**, who also works in a dingy basement office, is a fat, frowsy, shy woman who began her career when female academics were allowed to practice only on the fringes of research. Thus for twenty-five years she had been editing the journals of Ellen Ash when she would have preferred to focus on the great poet himself. Nevertheless, she has developed an appreciation and sympathy for the unintellectual but sensitive Ellen, and she is more conscious than any of the other scholars of the ''mystery of privacy.'' Professor Nest feels that the mysterious black box should remain where it is—that the couple's rest should not be disturbed.

With her loud voice, heavy body, and unconventional clothing, **Professor Leonora Stern**, an American from Tallahassee, Florida, is an especially vivid character. Energetic and outspoken, Leonora is a radical feminist lesbian who is not averse to sleeping with men on occasion and has, in fact, been married to two of them. Leonora's literary criticism—particularly on LaMotte—tends to emphasize the elements of female sexuality she discovers in any text she studies. Described by critic Jay Parini in the *New York Times Book Review* as ''a cross between Leon Edel [the noted biographer of Henry James] and Liberace,'' **Mortimer Cropper** is the obsessive author of *The Great Ventriloquist*, a biography of Randolph Henry Ash. A fastidious, pretentious Anglophile who works out of Robert Dale Owen University in New Mexico, Cropper lacks scruples and will apparently stop at nothing to collect Ash memorabilia for his university's collection. Cropper is comically thwarted when he tries to steal the black box buried in Ash's grave. **Fergus Wolff**, Maud's former lover, is a handsome, arrogant ''poststructuralist'' who becomes interested in the Ash-LaMotte letters as a means to advance his own career. But like Cropper, the novel's other disreputable academic character, Wolff is ultimately thwarted.

The characters from the Victorian segments of *Possession* are portrayed primarily through the letters and journal entries included in the novel. **Blanche Glover**, perhaps the most tragic of all the characters, is an obscure, frustrated painter who feels abandoned and betrayed by her friend (and possibly her lover) Christabel. Blanche drowns herself in the Thames River when the pregnant Christabel is in Brittany. Blanche's suicide letter is especially poignant in its passion for her art and her feelings of failure. She claims that her poverty, the collapse of her pact with Christabel, and her uselessness leave her no alternative but suicide. **Ellen Ash**, Randolph Henry's devoted wife, lacks intellectual depth but does reveal sensitivity and descriptive power in her journal entries. She was apparently visited by the distraught Blanche Glover during her husband's stay in Yorkshire and so probably knew of his liaison with Christabel, though she never says so. The fact that she had the final letter from her husband's lover buried with him—and mentioned this fact in her journal—suggests that she intended for it to be discovered some day. The novel also includes the journals of **Sabine de Kercoz**, a precocious adolescent who recounts the visit of her cousin Christabel to her home in Brittany and the birth there of Christabel's baby. The child born of Ash and LaMotte's liaison—named **Maia** but called, at her own insistence, May—is raised by Christabel's sister Sophie. She lives a happy, conventional existence, never knowing that the spinster aunt whose company she suffers is actually her mother or that the kind man she met one day in the garden was her real father.

Other characters in *Possession* include **Val**, Roland's dispirited girlfriend, who finds happiness with another man at the end of the book. **Sir George Bailey** and his wife, **Lady Bailey,** are the current owners of the Lincolnshire house in which Christabel spent her last years; stubborn, irascible, and devoted to his disabled wife, Sir George hopes that selling Christabel's letters will allow him to buy Lady. Bailey a wheelchair and refurbish Seal Court. Good-natured, handsome **Euan McIntyre**, Sir George's lawyer, falls in love with Val and helps the band of scholars resolve the Ash-LaMotte mystery.

Further Reading

Brookner, Anita. "Eminent Victorians and Others." *Spectator* Vol. 264, no. 8434 (March 3, 1990): 35.

Contemporary Literary Criticism. Vols. 19, 65. Detroit: Gale Research.

Dictionary of Literary Biography. Vol. 14. Detroit: Gale Research.

Hulbert, Ann. "The Great Ventriloquist." *New Republic* (January 7 & 14, 1991): 47–9.

Jenkyns, Richard. "Disinterring Buried Lives." *Times Literary Supplement,* no. 4535 (March 2, 1990): 213–14.

Karlin, Danny. "Prolonging Her Absence." *London Review of Books* 12, no. 5 (March 8, 1990): 17–18.

Parini, Jay. "Unearthing the Secret Lover." *New York Times Book Review* (October 21, 1990): 9, 11.

Rifkind, Donna. "Victorians' Secrets." *New Criterion* 9, no. 6 (February 1991): 77–80.

See, Carolyn. "At a Magic Threshold." *Los Angeles Times Book Review,* (October 28, 1990): 2, 13.

Raymond Carver
1938–1988

American short story writer, poet, and scriptwriter.

"Neighbors" (short story, 1976)

Plot: Bill and Arlene Miller, a thoroughly average couple who consider themselves happy, agree to care for the apartment of their more sophisticated neighbors, Jim and Harriet Stone, while the Stones are out of town. During several visits to the Stones' apartment to water their plants and feed their cat, Bill explores his neighbors' private lives by drinking their liquor, lying on their bed, pilfering their cigarettes and pills, and even trying on Harriet's clothing. Arlene also indulges herself in the Stones' apartment. Mutually aroused by this experience, the Millers enjoy an enhanced sex life. When Arlene tells Bill she has found some suggestive photos, they excitedly return to the apartment to discover that Arlene has locked the key inside. Dismayed, the Millers huddle together outside their neighbors' apartment.

Characters: Like all of Carver's stories, "Neighbors" (which appeared in his first short story collection, *Will You Please Be Quiet Please?*) portrays in spare, unadorned language and realistic detail the lives of ordinary people. This tightly structured story features the kind of negative epiphany found in much of Carver's early work—a moment when the characters realize that happiness they think they feel is fragile and may at any time be jarred out of place. Like many Carver protagonists, **Bill and Arlene Miller** do not seem to fully comprehend their own yearnings, despite their sense that the Stones live a "fuller and brighter life" than their own. The Millers' markedly mundane occupations—bookkeeper and secretary—help reinforce the dullness of their daily lives. Although they claim to need a vacation, they apparently never take one, whereas their neighbors travel frequently and generally seem more engaged with life. Entering the Stones' domain, the Millers briefly shed their own identities. Bill frequently watches himself in the Stones' mirrors (a common symbol for dissociation of identity in Carver's fiction) and also looks out the window while dressed in Harriet's clothing as he experiments with being someone else. Although the reader never learns what Arlene does in the Stones' apartment, her flushed face and lint-covered sweater on her return suggest similar behavior.

The Millers have always considered themselves happy and rarely argue, but neither do they talk much while sharing meals, and they spend most evenings in front of the television. The forbidden pleasures of invading the Stones' privacy, however, awaken their sexual interest. Their pleasure comes to an end when the Millers learn they are locked out of the apartment and, in an image much quoted and praised by critics, they "leaned into the door as if against a wind, and braced themselves." The story's ending is ambiguous, for the reader does not know what will happen next, yet it seems likely that the "wind" the Millers face—despite their closeness at this moment and mutual sense of loss—is an ill one. According to David Boxer and Cassandra Philips in their essay in the *Iowa Review*, Carver has effectively portrayed the Millers' "wistful identification with some distant, unattainable idea of self."

"Cathedral" (short story, 1983)

Plot: The narrator is annoyed to learn that his wife's old friend Robert, a blind man who once employed her as a reader, is coming to visit the couple. The wife has corresponded with her friend for years via cassette tapes, describing the details of her early marriage, divorce, and remarriage to her husband, the narrator. Uncomfortable with the prospect of having a blind person in his home, the narrator is surprised by Robert's appearance and behavior: his booming voice and full beard are not what he expected, and he eats, drinks, and smokes marijuana with relish. After dinner the three watch television. After the narrator's wife has fallen asleep, a program about cathedrals begins. The narrator asks Robert if he knows what cathedrals look like or represent, and Robert, admitting that he does not, asks the narrator to draw one. With Robert's hand lying on top of his own, the narrator traces roofs, spires, arches, and even people. Eventually Robert instructs the narrator to close his eyes and continue drawing. The narrator reports that this experience was "like nothing else in my life up to now."

Characters: The title story of Carver's 1983 volume, *Cathedral,* illustrates the shift in perspective that marks that collection. While the characters in Carver's earlier work are trapped in desolate (though not necessarily tragic) lives and lack the comprehension or ability to communicate that might help them escape, the stories in *Cathedral* feature a more hopeful, affirmative tone and more expansive narration. In fact, Carver noted in an interview that he realized before writing these stories that he had gone as far in the direction of minimalist as he could, "cutting everything down to the marrow, not just to the bone." One of the most acclaimed stories in the collection (which was nominated for the Pulitzer Prize and the National Book Critics Circle Award), "Cathedral" explores through its sometimes comically insensitive narrator the possibility that even the most ordinary sensibility can achieve deeper insight.

The narrator's irritation at having to entertain his wife's old friend may be attributed not only to his jealousy—for his wife has corresponded with Robert for years and shared many details of her life with him—but to his discomfort with blindness itself. He admits that his idea of blind people comes from the movies, where they always move slowly and silently. In a passage that reveals Carver's talent for black humor, the narrator muses on Robert's dead wife—how she was never seen by the man she loved and must never have received a compliment about her looks from him, "and she on an express to the grave." The narrator is surprised to learn that Robert not only behaves much like anyone else but also has a vibrant personality. Nevertheless, he treats his houseguest in a vaguely mocking, abrasive manner. During the exchange that develops between the two men while listening to the program about cathedrals, however, the narrator's defenses dissolve. He tries to describe to Robert the buildings being discussed on television, but he finds it difficult to explain their religious aspect; he says that he is "an agnostic or something." Significantly, then, he does undergo a kind of religious experience when, with the blind man's hand on top of his own, he draws the cathedral. The two share a rare moment of connection or fellowship that the narrator is reluctant to abandon; he keeps his eyes closed even after Robert has told him to open them and look at the drawing. The narrator's comment that this was "really something" indicates that he is no more articulate about his own feelings than before but also that he has undergone a profound, revelatory experience.

The blind man, **Robert**, is portrayed entirely through the narrator's rather jaded perspective, and the reader never receives many details about his personality or life. We do know that he has a job in social services and that he has recently lost his wife, to whom he was happily married. Despite the narrator's antagonism and insensitivity, Robert makes a positive impression through his cheerfully loud voice (in which he calls the narrator "Bub"), lack of self pity, and obvious pleasure in living. He eats, drinks, and smokes marijuana with gusto, chats amiably despite the narrator's sarcasm, and listens with real interest to the television program. By encouraging the narrator to draw a cathedral with him, he achieves a meaningful connection with his previously defensive host and helps him to broaden his vision. Despite his own disability and sorrow, he has remained engaged with life and with others.

The only other character in "Cathedral" is **the narrator's wife**, who is portrayed entirely through her husband's perspective. She is obviously fond of Robert, with whom she has faithfully maintained a correspondence over many years. She seems genuinely happy to see him and eager to make him comfortable in her home, and she disapproves of her husband's subtly antagonistic attitude toward their guest. In revealing that his wife occasionally writes poems, "usually after something really important had happened to her," the narrator suggests that she is more sensitive than he.

"A Small, Good Thing" (short story, 1983)

Plot: In anticipation of her son Scotty's eighth birthday, Ann Weiss goes to a bakery and orders a special birthday cake. The baker's abrupt manner bothers her, and she wonders why he does not seem to identify with the situation of a child's birthday. Two days later, on the morning of his birthday, Scotty is hit by a car while walking to school. Although he manages to make it home, he soon collapses and is taken to the hospital. The doctors assure Ann and her husband, Howard, that Scotty will recover, but he does not wake up for several days, and they wait anxiously by his bedside. When Howard returns home to bathe and feed the family's dog, he receives a telephone call concerning "a cake that wasn't picked up." Unaware that Ann had ordered a birthday cake and irritated by the caller's belligerent tone,

Howard hangs up. Later, Ann returns home and fails to recognize the baker's voice when he calls about "Scotty, that problem. Have you forgotten about Scotty?" After Scotty dies unexpectedly from a "one-in-a-million circumstance," the dazed and grief-stricken Weisses return home. Again the baker calls, asking, "Have you forgotten about Scotty?" Ann screams into the phone, calling him an "evil bastard." Finally Ann realizes the caller's identity, she and Howard drive to the bakery to confront him, even though it is the middle of the night. The scene is tense and potentially violent until Ann reveals that Scotty has died. Then the baker, acknowledging his insensitivity, invites the couple to sit down. He asks for their forgiveness and serves them bread and coffee, talking to them through the night about his own loneliness and doubt.

Characters: Because it is a revision of a story that appeared in an earlier collection ("The Bath" in *What We Talk about When We Talk about Love,* 1981), this story is a particularly illuminating example of Carver's shift toward more expansive, hopeful fiction. Frequently cited as one of his most successful stories, "A Small, Good Thing" ends on a note of redemption that contrasts strongly with the bleak existentialism of "The Bath." While the original story exhibited the stark realism and minimal characterization typical of Carver's earlier work, the revised version features, in addition to its more affirmative conclusion, many more details and expanded dialogue. Unlike the characters in Carver's earlier stories, those in "A Small, Good Thing" communicate successfully, thus forging a profound and healing connection that some critics have identified as Christian in tone.

Referred to only as "the mother" in "The Bath," **Ann Weiss** receives in the revised story not only a name but also more finely delineated emotions. As the story opens, she is perplexed by the baker's abrupt manner and wonders why he does not seem to realize how special birthdays are to children. The overwhelming anxiety and fear she feels as her son lies unconscious in the hospital are well portrayed, as are her feelings of connection and sympathy for the black family who are also waiting as their son hovers near death. Carver effectively conveys Ann's mingled sorrow, bewilderment, and rage in the wake of Scotty's death, culminating in the moment when she collapses into sobs after angrily confronting the baker. Ann's relationship with her husband is better developed in "A Small, Good Thing" than in "The Bath"; both admit that they have prayed for Scotty, and this revelation as well as their shared experience of loss seems to strengthen the bond between them. The character of **Howard Weiss**, Scotty's father, is similarly fleshed out in the later story. For example, in "The Bath," Howard is described merely as "lucky and happy," but in "A Small, Good Thing" his background is filled in: college, then marriage, followed by several years of business school, a good job with an investment firm, and fatherhood.

Although **the baker** is a central figure in both versions of the story, he is transformed from an almost abstract force of evil in "The Bath" to a flawed, pitiable human being in "A Small, Good Thing." He is the only character in the original story who receives a physical description: an older man, he has a thick neck and wet, staring eyes, and he wears a heavy apron knotted under his large belly. During his initial encounter with Ann, the baker is sullen and detached, and his belligerent and even menacing tone when he calls the Weisses is undoubtedly heightened by his failure to identify himself. When Ann and Howard confront him at the bakery, he is initially wary and defensive, picking up a rolling pin as a potential weapon. But as soon as he learns that Scotty is dead, the baker's manner changes. He becomes contrite and solicitous, bringing in chairs for the couple and insisting that they eat some rolls because eating is "a small, good thing in a time like this." Several critics, likening this offering of bread to the Christian ritual of communion, have identified it as a symbol of redemption. Whereas the reader learns nothing substantial about the baker in the earlier story, Carver gives us in the revised version a view into his emotional life. Claiming that he once was a different kind of person, the baker shares with Ann and Howard his loneliness and sense of futility and describes how it has felt to be childless for so many years.

Although some reviewers have found the baker's monologue unconvincing and the story's ending contrived, others claim that "A Small, Good Thing" evidences a positive development in Carver's fiction.

Further Reading

Adelman, Bob, and Tess Gallagher. *Carver Country: The World of Raymond Carver.* New York: Charles Scribner's Sons, 1990.

Atlas, James. "Less Is Less." *Atlantic,* (June 1981): 96–8.

Boxer, David, and Cassandra Phillips. "Will You Please Be Quiet Please?": Voyeurism, Dissociation, and the Art of Raymond Carver." *Iowa Review* 10, no. 3 (summer 1979): 75–90.

Bugeja, Michael J. "Tarnish and Silver: An Analysis of Carver's 'Cathedral.'" *South Dakota Review* 24, no. 3 (autumn 1986): 73–87.

Clark, Miriam Marty. "Raymond Carver's Monologic Imagination." *Modern Fiction Studies* 37, no. 2 (summer 1991): 240–47.

Contemporary Literary Criticism. Vols. 22, 36, 53, 55. Detroit: Gale Research.

Dictionary of Literary Biography:1984 and 1988 Yearbooks. Detroit: Gale Research.

Gorra, Michael. "Laughter and Bloodshed." *Hudson Review* 37, no. 1 (spring 1984): 151–64.

Howe, Irving. "Stories of Our Loneliness." *New York Times Book Review* (September 11, 1983): 1, 42–3.

Robinson, Marilynne. "Marriage and Other Astonishing Bonds." *New York Times Book Review* (May 15, 1988): 1, 35, 40–1.

Runyon, Randolph. *Reading Raymond Carver.* Syracuse, N.Y.: Syracuse University Press, 1992.

Saltzman, Arthur M. *Understanding Raymond Carver.* Columbia: University of South Carolina Press, 1988.

Short Story Criticism. Vol. 8. Detroit: Gale Research.

Skenazy, Paul. "Life in Limbo: Ray Carver's Fiction." *Enclitic* 11, no. 1, Issue 21 (fall 1988): 77–83.

Stull, William L. "Beyond Hopelessville: Another Side of Raymond Carver." *Philological Quarterly* 64, no. 1 (winter 1985): 1–15.

Towers, Robert. "Low-Rent Tragedies." *New York Review of Books* Vol. 28, no. 8 (May 14, 1981): 37–40.

Vander Weele, Michael. "Raymond Carver and the Language of Desire." *Denver Quarterly* 22, no. 1 (summer 1987): 108–22.

Weber, Bruce. "Raymond Carver: A Chronicler of Blue Collar Despair." *New York Times Magazine* (June 24, 1984): 36, 38, 42–6, 48–50.

Camilo José Cela
1916 –

Spanish novelist, poet, dramatist, travel writer, and nonfiction writer.

The Family of Pascual Duarte (*La familia de Pascual Duarte*; novel, 1942)

Plot: Most of the novel takes place at an unspecified time (but probably just before and after the Spanish Civil War) and is structured as the memoirs of Spanish peasant Pascual Duarte. Notes from a fictional "transcriber" are included at the beginning and end of the book, and two accounts of Pascual's death are added at the end. Pascual is about to be executed for the murder of Don Jesús González de la Riva, a wealthy landlord from his home village. Pascual first recounts his destitute, miserable childhood, describing the various members of his family. Both parents were alcoholics—his mother a bad-tempered nag and his father an abusive bully; his sister, Rosario, was attractive and intelligent but became a liar, a thief, and finally a prostitute; the youngest child, Mario, was mentally retarded and died at the age of ten after his ears were nibbled off by a hog. Pascual married a girl named Lola whom he first noticed (and raped) in the cemetery at his brother's burial. Lola miscarried the couple's first child after being thrown from a horse, and a vengeful Pascual duly killed the horse. He later also killed his beloved dog, because she seemed to be looking at him with reproach. Feeling a growing inclination to murder his own mother, Pascual left the village, spending two years in the seaside town of La Coruña. On his return he learned that Lola had an affair with a drifter nicknamed Stretch, who had also been his sister's lover. After admitting this liaison, Lola died. Pascual confronted Stretch, who challenged him to a fight; Pascual subsequently killed Stretch and was sentenced to a short prison term. When he returned home, he married a village girl named Esperanza, but his relative happiness ended when his old impulse to kill his mother returned and he actually performed the deed. This time Pascual was sentenced to a long prison term, but he was released early due to his good behavior. Pascual's final victim was Don Jésus, but no details about this murder are offered. A priest and a prison guard give varying accounts of Pascual's death.

Characters: Considered Spain's most important contemporary writer, Cela received the Nobel Prize for Literature in 1989. *The Family of Pascual Duarte* is his first novel and his best-known work; some contend that it is the second most widely read book in Spanish literature (the first is Cervantes's *Don Quixote*). Told in a deadpan, seemingly emotionless voice, the novel recounts the desperate conditions of life in civil war-era Spain and chronicles the bitterness and pessimism of that period. Although Cela fought on the Nationalist side in the war and was subsequently aligned with the government of Franco, Spain's fascist dictator, several of his books were banned in his own country due to their unflinching portrayal of the brutal conditions Cela saw around him. Cela is often credited with initiating the *tremendismo* movement, which emphasized structural innovation and brutal, even violent realism; yet Cela himself contends that a preoccupation with the grotesque has, in fact, always been a part of Spanish literature. *The Family of Pascual Duarte* was published several months after *The Stranger,* the existentialist classic by French author Albert Camus, and many scholars have noted such similarities between the two novels as the occurrence of meaningless murders and a pervading sense of spiritual void. Cela, however, seems less concerned than Camus with intellectual probing and more with creating a highly realistic portrait of what happens when a primitive mentality develops within a brutal environment.

In his introduction to his translation of *The Family of Pascual Duarte,* Anthony Kerrigan describes the novel as "the episodic tale of an unheroic outsider without direction or scruples, engaged in a one-man social war." **Pascual Duarte** is a simple, uneducated peasant whose murderous impulses are apparently the result of an inherently violent nature and a miserable upbringing in poverty and cruelty. In a matter-of-fact tone, Pascual explains how he raped his first wife, slaughtered several dumb beasts out of anger and paranoia, killed one man almost accidentally and his mother quite deliberately, and, finally—for a reason he does not disclose—murdered a kindly landlord. Unable to understand or explain his own behavior, Pascual blames not society but fate and his own sinfulness for his escalating violence. He acts without coherent moral or ethical notions, and he nurtures no expectations or hopes for himself or his future; thus he may be seen as a kind of antihero. In fact, many scholars have identified Pascual as the modern forebear of the picaresque figures of classic Spanish literature, who took their adventures and mishaps as they came and were often used to illustrate the flaws of their societies. Some reviewers have found implausible the idea that a destitute peasant could compose a memoir, but others felt that Cela succeeds in carrying off this unlikely premise by focusing not so much on Pascual's inner life as on the sheer horror of his circumstances and deeds, which in turn dramatize his horrific environment.

Pascual's descriptions of his family life give the reader insight into his development. His father, **Estaban Duarte Diniz**, was a drunken bully who regularly battered his wife and children; he died a suitably gruesome death, locked in a pantry after contracting rabies. **Pascual's mother** was a gaunt, sallow woman who always dressed in black. Bad-tempered, foul-mouthed, and dirty, she too was an alcoholic and abusive toward her children, who were all destined to meet bad ends. The fact that Pascual was obsessed with murdering her and eventually did so represents the epitome of human barbarity. **Rosario** is as much a victim as her brother, and her behavior was nearly as extreme. Endowed with intelligence and good looks, she took to lying, stealing, drinking, and prostituting, eventually contracting syphilis. But poor **Mario** is most unfortunate of the three siblings: born mentally retarded and completely helpless, he was neglected by his entire family. His ears were nibbled off by a hog, and eventually he drowned in a vat of oil.

Despite the fact that Pascual began his relationship with his wife **Lola** by raping her (during which encounter she eventually began to enjoy herself), the two achieved a few brief interludes of contentment together. These moments of happiness were invariably shattered by tragedy. First Lola miscarried the baby they had happily anticipated, then their infant son died, then Lola herself died (apparently of a heart attack) after admitting that Stretch was her lover while Pascual was in La Coruña. Pascual's relative happiness with his second wife, **Esperanza** (who claimed to have long harbored a secret passion for him), was also brief and ended when Pascual murdered his mother. **Paco Lopez**, or El Estirao (**Stretch**), was a tall, handsome, lazy drifter who easily attracted women; he was the lover not only of Pascual's sister but of his wife, and he died almost accidentally after challenging Pascual to a fight.

Don Jesús González de la Riva, Pascual's final victim, was the richest man in Pascual's village and was known for his kindness and generosity. Pascual dedicates his memoirs to Don Jesús, whom he claims called him Pascualillo and smiled when Pascual came to kill him. This may suggest that Pascual, emerging from jail during the bloody days of the Spanish Civil War, discovered the landlord dying of wounds inflicted by Republican torturers and agreed to put him out of his misery. On the other hand, the murder may have been inspired by antifascist sentiments aroused in Pascual by the brutalities he had witnessed. **Don Santiago Lurueña**, the prison chaplain, claims in a letter attached to Pascual's memoirs that the prisoner was in the end "a poor tame lamb" who repented his sins and died serene. By contrast, prison guard **Don Cesário Martín**, whose letter reveals his overzealous attention to regulations, claims that before being executed Pascual fainted, pleaded for mercy, and generally behaved in a cowardly manner, showing little consideration for those present to witness his death. These contradictory accounts consistent with the senselessness of Pascual's life. **Don Joaquín Barrera Lopéz** was the first recipient of the memoirs, chosen by Pascual because he was a respectable friend of Don Jesús. **The transcriber,** whose notes appear at the beginning and end of the novel, says that he found the memoirs in a pharmacy, that he cut out a few passages that were ''too crude,'' and that he hopes Pascual's account will serve as a model of behavior to be avoided—a negative example of how to live.

Further Reading

Bestsellers Vol. 90, no. 2. Detroit: Gale Research, 1990.

Carr, Raymond. ''Cold Comfort Hacienda.'' *Spectator* Vol. 264, no. 8428 (January 20, 1990): 27–8.

Contemporary Literary Criticism. Vols. 4, 13, 59. Detroit: Gale Research.

Donahue, Francis. Review of *The Family of Pascual Duarte. Southwest Review* (autumn 1978).

Feldman, David W. ''Camilo José Cela and 'La familia de Pascual Duarte.''' *Hispania* Vol. 44, no. 4 (December 1961): 656–59.

Foster, David. *Forms of the Novel in the Work of Camilo José Cela.* Columbia: University of Missouri Press, 1967.

Kerr, Sarah. ''Shock Treatment.'' *New York Review of Books* Vol. 39, no. 16 (October 8, 1992): 35–9.

Kerrigan, Anthony. Introduction to *The Family of Pascual Duarte.* Camilo José Cela. Boston: Little Brown, 1964.

Kirsner, Robert. *The Novels and Travels of Camilo José Cela.* Chapel Hill: University of North Carolina Press, 1964.

McPheeters, D. W. *Camilo José Cela.* New York: Twayne, 1969.

Ornstein, Jacob, and James Y. Causey. ''Camilo José Cela: Spain's New Novelist.'' *Books Abroad* Vol. 27, no. 2 (spring 1953): 136–37.

Arthur C. Clarke
1917–

English novelist, short story writer, essayist, nonfiction writer, and scriptwriter.

Childhood's End (novel, 1953)

Plot: The novel is divided into three sections. The first, ''Earth and the Overlords,'' chronicles the arrival on Earth of the Overlords, an extraterrestrial race with intelligence superior to humans'. They establish a benevolent dictatorship, halting the Cold War and further scientific development and banishing poverty, disease, and ignorance. The Secretary General of the United Nations, Rikki Stormgren, befriends the Overlord leader, Karellen, who, like all the Overlords, refuses to show himself to human beings. Through a trick, Stormgren manages to view Karellen, but he never reveals what he sees. Later in the book, when humans are judged ready to bear the shock, the Overlords allow everyone to see them in the form of devils.

The novels second section, "The Golden Age," illustrates the peaceful yet boring lives of such men as George Greggson and Jan Rodricks. The latter yearns to explore the stars, but the Overlords have declared space travel "not for man." Rodricks manages to leave Earth in an Overlord rocket ship by hiding himself in a model of a whale being taken to a museum on the Overlords' planet. Meanwhile, Greggson and Jean Morrel complete the social contract that replaces marriage, and the couple subsequently has two children, Jeffrey and Jennifer. These and other human children figure prominently in the novel's third section, "The Last Generation," in which the reader learns that the Overlords are competent but limited midwives to an evolutionary process that only the human race can fulfill. The children of Earth begin to develop telepathic powers that bring them into communion with the Overmind, the all-powerful being that oversees the universe. Rodricks returns from space eighty years after his departure, disabused of any desire for worlds other than his own. He witnesses the final transcendence of Earth's children as they abandon their material form, a process that also entails the destruction of Earth itself.

Characters: Considered a science fiction classic, *Childhood's End* was published just as this literary genre was gaining respectability and appealing to a wider audience. The novel reveals Clarke's mastery of science and metaphysical interests and suggests that, despite the threat of nuclear devastation, humanity may be destined for a positive future—even if it is not quite the future we imagine. A few critics regard the novel's mysticism as sentimental and its prose pretentious, and most find its characters wooden and conventional. Yet others laud Clarke for infusing *Childhood's End* with a compelling ambiguity. The reader must determine whether the author means to condemn or celebrate science and scientific development and whether or not Clarke's vision is hopeful or despairing.

Many critics note that characterization is not emphasized in *Childhood's End;* most of the book's characters, in fact, are similar in temperament: they are cool, rational, sensible, and impatient when they encounter foolishness. These qualities certainly characterize **Rikki Stormgren,** Secretary General of the United Nations and a central figure in the novel's first section. Stormgren does not resent the rule of the Overlords because they have rescued the human race from war, illness, and starvation. He does, however, wonder what their goal is; he wants to understand why the Overlords have come to Earth. This curiosity motivates his desire to see Karellen, whom he genuinely likes and trusts. When he manages to get a look, however, Stormgren reasons that the alien's devilish form means that earthlings and the Overlords must have had prior contact in the past in order to imprint their image on the collective human subconscious. Stormgren concludes that even though the Overlords take a shape that humans consider evil, they are actually guardian angels.

The novel's prime Overlord is **Karellen,** who develops a firm friendship with Stormgren. The Overlords are highly intelligent and technologically more advanced than human beings, to whom they refuse to show themselves. After fifty years the human race is judged advanced enough to withstand the shock, and Karellen reveals himself. Standing in the doorway of his ship, holding a human child in each arm, he appears in the classic form of the devil so prevalent in human mythology: he is huge, with horns on his head, leathery wings, and a barbed tail. Commentators differ on the meaning of the Overlords' appearance. Some agree with Stormgren that it signifies some long-ago encounter between the Overlords and humanity, while others contend that their appearance carries a premonition of apocalypse. Similarly, the presence of the children with Karellen may signify either that the Overlords have come to protect the children of Earth or to take them away. When Karellen and his fellow Overlords arrive, they seem almost godlike. They are able to travel through space, manipulate time, prevent nuclear war, and fashion utopia on Earth. Yet by the end of the book the Overlords are tragically limited. As Karellen realizes, his race is not capable of (and cannot comprehend) the evolutionary step that human beings are destined to take. The

Overlords' role is to shepherd humanity toward its fate—to serve as midwives as the inhabitants of Earth are transformed into a life-form no longer dependent on matter.

Jan Rodricks is a product of the "Golden Age" made possible by the Overlords' protection and guidance. Jan finds the serene, safe life on Earth boring, and he resents the limitations imposed on his curiosity. Jan longs to travel in space, but the Overlords have decreed that "the stars are not for man." Thus he stows away on an Overlord ship. His passage in the belly of a model of a whale evokes the biblical story of Jonah, who also found shelter from an alien environment inside a whale's belly. Rodricks ultimately fails to comprehend what he sees on the Overlords' planet. When he returns to Earth eighty years later, he has lost any desire to venture away from home. His disillusionment suggests that the longing for some idyllic life in the distant future may be misguided. Critic John Huntington contends that Jan's character gives us "a scale by which we can measure the sacrifice transcendence involves."

Whereas Jan Rodricks stands on a veranda above a spectacular African vista and longs to explore and discover, the same experience gives **George Greggson** a feeling of being lost and in need of human reassurance. George's alliance with **Jean Morrel** is supposed to be a more enlightened arrangement than conventional marriage, but it is marked by twentieth-century morality and roles. Jean, for instance, is the primary caretaker of the couple's two children, and George is the rather distant father. Somewhat clairvoyant, Jean foresees that the extinct volcano beneath their community is going to "reawaken and overwhelm them all"; something like this does happen at the end of the novel. The Greggson children are **Jeffrey**, the first human being to make contact (during mind excursions that occur while he is sleeping) with the Overmind, and **Jennifer,** or "**the Poppet,**" who exhibits a capacity for telekinesis. The evolution of Earth's children to a new, purely spiritual stage suggests that future generations of the human race, if not our own, will grow up to reach the stars. The novel implies, however, that their human form may change into something not yet imagined.

Other characters in *Childhood's End* include **Konrad Schneider** and **Reinhold Hoffmann**, who, in the novel's first section, react in contrasting ways to the Overlords' arrival. Schneider despairs because his personal ambitions have been crushed, while Hoffmann feels reassured by the Overlords' presence and is eager to share the secrets of the universe with other beings. **Rashaverak** is an Overlord who, during a seance at a party, unwittingly reveals the name of his planet's sun, thus illustrating that humans have greater psychic abilities than their protectors. **Professor Sullivan** operates an underwater research station that Jan Rodricks visits; although he can control his environment to some extent, Sullivan knows that the sea maintains its potentially deadly power over him, just as Rodricks's foray into space will reveal his own limitations.

2001: A Space Odyssey (novel, 1968)

Plot: The novel comprises three sections. The first, set on prehistoric Earth, involves a creature called Moon-Watcher who is apparently at some evolutionary stage between ape and man. He and his companions are slowly starving until they encounter a mysterious monolith that emits strange sounds and that singles out Moon-Watcher as the most intelligent of the band of man-apes. The monolith communicates such important survival knowledge as how to use a stone to kill prey and enemies. In the novel's second section, Dr. Heywood Floyd travels to the moon to investigate a report of a monolith found there. With Floyd present, the monolith emits radio waves aimed at Saturn. The third section of *2001* centers on the journey of astronauts David Bowman and Frank Poole aboard the spaceship *Discovery* en route to Saturn. They are accompanied by their H.A.L. 9000 computer, "Hal," as well as three hibernating scientists who will be awakened on arrival. During the trip, Hal tells Bowman and Poole that the *Discovery* antenna guidance system is going to fail. After investigating the problem, the astronauts begin to think that Hal has made a mistake. Because Hal controls the ship's life-support system, this computer malfunction may be life-threatening. Bowman and Poole decide to deactivate some of Hal's more advanced functions. The computer overhears their conversation and kills Poole while he is outside the ship. Hal's attempt to eliminate Bowman by cutting off the oxygen in the *Discovery* is thwarted when Bowman puts on his spacesuit, although the three hibernating scientists do perish. Bowman finally deactivates the computer's brain and continues flying the *Discovery* toward Saturn, eventually boarding a smaller "spacepod" vehicle. He approaches a monolith like those described earlier in the novel, and the object opens out to a "Star Gate." Passing through, Bowman finds himself in what looks like an ordinary hotel room, and there he becomes the Star Child.

Characters: Clarke's *2001: A Space Odyssey* is a novelization of the popular, critically acclaimed 1968 film directed by Stanley Kubrick. (Both were based on Clarke's short story "The Sentinel.") Although some critics contend that the stunning visual images in Kubrick's film dwarf any impact the novel might have, others claim that the novel provides a clearer presentation of Clarke's themes. Like Clarke's other important work, *Childhood's End, 2001* is infused with the concept of transcendence—the possibility that the human race is evolving to some higher life-form. The novel's premise is that some unidentified but benevolent extraterrestrial race has shepherded humanity's progress from prehistoric ignorance through space travel to eventual transformation into the "Star Child." Another strong theme of *2001* is man's relationship with machines and the inherent dangers, although some commentators suggest that Clarke posits the machine as an intermediary along mankind's route to becoming entirely free of "the tyranny of matter." In any case, both Kubrick's film and Clarke's book captured the public's imagination, and both will remain science fiction classics.

The central character in the novel's first section is **Moon-Watcher**, the leader of a group of prehistoric man-apes who is chosen by the monolith to receive its knowledge. Before the arrival of the monolith, Moon-Watcher's group is close to starvation and too preoccupied with individual survival to understand the advantage of communal values. The monolith imparts information about how to survive (and also, somewhat ominously, about how to kill one's fellow creatures) and thus allows Moon-Watcher and his companions to experience the benefits of peaceful family living. In this way, the monolith serves as guide and guardian to the developing human race. Clarke has been praised for his convincing portrayal of the rough but recognizably human emotions of Moon-Watcher, whose name refers to his lifelong wish to find a tree tall enough to allow him to touch the moon.

The second section of *2001* features **Dr. Heywood Floyd**, the chief space administrator of the United States. Floyd does not disclose to the press the true purpose of his visit to the moon, which is to investigate the report of a monolith found during excavation there. Contemplating the fact that the monolith has been on the moon for three million years, Floyd experiences a heightened awareness of time and of the loneliness and vulnerability of the human race—concepts prevalent in other parts of the novel as well. In addition, Floyd's awestruck reaction to the sophisticated technology that allows him to travel to the moon in comfort foreshadows the even greater (and notably dangerous) dependence of Bowman and Poole on their onboard computer. Also significant is Floyd's wariness of other nations, which recalls Moon-Watcher's fear of another group of man-apes and prefigures Hal's paranoia about the danger human beings pose to the computer's existence. A minor character in this section is **Dr. Dmitri Moisevitch**, a friendly Russian astronomer who tries to get some details about Floyd's mission, which has been kept secret even from the U.S.S.R.

En route to Saturn, astronaut **Frank Poole** receives a recorded birthday greeting from his family on Earth, to which he reacts with a sense of remoteness, of increasing withdrawal from the rest of humanity, which he finds somewhat unnerving. Yet even as he becomes less emotional, Poole is not entirely machine-like either; he may be in a transitional state on the path to transcendence. After Poole's death, Bowman consoles himself that his friend's floating body will reach Saturn before any other human being, so that even in death he will play a part in human development.

Like Poole, astronaut **David Bowman** is fluent in the robotlike "Technish" language in which the ship's functions are performed, and his daily routine is strictly regulated. Yet he too retains some of his humanity, even as he finds himself listening at night to the eerie, inhuman hum of Jupiter's radiation on his radio. Whereas at one time Bowman enjoyed recorded plays, he now prefers the orderly music of Bach; the human problems examined in drama are too remote to interest him. He is losing his capacity for emotion, but he never loses contact with Earth until he enters the Star Gate. Rather, he broadcasts back his account of what has occurred aboard the *Discovery*. Bowman and Poole rely completely on Hal to communicate with Earth, to complete their mission, and to maintain life support systems, and Bowman can only dominate Hal when—by donning a spacesuit—he too becomes a machine. He thus progresses from human being to machine to the final stage of the evolutionary process Clarke outlines: the Star Child. Described by critic Eliot Fremont-Smith as "a fetus of possibility in the womb, or mind, of God," Bowman apparently joins the extraterrestrials who have been overseeing humanity's progress for so long; in becoming one with a supreme being who resembles the Overmind in *Childhood's End,* Bowman overcomes the loneliness that has always plagued the human race. Bowman is not, however, the first astronaut to undergo such a transformation, for the rings of Saturn compose a kind of graveyard littered with abandoned spaceships from all over (and outside of) the solar system. Their astronauts also became Star Children.

The H.A.L. 9000 Computer—known as "**Hal**" is vital to the *Discovery* mission and its occupants' survival and is one of the most memorable mechanical characters in literature. With his cordial manner, idiomatic speech, and seemingly human emotions, Hal illustrates how humans interconnect with machines and how the line between the two may become blurred. When the computer realizes that the two astronauts suspect it of having made a mistake, Hal reacts with injured pride; when Bowman is about to deactivate its brain, the computer expresses fear. It is possible to view Bowman's victory over Hal as indicating the integrity of the human race over technology. Although this does seem to be the premise in Kubrick's film, in Clarke's novel Hal is a more sympathetic character—even more so, some critics say, than the *Discovery's* astronauts. The novel explains that Hal malfunctions when Mission Control enters two conflicting commands. Not programmed to process such conflicts, Hal shortcircuits and becomes "insane." The computer manifests a kind of likable personality in the novel, and—despite its killing four astronauts—it is a poignant moment when Bowman pulls Hal's plug.

Further Reading

Clareson, Thomas D. "The Cosmic Loneliness of Arthur C. Clarke." *Voices for the Future: Essays on Major Science Fiction Writers.* Edited by Thomas D. Clareson. Vol. 1. Bowling Green, OH: Bowling Green University Popular Press, 1976.

Contemporary Literary Criticism. Vols. 1, 4, 13, 18, 35. Detroit: Gale Research.

Hollow, John. *Against the Night, the Stars: The Science Fiction of Arthur C. Clarke.* New York: Harcourt Brace Jovanovich, 1983.

Huntington, John. "From Man to Overmind: Arthur C. Clarke's Myth of Progress." *Science Fiction Studies* Vol. 1 (spring 1974).

Maddox, Brenda. "Cosmic Thoughts." *New Statesman* Vol. 76, no. 1971 (December 20, 1968): 877–78.

Olander, Joseph D., and Martin Harry Greenberg, eds. *Arthur C. Clarke.* New York: Taplinger, 1977.

Rose, Lois, and Stephen Rose. In *The Shattered Ring: Science Fiction and the Quest for Meaning.* John Knox, 1970.

Slusser, George Edgar. *The Space Odysseys of Arthur C. Clarke.* San Bernardino, CA: Borgo Press, 1978.

J.M. Coetzee

1940–

South African novelist, essayist, and translator.

Waiting for the Barbarians (novel, 1980)

Plot: The novel is narrated by the Magistrate, an otherwise unnamed minor official who presides over a small town located between the civilization of the "Empire" and the untamed area inhabited by the nomadic "barbarians." The easygoing, comfort-loving Magistrate is increasingly appalled by the actions of Colonel Joll, a security officer who arrives in the town to investigate reports of barbarian banditry. Witnessing Joll's interrogation and cruel torture of innocent victims, the Magistrate becomes more and more sympathetic toward the barbarians. He eventually takes into his home a girl who has been brutally mutilated by the security police. When he returns from a long journey across the desert to return the girl to her people, the Magistrate is arrested for treason and tortured. Unable to subdue the barbarians, the army eventually leaves the town. Much altered by his experiences, the Magistrate resumes leadership, waiting with the rest of the villagers for the barbarians to arrive.

Characters: Coetzee is one of South Africa's best known and most accomplished contemporary novelists. Although his works portray the brutalities and contradictions inherent in apartheid, they also attain universality and impact through emphasizing the nature of human cruelty, the yearning for freedom, and the claims of the conscience. In *Waiting for the Barbarians*, Coetzee addresses oppression, torture, and individual responsibility. Despite its allegory, the novel is infused with chillingly, realistic details suggesting that cruelty exists in—and must be confronted and overcome by—each of us.

The unnamed **Magistrate** who narrates *Waiting for the Barbarians* is a petty official of the Empire who, for almost thirty years, has presided over this small town on the edge of the desert. Basically humane and easygoing, the Magistrate has ruled with benevolent paternalism, viewing the blackhaired barbarians with distaste but no particular hatred. Content to pursue his interests in food, wine, hobbies, and his favorite prostitute at the local brothel, the Magistrate anticipates his approaching retirement. Colonel Joll's brutal investigations alter the Magistrate's outlook, for he is shocked by the injustice and cruelty he witnesses and recognizes his own complicity in the Empire's paranoid, vicious excesses. Having lived so long in comfort and by rather loose ethics, however, the Magistrate finds himself at first too weak to oppose the system. Like other protagonists in Coetzee's work, he would prefer to exist *outside* history, with its menacing dangers and its demands for action. But eventually he sees that his obsession with the mutilated barbarian girl, whom he ritually bathes each night but whom he is unable to penetrate either psychologically or sexually, is a form of voyeurism. The Magistrate's decision to return the girl to her people is a deliberate protest against the Empire, and he is punished for it on his return. The torture the Magistrate endures (particularly when he is hung from a tree by his wrists, which were first tied together in back of him) helps him forge a bond of common humanity with the barbarians. Whereas the Magistrate had once thought the Empire would have to rid itself of the barbarian threat, he now sees that it is the Empire itself that deserves to fall. The Magistrate articulates one of the novel's central themes: "The crime that is latent in us we must inflict on ourselves." Faced with an unknown future, the Magistrate has nevertheless achieved a kind of victory in that he has expanded his own humanity.

Colonel Joll is an officer of the Empire's Third Bureau, the security police whose methods duplicate those formerly employed by the South African regime, particularly in its indefinite detention of prisoners who were never charged with any crimes. Paranoid that the barbarians are conspiring against the Empire, Colonel Joll interrogates and tortures them for information, symbolic of his nation's deepseated fear of the unknown. His dark glasses further denote his state of moral vacuum. In **Warrant Officer Mandel,** the man who tortures and humiliates the Magistrate, the same moral deficiency is represented by a cold, emotionless, impenetrable stare. After the Magistrate is released, he asks this man whether he finds it difficult to eat after he has done his work, or whether he wants to undergo some ritual washing of his hands; Mandel, of course, has no answer.

The Magistrate's feelings for the brutalized **barbarian girl** he takes into his home are a mixture of fascination, compassion, and guilt. The girl was tortured by the Empire police for information that she did not have; they broke her ankles and damaged her eyes with a hot poker. Uncomplaining and reticent, she offers only brief answers to the Magistrate's questions about her experiences, yet she seems hurt when he refuses her offers of sexual contact. The Magistrate becomes obsessed with the girl, spending his evenings in a ritualistic washing and examining of her body. Some critics have viewed this activity as a voyeuristic fascination with mutilation; indeed, the Magistrate eventually decides that he is trying to expiate his own guilt and that, in fact, he is no better than Joll and the others who have abused her.

Life and Times of Michael K (novel, 1983)

Plot: The first and last of the novel's three sections are told from the perspective of Michael K, a thirty-year-old colored (i.e., of mixed racial heritage) man living in Cape Town, South Africa. Born with a harelip that impairs his speech, Michael was labeled "slow" at an early age and grew up in an institution for disabled people. He is working as a gardener for the city government when civil war breaks out. Meanwhile, Michael's terminally ill mother, a former cleaning woman, expresses a desire to return to her warmly remembered childhood home, a farm in South Africa's Karoo region. Although she dies before Michael can take her to the farm, he takes her cremated ashes there. When a young army deserter—the white grandson of the farm's former owner—arrives and tries to make Michael his servant, Michael flees into the mountains. Nearly starved, he returns to the farm after the young man has left. From some seeds he finds in an abandoned building, Michael grows pumpkins and melons, hiding in an earthen burrow whenever guerrilla fighters pass through the area. Eventually he is discovered by a group of soldiers, who accuse him of supplying the guerrillas with food. Michael is sent to a work camp where rebels are "rehabilitated." The middle section of the novel, which centers on Michael's stay in the camp's hospital, is narrated by a doctor who philosophizes about Michael's life and wonders why the physically depleted young man refuses to eat. Michael finally escapes and, returning to the town from which he began his odyssey, lies in his mother's bed and plans his return to the farm.

Characters: Awarded England's prestigious Booker Prize, the novel combines a calm, dispassionate narrative tone with concretely rendered details, achieving not only a powerful indictment of South Africa's apartheid regime but a more universal tale of survival and the quest for freedom. With its location clearly identified as South Africa, *Life and Times of Michael K* is less allegorical than some of Coetzee's previous novels, but it features the same menacing atmosphere and meaningless or bizarre actions that have led critics to compare Coetzee's work with that of Franz Kafka. Although South African writer Nadine Gordimer detected in the novel a "revulsion against all political and revolutionary solutions," other critics have noted that the novel ends on a faint note of hope and affirmation.

Two-thirds of the novel is told through the perspective of **Michael K**, a colored (of mixed racial heritage) man of about thirty years who lives in Cape Town, South Africa. Michael's harelip, which distorts his speech, has shaped how others view him and how he views himself, and he tends to avoid communication. At an early age he was labeled dim-witted and placed in an institution for disabled people. Although Michael does often give an impression of stupidity, he displays ingenuity and perception during the odyssey related in the novel, and several critics consider his dullness a reaction to his oppressive environment. While readers may view Michael as symbolic of all South Africa's oppressed people, he himself spends no time analyzing politics. Victimized by social forces he can neither control nor understand, Michael simply does the best he can, whether trying to take his mother to her childhood home before her death or raising pumpkins on an abandoned farm. As the novel progresses, Michael reveals a quiet but astonishing stoicism and resilience. He experiences a brief period of contentment after he buries his mother's ashes and grows vegetables at the site. This close contact with the earth has a healing effect on Michael. It gives him a sense of identity that transcends the immediate circumstances of his war-torn environment: he is a gardener whose role is to maintain the link between human beings and the land. Although Michael's idyll is soon shattered by the soldiers who capture and imprison him, the book ends on a tentative note of hope with Michael dreaming of a return to the farm, where he will extract water from the earth spoonful by spoonful, "and in that way, he would say, one can live." Many critics believe that Michael K's name is a direct reference to Joseph K, the protagonist of Franz Kafka's *The Trial* (1925), another victim of a blindly repressive state who is punished for some never-disclosed crime. Some reviewers approve of this device, while others find it mannered and pretentious; still others contend that the connection with Kafka's character is unintended.

The novel's middle section is narrated by a **doctor** at the prison hospital to which Michael is taken after he collapses at the work camp. The doctor ponders the possible meaning of Michael's life, making silent speeches to his enigmatic patient and apparently viewing him as a key to his country's and his own future. Several critics have faulted this section as superfluous, asserting that the doctor's rather pat conclusions merely state the obvious and rob Michael of the mystery that is an important aspect of his character. It may be possible, however, that Coetzee intended the doctor as a satire of white liberalism and a reminder that attempts to define others' lives for them may prove patronizing and overly simplistic.

Michael's mother, **Anna K**, is a former cleaning woman whose son has remained loyal even though he spent most of his childhood apart from her, in an institution (further, his harelip prevented his nursing at her breast). As she lies dying, Anna dreams of returning to the farm of her youth, but during her journey there with Michael she dies. Anna's five-day sojourn in a hospital, where she is cruelly neglected, helps dramatize the plight of poor blacks in South Africa. After Anna is cremated—against her son's wishes—Michael buries her ashes on the farm she had longed to reach, and he eventually grows pumpkins and melons on that site. Thus Anna contributes to the healing process Michael undergoes during his days gardening.

Other significant characters in *Life and Times of Michael K* include the white **grandson of Visagie**, the farmer who owned the land on which Michael camps. A defector from the South African army, the young man is both arrogant and vulnerable and attempts to establish a master-servant relationship with Michael; ironically, the two are now leading parallel lives, as both are hiding from the authorities. Michael's fellow inmate at the work camp, **Robert**, is more politically aware and urges Michael to "wake up." Supplying the novel's only radical voice, he explains that this camp disguised as a charitable venture is actually intended to supply the country with cheap labor and to prevent able-bodied men from joining the guerrilla forces.

Age of Iron (novel, 1990)

Plot: The novel is structured as a long letter written by white South African Elizabeth Curren, a retired classics professor, to her daughter, who has denounced her country's racist government and moved to America. Mrs. Curren is dying of cancer and intends the letter to reach her daughter after her death. The novel begins with Mrs. Curren's discovery, on returning from her doctor's office, of a decrepit homeless man living in a makeshift shelter on her property. Although the man, Mr. Vercueil, is an uncommunicative alcoholic, Mrs. Curren tolerates his presence, particularly after he helps her start her car. The novel chronicles the developing relationship between the two unlikely companions, whose dependence on each other increases as Mrs. Curren's health deteriorates. Also part of Mrs. Curren's household are her efficient but unconfiding black maid, Florence, and Florence's children, a fifteen-year-old boy named Bheki and two girls named Hope and Beauty. Bheki, an antigovernment activist, is eventually killed in a riot in Guguletu, a shantytown where many destitute blacks live. Despite her disapproval of Bheki's methods, Mrs. Curren goes to Guguletu to find him and is shaken by the suffering she sees there. Her anger over her country's brutality is intensified when Bheki's friend John, to whom she has offered shelter, is killed in her home. The novel ends with Mrs. Curren, soon to die and desperately lonely, inviting Mr. Vercueil into her bed.

Characters: Although some critics view *Age of Iron* as Coetzee's most brutal and pessimistic work due to its detailed account of life under South Africa's apartheid system, others detect in the novel a suggestion that rebirth and human continuity may be possible. Certainly the novel is a more direct indictment of apartheid than Coetzee's previous works, and it incorporates such actual and recent events as the release of black activist Nelson Mandela from his long prison term.

The narrator of *Age of Iron* is **Elizabeth Curren**, an aging white South African widow and retired classics professor. Writing to her daughter, who has fled South Africa for the United States, Mrs. Curren relates the events of the last few months of her life as she slowly dies of cancer. She lives primarily alone, but several other people effect the tenor of her last months. Recounted in a sharp, laconic, and often lyrical voice, the novel chronicles Mrs. Curren's growing awareness of her country's true brutality and of her own complicity. Although she has always been a liberal and opposed to apartheid, only now does she witness its real tragedy herself. Although alerting a white woman to the horrors of the political system through her contact with black servants is a standard device in South African literature, Mrs. Curren's relationship with the homeless, decrepit Mr. Vercueil provides the novel with an unusual twist. She grows more dependent on this formerly alien person as she draws nearer to death; when she finally invites him into her bed, her earlier statement that "there are no rubbish people. We are all people together" gains deeper significance. Mrs. Curren's penchant for delivering moral lectures—such as when she admonishes Florence that children who are careless of themselves may eventually grow careless of others—do not make her less likable, because she is unsententious and goodnaturedly aware that the words of an old white woman will probably go unheeded. Mrs. Curren's visit to Guguletu

Township is pivotal, for there she witnesses firsthand the suffering under apartheid; her awareness is further deepened when young John is killed in her own house. She realizes that no one who lives in such a society can remain untouched by its brutality. Mrs. Curren claims that although she is a good person, she is neither activist nor hero, and this "age of iron" calls not for goodness but for heroism. But just as Mrs. Curren's excruciatingly detailed disease may be seen as a metaphor for the deterioration of her country, her relationship with Mr. Vercueil—forged on the most basic human level—may represent the possibility of connection and rebirth.

Mr. Vercueil is the homeless white man who camps on Mrs. Curren's property and, after refusing to leave, eventually becomes indispensable to her. A smelly, dirty alcoholic with long, greasy black hair and a crippled hand, Mr. Vercueil rarely speaks and is initially reluctant to do any work for Mrs. Curren. She comes to see this slovenliness, however, as symptomatic of his powerlessness and despair. As Mrs. Curren grows more weak and helpless, Mr. Vercueil becomes her constant companion, helping her with all of her day-to-day tasks. Their mutual dependence transcends all their differences. Critics have compared Mr. Vercueil to other primitive characters in Coetzee's fiction—those who exist on the fringe of civilized life and who are physically disabled or marred in some way (such as the barbarian girl in *Waiting for the Barbarians* and the title character in *Life and Times of Michael K*). In addition, many reviewers see Mr. Vercueil as an "angel of death," because he shepherds Mrs. Curren toward her demise.

Through Mrs. Curren's black housemaid, **Florence**, both she and the reader can view South Africa's oppressed black majority. Although she is a conscientious and efficient servant, Florence is reticent around her employer. She does, however, express pride in the angry black youth of South Africa, whom she claims are as tough as iron. Reverting to the language of her background in classics, Mrs. Curren refers to Florence as a strong "Spartan mother, iron-hearted, bearing warrior sons for the nation." Fifteen-year-old **Bheki** is such a son, one of the "iron" children who are killed for their antagonism toward the state. The sight of Bheki lying dead with his eyes open in both horror and victory affects Mrs. Curren powerfully; she says "Now my eyes are open and I can never close them again." Bheki's sisters **Hope** and **Beauty** make Mrs. Curren feel she is "living in an allegory," and it is suggested that these may not be the girls' true names. The murder of Bheki's friend **John** at Mrs. Curren's house, where he has been offered shelter, provides further proof of the madness of the apartheid system. Florence's brother (whom she initially claims is her cousin) **Mr. Thabane**, once a schoolteacher but now a shoe salesman, organizes the children's strike against South Africa's discriminatory education system, which leads ultimately to the deaths of Bheki and other young people. He also leads Mrs. Curren into Guguletu and demands that she acknowledge the township's suffering.

Further Reading

Annan, Gabriele. "Love and Death in South Africa." *New York Review of Books* Vol. 37, no. 17 (November 8, 1990): 8–10.

Contemporary Literary Criticism. Vols. 23, 33, 66. Detroit: Gale Research.

Gallagher, Susan V. *A Story of South Africa: J. M. Coetzee's Fiction in Context.* Cambridge,: Harvard University Press, 1991.

Gordimer, Nadine. "The Idea of Gardening." *New York Review of Books* Vol. 31, no. 1 (February 2, 1984): 3, 6.

Gornick, Vivian. "When Silence Speaks Louder than Words." *Village Voice* Vol. 29, no. 12 (March 20, 1984).

Lehmann-Haupt, Christopher. Review of *Life and Times of Michael K. New York Times* (December 6, 1983): C22.

Lewis, Peter. "Tales of Tyranny." *Times Literary Supplement,* No. 4049 (November 7, 1980): 1270.

Ozick, Cynthia. "A Tale of Heroic Anonymity." *New York Times Book Review* (December 11, 1983): 1, 26, 28.

Packer, George. "Manifest Destiny." *Nation* (New York) Vol. 251, no. 21 (December 17, 1990): 777–80.

Scrogin, Michael. "Apocalypse and Beyond: The Novels of J. M. Coetzee." *Christian Century* Vol. 105, no. 17 (May 18–25, 1988): 503–05.

Thornton, Lawrence. "Apartheid's Last Vicious Gasps." *New York Times Book Review* (September 23, 1990): 7.

Laurie Colwin
1944–1992

American novelist, short story writer, and essayist.

Happy All the Time (novel, 1978)

Plot: Set primarily in New York City, the novel follows the course of romantic love between two couples, Guido Morris and Holly Sturgis, and Vincent Cardworthy and Misty Berkowitz. Guido and Vincent are third cousins and close friends who are about thirty years old when the novel opens. A graduate student, Guido meets and falls in love with pretty, serene Holly, and the two are married. Three years later, Vincent is working at the Board of City Planning, where one of his colleagues is the intriguingly abrasive Misty. Strongly attracted to Misty, who differs dramatically from his previous girlfriends, Vincent gradually worms his way into her heart. Pessimistic and fatalistic, Misty is surprised and somewhat chagrined to find herself in love with the always upbeat Vincent. Meanwhile, the marriage of Guido and Holly progresses smoothly until Holly disrupts Guido's contentment by announcing that she plans to spend some time away from him so that neither takes their relationship for granted. Holly goes to France, returning after six weeks. After living together for some time, Vincent and Misty marry. After Holly discovers that she is pregnant, she spends several weeks in a monastery, which she has decided is the best place for her to accustom herself to the idea of having a baby. The novel's final section takes place six months after the birth of Juliana Sturgis Morris. Leaving the baby with her grandparents, Guido and Holly depart the city for a fishing weekend with Vincent and Misty and a cousin of Holly's. As the novel ends, the two couples are enjoying dinner together and making a toast to "a truly wonderful life."

Characters: Marked by elegant, witty prose and an abidingly optimistic tone, Colwin's fiction depicts attractive, well-educated, usually upper-class characters experiencing the ups and downs of romantic and familial love. Some critics have faulted Colwin for her limited range and for what Ross Feld terms "a sludgy buildup of adorableness," but she has also been compared with nineteenth-century author Jane Austen for her focus on manners and the quest for happiness in marital and family relationships. In *Happy All the Time*, the question of whether it is really possible to be constantly happy is explored by characters who, though generally well-adjusted, undergo periods of doubt and angst but finally are relatively contented.

Each partner in the two couples around which the novel is centered provides a counterpoint to his or her opposite number. When the novel opens, **Guido Morris** is a law school graduate who, having spent a few years working unhappily as a lawyer, has decided to return to graduate school to study Romance languages and literature. The scion of a wealthy family, Guido will one day take over the stewardship of a foundation that funds cultural projects. He first encounters Holly in a museum and is immediately entranced by her, despite her initial resistance to his charms. For her part, Holly comes to value Guido not only for his hazel eyes and pleasantly calloused hands but for his ability to do and say the right thing at the right time. Throughout their courtship and into their marriage, Guido agonizes over what the rather close-lipped Holly is thinking and whether she really loves him, and her insistence on spending short periods away from him continues to baffle and worry him. Commentators note that both Guido and Vincent are notably more old-fashioned about love and marriage than their mates, and indeed, Guido seems to find a traditional domestic bliss with Holly that is only disrupted by her departures first for France and then (soon after informing him that he is going to be a father) for a monastery. Guido will never thoroughly resolve the mysteries that make up Holly; despite his general happiness, he will never be "happy all the time."

Like Guido, **Holly Sturgis** is the product of a moneyed East Coast family. Slender, fine-boned, and elegant, she makes a strong impression on Guido with her black, well-cut hair and precision in all matters (she is described as someone who must fight the urge to straighten the pictures in other people's homes). Guido admires Holly's perfection but finds her unflappability and detachment unhinging, and he is constantly seeking reassurance about her feelings for him. During the course of the novel, Holly insists on three periods of separation from Guido: the first is a week spent at her grandmother's house, just after she has agreed to marry Guido; the second is six weeks in France, where she goes in order to gain perspective on and appreciation of her marriage; and the third is ten days in a monastery, where, presumably, she reflects on the impending arrival of her baby. Holly is the only one of the four friends who does not have a "career," devoting herself instead to making her home a domestic paradise. Unambitious in a worldly sense, she does many things well, such as flower arranging and cooking; Vincent says of her that "anything short of a transport carrier would crash under the weight of those accomplishments." Misty comments that her friend Holly fights "to keep the ugly, chaotic world at bay and to keep a sweet, pretty corner to live in."

Good-natured, old-fashioned, eternally optimistic **Vincent Cardworthy,** a graduate of the Massachusetts Institute of Technology, works for the New York Board of City Planning as a specialist in the sanitary engineering issues in which he is passionately interested. Before he meets Misty, tolerant, cheerful Vincent is in the habit of dating "raw-boned and healthy" blonde women who are married or otherwise unavailable in any permanent sense. Even though he has repeatedly advised Guido not to think and worry so much, Vincent gradually becomes aware of his own emotional immaturity. His attraction to the difficult, extremely intelligent Misty suggests that he is ready for a romantic challenge, and he sets out with his usual earnestness to court her. Misty is eventually won over by Vincent's inherent goodness and obvious devotion, and he eventually becomes irreplaceable in her life.

Small-statured, amber-haired, a wearer of small gold spectacles, and a perpetually scornful expression, **Misty Berkowitz** is a brilliant linguist who works with Vincent at the planning board. A native of Chicago, Misty graduated from a university in Paris, where she had an ill-fated affair with an American boy. Misty initially treats Vincent with hostility, informing him that she hates small talk, that rich people make her sick, and that she is, in fact, the "scourge of God." As she herself admits, however, Misty's prickly demeanor is like a sea creature's shell or a porcupine's quills, protecting a soft center where deep feelings reside. Misty is surprised and somewhat alarmed by her growing love for Vincent, and then by the contentment she finds in marriage. As pessimistic as Vincent is optimistic, Misty claims that like her Jewish ancestors she is constantly waiting for a "low blow" to fall. This explains her jealous reaction to Holly's breezy, athletic cousin Gem, whom she wrongly assumes Vincent will find attractive.

Happy All the Time is populated by a considerably sized cast of secondary characters, most of whom make brief but memorable appearances. **Betty Helen Carnhoops**, described as a square-shaped woman with piano legs, takes over as secretary at Guido's foundation and soon has the place humming along smoothly; highly efficient and seemingly, as Vincent says, "as bland as cream of rice," Betty Helen harbors a secret interest in spiritualism. **Maria Theresa Warner**, Misty's co-worker and ally, is a practical, plainspoken, witty woman who offers advice drawn from the writings of St. Theresa of Avila and who stands for Misty at her wedding. Misty's amiable, hippyish cousin **Stanley Berkowitz** takes a temporary job at Guido's foundation and stays on after the arrival of Betty Helen. Big, affectionate, generous **Uncle Bernie**, Misty's beloved relative, whose family has long assumed (wrongly, as it turns out) that he is involved with the mob, is the composer of a whimsical song called "Dancing Chicken." While visiting Misty and Vincent, Uncle Bernie meets Vincent's cousin, **Hester Gallinule**, a tall, flashy, forty-year-old former soap opera star who ends up going dancing with Uncle Bernie. Other characters in the novel include **Denton McKay**, the wealthy, vacuous, twenty-four-year-old head of the planning board; philosophy professor **Arnold Milgram** and his ethereal genius student (and, as it turns out, lover) **Doria Mathers**, whose sloppiness Holly comes to see as artful; and **Gem Jaspar**, Holly's wealthy, athletic, jet-setting cousin, who inflames Misty's jealousy.

Further Reading

Contemporary Literary Criticism Vols. 5, 13, 23, 84. Detroit: Gale Research.

Feld, Ross. Review of *Happy All the Time*. *Saturday Review* (October 10, 1978): 63-4.

Richlin, Amy. "Guilty Pleasures: The Fiction of Laurie Colwin." *New England Review and Bread Loaf Quarterly* Vol. 13, nos. 13–14 (Spring-Summer 1991): 296–309.

Romano, John. Review of *Happy All the Time*. *New York Times Book Review* (November 19, 1978): 14.

Spaulding, Martha. Review of *Happy All the Time*. *Atlantic Monthly* (October 1978): 114.

Taliaferro, Frances. Review of *Happy All the Time*. *Harper's* (April 1979): 83.

Noel Coward

1899–1973

English dramatist, scriptwriter, songwriter, short story writer, novelist, autobiographer, poet, actor, director, and editor.

Hay Fever (drama, 1925)

Plot: The play is set in 1920s England at the country estate of the Bliss family in "Cookham." Judith Bliss is a retired actress, and her husband, David, writes popular romantic novels; their children, Sorel and Simon, are both in their late teens or early twenties. Each member of the family has, without informing the others, invited a guest to the house for the weekend. Judith's guest is a good-looking athlete, Sandy Tyrell; David's is Jackie Coryton, a young woman he plans to feature as a character in his next book; Sorel has invited a respectable diplomat named Richard Greatham; and Simon's guest is Myra Arundel, a worldly woman whose beauty is fading. As the guests arrive, they are greeted with exaggerated warmth by the appropriate host and are ignored by the other family members. The guests' confusion mounts as they participate in a word game that results in a vociferous argument between the self-dramatizing Blisses. Judith is particularly theatrical and injects a melodramatic flourish into each encounter with her family and guests. By the next morning, the perplexed guests are thoroughly fed up with their hosts, so they all slip away in Sandy's car. The Blisses believe their guests to be awfully rude; David comments that "people really do behave in the most extraordinary manner these days . . . ''.

Characters: Coward, one of the most popular dramatists of the twentieth century, was also a noted actor, director, and composer. He frequently showcased the talents of his famous actor friends (such as Gertrude Lawrence, Alfred Lunt, and Lynn Fontanne) in his sophisticated comedies of manners, which feature witty repartee delivered by characters who are typically affluent, hedonistic, and entertainingly glib. Coward has been compared to late-nineteenth-century dramatist Oscar Wilde, whose plays revolved around clever insults, inversions, and non sequiturs and who often ridiculed social conformity and the conventions of Victorian romance. Coward maintained that he intended his work to entertain the audience, not to reform or instruct it, and his plays feature a strong infusion of frivolity. However, some critics detect an underlying cynicism in Coward's work, which has been interpreted as expressing the loss and blankness experienced by the post–World War I generation. One of Coward's earliest successes and among his best-known plays, *Hay Fever* features characters who—despite (or perhaps because of) their outrageous rudeness, self-involvement, and penchant for theatricality—appeal greatly to audiences.

Hay Fever was reportedly inspired by a weekend Coward spent at the country estate of actress Laurette Taylor, whose family delighted in parties and word games like the one featured in the play. *Hay Fever*'s hostess is also a retired stage actress, though she expresses a desire to act again. Beautiful, charming, flirtatious, and supremely self-dramatizing, **Judith Bliss** as an actress specialized in the role of the noble, long-suffering female—a part she continues to play with her family. She particularly enjoys the word game "Adverbs" (in which the participants act out words like "happily" and "winsomely") because it allows her to perform, and she has invited Sandy Tyrell to her home to be an adoring audience. Each of the play's scenes closes with Judith performing her melodramatic interpretations of grief or renunciation. At one point, much to the confusion of the guests, the whole family joins Judith in a reenactment of *Love's Whirlwind,* the play that brought her greatest success. Coward is at the top of his form in some of Judith's scenes, when she lapses into strings of sentimental cliches. For example, when Judith comes across David and Myra embracing, she immediately vows to "give" David to Myra, noting that "I may leave this house later on—I have a feeling its associations may become painful, especially in the autumn."

As real-life actress Laurette Taylor's husband, J. Hartley Manners, was a playwright, the character Judith's husband, **David Bliss**, is the author of romance novels with titles like *The Sinful Woman* and *Broken Reeds,* which he freely admits are "very bad." Frequently interrupted by his more vociferous wife and children, David is reading from his latest work as the curtain falls. The Bliss offspring comprise pretty, spoiled **Sorel** and inane, impudent **Simon,** who aptly summarizes the family's attitude when he says, "If people don't like it, they must lump it."

Each of the guests reflects the self-interest of his or her host. Young, handsome **Sandy Tyrell**, an unsophisticated boxer, is expected to be a worshipful audience for Judith. David describes **Jackie Coryton** as a "perfectly sweet flapper" who will furnish him with material for his next book. Naive, giggly, and foolish, Jackie protests in an amusing scene that she does not want to play ''Adverbs,'' yet she inadvertently acts out her assigned word, ''winsomely.''

Sorel invites the suave diplomat, **Richard Greatham**, so that some of his respectability will rub off on her. Likewise, Simon hopes to increase his own worldliness through association with cool, sophisticated **Myra Arundel**; he calls her ''awfully amusing,'' while his mother describes her as ''a self-conscious vampire.'' Shocked by her hosts' rudeness, Myra finally gains the others' attention amid all the chaos and declares that the Bliss home is ''a complete feather-bed of false emotions—you're posing, self-centered egotists, and I'm sick to death of you.''

A minor character in the play is the housekeeper **Clara**, who is out of sorts because the maid, **Amy**, is indisposed with a toothache.

Private Lives: An Intimate Comedy (drama, 1930)

Plot: The play's premise is that, five years after their divorce, Elyot Chase and Amanda Prynne encounter each other again by chance in Deauville, France. Both are honeymooning with their new spouses, Sybil and Victor. After meeting on the balcony outside their adjoining rooms, Elyot and Amanda decide they are still in love and run away together to Paris. Once ensconced in Amanda's flat there, however, they quickly resume their old pattern of alternating tender lovetalk and vicious quarreling. Victor and Sybil arrive at the flat to discover the other couple locked in battle on the floor. It seems that Elyot and Amanda are going to part company, but then Victor and Sybil engage in an increasingly violent argument that they find strangely pleasurable. Seeing their spouses mimic their own behavior, Elyot and Amanda slip away together.

Characters: Written over the four days that Coward toured Asia, *Private Lives* is considered one of the best light comedies of the twentieth century. Its witty dialogue and clipped conversations are hallmarks of Coward's work; in a much-quoted statement about the playwright, critic Kenneth Tynan declared that Coward ''took the fat off English comic dialogue.'' *Private Lives* examines the destructive potential of romantic relationships with both overt flippancy and an underlying seriousness or even pessimism. Thus the play anticipates later dramas, such as Edward Albee's *Who's Afraid of Virginia Woolf* (1962). Yet the brilliant talk featured in the play—particularly between the two leading characters—leads some critics to compare it to the Restoration dramas of eighteenth-century English playwright William Congreve.

Coward employs a repetitive technique in *Private Lives,* allowing the audience intimate knowledge of the parallels between the pairings first of Elyot/Sybil and Amanda/Victor, then of Elyot/Amanda and Victor/Sybil. Coward reportedly modeled **Elyot Chase** after himself, and this elegant, urbane, invariably flippant character is a mouthpiece for some of Coward's views. He favors frivolity over seriousness, appearances over substance, and he urges his friends to ''savor the delight of the moment.'' Although Elyot and Amanda are ever facetious and often bad-tempered, they generate excitement when they are together. They typically move from fond endearments, to shared memories that eventually prove dangerous, to exchanging outright insults. The play's balcony scene showcases their appealing (if occasionally violent) chemistry. At the beginning of the play, Elyot tells his new wife, Sybil, that he wants love to be ''wise, and kind, and undramatic,'' yet at the end of the play, he ironically chooses an entirely different fate with Amanda.

Coward fashioned the role of **Amanda Prynne** with his actress friend Gertrude Lawrence in mind. Whereas Elyot treats Amanda with flippancy, she takes a rather high-handed approach to him, resulting in some highly entertaining exchanges. After they reunite,

Amanda and Elyot recognize that they are slipping into their old love-hate pattern, so they vow to establish a truce by uttering the words "Solomon Isaacs" whenever things get out of hand. The couple's inability to accomplish a lasting peace is mirrored by their gradual shortening of the phrase to "Sollocks" and finally by their all-out battle on the floor of Amanda's flat. Just as Elyot tells Sybil that he wants an "undramatic" love, Amanda tells Victor that she loves him "calmly"—and Amanda's assertion proves just as ironic as Elyot's. Though frivolous Elyot and caustic Amanda are undeniably shallow and self-indulgent, the verbal sparks that fly between them ensure that the audience thoroughly enjoys their reunion.

Most commentators find **Victor Prynne** and **Sybil Chase** to be flat characters who are, according to critic Milton Levin, "only sufficiently real to provide momentary relief and ammunition for Elyot and Amanda." By paralleling the love-hate pattern enacted by the leading couple, Victor and Sybil satisfy the play's symmetrical structure. Calling their respective spouses by the nicknames "Mandy" and "Elli" fits into this framework, for Elyot and Amanda find these endearments annoying, which foreshadows the eventual switching of partners. Other passages of dialogue are similarly syncopated. At the play's beginning, Victor and Sybil are both insecure about their status with their spouses and frequently seek reassurance; by the end, they have adopted the other couple's destructive behavior. Eventually Victor tells Sybil, "It's a tremendous relief to me to have an excuse to insult you," and Sybil finds that she quite enjoys slapping Victor. Some reviewers believe that when Victor complains about Elyot's "incessant trivial flippancy," he is a stand-in for Coward's detractors, who accused the playwright of having the same shortcoming.

Further Reading

Contemporary Literary Criticism. Vols. 1, 9, 29, 51. Detroit: Gale Research.

Dictionary of Literary Biography. Vol. 10. Detroit: Gale Research.

Gill, Brendan. Review of *Private Lives. New Yorker* (December 13, 1969).

Kiernan, Robert F. *Noel Coward.* New York: Ungar, 1986.

Kissel, Howard. Review of *Hay Fever. Women's Wear Daily* (December 16, 1985).

Lahr, John. *Coward the Playwright.* London: Methuen, 1982.

Levin, Melvin. *Noel Coward.* Updated ed. Boston: Twayne, 1989.

Loss, Archie K. "Waiting for Amanda: Noel Coward as Comedian of the Absurd." *Journal of Modern Literature* Vol. 11, no. 2 (July 1984): 299–306.

Nathan, George Jean. "Noel Coward." In *The Magic Mirror: Selected Writings on the Theatre*. Edited by Thomas

Rich, Frank. Review of *Hay Fever. New York Times* (December 13, 1985): C3.

Harry Crews
1935–

American novelist, essayist, autobiographer, and short story writer.

A Feast of Snakes (novel, 1976)

Plot: Set in the small, economically depressed town of Mystic, Georgia, the novel centers on Joe Lon Mackey, a former high school football star whose life since graduation has lost all of its former glory. Unhappily married and the father of two small sons, Joe Lon sells moonshine liquor from the tiny store owned by his father, Big Joe Mackey, who also raises pit bull terriers. Each year, Mystic is the site of a rattlesnake roundup, and Joe Lon earns some extra income by renting chemical toilets to the assembled snake handlers and fanciers. Also arriving in time for the rattlesnake festival is Berenice Sweet, Joe Lon's high school girlfriend, who is now a student at the University of Georgia and with whom Joe Lon shares a night of brutal, illicit sex. As the novel progresses, Joe Lon grows increasingly desolate as he realizes that his bleak life will never change. His frustration leads to a fit of rage in which he kills four people; he experiences a moment of satisfaction before he is himself hurled into a pit full of writhing rattlesnakes.

Characters: Considered one of the most original and compelling of contemporary Southern writers, Crews sets his novels in impoverished locales (both rural and urban) that reflect his own Georgia upbringing. Often associated with the Southern Gothic style of such authors as Carson McCullers and Flannery O'Connor—both known for their grotesque characters acting out extremes of human behavior—Crews creates protagonists whose desperation frequently results in violence. In fact, some critics have found the violence in Crews' fiction gratuitous, whereas others contend that he is successful in conveying its causes within the milieu his characters inhabit and in their use of violence as a means of escape.

Once the ''Boss Snake'' of the Mystic Rattlers high school football team, twenty-one-year-old **Joe Lon Mackey** has come down in the world in the few years since his graduation. His illiteracy prevented him from accepting any of the more than fifty college football scholarships he was offered, and he was forced to stay in Mystic. Unhappily married and the father of two children, Joe Lon's only occupation is selling moonshine liquor to the local black population and renting chemical toilets to the tourists who come to town for the rattlesnake roundup. Although Joe Lon initially tries to accept the loss of his former glory (which, as he is constantly reminded, has been inherited by such younger figures as Willard and Hard Candy Sweet) by reminding himself that ''that's all right . . . . I had mine,'' his frustration gradually eats away at his sanity. Described by critic John Seelye as ''a trapped and savage satyr,'' Joe Lon takes refuge from his lack of prospects in heavy drinking, reckless driving, fighting with other men, and beating his wife. The outrage that seethes within him is common to many of Crews' protagonists, whose inability to alter their lives usually erupts, in the end, in some form of violence. After witnessing a cruelly staged fight to the death between two of his father's dogs, Joe Lon realizes ''that things would not be different tomorrow. Or ever. Things got different for some people. But for some they did not.'' The next day, Joe Lon murders four people and—before he is himself murdered—feels surging through him the power over his own life that has evaded him since he left the football field; ''Christ,'' the narrator says, ''it was good to be in control again.'' In the reader's last view of Joe Lon, he languishes in the rattlesnake pit with snakes hanging from his face. This gruesome image is particularly apt, for he is, like the snakes, a trapped creature who must kill or be killed (or, in his case, succumb slowly and agonizingly to despair). Although Crews portrays Joe Lon as at least partly the victim of his own limitations, critics have discerned in his story a suggestion that his fate is more universal, that everyone must eventually face the loss of joy and inevitable approach of death that Joe Lon experiences. In an essay published in the volume *Blood and Grits* (1979), Crews describes his interest in the case of Charles Whitman, who climbed a tower at the University of Texas and shot twelve passersby to death. Crews asserts that everyone is involved in a private struggle to resist the temptation to climb a similar tower. Thus while some commentators viewed Joe Lon's final act as a manifestation of insanity, others saw it as the inevitable, even logical result of his hopeless circumstances, from which only such violence affords him escape.

Joe Lon's deaf, brutish father **Big Joe Mackey** apparently treated his wife even worse than Joe Lon treats his, for she was driven to suicide. Big Joe's position as a deacon of the Church of Jesus Christ with Signs Following is ironic in view of his decidedly unreligious behavior, and he may be identified as an example of how religion provides no refuge from the world's harshness. Big Joe breeds and trains (using a particularly cruel treadmill method) the best-fighting pit bull terriers in Georgia, all named Tuffy and each killed by his son-successor when too old to defend himself. Like the snakes for which Mystic is famous, Big Joe's pit bulls provide an effective metaphor for Crews's vision of life as a constant battle in which the only alternative is to keep fighting until death finally wins. Unlike his son, Big Joe expresses no dissatisfaction with his own lot, a characteristic that has perhaps kept him from pursuing the violent course that Joe Lon chooses. Other members of Joe Lon's immediate family include his deranged sister **Beeder**, who was driven mad by her mother's death and spends all of her time watching television in a dark, feces-smeared bedroom. Joe Lon's abused wife **Elfie** spends her time caring for two bedraggled children in the couple's foul-smelling trailer home.

Commentators have noted that female characters in Crews's fiction tend to be either faceless sex objects or, like Beeder, repugnant and asexual. A member of the former category is Joe Lon's high school girlfriend, **Berenice Sweet**, who ends up as one of his victims. A champion baton twirler and student at the University of Georgia, Berenice returns to Mystic for the rattlesnake festival and has sex with Joe Lon before being murdered by him—apparently because their relationship is among the elements that have failed to rescue him from hopelessness. Berenice's sister **Hard Candy Sweet** is the Mystic high school's current baton twirler and the girlfriend of Joe Lon's friend, drinking partner, and successor, **Willard**, a football player who is determined to break all of Joe Lon's records.

Other significant characters in the novel include **Sheriff Buddy Matlow**, a one-legged Vietnam veteran who uses his powerful position to force black women into sex, and **Lottie Mae**, one of his victims. In one of the novel's most violent sequences, Lottie Mae is first raped by Buddy and then kills him by slashing off his penis, to which he has applied a condom crafted to resemble a snake that she feels compelled to destroy. Joe Lon's other victims are the ineffectual, whining deputy sheriff, **Luther Peacock**; the snake-handling preacher **Victor**; and a **tourist** who is not personally known to Joe Lon. To Victor—who Big Joe describes as stringing "diamondbacks in his hair like a lady strings ribbons"—the snakes are emblems of evil, and he views handling them as a means of conquering that evil. The sight of Victor holding a snake and preaching about good and evil sparks Joe Lon's violent eruption. The faceless tourist can be seen as a representative of the antagonistic, animalistic human mass that arrives every year for the rattlesnake festival and that wreaks its brutal revenge on Joe Lon by throwing him into the snake pit.

Further Reading

Contemporary Literary Criticism Vols. 6, 23, 49. Detroit: Gale Research.

Dictionary of Literary Biography Vol. 6. Detroit: Gale Research.

Jeffrey, David K., ed. *A Grit's Triumph: Essays on the Works of Harry Crews*. Associated Faculty Press: 1983.

Jeffrey, David K. "Murder and Mayhem in Crews's *A Feast of Snakes*." *Critique* Vol. 28, no. 1 (Fall 1986): 45–53.

Seelye, John. "Georgia Boys: The Redclay Satyrs of Erskine Caldwell and Harry Crews." *Virginia Quarterly Review* Vol. 56, no. 4 (Autumn 1980): 612–26.

Don DeLillo
1936–
American novelist, dramatist, and short story writer.

End Zone (novel, 1972)

Plot: The novel centers on Gary Harkness, a running back for the football team at Logos College in western Texas. Gary has previously attended and played football at four other universities—Syracuse, Penn State, Michigan State, and Miami—but was forced to leave each one for different reasons. At Miami a class in "disaster technology" awakened in Gary a compulsive fascination with nuclear war, which continues to preoccupy him at Logos. He attends his latest school out of a genuine love for football and a lack of anything better to do. The novel is a series of vignettes involving Gary and his unusually philosophical teammates; his overweight girlfriend, Myna; his famous but rapidly deteriorating coach, Emmett Creed; and Major Staley, an ROTC instructor who divulges his knowledge of nuclear technology to Gary. Due to its talented player Taft Robinson, the Logos College football team wins every game but the last one. The novel ends inconclusively, with Myna newly (and, to Gary, disappointingly) slim, the gifted Taft leaving to pursue his interest in mysticism, and Gary taken to the college infirmary suffering from a strange brain fever.

Characters: DeLillo's characteristic preoccupation with the tensions and paranoia of contemporary America is evident in his second novel, *End Zone,* which firmly established his reputation as a gifted stylist and chronicler of modern society. The novel de-emphasizes plot and focuses instead on language (both its pleasures and its inadequacies) and philosophical concerns. DeLillo's interest in the uses and misuses of language, his penchant for black humor, and his apocalyptic tone have led commentators to compare him to such "postmodernist" authors as Thomas Pynchon, John Barth, and Kurt Vonnegut. In *End Zone* DeLillo uses football as a metaphor for the American propensity for ritualized violence, with nuclear war as its ultimate consequence. While some critics consider the novel's characters mere vehicles for DeLillo's musings, others find them believable and likable figures whose obsessions, confusions, and philosophizing add both depth and humor to the story.

The central character in *End Zone* is **Gary Harkness**, a talented running back with philosophic tendencies (particularly about football) and apocalyptic gloominess. Before arriving at Logos College, Gary played football at four other, larger schools, leaving each for a different reason: at Syracuse University he was caught in a compromising position with a female student, at Penn State he refused to acknowledge the character-building quality of practice, at Michigan State he caused the death of an opponent, and at Miami he became obsessed with a class in "disaster technology." Gary's fascination with nuclear war complements his love for football, for each has generated an "elegant gibberish," illustrating how language may used to impose order to something that is essentially chaotic. Drawn to the "rationality in irrationality" that he discerns in the mechanics of nuclear holocaust—in which precise, advanced, abstract science is used to implement horrific destruction—Gary entertains detailed fantasies about the nuclear ruin to come. He discusses the subject with Major Staley, who teaches him technological jargon and explains how neither responsibility nor guilt would be assignable if a nuclear war were to occur. Gary's love for football is rooted in its simplicity, its links with the "ancient warriorship" of humanity's primitive past. The game's brutal physicality and violence, Gary asserts, allow players to reestablish contact with their basic humanness. Through Gary's philosophizing about football, DeLillo explores how the human need for order and closure is satisfied by both the definitive conclusion of the football game and, potentially, the irrevocable apocalypse of nuclear war. Although DeLillo uses Gary as a mouthpiece for the novel's concerns, he also gives his character such notably human quirks as a habit of reciting the names of the U.S. presidents and, after he has been appointed offensive captain of next season's team, an internal struggle over whether he should wear or carry his helmet during the coin toss that begins each game. At the end of the novel, Gary is suffering from a bizarre brain fever that has confined him to the infirmary, where he is being fed through tubes; his uncertain fate may feature either defeat or the possibility of revitalization. In any case, the novel's inconclusive ending is in keeping with DeLillo's portrayal of life as lacking the neat closure that human beings seem to crave.

Gary's teammates and classmates at Logos College have been characterized as amusingly unconventional (if also somewhat implausible) in their existential preoccupations and ascetic interests. One of the most colorful is **Anatole Bloomberg**, a Jewish New Yorker and defensive tackle who suffers from bed-wetting and a tendency to gain weight. He feels oppressed by his name, which he describes as too European and as smelling "like a hallway in a tenement where lots of Bulgarians live." Anatole informs Gary that he will adapt to his west Texas environment by "unjewing" himself, a process that involves consciously changing his speech and thought patterns. Gary is initially attracted to his girlfriend, **Myna Corbett**, whom he meets in a class on Mexican geography, because she has a mushroom cloud appliqued on her dress. An avid reader of science fiction, Myna keeps herself overweight because she wants to avoid the responsibility of beauty; at the end of the novel, however, she has become conventionally slim, thus disappointing Gary. **Taft Robinson**, a black athlete of extraordinary ability, is responsible for the team's winning all of it's games except the last one; he eventually abandons football for mysticism.

Major Staley, an ROTC instructor at Logos College, is the college's primary proponent for nuclear technology. A veteran of the World War II bombing of Nagasaki, Staley uses such terms as "super-ready status" and "collateral destruction" (Just as Gary speaks in equally arbitrary football terms, such as "Monsoon sweep" and "drill-9 shiver"). Staley elevates nuclear warfare to an abstract and thus guiltless plane, describing it as a "test of opposing technologies" for which no one has to take personal responsibility. Although **Coach Emmett Creed** has had an illustrious past in football, his career began a downslide two years earlier when he attacked the second-string quarterback of another college's team; he has been brought to Logos College as part of the school's attempt to build its prestige. By the end of the novel, however, Coach Creed has disintegrated even further, just as his team's winning season ends in failure. Critics have interpreted the coach's last name (as well as the name of Logos College) as symbolizing the human tendency to define reality through the imposition of ordered systems.

White Noise (novel, 1984)

Plot: The novel's central character is Jack Gladney, chair of Hitler Studies at the College-on-the-Hill in the midwestern town of Blacksmith. Jack lives with his third wife, Babette (who teaches an adult education course in posture), and their four children from various marriages: Heinrich, Denise, Steffie, and Wilder. Heinrich is a brilliant fourteen-year-old with a penchant for deconstructionism; the sweet, rather "dopey" baby, Wilder, has not yet begun to talk. Both Jack and Babette are obsessed with death—which at least partially explains Jack's interest in Hitler, who seemed to possess the ability to manipulate death. When a tank car accident at a nearby train yard releases a toxic cloud of a deadly chemical, Nyodene Derivative, the Gladney family is forced to evacuate their home. Jack is exposed to the poison cloud while refueling his car. At the evacuation camp he learns that exposure to Nyodene can be fatal, although the chemical effect may take thirty years. Meanwhile, Babette has answered a tabloid magazine advertisement for Dylar, a drug that supposedly eliminates the fear of death. The drug's manufacturers decide not to distribute it after all, but Babette manages to acquire some by sleeping with one of the company's representatives. Although Dylar does not relieve Babette's fear of death, Jack is desperate to take the drug himself and searches for Willie Mink, the man who supplied it to Babette.

Planning to murder Mink and make the shooting appear to be a suicide, Jack locates him in seedy hotel. After wounding Mink, Jack tries to place the gun in his victim's hand, but Mink manages to shoot Jack in the wrist. Now overcome with remorse, Jack takes Mink to a hospital, explaining to himself and Mink en route that Mink had actually fired the first shot. At the hospital Jack meets a German nun who claims she does not believe in God but merely serves others as a symbol of belief, which forces Jack to reevaluate his own perspective. Returning to his family, Jack finds himself gradually rejuvenated, especially after his beloved Wilder survives a harrowing excursion across a four-lane highway on his plastic tricycle. The novel ends with Jack, Babette, and Wilder standing on a freeway overpass, viewing a brilliant sunset with silent, awestruck appreciation.

Characters: DeLillo received the American Book Award for *White Noise,* which many critics and readers consider his most engaging and provocative work. Written in a vivid prose that blends a lighthearted, comic tone with some deeply serious concerns, the novel satirizes such aspects of American society as its rampant paranoia, its addiction to violence, and its fascination with and dependence on the media, especially television. The novel's title refers to the incessant, incoherent hum that permeates American life; composed not only of the sounds of expressway traffic, television, and radio call-in shows but also of images drawn from tabloid newspaper headlines, supermarkets, and automatic bank teller machines, "white noise" implies both banality and menace. Several notable detractors claim that *White Noise* is more political tract than novel and its characters mere mouthpieces for DeLillo's obsessions; its defenders, however, find the characters sympathetic and effective and praise the author for his willingness to tackle broad, serious problems. As one commentator noted, it is difficult to determine what DeLillo thinks of his characters—he allows the reader to come to his or her own conclusions.

The novel's protagonist, **Jack Gladney**—a big, bulky fifty-one-year-old man who wears thick glasses—chairs the Hitler Studies department at the College-on-the-Hill, where he consorts with other scholars of "American environments." Although Jack maintains an intellectually cool, ironic, detached tone in his conversations with the other characters, it becomes clear to the reader that he is not as much in control as he tries to appear. Jack's paranoia and fear of death dominate his inner life, even during his most intimate and gratifying moments with his wife, Babette. His interest in Hitler is apparently rooted in the German leader's near omnipotence at the height of his power, when he seemed capable of manipulating death itself. If Jack is an archetypal victim of contemporary life, paralyzed by both its dangers and its banality, Hitler may be seen as the ultimate aggressor; indeed, Jack's colleague Murray Siskind surmises that Jack became fascinated with Hitler because he is "larger than death. You thought he would protect you." Critics have found in much of DeLillo's work a preoccupation with Hitler and Nazism, which seem to embody for him the dark mystery at the core of human nature. After Jack is exposed to Nyodene Derivative (with vague long-term effects, including death), he desperately seeks the drug he believes will relieve his fear. The Mephisthophelean Murray tells Jack that humanity is divided into "killers and diers" and only the killers wield power over their circumstances. Jack's subsequent decision to shoot Willie Mink does give him a sense of power—until Mink shoots jack in the wrist. Jack is then overcome by compassion and remorse. Viewing himself as a kind of hero, Jack takes Mink to the hospital, but his encounter there with the pragmatic nun and her confession of faithlessness jars him. Jack returns to the small but significant refuge of his family, and by the end of the novel he seems to have reconciled himself with death as an inescapable but natural part of the unknowable universe. After witnessing Wilder's near miraculous tricycle ride across a busy freeway, Jack feels a mingled fear and elation as he stands with his wife and son (whose presence has always given him a strange sense of peace and contentment), admiring a magnificent sunset. Most commentators have viewed this passage as a redemptive, hopeful conclusion to the novel.

White Noise has been identified as the first of DeLillo's novels in which the family is portrayed as "the one medium of sense knowledge in which an astonishment of heart is routinely contained," a source of warmth and a welcome middle ground between dreary isolation and the confusion and dehumanization of mass culture. One of the novel's most prominent symbols of home and family is **Babette Gladney**, Jack's third wife, mother to the four children (two his, two hers) who live with them. Occupied most of the time with her child care duties, Babette also teaches an adult education course in posture, which critics regard as a comic example of the contemporary need for instructions on how to survive daily life (Babette plans future courses on eating and drinking). Although Jack sees the tall, "ample," basically guileless Babette as a comforting and dependable conduit of life, she too obsessively fears death, which leads her to seek a drug advertised in a tabloid newspaper. Babette is found to be one of the three most fearful applicants for Dylar, but after the manufacturers decide not to distribute the drug, she desperately agrees to sleep with its "project manager" in order to get some for herself; she calls the encounter a "capitalist transaction." Dylar does nothing to muffle Babette's fear of death, however, and she realizes well before Jack that such repression is, in any case, wrongheaded. Her reasoning to persuade Jack not to pursue the drug contrasts with Murray's suggestion that Jack not only repress his fear of death but become a "killer" to avoid being a "dier."

Of the Gladney children, **Wilder**, a sweet baby with a "dopey countenance," is Jack and Babette's primary refuge from their fears. His name complements his fearless, independent nature and his unusual—though nonverbal—intelligence. Wilder's inability to speak has been said to symbolize the inadequacy of language to embody or describe authentic experience, a concern that dominates all of DeLillo's fiction. For Wilder the world is "a series of fleeting gratifications." He encounters the exhilaration of *experience* and is unburdened by language and its obligations and deceptions, thus teaching his parents that preoccupation with dying may be borne through the experience of living. Many commentators find the scene in which Wilder maneuvers his tricycle across four lanes of a busy freeway (only to cry when he topples over on the embankment at the other side) particularly effective.

Jack gave his oldest son, fourteen-year-old **Heinrich**, a grand German name because he thought it would protect him, much as he sought his own refuge in a death-manipulating German leader. The highly precocious Heinrich is a typical adolescent in his surliness and reluctance to emerge from his room, but his receding hairline and deconstructionist philosophy suggest a psyche old beyond its years. In a much-quoted passage, Heinrich tries to persuade his father that the drops of water they see rolling down their car windshield do not prove that it is raining: "Our senses are wrong more often than right. . . . There's no past, present, or future outside our own minds." Heinrich is one of several brilliant and somewhat obnoxious adolescents in DeLillo's fiction; some critics maintain that he sounds more like a philosophy professor than a teenager. The other Gladney children include **Denise**, "a hard-nosed kid of eleven" who worries about her mother's diet pills and smoking and her father's exposure to Nyodene, internalizing the very adult fears contemporary children are burdened with; and **Steffie**, who (along with the rest of the family) watches televised disasters with absorption and mumbles "Toyota Celica" in her sleep, suggesting the extent to which the "white noise" of American life has affected her.

DeLillo employs Jack's colleagues at the College-on-the-Hill to satirize academia—particularly the "high-minded defenses of American culture," as noted by critic Thomas Di Pietro in *Commonweal*, which revere absurd or inherently shallow subjects. **Murray Jay Siskind**, a visiting professor of "living icons," is a New Yorker with stooped posture and menacing eyebrows who celebrates such aspects of American culture as car crashes in movies and generic food packaging. A former sportswriter, Murray is a glib manipulator of language who, with an air of scholarly detachment, remarks to Jack that human beings should repress their inescapable fear of death. One critic sees Murray as a satanic figure who, like Faust's Mephistopheles, encourages Jack to control death by becoming a "killer" rather than a "dier." Other scholarly characters in *White Noise* include **Alfonse "Junk Food" Stompanato**, the chair of the American Environments Department, who articulates the theory that because modern people suffer from "brain fade" caused by an overload of information, they crave televised catastrophes to break up the monotony; and **Dimitrios Cotsakis**, the college's resident expert on Elvis Presley, whose academic prowess is no protection against the elemental power of the surf off Malibu, in which he drowns during a holiday break.

Willie Mink, a project manager for the "small psychobiology firm" that manufactures Dylar, accepts Babette's offer of sex in exchange for a supply of the drug. When Jack locates him in a seedy motel in down-and-out Germantown, Mink is a pathetic sight: dressed in Budweiser-print shorts, he is stuffing handfuls of Dylar into his mouth and mumbling incoherently. Jack takes the injured Mink to the hospital, where he meets **Sister Hermann Marie**, a German immigrant with a pragmatic approach to her work, which apparently brings her into frequent contact with disreputable characters like Mink. The nun destroys the false sense of security Jack feels at the hospital when she tells him she does not believe in God but serves instead as a symbol of belief for others: "people find it necessary that *someone* believe. . . . Nuns in black . . . fools, children."

Further Reading

Bawer, Bruce. "Don DeLillo's America." *New Criterion* Vol. 3, no. 8 (April 1985): 34–42.

Bell, Pearl K. "DeLillo's World." *Partisan Review* Vol. 59, no. 1 (winter 1992): 138–46.

Contemporary Literary Criticism. Vols. 8, 10, 13, 27, 39, 54. Detroit: Gale Research.

Dewey, Joseph. "The Eye Begins to See: The Apocalyptic Temper in the 1980s; William Gaddis and Don DeLillo." In *a Dark Time: The Apocalyptic Temper in the American Novel of the Nuclear Age,* West Lafayette, IN: Purdue University Press, 1990, 180–229.

Dictionary of Literary Biography Vol. 6. Detroit: Gale Research.

Disch, Thomas. "Maximum Exposure." *Nation* Vol. 240, no. 4 (February 2, 1985): 120–21.

Edwards, Thomas R. "A Beautifully Made Football Novel about Thermonuclear War." *New York Times Book Review* (April 9, 1972): 1, 14.

Johnson, Diane. "Conspirators." *New York Review of Books* Vol. 32, no. 4 (March 14, 1985): 6–7.

Lehmann-Haupt, Christopher. Review of *White Noise. New York Times* (January 7, 1985): C18.

Lentricchia, Frank, ed. *Introducing Don DeLillo*. Durham, N.C.: Duke University Press, 1991.

————. *New Essays on White Noise*. Cambridge: Cambridge University Press, 1991.

Loose, Julian. "Shaping Up to Catastrophe." *Times Literary Supplement* No. 4613 (August 30, 1991): 20–1.

Mobilio, Albert. "Death by Inches." *Village Voice* Vol. 30, no. 18 (April 30, 1985): 49–50.

Oriard, Michael. "Don DeLillo's Search for Walden Pond." *Critique: Studies in Modern Fiction* Vol. 20, no. 1 (1978): 5–24.

Phillips, Jayne Anne. "Crowding Out Death." *New York Times Book Review* (January 13, 1985): 1, 30–1.

Yardley, Jonathan. "Don DeLillo's American Nightmare." *Washington Post Book World* (January 13, 1985): 3, 10.

Ding Ling
1904–1986

Chinese short story writer, novelist, editor, and essayist.

"Miss Sophie's Diary" (short story, 1928)

Plot: The diary's first entry is dated December 24 and the last March 28. Sophie is a young woman who lives alone in a dreary Beijing apartment, far from her family. She suffers from tuberculosis and does not attend the university, as do most of her friends. Sophie's condition requires that she spend the cold winter days inside, and her resulting boredom is relieved only by the few letters she receives and the visits of such acquaintances as Weidi, a young man who is in love with her. But Sophie does not reciprocate Weidi's affection, and she is often annoyed by his displays of emotion. Through her friends Yufang and Yunlin (a young couple in love) Sophie meets handsome Ling Jishi, a student from Singapore. Sophie spends her time fantasizing about Ling Jishi and is increasingly attracted to him. Despite her friends' disapproval, Sophie even moves to another, damper apartment in order to be closer to him. Although Sophie distrusts her own motives, she grows more determined to make Ling Jishi yield to her desire. He starts to pay visits to her apartment, but she acts aloof. When Sophie becomes very sick and has to spend some time in the hospital, both Weidi and Ling Jishi visit her. After she returns to her apartment, Sophie becomes better acquainted with Ling Jishi and learns that he is shallow and ambitious and lacks any social consciousness. Yet she still feels physically attracted to him. Yufang arranges for Sophie to recuperate in the Western Hills outside the city. The night before her departure, Sophie agonizes over her strong desire for Ling Jishi as she waits for him to visit her. He finally arrives, announcing that he wants to sleep with her; when he kisses her, Sophie feels a momentary sensation of victory, then is overcome by self-loathing. She sends Ling Jishi away and decides not to go to the Western Hills but to move to a city further south, where no one knows her.

Characters: "Miss Sophie's Diary" established Ding Ling as a prominent writer and is still considered one of her most accomplished works. Often associated with the "May Fourth Generation"—a movement of intellectuals (including Mao Zedong) who rebelled against traditional Chinese attitudes toward such issues as family, sex, language, and education—Ding Ling infused her fiction with a strong feminist orientation and an awareness of the dilemmas of self-analysis. Strongly influenced by her unconventional mother, a teacher, Ding Ling became a social activist at an early age. As a young woman she lived alone in Beijing, then married a poet named Hu Yepin. Ding Ling joined the Communist Party after her husband was executed by the Nationalist government, and she remained a loyal Communist even when, during the anti-intellectual purges of the late 1950s and 1960s, she was persecuted and jailed for her subversive views and writings. Most critics agree that the quality of Ding's writing declined dramatically after she complied with Mao's dictate that literature must serve the revolutionary cause rather than strive for any artistic excellence. But in her early stories focusing on the conflicts experienced by young, independent women—of which "Miss Sophie's Diary" (published in a collection entitled *Zai heianzhong,* or "In the Darkness") is considered the best example—Ding Ling explores with insight and power such themes as the difference and conflict between love and lust and the alienated, sensitive individual's quest for identity.

The story's protagonist and narrator is **Sophie**, a high-strung woman of about twenty who is suffering from advanced tuberculosis. Like other heroines in Ding Ling's fiction of the late 1920s, Sophie resembles her creator in some ways: she is an intelligent, sensitive young woman living far from her family, alone in a large, semimodern city. (In fact, such outward similarities between Sophie and Ding, in addition to Ding's audaciousness descriptions of Sophie's sexual fantasies, led Chinese government authorities to condemn Ding for immorality.) Ding's protagonists, such as Sophie and **Wendy**, take Western names, signifying their break with traditional Chinese culture; they are often impoverished or ill, and they live in drab, run-down urban dwellings. In her diary Sophie records the isolation and vulnerability of women resistant to the conventional bonds of marriage, work, and school. She learns that to be independent she must grapple with the question of her own identity and with her own weaknesses. Lamenting her desire for an unworthy man and the trouble it has caused her, Sophie says, "If a person's enemy is himself, how, oh heavens, can he seek vengeance and indemnity for all his losses?" Ding herself viewed women as victims not just of societal oppression but of their own shortcomings. The outcome of "Miss Sophie's Diary" is not romantic love but self-examination. Despite the immaturity she exhibits in pursuing Ling Jishi, Sophie elicits our sympathy because of the understanding she gains of her desires and motives. Sophie's complexity contrasts strongly with the characters Ding created later, after the Communist authorities demanded that literary characters be completely and identifiably good or evil.

Ding reportedly read *Madame Bovary*—the acclaimed novel by nineteenth-century French author Gustave Flaubert—many times, and her portrait of Sophie is said to have been strongly influenced by Emma Bovary. Like Sophie, Flaubert's heroine is a victim of romantic delusions and repressed desire who is doomed to die disappointed. Another literary precedent to "Miss Sophie's Diary" is Henrik Ibsen's 1879 drama *A Doll's House*, in which initially docile homemaker Nora Helmer ultimately abandons her conventional life and marriage to live independently. Some critics have interpreted Sophie as Ding's attempt to imagine the fate of a Chinese Nora. In any case, Ding's characterizations of Sophie and other heroines in her early fiction were a major innovation in Chinese literature, which regarded women as peripheral to the male characters.

Ling Jishi is the physically attractive young man whom Sophie desires despite his superficiality. Although he has the "handsome air of a medieval knight," Ling is shallow, greedy, and lustful. Lacking any social conscience, he is ambitious for personal gain and advancement, attributes the Chinese condemned as Western. Ling's birth in Singapore also signifies that he is not authentically Chinese, as do his full, red lips and pale skin that excite Sophie against her will. Ling precipitates Sophie's internal struggle, allowing Ding to explore the concept that love and sexuality may upset an individual's psychological balance and lead to intense self-examination. The kiss that signifies Sophie's victory in attracting Ling also elicits feelings of degradation, and she sends him away in disgust.

Other characters in "Miss Sophie's Diary" include her friends **Yunlin** and **Yufang**, students whose chaste love for each other seems to make them happy and whose concern for Sophie is manifested in their nursing her when she is overcome by illness; and **Weidi**, a lovesick, emotional young man Sophie tolerates for company but spurns for his courting and crying spells.

Further Reading

Barlow, Tani E. Introduction to *I Myself Am a Woman: Selected Writings of Ding Ling.* Boston: Beacon Press, 1989.

Brownmiller, Susan. "For Her Pains, She Was Called Old Shameful." *New York Times Book Review,*(September 3, 1989), 7–8.

Contemporary Literary Criticism. Vol. 68. Detroit: Gale Research.

"Ding Ling: A Spiritual Treasure." *Beijing Review* 29, no. 19 (May 12, 1986): 32–4.

Fueurwerker, Yi-tsi Mei. *Ding Ling's Fiction: Ideology and Narrative in Modern Chinese Literature.* Cambridge: Harvard University Press, 1982.

———."In Quest of the Writer Ding Ling." *Feminist Studies* 10, no. 1 (spring 1984): 65–83.

Gargan, Edward A. Obituary in *New York Times* (March 8, 1986), B6.

Mirsky, Jonathan. "Ding Ling: Setting the Record Straight." *Times Literary Supplement,* no. 4329 (March 21, 1986): 302, 315.

———."Stories from the Ice Age." *New York Review of Books* Vol. 36, no. 16 (October 26, 1989): 27–28, 30.

Wei, William. "From Miss Sophie to Comrade Wanxiang." *American Book Review* Vol. 12, no. 4 (September–October 1990): 31.

E. L. Doctorow
1931–
American novelist, short story writer, editor, essayist, and dramatist.

Billy Bathgate (novel, 1989)

Plot: The novel takes place in New York City (and several locations in upstate New York) in 1935. The title character is a fifteen-year-old whose father has abandoned the family and who lives with his insane mother in an East Bronx slum. Streetwise and resourceful, Billy rarely attends school and spends most of his time showing off his juggling prowess. Billy catches the eye of the notorious gangster Dutch Schultz, who is in the neighborhood checking on one of the warehouses he owns. Billy manages to ingratiate himself into Schultz's gang and becomes their apprentice, performing errands and gathering information. Otto "Abbadabba" Berman, Schultz's mathematical genius accountant, tutors Billy in such matters as shooting a gun and running a numbers racket. Billy witnesses several murders, including that of Bo Weinberg, a gang member who had conspired with Schultz's rival, Lucky Luciano. Weinburg's lover, Drew Preston, a beautiful young woman with a rich homosexual husband who does not keep tabs on her, then becomes Schultz's girlfriend. Assigned to chaperon Drew, Billy grows increasingly fond of her and, despite the differences in their ages and social backgrounds and the danger of incurring Schultz's wrath, the two eventually make love.

Ever paranoid and rightly sensing that his empire is crumbling, Schultz devises a plan to kill prosecutor Thomas Dewey, who is leading a crusade against the city's crime lords. Luciano distrusts this scheme, however, and has Schultz and his men gunned down in a restaurant. But Schulz does not die immediately. Hidden in his mentor's hospital room, Billy makes notes on the dying Schultz's rambling, nearly incoherent monologue, culling from it the location of a huge stash of money. Fifty years later, Billy reveals that he has used Schultz's wealth to establish his own corporate empire, though he does not state whether he has led a life of crime like his benefactor. As the novel comes to a close, Billy also reveals that soon after Schultz's death, a basket was delivered to the luxurious apartment in which he and his mother were then living. Inside was a baby boy, the product of Billy's liaison with Drew and, as the adult Billy notes, a living manifestation of his strange, thrilling days with Dutch Schultz.

Characters: As in his previous novels, in *Billy Bathgate* Doctorow draws on the resources of American history, weaving authentic, richly described details of 1930s New York City and several actual gangland figures into a book filled with both thrills and eloquence. As many reviewers have noted, the novel reflects America's ongoing fascination with gangsters, whose bravado and often violent power seem an alternative version of the American ideal of success. In fact, the similarities between organized crime and the American corporate world are explored in the book, and Doctorow seems to equate capitalist greed with underworld crime. Doctorow was lauded not only for the lush, often lyrical prose in *Billy Bathgate*—which some critics consider his masterpiece—but for the vivid characters it contains.

The novel's title character tells the story of his youth from a vantage point fifty years later. In 1935, when the action takes place, **Billy Bathgate** is a tough, streetwise, fifteen-year-old high school dropout living in an East Bronx slum and surviving on his considerable wits. He has taken his last name from his neighborhood's bustling, colorful market street, Bathgate Avenue. Billy's Jewish father abandoned the family long ago, and his Irish mother is mentally distracted, if not downright insane. Among Billy's many gifts is his talent for juggling, which catches the attention of the notorious gangster Dutch Schultz, whom Billy has already come to worship through newspaper accounts. Insinuating himself into Schultz's gang, Billy begins an apprenticeship that will instruct him in such worldly matters as money, murder, sex, and power and catapult him into adulthood. Schultz recognizes Billy's intelligence and resourcefulness and calls him a "capable boy," a phrase that, as the adult Billy reflects, refers to his capacity not only for learning but for worshiping Schultz's power and appreciating his menace. One of the most notable aspects of Billy's characterization is the narrative voice in which he speaks, which is both brisk and lyrical, highly descriptive and reflective, but also youthfully energetic. Several critics find this almost stream-of-consciousness narration mannered and too articulate to be spoken by a teenaged slum-dweller; others contend that the voice successfully blends Billy's verve and naivete at fifteen with his grown-up observations.

Deemed "a wonderful addition to the ranks of American boy heroes" by novelist Anne Tyler, Billy has been compared to such memorable protagonists as Ragged Dick (the title character of Horatio Alger's 1868 novel) and J. D. Salinger's Holden Caulfield (from *A Catcher in the Rye*, 1951). Billy is most frequently likened, however, to Mark Twain's Huckleberry Finn, a similarly self-reliant, parentless, and resilient teenager who, as described by critic John G. Parks, "miraculously fulfills his own charmed life." *Billy*

Bathgate may be viewed as a story of initiation or compared to an Arthurian quest tale: Billy sets out in search of adventure, success, love, and—perhaps most significantly—a father. Several commentators have called attention to the novel's Oedipal aspect, in which Billy seeks both to acquire and to supplant the father figure he finds in Dutch Schultz. Billy's conflicting loyalties are particularly evident in his liaison with Dutch's girlfriend Drew, who represents one corner of an Oedipal triangle. By the end of the novel Billy has witnessed several murders (to which he responds with too little emotion, according to several critics), learned how to shoot a gun and run a numbers racket, made love to Drew, and acquired Schultz's wealth. He informs us that he went on to receive an Ivy League education, served as an Army officer in World War II, built a corporate empire (the reader never learns whether or not it has a criminal basis); and earned a certain "renown." The matured, successful Billy remembers that with the arrival of his baby son (an event several reviewers found implausible and superfluous) he "felt a small correction in the universe and my life as a boy was over." This son now provides a living link with the brutal, exciting world of the 1930s.

The novel's central gangster character, **Dutch Schultz**, is modeled after an actual crime lord whose real name was Arthur Flegenheimer. Schultz specialized in racketeering, forcing taverns to buy his beer (even after Prohibition had ended), and running window washers' and waiters' unions. In *Billy Bathgate*, Schultz is portrayed as a hulking, mercurial presence who alternates between geniality and rage, growing even more capricious and prone to violence as he loses his hold on his criminal empire. Schultz exemplifies the unconditional power and shady impulses associated with the American gangster myth. Unlike his accountant, Abbadabba Berman, Schultz is impulsive and instinctual; a self-made man and an individualist, he is unable to adapt to the concept of conglomeration and cooperation that Berman knows will dominate the crime (and corporate) world of the future. His paranoia ultimately brings about his own death, because his rival Luciano stifles his grandiose plan to kill the New York City prosecutor. Schultz is a kind of father figure to Billy, shifting in his demeanor between fondness and detachment, benevolence and volatility. He ultimately (and unintentionally) bequeaths his fortune to the boy, informing him through his rambling deathbed monologue (based on what the real Dutch Schultz said while dying of gunshot wounds) of where his money was hidden.

Among the novel's memorable other gangster characters is **Otto "Abbadabba" Berman**, Schultz's dapper (though hunchbacked) accountant, a mathematical genius who runs the numbers racket for Schultz. Berman serves as a secondary father to Billy, whose apprenticeship he supervises; he slips Billy money and teaches him how to shoot a gun and how to manipulate numbers, which he sees as the basis of all existence and the key to the future. As rational and careful as Schultz is instinctual and impulsive, Berman tries to convince his boss that cooperation with men like Luciano (whose dominance Berman foresees) is necessary and beneficial. But Berman does not succeed in changing Schultz's approach, and in the end, he is gunned-down with Schultz on the floor of a New Jersey chophouse.

Other members of Schultz's gang include **Lulu Rosencrantz**, Schultz's dull but angry bodyguard; and taciturn, meticulous **Irving**, who makes the preparations for and cleans up after the gang's brutal murders but never kills anyone himself. **Bo Weinberg** is caught conspiring with Luciano and undergoes the classic "cement overshoes" execution of American gangster mythology. His pleas for a merciful bullet are ignored by Schultz's men, and he is further tortured when Schultz drags his lover, Drew Preston, off to an empty cabin—apparently to rape her. **Lucky Luciano**, Schultz's rival crime boss (historically as well as in the novel), represents the new, conglomeratic vision that will dominate organized crime in the future—a vision that Schultz is unable to adopt.

Called "Miss Lola" while she is Bo Weinberg's girlfriend, **Drew Preston** adapts without much fuss to becoming Schultz's lover after he murders Weinberg. A beautiful, wealthy twenty-two-year-old, Drew is married to a decadent homosexual named **Harvey** who does not mind where she goes or what she does. Drew behaves with casual insouciance in the face of great danger, and Billy admires her for "maintaining her being while in the grasp of others." A member of the elite upper class, Drew is apparently drawn to the illicit power and potential violence of the criminal underworld; but her assumption of privilege deceives her into believing that she can escape whenever she wants to. Despite his youth, the more streetwise Billy recognizes the foolishness of her attitude, and it is he who ultimately saves Drew from harm by arranging for her husband to liberate her. Drew has been identified as one corner of an Oedipal triangle in which Billy and his "father," Schultz, also figure; this image is reinforced when Drew's baby arrives at Billy's doorstep and is immediately taken in by Billy's mother. Proclaiming Drew the novel's least successful character, some critics see her as a mere vehicle for Billy's initiation into sex, money, and social divisions.

Billy's mother is a poor, mentally unstable, Irish laundry worker whose husband abandoned her. Although occasionally lucid, she indulges in such behavior as nailing her husband's suit, spread-eagled, to the floor of her room, lighting memorial candles for him, and pushing a doll around in a baby carriage. At the end of the novel, she places Billy's baby into this same carriage, accepting it immediately and with no questions. **Arnold Garbage**, Billy's friend from the neighborhood orphanage, is a scavenger who burrows through trash looking for treasure. He helps Billy recover Schultz's wealth, which is stashed in empty beer barrels. Arnold and Billy form a partnership that grows, according to the elder Billy, into a thriving corporate enterprise. **Thomas E. Dewey** is another of the novel's historically authentic characters: as New York City prosecutor, Dewey was famous for his crackdowns on gangsters; he also served as governor of New York and ran twice for president of the United States. Schultz's ill-advised plan to murder Dewey ultimately leads to his death, for Luciano recognizes its lunacy and has his rival killed.

Further Reading

Bemrose, John. "Growing Up in Gangland." *Maclean's Magazine* 102, No. 10 (6 March 1989): 58-9.

Bestsellers 89, Issue 3. Detroit: Gale Research.

Clifford, Andrew. "True-ish Crime Stories." *Listener* 122, No. 3131 (14 September 1989): 29.

Concise Dictionary of American Literary Biography: 1968-1988. Detroit: Gale Research.

Contemporary Literary Criticism, Vols. 6, 11, 15, 18, 37, 44, 65. Detroit: Gale Research.

Dictionary of Literary Biography, Vols. 2, 28. Detroit: Gale Research.

Eder, Richard. "Siege Perilous in the Court of Dutch Schultz." *Los Angeles Times Book Review* (5 March 1989): 3.

Harter, Carol C., and Thompson, James R. *E. L. Doctorow*. Boston: Twayne, 1990.

Kazin, Alfred. "Huck in the Bronx." *New Republic* 200, No. 12 (20 March 1989): 40-2.

Leonard, John. "Bye Bye Billy." *Nation* (New York) 248, No. 13 (3 April 1989): 454-56.

Morris, Christopher D. "'Fiction Is a System of Knowledge': An Interview with E. L. Doctorow." *Michigan Quarterly Review* 30, No. 3 (Summer 1991): 438-56.

Parks, John G. *E. L. Doctorow*. New York: Continuum, 1991.

Pease, Donald E. Review of *Billy Bathgate*. *America* 160, No. 18 (13 May 1989): 458-59.

Rushdie, Salman. "Billy the Streetwise Kid." *Observer* (10 September 1989): 51.

Tyler, Anne. "An American Boy in Gangland." *New York Times Book Review* (26 February 1989): 1, 46.

Wood, Michael. "Light and Lethal American Romance." *Times Literary Supplement* No. 4511 (15 September 1989): 997.

Roddy Doyle
1958–
Irish novelist and screenwriter.

Paddy Clarke Ha Ha Ha (novel, 1993)

Plot: Set in the late 1960s, the novel is composed of a series of anecdotes narrated by Paddy Clarke, a bright, energetic ten-year-old boy who lives in the working-class neighborhood of Barrytown, near Dublin, Ireland. Paddy describes his day-to-day life, including his adventures with his best friend Kevin, his clashes with his teacher Mr. Hennessy (or "Henno"), his increasing awareness of changes in his own and the wider world, and his efforts to torment his brother Francis, whom he calls Sinbad. Gradually the reader also learns of Paddy's anguish over the growing antagonism between his parents. He tries to will them back into harmony with each other, but near the end of the novel his father leaves the family.

Characters: Doyle won England's prestigious Booker Prize for *Paddy Clarke Ha Ha Ha*. Like his previous novels, *The Commitments* (1987), *The Snapper* (1990), and *The Van* (1991)—which are known collectively as the Barrytown Trilogy—this book is set in a working-class Dublin neighborhood similar to the one in which Doyle worked for several years as a teacher. Although some commentators faulted the novel as lacking a cohesive plot, most praised it for its comic, poignant exploration of such themes as friendship, religion, family relationships, and the joys and sorrows of growing up. Doyle was credited with creating an unusually realistic, unsentimental portrait of a particular character and milieu.

The novel's narrator is **Patrick "Paddy" Clarke**, an intelligent, inquisitive, high-spirited ten-year-old through whose eyes readers catch a glimpse of working-class Ireland during the 1960s. Doyle was praised for skillfully recreating the thought processes and chronicling the activities of a boy Paddy's age, although some critics found the novel's consequent disconnectedness confusing. Paddy's days are filled with inventing boyish rituals and playing games, committing petty thefts, participating in vandalism for the pure thrill of getting away with something, fighting with his friends, torturing his little brother, watching television, and asking his parents questions. Inside his quick mind is stored a considerable amount of random numerical data (such as that the life expectancy of a mouse is eighteen months), and he is fascinated by the story of Father Damien among the lepers of Hawaii and by the Native American leader Geronimo. As the novel progresses, however, Paddy's idyllic (if sometimes violent) world is darkened by the increasing tension between his parents. Well aware of the phenomenon of the broken family, Paddy dreads such a fate for his mother and father, both of whom he loves. Aware that their occasional arguments have become one long fight, he tries for a short time to stay awake through the night in order to ward off any eruption of enmity between them. But of course it is not within Paddy's power to heal his parents' relationship. By the end of the novel, he has lost some of his joy and honesty and become a more guarded, lonely figure who stoically endures his friends' taunting ("Paddy Clarke/has no da/ha ha ha!") because, unlike him, "They were only kids."

Doyle portrays with particular sensitivity the contradiction between the frequent harshness of boyhood and a boy's need for friendship and the love of his family. Providing the latter are Paddy's "Ma" and "Da," whose attention and regard Paddy craves. **Mr. Clarke** is thirty-three years old and holds an unspecified job in Dublin that allows him to support his family in reasonable comfort. He is an intelligent man whom Paddy describes as reading Norman Mailer's novel *The Naked and the Dead*, quoting poetry, and getting irate while watching the news on television. Although he is sometimes detached or annoyed, Mr. Clarke is basically warmhearted and Paddy looks forward to the times when he can keep his father engaged in talking to him and answering his questions. As the novel progresses, however, it becomes apparent that Mr. Clarke harbors a discontent that the naive Paddy (and consequently the reader) cannot fathom. He grows increasingly sullen and argumentative, takes to drink and even violence, and finally he leaves the family, returning on the book's final page to deliver Christmas presents to his sons. **Mrs. Clarke** is a more consistently benevolent character than her husband, a loving mother with the power to mend both physical and emotional hurts. Paddy likes to make her laugh by using grown-up phrases such as "I assure you," and he declares that she is the best mother in the neighborhood. Mrs. Clarke does grow somewhat more detached as her problems with her husband increase, and one morning she strongly signals her distress by not appearing for breakfast.

Another significant member of Paddy's family is his younger brother, **Francis**, whom he calls **Sinbad** due to his earlier resemblance (presumably when he was a chubby-cheeked baby) to the cartoon character. Described by critic Mary Flanagan as "a fine portrait of a bullied child who nevertheless possesses a mysterious inner strength," Sinbad endures some rather harrowing physical and psychological abuse from Paddy and his friends, including one incident in which the boys force a fuel capsule between his lips and then ignite it. Some commentators found this cruelty disturbing; others felt that Doyle had accurately depicted the tyranny and machismo of boyhood. Paddy states that he hates Sinbad because it is his obligation to do so, Sinbad being his brother, but that otherwise he might actually be proud of him, for example, for his soccer-playing ability. Toward the end of the novel, the boys' positions seem to change, as Paddy seeks reassurance from the much calmer Sinbad about their parents' problems. The other Clarke children include **Catherine** and **Dierdre**, babies quite close in age, who primarily serve to distract their mother from paying more attention to Paddy.

Other characters in the book include Paddy's teacher **Mr. Hennessy** (referred to by his students, among themselves, as **Henno**), who is strict and sometimes insensitive but who can also be kind, as when he escorts the very sleepy Paddy out of the classroom. Paddy's best friend **Kevin**, his cohort in starting fires with magnifying glasses and other misdeeds, impersonates Zentoga, a high priest of Ciunas (the Gaelic god of silence), in a ritual game that involves Kevin's whacking his friends with a poker until each produces a bad word by which he is called for the following week. Toward the end of the novel, Paddy rejects Kevin and beats him up so badly that the other boys "boycott" him. **Liam** and **Aidan O'Connell** are set apart from the other boys: Their mother is dead and that their grieving father has been known to howl outside during the night. He later acquires a girlfriend who scandalizes the neighborhood by staying overnight. A new arrival at school is **Charles Leavy**, one of the children from a nearby public housing project that Paddy and his friends have long regarded with a mixture of scorn and fear. Psychologically older and tougher than his schoolmates, Charles maintains a bored demeanor and smokes and swears freely, so that he is much admired (despite his plastic sandals) by Paddy.

Further Reading

Contemporary Literary Criticism Vol. 81. Detroit: Gale Research.

Donoghue, Dennis. "Another Country." *New York Review of Books* Vol. 41, no. 3 (February 3, 1994): 3–4, 6.

Flanagan, Mary. Review of *Paddy Clarke Ha Ha Ha*. *New York Times Book Review* (January 2, 1994): 1, 21.

Gallagher, John. "Tale of Troubled Irish Lad Lures American Audience." *Detroit Free Press* Sec. G (December 12, 1993): 7.

Kemp, Peter. "A Barrytown Boy." *Times Literary Supplement* no. 4706 (June 11, 1993): 21.

Lehmann-Haupt, Christopher. "A Window Into the Mind of a 10-Year-Old Irish Boy." *New York Times* (December 13, 1993): B2.

Morton, Brian. "Tar Baby." *New Statesman & Society* Vol. 6, no. 257 (June 18, 1993): 39.

Margaret Drabble
1939–

English novelist, critic, essayist, biographer, editor, short story writer, scriptwriter, journalist, and dramatist.

The Middle Ground (novel, 1980)

Plot: The central character in *The Middle Ground* is Kate Armstrong, a successful journalist in her early forties whose midlife crisis the book chronicles. As the novel opens, Kate is having lunch with her friend Hugo Mainwaring. She has recently suffered depression over job dissatisfaction and the issue of childbearing in later life. Kate's working-class background, childhood, and career are sketched in a long flashback: she is the child of sewer-system enthusiast Walter Fletcher and overweight, agoraphobic Florrie Fletcher; her brother, Peter, was also fat, and Kate often had to protect him from other children's taunts. After failing her grammar school examination (passing it would have led, under England's educational system, to college), Kate attended the Girl's Secondary Modern School, where she learned to disarm her classmates through humor. A boyfriend introduced Kate to London's bohemian art world, where she met and married Stuart Fletcher, an unsuccessful painter whom she has since divorced. After working for a short time for a photographer, Kate got a job as a secretary for a women's magazine. She advanced into editing and feature writing, eventually becoming a Sunday-newspaper columnist and popular freelance writer. Along the way, Kate and Stuart had three children, who are now essentially grown. Following her divorce, Kate had an affair with Ted Stennett, the husband of her best friend Evelyn. After discovering that Ted was also having an affair with someone else, Kate learned that she was pregnant. She first decided to have the baby and raise it alone, but chose an abortion when she found out that the fetus had spina bifida. This decision caused Kate a great deal of anguish and led to a year of promiscuity with a long series of unsuitable lovers.

Helping Kate return to normality was a new project: she agreed to return to her northern home town, Romley, to make a film contrasting the opportunities available to today's young girls with those open to her own classmates twenty-five years earlier. Kate also took a boarder into her home—an Iraqi student named Mujid who has challenged many of her assumptions about culture and politics. Kate has, in fact, asked Hugo to lunch in order to discuss Mujid. That same night, Mujid has an unpleasant confrontation with some Jewish friends of Kate's at a party she organizes. The next day, Kate goes to Romley to interview some of her old schoolmates. The novel concludes with another party, at which are gathered many of Kate's friends and extended family members.

Characters: Drabble is highly respected for her fiction chronicling the effects of the dramatic changes that have swept across contemporary British society, especially those affecting well-educated, socially conscious women. While Drabble's earlier novels featured protagonists in their twenties and thirties who were in the midst of establishing careers and families, *The Middle Ground* chronicles a later stage in its characters' lives. Like other Drabble novels, *The Middle Ground* exhibits what critic Lynn Veach Sadler has called a skillful blending of "the transcendent and the real." Although rooted in the mundane details of modern life, the novel is liberally sprinkled with literary allusions, symbolism, and authoritative asides to the reader, a characteristic of Drabble's writing in the eighteenth-century style. In addition to its somewhat apocalyptic portrait of late-twentieth-century Britain, the novel offers an engaging and affirmative exploration of such themes as the necessity of accepting one's destiny, the importance of family relationships, and the resilience and persistence of life and love even in the face of despair.

Drabble is consistently lauded for her sensitive portrayals of intelligent, educated women as they both enjoy and struggle with motherhood, careers, love, sex, and friendship. All of these concerns are present in the life of *The Middle Ground's* **Kate Armstrong**, a journalist in her mid-forties. Divorced for several years, Kate is the adoring mother of three well-adjusted, grown or nearly grown children, and she has a comfortable network of interesting, supportive friends. Although successful in her work, Kate has recently undergone a period of restlessness—a kind of midlife crisis. Long an advocate and voice for women in her writing, she has tired of women's concerns; nevertheless, her decision to write an exposè on the portrayal of women in advertising indicates that she will not abandon this realm. One of the most important dimensions of Kate's emotional crisis is her reaction to the abortion she had when she learned that the fetus had spina bifida. The importance of motherhood in women's lives is a major theme in Drabble's work, and her portrayal of Kate's anguish at ending her pregnancy has been particularly praised. All her life, Kate has used humor as a defense against hostility—sometimes at the expense of other people's feelings. The abortion brings Kate a deeper understanding of the need to use humor responsibly.

Another area in which Kate grows is in her attitude toward her past. She was brought up in a working-class environment (which, according to some critics, is not very convincingly illustrated) by two rather eccentric parents (an agoraphobic mother and a sewer-obsessed father), and she has long felt ashamed of her background. Kate's film project causes her to confront her past, and she has a Proustian memory sequence—brought on by the pleasantly familiar smell of sewage—that reaffirms her connection with her father and highlights the fact that her success in a more sophisticated world hasn't essentially changed her. Kate's worries about the breakdown of modern society are explored partly through her relationship with Mujid, who challenges her liberal assumptions about politics, religion, women's roles, and other issues. At the end of the novel, Kate is again cleaning her house and hosting a party—both signs of recovery; the party in particular is an emblem of the familial bonds and communal spirit that sustains Drabble's female protagonists through all their troubles. The novel ends on an affirmative if somewhat inconclusive note, with Kate still deeply engaged in living.

Some reviewers see Kate's social worker friend, **Evelyn Stennett**, as her alter ego; a few have even suggested that Drabble's portrayal of Evelyn is more effective than that of Kate, probably because Evelyn's background (especially her Quaker upbringing) and temperament are closer to Drabble's. Kate considers Evelyn a more balanced, "proper" woman than herself. Evelyn is apparently aware of the affair between her husband and Kate and may even welcome it, which suggests that she is already sexually estranged from Ted. Like Kate, Evelyn grows emotionally as a result of a traumatic experience. A maddened client throws ammonia in her face, temporarily blinding her, then sets himself on fire. While recovering in the hospital, Evelyn is astonished and uplifted by the show of concern she receives from her other clients, which affirms her belief in her vocation and in the value of doing good in the world, even if that world is chaotic and hostile. Evelyn tells Kate, "All we can do in this world is to care for one another, in the society we have."

Kate's close friend **Hugo Mainwaring** is thought to be Drabble's spokesperson in the novel, particularly in his belief that modern consciousness is crippled by the burden of the past; when Kate tells him that "the past is the past," Hugo responds, "If only it were." Hugo also comments that contemporary life is too fragmented and overloaded with information to be comprehensible. Yet Hugo makes other statements that counter those consistently stressed by Drabble. For example, Hugo feels that meaningful communication between people is ultimately impossible, whereas Kate (and other female protagonists in Drabble's fiction) relishes social occasions as opportunities to forge deeper connections with friends and family. Despite their very congenial relationship, Hugo and Kate do not become lovers, which has provoked comparisons with the situation in Henry James's acclaimed short story "The Beast in the Jungle," in which a couple's love is thwarted because the man believes that some calamitous fate awaits him.

A less sympathetically portrayed male character is **Ted Stennett**, Evelyn's husband and Kate's lover. He is also the father (although he never hears about it) of her aborted baby. Described as "not a nice man but he earned a lot," Stennett is a physician and microbiologist who studies tropical diseases for the World Health Organization. His belief in a massive worldwide epidemic with the power to destroy the human race—a notion that seems to excite him—foreshadows the AIDS crisis, which had not yet been identified at the time of the novel's publication.

A major thematic thread running through *The Middle Ground* is the importance of family and of resolving issues related to one's upbringing. Kate undergoes this process when she returns to her hometown to make a documentary film and experiences a flood of memories. Her father, **Walter Fletcher**, was a working-class intellectual whose two obsessions were atheism and the British sewer system, which he frequently proclaimed the best in the world. Kate's fat, agoraphobic mother **Florrie** bequeathed to her daughter a fear of flying and of traveling to foreign countries that has kept Kate perpetually confined to her own soil. Like their mother, Kate's brother, **Peter**, was overweight and rather odd, so that Kate had to protect him from other children's teasing. As an adult, Peter is jealous of Kate's success and sends her insulting, anonymous letters. Near the end of the novel, Kate signals her progress in making peace with her family by inviting them to her home for Christmas dinner, thus avoiding the kind of dreary meal in Romley that she has always hated.

Drabble apparently modeled Kate's Iraqi houseguest, **Mujid,** after an Arab student boarder she took into her own home. Mujid instills some self-doubt in Kate during their discussions about Marxism; he criticizes British television for its inadequate, dominantly pro-Israeli coverage of Middle East affairs and British fruits and vegetables for their poor quality. At one of Kate's parties, Mujid offends some Jewish friends of hers with an anti-Semitic joke, yet he also touches Kate's heart with his eloquently voiced gratitude for her kindness. At the end of the novel, Mujid returns to Iraq.

Other characters in *The Middle Ground* include Kate's former husband, **Stuart Armstrong**, a talented but self-defeating painter; Kate remains grateful to Stuart for fathering their three children and for the warmer, more physical style of family life she learned from him and his family. Hugo's former wife, **Judith**, is so aggrieved when their son suffers brain damage due to a hospital mishap that she becomes obsessed with suing for damages. Among Kate's sometimes comically inadequate lovers during her year of promiscuity are **Patrick**, a womanizer who subjects Kate to embarrassing babytalk in bed; **Kevin**, who expects her to do his laundry; and **Adrian**, who is offended when Kate—who pays for all of the couple's expenses—books hotel rooms in her own name.

The Radiant Way (novel, 1987)

Plot: This loosely plotted novel takes place in England in the first half of the 1980s, centering on three middle-aged women who have been friends since all attended Cambridge University on scholarships. Liz Headleand is a psychiatrist who specializes in adoption issues, Alix Bowen teaches English part-time at a women's prison, and Esther Breuer is an art historian. The novel focuses on the characters as they struggle with various political, social, and personal concerns. While emphasizing to her patients the importance of resolving family mysteries, Liz has avoided confronting her own upbringing by an odd, agoraphobic mother and a father who may have sexually abused her. Alix's parents are earnest socialists, while she herself loses her old idealism in the face of England's increasingly desolate economic, political, and social situation. Unlike her two friends, Esther remains detached from deep commitments to others, including her eerie Italian lover, Claudio Volpe. Esther is horrified to learn that her quiet young neighbor, Paul Whitmore, is the "Horror of Harrow Road," a gruesome serial murderer. Alix also has a connection with the murderer; he kills one of her students and leaves his victim's head on the front seat of Alix's car. During the course of the novel, Liz returns to her old home in northern England to see her mother before she dies and to reconnect with her sister, Shirley Harper, a middle-class housewife. Other significant events include the breakup of Liz's marriage; Alix's near-affair with a friend of her husband, Brian; and Esther's plan to move to Italy to live with Claudio's sister, a radical lesbian feminist. The novel ends with the three friends enjoying another of their monthly outings together.

Characters: *The Radiant Way* expands on the exploration of social decline that characterized Drabble's earlier novel, *The Middle Ground,* portraying the disillusionment of England's liberals during the 1980s. The novel is pervaded by images of madness and death and features less of the humor that lightened Drabble's previous works. Although *The Radiant Way* may be defined as a realistic novel due to its anecdotal structure and detailed portrayal of its characters' lives, it is also infused with mythological references and symbolism and displays Drabble's considerable knowledge of history and literature. Although sometimes faulted for its unconvincing portraits of working-class characters, *The Radiant Way* is praised for its penetrating look into the connection between the past and the present, the influence of destiny on people's lives, the responsibility of the individual for promoting collective progress, and the roots of the irrational in human behavior.

In *The Radiant Way,* the narrative perspective is split between three central protagonists, all of them middle-aged, professional women who have been friends since they attended Cambridge University together. **Liz Headleand** seems to be the most successful of the three: she has a brilliant career as a psychiatrist, a husband, children, and a big house on fashionable Harley Street. Yet Liz's life is not as orderly as it appears, for her husband suddenly announces his desire for a divorce, and she must finally confront some important aspects of her past. Liz is an expert on family issues who has never resolved for herself the same kinds of problems on which she counsels her patients. Recognizing this failing, she compares herself to a "faithless priest" who continues to minister to his flock despite his own spiritual doubt. What Liz describes as her "family romance" involves a reclusive, strange mother and a father about whom Liz has nagging sexual memories. During the course of the novel, Liz eventually practices her belief that understanding the past can benefit an individual's present life. She returns to her hometown to visit Rita, the now bedridden, obese mother whose loneliness she has always dreaded, and she emerges with more compassion for her as well as a renewed connection with her sister Shirley.

The theme of disillusioned liberalism is explored through **Alix Bowen**, the daughter of an old-style socialist couple who was brought up in a northern England town. Alix is depressed about her country's current malaise and embarrassed by her husband's idealism, which she considers outdated. She has the most rigorous intellectual perspective of the three friends and consistently tries to apply the lessons of her Cambridge education and subsequent scholarship to her current life, thus giving Drabble an opportunity to weave many literary allusions into the story (as well as reflecting her recent editorship of *The Oxford Companion to English Literature*). Alix's desire, to develop a "comprehensive vision" that somehow draws together into a meaningful whole the many disparate perspectives that surround her, reflects a similar desire on Drabble's part, which is demonstrated in all of her fiction.

Petite, vaguely exotic **Esther Breuer** is an art historian whose Jewish heritage (she was born in Berlin but brought to England as a baby by her refugee parents) is part of what makes her the least typically British of the three friends. Faulted by some critics as the novel's least successfully drawn character, Esther is consistently associated with the image of a dying potted palm, symbolizing her avoidance of any deep or meaningful relationships with others. A specialist in Italian art whose scholarly style is noted for its "startling, brilliant connections," Esther claims that she wants only "to acquire interesting information." Thus she keeps herself detached from love and political commitment and also from the kind of self-questioning that Liz and Alix engage in. Esther's plan to leave England manifests her wish to escape the evil manifested by Paul Whitmore, the neighbor she thought to be harmless.

None of the novel's male characters have flattering portrayals. Liz's husband, **Charles Headleand**, who leaves her for a shallow aristocrat, is a former idealist who once made a documentary film promoting educational reform (with the same title as the novel) but who has since become greedy for power and money. Alix's husband, **Brian Bowen**, who teaches at a local college, is basically decent, but Alix is embarrassed by his "outdated faith" in the possibility of social progress. Brian has retained his ardent political interests despite his increasingly bourgeois lifestyle, but it does not seem likely that he will ever live up to his early promise and write the definitive working-class novel. Esther's lover, **Claudio Volpe**, is a married Italian anthropologist with a strong belief in the supernatural; he claims to have seen a werewolf (in fact, his surname hints that he may be one himself) and insists that Esther harbors untapped spiritual powers.

One of the novel's most sympathetically portrayed characters is **Shirley Harper**, Liz's sister. Whereas a teenaged Liz had applied herself to her studies, won a scholarship to Cambridge, and escaped their dreary northern town, Shirley chose early marriage and a bleak life as a homemaker. Though weary of her surroundings, Shirley takes comfort in her safe, circumscribed life and in the sustaining communal spirit of her small town. Commentators have asserted that this character allows Drabble to create a more comprehensive vision of England in the 1980s: while Liz represents the more lively and economically viable south, Shirley serves as a link to the depressed north.

During their childhood, Liz and Shirley's mother, **Rita Ablewhite**, was eccentric, stingy, agoraphobic, and unaffectionate and consequently not much loved by her daughters. But as in all of Drabble's works, the importance of family connections is a strong theme in *The Radiant Way*, and Liz will not be allowed to shirk hers with her mother. During her visit to the dying, obese Rita, Liz recalls that despite her faults, her mother always read good books and encouraged her daughters to accomplish as much as they could. In this novel's sequel, *A Natural Curiosity*, Liz makes a discovery that deepens her compassion for Rita.

Another character who receives even more attention in *A Natural Curiosity* is **Paul Whitmore**, the "Horror of Harrow Road." Described by critic Ann Hulbert as an "emblem of the banality of England's evil," Whitmore is an ordinary young man who shocks everyone with his homicidal impulses. Whitmore decapitates his victims, and the novel is infused with images of severed heads, which seem to symbolize the dark, irrational side of human nature. One of Whitmore's victims is Alix's student **Jilly Fox**, a rather threatening drug addict whose head is found on the seat of Alix's car.

Other characters in the novel include Charles Headleand's superficial, exploitative lover, **Henrietta Latchett**, an aristocrat (and said to be Drabble's first aristocratic character) who is only sketchily portrayed. Academician **Otto Werner**, Brian's friend, and Alix fall in love but never consummate their feelings; instead, Otto takes his wife and children to the United States.

A Natural Curiosity (novel, 1989)

Plot: The novel is a sequel to *The Radiant Way* and continues the chronicle of many of the characters in that work. *A Natural Curiosity* centers on the efforts of former prison teacher Alix Bowen to explore the background of Paul Whitmore, the serial murderer called the "Horror of Harrow Road," who is now serving a life sentence in prison. Alix has always been deeply interested in prisons, violence, and the criminal mind and is curious about the roots of evil in human behavior. Psychiatrist Liz Headleand, Alix's friend from college days, is also fascinated by the mysteries of the past and how they impinge on her patients' lives and hers. Committed to the "nurture" side of the nature/nurture debate— that is, whether character is determined by genetics or environment—Alix discovers evidence from Paul's upbringing that seems to verify her thesis. She manages to locate Paul's mother, Angela Whitmore Malkin, who psychologically abused her son and now wants nothing to do with him. Alix engages in a mock-epic battle with Angela and emerges victorious. She subsequently reports Angela, who is a dog breeder, to the authorities for cruelty to animals. Meanwhile, Liz and her newly widowed sister, Shirley Harper, meet Marcia Campbell, who turns out to be their half-sister. They learn that their mother gave Marcia up to be adopted after becoming pregnant by an aristocrat, who paid her to give up the baby and marry Liz's father. This insight gives Liz new sympathy for her mother.

Characters: In an interview, Drabble claimed that *A Natural Curiosity* is "about how we cling to normalcy in a world which at a national, international and personal level seems fairly odd these days." Infused with images of severed heads, death, and brutality, the novel focuses on its characters' efforts to find clues to the persistence of evil. A major concern is the ultimately unresolvable question of whether the propensity for violence is rooted in childhood trauma or genetically programmed, that is, the nature versus nurture debate. Drabble incorporates many references to anthropology, Greek and Latin mythology, and the ancient history of Britain, suggesting that the human tendency toward brutality is a constant, thereby testing readers' assumptions about what is normal and what is deviant.

In *The Radiant Way*, **Alix Bowen** taught English to incarcerated women, one of whom was murdered by the "Horror of Harrow Road." In *A Natural Curiosity,* Alix probes deeper into the criminal mind as she develops a relationship of sorts with the now imprisoned serial killer Paul Whitmore. Always fascinated by crime, violence, and prisons (and haunted during her childhood by feelings of guilt and dreams of criminal activity), Alix seems obsessed with identifying the origins of Paul's deviancy. She believes that environment is more important in determining behavior than genetics—that one can identity the roots of criminality in the criminal's past. By the end of the novel, Alix believes she has found the source of Paul's troubles: his neglectful, cruel mother. But she also admits that she has merely confirmed her own bias. Although a few critics feel it is unconvincing, Alix's mock-epic battle with Angela Whitmore Malkin is an important and symbolic event in the novel. Alix takes on the role of Paul's surrogate or adoptive mother as she battles the Medusa-like monster who has warped the young man's life. Alix emerges victorious from the confrontation, and her subsequent bath in a river, during which she sees a rare Kingfisher bird and receives a kind tribute from an old man, may be a kind of ritual cleansing or benediction. She may not have solved the ultimately unfathomable mysteries of human behavior, but she has made a stand (however minor) for the suffering innocents of the world and symbolically avenged the damage done to Paul Whitmore.

Psychiatrist **Liz Headleand**, whose professional specialty is helping adopted children resolve the mysteries associated with their birth families, shares with her friend Alix an interest in the roots of evil in human behavior. She often wonders whether the human race is sinking deeper and deeper into collective psychosis and not developing the understanding that might lead to decreased deviancy. A survivor of child sexual abuse, Alix shocks the audience of a television show when, during a panel discussion on the topic, she suggests that the desire of some adults for sex with children may be more normal than is currently assumed. Liz's listeners overreact to her purely speculative comments, which reflect her ambivalence about her own childhood experiences with her father. Liz's quest to plumb her past and "heal" herself—a process she begins in *The Radiant Way*—is facilitated by her discovery, through her newfound half-sister, Marcia Campbell, of her family's real history. Imagining the grief and isolation her mother must have felt after relinquishing a child and marrying a man she did not love helps Liz develop a deeper sympathy for the agoraphobic woman. She also comes to see her father not as a fiend but as a timid, pitiable man with sexual and emotional problems. Liz is not as sure as Alix that the roots of human evil lie in childhood, for she notes that Paul Whitmore grew up with a decent father and that many abused and neglected children become well-adjusted adults. Nevertheless, she acknowledges that science can provide no pat solutions or definitive answers to the riddles of human behavior.

Paul Whitmore, the "Horror of Harrow Road," plays a central role in *A Natural Curiosity*, for he is the focus of Alix's quest for answers about human evil. Now serving a life sentence for the ritualized serial killings that are chronicled in *The Radiant Way*, Paul is a mild-mannered, studious, seemingly reasonable young man interested in botany and ancient British history. The son of a butcher, he is himself a vegetarian, which is somewhat ironic in view of his grisly treatment of his victims' corpses. Through her discussions with Paul, Alix decides that the source of Paul's deviancy is his emotionally abusive mother. Thus Paul's character undergoes a shift from a figure of revulsion in *The Radiant Way* to one deserving sympathy in *A Natural Curiosity*.

Whereas Paul is the central villain of *The Radiant Way*, his fittingly named mother, **Angela Whitmore Malkin**, takes up that role in *A Natural Curiosity*. With her ringletted red hair and violent temper, Angela resembles Medusa, the snake-haired Gorgon monster of Greek myth; in fact, some critics fault this character as rather overblown. After her divorce from Paul's father, who confirms that Angela consistently teased and tormented their son and encouraged his obsession with death and sacrifice, Angela remarried and became a breeder of bull mastiffs. When Alix visits Paul's mother to confront her about how she treated her son, Angela reacts with rage, denouncing Paul and threatening Alix. On her second visit to Angela's home, Alix is horrified to discover a heap of dead and dying dogs with a rotting slab of meat hanging just out of their reach. She manages to repel Angela's subsequent attack, then reports her to the authorities for animal abuse. Subsequent information reveals that even Angela harbors a past trauma that sheds light on her wicked behavior: Paul had a twin sister whose death so unhinged their mother that she mistreated her surviving child. Thus, like her son, Angela transforms from monster to pitiable human being.

Many of the secondary characters in *The Radiant Way* also have roles in *A Natural Curiosity*. Art historian **Esther Breuer** is a much less central figure in this novel; she moves to Italy to live with **Elena Volpe**, the radical-lesbian-feminist sister of her former lover, but finally returns to England. Esther is one of several characters in Drabble's fiction whose intellects are disengaged from their bodies and who avoid normal relationships with others, in contrast to the life-affirming personalities Drabble seems to prefer. Liz's ex-husband, **Charles Headleand**, now divorced from his aristocratic second wife, is treated more sympathetically in this novel than in *The Radiant Way*. He lives in a small flat, studying the Koran and a stolen Gideon Bible for clues to life's mysteries. Liz's sister, **Shirley Harper**, undergoes a kind of hysterical episode after her debt-ridden husband, **Cliff**, commits suicide. She spends a month in Paris with womanizing, neurotic **Robert Holland**, whom she discards after he infects her with a venereal disease. Near the end of the novel, Liz and Shirley learn that they have a half-sister, **Marcia Campbell,** their mother's daughter by an aristocrat who paid her to give up her baby and marry someone else. The wise, generous, life-affirming Marcia is a very positively portrayed character. **Clive Enderby**, Liz's family solicitor, proves to know more about their history than Liz.

Further Reading

Brookner, Anita. "Too Much of a Muchness." *Spectator* Vol. 258, no. 8286 (May 2, 1987): 29–30.

Campbell, Jane. "'Both a Joke and a Victory': Humor as Narrative Strategy in Margaret Drabble's Fiction." *Contemporary Literature* Vol. 32, no. 1 (spring 1991): 75–99.

Contemporary Literary Criticism. Vols. 2, 3, 5, 8, 10, 22, 53. Detroit: Gale Research.

Dictionary of Literary Biography. Vol. 14. Detroit: Gale Research.

Duguid, Lindsay. "Icons of the Times." *Times Literary Supplement* No. 4387 (May 1, 1987): 458.

Elkins, Mary Jane. "Facing the Gorgon: Good and Bad Mothers in the Late Novels of Margaret Drabble." In *Narrating Mothers: Theorizing Maternal Subjectivities.* Edited by Brenda O. Daly and Maureen T. Reddy. Knoxville: University of Tennessee Press, 1991.

Greene, Gayle. "The End of a Dream." *Women's Review of Books* Vol. 5, no. 4 (January 1988): 4–5.

Hannay, John. *The Intertextuality of Fate: A Study of Margaret Drabble.* Columbia: University of Missouri Press, 1986.

Myer, Valerie Grosvenor. *Margaret Drabble: A Reader's Guide.* New York: St. Martin's Press, 1991.

Rifkind, Donna. "No Way Out." *New Criterion* Vol. 6, no. 3 (November 1987): 70–73.

Rose, Ellen C. *The Novels of Margaret Drabble: Equivocal Figures.* London: Macmillan, 1980.

Rubenstein, Roberta. "Severed Heads, Primal Crimes, Narrative Revisions: Margaret Drabble's A Natural Curiosity." *Critique: Studies in Contemporary Fiction* Vol. 33, no. 2 (winter 1992): 95–105.

Sadler, Lynn Veach. *Margaret Drabble.* Boston: Twayne, 1986.

Updike, John. "Seeking Connections in an Insecure Country." *New Yorker* Vol. 63, no. 39 (November 16, 1987): 153–59.

André Dubus

1936–

American short story writer and novelist.

"A Father's Story" (short story, 1983)

Plot: The story is narrated by middleaged divorcée Luke Ripley, who owns a horseback-riding stable in northeastern Massachusetts. He describes his quiet, orderly, pleasant daily routine and the comfort he derives from his Catholic faith and his friendship with a compassionate priest, Father Paul LeBoeuf. Luke was devastated by the departure of his wife and four children but has since reconciled himself to a solitary existence. He then relates what happened during his twenty-year-old daughter Jennifer's recent visit. While driving home after an evening of drinking beer with her girlfriends, Jennifer hit someone with her car. Panicked, she did not stop but drove home and tearfully told her father what she had done. Determined that Jennifer should not bear the responsibility for what had happened, Ripley went to the scene and finally located the victim, a young man who was unconscious and obviously badly hurt but possibly not quite dead. Instead of phoning the police or even his priest friend, Luke returned home and comforted Jennifer. The next morning, he deliberately drove into a tree in order to provide an explanation for the damage to the car. Luke has since had several imaginary conversations with God about the incident and his own actions, during which he maintains that he would do the same thing again to protect his daughter and that God cannot understand what it is like to be "the father of a girl." He admits that he has lost his old sense of peace but claims that he prefers this new condition.

Characters: Described as a "geographer of the sadness of ordinary life" by critic Judith Levine, Dubus is acclaimed for his well-plotted, realistic fiction, in which characters (most of whom are working- or middle-class New Englanders) struggle with self-doubt, loneliness, the pain of broken relationships, and other dilemmas of contemporary life. Considered one of the most accomplished stories in the collection *The Times Are Never So Bad*, "A Father's Story" centers on the joy and anguish of fatherhood, which some commentators have identified as a strong thematic thread throughout Dubus' work. Another quality that makes this a typical Dubus story is its presentation of Catholicism as a strong and generally positive force in the life of the protagonist, who demonstrates how the rituals of both religion and daily routine have healing power.

The story's central character and narrator is fifty-four-year-old **Luke Ripley**, who offers riding lessons and boarding at his stable of thirty horses. Divorced for some years, Luke is the father of four grown children. In the first part of the story, Luke describes how he has found comfort (particularly after the devastating break-up of his marriage and the overwhelming solitude that followed his family's departure) in his Catholic faith and in his daily routine. Every morning, he forces himself to get up early for an hour of silence, contemplation, and prayer, and every night he is a "big-gutted, grey-haired guy, drinking tea and smoking cigarettes" while listening to opera. Luke's Catholicism is an important part of his life, although he warns the reader not to interpret his daily attendence at Mass as a sign that he is "a spiritual man;" rather, he maintains, he appreciates "the necessity and wonder of ritual." With his priest friend, Luke debates the more troubling aspects of his faith, such as the prohibition against remarriage after divorce. Luke's initial narration prepares the reader somewhat for his reaction to what happens when his daughter accidentally kills a pedestrian with her car, and his rationalization of his own subsequent behavior. By deciding not to divulge Jennifer's involvement in the accident either to the police or to Father LeBoeuf, Luke essentially assumes her guilt. Although he now has a secret from his best friend—as well as from Jennifer, with whom he does not share the information that the young man may not have been killed instantly—Luke shares his thoughts and reasoning with God in imaginary conversations. Both humble and defiant, Luke tells God that if he had to make the choice again he would still choose to protect Jennifer, simply because she is a girl. "You never had a daughter," he reminds the Creator, "and if You had, You could not have borne her passion." Luke now experiences a diminishment in the peace he once felt, but because he feels he never really earned that peace, he prefers his current state. In the story's last lines, God tells Luke that he loves his daughter "in weakness," and Luke compares this love with that of God for him.

Luke describes his friend **Father Paul LeBoeuf** as "another old buck." Big and balding with a ruddy face, the French-Canadian priest is an outdoorsman who seems younger than his age, which is about ten years older than Luke. Father LeBoeuf demonstrated the compassion of both a man of God and a friend when he continued to arrive at Luke's house for dinner every Wednesday night even after Luke's wife and children had left, and he has since helped Luke endure this loss and puzzle out the mysteries of the Catholic faith. Luke appreciates the fact that Father LeBoeuf is not as concerned as other priests with sin and guilt but focuses instead on the comfort and strength to be derived from faith.

The story's only other character is Luke's twenty-year-old daughter **Jennifer**, his youngest child and the only one who lives close enough to visit fairly frequently. An athletic college student, Jennifer has retained many friends from her girlhood with whom she gets together while staying with her father. Luke has watched with awe the transformation of Jennifer and her friends from girls into women, and he claims that his daughter's entrance into "the deep forest" of womanhood "renders me awkward." Luke admits that if Jennifer had been a boy he would have stood by in resignation and even pride as his son faced the consequences of his act, but that as "the father of girl" he had no choice but to spare her that trauma. Critics have noted in Dubus' fiction a tendency to portray female characters as distinctly "other;" they are either dangerous or, as in "A Father's Story," in need of protection.

Further Reading

Contemporary Literary Criticism, Vols. 13, 36. Detroit: Gale Research.

Johnson, Greg. "Three Contemporary Masters: Brodkey, Carver, Dubus." *Georgia Review* (Help! Need rest of info.!)

Kennedy, Thomas E. *André Dubus: A Study of the Short Fiction*. Boston: Twayne Publishers, 1988.

Levine, Judith. Review of *The Times Are Never So Bad*. *VLS* No. 23 (February 1984): 3-4.

Oates, Joyce Carol. "People to Whom Things Happen." *New York Times Book Review* (26 June 1983): 12, 18.

Stonehill, Brian. "Memory, the Lens to Look at Life." *Los Angeles Times Book Review* (14 August 1983): 5.

Henry Dumas
1934–1968
American short story writer and poet.

"Ark of Bones"(short story, 1970)

Plot: Set in the rural American South, the story is narrated by a black youth named Fishhound. On his way to fish in the nearby Mississippi River, Fishhound meets his friend Headeye, who announces that he has a mojo bone that gives him supernatural powers. Headeye reminds Fishhound that in the Old Testament, Ezekiel prophesied that the dry bones in the valley will be bound up to rise again. While Fishhound fishes, Headeye keeps watch for Noah's Ark, which he claims will reappear. When Fishhound sees a huge boat approaching (which also seems to be standing still), he believes that he and his friend have died and are about to be ferried to heaven. A rowboat takes them to the Ark and they meet its old, black captain clad in skins and sandals. Fishhound and Headeye then visit the ship's hold, which is filled with bones. Attendants are handling them with great reverence. Men are bringing in fresh bones from the river, the bones of those who either died during the infamous Middle Passage, when enslaved blacks crossed from Africa to America by ship, or were lynched by hateful whites. The old man explains that Headeye is to be anointed and charged with the mission of setting his brothers free. After a ritual involving the mojo bone, Fishhound and Headeye leave the Ark. Some days later Headeye sets out on his own, promising to return and leaving Fishhound as his witness. When people ask Fishhound where Headeye has gone, he does not mention the Ark but tells about Ezekiel and the dry bones, so that he gains a reputation for lunacy.

Characters: A gifted writer, Dumas gained widespread critical acclaim only after his death at thirty-four (he was shot by a policeman in a Harlem subway station in what the authorities called a case of mistaken identity). His works of fiction and poetry are distinguished by complex symbolism, deft blending of African mysticism and Christian mythology, and authentic rural southern and urban northern settings. Critics sometimes regard him as a link between the prominent African-American authors of the early twentieth century—such as Jean Toomer and Langston Hughes—and contemporary black authors like Alice Walker and Toni Morrison. Dumas balanced his artistic and political concerns through lean but flowing, image-laden prose, noted for being lyrical but never didactic. One of Dumas's most accomplished stories, "Ark of Bones" is an African-American parable recounting both injustice and the promise of deliverance. It is at once a fable, a morality tale, and a chronicle of black experience in America.

The protagonists of Dumas's short stories are often southern black adolescents who undergo mythic experiences. The events that emphasize their kinship with the natural world provide strength and the courage to fight racism. **Headeye**'s anointing, which confers on him the responsibility for freeing his people, gives birth to a twentieth-century black folk hero. Headeye is a mysterious figure–something of a misfit, apparently, in his local community– who claims that his mojo bone is the world's only key to African American experience. Several critics have commented on the symbolism of bones in the story. Headeye relies on the mojo bone, encounters the ark ferrying his people's bones, and narrates the biblical story of Ezekiel and the valley of dry bones, which all suggest that he will deliver his people after he is anointed as a savior. Thus bones represent power, hope, and the promise of freedom. Also symbolic is Headeye's name, which Fishhound explains as coming about because "on Headeye, everything is stunted cept his eyes and head." Commentators have noted that his name denotes his vision of the future or his vision into the very heart of the African American experience, even if others are blind or turn away.

Dumas has been lauded for rendering the speech rhythms and idiom of southern, uneducated black youth with skill and sensitivity. In "Ark of Bones," the narrator **Fishhound** also laces his speech with biblical rhythms. The story blends the profane and the sacred and subtly evokes the African chanting echoed in the storytelling and music of American blacks. Ordinary, literal-minded, and peripheral to the story's action, Fishhound witnesses the events and awkwardly tries to make sense of what he sees. His name emphasizes his ties to the natural world and his community and may connote the Christian symbols of the fish and the "Fisher of Men."

The story's other significant character is the **ark's captain**, who some critics regard as a priest because he ordains Headeye to save his people. He tells Headeye: "Son, you are in the house of generations. Every African who lives in America has a part of his soul in this ark." Fishhound notes how similar the captain is to the biblical Noah, for the captain of the ark is black and dressed in skins and sandals and performs his ritual through an African-style chant.

Further Reading

Baraka, Amiri. "Henry Dumas: Afro-Surreal Expressionist." *Black American Literature Forum* Vol. 22, no. 2 (summer 1988): 164–66.

Browne, W. Francis, and J. Launay. "Henry Dumas: Teaching the Drunken Earth." *Centerpoint* Vol. 1, no. 3 (spring 1975): 47–55.

Collier, Eugenia. "Elemental Wisdom in Goodbye, Sweetwater: Suggestions for Further Study." *Black American Literature Forum* Vol. 22, no. 2 (summer 1988): 192–99.

Contemporary Literary Criticism Vols. 6, 62. Detroit: Gale Research.

Deck, John. "A Rich Talent." *New York Times Book Review* (October 24, 1974): 36.

Dictionary of Literary Biography Vol. 41. Detroit: Gale Research.

Jackson, Angela. Review of *Ark of Bones, and Other Stories. Black World* Vol. 24, no. 3 (January 1975): 51–52.

Rampersad, Arnold. "Henry Dumas's World of Fiction." *Black American Literature Forum* Vol. 22, no. 2 (summer 1988): 329–32.

Redmond, Eugene B. Introduction to *Goodbye, Sweetwater: New and Selected Stories* by Henry Dumas, ed. Eugene B. Redmond. New York: Thunder's Mouth Press, 1988, xi–xx.

Smith, Barbara. "Combining Traditions of the Black Experience." *Freedomways* Vol. 15, no. 1 (first quarter, 1975): 52–55.

Daphne du Maurier
1907–1989

English novelist, dramatist, nonfiction writer, and editor.

Rebecca (novel, 1938)

Plot: The novel takes place primarily on England's windswept, rocky Cornish coast. An unnamed young girl, poor and serving as a companion to the vulgar Mrs. Van Hopper, travels with the old lady to Monte Carlo. There she meets a romantically somber, mysterious, and wealthy older man named Maxim de Winter. To the girl's surprise and delight, Maxim asks her to marry him. After their marriage, the couple return to Manderley, Maxim's stately home, where the new Mrs. de Winter learns all about her husband's first wife, Rebecca, from the ghoulish housekeeper, Mrs. Danvers. The second Mrs. de Winter feels inferior to her beautiful, sophisticated predecessor until she learns the truth about Rebecca. Maxim actually hated his glamorous first wife, who frequently engaged in sexual escapades with other men, and he murdered her when she told him she was pregnant with her lover's child. The murder was never discovered, and she was presumed drowned. A last-minute discovery proves that Rebecca would have soon died from cancer even if she had not been murdered, and Maxim is cleared of any wrongdoing at a trial. Returning to their home, Maxim and his young wife discover that Manderley is on fire, set alight by a jealous Mrs. Danvers. The de Winters leave England and spend the rest of their lives traveling around Europe, never completely free of their memories of Manderley and the legacy of Rebecca.

Characters: *Rebecca* is one of the most widely read of all English novels, and its popularity was enhanced by the acclaimed screen version (starring Joan Fontaine and Sir Laurence Olivier), which won the Academy Award for Best Picture in 1940. Although du Maurier's critical standing has never attained the level of her popularity with readers, many scholars place her well-told gothic novels solidly within a tradition established in the late eighteenth century by such authors as Ann Radcliffe (*The Mysteries of Udolpho*, 1794) and continued into the nineteenth with Charlotte Brontë's *Jane Eyre*. *Rebecca* opens with one of the most famous lines in English literature: "Last night I dreamt I went to Manderley again." The novel incorporates all of the mystery, suspense, and melodrama of the gothic tradition but also offers a study of an obsessive personality and the long-term effects of strong emotion.

As many critics have pointed out, *Rebecca* follows the model of the Cinderella story that has so dominated the mythology of Western culture. It is something of a *bildungsroman* (a novel of initiation into adulthood) in that it chronicles young **Mrs. de Winter**'s progress from her initial state as Mrs. Van Hopper's toady, to her precarious position in the shadow of Rebecca, to her eventual assumption of the role of Maxim's wife. By the end of the novel, the unnamed protagonist has gained confidence and knowledge—albeit tinged with tragedy. When she first meets Maxim in Monte Carlo, Mrs. de Winter is a poor, dependent, naive young girl with a shy, meek demeanor. Described as "devastatingly plain," she has short hair and wears ill-fitting clothing and no makeup. Still, Maxim is attracted to her (he later claims that he cherished her innocence), and he rescues her from the clutches of Mrs. Van Hopper. Dazzled by and grateful to her mysterious new husband, Mrs. de Winter longs to be a true companion to him and a worthy mistress of his magnificent home. Already prone to romantic fantasy, she is much affected by Manderley. She soon senses, however, that Maxim is still grieving his first wife, Rebecca, to whom she feels hopelessly inferior. The malicious intrusions of Mrs. Danvers—who idolized her old mistress and resents her new one—exacerbates her distress, culminating in disaster when she appears (egged on by the housekeeper) dressed as Rebecca at a costume ball. Several critics consider Mrs. de Winter's subservient adoration of Maxim (who is twice her age) a reflection of du Maurier's relationship with her often distant father, and they see Oedipal overtones in the young woman's selfish joy and apparent lack of censure upon learning that Maxim not only never loved but also killed Rebecca. Although Mrs. de Winter may be said to triumph in the end by achieving marital happiness with Maxim, the two are also punished when they lose Manderley and must spend their lives wandering outside of England.

When the young woman who will become his second wife first meets **Maxim de Winter**, he strikes her as "arresting, sensitive, medieval in some strange inexplicable way." The charismatic, unhappy Maxim plays the role of the tortured hero so vital to gothic fiction, as well as its obsessed personality. Having managed to hide Rebecca's murder from the world, he is gnawed by guilt and constantly preoccupied, so that the second Mrs. de Winter assumes he is still in love with and pining away for Rebecca. A wealthy aristocrat, Maxim cherishes his home—the symbol of his social standing—and will do anything to protect it from scandal, even murder. When Maxim learns that Rebecca was suffering from terminal cancer at the time of her death, he concludes that she actually wanted him to kill her, and he feels absolved of guilt. Nevertheless, he ultimately loses Manderley, suggesting that he pays for his crime. Several critics have noted the paternal aspects of Maxim's relationship with his second wife: he is twice her age, he values her innocence above all else, and he treats her as a charming child. Those who find an Oedipal theme running through *Rebecca* contend that du Maurier projected her own desire for her father's attention into her portrayal of Maxim. Significantly, Maxim ultimately provides the second Mrs. de Winter with a satisfying Oedipal victory when he reveals that he loves her, not her threatening rival.

Although she is dead by the time the action in the novel takes place, **Rebecca de Winter** seems a living force to readers and to the young Mrs. de Winter, who feels she will never be able to compete with her glamorous predecessor. Extremely beautiful and sophisticated, Rebecca was adored by everyone she knew—or so Mrs. Danvers leads Mrs. de Winter to believe. The inscription Mrs. de Winter finds in a book Rebecca had given Maxim seems to characterize her and highlights the differences between the two women: ''That bold, slanting hand, stabbing the white paper . . . so certain, assured.'' By the novel's end, Rebecca is found to be the corrupt one, engaging in adultery and then taunting Maxim that she was pregnant with another man's child. That Rebecca was actually suffering from a terminal cancer that mimicked pregnancy has been interpreted to mean that perverted sexuality leads only to sterility and death. Rebecca is a demon that both Maxim and his new wife must exorcise, but the fact that Mrs. de Winter's imagination continually returns to Manderley suggests that Rebecca will never entirely disappear from their lives.

Mrs. Danvers, the housekeeper at Manderley, makes it clear to the second Mrs. de Winter that she idolized her former mistress, whom she saw as a courageous free spirit who could be beaten by no human being—only by the sea in which she drowned. The tall, gaunt, black-draped Mrs. Danvers is an ominous, macabre figure with a skeletal white face and a cold voice. Playing the role of death or an evil witch, she prevents Mrs. de Winter from assuming her full, mature role as Maxim's wife. Determined to protect Rebecca's memory by discrediting Mrs. de Winter, Mrs. Danvers convinces the unwitting young woman to dress as her predecessor for a costume ball, and she responds with malicious glee to the disastrous result. She encourages Mrs. de Winter to end her misery by jumping out of a window and, through the hypnotic power of her voice, almost succeeds. Critics have characterized Mrs. Danver's fascination with Rebecca as a projection of her own ambition and sexual drive, and possibly even of a lesbian relationship between the two. In any case, Mrs. Danvers apparently has a sexual connection with Jack Favell, Rebecca's former lover, and it is thought that she flees with him after setting fire to Manderley.

Other characters in Rebecca include **Jack Favell**, Rebecca's first cousin and lover, a wicked man who threatens Maxim with blackmail and who is said to accompany Mrs. Danvers in her escape at the end of the novel. **Frank Crawley**, Maxim's agent, tells the second Mrs. de Winter about Rebecca's death, corroborating—to the young woman's dismay—her predecessor's great beauty. **Mrs. Van Hopper**, the vulgar old American woman for whom Mrs. de Winter serves as a companion, is wealthy but a tasteless, foolish, overbearing, insensitive social climber. Du Maurier's biting portrayal of this character evidences her snobbish dislike of Americans.

Further Reading

Bakerman, Jane S. ''Daphne du Maurier.'' In *And Then There Were Nine . . . More Women of Mystery*. Bowling Green, OH: Bowling Green State University Popular Press, 1985, 12–29.

Conroy, Sarah Booth. "Daphne du Maurier's Legacy of Dreams." *Washington Post* (April 23, 1989): F1, F8.

Contemporary Literary Criticism Vols. 6, 11, 59. Detroit: Gale Research.

Davenport, Basil. "Sinister House." *Saturday Review* (September 24, 1938): 5.

Forster, Margaret. "Queen of Menacing Romance." *Sunday Times* (London) (April 23, 1989): G8.

Kelly, Richard Michael. *Daphne du Maurier.* Boston: Twayne Publishers, 1987.

Major 20th-Century Writers Vol. 1. Detroit: Gale Research.

Shallcross, Martyn. *The Private World of Daphne du Maurier.* London: Robson, 1991.

Marguerite Duras

1914–

French novelist, playwright, scriptwriter, short story writer, and essayist.

The Vice-Consul (*Le Vice-Consul;* novel, 1966)

Plot: Set in colonial India, the novel interweaves events that take place at the French Embassy in Calcutta with the story of a destitute, pregnant Asian girl, who is the subject of a biography or novel by Peter Morgan, a friend of the French ambassador. The ambassador's beautiful, charming, promiscuous wife, Anne-Marie Stretter, is the center of social life in the diplomatic community. The vice-consul of the novel's title is Jean-Marc de H., who was stationed at Lahore when, for no apparent reason, he discharged a firearm into a public park where a number of lepers and dogs were sleeping. Several deaths occurred, and the vice-consul was sent to Calcutta to await his next posting. Unable to explain his actions, he is ostracized by the French and other diplomats of Calcutta. At an embassy dance, Anne-Marie not only drinks and talks with the vice-consul but dances with him, despite the shocked disapproval of her friends. Eventually, however, she rejects the vice-consul, and he cries out in despair. The novel ends inconclusively, with life promising to continue as before in Calcutta after Jean-Marc de H. leaves for Bombay.

Characters: Duras is one of France's most acclaimed and controversial writers. Categorized with the novels of her third, highly experimental literary period (sometimes called the India Cycle), *The Vice-Consul* is an impressionistic, nearly abstract work that explores the boundaries of narration, fiction, and fantasy and delves, like much of Duras's writing, into the mysteries of memory and language. Some critics maintain that the stark prose, fragmentary structure, and rather hopeless tone of *The Vice-Consul* are qualities of the "antinovels" often associated with France's New Novelists. Juxtaposing India's most physically destitute people with the spiritually impoverished European diplomatic community, Duras trains her focus on the exclusion and exploitation of that colonial period. While some commentators fault Duras for not resolving the situations presented in *The Vice-Consul,* others find its lack of closure in keeping with its impressionistic nature.

The novel's title character is **Jean-Marc de H.**, who was the French vice-consul to Lahore (a city now located in Pakistan) when he apparently became mentally unhinged and discharged a gun into the Shalimar Gardens, killing several lepers who slept there. Sent to Calcutta to await his next assignment, the vice-consul is constantly questioned by French embassy officials. Although he is perfectly cordial and polite and does not wish to be uncooperative, the vice-consul has no explanation for his behavior. The ambassador describes the vice-consul's condition as ''nervous depression,'' and he does to seem to have suffered from a kind of hysteria. As the novel progresses, it seems that the vice-consul was unable to adapt to the overpowering misery around him, leading to the shooting incident. He therefore unsettles the rest of the diplomatic community, who ostracize and avoid him as they do India's lepers. Like all of the men in the novel, Jean-Marc de H. is attracted to Anne-Marie, but his feeling for her goes beyond passion; it is a special sympathy, a conviction that she shares his awareness of suffering but is unable to speak of it. When Anne-Marie pulls away from the inebriated vice-consul at the embassy reception, he wails, ''Don't leave me!'' Commentators believe his lament emerges from his subconscious and protests not just Anne-Marie's rejection but all the unbearable pain the vice-consul has witnessed and felt.

One of the most compelling characters in the novel is **Anne-Marie Stretter**, the wife of France's ambassador to Calcutta. Indulged by her husband and constantly surrounded by admirers, the aging but still beautiful Anne-Marie maintains an aloof, indifferent manner as she reigns over the diplomatic community's social life. Men are invariably attracted to her, and the English tourist Michael Richard is her current lover. The vice-consul too feels drawn to Anne-Marie, and he believes that she shares his heightened awareness of India's suffering and his inability to articulate this awareness. Anne-Marie surprises the shunned vice-consul by personally inviting him to the embassy reception and treating him as if she may accept him into her circle, even though the shooting incident has estranged him from the rest of the community. She even dances with Jean-Marc de H., which seems to bode well for him, but she rejects him in the end. Anne-Marie's links with the bald, filthy, crazed mendiante (beggar-woman) also figure in the novel. She tells Peter Morgan that she first noticed the woman—who was then trying to sell her baby—while traveling up the Mekong River to meet her husband. The incident seemed to affect her strongly, for her husband began to fear that she would never adapt to the misery so common in India. The two women also share the bond of female sexuality, yet while the beggar-woman is punished for her sexuality with banishment and destitution, Anne-Marie carries on her indiscretions with no apparent consequences. Duras reportedly modeled Anne-Marie after Elizabeth Striedter, the wife of a diplomat she met during her childhood in French Indochina (now Vietnam). Striedter's lover supposedly committed suicide, and Duras was fascinated that a quiet, ordinary woman could inspire such passion.

The seventeen-year-old **mendiante** or **beggar-woman,** is a character in both Duras's novel and the narrative Peter Morgan is writing. A native of southeast Asia who does not speak Hindi, the woman is homeless, starving, and filthy and repeats only one apparently meaningless word: ''Battambang.'' Morgan's biography creates a history for her—that she was born in Cambodia and banished by her mother when she became pregnant out of wedlock, that she made an improbable walking journey across Cambodia and Thailand to reach Calcutta, and that utter destitution precipitated in sanity. For Morgan, the pathetically bald woman with an infected foot exemplifies India's suffering, which he wishes to comprehend. Duras garnered praised for her portrait of this mysterious character, whose sexuality—like that of other Duras protagonists—is closely linked with violence and death and whose madness has overtaken memory and language.

Duras explores the art of writing and the boundaries of fiction through **Peter Morgan**, a friend of the French ambassador who is writing a kind of the biography of the beggar-woman he has seen wandering, filthy and crazed, through the streets of Calcutta. In imagining the woman's biography, Morgan invents facts and circumstances about which he actually knows nothing. He does so out of a strong desire to understand the misery he sees around him, so thus Morgan exemplifies the idea that storytelling is motivated by the wish to know and is ultimately narcissistic (as Michael Richard points out), because it replaces real experience with fabrication and denies the true humanity of its subject. **Michael Richard**, Anne-Marie's lover, is an English tourist living in Calcutta who was first drawn to the ambassador's wife when he heard her playing piano and recognized the passion and pain she expressed. **Charles Rosset**, a close associate of the French ambassador, has found it difficult to adjust to life in India; as the vice-consul notes, however, Rosset will probably ultimately adapt because he is not "accident-prone."

The Lover (*L'Amant*; novel, 1984)

Plot: The narrator is a sixty-year-old French writer recalling her youth in Vietnam (once called French Indochina) and her first love affair. In the face of a number of setbacks, her widowed mother struggled to relieve the family's financial decline and to help her children achieve success. The narrator's older brother was a selfish, irresponsible lout whom the mother nonetheless favored and who dominated and brutalized their gentler younger brother, whom the narrator adored. While crossing the Mekong River on a ferry, the fifteen-year-old narrator met a wealthy, twenty-seven-year-old Chinese millionaire who was fascinated by the tiny but knowing French girl. Hoping he will give her money to help her mother, the girl initiates an affair with the man, and the two become passionate lovers. Their relationship lasts for a year and a half, during which time the narrator's family treats her lover with contempt. Eventually the man's father insists that he marry a Chinese girl, and the narrator leaves Vietnam to attend the Sorbonne in Paris. Many years later she meets her first lover again in France; he reveals that he has continued to love her.

Characters: Based on Duras's own experiences as an adolescent in Vietnam, *The Lover* was awarded the 1984 Prix Goncourt and brought Duras international acclaim. Considered more accessible than her previous work, the novel explores in austere but emotionally intense, even poetic prose the connections between desire, death, and memory. Duras is often identified as one of France's New Novelists, whose work is characterized by experimentation with form, repetition, and fragmentation; in addition, her novels are strongly visual and cinematic, reflecting her interest and work in the film medium. The narration in *The Lover* shifts between past and present and from a first-person to third-person perspective, creating a haunting, erotic portrait of its Asian setting and the passionate relationship that takes place there. Duras's penchant for challenging the boundary between fact and fiction is noticeable in the novel's apparent blending of autobiography with fabrication, and her leftist orientation is expressed through the unflattering view of French colonialism she presents. Her primary subject, however, is love—its power to create happiness as well as to destroy, and its connection with death and alienation.

The narrator is a successful, sixty-year-old French writer who recounts her experiences as a fifteen-year-old schoolgirl in Vietnam, where she lived with her schoolteacher mother and two brothers. She describes her adult face as lined and ravaged by time and hard living, particularly drink, which critics claim duplicate Duras's own appearance and alcoholic history. At the time of the action in the novel, however, the narrator is a strangely beautiful, slender, dreamy young woman perched on the edge of adulthood. "At the age of fifteen," her older self remembers, "I had the face of pleasure and did not know pleasure." The virginal girl is nevertheless ready to explore her sexuality, a fact that is communicated by the clothing she is wearing when she first meets the man on the ferry: a thin silk dress, high-heeled lamé shoes, and a man's fedora that she wears because when she puts it on, "Suddenly I see myself as another . . . available to all, available to all eyes." The Chinese man is entranced by this child-woman who actually seduces *him,* astonishing him when she commands that he treat her as he has treated other women. The girl initiates the affair out of curiosity and the need for money, but as it progresses she comes to love him passionately. When she is with her family, however, she treats him as they do—as an alien worthy only of contempt for trying to buy their respect—thus illustrating the racism of the colonial environment. Duras has been praised for her haunting, erotically charged descriptions of the encounters between the girl and her lover, during which the girl discovers the depths of desire within herself and her own ruthlessness in expressing that desire. The voice of the older woman who remembers herself as this young girl maintains a tempered detachment as she turns the memories over and over in her mind, plumbing the past for its connections with the present.

As several critics have noted, **the Chinese lover** is only sketchily portrayed, suggesting that Duras means to focus not on *why* the girl loves him but on the *nature* of the passion itself. He is a twenty-seven-year-old, Paris-educated millionaire who drives around Saigon in a long, black limousine. Attracted by the girl's odd beauty and simultaneous innocence and sensuality, he loves her intensely but futilely, because she is a racially scorned outsider, and there is no possibility that they can have a future together. The man's passion puts him at the mercy of the girl's family, whose racist contempt he endures when he takes them on a social excursion. At the end of the novel, he visits the narrator in Paris many years after their affair has ended. Although he obeyed his father's command and married a Chinese girl, he now admits that he never stopped loving the narrator. Various critics have claimed that the Chinese lover actually represents either Duras's father or her brother, thus replacing the concept of miscegenation with the possibility of incest.

The narrator's widowed **mother** is living an impoverished, rootless existence with her three children, drifting between brief stays in France and her work as a schoolteacher in Vietnam. The narrator's feelings toward this important figure in her life are ambivalent; she loves her mother but resents her for exposing her children to her own despair and for blindly favoring her undeserving elder son. The mother's schemes to make money (including the purchase of some rice paddies, about which the authorities gave her the wrong information) invariably fail, yet somehow she manages to send her daughter to the prestigious French lycée in Saigon and eventually the Sorbonne in Paris. Desperate to escape poverty and for her children to succeed, the mother tries to maintain an aura of gentility in their household by retaining a houseboy to serve them their small meals and a maid to incompetently sew her daughter's dresses. The narrator's **older brother**, like Duras's own, is an irresponsible reprobate who gambles away his family's money, lies, cheats, and steals and even, as an adult, collaborates with the Germans during the occupation of France in World War II. Brutal and oppressive, he dominates his weaker **younger brother**, and the narrator holds him responsible for the other's death. The younger brother also had a counterpart in Duras's own family; gentle and much loved by his sister, he dies of illness during Japan's occupation of Indochina during World War II.

Another notable character in *The Lover* is **Hélène Lagonelle**, an apparently desirable but still-innocent school friend of the narrator about whom she has erotic fantasies, imagining a ménage à grave trois with her lover.

Further Reading

Brée, Germaine. "Contours, Fragments, Gaps: The World of Marguerite Duras." *New York Literary Forum* Vols. 8 & 9 (1981): 267–76.

Cismaru, Alfred. *Marguerite Duras* New York: Twayne, 1971.

Contemporary Literary Criticism. Vols. 3, 6, 11, 20, 34, 40. Detroit: Gale Research.

Dictionary of Literary Biography. Vol. 83. Detroit: Gale Research.

Glassman, Deborah N. *Marguerite Duras: Fascinating Vision and Narrative Cure.* London: Associated University Presses, 1991.

Gornick, Vivian. "Memory and Desire." *Village Voice* Vol., no. 31 (July 30, 1985): 47.

Hill, Leslie. "Marguerite Duras and the Limits of Fiction." *Paragraph: The Journal of the Modern Critical Theory Group* Vol. 12, no. 1 (March 1989): 1–22.

Hoffman, Eva. Review of *The Lover. New York Times* (June 10, 1985): C17.

Hofmann, Carol. *Forgetting and Marguerite Duras.* Niwot: University Press of Colorado, 1991.

Johnson, Diane. "First Love and Lasting Sorrow." *New York Times Book Review* (June 23, 1985): 1, 25.

Koch, Stephen. "Saigon, Mon Amour: Duras's Novel of Passion and Memory." *Washington Post Book World* (July 21, 1985): 3, 13.

Margaronis, Maria. "The Occupying Passion." *Nation* (New York) Vol. 243, no. 15 (November 8, 1986): 493–96.

Murphy, Carol J. *Alienation and Absence in the Novels of Marguerite Duras.* French Forum, 1982.

Schmidt, Joanne. "Marguerite Duras." *Belles Lettres: A Review of Books by Women* Vol. 4, no. 2 (winter 1989): 12–13.

Seymour, Miranda. "The Only Fedora in Saigon." *Spectator* Vol. 256, no. 8217 (January 4, 1986): 29.

Solomon, Barbara Probst. "The Politics of Passion: Marguerite Duras." In *Horse-Trading and Ecstasy.* San Francisco: North Point Press, 1989, 3–11.

Willis, Sharon. *Marguerite Duras: Writing on the Body.* Urbana: University of Illinois Press, 1987.

Umberto Eco

1932–

Italian novelist, scholar, essayist, and editor.

Foucault's Pendulum (*Il pendolo di Foucault*; novel, 1989)

Plot: The novel takes place in contemporary Milan, Italy. Belbo, Casaubon, and Diotavelli are editors employed by a vanity publisher who are often required to read crackpot manuscripts on occult topics. They receive a visit from a strange man named Colonel Ardenti, who claims to have discovered a coded message about a plan formulated by the Knights Templar—a medieval secret society—identifying a source of energy that would give whoever tapped into it the power to rule the world. The three bored editors decide to concoct a plan of their own, which they begin to generate on their computer. Gradually gaining steam and interest, they incorporate a plethora of hermetic information and weave together many of history's greatest mysteries, movements, and personages. The Plan is based on the assumption that the Templars have survived into the twentieth century and are still in search of the missing link that will allow them to attain world dominance. Although the editors' project begins as a joke, it gathers seriousness as they find themselves drawn into its web and as they gradually learn that certain individuals are intensely interested in their conjectures and connections. The story culminates in a scene of human sacrifice, during which Belbo is killed by occultists, and ends with Diotavelli dead of cancer and Casaubon waiting to be assassinated.

Characters: Like Eco's earlier novel, *The Name of the Rose, Foucault's Pendulum* combines popular appeal with erudition, and it was an instant best-seller on its publication. Multilayered and postmodernist in its structural innovation and blending of genres, the novel is at once satire, fantasy, history of Western mysticism, and detective story. It is heavily weighted with scholarly material, which, according to some reviewers, makes it boring and inaccessible; others find *Foucault's Pendulum* entertaining despite its difficulty. Most of the historical and religious mysteries of the last 2,000 years are explored, from Stonehenge to the Freemasons to Adolph Hitler to contemporary Brazilian voodoo rituals. The novel lends itself to a variety of interpretations: it may be seen as an elaborate, even laborious joke; a metaphor for the arrogance of Western thought and science; or a cautionary tale about the dangers of poor logic and faulty reasoning. It also contains elements of realism with its account of Italy during World War II and the student revolution of the 1960s, and comedy in its portrayal of the Milan publishing scene.

Although several critics pointed out that the large amount of scholarly material in *Foucault's Pendulum* leaves little room for character development, the three editors who mastermind ''the Plan'' on their computer provide the story with some human interest. The narrator is **Casaubon**, an occult expert (particularly on the Templar movement) who provides much of the voluminous background information on mysticism throughout history. His name is one of the novel's many allusions: in George Eliot's 1872 novel, *Middlemarch,* Casaubon is a stuffy, pedantic scholar who is writing a never-finished key to the mythologies of the world. Although Casaubon claims that he does not tend to be carried away by passion, he *is* looking for answers of some kind, and he finds himself, along with his friends, half-believing the elaborate joke they have concocted as the pieces fall into place one after another. After the Plan has attracted the murderous attention of some occult fanatics, however, Casaubon reflects (while waiting calmly for almost certain death) that there is really nothing to understand—that it is during such acts as eating a peach or playing a trumpet that we are at one with ''the Kingdom,'' and that ''the rest is cleverness.''

Editor **Jacopo Belbo** (whose name alludes to Bilbo, the hero of J. R. R. Tolkien's classic fantasy trilogy *The Lord of the Rings;* 1954–56), has been identified as an autobiographical figure. Like Eco, he was born in 1932 in Italy's northern Piedmont region, making him too young to have participated in World War II and too old to have joined the student movement of the 1960s. And Belbo is an editor who would really like to write, which at least partly explains his enthusiasm for constructing the plan—an activity that some critics have viewed as a metaphor for the writing of a novel. Casaubon discovers Belbo's autobiographical writings on a computer disk, thus providing the reader with realistic glimpses into life in Italy during World War II, the student riots of the early 1970s, and contemporary Italian politics. Belbo also resembles his creator—a noted scholar of semiotics (the study of signs and symbols and how they are interpreted)—in his obsession with texts; at one point, he performs a kind of ''deconstruction'' of Shakespeare's *Hamlet* as he imagines himself advising the playwright to change the drama in various ways. In a vivid scene of occultist fervor, Belbo is hanged from the pendulum that is supposed to mark the earth's navel, but his death is strangely dignified because he does not divulge the secret for which his captors are looking.

Belbo's assistant, **Diotavelli,** is the least developed of the three editor characters. His irrational conviction that he is Jewish and his death from cancer, which he believes was somehow generated by the intellectual tampering in which he and his friends had been indulging, help to illustrate the theme that faulty reasoning may have dire consequences.

Casaubon's girlfriend, **Lia**, who helps him with his research, is the novel's anchor of sanity and earthbound wisdom. First, she gives birth to a baby during the course of the novel, reminding Casaubon of the more primal forces of life. Second, it is Lia who finally interprets the Templar message as a medieval laundry list rather than a key to universal power. She points out that the Western mind (and particularly the Western *male* mind) cannot seem to tolerate the idea that the world's mysteries are ultimately unknowable. Other characters in the novel include the flagrantly unfaithful, flighty, pinball-playing **Lorenza**, Belbo's girlfriend; **Colonel Ardenti**, who has artificially black hair and a dramatic mustache and who introduces the mysterious manuscript that initially inspires the three editors; and **Signore Garamond** (named for a famous typeface design), the semiliterate owner of the vanity press (which requires authors to finance the publication of their own works) that employs the three editors and allows Eco to create a comic portrait of an unscrupulous publishing operation.

Further Reading

Adams, Robert. "Juggler." *New York Review of Books* Vol. 36, no. 17 (November 9, 1989): 3–4.

Bayley, John. "Let the Cork Out." *London Review of Books* Vol. 11, no. 20 (October 26, 1989): 15.

Bestsellers. Vol. 90, no. 1. Detroit: Gale Research, 1990.

Contemporary Literary Criticism. Vols. 28, 60. Detroit: Gale Research.

Eder, Richard. "Umberto's Truffle-Hunt." *Los Angeles Times Book Review* (November 5, 1989): 3, 15.

"Lesson Zero." *VLS* No. 80 (November 1989): 29–30.

Mitgang, Herbert. "Inside Jokes from the Knights Templar to Snoopy." *New York Times* (October 11, 1989): C21.

Rushdie, Salman. "Cabbalistic Babble and Gobbledygook." *Observer* (October 15, 1989): 49.

Stille, Alexander. "The Novel as Status Symbol." *Atlantic Monthly* Vol. 264, no. 5 (November 1989): 125–29.

Updike, John. "In Borges's Wake." *New Yorker* Vol. 65, no. 51 (February 5, 1990): 116–20.

Stanley Elkin

1930–

American novelist, short story writer, scriptwriter, and editor.

George Mills (novel, 1982)

Plot: The novel takes place over 1,000 years and focuses on the activities of four characters named George Mills. The first is Greatest Grandfather Mills, a stable boy who accompanies Guillalume, the fourth son of a nobleman, to the Crusades. Guillalume has no intention of fighting, however, hoping instead that all his brothers will be killed in the Crusades so that he will inherit the family fortune. Thus he leads Greatest Grandfather Mills off track, and the two are captured and forced to work in a Polish salt mine. They finally escape, only to be confronted by a hoard of barbarians. Greatest Grandfather saves their lives by improvising a sermon that extols pacifism and disarms their aggressors. When they finally reach home, however, he must resume his stable duties, while Guillalume learns that his brothers have indeed died and he is now wealthy. Greatest Grandfather pities the future generations of Millses, who are doomed to inherit from him the family curse of mediocrity.

Another significant portion of the novel is devoted to the forty-third George Mills, a nineteenth-century Londoner who hopes to improve his position in the world. He takes a letter of reference to King George IV, who mistakenly believes the writer is one of his enemies and thus sends Mills on a doomed mission to the Turkish sultan. There Mills encounters a band of tough soldiers called Janissaries whose discipline he meekly accepts, unintentionally earning legendary status among them. Sent on another suicide mission, George and his friend Bufuesque manage another unintentionally ingenious escape and land in the sultan's harem. For a while Mills successfully pretends to be a eunuch, but he finally flees to the British embassy and from there goes to America.

The remainder of the book concerns the contemporary George Mills, a St. Louis furniture mover. (It also includes a long flashback chronicling the life of his father, the previous George Mills). Mills accompanies a dying woman named Judith Glazer to Mexico, where she is seeking a cure for her cancer and where she endangers the life of her long-suffering companion through her attempts to achieve martyrdom. Mills also develops a kind of relationship with Cornell Messenger, a college professor with troubled children and a dependence on marijuana who is constantly gossiping about his academic colleagues. Mills's attempts to parlay his service to Judith into some material advantage fails, thus dooming him to the second-rate status he has never been able to rise above. The novel's "Cassadega" section relates the struggles of the father of the contemporary George Mills, who moved his family from Milwaukee to a spiritualist community in Florida in order to evade the Mills curse. By the end of the novel, the contemporary George Mills has decided that he is "saved" because he knows that nothing more will ever happen to him; in a revelatory sermon to the congregation of a small church, he affirms his connection with others who suffer from Mills-like mediocrity. The Mills curse will end with him because he will not pass on his genes.

Elkin received the National Book Critics Circle Award for *George Mills,* which is considered the most ambitious work by this author who is critically acclaimed but not known to a wide readership. Characterized by the exuberant prose and inventive imagery for which Elkin is noted, the novel comprises seven narrative sections, focusing on four characters who share the same name and the same genetic heritage as "God's blue collar worker." *George Mills* spans 1,000 years, combining comedy and tragedy in its chronicle of how the title characters attempt to beat the mediocrity that is their family curse. Several critics believe Elkin occupies a literary position somewhere between such realist novelists as Saul Bellow and William Faulkner and such experimentalists as Thomas Pynchon and William Gass, and they laud Elkin for his fresh, energetic approach to language and, in *George Mills,* for his eloquent, darkly humorous ruminations on the theme of limitations and lost opportunities.

Characters: It is the eleventh-century **Greatest Grandfather Mills,** who first receives the family curse of perpetual second-rate status. He articulates the metaphor of the "tapestry condition" that describes how the Millses and others like them are viewed by their social superiors: as fixed figures in a natural hierarchy that is as permanently woven as a medieval tapestry. Yet during his journey with Guillalume, Greatest Grandfather does briefly rise above his customary lowliness, experiencing for a short time how it feels to manipulate power and initiate action rather than to be swept along in their wake. His desperately improvised, cliche-loaded sermon to the barbarians ("God hates hitters. . . . He told me to tell you you musn't hit"), one of many such entertaining discourses delivered by Elkins's characters, saves him and his employer from death. Yet on their return, Greatest Grandfather again finds himself relegated to the stables. His desire to terminate the Mills curse by not leaving any heirs is thwarted by the fact that he has impregnated a young wench before leaving for the Crusades. Resentful of his social immobility but lacking the wherewithal to alter his circumstances, Greatest Grandfather grieves for the future Millses who will inherit his bleak legacy.

Forty-three generations later, **the nineteenth-century George Mills** undergoes a similar journey and brush with greatness, only to end up as second-rate as his disappointed forebear. This George Mills also adapts to the unusual circumstances in which he finds himself, accepting the disciplinary rigor of the Janissary lifestyle with his genetically programmed, "blue-collar habit of obedience" and thus accidentally gaining legendary status among them. His spectacular escape from the Janissaries is also due more to desperation than ingenuity or courage. When he lands in a Turkish harem, Mills again adapts, this time by reining in his natural impulses in order to appear to be a eunuch. Then Mills has the good (or just lucky) sense to study court protocol, which facilitates his escape to the British Embassy. In the end, however, the nineteenth-century George Mills receives for his efforts only disillusionment and no higher a position in the social hierarchy—even after his removal to America—than that of any other George Mills.

The long portion of the novel recounting the experiences of the **contemporary George Mills** also includes a section, presented as a kind of flashback, about his father's efforts to evade the Mills curse. The modern-day George Mills is a fifty-one-year-old St. Louis resident whose job is moving furniture from the dwellings of evicted tenants. Like his forebears, this Mills undergoes an odyssey that proves he is capable of limited heroic action. He is hired to accompany the dying heiress Judith Glazer to Mexico, where she will receive a last-ditch laetrile treatment for her cancer. Mills responds to his employer's needs with selfless patience, even though—in a contemporary demonstration of the "tapestry condition"—she is oblivious to his troubles or fears. On his return, however, Mills feels himself sliding back into mediocrity, a circumstance he combats by attempting to parlay his connection with Judith into some kind of material reward from her heirs. This attempt fails, of course. The flashback to Mills's childhood, entitled the "Cassadega" section after the Florida town in which his family lived, features a reconstruction of events that critics consider Faulknerian in technique and effect. Through his conversations with a spiritualist, Reverend Wickland, the young Mills learns that his father (**the previous George Mills**) tried to terminate the family curse by hiding in a Milwaukee basement, vowing not to procreate. But this George Mills also became a "myth victim," eventually marrying and fathering a son. That son—the contemporary George Mills—also obtains from the spiritualist the information that his mother gave birth to a girl, his half-sister. The existence of this sister and the thought that she is living somewhere happily gives hope to Mills that escape from the Mills curse is possible. But after his odyssey with Judith Glazer ends, Mills decides to accept his second-rate status and to view himself as "saved," in that "he is the man to whom everything has happened that is going to happen." At least the Mills curse—which he now realizes is not limited to his family but affects others as well—will end with him. Some critics interpret Mills's essentially passive resolution as a suggestion that human beings need not be entirely victimized by destiny or fate but may, at least to some extent, contribute to the shape their own lives take. At the end of his sermon to Reverend Coule's congregation, Mills affirms his brotherhood with his audience and proclaims that the point of existence is "to live long enough to find something out or to do something well."

Many commentators note similarities between the character of **Cornell Messenger** and Elkin: both are St. Louis college professors and novelists whose books are not widely read, both have survived heart attacks, and both are the sons of dynamic salesman from whom they inherit the obsessive need for storytelling, verbalization, and confession. Pot-smoking and sentimental (he weeps over the annual Jerry Lewis Telethon for Muscular Dystrophy), Messenger meets Mills at the deathbed of Mills's father-in-law; Messenger is there because he has taken over Judith Glazer's Meals-on-Wheels route. The two strike up a relationship that consists primarily of Messenger's gossiping about his academic cronies while offering Mills no outlet to tell his own pathetic story. This provides yet another example of the "tapestry condition": those to whom things happen, whose lives are dynamic, seem unaware of the bleak, static existences around them. It is easy for Messenger to repeat the phrase "the horror, the horror" (the last utterance of Kurtz in Joseph Conrad's 1902 novella, *Heart of Darkness*) or to conclude that "things happen, that's all," because for him the tenor of life changes. At the end of the novel, he is revitalized and lifted from his former despair by a number of happy circumstances involving his troubled friends and family members, whereas Mills has had to accept the unvarying mediocrity of his life.

Reviewing her life, **Judith Glazer** says, "No one loved me enough, and I never had all the shrimp I could eat." The mingled poignancy and petulance of this statement reflects the contradictions of this complex figure, who is one of the most successful and compelling characters in the novel. Judith has an eleven-year history of mental illness, a loss of precious time she resents even more strongly because she is now dying of pancreatic cancer. In many ways, Judith is unappealing and even repellent: she is selfishly obsessed with her own problems and indignant that other people enjoy good health, and she frequently lashes out at those closest to her. With characteristic vindictiveness, she attempts to torment her wealthy father by giving his phone number to her Meals-on-Wheels clients. Yet Judith also displays courage and even heroism when, in order to buy some time in which her daughter, **Mary**, may come to accept her death, she breaks her vow not to seek a quack cure for her cancer. At the same time, however, Judith rather selfishly pursues martyrdom by deliberately making herself available to robbery and bodily harm—actions that also endanger her companion, George Mills. The qualities of dignity and pettiness, life-affirmation and self-destructiveness co-exist in Judith, making her one of the novel's nobility—those whose lives are dynamic rather than (like all the George Millses of the last 1,000 years) static.

The curse of the Mills family is first articulated in the fourteenth century by **Guillalume**, the fourth son of a baron, who employs Greatest Grandfather Mills on a trek to join the Crusades. Guillalume's true goal, of course, is neither to prove his own mettle or to recover the Holy Grail but to wrest the family fortune from his older brothers by outliving them, at which quest he succeeds. Guillalume tells Greatest Grandfather that a natural hierarchy predetermines the roles of every human being, noble or lowly, and that "the brick walls of some secret, sovereign architecture" keep both he and Greatest Grandfather in their respective places.

Other characters in George Mills include **Bufuesque**, the nineteenth-century George Mills's friend and companion in his exploits, who suppresses his natural instincts in order to stay within the pleasurable confines of the **Sultan's** harem. The **Reverend Wickland** of Cassadega, Florida, is the spiritualist who helps the contemporary George Mills reconstruct the story of his family's past. Like Cornell Messenger, Wickland holds that destiny rather than choice determines the course of human lives; he says, "Our lives happen to us. We don't make them up." **Reverend Coule** is a former televangelist whose interest in Mills's state of "grace"—which Mills's wife, Louise, has described to him—leads him to invite Mills to speak to his congregation. **Mr. Mead**, Louise's father, provides a link between Messenger and Mills; his dignified death scene foreshadows Judith's passing.

Further Reading

Bailey, Peter J. *Reading Stanley Elkin.* Urbana: University of Illinois Press, 1985.

Bargen, Doris G. *The Fiction of Stanley Elkin.* Lang, 1979.

Charney, Maurice. "Stanley Elkin and Jewish Black Humor." In *Jewish Wry: Essays on Jewish Humor.* Edited by Sarah Blacher Cohen. Bloomington: Indiana University Press, 1987.

Conarroe, Joel. "Stanley Elkin's St. Louis Everyman." *Book World—The Washington Post* (October 10, 1982): 1, 11.

Contemporary Literary Criticism. Vols. 4, 6, 9, 14, 27, 51. Detroit: Gale Research.

Delta No. 20 (February 1985). Special Elkin issue.

Dictionary of Literary Biography. Vols. 2, 28, and 1980 Yearbook. Detroit: Gale Research.

Dougherty, David C. "A Conversation with Stanley Elkin." *Literary Review* Vol. 34, no. 2 (winter 1991): 175–95.

————. *Stanley Elkin.* Boston: Twayne, 1990.

LeClair, Thomas. "The Obsessional Fiction of Stanley Elkin." *Contemporary Literature* Vol. 16, no. 2 (spring 1975): 146–62.

————. Review of *George Mills. New Republic* Vol. 187, no. 3545 (December 27, 1982): 37–38.

Taliaferro, Frances. "Lyrics of the Lunchpail." *Harper's* Vol. 265, no. 1590 (November 1982): 74–75.

Bret Easton Ellis

1964–

American novelist.

Less than Zero (novel, 1985)

Plot: The novel is narrated by Clay, an eighteen-year-old freshman at a New Hampshire college who returns to his Los Angeles home for a four-week Christmas holiday. Reunited with his old high school friends—who, like him, are the children of wealthy parents, many involved in the Hollywood film business—Clay passes his days in bored inactivity and his nights in drug- and alcohol-saturated visits to restaurants and nightclubs. He also occasionally dines with one or the other of his separated parents and talks to his ineffectual psychiatrist. Clay learns that his friend Julian has become a male prostitute in order to support a heroin addiction. The sordid situations Clay finds himself in include visiting one of Julian's clients with Julian, gawking with others at the corpse of a young man who has apparently died of a drug overdose, and witnessing the gang rape of a drugged twelve-year-old girl. Clay's already faltering relationship with his girlfriend, Blair, comes to an end just before he returns to New Hampshire.

Characters: *Less than Zero* received a great deal of attention on its publication not only because of the youth of its author, who was a twenty-one-year-old Bennington College undergraduate at the time, but because of the disturbing portrait it presents of the wealthy, bored Los Angeles teenagers who populate its few pages. Writing in an economic, deadpan style, Ellis creates a present-tense, highly visual narrative through which occasional reminiscences of the past are woven. Although most critics were impressed by Ellis's convincing and consistently maintained tone and his gift for relaying realistic details and dialogue, some maintained that the carefully constructed atmosphere of inertia, which so closely mirrors the characters' attitudes, ultimately bores the reader as well. In chronicling his characters' cycle of drinking, drug-taking, shopping, and keeping their bodies in shape and tanned, Ellis peppers his novel liberally with a wide variety of trade names, including those of restaurants (such as Chasen's and Spago), nightclubs (The Edge and The Roxy), recreational drugs (cocaine and Quaaludes), and rock performers and groups (Elvis Costello and X). *Less than Zero* has been termed one of the first artistic documents of the "video generation"—those whose teenaged years are dominated by the music videos played twenty-four hours a day on the MTV cable television channel. The novel's episodic structure mimics the brevity and vivid imagery of music videos, portraying in lurid (or even sensational) detail the characters' shallowness, moral bankruptcy, and tendency toward violence.

The disturbing account of alienation and spiritual emptiness in *Less than Zero* is delivered in the flat, unemotional voice of **Clay**, an eighteen-year-old who has returned to his Los Angeles home after four months at an eastern college. Describing his own, his family's, and his friends' activities during his four-week Christmas holiday, Clay's tone is almost uniformly blase and passive. He smokes cigarette after cigarette, drinks, takes drugs, has sex, argues with his sisters, lunches with his oblivious parents, and reveals almost nothing of his feelings about any of it. Some critics found him a repellent character in his extreme lack of energy and self-absorption; he relates a number of particularly appalling things without comment or judgment. Whatever faint degree of superiority Clay displays over those around him is based on such flimsy factors as his declining to use heroin, walking out of a "snuff" movie (in which, supposedly, someone is actually murdered at the end), and turning down a friend's invitation to rape a drugged twelve-year-old girl. Clay does realize that his psychiatrist is incompetent and eventually disengages him. At the end of the novel, Clay delivers a commentary that, unlike the rest of the narration, does seem to take a moral stand on the world it describes. In a tone of condemnation, Clay characterizes the parents of these Los Angeles youths as "so hungry and unfulfilled they ate their own children" and claims that the "violent and malicious" images he has just described have stayed with him for a long time. Although many critics have assumed that Clay is an autobiographical creation, Ellis—despite his admission that the novel had its genesis in a diary he kept during his high school years—claims that Clay does not represent his creator. Most commentators have also scoffed at attempts to compare the jaded, emotionless Clay with Holden Caulfield, the alienated but innately passionate and compassionate protagonist of J. D. Salinger's 1951 novel, *The Catcher in the Rye*.

None of the secondary characters in *Less than Zero* are portrayed in much detail; rather, they form a kind of composite portrait of young people who have received very early in their lives a surfeit of material advantages and sensory stimuli (e.g., drugs and sex) but, apparently, very little love and few values. Clay's best friend, **Julian,** represents an extreme consequence of this skewed existence: addicted to heroin, he works as a male prostitute (for the repellent pimp **Finn**) in order to support his habit. Clay witnesses an encounter between Julian and a client and even plays a role in the sex act himself by serving as a paid observer. Later, Clay is present when Finn forces a heroin injection on Julian, who has just expressed a desire to quit the business. Clay's girlfriend, **Blair**, the daughter of a famous and wealthy movie producer, picks him up at the airport at the beginning of the novel and accompanies him to various restaurants and nightclubs as the story progresses. Near the end of the novel, complaining that Clay never called her during his four months at college, (Blair gets him to admit that he never loved her, though she claims that she did once feel love (or something like it) for him. Clay's exchanges with Blair reveal the same lack of commitment, emotion, and ability to communicate that also characterize Clay's other friends. **Trent**, with whom

Clay goes to various parties and movies, is a narcissistic male model who reveals to Clay that his flawless tan is chemical and urges that Clay not divulge the information to anyone.

Other characters in *Less than Zero* include several with typically abbreviated and often androgynous names, such as **Kim**, **Rip**, and **Spin** (who offers Clay a chance to rape a pretty, tied-up twelve-year-old girl who has been plied with heroin). **Clay's psychiatrist**, a scruffy-looking but actually successful, wealthy doctor whose exchanges with Clay tend to center on his own concerns, is typical of other adults in the novel in that he fails those who depend on him for guidance.

Further Reading

Contemporary Authors. Vol. 123. Detroit: Gale Research.

Contemporary Literary Criticism. Vol. 39. Detroit: Gale Research.

Fremont-Smith, Eliot. "The Right Snuff." *VLS* Vol. 35 (May 1985): 20–1.

Jenkins, Alan. "Back Home with the Tan Blonde Boys." *Times Literary Supplement* No. 4326 (February 28, 1986): 216.

Milliken, James M., Jr. Review of *Less than Zero*. *BestSellers* Vol. 45, no. 5 (August 1985): 166.

Pinckney, Darryl. "The New Romantics." *New York Review of Books* Vol. 33, no. 9 (May 29, 1986): 30–4.

Rechy, John. Review of *Less than Zero*. *Los Angeles Times Book Review* (May 26, 1985): 1, 11.

Review of *Less than Zero*. *New Republic* Vol. 192, no. 23 (June 10, 1985): 42.

Salter, Mary Jo. Review of *Less than Zero*. *New York Times Book Review* (June 16, 1985): 24.

Shusaku Endo

1923–

Japanese novelist, dramatist, short story writer, essayist, and biographer.

Silence (*Chinmoku;* novel, 1966)

Plot: The novel begins with a prologue describing the activities of Christian missionaries in seventeenth-century Japan and the case of Christavao Ferreiro, a Portuguese priest who promoted Catholicism in Japan for thirty years, then capitulated to official persecution and renounced his faith. Finding the report of this betrayal difficult to believe, three of Ferreiro's former students travel to Japan to investigate. When they arrive in the country, they learn more about the persecution of Catholics there. They hire a disreputable guide named Kichijiro to take them inland; one of the seminarians, Sebastian Rodrigues, immediately distrusts this man, who he later learns is a former Christian. When one of the young Portuguese priests falls ill, Rodrigues and Francisco Garrpe continue their journey without him.

At this point, the narration shifts to the form of letters written by Rodrigues to his superiors in Portugal. The priest is initially firm and confident in his faith and in his belief that he will have the strength, unlike his teacher, to become a martyr. Yet as he witnesses the suffering of those who refuse to trample on the fumie—the crude wooden representation of Christ's face that captured Christians must either tread upon or face torture and death—his confidence wavers and his compassion increases. Eventually Rodrigues is captured, while Garrpe drowns while attempting to reach a boat full of Catholics about to be put to death. Rodrigues then encounters Ferreiro, who tells him that it is not possible to spread the message of Christianity in Japan, which invariably twists that message into something unrecognizable to Westerners. Finally Rodrigues is brought before the fumie and must decide whether to renounce his faith or become a martyr. But the face of Christ urges him to trample the fumie, and thus perform an act of sacrificial love that will save others from death. He tramps across the image, outwardly giving up his religion but inwardly strengthening his faith. As the novel ends, Rodrigues absolves the formerly reviled Kichijiro, recognizing that his apostasy too was an act of charity to benefit others.

Characters: Endo is one of Japan's most highly respected contemporary authors and among those best known to Western readers. The first of his works to be translated into English, *The Silence* is widely regarded as his best novel. Its exploration of Catholicism in Japan reflects Endo's own background: converted as a child to Catholicism, Endo has since struggled to reconcile his faith with his cultural identity, a process he has compared with transforming an ill-fitting Western suit into more comfortable Japanese garb. *The Silence* depicts the clash between Christianity and the Japanese temperament, a rift that can only be bridged, Endo suggests, by changing the stern, paternal image of the Western God into an all-forgiving, maternal version that conforms more closely to the Buddhist concept of universal compassion. Endo's novel is often compared to Graham Greene's *The Power and the Glory*, which treats similar themes and features several characters like the protagonists of *The Silence*. The French Catholic novelists Francois Mauriac and Georges Bernanos, whose work Endo studied while attending graduate school in France, are also said to have influenced his work.

The novel chronicles the spiritual odyssey of **Sebastian Rodrigues**, a Portuguese priest who travels to Japan to learn why his former teacher has bowed to official repression and renounced his faith. When he arrives in Japan, Rodrigues is puffed up with certainty of his own belief and confident that a glorious martyrdom awaits him. He is arrogant about his own spiritual strength and scornful of others' weakness, as evidenced by his contempt for the cowardly Kichijiro. Endo uses the device of first-person narration in the form of Rodrigues's letters to convey the priest's arrogance, and the later shift to an omniscient narrator signals his gradual humbling. The image of God Rodrigues carries with him is initially triumphant, all powerful, and judgmental. By the novel's end, this image has been replaced by that of the earthy face represented on the fumie—a weak, powerless, but compassionate God who joins with and sustains his followers in their suffering. Rodrigues's transformation from aggressive self-assurance to the self-abnegation represents a more profound faith and parallels his physical journey from the mountains to the prison cell in which he is eventually incarcerated. His exalted sense of mission becomes a compassionate awareness of human weakness; his betrayal of belief is really a deepening of belief. As he witnesses the suffering and deaths of Catholic martyrs and sees that he can spare some of their lives by renouncing his faith, Rodrigues begins to identify with the sufferers and to realize the bond of human weakness he shares with them. This bond is especially manifest in the relationship between Rodrigues and Kichijiro, whom he had previously reviled but whom he now sees that he resembles. The act of trampling the fumie causes Rodrigues much pain and anguish, but he recognizes that it is an act of love; his faith not only remains in his heart but has been increased. The novel's conclusion reveals that Rodrigues was ultimately placed in a home for reformed Catholics and given a Japanese name and even a Japanese wife; but while his public persecution thus continues, his private victory remains intact.

123

Christavao Ferreiro is a renowned theologian and missionary priest who spent thirty years attempting to establish the Catholic church in Japan before finally renouncing (outwardly, though apparently not inwardly) his faith. Brought together by the authorities after Rodrigues's arrest, Ferreiro and his former student debate the viability of Christianity in Japan. Ferreiro holds that because Japan is a "mud swamp" that destroys, absorbs, or changes everything it confronts, the Church has no future here. Describing the failure of Catholicism to take root in Japan, he says, "The seedlings which we brought to this country eventually began to rot." Ferreiro also compares Japanese Christianity to a butterfly caught in a spider's web: the body and wings have been eaten away, and only the skeleton remains. For Rodrigues the opposite has occurred—the exterior framework of faith has disappeared but its substance remains.

Cowardly, groveling **Kichijiro** is the guide Rodrigues and his two colleagues hire after they arrive in Japan. A former Christian who assumedly trampled the fumie to avoid torture and death, he eventually betrays them to the authorities. Initially Rodrigues finds Kichijiro repulsive and he scorns his weakness, but by the end of the novel the priest understands the guide's motivation. One the surface, Kichijiro appears to be a Judas figure, but his compassion for the suffering Catholic martyrs causes him to betray the priests. Kichijiro helps to illustrate the theme of the need for a maternal, all-forgiving, and thus more Japanese image of God.

Francisco Garrpe, Rodrigues's fellow seminarian, accompanies him into the interior of Japan after the third priest in their party becomes ill. Garrpe drowns trying to reach a boat of Catholics about to be thrown overboard. Rodrigues is deeply affected by the martyrdom of **Yuki**, a young woman who places her head on the fumie in order to prevent her lover (a non-Catholic) from stepping on it; he refuses to trample her, so both are executed. **Inoue** is the cool, detached Japanese magistrate before whom Rodrigues appears. Like Ferreiro (and like many Japanese intellectuals), Inoue holds that Christianity is fundamentally unsuited to Japan.

Further Reading

Contemporary Literary Criticism. Vols. 7, 14, 19, 54. Detroit: Gale Research.

Gallagher, Michael. "Exploring a Dark and Cruel Period: A Japanese-Catholic Novel." *Commonweal* (November 4, 1966): 136–38.

Gessel, Van C. "Salvation of the Weak: Endo." In *The Sting of Life: Four Contemporary Japanese Novelists.* New York: Columbia University Press, 1989.

———. "Voices in the Wilderness: Japanese Christian Authors." *Monumenta Nipponica* Vol. 37, no. 4 (winter 1982): 437–57.

Higgins, Jean. "The Inner Agony of Endo Shusaku." *Cross Currents* Vol. 34, no. 4 (winter 1984–85): 414–26.

Mathy, Francis. "Shusaku Endo: Japanese Catholic Novelist." *America* Vol. 167, no. 3 (August 1, 1992): 66–71.

Updike, John. "From Fumie to Sony." *New Yorker* Vol. 55, no. 48 (January 14, 1980): 94–102.

Wills, Garry. "Embers of Guilt." *New York Review of Books* Vol. 28, no. 2 (February 19, 1981): 21–22.

Louise Erdrich
1954–

American novelist, poet, and short story writer.

Love Medicine (novel, 1984)

Plot: The fourteen-chapter novel features the stories of various narrators living on and around the Chippewa reservation over three generations in North Dakota. Set in 1981, the first chapter, "The World's Greatest Fisherman," establishes the identities of the novel's main characters. It begins with the Chippewa June Kashpaw, an aging, attractive woman who has died in a snowstorm after picking up a white man in a Williston, North Dakota bus station. The narrative then shifts to Albertine Johnson, June's niece. A Chippewa of mixed race, Albertine, a nursing student, who recounts June's life and her own return to the reservation after her aunt's death, when she interacts with her mother Zelda, aunt Aurelia, grandparents Marie and Nector Kashpaw, great-uncle Eli Kashpaw, and other relatives. Albertine's grandmother narrates the next chapter and recalls her unhappy stay in a nearby convent when she was fourteen years old. Then Nector tells how he first met Marie as she was fleeing from the convent. Their ambiguous sexual encounter led eventually to their marrying, even though he was in love with another girl, Lulu Lamartine. Nestor and Marie had several children and also took in many parentless children, including June, Marie's sister's orphaned daughter. June later lived with her uncle Eli in the woods.

"Lulu's Boys," set in 1957, focuses on warmhearted and accommodating Lulu Lamartine, whose eight adoring sons all have different fathers. "The Plunge of the Brave" also takes place in 1957 and tells of Nector Kashpaw's affair with Lulu after seventeen years of marriage to Marie. Those intervening years saw him work hard, drink too much, and—with Marie's help—become tribal chairman. Marie finds out about Nector's affair, but the couple stay together. Other chapters feature the younger characters, including Albertine and three of Lulu's sons, Henry Lamartine, Jr., Gerry Kashpaw, and June's husband, Gordie Kashpaw. The central figure in "Love Medicine" is Lipsha Morrissey, who was raised by Marie after his mother abandons him. Believing that he possesses healing powers, Lipsha concocts a potion that Marie will use to win Nestor's heart back from Lulu. Though the "love medicine" should ideally be made from the hearts of geese, which are monogamous, Lipsha must settle for supermarket turkey hearts. Nestor chokes on the resulting concoction and dies. Later Marie claims that Lipsha's potion has caused her husband's spirit to return, but Lipsha assures her that Nestor's love has brought him back, not the love medicine. At the end of the novel, Lipsha learns that June was his biological mother. He travels to Minneapolis to confront his father, Indian rights activist and escaped convict Gerry Kashpaw. Then in a poker game, he wins the sports car that June's other son, King, bought with the money she had left him.

Characters: Erdrich is an acclaimed contemporary author whose fiction is rooted in the harsh landscape and traditions of her cultural identity. The daughter of a German American father and a Chippewa mother, Erdrich grew up on the Turtle Mountain reservation in North Dakota. *Love Medicine* won the National Book Critics Circle Award and contains lyrical prose and beaten yet memorable characters that portray the mingled beauty and brutality of America's indigenous peoples. Erdrich's style is often likened to that of William Faulkner due to its regional focus, fragmentary structure, and multiple narrative viewpoints; indeed, some critics found the novel's shifts in perspective and time confusing. Most, however, lauded Erdrich for her vivid evocation of the native milieu and the confused, courageous, lovesick people who inhabit it.

The most prominent among the first generation characters in the novel are **Nector Kashpaw** and his wife. Several critics contend that *Love Medicine* portrays the breakdown of traditional structure in Native American life. For her part, critic Louise Flavin believes that the indecisive Nector exemplifies "the ineffectuality of male leadership on the reservation." Nector's mother, Rushes Bear, sent him to boarding school where he learned to read and write English, which propelled him at an early age away from traditional ways and toward the white society around him. Nector's loyalties were further divided when he felt obliged to marry Marie, even though he loved Lulu. Marie enables him to rise to tribal chairman, which she nominated him for and kept him sober enough to get it and keep it. Nector stays with and apparently, loves Marie, but he never loses his feelings for Lulu and has an affair with her even after he is at least partially senile. Marie claims that Nector's spirit visits her after his death, and Lipsha tells her that it was not the turkey-heart love medicine that brought him back but the fact that "he loved you over time and distance, but he went off so quick he never got a chance to tell you how he loves you, how he doesn't blame you, how he understands."

Though Nector may embody the negative side of the contemporary native personality, his stalwart wife, **Marie Lazarre Kashpaw**, manifests its positive persona. Born to slatternly, disreputable parents, fourteen-year-old Marie believed the convent would save her from her home life, but once there she found herself at the mercies of Sister Leopolda, who regarded the girl as filled with evil impulses. After Marie escapes from the convent, she discovers that she pities Sister Leopolda, expressing the compassion that marks the rest of her life. Marie's strange sexual encounter with Nector seems to be a rape, but it is unclear who is raping whom; in any case, Nector feels obligated to marry her. Due mostly to Marie's generosity, the couple raises not only their own offspring but many abandoned or otherwise parentless children. (Reviewers comment that informal adoption is common among Native American families and reflects a strong concern for the good of the community as a whole.) Marie's many small and large acts of caring for others and her ability to recover from adversity make her a heroic figure, and critic Louise Flavin calls her "the priestess of love—the saint in the story."

Another heroic figure in *Love Medicine* is **Lulu Lamartine**, compassionate and sensual, the lover of many men and the mother of eight sons, all of whom adore her. Lulu's relationships with men are portrayed as natural extensions of her loving nature and enjoyment of life. Lulu's connection with Nector—and thus with Marie—lasts for forty-eight years and continues even when all three move into a residence for the elderly. After Nector's death, Lulu and Marie wield considerable power over their senior citizens' housing complex.

Another significant member of the novel's older generation is Nector's twin brother **Eli Kashpaw**, who stays on the reservation when Nector boards as school. Eli lives in the woods according to Chippewa tradition, which he passes on to his informally adopted and similarly inclined "daughter" June. Later he teaches the traditional ways to June's son Lipsha. **Sister Leopolda** personifies the troubled union of Catholicism and Native American culture. Although of Indian heritage herself, she can neither accept her native identity nor fully adapt to her adopted faith. Instead Sister Leopolda becomes a sadistic religious fanatic and projects her own self-loathing onto Marie. **Beverley Lamartine**, Lulu's one-time brother-in-law and occasional lover (and possibly the father of one of her sons), is a Chippewa intent on rejecting the traditional ways. He lives off the reservation and is married to a white woman, who takes him to visit her relatives only in the summer so that they can admire his "tan."

Central among the second-generation characters in *Love Medicine* is **June Kashpaw**, and the novel chronicles how her death affects the other characters. June was living in an isolated cabin in the woods when her mother died, and she survived by eating pine sap before being taken in by Marie and Nector. She found that she had more in common with her nature-oriented uncle Eli and moved into his cabin. June is described by her sympathetic niece Albertine as a long-legged, attractive woman who reveals her vulnerability only in rare moments of emotional desolation. June is a tragic figure, for she is never able to achieve the kind of life she desires. After leaving her alcoholic, abusive husband, Gordie, June has a long series of degrading liaisons with men in various oil boomtowns. She is returning to the reservation when she encounters a relatively amiable white man who she hopes will prove different from the rest. But during their lovemaking, the man falls asleep, and June leaves his truck and walks into a brutal snowstorm. Her death from exposure is not technically a suicide, but her family members know that she was familiar enough with the potential deadliness of North Dakota snowstorms to understand what would happen to her.

The most notable of Lulu's eight sons is probably **Gerry Nanapush**, who is dedicated to communal life and tradition. Gerry is physically imposing but gentle and nonviolent; nevertheless, he spends much of his life in jail and ultimately kills a state trooper. Gerry seems to personify the role of the trickster through his many escapes from prison, which extend his stay far beyond his original three-year sentence. His people admire Gerry both for his bravado and for the value he recognizes in native tradition, and he becomes a hero of the Indian Rights Movement. At the end of the book, after Lipsha learns that Gerry is his father and confronts him in Minneapolis, Gerry is again about to be captured, but he evades arrest and disappears without a trace.

Lulu's sons also include **Gordie Kashpaw**, June's alcoholic husband, whose hopeless floundering and feeling of victimization typify the male characters in Erdrich's fiction. After June's death, the drunken Gordie hits a deer and loads the animal into his car; when the stunned creature awakens and Gordie smashes it in the head, he becomes convinced that it is June he has killed. The once serene **Henry Lamartine, Jr.**, whose spirit is broken when he returns from the Vietnam war and who finally kills himself, illustrates the devastating effects of this conflict on young Indian men.

Unlike his cousin Albertine, another member of *Love Medicine*'s youngest generation, **Lipsha Morrissey** remained on the reservation after reaching adulthood. Lipsha is ''more a listener than a talker, a shy one with a wide, sweet face.'' He admits that his grandmother's claim that he is ''the biggest waste on the reservation'' is not entirely untrue, for he leads a rather aimless life and often seems naive or even simpleminded. Many reviewers, however, find Lipsha likable in his compassion for others—especially his grandparents—and his attempts to salvage something of value from his people's tradition. Although Lipsha absorbs little of what Eli tries to teach him about traditional ways, he feels he has inherited some mystical healing power, and he regrets that his people have strayed from their own religion into the murkier realm of Catholicism. Lipsha's attempt to reunite his grandparents with ''love medicine'' comes to a tragicomic end when Nector chokes on the turkey-heart concoction (or perhaps, as Lipsha suggests, on something less tangible). Yet Lipsha does succeed in working a kind of cure, for his loving interpretation of his grandmother's vision helps lessen her grief. By the end of the novel, Lipsha is closer to understanding his own past, for he has learned that June was his mother and Gerry Nanapush his father. Confronted by Lipsha, Gerry tells him that both suffer from ''this odd thing with our hearts'' that prevents their serving in the military; indeed, both share an aversion to violence and pain and a capacity for deep connections with others.

Lipsha's cousin **Albertine Johnson** is a mixed-race Chippewa who has left the reservation. A nursing student who decides to become a physician, she identifies with her native heritage. Albertine explores the past by asking many questions of the older people around her, even as she (according to critic Marco Portales) ''represents the modern Chippewa woman faced with an undefined life she must determine.'' **Howard ''King'' Kashpaw**, the legitimate son of June and Gordie, is wild and independent, like his mother. His move to Minneapolis and marriage to a white woman also express his mother's same desire to leave the reservation, as does his inability to create a successful life: he drinks excessively, fights with his wife and others, and is unable to hold a job. King's overweight wife, **Lynette**, a white woman, endures both physical and verbal abuse from her husband and feels unwelcome among his family members.

Further Reading

Contemporary Literary Criticism Vols. 39, 54. Detroit: Gale Research.

Flavin, Louise. "Louise Erdrich's *Love Medicine*: Loving over Time and Distance." *Critique* Vol. 31, no. 1 (fall 1989): 55–64.

Jahner, Elaine. Review of *Love Medicine. Parabola* Vol. 10, no. 2 (May 1985): 96, 98, 100.

Major Twentieth-Century Writers Vol. 2. Detroit: Gale Research.

Portales, Marco. "People with Holes in Their Lives." *New York Times Book Review* (December 23, 1984): 6.

Schultz, Lydia A. "Fragments and Ojibwe Stories: Narrative Strategies in Louise Erdrich's *Love Medicine*." *College Literature* Vol. 18, no. 3 (October 1991): 80–95.

Towers, Robert. "Uprooted." *New York Review of Books* Vol. 32, no. 6 (April 11, 1985): 36–37.

Wong, Hertha D. "Adoptive Mothers and Throwaway Children in the Novels of Louise Erdrich." In *Narrating Mothers: Theorizing Maternal Subjectivities*. Edited by Brenda O. Daly and Maureen T. Reddy. 174–92.

Nuruddin Farah

1945–

Somalian novelist, dramatist, short story writer, and translator.

Variations on the Theme of an African Dictatorship (trilogy of novels comprised of *Sweet and Sour Milk*, 1979; *Sardines*, 1981; and *Close Sesame*, 1982)

Plot: Each of the trilogy's novels is set in the East African country of Somalia in the years following the 1969 revolution. When the novels were published, Somalia's government was headed by General Muhammed Siyad Barre (referred to in the novels as "the General"), whose regime was a quasi-military dictatorship disguised as a "socialist republic." In *Sweet and Sour Milk,* a young man named Loyaan investigates the death of his twin brother, Soyaan, a government economist who secretly opposed the General's regime. Their father, Keynaan, is a government informer and torturer now on a pension; he is typical of the patriarchs of many Muslim Somalian families—tyrannical and unbending. Keynaan is behind an official campaign to fashion his dead son into a "Hero of the Revolution." Loyaan knows Soyaan's true beliefs (and increasingly concurs with them), so Loyaan considers his father's campaign a travesty. In the end, however, Loyaan can do nothing to change the situation, and the government exiles him by making him Somalia's councillor in Belgrade.

Sardines centers on the conflicts between several strong female characters. Medina is a cosmopolitan, Western-educated journalist who lives with her husband, Sameter; eight-year-old daughter, Ubax; and mother-in-law, Idil. Medina takes her daughter and leaves home not only because Sameter caves in to threats against members of his clan and becomes a government minister, but because Idil is pressuring her to submit Ubax to the traditional circumcision ritual. Eventually Idil's meddling diminishes her considerable power over her son. Meanwhile, Medina loses her important job as editor of Somalia's only daily newspaper when she objects to publishing the General's speeches verbatim every day.

The central character in *Close Sesame* is Deeriye, an elderly man who has spent many years as a political prisoner for opposing first the colonial rule of the Italians and English and then the General's regime. Now living a quiet, devout Muslim life with his family, Deeriye is protected by his devoted children. Nevertheless, he becomes convinced that his son Mursal is conspiring with three other young men to overthrow the General. Deeriye fears that his own political history has unduly influenced and thus endangered his son, but he allows Mursal to pursue his own aims. The conspirators bungle several assassination attempts, and Mursal is killed. In revenge, Deeriye tries—but fails—to kill the General; at the end of the novel, Deeriye's body lies riddled with bullets at the gates of the leader's residence.

Characters: An important figure in African literature, Farah is lauded for his insightful portrayals of contemporary Somali society. Because of his vocal opposition to General Muhammed Siyad Barre, Somalia's dictator until the bloody civil war in 1991, Farah has lived in exile for almost twenty years. The concerns expressed in Farah's fiction include the plight of women living in an autocratic patriarchal society; the role of the Western-educated elite; and political corruption and repression. Several commentators detect in Farah's work the suggestion that the communal aspect of traditional African culture should not be mythicized or over-glorified at the expense of individual freedom, but that instead Africans should sift through and analyze their heritage to separate the positive from the negative.

In *Sweet and Sour Milk* Farah projects the viewpoint that the traditional Somali social structure impedes the country's progress. Although Farah does not completely reject the Islamic religion, in this novel he equates its patriarchal rigidity with Somali's authoritarian government. Through the story of **Loyaan**'s efforts to learn the truth about his brother **Soyaan**'s death, Farah portrays a society in which tradition is manipulated to serve power and oppression. Aware that Soyaan is not a "Hero of the Revolution" but an enemy of the regime, Loyaan seeks to vindicate his brother's name. Though his mission is initially personal, Loyaan becomes more sympathetic to Soyaan's politics as he learns more about the workings of Somalia's government. Yet Loyaan is only an ordinary man, and he never succeeds in acting on his principles. The government wins out when it forces Loyaan to take a diplomatic post far from his own country.

If the traditional Somali family structure is likened in the novel to that of the country's government, then the patriarch **Keynaan** may be equated with the General. A tyrant, Keynaan wields absolute power over his family, proclaiming: "I am the father. It is my prerogative to give life and death as I find fit. . . . I am the Grand Patriarch." **Qumman**, the wife of Keynaan and mother of Soyaan and Loyaan, upholds the role expected of her as a Muslim woman: loving, patient, and self-sacrificing, she endures physical abuse from her husband and devotes herself to her children. Qumman and other conservative religious female characters in Farah's fiction are cast as helping to hold back the tide of change as they maintain a lifestyle that, if oppressive, is at least familiar.

Two additional characters in *Sweet and Sour Milk* include Keynaan's second wife, **Beydan**, and Soyaan's mistress, **Margaritta**. Keynaan uses the utterly dependent Beydan as a wedge to enhance his own power over his family, and Qumman hates and victimizes her. When Beydan is in labor, she is helpless and abandoned and dies in childbirth. In contrast to both Beydan and Qumman, Margaritta represents a new breed of Somali woman. Independent and with her own ideas about society, politics, and love, she has no desire for a permanent relationship with a man and does not even demand from Keynaan support for her child by Soyaan.

Sardines is particularly noted for its sensitive portrayal of several compelling female characters; in fact, some critics consider Farah to be Africa's first feminist author. Farah asserts throughout his fiction that there can be no real emancipation for Somali until its women are freed from the bonds of tradition. The struggle for emancipation is illustrated in *Sardines* by **Medina**, who finds herself in conflict with her autocratic government and her repressively religious mother-in-law. Medina is the archetypal westernized African (a category to which Farah himself is said to belong): the daughter of a diplomat, she has lived in numerous African and European capitals, has attended an Italian university, speaks four languages, and holds (at least for a time) an important job. She is cosmopolitan in outlook and, in many ways, highly privileged. Like Margaritta in *Sweet and Sour Milk,* Medina is one of Somali's new women—educated, economically self-sufficient, and a confident participant in life outside the home. Yet Medina complains that she feels like a guest in her own country, where such brutal repressions as female circumcision are still practiced. That Medina considers herself an enemy of both the General's regime and of the traditions her mother-in-law espouses is dramatized when she leaves home with Ubax. She intends to protect her daughter against circumcision and protest her husband's capitulation to government pressure.

Like other matriarchal characters in Farah's fiction, Medina's mother-in-law, **Idil**, is extremely conservative—an enthusiastic supporter of the General's regime and an upholder of Islamic tradition. Allowed no other outlet, Idil focuses her domineering personality on her children. Her emotional manipulation backfires, however, when Idil attempts to wed Sameter to a more docile wife during Medina's absence, which leads to estrangement from her son. **Sameter** earns his wife's disapproval by agreeing to become a government minister in order to protect members of his clan from harm; Farah consistently portrays this loyalty to clan or tribe as an impediment to positive change in Somalia. **Xaddia**, Sameter's sister, also suffers from their mother's interference. Idil is eager for a grandchild and consults a herbalist to try to enhance Xaddia's fertility; she is later enraged to learn that her daughter is taking birth control pills.

Medina's quiet, docile mother, **Fatima Bint Thabit**, exemplifies the economic dependence of Somali women on their men and their reluctance to embrace change. Fatima can conceive of no suitable alternative to traditional Somali culture. Nevertheless, Medina raises her daughter, **Ubax**, to forge just such an alternative some day. Medina refuses to allow her daughter to be circumcised and treats the girl as an equal and friend, which shocks her mother-in-law.

Through the musings of Medina's friend **Sagal**, an ambitious swimming champion, Farah articulates the idea that the head of the traditional Islamic family is tantamount to the head of the authoritarian state, and that as long as the Somali father wields absolute power over his family, the General will wield the same power over Somalia. Sagal is intelligent but in some ways rather naive and superficial, which one critic considers typical of the confusion and rootlessness of many young characters in Farah's fiction.

Commentators agree that **Deeriye**, the protagonist of *Close Sesame,* is the trilogy's most successful character. Elderly, asthmatic, and deeply humane, Deeriye is a veteran of political struggle who has spent many years in prison for his beliefs. Opposed to government oppression and tribalism, he believes in individual freedom and a state that administers justice evenhandedly. Physically frail after his difficult life, Deeriye is now sheltered and protected by his children; he spends his time telling the traditional Wiil-Waal stories to his grandson, **Samawade**, and dreaming of his dead wife, **Nadiifa**. Several critics note that Farah does not portray this character as an extremist; though a devoted Muslim, Deeriye is not an authoritarian father-figure. He exhibits a much greater awareness of the poverty and starvation that plague his country than some of the younger, more self-involved characters in Farah's fiction. Deeriye's suspicion that his son is involved in a plot against the government causes him a great deal of anxiety, for he fears that he may have instilled his own political ideology in his children, thereby endangering their lives. He warns **Mursal** about the different tribal loyalties of one of his colleagues but later feels ashamed when this same young man, **Mukhtaar**, is killed in the defense of his beliefs. Though he has long held to nonviolent opposition, Deeriye now acts on the traditional right of the victim to exact revenge on the state in the person of the leader of that state. His attempt on the General's life fails, and the oppressive, bloodthirsty regime claims yet another victim.

Further Reading

Bardolph, Jacqueline. "Time and History in Nuruddin Farah's *Close Sesame.*" *Journal of Commonwealth Literature* Vol. 24, no. 1 (1989): 193–206.

Black Literature Criticism. Vol. 1. Detroit: Gale Research.

Contemporary Literary Criticism. Vol. 53. Detroit: Gale Research.

Dasenbrock, Reed Way. "Creating a Past: Achebe, Naipaul, Soyinka, Farah." *Salmagundi* Nos. 68–69 (fall–winter 1986): 312–32.

Durix, J. P. "Through to Action." *Times Literary Supplement* No. 4211 (December 16, 1983): 1413.

Lewis, Peter. "Closing the Cave." *London* magazine n.s. Vol. 23, no. 11 (February 1984): 101–05.

Mnthali, Felix. "Autocracy and the Limits of Identity: A Reading of the Novels of Nuruddin Farah." *Ufahamu* Vol. 17, no. 2 (spring 1989): 53–69.

Okonkwo, J. I. "Nuruddin Farah and the Changing Roles of Women." *World Literature Today* Vol. 58, no. 2 (spring 1984): 215–21.

Petersen, Kirsten Holst. "The Personal and the Political: The Case of Nuruddin Farah." *Ariel: A Review of International English Literature* Vol. 12, no. 3 (July 1981): 93–101.

Pullin, Faith. Review of *Sardines. British Book News* (spring 1982): 320.

Sparrow, Fiona. "Telling the Story Yet Again: Oral Traditions in Nuruddin Farah's Fiction." *Journal of Commonwealth Literature* Vol. 24, no. 1 (1989): 164–72.

Turfan, Barbara. "Opposing Dictatorship: A Comment on Nuruddin Farah's Variations of the Theme of an African Dictatorship." *Journal of Commonwealth Literature* Vol. 24, no. 1 (1989): 173–84.

Jessie Redmon Fauset

1882-1961

American novelist, editor, short story writer, critic, essayist, and poet.

Plum Bun (novel, 1929)

Plot: The novel's central character is Angela Murray, an African American artist who grows up in a black, working-class neighborhood in Philadelphia. Because she and her mother are very light-skinned, they are able to "pass" as white and thus gain entrance to theaters and restaurants from which blacks are excluded; Angela's sister Virginia (called Jinny) has much darker skin. Angela deeply resents the limitations that white-dominated society imposes on African Americans. After the deaths of both of her parents, she decides to move to New York and attend art school, while Jinny chooses to remain in Philadelphia. In New York, Angela changes her name to Angèle Mory and establishes herself among a group of predominantly white fellow students, none of whom know she is black. She becomes involved with a rich, suave white man named Roger Fielding and determines to achieve economic security and social status by marrying him. Meanwhile, Angela rejects the love of artist Anthony Cross despite her admiration for his compassionate character. Jinny decides to move to New York, but Angela denies that they are sisters because she does not want to reveal her true racial heritage.

After persuading Angela to become his mistress, Roger (who never intended to marry a girl from a lower social stratum than himself) grows tired of her and ends their relationship. Angela seeks out a reconciliation with Jinny, who has entered happily into the black community of Harlem, where she teaches music. Angela would also like to earn back Anthony's love and is dismayed to learn that he and Jinny are engaged. When Angela's fellow student Rachel Powell is denied a scholarship because she is black, her friends gather to organize a protest. At this meeting, Anthony reveals that he too is of mixed black and white blood. All of these factors contribute to Angela's dawning realization that she must confront and embrace her black heritage. In a public defense of Rachel, Angela announces that she too is black. She is later reconciled with Anthony, while Jinny returns to an earlier sweetheart.

Characters: Fauset was an integral figure in the Harlem Renaissance, the post-World War I period of great achievement in African American art and literature. Although she is most widely known as the literary editor of the pioneering journal *Crisis*, published by the National Association for the Advancement of Colored People, Fauset is also lauded for her fiction. Once viewed as essentially conservative romances or melodramas, her novels have more recently been identified as groundbreaking affirmations of feminism and civil rights. Considered her finest literary achievement, *Plum Bun* dramatizes not only the racism in American society but the folly of denying one's own identity. It blends an emphasis on values that blacks and whites have in common with an appreciation for African American culture.

Plum Bun is one of several significant novels of the Harlem Renaissance (others include William White's *Flight* and Nella Larson's *Passing*) that feature a mulatto or light-skinned heroine who yields to the temptation to "pass" as white but eventually affirms her African American identity. Fauset's other novels also center on light-skinned heroines who seek economic security and social status by pretending to be white, a decision that invariably leads to emotional anguish and confusion and a renewed commitment to their true ethnic identities. *Plum Bun* chronicles the development of **Angela Murray**'s consciousness as she gradually recognizes the error of her early ambitions. An attractive and idealistic young girl, Angela is deeply hurt by the rejection of her white friends when they learn she is black, and she resents the fact that so many liberties and opportunities are available only to whites. Aware from her experiences with her equally light-skinned mother that she can easily "pass," Angela takes on a new identity when she goes to New York to attend art school. Neither the other students nor her rich white boyfriend know that she is really black, and she carries on the charade successfully for some time. But events conspire to expose Angela's folly: She is rejected by the class-conscious Roger, she witnesses her sister's happiness living within the black community, and she learns that Anthony is part black. Finally recognizing her own self-absorption and the superficiality of her ambitions, Angela takes a definitive step toward establishing her identity when she publicly announces her racial heritage. She has always harbored within her a sympathy for her fellow African Americans that was eclipsed by her own materialism, but now her ethnic pride and appreciation for the endurance and accomplishments of blacks can blossom. In addition, by defending Rachel and rejecting her own fellowship (which she knows was granted in ignorance of her race), Angela aligns herself with those fighting against the persecution of blacks.

Virginia "Jinny" Murray serves as a foil to Angela in both appearance and ambition. With her dark skin, Jinny does not have the opportunity to pass as white, but neither does she have the inclination. Instead, she embraces her black heritage by joyfully entering into the lively community of Harlem, where black artists and intellectuals are active in the Harlem Renaissance. Instead of pursuing materialistic interests, as Angela does, Jinny chooses to serve others by becoming a music teacher. Critics have seen Jinny as a manifestation of Angela's black self, whereas **Roger Fielding**, a wealthy, sophisticated, self-centered playboy, represents the artificial values she ultimately rejects. The highly class-conscious Roger never intends to marry Angela, and after making her his mistress he grows tired of her possessiveness and leaves her.

A much more worthy partner for Angela is **Anthony Cross**, a handsome, talented portrait painter from South America. Although she finds Anthony's sensitivity and sympathy for the struggles of African Americans admirable, Angela spurns his love in favor of the false passion expressed by Roger. Later, the bond between Angela and Anthony deepens when he reveals that he is of mixed race and has undergone an awakening of race consciousness similar to her own; the novel ends with their reconciliation. Some critics found the revelation of Anthony's racial heritage unconvincingly coincidental. The struggles of their fellow art student **Rachel Powell**, denied a scholarship because she is African American, inspire epiphanies in both Anthony and Angela. A quietly persistent, dedicated artist, Rachel projects a pride and confidence in herself and her talent that Angela lacks. When Rachel tells her friends that she wants no part of a loud public fight to regain her scholarship, Anthony explains that blacks are sometimes reluctant to risk losing those gains and privileges they do have in order to win "the trimmings of life."

Unlike Angela, her honest, hardworking, affectionate parents **Mattie** and **Junius Murray** are content with their little house they have managed to attain and with their harmonious family life. Mattie sometimes amuses herself by passing as white to enter public places that would otherwise be off-limits, but she always retains a sense of her black identity, suggesting that she has achieved the balanced identity that Angela lacks. Junius dies suddenly of a heart attack after a disturbing racial confrontation, and Mattie's demise soon follows; some critics have found these rather convenient deaths—which free Angela to use her inheritance for art school in New York—another example of Fauset's excessive use of coincidence. Other characters in the novel include **Ralph Ashley**, a shy, introverted young white man who wants to marry Angela; **Martha Burden**, a liberal white art student who hosts the meeting at which Rachel's friends plan to defend her; **Rachel Salting**, a supposedly idealistic Jewish woman who turns out to be prejudiced against blacks; and

Elizabeth and Walter Sandburg, a white couple who prove good friends to Angela and other blacks.

Further Reading

Feeney, Joseph J., S.J. "A Sardonic Unconventional Jessie Fauset: The Double Structure and Double Vision of Her Novels." *CLA Journal* Vol. 22, no. 4 (June 1979): 365–82.

McDowell, Debra E. "The Neglected Dimension of Jessie Redmon Fauset." In *Conjuring: Black Women, Fiction, and Literary Tradition*, edited by Marjorie Pryse and Hortense J. Spillers. Bloomington, IN: Indiana University Press, 1985, 86–104.

Review of *Plum Bun. New Republic* Vol. 58, no. 749 (April 10, 1929): 235.

Sato, Hiroko. "Under the Harlem Shadow: A Study of Jessie Fauset and Nella Larsen." In *The Harlem Renaissance Remembered*, edited by Arna Bontemps. Dodd, Mead, 1972, 63–89.

Singh, Amritjit. "'Fooling Our White Folks': Color Caste in American Life." In *The Novels of the Harlem Renaissance: Twelve Black Writers, 1923–1933*, University Park, PA: Pennsylvania State University Press, 1976, 89–104.

Sylvander, Carolyn Wedin. *Jessie Redmon Fauset: Black American Writer.* Troy, NY: Whitston, 1981.

Penelope Fitzgerald
1916–
English novelist, biographer, and journalist.

The Beginning of Spring (novel, 1988)

Plot: *The Beginning of Spring* takes place in Moscow over a few weeks in 1913, chronicling the first signs of the city's emergence from the long, cold Russian winter. Frank Reid is an English expatriate who has lived in Moscow most of his life; he runs the printing business established nearly forty years earlier by his father. As the novel begins, Frank learns that his wife, Nellie—leaving only a note that does not explain her motives—has taken the children away with her, presumably to England. The next day, the children return to Moscow, sent by their mother who continued on her way alone. Distraught but determined to maintain calm in his household, Frank tries to find someone to care for his children. His company's accountant, Tolstoy enthusiast and part-time poet Selwyn Crane, suggests a girl of peasant origin whom he has found crying at her post as a clerk in a department store. Frank hires the beautiful, placid, and enigmatic Lisa Ivanovna, who establishes order in the household and whom the children love. Frank too begins to fall in love with Lisa, who appears to have some connection to the hapless student who enters the print shop after hours and, discovered by Frank, fires two gunshots that miss Frank but destroy some equipment. Then Nellie's brother Charlie Cooper arrives in Moscow, ostensibly to help resolve the mystery of her disappearance; he enjoys his visit but offers no insights into where Nellie might be. The Reid children convince Frank to let them travel with Lisa to the family's dacha (country home). The night before they leave, Frank makes love to Lisa. After only a few days at the dacha, Lisa sends the children back to Moscow and herself disappears, leading to speculation that she is involved in the revolutionary movement then growing in Russia. Meanwhile, Selwyn has admitted to Frank that he and Nellie planned to run away together but that he lost his nerve at the last moment. On the novel's last page, the Reid family begins the much-relished yearly ritual of unsealing the house's windows. In the midst of this activity, Nellie walks through the front door.

Characters: Fitzgerald is lauded for her economically written, well plotted novels, which often feature somewhat eccentric characters in confrontation with unexpected events or conflicts in their circumstances. *The Beginning of Spring* earned critics' praise for its vivid evocation of Russia in 1913, when that "magnificent and ramshackle country" was perched on the edge of cataclysmic change.

The novel's central character is **Frank Reid**, an Englishman born and raised in Russia after his father established a printing company in Moscow. The novel chronicles Frank's reaction to the unexpected departure of his wife, of whose unhappiness or dissatisfaction, he realizes in retrospect, he had been only vaguely aware. Frank is a good, kind man whose basic decency is thrown into relief by the shadowy dealings of those around him—particularly the seemingly benevolent Selwyn, who finally admits to a love affair with Nellie. Frank is honest and loving with his children and treats his employees with consideration, aided in the latter task by his knowledge of the Russian temperament and culture. He does not so much love Russia as feel it part of himself, even though he realizes that there may be political and social turmoil to come that would force him to return to England; the country's "history, since he was born, had been his history, and [its] future he could hardly guess at." In addition to his worries about what may happen to the life and business he and his family have established in Russia, Frank is plunged into confusion and anguish by Nellie's departure. His sense of responsibility to others, however, leads him to hide his pain and carry on more or less as usual. Frank's brief liaison with Lisa seems motivated by a combination of factors, including both a sexual attraction and a need for the sense of nurturing calm she embodies. He seems nearly as surprised by Lisa's sudden exit as he had been by Nellie's, and the reader can only wonder how he will react to the latter's just-as-unexpected return in the novel's last line. The fact that he has consistently exhibited a deep regard for his wife and expressed sympathy for her regarding her abandonment by Selwyn suggests that the two will reconcile.

Although she appears only in a flashback scene, Frank's wife **Nellie** is a pivotal character in the novel, for it is her unexpected departure that precipitates the action. Frank had met Nellie while he was in England training for his profession. A twenty-six-year-old schoolteacher, she was eager to escape her spinster's life in her brother's dull home. Frank was initially attracted to Nellie's "disapproval of life's compromises," and she has continued to exhibit her strong will and determination. She despises the idea of being "got the better of" by anyone, which is why—intent on thwarting the assumptions of her smallminded neighbors—she slept with Frank before their wedding. Frank describes Nellie as a "jumper up and walker about" who once talked a lot, although he reflects that she has perhaps been more quiet recently. Toward the end of the novel, Selwyn offers a secondhand explanation of what happened to Nellie, although her motivations and her own feelings about what she has done are never delineated: She had planned to take the children and run away from Russia with Selwyn, but when he lost his nerve and failed to meet her at the agreed-upon railroad station, she sent the children back and continued on her way. She did reach England and spent some time at a Tolstoyan settlement, but this communal life apparently did not agree with her. Eventually Nellie finds her way back to Moscow, arriving on that joyful, momentous day when the winter-sealed windows are opened and the cold spring winds allowed to blow through the house.

The oldest of the Reid children is eleven-year-old **Dolly**, who approaches the encroachment of adulthood with the confidence that "there was in store for her some particular greatness." Allowed by her understanding father to freely express her own opinions and to keep her own counsel, she writes a letter to her absent mother about which Frank knows only that it contains the word "irresponsible." Like her father, Dolly is deeply hurt by Nellie's departure but hides her feelings by delving determinedly into her homework. Losing Lisa, however, proves more than even tough little Dolly can take, and she uncharacteristically clings to her father at their reunion. Nine-year-old **Ben** is also precocious, but he seems more intrigued by motor cars and fountain pens than particularly worried about his mother's absence. **Annushka**, who is almost three, is a stout, affectionate little girl who adapts easily to the change in the family's circumstances.

Described by critic Margaret Walters as "gratingly benevolent," middle-aged **Selwyn Crane** is Reidka's chief accountant. A vegetarian and would-be poet (his volume *Birch Tree Thoughts* has just been published by Frank's company), Selwyn is an enthusiast of the great Russian author Leo Tolstoy, who condemned capitalism and extolled the virtues of physical labor. Tall and thin, Selwyn dresses oddly, wearing (like Tolstoy) a Russian peasant's blouse beneath his English frock coat. Frank maintains that Selwyn has a "reserve of good sense" that allows him to perform his work competently, but he is otherwise a rather flighty moralist who, as Frank's servant points out, is "always on his way from one place to another, searching out want and despair." By the end of the novel, Selwyn's apparent earnestness has been revealed as deceptive, for he admits to Frank that he and Nellie were lovers and that only his own cowardice prevented him from running away with her.

Knowing that Frank needs someone to take care of his children after Nellie leaves, Selwyn suggests that he hire **Lisa Ivanovna**, a carpenter's daughter whom he had found crying near her post at a department store. Described by Selwyn as an "unfortunate," Lisa turns out to be a beautiful young woman with a "pale, broad, patient, dreaming Russian face" and thick, fair hair that she cuts in an unattractive way in an apparent effort to please Frank. Although Lisa exhibits glimmers of intelligence and even humor, her extreme placidity and self-possession prevent either Frank or the reader from learning much about her. She may be involved in the fomenting revolutionary movement that will transform Russia in four years, but this suggestion is never confirmed. In any case, Lisa brings order to the Reid household and the children adore her, while Frank falls in love with her and manages to spend one night making love to her before she disappears. Neither the strange tryst in the forest—which some critics have called an unconvincing scene—nor Lisa's real motivations or connections are delineated.

Fitzgerald's deftness in creating memorable characters is evident in such figures as **Mrs. Graham**, the sharp-tongued, chain-smoking, interfering wife of the English community's chaplain, who is described as "a student . . . of other people's troubles." One of the tortured souls Mrs. Graham undertakes to assist is Miss Muriel Kinsman, a lonely governess recently dismissed from her position with a wealthy Russian family due to a mysterious "matter of the bath house." Reluctant to hire this excessively dowdy Englishwoman to care for his own children, Frank evades her dogged efforts to reach him but later regrets his unkindness. The Reid family receives a visit from Nellie's brother, **Charlie Cooper**, a highly provincial widower and retired solicitor's clerk who implies he is going to help them resolve the problem of Nellie's disappearance. All are surprised when Uncle Charlie thoroughly enjoys his visit to Moscow, although he provides them with no new insights into his sister's behavior. Amiable, naive, and not very perceptive, Uncle Charlie finds Mrs. Graham gracious and friendly, relishes his harrowing drive with Kuriatin, and finally proposes to take the children—along with Lisa—back to England with him.

Frank's Russian merchant friend **Arkady Kuriatin** is a vividly drawn, extravagant personality. After the Reid children spend one disastrous afternoon in his "half-savage" household, Frank reconsiders his plan to leave them there for a short period every day. Capricious and prone to lying if it serves his own ends, Kuriatin considers life a game that he has "arranged to win" by making up his own rules. Other notable Russian characters in the novel include Reidka's new cost accountant, the ambitious, sharp **Bernov**, who thinks the company should give up small jobs and print more newspapers and who begrudgingly accompanies Charlie on a motoring excursion with Kuriatin; and **Volodya Grigorivich**, whose assault on the printshop proves to have been motivated by his love for Lisa rather than, apparently, any revolutionary intent. Reidka's compositor, the dedicated, meticulous, and competent **Yacob Tvyordov**, utterly abandons his specialty of hand-printing after the shots Volodya fires destroy some of his beloved equipment. **Toma**, the Reids' main house servant, is in charge of unsealing the windows after the long winter.

Further Reading

Brookner, Anita. "Moscow Before the Revolution." *Spectator* Vol. 261, no. 8360 (October 1, 1988): 29-30.

Chamberlain, Lesley. "Worried, Norbury." *Times Literary Supplement* no. 4460 (September 23–29. 1988): 1041.

Contemporary Literary Criticism Vols. 19, 51, 61. Detroit: Gale Research.

Dictionary of Literary Biography Vol. 14. Detroit: Gale Research.

Eder, Richard. "A Morris Dance at Russian Easter." *Los Angeles Times Book Review* (April 23, 1989): 3.

Penner, Jonathan. "Moscow on the Eve." *Book World—The Washington Post* (June 11, 1989): 1, 14.

Plunket, Robert. "Dear, Slovenly Mother Moscow." *New York Times Book Review* (May 2, 1989): 15.

Walter, Margaret. "Women's Fiction." *London Review of Books* Vol. 10, no. 18 (October 13, 1988): 20–1.

Janet Frame
1924–

New Zealand novelist, autobiographer, short story writer, and poet.

Owls Do Cry (novel, 1957)

Plot: The novel, which takes place in the small New Zealand town of Waimaru, centers on the lives of a working class family. Bob Withers is a rather narrow-minded millworker; his wife, Amy, is a little more imaginative but preoccupied with her home and children. The Withers children include teenaged Francie; Daphne (the narrator), a sensitive, imaginative girl; Toby, an epileptic; and Teresa, or "Chicks," a tiny child who trails behind the others. In the novel's first section, Daphne and her siblings find refuge from the dreariness and ridicule they experience in the adult world in their favorite playground, a local garbage dump. There they find the "treasures" that others have discarded—such as a dusty, worm-eaten book of fairy tales. Because Francie is almost an adult, she is most threatened with having to leave their imaginary realm. When her father announces that he has found a job for Francie at the local woollen mill, all of the children take a Saturday excursion to the dump. A fire starts while they are there, and Francie burns to death.

In the novel's second section, the surviving Withers children have reached adulthood. Despite his disability, Toby has achieved some success as a demolition and scrap metal entrepreneur; he continues to live with his parents. Chicks, now called Teresa, is the socially ambitious wife of successful businessman Timothy Harlow. Daphne has been committed to a mental hospital, where she is scheduled to receive a lobotomy to eliminate her abnormal thoughts and equip her for life in the outside world. The final section of the novel chronicles Daphne's hospital experiences, as she attempts to avoid electric shock treatment and lobotomy. Her father and brother (her mother is now dead) visit her in the hospital: although Bob finds the sight of Daphne's shaven head disturbing, he agrees to the operation; Toby has an epileptic fit during the visit. The novel's epilogue—entitled ''Anyone We Know?''—indirectly suggests the fates of the main characters through newspaper accounts of anonymous individuals. If these people are indeed the Withers children, Teresa has been murdered by her husband, Toby has become a homeless vagrant, and the lobotomized Daphne is commended for her exemplary work at the woollen mill, while Bob Withers ends his life as a senile old man confined to a geriatric hospital.

Characters: Considered one of the first important novels by a New Zealand writer, *Owls Do Cry* was produced while Frame was a patient in a psychiatric hospital; she was, in fact, saved from undergoing a lobotomy when the book received a literary award. Diagnosed as schizophrenic, Frame spent most of her twenties in and out of psychiatric institutions, and her characters are often lonely, alienated individuals whose sensitive imaginations are interpreted as madness by a society that punishes nonconformists. Several commentators regarded Frame's suggestion—that ''insanity'' may actually represent heightened insight—as anticipating the publications of R. D. Laing, who viewed madness as a means to integrating the ''divided self.'' Although some critics called the novel overwritten and self-consciously profound, most praised its inventive narrative structure and effective blending of lyrical language, naturalistic details, and metaphor.

In creating the novel's narrator, **Daphne Withers**, Frame drew not only from her own experience but from that of her friend and fellow psychiatric patient Nora, who lived in a dimmed world of half-experience after undergoing a lobotomy. In the novel's first section Daphne is a sensitive, introspective child who loves poetry and who, along with her siblings, escapes a drab, cruel life by fleeing to a ''treasure'' land, which is how her strong imagination sees the local dump. Francie's death, which represents the ultimate limit that life can impose, affects Daphne profoundly. Her poetic language contrasts markedly with the predictable, cliche-ridden speech considered to be normal, marking Daphne as someone beyond the boundaries of sanity. The novel's third section is based on Frame's years of psychiatric treatment, particularly her efforts to avoid ''the dreaded ECT,'' electric-current therapy. Unlike Frame, however, Daphne is lobotomized. The epilogue's revelation that Daphne is eventually commended for her work in the woollen mill—the novel's symbol of societal restriction and death of the imagination—means that the operation is successful. Her capacity for fantasy, introspection, and poetry now suppressed, Daphne is allowed to rejoin society, cured of madness and made ''normal.''

Daphne's sister **Francie Withers** also seeks refuge from the outside world in the garbage dump. Threatened by impending adulthood, her father has already found her a job in the woollen mill, a place that promises to destroy her individuality and restrict her imagination. Yet Francie is also attracted by some of the possibilities of adulthood, such as the love she romanticizes in her relationship with an ordinary neighborhood boy. Francie's death in the garbage dump fire (foreshadowed by her appearance as Joan of Arc in a school play) represents the limitations that life and time may impose; it may also symbolize the power and potential destructiveness of the imagination (which has drawn her toward the dangerous dump), or an escape from the class divisions and hatred she would have experienced in her later life as a millworker. In addition, Francie's actual death corresponds to Daphne's metaphorical death in the mental hospital, where she is confined to a ''dead-room'' of alienated silence.

His reactions slowed by his epilepsy, **Toby Withers** depends on his mother and sisters to help him navigate through the callous outside world, where he is considered "a shingle short." Lacking the imaginative gifts that Daphne possesses, Toby is trapped in a lonely, private world from which he cannot seem to venture. In the novel's second section, Toby has become a fairly successful businessman and suffers from fewer epileptic fits, but he is still considered odd and still lives with his parents. His wish to marry Fay is dashed when she accepts another man's proposal, a decision he accepts with customary passivity, settling back into isolation and loneliness. Critics see Toby as an intermediate figure between the highly imaginative Daphne and the very conventional Teresa, whom he resembles when he uses such cliches as "I've got to get going in life" and "I've got commitments."

Called **"Chicks"** as a child because of her position as the "littlest chicken" in the family and her tendency to toddle along after the others, **Teresa Withers** does not play a major role in the first section of the novel. In the second part, however, she exemplifies social normality and materialism, contrasting with Daphne's retreat into imagination. Just as the child Chicks always struggled to catch up with her brother and sisters, the adult Teresa is a social climber who tries to emulate those she considers successful; she writes in her diary, "What more can one ask of life than to be popular and sought after?" Compared to her siblings' retreat from the world at large, Teresa embraces society and its shallow values, such as elevating the importance of money and esteeming "normality" above imagination. Teresa equates love with money in her announcement that she intends to buy her daughter anything she wants. She displays insensitivity when she misinterprets the "Help help help" Daphne writes at the bottom of her letter from the psychiatric hospital, pleading for rescue. Instead, Teresa decides that Daphne wants the lobotomy. After Daphne's operation, Teresa makes the ludicrous gesture of giving Daphne an iron to help her establish herself in the conventional world, which Teresa herself inhabits. The novel's epilogue suggests, however, that Teresa's conformity leads to no more happiness than her siblings attain: she is killed by her husband, the successful businessman **Timothy Harlow**.

The childrens' father, **Bob Withers**, is a member of the working class whose views have been narrowed and hardened by the routine and hardships of his life. His affection for the weather report illustrates that being *told* something is preferable to thinking about it himself. Bob is disturbed by the sight of Daphne's shaven head as she awaits a lobotomy; he weeps in remembrance of his dead daughter Francie, but he never realizes that Daphne is also about to undergo a kind of death and he is contributing to it by allowing the operation. **Amy Withers** is gentler and somewhat less prosaic than her husband, to whom she dutifully defers. Her pseudonymous letters to newspapers express a literary inclination of sorts, but she is too entwined in the routines of homemaking (particularly her obsessive baking) to further develop this aspect of herself.

Other characters in *Owls Do Cry* include **Fay Chalkin**, the girl Toby wanted to marry but who accepts instead the proposal of **Albert Crudge**. The novel's epilogue informs the reader that Fay kills herself after her husband's conviction for embezzlement. **Flora Norris**, a nurse at the psychiatric hospital to which Daphne is committed, is an authority figure herself notably fearful of life outside the hospital; defining herself by her social role only, she cannot imagine any other, broader existence.

The Carpathians (novel, 1988)

Plot: The novel concerns a rich, middle-aged American woman, Mattina Brecon, who habitually travels to exotic areas of the world to live and get to know the inhabitants. Her husband, Jake, is a novelist whose first work was very successful but who has struggled for thirty years to produce a second novel; Mattina hopes her long separations from her husband will provide him with material and revitalize their relationship. She visits New Zealand after hearing that a small town there, Puamahara, marks the location of the Memory Flower, a repository of "land memory" mentioned in Maori (the indigenous people of New Zealand) legend and now used as a promotional gimmick to draw tourists. Arriving in Puamahara, Mattina rents a house on quiet Kowhai Street and gets to know her neighbors. These include elderly Hercus Millow, a former prisoner of war; Ed and Renée Shannon, who operate a computer store; and Hene Hanuere, a Maori storekeeper. Mattina also meets an eccentric old woman, Dinny Wheatstone, who calls herself an "imposter novelist." The second part of the novel, written by Dinny, in Mattina's "point of view," records Mattina's observations about Puamahara.

The Memory Flower intrigues Mattina, but so does the Gravity Star, a recent scientific discovery that bodes ill for the human population because it destroys conventional perceptions of time and space, making what is near seem far away and vice versa. At the close of the novel's second section, Dinny's manuscript ends and Mattina's perspective again becomes dominant. She reviews the course of her life and especially her marriage— including the early years with Jake in Paris; the birth and growth of their son, John Henry; and several vacations—and she also ponders the lives of her Puamahara neighbors. Near the end of her stay in New Zealand, Mattina becomes aware of an unexplained but distinct presence in her bedroom, and one night some bizarre circumstances evolve that seem connected with the Gravity Star. She is awakened by the collective, wordless screaming of all of her neighbors, who stand outside of their houses, wailing but otherwise speechless. A rain of dried-up, crusted letters is also falling from the sky, as if language has been shattered and scattered in the wind. The next day Mattina's neighbors have all disappeared, and no one can explain their absence, not even Albion Cook, the real estate agent who arranges Mattina's subsequent purchase of all the street's houses. After she returns to New York, Mattina learns that she has a terminal illness. During her last few months, she talks incessantly to Jake about Puamahara, the Memory Flower, and the Gravity Star, insisting that he visit there himself. After her death, Jake does go to Puamahara and is as mystified by the disappearance of the Kowhai Street residents as Mattina was. He vows to share his and Mattina's experiences with John Henry—whose first novel, published before Mattina's death, received enthusiastic reviews—so that he can write a novel about them. The novel's final paragraph reveals that John Henry is the real author of this novel and that his parents died when he was seven years old.

Characters: Winner of the Commonwealth Literary Prize, *The Carpathians* is a complex, ambitious novel featuring several conscious shifts in point of view and, like Frame's earlier fiction, artfully juxtaposing the mundane and the surreal. Although some critics found the novel overburdened with ideas and difficult to untangle, most praised Frame for her strong yet graceful prose and unconventional use of a narrative-within-a-narrative structure. The images of both the Memory Flower and the Gravity Star refer to consistent themes in Frame's fiction: the power and danger of language and its link with the past as well as the inadequacy of words to fully capture the truth. In addition, Frame explores some interesting aspects of New Zealanders' sense of themselves, such as their anxiety about how other parts of the world view their remote country, their feeling that they are still "settlers" there, and their struggle to sift through their native Maori traditions, colonial heritage, and foreign influences (especially American) to forge their own cultural identity.

Frame explores the relativity of distance through the rather surreal concept of the Gravity Star and the novel's central character, a traveler from a faraway country who intends to familiarize herself with this new place and people and who also reviews her own faraway personal life. The traveler is **Mattina Brecon**, a wealthy, middle-aged, urban New Yorker whose life has been cushioned by the ability to purchase whatever she wants. She has made a habit of traveling to remote areas of the world (such as Nova Scotia, the Bahamas, Hawaii, and Portugal) to live for several months at a time and get to know the people there as intimately as possible. Mattina's desire to know people and places is so strong that it sometimes seems greedy, as if she wants to possess them. Indeed, she often uses her money not only to travel by airplane and to rent or buy homes but also to purchase experience and approval. Although she gives freely to people in need (such as the struggling writers she encounters through her work as a publisher's reader), she seems to have ulterior motives for her generosity and is somewhat deluded about the approval she thereby earns. Mattina's motivation for traveling seems to be to help her husband, Jake, write his second novel by leaving him alone for extended periods of time and by bringing back information and ideas that may inspire him. In addition, Mattina always feels their love renewed, however briefly, by these periods of separation. In Puamahara, Mattina reaches no definite conclusions about the Memory Flower, the Gravity Star, or her Kowhai Street neighbors, most of whom seem eager to categorize her in terms of her American origin or as a writer (which, unlike so many of those around her, she isn't). Yet Mattina is profoundly affected by her experiences there. The bizarre midnight rain, during which she sees the letters of the alphabet falling from the sky, is particularly mystifying; her previous perception that the people around her were two-dimensional paper cutouts floating between the pages of a book seems verified when their loss of language causes them to die or disappear. Having first "surrendered her point of view" when Dinny Wheatstone took over the narrative, Mattina surrenders it again—for the last time—when she dies of cancer. Before she dies, however, she talks incessantly to Jake about Puamahara, thus highlighting the powerful, if flawed, human tendency to try to recreate memories and experience through language.

Dinny Wheatstone, one of the residents of Kowhai Street whom Mattina meets during her stay there, is an eccentric woman of about sixty who defines herself as an "imposter novelist." She claims that because she has no point of view herself she can appropriate those of other people, and she proves it by taking over Mattina's project—i.e., the novel. The novel's second section is composed of Dinny's manuscript, which Mattina is supposedly reading and which chronicles her continuing explorations of Puamahara; occasional interjections pointedly remind the reader that the novel is now being written by Dinny. In the course of her narrative, Dinny makes the important point that language can never fully capture the truth, but that human beings nevertheless survive within this "inevitable deceit." After Mattina comes to the end of the manuscript, the novel shifts back to her perspective. She informs Dinny that she finds the manuscript "interesting" in that "you've taken all points of view, all time—it's dreamlight robbery," but that she does not believe the publisher she works for would be interested in it. Although Mattina ultimately concludes that Dinny is crazy, the reader cannot help but note that the strange "imposter novelist" did succeed in stealing Mattina's point of view.

Frame's descriptions of Mattina's Puamahara neighbors supply an element of mundane reality that provides an effective contrast to its poetic or surreal passages. The first neighbor Mattina meets is **Dorothy Thompson**, who works in the town's famous horticulture industry. She explains that she and her husband, **Rex**, a "Full Gospel" (a much-repeated term that is never explained) businessman and wool dyer, and children, **Hugh** and **Sylvia**, are quiet people who keep to themselves; originally from England, the Thompsons—like the other New Zealanders Mattina encounters—feel that they are still strangers here. **Connie Grant**, Dorothy's mother, who has recently been brought to live with them, feels lonely, unwanted, and confused about why they insisted she leave her home in England. Just before Mattina arrives in Puamahara, a woman is murdered on Kowhai Street, and this circumstance provides a lingering note of dread throughout the rest of the novel. The victim—killed in her sleep by a resident of the Manuka Home for the mentally deranged— is **Madge McMurtrie**, a widow dying of cancer who is consistently referred to as "the penultimate Madge" because she feels she must be the last person on earth with that name. The novel chronicles the last day of Madge's life, when she receives a visit from her niece Olga and grand-niece Sharon. Madge feels alienated from her relatives, who she believes are hoping to be remembered in her will, and she notes (significantly, in view of the novel's preoccupation with language) that she speaks a different language than they do, the speech of a now-distant age.

George Coker is a spry ninety-three-year-old who loves gardening and especially delights in being told that at his age he should refrain from this activity. Toward the end of Mattina's stay in Puamahara, Coker dies, and his possessions—including some silver cups for egg-laying he won when he was a poultry farmer—are auctioned off; many of the Kowhai Street neighbors are drawn by a morbid curiosity to walk through his empty house. Another elderly widower, **Hercus Millow**, tells Mattina that he is really a stranger to Puamahara, having moved here from another small New Zealand town several years ago when his wife died. The central experience of his life was his internment as a prisoner of war in Germany during World War II. His memories of this time are so vivid that he feels it is "still here, but distant," an observation that evokes the image of the Gravity Star. **Ed Shannon** manages a computer store in the local mall; although he maintains an outwardly composed, controlled manner, he harbors many vague fears about every aspect of his life. His wife, **Renée**, is described as a "more tousled," emotional person. She considers Puamahara a "dump" and wants to move back to the larger city of Auckland, where she was raised. The Shannons' son, **Peter**, is a quiet, ordinary though unusually thoughtful ten-year-old who is more skilled on the family computer's flight simulator than his father. The Shannons decide to move to Auckland just before the midnight rain that seems to cause the Kowhai Street residents to vanish.

Gloria James—who Mattina regards as a strong, healthy, but rather bland midwestern American—explains that although her husband, **Joseph**, is a piano tuner and has "perfect pitch, of course," he is not a pianist. The James' fifteen-year-old daughter, **Decima**, is autistic and has never spoken; this lack of language makes her, according to her mother, "unknown" and "new." Decima lives at the Manuka Home, where Jake visits her when he travels to Puamahara after Mattina's death. Through **Hana and Hene Hanuere**, shopkeepers who befriend Mattina, Frame touches on the issue of New Zealand's Maori element in the country's cultural identity. Many contemporary Maoris, including the Hanueres, have only recently begun to learn their native language and explore their own cultural traditions. The Hanueres take Mattina to a Maori encampment on a river a distance from town, where she shares in a pleasant evening of eating and singing. **Albion Cook**, the real estate agent who arranges Mattina's purchases of the Kowhai Street houses and who gives Jake a tour of the properties, claims ignorance about what has happened to all the residents. Oddly, Mattina describes Cook's facial expressions as constantly changing, but Jake finds his face completely immobile.

A significant portion of *The Carpathians* recounts the marriage and relationship of Mattina and her husband, **Jake Brecon**. They meet in Paris, where Mattina travels on an inheritance from her aunt and where Jake's successful first novel makes him the toast of the literary establishment. They marry, and throughout the next thirty years—as they establish a home in New York City and vacation at Lake George, as their son John Henry is born and grows up, as Jake writes well-received literary essays and Mattina works as a publisher's reader and travels to exotic locations—Jake is supposedly working on his second novel. The fact that he is unable to produce this work is a source of worry, embarrassment, and sorrow to both Jake and Mattina, which explains Mattina's joy when a telegram she receives in Puamahara announces that the novel has been finished. She later learns that John Henry has written the novel, not Jake. Jake then declares his vocation to be a scholar and lover of literature and not a novelist. He feels deeply gratified that his love for literature has borne fruit in his son. His visit to Puamahara after Mattina's death causes Jake to resolve to share his experiences—inconclusive as they may be—with his son so that John Henry can write a novel about them.

Exposed during his youth to many different forms of language—from his father's beloved literature to his mother's "chittering" conversations and storytelling—**John Henry Brecon** ultimately produces a novel of his own. The reader learns at the end of *The Carpathians* that John Henry has in fact been the true creator of this novel and the inventor of Mattina, Jake, and the other characters. Although in keeping with the novel's narrative-within-a-narrative structure, some readers regard such an admission skeptically. Critics suggest that Frame designed the ending to challenge our notions about truth, language, and storytelling itself.

Further Reading

Adcock, Fleur. "An American in New Zealand." *New Statesman and Society* Vol. 1, no. 17 (September 30, 1988): 42–3.

Armstrong, T. D. "Janet and Jason." *London Review of Books* Vol. 7, no. 21 (December 5, 1985): 26.

Ashcroft, W. D. "Beyond the Alphabet: Janet Frame's *Owls Do Cry.*" *Journal of Commonwealth Literature* Vol. 12, no. 1 (August 1977): 12–23.

Contemporary Literary Criticism. Vols. 2, 3, 6, 22, 66. Detroit: Gale Research.

Evans, Patrick David. *Janet Frame.* Boston: Twayne, 1977.

Farr, Cecilia Konchar. Review of *The Carpathians. Belles Lettres: A Review of Books by Women* Vol. 4, no. 3 (spring 1989): 21.

Leiter, Robert. "Reconsideration." *New Republic* (May 31, 1975): 21–2.

Nokes, David. "Lexical Fall-out." *Observer* (October 23, 1988): 42.

Pilling, Jayne. "Relativities." *Times Literary Supplement* No. 4470 (December 2–8, 1988): 1350.

Review of *The Carpathians. Publishers Weekly* Vol. 234, no. 9 (August 26, 1988): 76.

Review of *Owls Do Cry. New Yorker* Vol. 36, no. 26 (August 13, 1960): 104–3.

Rutherford, Anna. "Janet Frame's Divided and Distinguished Worlds." *World Literature Written in English* Vol. 14, no. 1 (April 1975): 51–68.

Wartik, Nancy. Review of *The Carpathians. New York Times Book Review* (January 22, 1989): 22.

Brian Friel

1929–

Irish dramatist, short story writer, and scriptwriter.

Aristocrats (drama, 1979)

Plot: The play takes place at historic Ballybeg Hall in Ireland's County Donegal, where the aristocratic O'Donnell family has gathered for the wedding of the youngest daughter, Claire, to a widowed greengrocer much older than she. The other O'Donnell children include Judith, who cares for her senile, ailing, but still tyrannical father, Justice O'Donnell; Casimir, who lives in Hamburg, Germany with—he claims—a wife and three children;

Alice, a childless alcoholic who lives in London; and Anna, who has been a missionary in Africa for seventeen years (she is not present at the reunion but sends a taped message to the family). Other characters in the play include Eamon, Alice's husband, a native of the nearby town of Ballybeg; and Tom Hoffnung, an American scholar researching the history of Ireland's Catholic aristocracy, who interviews the various family members. As the play progresses, the audience learns how the O'Donnells' aristocratic legacy has shaped their lives. Despite his infirmity and dementia, Justice O'Donnell maintains his iron grip on his children as he croaks commands through a baby intercom system. Casimir, the only son and perhaps most unhinged by the sound of his father's voice, fails in his attempt to perpetuate the family's line of successful lawyers. Although he lives in Germany, he holds onto the myth of the O'Donnells' past glories. Eamon sees as outmoded the notion of an Irish aristocracy, but he also feels nostalgic for the vanished world he knew as the son of a maid at Ballybeg Hall. The other characters reveal various secrets about themselves, such as the outwardly patient Judith's real feelings about her caretaker role and about the illegitimate baby she gave to an orphanage years ago; Claire's manic-depression; and Alice's disguised bitterness toward her father. As the play draws to a close, Justice O'Donnell dies, his demise brought on by the sound of his absent daughter Anna's voice on tape. Their father's death proves liberating for the O'Donnell children, who show signs that they will now relinquish the burden of their aristocratic heritage.

Characters: One of Ireland's most acclaimed contemporary dramatists, Friel earned the New York Drama Critics Circle Award for Best Foreign Play for *Aristocrats*. Set in Ballybeg (the rural village featured in many of Friel's works) in the socially depressed but geographically beautiful County Donegal, *Aristocrats* provides a glimpse of the declining Irish aristocracy. The characters gradually reveal their delusions and failures as well as their feelings about their family's glorious past. Like nineteenth-century Russian playwright Anton Chekhov (whose work is often cited as an influence on Friel's), Friel emphasizes character over plot, treats his characters with sympathy and compassion, and skillfully blends humor and psychological insight. Although the conflicts and struggles Friel's characters face mirror Ireland's larger cultural and social problems, political matters are de-emphasized in *Aristocrats*. The play's conclusion suggests that the characters may overcome their self-deception and experience a brighter future.

The patriarch of the family featured in *Aristocrats* is retired **District Justice O'Donnell**, the last in a long line of distinguished judges—last, because his son Casimir failed to qualify to practice the law. Although left helpless and senile by a stroke, Justice O'Donnell maintains his tyrannical hold on his household. Bedridden, he communicates through a baby-intercom system, croaking out harsh commands that have a profoundly withering effect on his children. The death of Justice O'Donnell near the end of the play symbolizes the final collapse of the family's aristocratic illusions about itself and also seems to offer the O'Donnell children an uncertain but possibly liberating future.

A social activist once involved in the conflict in Northern Ireland, **Judith O'Donnell** has spent much of her adulthood caring for her domineering, invalid father—a role she performs with apparent devotion and patience. As the play progresses, however, Judith reveals her true feelings about her responsibilities and about the child she bore long ago and relinquished to an orphanage. At the close of the play, Judith is planning to visit this now-grown child. Judith's sister **Alice**, an alcoholic whose marriage to Eamon has produced no children, lives in a damp basement apartment in England. Her voice shifts from sweetness to hostility, exposing the bitterness she feels toward her heritage; it is only after Justice O'Donnell no longer recognizes her that Alice achieves a kind of reconciliation with him. **Anna O'Donnell**, who is represented in the play only by her taped voice, has been a missionary in Africa for the last seventeen years. Her message reveals both her smug piety (she assures her father and siblings that she is "praying for them") and her illusions about the O'Donnell family's life.

Youngest daughter **Claire**'s planned wedding to marry an elderly greengrocer brings her siblings home to Ballybeg Hall. Pretty, sensitive, and musical, Claire once dreamed of becoming a concert pianist, but her tyrannical father "stifled" this dream. Her engagement to a man twice her age who drives a white truck with a huge plastic banana on its roof signifies not only a bleak future for Claire (the couple will live with the groom's two children in his sister-in-law's house) but the family's social decline. Initially energetic, Claire lapses into a depression similar to that suffered by her mother, an actress whose response to her repressive environment was suicide.

The family's only son is energetic, talkative, somewhat effeminate **Casimir**, who has failed to qualify as a lawyer and thus carry on the O'Donnell legacy. Supposedly proud of his aristocratic heritage, Casimir lives in exile in Hamburg, Germany, where he works in a food-processing factory and has, he claims, a wife and three children. Eamon notes, however, that Casimir's boasting about his domestic situation has "the authentic ring of phony fiction"; indeed, Casimir's attempts to reach his family by phone all fail. Eccentric and irrepressible, Casimir subscribes to the fantasy that every piece of furniture at Ballybeg Hall was dented or somehow marked by a visiting celebrity, such as a chair in which the poet Gerard Manley Hopkins once sat. Preferring to fabricate a glorious past for his family rather than face the truth is evident in Casimir's inability to supply accurate fact for Tom Hoffnung's questions. Brought to tears by the sound of his father's voice, Casimir is perhaps the most wounded of the O'Donnell children, and the best example of how a family's public image can trap its individual members in faulty, damaging misconceptions.

Alice's husband, **Eamon**, a native of the village of Ballybeg and the son of a former maid at Ballybeg Hall, is a product of the working class who married into the gentility that the O'Donnell family once represented. Educated and intelligent, Eamon maintains that the aristocracy is now irrelevant and exists "only in its own concept of itself," Yet he feels somewhat loyal to the past and to a life of privilege he knew only as an outsider. Despite his cynicism, he is the most nostalgic of the play's characters. Once a low-level civil servant in the Irish diplomatic service, Eamon was fired for his political sympathies. Now he seems committed to a new job as a probation officer. In his solicitude toward the O'Donnell sisters and his kindness to Uncle George, Eamon exemplifies the interconnectedness and concern that promises to replace the loss of a privileged and aloof aristocracy.

Tom Hoffnung is a scholar from Chicago who is visiting Ireland to study the Irish Catholic aristocracy. As the play progresses, he interviews the various family members at Ballybeg Hall, revealing his dispassionate skepticism and treating the O'Donnells not as complex individuals but as "fossilized objects." He prefers facts and statistics to developing deep insight into the family's struggles. As Eamon perceptively points out, certain matters are beyond his clinical method of scrutiny. Some reviewers considered Hoffnung a rather awkward theatrical device present only to prompt expository monologues by the other characters. Also appearing in *Aristocrats* are elegantly white-suited **Uncle George**, who is mute until the end of the play, when his speaking symbolizes the family's new freedom after the death of its tyrannical patriarch; and **Willie Diver**, an accommodating handyman who helps Judith care for Justice O'Donnell—despite having grown up alongside the O'Donnell siblings, he has little in common with them.

Dancing at Lughnasa (drama, 1991)

Plot: The play is set in Ireland's County Donegal in late summer 1936. The adult narrator, Michael, recalls an interlude from his childhood when he was seven years old and living in a small cottage with his mother, Chris, and her four sisters, Kate, Maggie, Agnes, and Rose

Mundy. The memory is so vivid because the family had recently acquired a radio (albeit an unreliable one); his uncle Jack, a Catholic priest, had returned from missionary work in Africa; and the Feast of Lughnasa (honoring Lugh, the Celtic god of the harvest) was taking place in the surrounding countryside. None of the women in the family is married; Michael is the illegitimate child of Chris and Gerry, a Welsh n'er-do-well who visits the cottage about once a year. Kate is a proper, morally rigid schoolteacher; Maggie is the family wit; kind Agnes and simple-minded Rose support themselves by knitting gloves. Michael is adored by all the household's women and by Uncle Jack, who was sent home from Africa ostensibly for failing health but actually for adopting African beliefs. Jack regales his sisters of such customs as the popularity of "love children" and the festival of the yam, which, with its three days of dancing, resembles the Feast of Lughnasa. As the play closes, the adult Michael reveals the changes that occurred after that period. Agnes and Rose lost their livelihood when a factory replaced their cottage industry, and both moved away and died in poverty; Chris spent her remaining years working at a dreary factory job; Gerry went off to fight in the Spanish Civil War; and Jack died within a year.

Characters: In *Dancing at Lughnasa*, the act of dancing is portrayed as containing "the very heart of life and all its hopes." Praised for its vivid characterizations and lyrical language, the play focuses on such themes as joyful paganism versus staid Christianity, the damaging effects of industrialization, the conflict between romance and reality, disappointment, and dissolution. Although a few critics found the characters in *Dancing at Lughnasa* too resigned, tame, or stereotypical, others lauded Friel's loving tribute to their courage and spirit.

The play's narrator, **Michael,** relates from an adult vantage point his memories of several weeks in 1936, when he was seven years old. Often compared to Tom Wingfield—the narrator of Tennessee Williams's 1944 play, *The Glass Menagerie,* who recounts his memories of his family—Michael's role is to call attention to an isolated interlude in time, encouraging the audience to focus on these events and plumb from them a profound insight into the characters' lives. Although he obviously basked in the love of his mother and her sisters, Michael claims he was eager to escape from the matriarchy and succeeded in doing so. He remains tied to that earlier time and place through the dancing which crystallizes the essence of life for him. Some reviewers found much of Michael's adult commentary gratuitous, claiming that it includes too many events outside the scope of the play.

Friel dedicated *Dancing at Lughnasa* to his mother and her sisters, "those five brave Glenties women," and the five Mundy women in the play communicate the playwright's love and respect. Michael's mother, **Chris,** has a rather breathless, distracted manner that suggests hidden depths of feeling, as does her romantic dance to the song "Dancing in the Dark" with Gerry, her son's father. At the end of the play, we learn that Chris spent the remainder of her life toiling at a factory job that she hated. **Aunt Kate,** a schoolteacher who reads stories to her beloved nephew every night, is extremely proper and moralistic. In response to Jack's assertion that "love children" (i.e., illegitimate offspring) are status symbols among his African friends, Kate demurs that as "much as we cherish love-children here they are not exactly the norm." Although she has previously called those who are celebrating Lughnasa "savages," Kate participates with her sisters in a wild Irish dance that represents a joyous, pagan release from the generally stultified Irish society.

Hearty, buoyant **Aunt Maggie** is the family joker, constantly regaling her adored nephew with riddles, puzzles, and brain-teasers and otherwise lifting everyone's spirits. Her determined good cheer in the face of poverty and uncertainty are a sign of stamina that protect her family from a withering fatalism. Solid, matronly **Aunt Agnes** treats her dependent sister Rose with love and tenderness. Mentally deficient **Aunt Rose** has only a frail grasp on reality and depends on her sister's vigilant guidance. The two earn money through piecework, knitting gloves in a cottage industry that loses its business to a faraway factory.

Dancing at Lughnasa chronicles **Uncle Jack**'s return to Ireland from Africa, where he served as a Catholic missionary priest for twenty-five years. Although Jack's removal from his post was ostensibly for failing health, his supervisors actually suspected him of "going native." Indeed, Jack is so accustomed to speaking Swahili that he has trouble remembering the English words for things, and he no longer says mass. His enthusiasm for African customs and beliefs suggests either a loss of faith or an expanded perspective in which culturally distant elements are relevant to his own life. For instance, Jack recommends the Ryangan enthusiasm for "love children"—a category that includes his beloved nephew Michael. Parallels between the African and Irish reverence for magic and ritual are obvious in the prolonged, joyous dancing found in both the African feast of the yam and the Celtic Feast of Lughnasa.

Michael's father, **Gerry**, is a handsome, charming Welsh n'er-do-well and an irresponsible father. A traveling salesman and ballroom dance instructor, he visits the family only about once a year, and he never fails to cause tension between the Mundy sisters. Like the other major male character in *Dancing at Lughnasa,* Uncle Jack, Gerry contributes little to the family's material well-being and is obviously not essential to its daily life or happiness. At the end of the play, Michael reports that Gerry soon left to fight in the Spanish Civil War.

Further Reading

Barnes, Clive. "Rituals of Death and Transfiguration." *New York Post* (April 26, 1989).

Billington, Michael. Review of *Aristocrats*. *Guardian* (June 4, 1988).

Brustein, Robert. "The Dreaming of the Bones." *New Republic* (January 27, 1992): 28–30.

Contemporary Literary Criticism. Vols. 5, 42, 59. Detroit: Gale Research.

Deane, Seamus. "Brian Friel: The Double Stage." In *Celtic Revivals: Essays in Modern Irish Literature, 1880–1980.* London: Faber & Faber, 1985, 166–73.

Dictionary of Literary Biography. Vol. 13. Detroit: Gale Research.

Feingold, Michael. "The Plough and the Tsars." *Village Voice* Vol. 33, no. 18 (May 29, 1989): 18.

Hornby, Richard. Review of *Dancing at Lughnasa. Hudson Review* Vol. 45, no. 1 (spring 1992): 115–16.

Kramer, Mimi. "The Theatre: Five Sisters." *New Yorker* Vol. 67, no. 37 (November 4, 1991): 95–7.

Maxwell, D. E. S. *Brian Friel.* Cranberry, NJ: Bucknell University Press, 1973.

O'Brien, George. *Brian Friel.* Boston: Twayne, 1990.

Oliver, Edith. "At Ballybeg Hall." *New Yorker* Vol. 65, no. 12 (May 8, 1989): 104.

Pine, Richard. *Brian Friel and Ireland's Drama.* London: Routledge, 1990.

Rich, Frank. "A Family as Symbol of Ireland's Troubles." *New York Times* (April 26, 1989): C15.

Spillane, Margaret. Review of *Dancing at Lughnasa. Nation* (January 27, 1992): 102–4.

Weales, Gerald. "The Music of Memory: 'Dancing' and 'Borrowed Time.'" *Commonweal* (December 6, 1991): 718–19.

Carlos Fuentes
1928–

Mexican novelist, dramatist, short story writer, scriptwriter, essayist, and critic.

The Old Gringo (*Gringo viejo*; novel, 1985)

Plot: The novel takes place in Mexico in 1913, during the Mexican Revolution. The title character is a seventy-two year-old American journalist who has grown bitter and disillusioned after the tragic deaths of his two sons and his estrangement from his wife and daughter. The old gringo decides to seek an honorable death by joining Pancho Villa's men in their struggle against the Mexican government. He allies himself with the self-appointed general, Tomás Arroyo, who has installed his brigade at the Miranda hacienda on which he, an illegitimate son of the owner, was brought up in poverty and ignorance. Thirty-year-old Harriet Wilson, a native of Washington, D.C., who has been hired to teach the Miranda children, also arrives at the ranch, which is being destroyed by Arroyo's men. Both Arroyo and the old gringo are attracted to Harriet, who eventually becomes Arroyo's lover. The tension between the two men causes Arroyo to kill the old gringo, who in turn is killed himself when Villa decides that the young man has taken too much power from him. Returning to Washington, Harriet buries the old gringo in her father's empty grave; many years later, she composes this narrative of her Mexican experiences.

Characters: Considered Mexico's leading novelist, Fuentes employs a colorful, densely metaphoric prose style, frequently intertwining myth, legend, and history to examine both the past and the present. Fuentes is one of the most prominent writers of the Latin American "boom" that began in the 1960s, when Latin American authors began to gain international prominence. In *The Old Gringo*, Fuentes imagines what might have happened to American writer Ambrose Bierce, who disappeared in Mexico in 1913. A political parable, a love story, and a murder mystery in one, the novel is also regarded as an allegory of contemporary U.S. policy toward Central America, and several critics have detected in it a strong vein of anti-Americanism. *The Old Gringo* certainly exhibits Fuentes's characteristic preoccupations with history and Mexican identity.

The novel's lean, cynical title character is based on the misanthropic Ambrose Bierce, a turn-of-the-century muckraking journalist and short story writer who wrote, shortly before he disappeared, that dying in Mexico was preferable to any other fate: "To be a Gringo in Mexico—ah, that is euthanasia." Some historians believe that Bierce, author of "The Occurrence at Owl Creek Bridge" and other works, joined Pancho Villa's soldiers, was killed in battle, and was buried anonymously; Whatever the facts, he was never heard from again. Fuentes's **old gringo** arrives in Mexico with a suitcase that holds two of books he has authored, a copy of *Don Quixote* (the protagonist he is said to resemble), and his firearms, a Colt .44. The old gringo grimly proclaims his disdain for the corruption, hypocrisy, and ignorance pervading American society. (Some critics find some of the comments credited to the old gringo, such as "We are caught in the business of forever killing people whose skin is of a different color," to be anachronistic, reflecting not so much what Bierce might actually have said, but Fuentes's own views on American foreign policy.) The old gringo is also embittered over his personal life, for two of his sons are dead—one was an alcoholic who committed suicide, the other the victim of a senseless shooting—and his daughter and wife refuse to have anything to do with him. Reluctant to simply fade away, the old gringo decides to die in style as a fighter in the Mexican revolution. He performs bravely in his first battle; this kindles the jealousy of Tomas Arroyo, who already objects to the attentions the old gringo showers on Harriet Wilson. Indeed, the old man seems to goad his young competitor into killing him. Arroyo shoots the old gringo in the back, and when Harriet Winslow asks to take the body to Washington for burial, Villa's men disinter it and shoot it in the chest to make the killing appear more honorable (an incident based on an actual occurrence of an Englishman killed by Villa's troops). Commentators familiar with Bierce's work compare the death-seeking old gringo to the character of the father in "The Horseman in the Sky," a Confederate officer who seems to want to be killed by his own son, who is serving in the Union Army. In a variation on this theme, the old gringo resents his own father, a rigid Calvinist who sided with the Confederacy in the Civil War.

The Old Gringo is narrated partly through the attractive, 30 year-old Washington D.C., native, **Harriet Winslow,** who comes to Mexico to teach the Miranda children, a job circumvented by the Mexican Revolution. Talking to Tomás Arroyo and the old gringo, teaches Harriet about Mexico's troubled history and its relationship with the United States, which both men believe has exploited its southern neighbor. An ardent American patriot when she first arrives in Mexico, Harriet eventually denounces U.S. foreign policy in Mexico. At the same time, the prim schoolteacher loses her sexual inhibitions through her affair with Arroyo; some critics judge Harriet's excessive delicacy as stereotypically spinsterish and the sexual heat between her and Arroyo anachronistic. Despite the passion she feels, Harriet realizes all along that the differences in their cultural backgrounds and orientations doom the affair. At the end of the novel, the reader learns that Harriet has lied about her father being a brave soldier who died in Cuba, that instead he abandoned her mother for a mistress and never reappeared. In arranging for the old gringo to occupy the Arlington Cemetery grave originally intended for her father, Harriet implies that she has assigned to the old gringo a paternal role in her life.

The young, self-proclaimed rebel general, **Tomás Arroyo,** gives voice in the novel to the revolutionary viewpoint and personifies Mexico's tormented history. The illegitimate son of a peasant and her wealthy employer, Arroyo grows up on the Miranda ranch but is never acknowledged as its heir. Now he belongs to the movement to restore Mexico to those who feel it is theirs by right, and he is determined to avenge centuries of the rich exploiting the poor just as he avenges himself against his father. Thus he sets himself up in a luxuriously appointed railway car to supervise the destruction of the Miranda ranch by his soldiers, who live in extremely primitive conditions. Some critics fault Fuentes for reinforcing the stereotype of the Latin American male through his insistent emphasis on Arroyo's virility.

Further Reading

Brody, Robert, and Charles Rossman, eds. *Carlos Fuentes: A Critical View.* Austin: University of Texas Press, 1982, pp. 121–31.

Contemporary Literary Criticism. Vols. 3, 8, 10, 13, 22, 41. Detroit: Gale Research.

Eberstadt, Fernanda. "Montezuma's Literary Revenge." *Commentary* Vol.81, no. 5 (May 1986): 35–40.

French, Sean. "Shouting from the Backyard." *Times Literary Supplement* No. 4344 (July 4, 1986): 733.

Grossman, Anita Susan. Review of *The Old Gringo. American Spectator* Vol. 19, no. 2 (February 1986): 48–51.

Kearns, George. "Revolutionary Women and Others." *Hudson Review* Vol. 39, no. 1 (spring 1986): 121–34.

Norris, Gloria. Review of *The Old Gringo*. *America*. Vol. 154, no. 19 (May 17, 1986): 416.

Pickering, Paul. "Down Mexico Way." *Punch* Vol. 290, no.7588 (May 28, 1986): 56–7.

Raskin, Jonah. "Borderline Case." *Village Voice* Vol 31, no.13 (April, 1986): 57–8.

Athol Fugard
1932–
South African dramatist, novelist, and scriptwriter.

The Blood Knot (drama, 1961)

Plot: The play is set in a one-room shack in Korsten, a black community near Port Elizabeth, South Africa. The shack is the home of the dark-skinned Zachariah, who works as a gatekeeper at a nearby factory, and his much lighter-skinned brother, Morris, called Morrie, who keeps house. Morrie had been away, able to "pass" as a white man, but had returned about a year ago. The play consists entirely of dialogue between the brothers and their interdependency and their differing roles in their racially divided society. Morrie encourages Zach, who is starved for female companionship, to answer an advertisement for a pen-pal but is shocked when the pen-pal, Ethel, turns out to be white. Nevertheless, he agrees to stand in for his brother with the girl, posing as a white man, and to use the brothers' savings—with which he had hoped they could buy an out-of-the-way farm–for clothing that will make the charade more believable. At the last minute, however, Ethel's visit is canceled. Then the brothers play a game enacting scenes from their own past and encounters between white and black men. Their play begins playfully but ends in violence. In the end, however, Morrie and Zach abandon their shadowy dreams of a better future and acknowledge the bonds of their brotherhood.

Characters: Due to its overt discussion of racism and apartheid, *The Blood Knot* sent shock waves through South Africa when it premiered in Johannesburg in 1961. By the time of its 1985 revival in New York, Fugard had become his country's foremost dramatist. He is respected for his ability to expand the boundaries of social protest, which gives his plays universal appeal despite their focus on apartheid. Fugard stated that his purpose in *The Blood Knot* was to explore not so much racial divisions as human ones, and that South Africa had merely given him a suitable dramatic context "for showing how different two men are." Like the characters in Fugard's other plays, the two brothers in *The Blood Knot* suffer from alienation, isolation, and powerlessness, which are natural outcomes of South Africa's racist policies as well as of the human condition itself. The bond of brotherhood they ultimately forge is presented as humanity's only defense against despair.

The son of a black mother and white father, **Morris**, called **Morrie**, has skin much lighter than his half-brother's, which has enabled him to enjoy social advantages. The game in which the brothers reenact scenes from their childhood reveals that Morrie received more attention and love from their mother, and he later availed himself of opportunities for self-education. For a time he also "passed" as a white man, an illegal act in South Africa. Though he was never found out Morrie suffered guilt for abandoning his family and heritage. He returned to live with Zach, motivated by a need to atone and by a hatred of the white world. Morrie hates white society even more than Zach does—at least Zach eventually attains a sense of identity. Morrie's behavior offers clues to his insecurity: He is overly cautious and nervous, he constantly nags his brother to live frugally and save money, he is obsessed with order—the ring of an alarm clock marks the correct times for his various household tasks—and he has imposed on his brother an unpleasantly monastic lifestyle. All of this is based on Morrie's dream that the brothers will one day buy a farm, a dream Zach does not share. Whereas Zach is rooted in the present, Morrie believes in delaying gratification. Nevertheless, he agrees to pose as a white man and entertain **Ethel**, a sign that his unrealistic focus on the future may be changing. During the brothers' subsequent gameplaying, Morrie comes to terms with the limits of his life and agrees to live in the present; he comments that after all "there's quite a lot of people getting by without futures these days." Some critics regard this outcome overly pessimistic, but others maintain that in so resigning himself Morrie is expressing a universal human plight. These same critics contend that Morrie has exchanged his former illusions for a heightened consciousness, including a deeper awareness of his abiding connection or "blood knot" with his half-brother.

Employed as a lowly gate attendant, **Zachariah**, called **Zach**, is crude and illiterate, exemplifying the social role imposed on him. Though Morrie dreams about buying a farm, Zach craves more immediate gratification. The sexual contact he enjoyed with his friend Minnie before Morrie arrived sustains him, even though he has been worn down and sapped of energy and passion by Morrie's nagging and manipulation. Whereas Morrie deludes himself about buying property, Zach dreams of having a white woman, and by the end of the play both men have had to accept the true limitations of their lives. His resentment of whites explodes into violence against Morrie, then Zach eventually comes to terms with his own blackness—an acceptance that may even give him an advantage over Morrie, whose identity is not so secure, despite appearing to have wider opportunities. Several critics complained that Zach is too stolid and dumb to personify South African blacks, while others proposed that such qualities might make Zach less visible to hostile whites. Some commentators deplored the resignation with which the play ends, noting that Zach expresses no intention to resist his society's injustice. Yet Zach's self-acceptance and affirmation of the "blood knot" he shares with Morrie make him, for most reviewers and audiences, an admirable character whose plight may be viewed not just as South African but as universally human.

Boesman and Lena (drama, 1969)

Plot: The action takes place on the desolate mudflats of South Africa's Swartkops River, where a coloured (mixed race) couple, Boesman and Lena arrive dirty and weighed down with all their belongings. Earlier in the day, Boesman and Lena were evicted from their squatter's shanty when bulldozers driven by white men came to destroy the community. Their relationship is a degrading and brutal one: Boesman is either silent, ridiculing, or physically violent toward Lena, and she constantly harangues him with chatter and questions. An old, exhausted black man arrives at their campsite seeking shelter. Calling him Outa, Lena gives him food and spends the night talking to him, although she does not understand the language he speaks. The old man then dies, and the bewildered Boesman pounds the body with his fists. Lena comments that he will probably be considered Outa's murderer. Boesman prepares to leave, and Lena, after briefly considering going off on her own, follows him.

Characters: *Boesman and Lena,* which earned the prestigious Obie Award for best foreign play, conclusively established Fugard not only as South Africa's leading playwright but as one of the most accomplished in the world. Its portrayal of a bleak, apparently orderless world with alienated, despairing characters shares the existential concerns of Samuel Beckett's *Waiting for Godot* (1952). Fugard's play recounts a journey of self-discovery that ends with both an acknowledgment of human interdependency and an awareness that humanity's questions about existence and identity may never be answered. Critics praised Fugard for exploring in *Boesman and Lena* not just the immediate dilemma but the broader, universal themes of alienation and powerlessness.

Boesman is of mixed race. In South Africa, these lighter-skinned people, known as "Coloured," had only slightly higher status than blacks had under apartheid. Destitute, Boesman and his companion live temporarily in various shantytowns; on the morning of the day on which the play takes place, they have been evicted from one such makeshift dwelling. The first impression the audience forms of Boesman is that he is brutal and insensitive, for he answers Lena's questions only with ridicule and she is bruised from his beatings. It is soon obvious that Boesman's cruelty toward Lena results from his self-hatred and resentment toward his social conditions: he treats her as the white man has treated him. He tells Lena: "We are the white man's rubbish. . . . He can't get rid of us. . . . We're the white man's dog, with our tail between our legs." As if to gain some control over events he is powerless to alter, Boesman claims that the white men who destroyed the couple's shanty did them the favor of propelling them into "freedom." Of course, this freedom is only the liberty to continue wandering. Lena's kind treatment of Outa angers Boesman, who calls the old man a "kaffer" (a derogatory term for South African blacks), and he demands that Lena send him away. Just as he has beaten his woman, Boesman brutalizes the black man—the only other member of society who is weaker than he. Yet Outa represents more than an insult to Boesman's sense of racial superiority; Boesman is jealous of the attention Lena pays the old man. Where at first Boesman seemed utterly insensitive, he reveals greater depth of feeling as he drinks wine and becomes more loquacious. His dependence on Lena is obvious and pathetic. After Outa dies, Boesman responds physically, as Lena says he typically does when he doesn't understand something: he pounds the corpse with his fists. Yet Lena laughs at him and predicts that he will be accused of murdering Outa. This brings Boesman to his senses, and he meekly complies with Lena's request to recite the litany of places where the two have been. Her hospitality to the old man and her threatened independence increase Lena's stature, even though she chooses to stay with Boesman.

Lena's ragged, filthy appearance and bruises testify to her poverty, social alienation, and her violent companion, Boesman. Lena talks incessantly, and the exasperated Boesman never responds to her. Fugard remarked in his notes about the play that the couple do not exemplify a simple victim-oppressor relationship, because Lena and Boesman are both victims and each aggravates the other's problems. As the play opens, Lena is confused and trying to order the events of the past, a state that symbolizes her uncertain identity. Lena craves some connection with others to affirm that she exists, and the uncommunicative Boesman cannot provide this connection. When Outa appears, Lena recognizes him as a witness to her existence. She offers him food and warmth and, as the night passes, she tells him the story of her life, including a moving account of the death of her baby. Lena's insistence on sheltering the old man and sharing her experiences with him are signs of independence that Boesman finds troubling, and he is even more worried when she tells him that he will be suspected of murdering Outa. He then complies to her request to recite the order of events the two have been through. The recitation causes Lena to realize that her questions will remain unanswered and that life will always be incomprehensible, but she also gains the strength to move on. While the process of accepting limitations seems more negative than affirmative, it allows Lena to avoid the disappointment and frustration of unanswered hopes. Saying "you can't throw yourself away before your time," Lena stays with Boesman, but she is neither wholly dependent on her companion nor wholly separate. Asserting her own existence, she also asserts that her continuing existence depends on others.

The play's only other character is the very dark-skinned, old, and ailing **Outa** (a nickname that means "old man"), who wanders into the couple's campsite and is offered shelter by

Lena. Although she does not understand him (he speaks an African language identified by some critics as Xhosa, a common language of the region), Lena talks to him throughout their night together. She admits that she is helping Outa for her own sake, not his—she needs a sounding board to verify that she exists. She projects her own meanings onto the old man's words, with the conversation between them becoming a stream-of-consciousness monologue spoken by Lena. Outa's death reminds Lena of her own mortality. To the acceptance of the past and present Lena has just developed, she adds the future, which may hold for her an end as bleak as the old man's.

Further Reading

Cohen, Derek. "Drama and the Police State: Athol Fugard's South Africa." *Canadian Drama/L'Art dramatique canadien* Vol. 6, no. 1 (spring 1980): 151–61.

Contemporary Literary Criticism Vols. 5, 9, 14, 25, 40. Detroit: Gale Research.

Fugard, Athol. Introduction to *Three Port Elizabeth Plays,* by Athol Fugard. New York: Viking Penguin, 1974, vii–xxv.

Gray, Stephen. *File on Fugard.* London: Methuen Drama, 1991.

Kauffmann, Stanley. *Review of Boesman and Lena. New Republic* (July 25, 1970).

Oliver, Edith. *Review of Boesman and Lena.* New Yorker Vol. 67, no. 51 (February 10, 1992): 86–7.

Rich, Frank. *Review of Blood Knot. New York Times* (December 11, 1985): C23.

Simon, John. "Houses Divided." *New York Magazine* Vol. 19, no. 1 (January 6, 1986): 50, 52–3.

Torrens, James S. Review of *Boesman and Lena. America* Vol. 166, no. 10 (March 28, 1992): 250–51.

Vandenbroucke, Russell. *Truths the Hand Can Touch: The Theatre of Athol Fugard.* New York: Theatre Communications Group, 1985.

Walder, Dennis. *Athol Fugard.* London: Macmillan, 1984.

Charles Fuller

1939–

American dramatist, short story writer, and scriptwriter.

A Soldier's Play (drama, 1981)

Plot: Set in 1944, the play's action focuses on the mysterious murder of Tech/Sergeant Vernon C. Waters at Fort Neal, Louisiana, where all the noncommissioned officers and enlisted men are black. The white officers at the army base suspect that Waters's killer is white. Because the fear conflict between the soldiers and the white residents of nearby Tynan, they order an investigation. Captain Richard Davenport, a black officer and lawyer, is assigned to the case and sent to Fort Neal, where he is assisted by a white captain, Charles Taylor. Taylor confides to Davenport that, because everyone assumes Waters's assailant is white, the inquiry will be stonewalled. Nevertheless, Davenport continues his investigation, initially suspecting that two white officers who encountered Waters the night of the crime are responsible for his death. Taylor eventually supports this theory and is eager to charge the officers, but then Davenport decides that the case is more complicated than he had suspected. Through interviews with the black soldiers, Davenport learns more about Waters's difficult personality and reputation among the men he commanded. A veteran of World War I, Waters was a strict disciplinarian who insisted that his men meet his high standard of comportment in order not to shame their race. Southern blacks especially annoyed him, because he felt their habits affirmed white stereotypes about blacks. He made a special victim of C. J. Memphis, a goodnatured, rather slow-witted Mississippian who excelled at baseball and blues singing. Davenport learns that Waters plotted to get rid of Memphis by framing him for a crime and having him thrown in the stockade. But Waters's plan backfired when Memphis committed suicide in jail, which intensified the other soldiers' resentment of their sergeant. Davenport finally determines that Waters was killed not by any white assailant but by two of his own men, Private First Class Melvin Peterson and Private Tony Smalls. At the end of the play, Davenport reveals that the case received little publicity and that all of the soldiers in Waters's company were subsequently killed in a battle in Germany.

Characters: Fuller won the Pulitzer Prize for *A Soldier's Play*, the second African American to achieve this recognition. He also received an Academy Award nomination for his film version of the play, which was produced as *A Soldier's Story* in 1984. Modeled in some measure after Herman Melville's novel *Billy Budd* (which also features an innocent figure who is tormented by a superior officer), *A Soldier's Play* is structured as a murder mystery, but one that forces audience members to examine their own prejudices as they search not only for the murderer's identity but for insights into the victim's psyche. Fuller has said that he sought to challenge the traditional portrayal of black men as ineffectual, lustful, overly emotional, and nonintellectual, and most critics praised him for creating characters who represent, according to Richard Gilman, "American reality in its widest sense." The play provoked controversy among some commentators—dramatist Amiri Baraka claimed that Fuller had made a reprehensible capitulation to white expectations of blacks. Others lauded the dramatist for lending universality and accessibility to the important social issues of racism and prejudice.

Tech/Sergeant Vernon C. Waters is the most compelling figure in *A Soldier's Play* and one of the most complex, interesting characters in Fuller's entire body of work. Fuller's portrayal of Waters emerges gradually, through the flashbacks that occur as Davenport interviews the various members of the company. Waters is a career army man, a veteran of World War I who was decorated for bravery but who, as the play's conclusion reveals, has never felt fully appreciated for his efforts. Through Waters, Fuller shows how racism warps both perpetrator and victim; thus Waters, whose basic motive is to help his race advance, ultimately hurts his fellow blacks. Waters has fashioned himself as a model soldier and strict disciplinarian—complete with gravelly voice, an exaggeratedly stiff bearing, and a pointed disdain for those beneath him. Waters believes that black soldiers must perform not just well but superbly in order to beat whites at their own game. He frequently criticizes and ridicules his men, particularly those who display the "ignorant colored" characteristics he most despises. Indeed, he treats them much more harshly than the white officers. Yet his anguish after C. J.'s suicide, when he realizes that his plan to remove "a detrimental element" has backfired, underscores his ultimate failure. Just before his death he laments: "You got to be like them. But the rules are fixed. It doesn't make any difference. They still hate you." Nevertheless, Waters is not inherently evil: he expresses concern about his own children's future; he wants them to attend white colleges so that they will be able to succeed in the white world. Although Waters's meanness and pomposity render him unlikable, the fact that he causes his own downfall and is victimized by racism make him a tragic figure.

In the American South of 1944, **Captain Richard Davenport** is a rarity: a black army officer with a law degree. His arrival at Fort Neal is much savored by the black noncommissioned officers and soldiers there. Davenport has undoubtedly had to overcome many obstacles to achieve success, but he states that he wishes to be judged on his own merit and on an equal basis with whites. Through his cool, rather distant manner and cautious rationality, he personifies the universal standard of soldierliness, and some critics even detect in him a faint resemblance to the man whose death he is investigating. Assisting Davenport in the investigation is **Captain Charles Taylor**, a graduate of West Point who acknowledges that he never encountered a black person until he was twelve or thirteen years old. His fascination (and even discomfort) with the idea of an African American officer suggests that his attitude toward blacks is still ambiguous. In theory Taylor is a liberal who considers blacks human beings and wishes them well, but he reveals some racist assumptions when, for example, he tells Davenport that "colored soldiers aren't devious." Initially impatient with Davenport's meticulous investigative methods, Taylor eventually leaps to conclusions and wants to charge the two white officers with murder even when the evidence against them is inadequate.

The victim of Waters's abuse is **Private C. J. Memphis**, an affable but slow-witted young soldier from Mississippi who is the company's star baseball player as well as a talented blues guitarist and singer. These attributes fail to impress Waters, however, who sees in C. J. all the personality traits for which whites have abused blacks in the past. Like the protagonist of Melville's *Billy Budd,* C. J. is handsome, athletic, and inherently innocent, which incites the antagonism of the older, jaded superior. Waters succeeds in getting C. J. thrown in jail, claiming there is now "one less fool for the race to be ashamed of." However, C. J. despairs of ever getting out of jail and commits suicide, and this unexpected turn of events shocks Waters into recognizing the flaws in his reasoning.

Unlike most of his fellow soldiers at Fort Neal, **Private First Class Melvin Peterson** manages to resist oppression from whites as well as from Sergeant Waters. Ironically, Peterson exhibits some qualities that Waters admires: he is strong and opinionated, and, despite his origin in the South, he is much more sophisticated and streetwise than C. J. Unlike Waters, Peterson appreciates C. J.'s talents. He holds Waters responsible for his friend's suicide, and added to the consistently harsh treatment he and the others have long received from the sergeant, he kills Waters. Critics regard Peterson as a precursor to the militant figures whose anger was expressed in the Black Nationalist movement of the 1960s.

Also notable among the black soldiers at Fort Neal are **Private James Wilkie**, who is demoted from sergeant (a rank it took him ten years to attain) after Waters discovered him drunk while on duty— Wilkie nevertheless treats Waters deferentially and even goes along with his scheme to frame C. J.; and **Private Tony Smalls**, Peterson's accomplice in murder. **Lieutenant Byrd** and **Captain Wilcox** are the two white officers who Davenport and Taylor suspect have murdered Waters. During their questioning they express some bigotry in their views of blacks, as when they first complained that Waters violated military protocol by refusing to show them respect, but they later revealed that they resented such treatment from a black man.

Further Reading

Asahina, Robert. "Theatre Chronicle." *Hudson Review* Vol. 35, no. 3 (autumn 1982): 439–46.

Baraka, Amiri. "The Descent of Charlie Fuller into Pulitzerland and the Need for African-American Institutions." *Black American Literature Forum* Vol. 17, no. 2 (summer 1983): 51–54.

Black Literature Criticism Vol. 1. Detroit: Gale Research.

Demastes, William W. "New Voices Using New Realism: Fuller, Henley, and Norman." In *Beyond Naturalism: A New Realism in American Theatre*. Westport, CT: Greenwood Press, 1988.

Contemporary Literary Criticism Vol. 25. Detroit: Gale Research.

Dictionary of Literary Biography Vol. 38. Detroit: Gale Research.

Gilman, Richard. Review of *A Soldier's Play*. *Nation* Vol. 234, no. 3 (January 23, 1982): 90–91.

Hughes, Catherine. "Soldiers at Sea." *America* Vol. 147, no. 17 (May 1, 1982): 343.

Hughes, Linda K., and Howard Faulkner. "The Role of Detection in *A Soldier's Play*." *Clues* Vol. 7, no. 2 (fall/winter 1986): 83–97.

Kerr, Walter. "A Fine New Work from a Forceful Playwright." *New York Times* (December 6, 1981): 3.

Oliver, Edith. "A Sergeant's Death." *New Yorker* Vol. 57, no. 42 (December 7, 1981): 110, 113–14.

Mavis Gallant

1922–

Canadian short story writer, novelist, and dramatist.

"Varieties of Exile" (short story, 1981)

Plot: Most of the story takes place during the third summer of World War II, when the narrator and protagonist, eighteen-year-old Linnet Muir, is working as a newspaper reporter in Montreal. Dissatisfied with her job and surroundings, Linnet spends her free time writing fiction and reading. She is particularly interested in Socialism and in the European refugees who have come to Montreal. On her commuter train, Linnet meets Englishman Frank Cairns, whom she identifies as a "Remittance Man." These are sons banished to various English colonies after serious disagreements with their fathers, supported by allowances from home, and doomed to live marginal, unfulfilling lives. Frank's claim that he is a Socialist is of particular interest to Linnet, who suspects that his convictions are based on second-hand knowledge. Linnet carries on a brief, apparently non-romantic relationship with Frank until she moves into Montreal and ceases riding the commuter train. When she later meets him in the city, Linnet learns that Frank is about to go overseas as an army officer. After telling him that she plans to marry, Linnet inexplicably begins to cry. Some time later, the now-married Linnet is living in Montreal with a friend (her husband having also gone overseas to fight) when she reads in a newspaper that Frank had been killed in the war. Linnet burns all of the fiction she had been writing during this period, and later concludes that her habit of manipulating reality in this way was another "variety of exile."

Characters: Gallant is an important contemporary writer acclaimed primarily for her finely crafted short stories, many of which have appeared in the *New Yorker* magazine. Critics uniformly praised *Home Truths*, the collection of stories in which "Varieties of Exile" appears, citing Gallant's characteristic attention to detail, precise prose, and sophisticated wit. Sometimes likened to the nineteenth-century Russian author Anton Chekhov for her ability to authentically create a slice of life in just a few pages, to blend comedy and despair, and to be sympathetic without sentimentality, Gallant often writes from the perspective of a character who is detached or alienated from what was once familiar. The problems and ambiguity of the Canadian identity are also particular concerns in her work.

The protagonist of the final six stories in *Home Truths* is **Linnet Muir**, whom many commentators have identified as an autobiographical character. An ardent writer of fiction, she is working as a reporter in Montreal after spending a portion of her childhood in the United States—circumstances that correspond with the facts of Gallant's early life. Eighteen years old when the story begins, Linnet is intelligent, independent, and obviously hungry for experience and understanding. Having been educated in New York, she feels out of place in Canada, where, she contends, respectability and the capacity to suppress feeling are valued above all else. She is dissatisfied by conventional romance because she feels too little is expected from the woman; she considers traditional wives frustrated "Red Queens" (a term taken from Lewis Carroll's *Through the Looking-Glass*) who constantly harangue their husbands and children; and she has come to realize that the men she works with do not consider her their equal. Meanwhile, Linnet has immersed herself in the literature of Socialism, reading the works of Lenin, Freud as well as such Russian authors as Fyodor Dostoyevsky. She is fascinated with the refugees who have been streaming into Montreal from various war-torn European countries. Linnet views these people as "prophets of a promised social order" in which justice and equality will prevail, and she incorporates them into her fiction, which she uses to untangle mysteries and work out her confusion. Thus it is not surprising that Linnet begins a story called "The Socialist RM" after meeting Frank Cairns, who embodies for her the type of the black sheep Englishman banished to the colonies. Just as she has fashioned the refugees after her own idea of how they should behave, she has a fixed idea of what Frank's life means. Later, however, in the wake of her shock at hearing that Frank has died in the war, Linnet burns this story and others written at around the same time, indicating her awareness that she may not have seen either Frank or the refugees she idealized with accuracy. Indeed, the older Linnet admits that she knew even then that "all this business of putting life through a sieve and then discarding it was another variety of exile."

Linnet claims that she only notices **Frank Cairns**, who she guesses is in his early thirties, on the computer train because he is so "hopelessly English" and fits the mold of what she has identified as the "Remittance Man." Critic Ronald Hatch lauded Gallant for her "particularly trenchant sociological analysis" of this type of individual, who apparently became obsolete after World War II. Linnet explains that Remittance Men are sent to Canada, South Africa, New Zealand, or Singapore in disgrace after offending their fathers in one of six ways (including refusing to enter a prescribed profession and homosexuality) and are supported by an allowance from home that precludes their having to work, although they sometimes do. Remittance Men have no particular sense of adventure, ability to fit in with their surroundings, or fitness to do anything; they seldom marry or reproduce and often spend their lives drifting or succomb to alcohol. Frank Cairns is married but childless and spent a short time in Ceylon before being sent home—ostensibly with malaria, but Linnet speculates that homesickness was the real cause—from whence he was shipped off to Canada. Linnet remembers Frank as a neat, small man with a brisk step who interested her primarily because he claimed to be a Socialist. This inclination seems to have been influenced by some more brilliant, philosophical friend from the past. Frank often refers reverently to the poor of England, although Linnet suspects he has no personal knowledge of or contact with them; his attitude is that their lot will never be improved but that they are happy as they are. Linnet considers Frank's unemphatically intoned comment that "Life has no point" his "true voice." The older Linnet admits that she treated Frank as a curio cabinet, the contents of which she blithely investigated without comprehending their true ambiguities or depth. The news of Frank's hero's death stuns Linnet, whose musings have not encompassed such a possibility and who later burns the story she had begun about this Socialist Remittance Man.

Further Reading

Abley, Mark. "Home Is Where Complacency Is." *Maclean's Magazine* 94, No. 45 (November 9, 1981): 74, 76, 78.

Contemporary Literary Criticism, Vols. 7, 18, 38. Detroit: Gale Research.

Grosskurth, Phyllis. "Close to Home." *Saturday Night* 96, No. 10 (November 1981): 68.

Hatch, Ronald. Review of *Home Truths: Selected Canadian Stories. Canadian Fiction Magazine* 43 (1982): 125-29.

Howard, Maureen. "When the Identity Is the Crisis." *New York Times Book Review* (May 5, 1985): 1.

Motion, Joanna. "Warfare in the Hinterland." *Times Literary Supplement* (February 2, 1986): 216.

Spencer, Elizabeth. "Mavis Gallant and the Canadian Scene." *Washington Post—Book World* (April 14, 1985): 1, 14.

Gabriel Garciá Márquez
1928–

Columbian novelist, short story writer, journalist, critic, scriptwriter, and dramatist.

Love in the Time of Cholera (*El amor en los Tiempos del colera;* novel, 1985)

Plot: Set in an unnamed town on the coast of Colombia, the novel spans the years 1880 to 1930. As it opens, septuagenarian Dr. Juvenal Urbino is examining the body of his friend Jeremiah de Saint-Amour, who committed suicide rather than face the pain and indignities of old age. Later that day, Urbino—a well-to-do, beloved physician who successfully battled the town's cholera epidemic—dies in a freak accident: chasing an escaped pet parrot, he falls out of a mango tree. At his funeral, his grieving widow, Fermina Daza, receives Florentino Ariza, an old suitor who informs her that his love for her is as strong as it was over fifty years ago. Fermina angrily dismisses Florentino from her home. Now the novel shifts back in time to the romance between Florentino and Fermina. A voracious reader with an extremely romantic nature, Florentino courts the beautiful young Fermina (daughter of a wealthy but disreputable mule dealer), sending her voluminous, ardent letters to which she responds with innocent passion. Determined that his daughter should not become the wife of a lowly telegraph operator, Lorenzo Daza sends Fermina on a long journey with her cousin Hildebranda. Upon her return, Fermina decides that she does not love Florentino after all, and she spurns him. She subsequently accepts the proposal of the town's most eligible bachelor, Dr. Juvenal Urbino, even though she is not in love with him either Florentino, meanwhile, decides that he will love Fermina for the rest of his life; nevertheless, he embarks on a series of 622 sexual liaisons—a number that does not include casual encounters. Having completely forgotten Florentino, Fermina settles into her role as the wife of a wealthy, prominent citizen and the mother of two fine children.

The narrative now returns to the time of Urbino's death. Despite Fermina's rejection, Florentino renews his attack on her heart, sending her letters in which he ruminates with mature eloquence on life, death, love, and aging. He finally wins Fermina's love, and the novel ends as the two septuagenarian lovers drift down the Magdalena River on a boat that, in order to protect their privacy, flies the yellow flag of cholera.

Characters: Winner of the Nobel Prize in literature in 1982, García Márquez is closely associated with the Latin American "boom" of the 1960s and 1970s, when a large number of significant works were translated into English and came to the attention of American critics and readers. In his highly acclaimed 1970 novel, *One Hundred Years of Solitude,* García Márquez employs the celebrated "magic realism" technique, which blends the mundane and the fantastic. *Love in the Time of Cholera,* which features less surrealism than its predecessor and more psychological revelations about its characters, was also critically lauded. Combining such realistic elements as war, disease, and environmental decay with a strong infusion of romance, the novel explores many manifestations of love, including the sexual, platonic, loveless, marital, and obsessive varieties. It also portrays love and eroticism in old age with humor and compassion. A few critics object to the self-indulgence and social irresponsibility of the main characters, but most find *Love in the Time of Cholera* a lyrical, compelling, and essentially optimistic tribute to long-lasting, ageless love and vitality.

The novel's principal romantic is **Florentino Ariza**, who lives out the very unmodern concept of a constant heart. A telegraph operator with a passion for music and books (he is a voracious reader of both classic and popular literature but especially of poetry), Florentino falls in love with the teenaged Fermina, who is teaching her aunt to read. And for the next fifty-one years, nine months, and four days—for the rest of his life, in fact—he continues to love her. García Márquez based this couple on his own parents, whose courtship took a similar course; indeed, the author's father was a telegraph operator who, like Florentino, sent his sweetheart telegrams while she was on a journey that was supposed to make her forget all about him. But whereas García Márquez's parents married, Florentino is spurned by his beloved, who then marries someone else. On the second of the three boat voyages that shape his life (the first is Fermina's, and the third is the final one they take together), Florentino resolves to love Fermina for the rest of his life. He then loses his virginity to another woman, which begins an erotic career that will include more than 622 liaisons. Florentino's irresistibility to women is described by Fermina's cousin Hildebranda, "He is ugly and sad, but he is all love." Florentino is so ruled by love that he finds himself unable to compose the simple business letters required for his job at the River Company of the Caribbean; he does, however, develop a comfortable sideline writing letters for the lovelorn. Despite his deficiency with business letters, Florentino has a highly successful career with the riverboat company, which he accomplishes in order to make himself worthy of Fermina's love. Florentino waits more than fifty years—until Urbino dies—to win Fermina back. Not deterred by Fermina's vehement rejection, he returns to his old habit of writing her long letters (with the important distinction that whereas his adolescent missives were effusively ardent and handwritten, these are typewritten and reflect the contemplative wisdom of a mature man). These ruminations on life and love prove to be what Fermina needs to hear, and she finally succumbs. When they consummate their affections, Florentino tells Fermina that he has remained a "virgin" for her, and despite his voluminous sexual history he has been faithful. For her part, Fermina recognizes this fidelity even though she knows very well that Florentino is no virgin. Critics praise García Márquez enthusiastically for his compassionate portrayal of love between these two aged protagonists. The persistent Florentino attests to the existence of undying love and that love may be most intense at the end of life, in defiance of the infirmities and indignities of old age.

When Florentino first sees **Fermina Daza,** she is the beautiful, haughty young daughter of a wealthy but disreputable horse dealer. Initially dazzled by Florentino, Fermina is sent on a journey by her father in the hope that she will become disenchanted with her suitor, and indeed his behavior now strikes her as exaggerated. Fermina's reasons for marrying Urbino, whom she does not love, are somewhat ambiguous and impress some critics as selfish or calculating: her father has informed her that he is financially ruined, so she may be looking out for her own material well-being; in addition, she has also told herself that she must be married by the age of twenty-one. In any case, her marriage begins without love but acquires it over time, and critics laud García Márquez's insightful portrayal of this ordinary yet successful union. Fermina demonstrates pride and stubbornness in the two episodes that bring about separations from her husband. The first involves her refusal to admit that she did not place soap in the bathroom; Urbino finally concedes to her. The second and longer separation occurs when her husband has an affair with another woman, but Fermina seems angriest that he took a black lover. Over the years with Urbino, Fermina admirably fulfills her role as ornament, companion, and mother of his children, even becoming something of the "great lady" her father envisioned. Yet she remains modest in her tastes and resistant to social hypocrisy, exhibiting a trace of populism or even of rebelliousness that may derive from her own never–specified origins. After Urbino's death, Fermina admits to herself that her life was borrowed from her husband, that she was essentially a highly paid servant in his house, a commentary on the options available to women of Fermina's time, place, and culture. By contrast, the elderly Fermina undertakes her relationship with Florentino in answer to her own needs and in defiance of social stereotypes.

Soon after Fermina returns from her journey and spurns Florentino, she is courted by the town's most eligible bachelor, **Dr. Juvenal Urbino**, a wealthy, refined physician who spent time overseas and prefers European ways. Wellborn and dapper, Urbino typifies the typical hero of a nineteenth-century romantic novel, and when Fermina does not respond, Urbino is inflamed. Just as Fermina has other reasons than love for deciding to marry him, Urbino is rational and unromantic in his desire to acquire Fermina as his wife. He knows that this lovely, charming, somewhat haughty young woman will make an appropriate mate for a prominent, upstanding citizen like himself. Although he is undoubtedly conceited, often weak, and chauvinistic in his attitude toward domestic arrangements, Urbino has significant positive qualities. His civic-mindedness and sincere desire for progress lead him to make a heroic, ultimately successful effort to combat cholera in his community. On a personal level, he treats the frightened Fermina with great tenderness during the first days of their marriage, which provides a solid foundation on which love may grow. She does come to love Urbino, and on the day of his death—which occurs in a decidedly ridiculous way for such a dignified man—he manages to stay alive long enough to tell her how much he has loved her. Many critics contrast Urbino with Florentino, particularly in regard to reading: while Urbino owns a set of identically and finely bound classics that he reads because he is supposed to read them, Florentino devours a wide variety of books with great gusto, whether they are ancient Greek poetry or the latest pulp novel, an approach García Márquez clearly sides with.

A number of minor characters animate the pages of _Love in the Time of Cholera_. The story begins with the self-inflicted death of **Jeremiah de Saint-Amour**, a photographer and chess enthusiast, which shocks his good friend, Dr. Urbino. After Saint-Amour commits suicide, keeping a promise he made to himself long ago to spare himself the troubles of old age, Urbino discovers that his friend was an escaped convict who once committed a brutal crime and secretly maintained a mulatto mistress in a ghetto hovel. Several critics note that the story of Saint-Amour and his devoted (if exploited) lover rehearses the themes of love, devotion, and aging that are explored in the course of the novel. The townspeople suspect **Lorenzo Daza**, Fermina's father, of being some kind of gangster or horse thief, but Daza turns out to be a dealer of illegal guns. Lorenzo wants Fermina to become a "great lady" and sends her on a long journey so she will forget about Florentino. With Fermina on this trip is her cousin **Hildebranda**; together they visit various telegraph offices to retrieve Florentino's messages to his sweetheart. The children of Fermina and Urbino are **Ofelia** and **Dr. Urbino Daza**. Ofelia is more snobbish and morally rigid than her mother, and she banishes Fermina from her home over her mother's relationship with Florentino. Although Dr. Urbino Daza (a physician like his father) is not as intolerant as his sister, he observes that the elderly should be segregated so that they are shielded from the sadness they must feel when they are around young people. The devotion of Florentino's mother, **Transito Arizo**, a pawnbroker who gave birth to him after an illicit affair, seems to veer into eroticism. She advises him not to overwhelm young Fermina with so many ardent letters, and she later helps him recover from the cholera-like symptoms of thwarted love. Another significant character in Florentino's life is his uncle **Leo XII Loayza**, who comes from a family in which all the male children were named after popes. Leo XII owns the riverboat company for which Florentino works. When his nephew claims that he is only interested in love, Leo XII observes that "without river navigation, there is no love."

Among the 622 women Florentino has had love affairs with, some of the most notable are the **Widow Nazaret**, whose tenderness over their thirty-year-relationship he appreciates greatly; **Olimpia Zuleta**, whose husband kills her when he learns of her infidelity with Florentino; **Sara Noriega**, who is eventually committed to a lunatic asylum where she sings obscene songs; and **America Vicuna**, the fourteen-year-old schoolgirl with whom the seventy-some-year-old Florentino is involved just before his reunion with Fermina and who commits suicide upon learning that he has left her. Other characters in the novel include **Escolastica**, Fermina's spinster aunt, who aids and abets the romance between her niece and Florentino and is ultimately banished from her brother's house. Escolastica also exemplifies the limited options open to women of this time and place. **Leona Cassini**, Florentino's devoted assistant, facilitates his ascent in the riverboat company by taking charge of many practical matters; his deepest fidelity is to Fermina, and she resists his sexual advances. **Barbara Lynch** is the black woman with whom Urbino has an affair, which causes a two-year rupture in his marriage.

Further Reading

Bell-Villada, Gene H. *Garciá Márquez: The Man and His Work.* Chapel Hill: University of North Carolina Press, 1990.

Bestsellers 89. Issue 1. Detroit: Gale Research, 1989: 19–21.

Carter, Angela. "Garciá Márquez: Sick with Love and Longing." *Book World—The Washington Post* (April 24, 1988): 1, 14.

Columbus, Claudette Kemper. "Faint Echoes and Faded Reflections: Love and Justice in the Time of Cholera." *Twentieth Century Literature* Vol. 38, no. 1: 89–99.

Contemporary Literary Criticism. Vols. 2, 3, 8, 10, 15, 27, 47, 55. Detroit: Gale Research.

McNerney, Kathleen. *Understanding Gabriel Garciá Márquez.* Columbia: University of South Carolina Press, 1989.

Oberhelman, Harley D. *Gabriel Garciá Márquez: A Study of the Short Fiction.* Boston: Twayne Publishers, 1991.

Pynchon, Thomas. "The Heart's Eternal Vow." *New York Times Book Review* (April 10, 1988): 1, 47, 49.

Simons, Marlise. "Garciá Márquez on Love, Plagues and Politics." *New York Times Book Review* (February 21, 1988): 1, 23–25.

Simpson, Mona. "Love Letters." *London Review of Books* Vol. 10, no. 15 (September 1, 1988): 22–24.

Wood, Michael. "Heartsick." *New York Review of Books* Vol. 35, no. 7 (April 28, 1988): 6, 8–9.

Ellen Gilchrist

1935–

American short story writer, novelist, poet, and scriptwriter.

"In the Land of Dreamy Dreams" (short story, 1981)

Plot: The story takes place in May of 1977 in New Orleans. As it opens, LaGrande MacGruder has driven onto the Huey P. Long Bridge, from which she drops three tennis rackets and a can of tennis balls, resolving never to play tennis again. The story then backtracks to recount the events that have led to this action. LaGrande is at least a third-generation member of the once-exclusive New Orleans Lawn Tennis Club, which has recently been infiltrated by players deemed nouveau-riche by its longtime members. One such intruder is Roxanne Miller, who is not only newly wealthy but Jewish and who has a slight physical disability. Roxanne finally talks LaGrande into a tennis match, and is in the process of beating her when LaGrande intentionally miscalls one of Roxanne's serves. Rattled, Roxanne loses the next twelve games and LaGrande takes the match. Watching this sequence of events is elderly, aristocratic Claiborne Redding, who has been harboring a simmering antagonism toward Roxanne and the changes she represents. After discarding her tennis rackets and balls, LaGrande goes on a shopping spree to cheer herself up, then heads for the Country Club to find someone to have sex with.

Characters: Gilchrist is critically acclaimed for her short stories chronicling the decline of the Southern aristocracy, often from the perspective of upper-class female characters. Like much of Gilchrist's fiction, the title story of her much-praised volume *In the Land of Dreamy Dreams* is set in New Orleans and features a narrative voice that is revealing but also maintains an ironic distance.

The story's central character is **LaGrande MacGruder**, a member of a New Orleans family that has (unlike that of Roxanne Miller) been wealthy for many generations. Tennis is also a long-standing family pursuit: LaGrande's grandfather was once the president of the U.S. Lawn Tennis Association, and she herself has been playing for four or five hours a day, whenever possible, since she was very young. Clearly, tennis is an important part of her life, which is otherwise occupied mainly with shopping, lunching at the New Orleans Country Club, and sexual liaisons with a variety of partners. Like other characters in Gilchrist's fiction, LaGrande is a snob who resents the encroachment of people like Roxanne on the territory formerly dominated by her and her fellow WASPish New Orleans aristocrats. LaGrande agrees to a tennis match with Roxanne only because she wants to impress a potential lover with her largesse toward someone they both recognize as an intruder. LaGrande goes into the match assuming she will win, but planning not to hit any of the overhead lobs that the disabled Roxanne might not be physically capable of reaching. She is shocked to find that Roxanne is an excellent tennis player, and that even resorting to lobs won't ensure a victory. Determined not to be beaten by this interloper, LaGrande violates the code of honor that has been a mainstay of her society, calling out a serve that both players know is within bounds. Although this action leads to LaGrande's winning the match, it also seems to produce an upheaval in her psyche, for she not only gives up tennis but drives around for a while "thinking of things to do with the rest of her life." At the end of the story, however, LaGrande has consoled herself with an extravagant shopping excursion and the anticipation of a sexual dalliance.

Referred to by LaGrande as "the crippled girl," **Roxanne Miller** is actually only slightly disabled, with one leg slightly shorter than the other. Her husband's recently acquired wealth and influence in the financial community led to the couple's being allowed to join the tennis club, which had previously had only one rarely present Jewish member. Roxanne has since made a massive effort to become an integral part of this exclusive realm. She not only spends much of her time organizing new activities but much of her money on equipment and lessons. Envisioning herself as "a sort of Greek figure of justice" and apparently motivated by a desire for both revenge and acceptance, Roxanne plots to beat the other, aristocratic tennis players one by one. Overjoyed when she finally corners the unusually resistant LaGrande into a match, Roxanne fantasizes about first beating LaGrande and then having a comradely lunch with her. Thus she is profoundly shocked—as evidenced by the immediate decline in her skill—to learn that LaGrande has no intention of losing to someone like her and will even resort to cheating to avoid such a loss.

Elderly **Claiborne Redding** is a denizen of the old southern aristocracy who sees LaGrande (the daughter of his long-ago doubles partner) as defending that rapidly disappearing order. Having been persuaded into allowing the Millers to join the tennis club by cronies cognizant of their wealth and influence, Claiborne deeply resents Roxanne's presence and her presumptuous interference in how the club operates. When he sees that LaGrande is losing her match with Roxanne, he debates whether his appearance on the balcony above the court will help or hinder LaGrande. He chooses to appear and thus witnesses LaGrande's breach of honor, to which he feels he was a party. Despite his deep desire for LaGrande to win the match, Claiborne is dispirited enough by her action to reflect that he has outlived his time and place and that his familiar society is now being "besieged by the children of the poor carrying portable radios and boxes of fried chicken."

Other characters in the story include **Semmes Talbot**, a witty, well-connected psychiatrist and tennis player from Washington who agrees with LaGrande that Roxanne "certainly has her nerve!" and who sleeps with LaGrande but leaves New Orleans without planning to see her again; and **Nailor**, the elderly black man who has been the club's groundskeeper, "arbiter of manners," and tennis expert (even though he has himself never played) for many years and who hates the new members even more than Claiborne.

Further Reading

Allen, Bruce. "American Short Fiction Today." *New England Review* Vol. 4, no. 3 (Spring 1982): 478–88.

Contemporary Literary Criticism Vols. 34, 48. Detroit: Gale Research.

Crace, Jim. "The Cold-Eyed Terrors." *Times Literary Supplement* no. 4150 (October 15, 1982): 1142.

Smith, Wendy. Interview with Ellen Gilchrist. *Publisher's Weekly* Vol. 239, no. 12 (March 2, 1992): 46–7.

Thompson, Jeanie, and Garner, Anita Miller. "The Miracle of Realism: The Bid for Self-Knowledge in the Fiction of Ellen Gilchrist." *Southern Quarterly* Vol. 22, no. 1 (Fall 1983): 101–14.

Wood, Susan. "Louisiana Stories: The Debut of Ellen Gilchrist." *Book World—Washington Post* (March 21, 1982): 4, 13.

Natalia Ginzburg
1916–

Italian novelist, short story writer, critic, essayist, biographer, autobiographer, journalist, and dramatist.

All Our Yesterdays (*Tutti i nostri ieri,* translation published as *Dead Yesterdays* and *A Light for Fools*; novel, 1953)

Plot: Set in a provincial town in northern Italy, the novel begins in the late 1930s (during the years of Mussolini's fascist dictatorship) and ends in 1945, after World War II. It centers on the adolescent members of two families who live on the same street and who become close friends. Ippolito, Giustino, Concettina, and Anna are the motherless children of a well-to-do lawyer who quits his profession to write a book condemning the fascists. The father eventually grows frustrated with his efforts and burns his manuscript before he dies. After his death, the children are cared for by Signora Maria, once their mother's companion. The other family's children—whose now-dead father was a wealthy factory owner—are Amalia, Emmanuele, and Giuma.

When sixteen-year-old Anna becomes pregnant by the carefree Giuma, he flees the scene, recommending that she have an abortion. Reluctant to do so but also unwilling to reveal her pregnancy to her family, the desperate Anna is finally rescued by Cenzo Reno, an eccentric friend of her father's who offers to marry her. The couple move to southern Italy, where Cenzo is a well-liked, philanthropic landowner who sympathizes with the peasants rather than the fascists. In her new home, Anna must adjust to an unfamiliar culture; she must also overcome her childish lack of connection with the world in which she lives. She is aided by her warmhearted husband, whom she grows to love.

When war breaks out in Italy, Anna's brother Ippolito commits suicide as a protest against the fascists. After the Germans march into the country, a German soldier is accidentally killed in Cenzo's house by an Italian army deserter who had been offered shelter there. In order to save others' lives, Cenzo takes responsibility for the death and is executed by the Germans. When the war ends, Anna returns with her child to her old home in the north. Despite their many losses, she and her brother Giustino find comfort in each other's presence and in their memories of the past.

Characters: Ginzburg is among Italy's most respected contemporary authors, and *All Our Yesterdays* is considered one of her finest achievements. It provides a portrait of Italian life from the mid-1930s to 1945, chronicling the experiences of a strongly antifascist family during the turbulent years of Mussolini's dictatorship and World War II. Ginzburg's spare, disarmingly direct style results in an understated narrative through which sudden violence or tragedy occasionally flashes. She builds her characterizations not so much through direct description as through accumulated details and the observations of other characters, creating personages who, though often flawed, are quite memorable. Ginzburg's sad but likable characters—with their pathetic tendency to hope that happiness will arrive at some distant, future time—have been compared to those of nineteenth-century Russian dramatist and short story writer Anton Chekhov. In the face of the social and political upheaval that has affected their world so drastically, the characters in *All Our Yesterdays* attempt to live decently and to defend themselves by shoring up the memories they hold in common.

Identified as Ginzburg's alter ego, quiet, passive **Anna** is an observant though inarticulate young woman whose passage to adulthood is chronicled in the novel. When the story begins, Anna is a plump, pale, rather lazy teenager dazzled by talkative, art- and poetry-loving Giuma, who abandons her as soon as she becomes pregnant. Never adept at expressing herself, frightened Anna is no more able to tell her family about her pregnancy than to seek an abortion; thus they are surprised and dismayed when she agrees to marry the much older Cenzo Rena. But Cenzo rescues Anna from a disastrous situation, and through this and many other acts of kindness he eventually gains her love. Cenzo also attempts to prod Anna into a broader awareness, scolding her about being an "insect" who sees only the branch on which she is perched. He encourages her to develop convictions and become a "real person." Anna is forced to take a more realistic and active role in life as the outside world alters her own. Cenzo is killed by the Germans, Giustino goes off to fight with the Italian Resistance movement, Ippolito commits suicide, and Signora Maria is killed in a bombing raid. Nevertheless, when the war finally ends and Anna returns with her baby to her old home in the north, she finds solace with Giustino, sharing memories of the loved ones now gone and of the old days. With a frail hope centered—as in much of Ginzburg's work—in the remnants of a family, Anna rediscovers refuge in a fragmented world.

Cenzo Rena has been judged one of the most admirable of all Ginzburg's characters and certainly as one of her very few admirable men. An eccentric, wealthy landowner in southern Italy, Cenzo is a benevolent patriarch to the peasants of his village, siding with their interests against the fascist government. He extends his generosity to the desperate, abandoned Anna when he offers to marry her, and he performs many small acts of caring for his friends, relatives, and acquaintances. He even pities the German soldiers, perceiving the humanity beneath their uniforms and commenting that most were probably humble waiters before the outbreak of war. Cenzo figures in Anna's personal growth by rescuing her from her unwed mother status and urging her to expand her outlook. He encourages her to develop courage and a skeptical awareness of politics, which inevitably effects everyone. Cenzo disapproves of Ippolito's suicide, whatever the young man's convictions. Believing that human beings are obliged to endure their lives, no matter how bleak their circumstances, Cenzo regards suicide as a negative, meaningless act. Yet Cenzo sacrifices himself so others may be spared, reflecting his positive approach to social problems. The death of this good man attests to the blind slaughter of war.

The other members of Anna's family include her **father**, a Jewish lawyer and antifascist. Prone to sudden mood changes, he abandons the law to write a book, which he eventually tosses into the fire. Like other fathers in Ginzburg's work, this one is thought to have been modeled after her own, whose kindness alternated with frightening spells of violent anger. **Signora Maria**, once a companion to Anna's mother, raises the four children after her mistress's death. Often overwhelmed by this difficult role, she takes solace in remembering the more luxurious life she once led. Signora Maria becomes another casualty of war when she is killed during an American air raid while trying to save some household items. Anna's siblings include **Concettina**, the older sister who teaches her what the world expects of women; and **Giustino**, a resistance fighter during the war. Later he finds university studies and work difficult to adjust to. At the end of the novel, Anna and Giustino take comfort from their shared memories. Anna's other brother, **Ippolito**, kills himself in despair when the fascists gain power. this hopeless act of rebellion highlights the need to express personal feelings, as Ippolito's grieving siblings discover when they search the past for some clue to their brother's despair.

Across the street from Anna and her siblings are their teenaged friends **Amalia, Emmanuele,** and **Giuma**. Talkative, self-important Giuma becomes Anna's lover, dazzling her with his interest in movies, art, and poetry. When she learns she is pregnant, he recommends an abortion, and when Anna refuses, Giuma abandons her. After the war, Giuma feels guilty for having fled to Switzerland to avoid fighting, but he is comforted by a psychiatrist who assures him that Italians were not meant to take sides in such conflicts. Giuma eventually marries an American woman with a passion for social reform.

No Way (*Caro Michele*, translation published as *Dear Michael*; novel, 1973)

Plot: Set in the early 1970s, the novel is composed of thirty-six letters to and from a young Italian named Michele. The product of an upper-middle-class family, Michele is forced to leave Rome for England due to his leftist political activism. During his year of exile he writes to his mother, Adriana, and his sometime girlfriend, Mara, who has given birth to a baby that may or may not be Michele's. *No Way* chronicles a series of events and episodes, including Michele's short marriage to an alcoholic American physicist. As the novel ends, the reader learns that Michele has been killed by fascist terrorists during a student demonstration in Bruges, Belgium.

Characters: Written in an epistolary style that interweaves the perspectives of a number of different characters, the novel portrays the last year in the life of an exiled artist. *No Way* is considered one of Ginzburg's most pessimistic works, for the fiction of this highly acclaimed Italian writer is infused with the damage wrought by social upheaval on human relationships. Despite being passive and unable to commit to anything or anyone, Ginzburg's characters arouse in the reader interest and affection, and the writer's compassion for them is evident. As many critics have noted, these hopeless but likable characters resemble those created by renowned nineteenth-century Russian writer Anton Chekhov. In Ginzburg's earlier works the family was portrayed as potentially stifling, but as a necessary, stabilizing force, whereas *No Way* highlights the debilitating effects of divorce and generational conflict and suggests that reminiscence is the human race's only refuge in the face of suffering.

Although **Michele** is the central figure in *No Way,* he persists throughout as an ambiguous, enigmatic character. He is portrayed almost entirely through the letters written by others, and his own correspondence is brief and reticent. A young Italian from an upper-middle-class family, Michele becomes involved in some unspecified left-wing activities, which result in having to escape from Rome to London to avoid arrest. He is an artist of minimal talent—he paints only collapsing houses with owls watching over them. Although briefly married to an alcoholic American nuclear physicist, Michele is suspected of being homosexual—as a child he often preferred female roles in games, his interests were more domestic than his wife's, and he is uncomfortable with traditional male ambitions. Michele's inability to commit wholeheartedly to work, relationships, or even the political cause that ended in his exile typify the "curdling of aspirations and enfeebling of powers" (according to L. E. Sissman in the *New Yorker*) that all of the novel's characters experience. Michele's violent death symbolizes the death of their hopes and their misperception of him as stronger than he was ever capable of being. In the end, they have only their memories of Michele to comfort them.

In her letters to Michele, his beautiful, aging mother, **Adriana**, blends inquiring messages of concern for him with accounts of events in her own life, such as her failed love affair. Critics have noted that she differs from the female characters in Ginzburg's earlier novels by being exuberant and bold, reflecting the shift in Italian women's roles from the background of society to the foreground. Adriana voices the angst of the generation that came to maturity during and after World War II when she says that people her son's age "have never been young, so how can they grow old?" The only one of Michele's correspondents who remains in one place, Adriana represents the last remnant of stable family life. After Michele has died, she writes to her former lover to ask him to send her the words of an old song she once heard him singing with her son, as if collecting the sweet memories of the past against the suffering of the present.

Mara has been Michele's girlfriend at some point or points in the past, and her baby may or may not be his. A rootless "flower child," Mara lives a nomadic life, moving from apartment to apartment, carrying with her a plastic suitcase in which her baby sleeps. The infant's fatherlessness (its parentage is never settled) may symbolize the breakdown of the family, a development Ginzburg laments in several of her recent novels. In one of her letters to Michele, Mara expresses with honest stoicism one of the novel's major themes: "The important thing is to keep walking and to distance ourselves from the things that make us cry."

Other characters in *No Way* include Michele's friend (and possibly his lover) **Osvaldo**, a gentle but exploited bookseller; Osvaldo's domineering and wealthy, socially prominent wife, **Ada**; **Angelica**, Michele's sister, who dutifully disposes of a gun for him after he leaves Rome; and **Viola**, his other sister, the only member of the family who believes he is homosexual.

Further Reading

Bowe, Clotilde Soave. "The Narrative Strategy of Natalia Ginzburg." *Modern Language Review* (October 1973): 788–95.

Bullock, Alan. *Natalia Ginzburg: Human Relationships in a Changing World.* New York: St. Martin's Press, 1991.

Contemporary Literary Criticism. Vols. 5, 11, 54. Detroit: Gale Research.

Cunningham, Valentine. "Griding Mistress." *New Statesman* Vol. 89, no. 2293 (February 28, 1975): 284.

Harris, Daniel. "To the Letter." *Nation* (New York) Vol. 247, no. 17 (December 5, 1987): 686–88.

Lobner, Corinna del Greco. "A Lexicon for Both Sexes: Natalia Ginzburg and the Family Saga." In *Contemporary Women Writers in Italy: A Modern Renaissance.* Ed. Santo L. Aricò. Amherst: University of Massachusetts Press, 1990, 27–42.

Merry, Bruce. *Women in Modern Italian Literature: Four Studies Based on the Works of Grazia Deledda, Alba de Cespedes, Natalia Ginzburg and Dacia Maraini.* Townsville, Queensland, Australia: James Cook University of North Queensland, 1990.

O'Healy, Anne-Marie. "Natalia Ginzburg and the Family." *Canadian Journal of Italian Studies* nos. 9, no. 32 (spring 1986): 21–36.

Piclardi, Rosetta D. "Forms and Figures in the Novels of Natalia Ginzburg." *World Literature Today* Vol. 53, no. 4 (autumn 1979): 585–89.

Signorelli-Pappas, Rita. "Lives in Letters." *The Women's Review of Books* Vol. 5, no. 3 (December 1987): 14.

Sissman, L. E. Review of *No Way. New Yorker* (October 21, 1974).

Slonim, Mark. "Wreckage of War." *New York Times Book Review* (January 6, 1957): 5.

Spice, Nicholas. "Ashes." *London Review of Books* Vol. 7, no. 22 (December 19, 1985): 17–18.

Thompson, John. Review of *No Way. New York Review of Books* (January 23, 1975).

Gail Godwin
1937–
American novelist, short story writer, and essayist.

A Mother and Two Daughters (novel, 1982)

Plot: Set primarily in North Carolina, most of the novel takes place between December 1978 and summer 1979, with the final section taking place in 1984. As the novel opens, Nell and Leonard Strickland, residents of Mountain City, North Carolina, attend a party at the home of their friend Theodora Blount. Shortly thereafter, Leonard dies of a heart attack, and the Strickland daughters arrive for the funeral. Older daughter Cate Galitsky is a twice-divorced English professor at a near-bankrupt college in Iowa, and her sister, Lydia Mansfield, is a homemaker and mother of two boys who has just left her husband and entered college. The novel chronicles these three women as they adjust to the changing circumstances of their lives. The widowed Nell must redefine her position in her community and determine how to fill her days, while Cate deals with tenuous employment and a wealthy man's desire to marry her. Meanwhile, Lydia excels in her studies, acquires a lover, and lands a good job as a television personality. The next summer Nell and her daughters converge at the family's cottage on North Carolina's Ocracoke Island. Nell experiences renewed grief, old resentments between Cate and Lydia explode into an argument, and the cottage burns down. The novel's final section takes place five years later at a party; the sisters have reconciled, and all three women have taken important steps in their lives: Cate teaches on a free-lance basis, Lydia enjoys success in her television career, and Nell remarries and resumes her nursing professions.

Character: Godwin is lauded for her convincing portrayals of intelligent, sensitive characters who adjust to personal and social changes and develop their individual identities. Considered an improvement on her earlier novels due to its expansiveness and compassionate tone, *A Mother and Two Daughters* considers the question—as voiced by one of the protagonists in a discussion about Nathaniel Hawthorne's 1850 novel *The Scarlet Letter*— "Can the individual survive in the society in which it has to live?" Infused with a sense that family is the source of both stability as well as conflict, the novel affirms the values of connecting with others and meeting life's challenges with enthusiasm.

Although Godwin divides her attention between three central characters, **Cate Galiskey** dominates the narrative. She does not garnish the most sympathy, however. Two divorces attest to fierce independence and resistance, symbolized (somewhat too obviously, according to some commentators) by her persistently uplifted chin. Cate also has occasional bouts of self-righteousness and self-pity and has been known to reject love and comfort. Cate differs significantly from her mother and sister. Whereas Nell favored social conformity, idealistic Cate was jailed in 1970 for demonstrating against the U.S. invasion of Cambodia and continues to "sacrifice people to ideals." Unlike Lydia, Cate is intuitive in approach and often strikes out impetuously. After her argument with Lydia, Cate takes a long walk on the cold, windy beach and consequently contracts Bell's Palsy, a temporary numbing of the facial muscles. This sobering experience reminds her to temper her idealism and impulsiveness with self-control. At the end of *A Mother and Two Daughters*, Cate reconciles with her sister and resolves her employment dilemma; free-lancing requires her to market her teaching skills, and seems better suited to her personality than her previous position.

Nell Strickland has lived in Mountain City for most of her life and is a well-liked member of her community, but she has always viewed her surroundings with something of an outsider's eye. Out of respect for her gentle husband, Nell suppresses her sense of satire and refrains from being too critical, just as she realizes that Leonard also protects her. After Leonard's death, Nell must review their life together and judge to what extent her personality was shaped by their union and how she will conduct herself on her own. As the novel draws to a close, Nell begins to become more involved with others: after helping her old friend Merle through the final stages of cancer, Nell decides to return to nursing, and she also marries her friend's widower.

In contrast with her older sister, **Lydia Mansfield** has always seemed practical, conventional, always conforming to social expectations. Pretty, feminine, and nurturing, Lydia ran her domestic life efficiently for sixteen years, the only symptom of any deep-seated discontent being her need for frequent naps. Significantly, after Lydia leaves her husband, returns to college, and establishes a career, she no longer needs naps. Although successful in her studies, relationships, and employment, Lydia is still insecure at the conclusion of *A Mother and Two Daughters*. She resents it when Cate criticizes her for wanting to be "admired and influential" within traditional society, and Lydia still feels inadequate before her bold, independent sister. Nevertheless, she has a supportive, devoted lover and an interesting, challenging job, and she seems well equipped to cope with whatever life may bring her.

Several critics note that *A Mother and Two Daughters* features several positively portrayed male characters. One of the most prominent (though he dies at the beginning of the novel) is the gentle, **Leonard Strickland**, the husband of Nell and the father of Cate and Lydia. An introspective, idealistic lawyer, Leonard instills in his wife and daughters the importance of family connections. Another supportive male is podiatrist **Stanley Edelman**, Lydia's lover. The Stricklands' eccentric, disfigured **Uncle Osgood**, who lost his nose in World War I, is a good-hearted person who plays a redemptive role in the novel. Cate evades the pressure of pesticide manufacturer **Roger Jernigan**, to marry him; his personality is as strong and independent as hers. By contrast, Nell marries **Marcus Chapin**, a retired Episcopal priest and the widower of her old school friend, **Merle Chapin**, whose dying Nell eases. Lydia's husband, **Max Mansfield**, is an upwardly mobile, rather stuffy, but pleasant banker.

Other characters in *A Mother and Two Daughters* include the overbearing, nosy **Theodora Blount**, a leading social force in Mountain City and a repository of traditional, conservative southern values. Theodora's protegee and, as it turns out, distant cousin **Wickie Lee** is a country girl whose out-of-wedlock pregnancy hints at the fading of the old values but who eventually achieves respectability. Also reflecting the changing social atmosphere of the South are Lydia's son **Leo Mansfield** and his black fiancee, **Camilla Peverall-Watson**, whose relationship would not previously have been sanctioned.

A Southern Family (novel, 1987)

Plot: Set primarily in the town of Mountain City, North Carolina, the novel begins with the Quick family gathering to celebrate the birthday of its matriarch, Lily. Present are Lily's husband, Ralph, her daughter (from a previous marriage), Clare Campion, who is a successful novelist who lives in New York, sons Theo and Rafe, and Clare's longtime friend Julia Richardson Lowndes. Twenty-eight-year-old Theo has failed at in both career and marriage and has recently returned to his parents' home with his three-year-old son, Jason; Rafe, twenty-six, is a "professional" graduate student who drinks too much. The day after the party, Theo dies with his current girlfriend in an apparent murder-suicide. The novel chronicles how each of Theo's stunned family members reacts to his death, and there are also observations by Julia and Snow Mullins, Theo's ex-wife. Clare recalls Theo's comment, made the night of the birthday party, that she always neatly resolves her characters' problems. Almost as if he were alluding to himself, Theo had asked "Why don't you write a book about something that can never be wrapped up?" Clare returns to New York and destroys the novel she had been working on. She eventually returns to North

Carolina, and visits Snow's family, her own parents, and Julia, all the while searching for the meaning of her brother's life and death and her own narrative voice. Eventually Clare writes a letter to the deceased Theo describing her new novel, which closely resembles *A Southern Family*.

Characters: Cited by many critics as one of Godwin's most successful novels, *A Southern Family* receives praise for realistic detail and psychological depth. The novel's complex structure and extensive cast cause it to be compared to the novels of the Victorian period. Godwin employs multiple narrative perspectives of the various family members and friends on the death of Theo, each mirroring an intensely personal viewpoint. Like Godwin's previous novels, *A Southern Family* presents family as an entity both close and divided, both nurturing and constrictive, emphasizing that each member must be allowed to achieve personal fulfillment rather than conform to the expectations of others. Godwin also reflects on such aspects of the writer's vocation as the relationship between art and real life and the storyteller's struggle to locate his or her "true subject."

Forty-two-year-old **Clare Campion** is a writer who flees the South where she grew up, yet achieves success writing novels about the eccentric charm of southern life and people. Clare is autobiographical in her approach to fiction and in the circumstances of her personal life; like Godwin, she is the daughter of a woman who once aspired to be a writer and the half-sister of a troubled young man who killed himself and his girlfriend. Theo's death sparks Clare's search for insight into her profession and her brother, which emerge as central concerns in the narrative, to which other characters contribute their perspective. Clare resents Theo's remark that her novels have neat resolutions, she says she has always aspired to write fiction that is "deep-breathing, reflective, and with that patience for detail I admired in those medieval stone-carvers who would lavish their skills on the lowliest gargoyle because . . . that was their job for the day, and every day's work was done for the glory of God." Theo's remark makes Clare wonder if she has modeled her novels not after the realities of life but after her wishes about life. Clare also realizes that she had shut her troubled brother out of her consciousness because he didn't fit into her vision of life. She ponders that Theo became what she might have become had she stayed in Mountain City, and she feels guilty for having left him there to serve as their parents' "battleground." Near the end of the novel, Clare begins a new novel that resembles this one—with complex human problems and issues that can be explored but not resolved. In addition, Clare's exchange with Felix's daughter—in which she refrains from voicing her own reservations about **Lizzie**'s decision to marry a Hasidic Jew and become a traditional, obedient wife—suggests that in personal matters she has learned to allow others their true, particular natures.

Like Godwin's own mother, **Lily Quick** is an intelligent woman who, as a young widow, supported herself through her writing (Lily was a newspaper reporter, while Godwin's mother wrote romance novels), but she abandoned this activity after her second marriage. Although Clare contends that Ralph steals Lily's independence, the truth seems to be that Lily relinquishes it voluntarily in favor of material security. Lily's relationship with Ralph is initially quite passionate, but as that early ardor fades the differences in their backgrounds and interests become prominent and their antagonism grows. From a more genteel background than her husband, Lily becomes the kind of snobbish, censorious woman she once scorned, complete with a detached, imperious manner. Her habit of driving around with her car's gas tank nearly empty is an apt metaphor for her life: in becoming someone who would never pump her own gas at the self-service gas stations that now dot America, Lily is spiritually and emotionally "running on empty." Theo's tragic death leads her to confront this truth about herself; as she trudges up the hill toward her house after running out of gas, she wishes for a "spiritual second wind" and for the power to "die" and let others be themselves and not expect them to conform to her vision. Toward the end of *A Southern Family*, Lily again climbs up the hill, this time in the company of Sister Patrick, and their conversation reveals that she is beginning to allow those around her to exercise their own perspectives.

Whereas Lily comes from southern gentility, **Ralph Quick** was raised in poverty in the North Carolina mountains. At the same time that he aspires to higher social status, he flaunts his crude manners and keeps his driveway strewn with junk. Interviewed for a local newspaper soon after he returned from World War II, Ralph expressed his goals: to marry, raise children, and live in a big house on top of a hill. Although he achieves all of these things, he is not content, and Ralph expresses his lingering unhappiness through his provocative behavior. Several critics note that Ralph is a sympathetic character despite his unpleasant qualities; for example, Clare blames Ralph for Lily's crushed hopes and loss of independence, but it turns out that Lily begged Ralph to take care of her, and he has felt cheated of his youth ever since.

One of the novel's most important characters, despite his death very early in the story, is Clare's twenty-eight-year-old half-brother, **Theo Quick**. Like Godwin's own half-brother, Theo dies violently, apparently at his own hand and after killing his estranged girlfriend. His death throws the family into emotional turmoil, and through Theo, Godwin explores the tendency families have of categorizing its members, fixing them in molds that may not reflect their true nature or aspirations. In life Theo was thought to be charming but inept, a perpetual failure, and less attractive and intelligent than either of his siblings. A misfit in the Quick family, Theo both rebelled against them and sought their approval; as his ex-wife, Snow, points out, he could neither push himself to succeed nor separate himself from his family and their ideas of success.

Clare's best friend, **Julia Richardson Lowndes**, a history professor in her early forties, suggests to Clare that perhaps Theo's death can bring her heightened insight. She observes that the Quicks "didn't give life a chance to express itself; they were busy making it over into what they'd rather see." Julia is the dutiful southern girl who sacrificed herself for the benefit of her ailing parents and now wonders if she has given up too much. She is portrayed, however, as a nurturing, responsible person, very different from her selfish, status-conscious mother. Some critics feel that the unfailingly trustworthy, supportive Julia lacks dimension and is present primarily as a sounding board for Clare.

Many commentators single out the section of the novel narrated by **Snow Mullins**, Theo's former wife and the mother of his young son, as particularly effective. Pretty, aloof, and self-assured, Snow is uneducated but smart, the proud daughter of a big clan of mountain people who live in tiny, remote Granny Squirrel, North Carolina. During her marriage to Theo, Snow has refused to accommodate herself to the ambitions of the Quick family and particularly to the efforts of Lily—whom she terms the Queen Mother—to fashion her into a more suitable mate for her son. As an outsider, Snow has developed some highly perceptive observations about the Quicks. She recognizes their self-dramatization, noting: "It's like they're all acting in a play or something. Each one's got himself a part, and they have to stay in that part as long as they're around the others." As for the troubled Theo, Snow recognizes that she has seen him as he really was, unlike his family, who "never allowed [him] to live his own life or be his own self." Snow also has opinions about Clare's fiction: "She makes up lies about real people and writes them down in books and makes lots of money off the lies."

Other characters in the novel include Clare's older, amiable lover, **Felix Rohr**, who voices an important theme of the novel when he describes the artist's "true subject" as "the truth he can no longer escape rather than the illusions he has been longing to make true." Clare's other half-brother, **Rafe**, is a good-looking, arrogant, possibly alcoholic graduate student who has always been considered the "smart" brother; after Theo's death, Rafe expresses to his psychiatrist his shame over his brother's steady "sinking" into failure. The Quicks' elderly neighbor, **Alicia Gallant,** represents the fast-disappearing southern gentility to which she and even Ralph—who certainly never belonged to it himself—still nostalgically cling. **Sister Patrick**, a friend of the family who taught several of the Quick children in the local Catholic school, provides another perspective on the events in the novel. The energetic, good-humored nun interprets Lily's dream about walking up the hill to her school with Theo, who explains that he wants to wash his hands; Sister Patrick assures Lily that the dream is a sign that Theo wants his loved one to forgive him. Theo's three-year-old son, **Jason**, is the subject of a bitter custody dispute between the Quicks and his mother, which Snow finally wins; he has the ability to move easily between the very different worlds of Granny Squirrel and his grandparents' home.

Further Reading

Allen, John Alexander. "Researching Her Salvation: The Fiction of Gail Godwin." *Hollins Critic* Vol. 25, No. 2 (April 1988): 1–9.

Breslin, John B. Review of *A Mother and Two Daughters. America* Vol. 146, no. 15 (April 17, 1982): 305.

Contemporary Literary Criticism. Vols. 5, 8, 22, 31, 69. Detroit: Gale Research.

Dictionary of Literary Biography Vol. 6. Detroit: Gale Research.

Heeger, Susan. "Write What You Can't Know." *Los Angeles Times Book Review* (October 4, 1987): 1, 13.

Hendin, Josephine. "Renovated Lives." *New York Times* (January 10, 1982): 3, 14.

Hill, Jane. *Gail Godwin.* Boston: Twayne Publishers, 1992.

Lowry, Beverly. "Back Home in Carolina." *New York Times Book Review* (October 11, 1987): 1, 28.

Rogers, Kim Lacy. "A Mother's Story in a Daughter's Life: Gail Godwin's *A Southern Family*." In *Mother Puzzles: Daughters and Mothers in Contemporary Literature.* Ed. Mickey Pearlman. Greenwood Press, 1989, pp. 59–66.

Taliaferro, Frances. "'Dream Daughter' Grows Up." *New York Times Book Review* (January 27, 1985): 7.

Tyler, Anne. "All in the Family." *New Republic* Vol. 186, no. 7 (February 17, 1982): 39–40.

Yardley, Jonathan. "Gail Godwin: Reflection and Renewal." *Book World—The Washington Post* (September 13, 1987): 3.

Isaac Goldemberg
1945–
Peruvian novelist and poet.

The Fragmented Life of Don Jacobo Lerner (novel, 1976)

Plot: The novel opens in 1935 on the night before the title character's death and recounts his experiences during the twelve preceding years. Lerner fled Russia for Peru in 1923 to escape the pogroms against the Jews. Initially he planned to marry a Jewish girl and become a prosperous member of Lima's Jewish community, but instead he joined his friend León Mitrani in the small town of Chepén. He then learned that Mitrani's marriage to a local Catholic woman made Mitrani feel alienated from his wife's society and his own faith. Jacobo established himself in Chepén and was even sought as a son-in-law by the family of Bertila Wilson, but his fear of repeating Mitrani's experiences caused him to jilt Bertila and flee. He initially worked as a peddler, but eventually became a partner in ownership of a brothel. This business venture was highly successful, but Jacobo still lacked the wife and children he had planned to acquire. Since the woman he really loved, Sara, was married to his brother, he proposed to her sister, Miriam Abramowitz, but she rejected him when she learned about his brothel. Lerner can not even marry his faithful mistress, Juana Paredes, because she is not Jewish. In the end, Lerner believes that he has been possessed by the dybbuk (malevolent spirit) of the now-dead Mitrani. After an exorcism, he dies. Meanwhile, Ephrain, the illegitimate son of Lerner and his former lover Bertila, has grown up in Chepén's hostile environment; he is unaware of his father's identity and becomes increasingly insane. After attacking a statue of the Virgin Mary in a local church, Ephraín is confined to an empty room, where he talks only with spiders.

Characters: *The Fragmented Life of Don Jacobo Lerner* brought Goldemberg a wider audience than he had previously known. The novel is written in a disjointed style in which quotes from public records and a newspaper alternate with third-person narration and dramatic monologues, effectively creating the rootlessness and loss of identity experienced by Jewish immigrants to Peru.

The novel chronicles the twelve years of **Jacobo Lerner**'s life in Peru and documents how his sense of self is gradually eroded. The novel's fragmented structure portrays Lerner as pieced together and varied; from one perspective he seems dishonest, from another a victim, and from yet another a generous benefactor. Also significant: Lerner never addresses the reader, and according to critic Jonathan Tittler, "His silence bespeaks eloquently the essential absence at the heart of the novel." Through Lerner, Goldemberg shows that relief from poverty, war, and oppression available in the New World was not without its tradeoffs. Lerner never marries a Jewish girl and never establishes a home, although he does make a surrogate family of the employees of his prosperous brothel. However, his profession causes Lerner to lose his chance of marrying Miriam Abramowitz. Even when his business is thriving and he has a loving, devoted mistress, Lerner is dogged by loss and discontent, and he fears that death is near. Unlike other people he knows, Lerner finds no satisfied with the superficial accoutrements of success; he longs for an ever-elusive, deeper meaning in life. Goldemberg makes a wandering Jew out of Lerner, but Lerner also expresses modern alienation and spiritual emptiness.

Jacobo's illegitimate son, **Efraín Wilson,** seems to inherit his father's alienation, although more acutely pathetic. Like Goldemberg, Efraín is the son of a Peruvian Catholic mother and a Russian Jewish father; but whereas Goldemberg was taken as a child to live with his father in Lima's Jewish community, **Efraín** is abandoned by his father and left in a hostile environment. He is neglected by his mother and shunned by the largely Catholic community, highlighting the anti-Semitism of small-town Peru, and he never knows the identity of his father. When he attacks a statue of the Virgin Mary, Efraín loses his only two allies, his aunt Francisca and the local priest. The novel ends with Efraín confined to a bare room babbling to spiders.

Jacobo never fulfills his plan to marry a Jewish woman. He rejects **Bertila Wilson,** who is not Jewish, for fear of repeating the unhappy fate of his friend Mitrani; abandoned and pregnant Bertila may be a victim, or she may be a schemer who had planned to trap a prosperous husband. Jacobo claims to love the, unavailable **Sara Lerner,** his brother's wife, who is prominent in Lima's Jewish community and who turns out to be superficial and obsessed with her own image above all else. When Jacob pursuers Sara's widowed sister,

Miriam Abramowitz (whose husband committed suicide), she rejects him admitting that she wanted to marry Jacobo only for his money. All the while his mistress, **Juana Paredes**, truly loves him and would have been glad to marry him and establish a stable home, but Jacobo feels he must marry a Jewish woman.

Soon after his arrival in Peru, Jacobo relocates to the small town of Chepén, to be near his friend **Léon Mitrani** who owns a thriving business. As it turns out, Mitrani's home life is desperately unhappy. He feels lost among his Catholic wife's people and among his fellow Jews, and he is consumed by the same fear he felt in the Old World. When Mitrani dies and Jacobo finds that he feels the same unhappiness and fear within himself, he believes that Mitrani's dybbuk has possessed him. Other characters in the book include Jacobo's brother **Moisés Lerner**, whose swindling forces Jacobo to become a peddler and who later becomes the highly respected president of Lima's Hebrew Union; Jacobo's friend and fellow peddler **Samuel Edelman**, whose contentment in marrying a Peruvian woman and raising a family contrasts with Mitrani's experience; and **Francisca Wilson**, Bertila's sister, who fills in lovingly as Efraín's surrogate mother until he defaces a religious statue which offends her.

Further Reading

Contemporary Literary Criticism. Vol. 52. Detroit: Gale Research.

Irwin, Michael. "As Hope Lies Dying." *Times Literary Supplement* No. 3963 (March 10,1978): 274.

Jefferson, Margo. "Wandering Jew." *Newsweek* Vol. 89, no. 19 (May 9, 1977): 103.

MacShane, Frank. "American Indians, Peruvian Jews." *New York Times Book Review* (June 12, 1977): 15, 33.

Speck, Paula K. "Fragments of a Vanished World." *Americas* (May–June 1982): 63.

Tittler, Jonathan. *"The Fragmented life of Don Jacobo Lerner*: The Esthetics of Fragmentation." Ithaca: Cornell University Press, 1984: 172–85.

Nadine Gordimer

1923–

South African novelist, short story writer, critic, essayist, and editor.

My Son's Story (novel, 1990)

Plot: The novel takes place in South Africa during the waning years of apartheid, the political system that denied full civil rights to the country's black and colored (mixed race) residents. Parts of the novel are narrated directly by Will—whose father, Sonny, is a leader of the resistance movement. An omniscient narrator relates the episodes in Sonny's life. A former schoolteacher, Sonny became politically active and spent two years in prison for his dissidence. As the novel opens, Will unexpectedly encounters his father leaving a suburban movie theater with a white woman, whom Will recognizes as Hannah Plowman, the human rights organization member who visited Sonny in prison. Flashbacks relate that Sonny and Hannah were attracted by their commitment to a common cause, just as Sonny was growing away from his quiet, submissive wife, Aila. Shocked about his father's unfaithfulness, Will nevertheless complies with Sonny's unspoken plea to keep quiet about the affair. While the studious Will spends most of his time at home with his beloved mother, his sister, Baby, experiments with drugs and sex and even attempts suicide. Finally Baby informs her family that she is moving to Zambia to be trained as a guerilla. Aila subsequently acquires a passport and visits Baby in her new home, returning to report that her daughter is married and expecting a baby. Neither Sonny, who is busy with political work and his obsession with Hannah, nor Will, who constantly broods about his father's involvement with a white woman, pays much attention to Aila's frequent trips to Zambia. Thus both are stunned when the security police arrive at their door, arrest Aila, and retrieve a cache of explosives from the house; they learn that Aila has been acting as a courier for the Zambian-based guerrillas. Meanwhile, the liaison between Sonny and Hannah ends when Hannah accepts a job in another country. Aila is eventually forced to join her daughter and grandson in exile in Zambia, while Sonny continues to participate (albeit in a much-diminished role) in the resistance movement. At the end of the novel, Will reveals that Sonny has again been detained and that he (Sonny) has written this story of his family's lives but can never publish it.

Characters: Awarded the Nobel Prize for Literature in 1991, South African writer Gordimer provides through her fiction an important and expertly rendered social history of a country in the midst of profound, wrenching change. She is lauded for portraying with skill and sensitivity—and in prose that is sometimes extravagant or demanding—the situations and personalities that comprise that struggle. Gordimer's works demonstrate the detrimental consequences of apartheid on both whites and blacks, focusing not so much on its political permutations as on its effects on the human psyche and on interpersonal relationships. In *My Son's Story,* she explores the personal price paid by those who fight for a political cause, and she examines the role of the novel, which both shares experience and invades privacy.

The novel is largely narrated by **Will**, who seems to be in his late teens or early twenties when most of the action takes place. Will's book-loving father named his son after his favorite author, William Shakespeare, and Sonny's apparent hope seems realized by the novel's ending, when Will reveals he has become a writer. Will also admits that he is the author of those passages in which his parents lives and thoughts are intimately described, basing his narrative on his own observations and conjecturings. The novel chronicles Will's reaction when he discovers that his father is having an affair with a white woman and his gradual evolution from disgust and sexual jealousy to a somewhat more thoughtful analysis. Initially perplexed, Will grows cold and scornful, resenting that his father expects him to keep his discovery secret, noting the irony of his father's public image of high integrity. Unlike Sonny, Will is not political by nature. Preferring to stay at home and read or brood about what his father does with Hannah in her little cottage, Will has always identified more with his mother, while Sonny's affinity was more toward his daughter. Yet Will is bound to his father, and Gordimer portrays the complex elements of their relationship. Both father and son are startled to learn of Aila's secret life, and they do lend each other support during her arrest and trial. By the end of the novel, Will gains maturity in his views of his parents and his country. His feelings about his role as a writer are ambiguous, for he laments: "I wish I didn't have imagination. I wish that other people's lives were closed to me." Yet, due to South Africa's oppressive political system, Will's narrative can never be published.

Through Will's father, **Sonny**, Gordimer explores some of the consequences of political commitment and illustrates that, although heroic, activists are as fallible as anyone else. A former teacher, Sonny is a conscientious, bookish man whose sense of justice draws him into the fight against apartheid and propels him from obscurity to celebrity. Spending two years in jail for his ideals earns Sonny the rank of an honored leader of the liberation movement, and he becomes a renowned public speaker. Before his imprisonment, Sonny was faithful to his gentle wife, with whom he fell in love when both were quite young. But gradually Sonny's political work creates a gulf between them that has persisted since his prison stay. His relationship with the politically compatible Hannah Plowman is, by contrast, sexually passionate and involves constant sharing of thoughts and ideas. Sonny, who tells Hannah that she is his only friend, admits that before the repeal of South Africa's law banning interracial sexual relationships he would have resisted forming such a tie, in deference to his role in the anti-apartheid struggle. His affair has complications, however. When his son discovers it, Sonny wants Will's silence to preserve his image of having a respectable marriage. Sonny is also drawn into the in-fighting among the radical party elite. Together with his absorption in his affair with Hannah, he fails to notice Aila's increasing absences from home. Thus he is shocked to learn that he was wrong about Aila's apolitical nature and the stable home life he had taken for granted. The costs are great, for Sonny loses prominence in the movement and suffers personally as well; Hannah accepts a job in another country and Aila is forced into exile with Baby. At the end of the novel the government still considers Sonny a threat and detains him again.

Whereas Gordimer conveys in some detail the thoughts and motives of both Will and Sonny, **Aila** remains a rather shadowy character whose perspective, some critics contend, is not well represented. Beautiful, dignified, and always impeccably dressed, Aila is even respected by the family's white neighbors, who exempt her from their general denigrations of blacks. Quiet and submissive, Aila supports Sonny's political commitment but is not outwardly political herself. The distance between Aila and Sonny increases after his release from prison—an experience that, he seems to feel, she cannot possibly comprehend. Sonny takes little notice of Aila's activities during his affair with Hannah and thinks nothing of her new, short haircut, which Will recognizes as a sign that his mother has undergone some profound change. Arrested for acting as a courier for the Zambian-based guerrillas, Aila serves a jail sentence, bearing the experience with a stoicism that stuns her husband. Just as Sonny displays the weaknesses that heroes are subject to, Aila demonstrates the hidden strengths of those assumed to be weak.

Hannah Plowman, a white South African member of an international human rights organization, visits Sonny in jail to check on his conditions, then becomes his lover. The granddaughter of a Lesotho-based missionary, Hannah is a sensitive, sincere opponent of apartheid, yet, when Will discovers his father and Hannah together, he calls her a "pink pig" whose race is an affront to his own family's honor. Sonny loves Hannah for the intellectual and sexual expansion she offers, which is lacking in his relationship with Aila. Commentators note Gordimer's consistent interest in the possibilities and difficulties of interracial love. Near the end of the novel, Hannah accepts a high-level job despite her knowledge that it means ending her affair with Sonny.

Unlike her studious, brooding brother, **Baby** is a demonstrative, often flamboyant teenager who experiments with drugs and sex but who also exhibits deeper concerns when she attempts suicide. Some critics find Baby's conversion to political commitment and self-exile to Zambia for guerilla training a rather contrived solution to her youthful rebelliousness and depression.

Further Reading

Clingman, Stephen. *The Novels of Nadine Gordimer: History from the Inside*. London: Allen & Unwin, 1986.

Coles, Robert. "A Different Set of Rules." *New York Times Book Review* (October 21, 1990): 20–21.

Contemporary Literary Criticism. Vols. 3, 5, 7, 10, 18, 33, 51. Detroit: Gale Research.

Cooke, John. The Novels of Nadine Gordimer: *Private Lives/Public Landscapes*. Baton Rouge: Louisiana State University Press, 1985.

Eckstein, Barbara J. "Nadine Gordimer: Nobel Laureate in Literature, 1991." *World Literature Today* Vol. 66, no. 1 (winter 1992): 6–10.

Packer, George. "Manifest Destiny." *Nation* Vol. 251, no. 21 (December 17, 1990): 777–80.

Papineau, David. "Of Loyalty and Betrayal." *Times Literary Supplement* No. 4565 (September 28–October 4 1990): 1037.

Parrinder, Patrick. "What His Father Gets Up To." *London Review of Books* Vol. 12, no. 17 (September 13, 1990): 17–18.

Smith, Rowland, ed. *Critical Essays on Nadine Gordimer.* Boston: G. K. Hall, 1990.

Wachtel, Eleanor. Interview with Nadine Gordimer. *Queen's Quarterly* Vol. 98, no. 4 (winter 1991): 899–910.

Mary Gordon
1949–
American novelist.

Final Payments (novel, 1977)

Plot: The novel's narrator and central character is thirty-year-old Isabel Moore, who has spent the last eleven years caring for her invalid father, a college professor. As the novel opens, Joe Moore has died and, at his funeral, Isabel reflects that she must now "invent a new existence" for herself. Her life has been confined to the conservative Catholic realm of her Queens neighborhood, where her only frequent visitor during her father's long illness was the kindhearted Father Mulcahy. With the help of her childhood friend Liz Ryan, Isabel moves to her own apartment and begins a job as project director of a home-care study. Her work requires her to interview elderly patients and those who care for them, which leads her to meditate on the meaning and motivation of her own devotion to her stroke-afflicted father. She wonders whether she made this sacrifice out of love or guilt because her father had caught her in bed with his favorite student. Isabel embarks on a brief and soon-regretted affair with Liz's callous, womanizing husband, John Ryan; Liz, meanwhile, is involved with another woman. Then Isabel falls in love with kindly Hugh Slade, a married veterinarian with whom she finds happiness until his vindictive wife confronts and humiliates her about the affair. Stricken by guilt and determined to achieve a selfless love, Isabel moves in with the unkempt, cantankerous Margaret Casey, who once kept house for Isabel and her father until Isabel (then only thirteen) perceived her romantic interest in Joe and fired her. Isabel cares for the arthritic Margaret while allowing her own physical and emotional state to deteriorate: she chops off her hair, gains weight, and loses interest in and connection with the outside world. Finally, however, with the help of several friends as well as her own returning good sense, Isabel decides to shape a real existence for herself. Leaving Margaret the $20,000 profit from the sale of her father's house, Isabel moves out to begin her new life.

Characters: The widely praised *Final Payments,* Gordon's first novel, reflects her Irish Catholic upbringing and continuing interest in broader matters of faith and spirituality. The novel explores the limitations of human love—what novelist and critic Francine du Plessix Grey calls "the universal religious problem of the search for perfect charity"—as well as the changing roles of women in the family and society and the importance of friendship. Some critics detect in _Final Payments_ a tension between the desire to escape the stifling confines of the "Catholic ghetto" and nostalgia for the lost comforts of religious certainty. Although reviewers fault Gordon for her lack of skill in creating male characters, most commentators find the novel an eloquent plea for freedom over stagnation.

Isabel Moore is one of Gordon's most interesting protagonists. Physically attractive and intelligent, she is at once vulnerable, sensuous, frank, and frequently smug. Contemplative and articulate, she is perceptive about other people's motives and fairly honest about her own. For example, she admits to herself that she may have wanted her father to discover her in bed with his student in order to assert herself to him. But then Isabel spends eleven years as the ever-devoted daughter—perhaps out of guilt for (possibly) causing her father's stroke, or perhaps for the narcissistic pleasure of self-sacrifice. The job she takes after her father's death invites her to contemplate on her own years in his service and the relationship between the ailing patient and the self-abnegating caretaker. At the same time, Isabel attempts to escape her suffocating Catholic environment through affairs with two men, both of them married. These relationships, for their different reasons, end badly, and Isabel retreats again into her dreary, sheltered life, reclaiming her role as selfless caretaker by moving in with the sanctimonious, malicious Margaret Casey. Isabel hopes to attain the kind of universal, impersonal love that, unlike ordinary human love, can never leave a person bereft; Isabel reflects that if she can succeed in loving the unlovable Margaret, "then it's a pure act, love; then we mean something, we stand for something." During her miserable months with Margaret, Isabel begins to shed her identity as she allows her appearance and mental state to deteriorate. Isabel does emerge from this dismal cocoon, sparked by a gentle comment from Father Mulcahy that she is slowly killing herself, by Margaret's attack on her beloved Charlotte Brontë (which she cannot allow to go unchallenged), and by her loyal friends Liz and Eleanor. Thus the novel is one individual's struggle for identity, although the conflict between older and younger generations and the problems of women in a patriarchal society are strong themes.

Isabel comments that she has spent her life surrounded by priests. Although her widowed father, **Joe Moore**, is not a clergyman, he is priestlike in his devotion to his faith and in his celibacy. A professor of medieval literature at a small Catholic college in Queens, Moore is a fiercely conservative absolutist whose fiery joy in his faith Isabel envies but does not share. She describes his belief as "gladiatorial," a quality that is distinctively male, and he represents the essentially authoritarian, patriarchal power structure not only of the Catholic church but, by extension, of the Catholic family. At the same time, Isabel recognizes and appreciates her father's deep love for her, and she values his teaching her the importance of the intellect. Commentators hold that Gordon modeled Moore after her own much-loved father, a conservative and scholarly Catholic who died when she was eight years old. The other cleric in Isabel's young life is her longtime parish pastor and friend, **Father Mulcahy**. Gordon's portrait of this gentle Catholic priest is mostly affectionate, if not particularly vivid. Father Mulcahy initiates Isabel's recovery when he tells her that by neglecting herself she is violating the Fifth Commandment ("Thou shalt not kill"), which "means slow death, too."

Margaret Casey is a quintessentially unlovable figure: cantankerous, penurious, and malicious, she disguises her complaints with false piety. Isabel's connection with this embittered woman goes back to the time when Margaret performed housekeeping duties for them and apparently schemed to marry Joe Moore. An important aspect of Margaret's character is that she shares the same Irish Catholic background as Isabel, devoted to the service of others. Thus Margaret is Isabel's double, the dark side of self-denial. Isabel's determination to love Margaret selflessly reflects Gordon's stated respect for—if not the church itself—Catholicism's "very high ethic of love." Yet Isabel fails to love Margaret and instead gives her a "final payment" that is apparently supposed to discharge her obligations; a few critics find this outcome disappointing, since it seems to preclude the possibility of transcendent love for someone like Margaret.

Two of the most important people in Isabel's life are her childhood friends Liz and Eleanor, who provide her with both a connection to the past and loving support for the future. Dark-haired, tough-talking **Liz Ryan** is vital, passionate, and active; she engages in numerous sporting activities and is single-handedly building a barn on her country estate. Her marriage to politician John Ryan was apparently contracted only as a convenience for producing and raising the couple's two children, and Liz is happy with her lesbian lover, **Erica**. Liz has a precise, sometimes cutting wit that makes the more fragile, passive **Eleanor** uncomfortable. Gentle, blonde, and sexually squeamish, the divorced Eleanor maintains a meticulously neat apartment and sheltered life that appeal to Isabel in a different way than Liz's more engaged manner. Indeed, Liz and Eleanor do not particularly like each other, so it is significant that they join forces at the end of the novel to help Isabel escape from Margaret. When she sees the overweight Isabel with her unattractive haircut, Liz asks sardonically, "Who did your hair, Annette Funicello?" The question invokes relieved, joyful laughter from all three women, depicting the strong bond between them. Indeed, critics note that Gordon consistently denies that sexual love is life's most dominant emotion, as the romantic writers held, and maintains that friendship is ultimately more sustaining.

Most critics agree that Gordon has trouble depicting believable male characters, and Gordon herself admits that she does not understand how men think. The crude, selfish politician **John Ryan**, to whose advances Isabel submits in a moment of weakness, is a contemptible womanizer who, Isabel is forced to admit, does do some good in his job as overseer of his country's welfare programs. Although he is more positively portrayed, veterinarian **Hugh Slade** is too saintly to be convincing; a Protestant, he refers to the Catholic background of Isabel and her friends as "barbarous" and offers a more tolerant approach to life and love. Isabel's affair with Hugh brings her joy (and it does appear at the end of the novel that she will go back to him) as well as pain and guilt. The latter emotions are inspired primarily through **Cynthia Slade**, Hugh's vulgar, self-pitying wife, who reportedly tricked him into marriage and now humiliates his lover in public. The fact that the affair between Hugh and Isabel, which causes Isabel such guilt, breaks up an unhealthy marriage is presented positively. Notable among the caretakers and patients that Isabel interviews are **Patricia Kiley** and her mother, who live in a dirty, dilapidated house that smells of cat feces. Patricia has no front teeth, lifeless eyes, blemished skin, and hanging breasts—signs that she has abnegated her own identity in order to care for the hopelessly paralyzed **Mrs. Kiley**. Isabel understands how this kind of deterioration can occur and considers it "only luck" that it did not happen to her during her father's long illness; she does, of course, undergo a similar transformation later in the novel.

The Company of Women (novel, 1981)

Plot: The novel comprises three sections that recount different periods in the life of the central character, Felicitas Taylor. Part 1 takes place in 1963 in the western New York town of Orano, where Felicitas's mother, Charlotte, and four other women gather every year to visit their good friend and spiritual adviser, Father Cyprian Leonard. The highly conservative Cyprian was once a member of the Paracletist monastic order but left because he felt it was becoming too liberal, and he now fills in for other priests when they are ill or on vacation. Fourteen-year-old Felicitas (whose father died when she was a baby) is the only child born to any of the group members, and she is the focus of their hopes for the future. Cyprian is even grooming her to be a kind of spiritual warrior against the evils of the secular modern world. But in Part 2, set in 1969, Felicitas rebels against this imposed role. A sophomore at Columbia University in New York City, she has an affair with her political science professor, Robert Cavendish. An enthusiastic participant in the counterculture of the 1960s, Cavendish is an insensitive manipulator who has—Felicitas learns when she moves in with him—two other women already living in his apartment. Eventually Robert tires of Felicitas and suggests she sleep with their neighbor, Richard. Felicitas becomes pregnant and, not knowing whether the baby's father is Robert or Richard, seeks an abortion. But after a harrowing experience at an abortion clinic, she returns to her mother and old friends to give birth to her child. Part 3 takes place in 1977. Felicitas, Charlotte, and their friends have all moved to Orano to be near the dying Cyprian. Felicitas's daughter, Linda, now seven years old and cherished by her extended family, has been told that her father is "one of two people." The individual monologues that end the book reveal that Cyprian has softened his views in recognition of the value of human love, and that Felicitas plans to marry the silent but dependable Leo Byrne, owner of the local hardware store.

Characters: Like *Final Payments,* Gordon's previous novel, *The Company of Women* draws on the author's Catholic upbringing and may attempt to salvage the cherished elements of that heritage and reject its negative aspects. Following the protagonist's maturation, the novel promotes the idea of redemption through "ordinary human love," which is cast as an antidote to despair with distinct religious value even without strict adherence to religious doctrine. Critics identify a number of central themes in the novel, including the subservient role of women within patriarchal institutions, the relationships between parents and children, and the importance of friends rather than lovers. In her first novel, Gordon affirmed the value of friendship over the romantic notion of sexual or marital love, and *The Company of Women* makes a similar case. Despite giving the novel mixed critical reviews (with negative commentary centering on the weakness of some of the male characters and the sentimentality of the final chapters), commentators generally praise its unique, compelling perspective on contemporary life.

The novel chronicles **Felicitas Maria Taylor** at three stages of her life: a naive fourteen-year-old, a rebellious twenty-year-old, and a twenty-seven-year-old mother. Named after "the one virgin martyr [mentioned in the Canon of the Catholic mass] whose name contained some hope for ordinary human happiness," the teenaged Felicitas is the vessel of hope for the entire "company of women" (none of whom has any other children) and Father Cyprian Leonard. Trained by Cyprian in religious doctrine and ritual, Felicitas knows she is his spiritual prodigy and is rather arrogant about this special status. After a year in the heady secular atmosphere of Columbia University, however, she sheds the role. Felicitas decides that the lives of her mother and her friends are empty and based on lies, and that Cyprian is a hypocritical tyrant. Like Isabel Moore, the protagonist of *Final Payments* (and a more interesting, complex heroine, according to several critics), Felicitas chooses sex to escape her sterile existence. Gordon's portrait of the 1960s counterculture that is the setting for this character's rebellion has been cited as the weakest part of the book—a judgment due particularly to Gordon's unconvincing characterization of Felicitas's caddish lover, Robert Cavendish. Felicitas is exploited and then discarded by the professor, who may or may not be the father of her baby. Her decision to return to the shelter of her extended family, as well as her later plan to marry a stolid storekeeper, receives several interpretations. Some commentators view Felicitas's acceptance of an ordinary life in a positive light; they contend that she is affirming the values of unselfish love and friendship over shallow glamour and fleeting passion. Other critics, however, detect in the novel's conclusion a sense of loss and a regrettable lack of engagement with life. Some reviewers see Felicitas's decision to marry Leo as a rejection of feminism (particularly in view of her comment that "it is for shelter that we marry and make love"), while others contend that she rejects both a rigid Catholicism and the falseness of sexual "liberation" in favor of an alternative viewpoint that is essentially feminist.

Although Gordon is generally faulted for her portrayals of male characters, **Father Cyprian Leonard** is a fairly successful creation. As a young and spiritually inspired man, Cyprian rejected his crude nuclear family and joined a monastic order, shedding his birth-given name of Philip for the name of a Catholic martyr. A conservative, absolutist Catholic (not unlike Joe Moore in *Final Payments*), Cyprian abandoned the Paracletist Order when it became too liberal for his tastes, choosing instead a rather depressing life as a substitute priest with no parish of his own. His dominant status over "the company of women," who began attending his weekend retreats many years ago and remain his friends and followers, is one of Gordon's most vivid illustrations of the patriarchal nature of the Catholic church. She consistently portrays male authoritarian figures who show little understanding of the subordinate women around them. Thus Cyprian sees the naive, sheltered Felicitas as the spiritual warrior who will promote his own agenda, combating what he calls "the whole sewer of the modern world," never suspecting that she may not wish to assume such a role. Significantly, though, Cyprian undergoes a transformation by the end of the novel. Convinced that his priesthood has failed, he is finally rescued by "the enduring promise of plain human love." As he lies dying, he admits that he "had to be struck down by age and sickness to feel the great richness of the ardent," which is embodied in the tender care of his "company of women." Although Cyprian may be likened to Cavendish in his unyielding defense of his ideas and his frequent selfishness, he is ultimately redeemed. Francine du Plessix Gray praises Gordon for Cyprian's "subtle balance of emotional violence and capacity for love, the pathos of his exile, the eccentric complexity of his conservatism."

The novel's title refers to five Catholic women who have been friends for many years and possess more identity as a group than as individuals, embodying the kind of "ordinary human love" and friendship the novel strongly affirms. **Charlotte Taylor**, Felicitas's widowed mother, is the only member of the group who has had a child. She articulates the group's peculiar collective identity by saying that "when they all came together, they were something." Resilient, tough-talking, and fiercely supportive, she is reportedly modeled after Gordon's own widowed mother, who was disabled by polio but worked in a law firm to support her family. The other group members include practical **Clare**, emotional **Elizabeth**, flighty **Mary Rose**, and possessive **Muriel**.

Critics roundly fault Gordon for her weak portrayal of **Robert Cavendish**, typical of her usual trouble in creating convincing nonclerical men. A political science professor at Columbia University, Robert takes over the role of authoritarian father-figure once held by Cyprian (and indeed, his "harem" of hippyish women is a kind of parody of Cyprian's female followers). Manipulative and egotistical, Robert mouths radical views but displays profound insensitivity to the people around him. Gordon satirizes 1960s counterculture shallowness through Robert (who has a son named Mao and who wishes that he had been born in a Third World country). Robert enjoys the freedom from conventional morality promoted during that period and exhibits the irresponsibility that was, Gordon seems to contend, its result. Critic Brenda L. Becker claimed that "this turkey is no character at all, but a caricatured grotesque of the sixties."

Other characters in *The Company of Women* include **Richard**, Robert's neighbor, to whom he passes Felicitas when has tired of her; stolid, silent, but apparently comforting **Leo Byrne**, the hardware store owner Felicitas plans to marry; and **Linda**, Felicitas beloved daughter, who knows that her father is "one of two people."

Men and Angels (novel, 1985)

Plot: The novel takes place in a small northeastern college town. Anne Foster is the thirty-eight-year-old wife of a French professor and the mother of two adored children. At the same time that her husband is scheduled to spend a year teaching in France, Anne is given an opportunity to prepare a catalog for an exhibit of the works of Caroline Watson, an impressionistic painter of the early twentieth century who never received the attention she deserved during her own lifetime. Anne hires a babysitter named Laura Post to care for her children while she is working on the project. Laura's monologues, which comprise alternating chapters of the novel, reveal that as a child she was a unloved and turned to evangelical Christianity for solace; although sexually exploited by a cult leader, she continues in her religious fanaticism. Laura believes that she has been sent to save Anne and her family from their corrupt ways. Anne finds herself unable to like this strange, self-righteous girl. Meanwhile, as she investigates the life of Caroline Watson, she finds out that the painter neglected her son, Stephen. Anne, passionately devoted to her own children, is troubled by her finding. Then Laura allows the Foster children to walk on the thin ice of a pond. When Anne, whom she had assumed sincerely liked her, fires Laura, Laura commits suicide by slitting her wrists in the family's bathtub. Only then does Anne realize the extent of Laura's need for love and her own inability to give it.

Characters: Like both of Gordon's previous novels, *Men and Angels* is deeply infused with the notion of how to love the unlovable and the need to be nourished by ordinary human love. Gordon also explores here the importance of motherhood in women's lives and the mingled power, guilt, joy, and vulnerability that it brings. In her review of *Men and Angels,* critic Ruth Perry calls Gordon ''perhaps the first feminist novelist of our generation to explore deeply in her fiction what it feels like to be a mother and an intellectual or writer.''

Several critics note that whereas the protagonists of *Final Payments* and *The Company of Women* exhibit both ''good'' and ''bad'' behavior, in *Men and Angels* Gordon splits these extremes between two characters. Thus **Anne Foster** is the ''good'' mother, while troubled Laura Post exhibits only ''bad'' qualities. Indeed, reviewers even note that Anne and Laura share a physical resemblance—both have white skin, blue eyes, and red or reddish hair—thus suggesting that they are two sides of the same coin. A thirty-eight-year-old art historian, Anne lacks the strong Catholic background of Gordon's previous heroines (her mother claims to have had her fill of Catholicism during her own upbringing) and has no religious inclination, but she does share with them a capacity for self-scrutiny, an insecurity about her own talents and achievements, and a fear that she will be punished for her good fortune. Gordon has been particularly praised for her eloquent portrayal of Anne's feelings for her children, which include fear and guilt as well as a profound delight that is both physical and emotional. Yet Anne also highly values her intellectual work, which is described as inducing a euphoric weightlessness that contrasts with the heavy, earthbound (and, in Anne's case, welcome) sensation of being a mother. The values of both work and mothering are affirmed in the novel, although the sometimes troubling issue of handing responsibility for one's children over to someone else is also present through the character of Laura Post. Anne's rage when she learns that Laura has endangered her children's lives is overwhelming; she feels fully capable of strangling the babysitter with her own hands. After Laura's suicide, however, Anne must come to terms with the misery of the girl's life and the fact that Anne might have overcome her dislike and found a way to help her. At the same time, Laura's death permanently shatters Anne's illusion that she can function as the ideal, ''omnipotent'' mother, always sheltering her children from the world's dangers and pain.

In her lack of social skills and extreme self-righteousness, twenty-one-year-old **Laura Post** is profoundly unlikable. Her monologues reveal her religious fanaticism and some reasons for her mental state. Born to a seventeen-year-old mother who resented her lost freedom, Laura grew up mistreated and unloved. Her mother left used sanitary pads around the house and conducted illicit affairs during the day. When her mother physically attacked Laura, Laura joined an evangelical cult headed by a corrupt manipulator who sexually exploited her. Nevertheless, she continues to cling to the idea of an omniscient spirit who will give her unconditional love. Laura is an inarticulate, totally isolated character whom no one can ever know. Because the two women physically resemble each other, several critics see Laura as Anne's "bad" double, despite the great differences in their backgrounds and perspectives. Whereas Anne represents the positive values of care and devotion, Laura embodies the misery and neglect that are also real aspects of life and sometimes of motherhood. Laura's suicide is both a tragedy and something of a relief that her neurosis did not result in violence against those she felt she had to "save."

Gordon has been lauded for her convincing creation of painter **Caroline Watson**, whom she modeled after a number of celebrated female impressionists of the early twentieth century, including Mary Cassatt, Cecelia Beaux, and Suzanne Valadon. A talented, passionate artist who continually struggled for recognition, Watson was faced with an agonizing choice: she could not legally take her son out of the United States, and she could not paint in the United States. Watson chose her work over her child, leaving young Stephen in the care of others and thus giving him permanent emotional scars. Although tremendously moved by Watson's paintings, Anne is angered at the painter's mistreatment of her son, which threatens her objectivity. Eventually Anne must ask herself whether there is any excuse for being a bad mother—such as the conviction that one is a great artist and must sacrifice all else to that—and whether it is just that women are consistently judged not for their accomplishments but for their ability to mother children.

Ironically, Watson's inability to adequately mother **Stephen**, who died at the age of twenty-eight, did not extend to her beloved daughter-in-law **Jane**, who found the painter an ideal mother-figure. In the course of preparing the catalog, Anne meets and interviews Jane, an attractive, intelligent, proud old woman. Jane describes her guilt about her own mistreatment of Stephen, which led to a religious conversion. Like several other notable Protestant characters in Gordon's fiction (such as Hugh Slade in *Final Payments*), Jane projects a comfortable, tolerant spirituality that contrasts strongly with the rigidity of Catholicism. Jane claims to value Christianity for its promise of "forgiveness for the unforgivable," a concept related to the novel's theme of love for the unlovable. It is Jane who, in discussing Laura's death, points out that the message of the Gospels was lost on this troubled girl because God's love "means nothing to the heart that is starved of human love."

Anne's husband, **Michael Tucker**, plays only a small role in the novel, because he is on sabbatical in France during most of the action. Michael's mother, who was abandoned by her husband and subsequently relinquished her domestic responsibilities to her very young son, is another of the novel's deficient parents. In this case, however, Michael creates a loving relationship with his wife and children (though there are intimations that he has a brief extramarital affair in France). Another minor character in the novel is art dealer **Ben Hardy**, an old friend of Anne's, who presents her with the opportunity to write the catalogue for the Watson exhibit.

Further Reading

Becker, Brenda L. "Virgin Martyrs." *American Spectator* Vol. 14, no. 8 (August 1981): 28–32.

Contemporary Literary Criticism. Vols. 13, 22. Detroit: Gale Research.

Dictionary of Literary Biography. Vol. 6, 1981 Yearbook. Detroit: Gale Research.

Gilead, Sarah. "Mary Gordon's *Final Payments* and the Nineteenth-Century English Novel." *Critique* Vol. 27, no. 4 (summer 1986): 213–27.

Gray, Francine du Plessix. "A Religious Romance." *New York Times Book Review* (February 15, 1981): 1, 24, 26.

Howard, Maureen. "Salvation in Queens." *New York Times Book Review* (April 16, 1978): 1, 32.

Iannone, Carol. "The Secret of Mary Gordon's Success." *Commentary* Vol. 79, no. 6 (June 1985): 62–65.

Lardner, Susan. "No Medium." New Yorker Vol. 57, no. 7 (April 6, 1981): 177–80.

Lodge, David. "The Arms of the Church." *Times Literary Supplement* (September 1, 1978): 965.

Mahon, John W. "Mary Gordon: The Struggle with Love." *In American Women Writing Fiction: Memory, Identity, Family, Space.* Edited by Mickey Pearlman. Lexington: University Press of Kentucky, 1989: 47–67.

Morey, Ann-Janine. "Beyond Updike: Incarnated Love in the Novels of Mary Gordon." *Christian Century* Vol. 102, Iss. 36, no. 20 (November 20, 1985): 1059–63.

Perry, Ruth. "Mary Gordon's Mothers." In *Narrating Mothers: Theorizing Maternal Subjectivities.* Edited by Brenda O. Daly and Maureen T. Reddy. Knoxville: University of Tennessee Press, 1991: 209–21.

Sheed, Wilfrid. "The Defector's Secrets." *New York Review of Books* Vol. 25 (June 1, 1978): 14–15.

Wolcott, James. "More Catholic than the Pope." *Esquire* Vol. 95, no. 3 (March 1981): 21, 23.

Henry Green
1905–1974
English novelist.

Loving (novel, 1945)

Plot: The novel takes place during World War II in Ireland, where—despite that country's neutrality—some of the war's repercussions are felt by a group of English servants sent to their aristocratic master's country estate. On the death of the old butler, Eldon, forty-year-old Charley Raunce is suddenly promoted, and he wavers between pomposity and meekness as he takes over Eldon's duties. One of the housemaids, pretty Edith, accidentally discovers Mrs. Jack (the daughter-in-law of the estate's mistress, Mrs. Tennant) in bed with a neighbor, Captain Davenport. This experience prompts Edith to try to attract the amorous attention of the new butler, Charley, at which task she succeeds. Soon the two are in love, and their romance is chronicled, as well as several mysteries surrounding some lost peacock eggs and Mrs. Tennant's ring. At the end of the novel, Edith's other suitor, the ardent but ineffectual young Albert, joins the Royal Air Force; Edith's fellow maid and close friend Kate finds happiness with an Irish servant; and Edith and Charley leave for England to be married and to "live happily ever after."

Characters: Although many readers are unfamiliar with Henry Green, he is known as the "writer's writer's writer"; such acclaimed authors as T.S. Eliot, W. H. Auden, Eudora Welty, and John Updike have praised his inventive approach to style and character and his unusual and successful rendering of ordinary conversation. Most critics consider *Loving* Green's best novel, discerning in it the skillful use of symbolism, expertly conveyed colloquial speech, and the mingled comedy and tragedy that are hallmarks of his writing. Like several of Green's other novels, *Loving* focuses on a small group of people in isolation, exploring not so much their individual psychologies as their interactions with each other. Everyone in the book either loves or seeks love, and a wide variety of affections are present, from the conventionally romantic to the adulterous to the platonic. Lauded for depth, creating characters of Green finds even the most mundane personalities capable of the unexpected.

Loving, which begins with the words "Once upon a time" and ends with "happily ever after," is meant to either conform to or ironically reverse the classic model of the fairy tale. The novel's leading male character—through whom Green conveys the ideal, conventional love for which fairy tales are known—seems unlikely for the traditional role of the prince. **Charley Raunce** is forty years old, undistinguished, and not particularly healthy; never married, he remains solicitous of his unresponsive mother, writing her letters first in pencil, then copying over the words in ink. Charley is unexpectedly promoted to butler when old Eldon dies, and he inherits with this post his predecessor's chair of honor at the servants' dinner table as well as Eldon's tradition of pilfering small amounts of cash from the estate's weekly accounts. Unsure whether he really deserves this new status, Charley is alternately bold and cowardly toward the other servants, treating them dictatorially or with meekness. Charley's behavior exemplifies Green's portrayal of characters through personality and role conflicts, rather than through introspective probing. Charley's growing love for the pretty Edith, who forces herself into his line of vision, surprises him and seems another manifestation of a good fortune he may not deserve. This may explain why Charley's always dyspeptic health seems to decline even further as the courtship progresses. Some critics suspect that the "happily ever after" ending is actually ironic, and that Charley will meet the same fate as Eldon, who moaned "Ellen" on his deathbed just as Charley moans "Edie!" when he sees his beloved surrounded by birds. Most commentators, however, believe that Charley and Edith really will depart for England to achieve married happiness, and that their successful "loving" signifies another triumph of the life force in all its insistence and variety.

Edith is the lovely upstairs maid who captivates Charley with her huge, dark eyes, which are described as resembling "plums dipped in cold water." Discovering her employer's daughter-in-law in bed with a neighbor seems to awaken Edith's own yearning for a mate, and Charley is the most eligible man around. Although Edith's romantic style may be devious, she is an affectionately portrayed character who gives and receives a generous portion of the love connoted by the novel's title. The self-possessed, calculating Edith— despite her youth and beauty—may seem an unlikely choice for a fairy tale princess, but she does embody a strong, wholesome life force that ultimately triumphs over isolation and loneliness. Many critics found as especially effective the novel's final scene, in which Edith, her face aglow with happiness, is engulfed in a cloud of doves and peacocks—birds used throughout *Loving* to symbolize sensuality, beauty, and pride.

Several reviewers commented on Green's skill in portraying a wide range of characters, from the humble to the aristocratic, but the servants, not the masters, dominate *Loving*. Housemaid **Kate** is only a little less pretty than her close friend Edith, with whom she shares an intimacy that (as several critics have noted) is sometimes expressed physically. And like Edith, Kate feels a need for love, which is answered by the uncouth, grimy Irish lampman, **Paddy O'Conor**. Paddy's heavy brogue is virtually indecipherable to all the English servants except Kate, whose love facilitates her understanding.

The household staff also includes the housekeeper, **Miss Burch**, an elderly, gossip-loving spinster who dearly loves the young housemaids she supervises; **Miss Welch**, the gin-tippling cook who loves her pots and pans and her obnoxious, precocious nephew **Albert** (rumored to be her son), a Cockney boy who has been evacuated from blitz-torn London and whom the other servants call "little 'itler' "; and **Nanny Swift**, laughably naive but devoted to her unappreciative charges (Mrs. Jack's two children). In his quest to win Edith's heart, Charley's eighteen-year-old assistant, **Albert**, plays the fairy tale role of the courtly lover. The only affection he succeeds in winning, however, is from the children's donkey. At the end of the novel, Albert goes to England to join the Royal Air Force—thus sorely grieving Charley, who claims he has always treated the boy as a son (dispensing such advice as "always to clean your teeth before you have to do with a woman"). The death of the household's former butler, the somewhat dishonest but reliable old **Eldon**, marks Charley's ascension in status. While dying, Eldon keeps repeating the name "Ellen," revealing hidden depth and sorrow in his apparently mundane life and reinforcing the novel's themes of love and loneliness.

Although the aristocratic characters play less important roles than the servants, they help to widen the range of different kinds of "loving" with which the novel is concerned. **Mrs. Tennant**, the estate's owner, represents the old aristocracy whose influence is fading as the twentieth century progresses. Unable to view her servants as actual human beings, Mrs. Tennant is also pitiably lonely. She struggles to manage the estate alone, while her beloved son, **Jack**, is off to the war or unwilling to help her when he is home. **Mrs. Violet Tennant,** or "Mrs. Jack," is Mrs. Tennant's daughter-in-law who relieves her boredom and sexual frustration during her husband's absence through an affair with an Irish neighbor, **Captain Davenport**, providing the novel's adulterous love, depicted as inferior to the conventional union shared by Charley and Edith. Mrs. Jack is spoiled and indecisive—she cannot quite make up her mind whether to end her affair with the captain—and violating her society's moral code results in guilty worries that her mother-in-law will discover her secret. Although they cannot hope to receive their selfish mother's whole attention, Mrs. Jack's children, **Evelyn and Moira**, are blessed with the complete devotion of Nanny Swift.

Concluding (novel, 1948)

Plot: Set in the future in an impersonal totalitarian state, the novel takes place during eighteen hours of the same day at a school where young girls are trained to become efficient bureaucrats. In recognition of a great discovery made early in his career, the elderly scientist Mr. Rock is allowed to live in a cottage on the school grounds. This circumstance rankles Miss Edge, one of the institution's directors, who would like to control both the cottage and the independent old man. Mr. Rock's granddaughter, who is living with him since suffering a nervous breakdown, has fallen in love with one of the school's few male teachers, Sebastian Birt. As the book opens, two of the school's students are reported missing. Determined to keep this alarming news a secret for as long as possible, Miss Edge and her co-director, Miss Baker, search secretly while at their normal business. One of the girls turns up in the woods, but the other, Mary, cannot be located. The school's annual dance is scheduled for that evening, and the girls and adults look forward to the event with pleasure. Rock and his granddaughter decide to attend the dance, and Elizabeth persuades her grandfather to try to cajole Miss Edge into allowing them to keep the cottage. During their encounter, Miss Edge becomes intoxicated by cigarette smoke and proposes to Rock, who scorns her and departs in triumph. After a harrowing journey back through the dark, Rock reaches his cottage and goes to bed, relatively satisfied with the day's events, while Elizabeth returns to the dance and her lover.

Characters: Often compared to George Orwell's *1984*, which was published around the same time, *Concluding* also provides a sinister portrait of totalitarianism, but critics have found Green's novel less didactic and more optimistic than Orwell's. Green has been lauded for his success in creating a highly symbolic, nearly hallucinatory atmosphere, particularly through his lush, impressionistic descriptions of the mansion's natural surroundings. In exploring such themes as the rivalry between youth and age, the problems of communication, and the human need for love, Green infuses *Concluding* with mingled joy and sorrow, beauty and ugliness, sanity and madness, change and stasis. The novel's title may refer to the end of Mr. Rock's life, or it may reflect the wealthy Green's fear (inspired, commentators believe, by the Labour Party's rise to power in late 1940s England) that his country was on the verge of a bureaucratic nightmare. The inconclusive ending of *Concluding* suggests that in spite of the human desire to impose structure, life is essentially unsettled and—as is emphasized in much of Green's work—that the richness and endless variety of existence can overcome even the greed for closure and loss of individuality inherent in totalitarianism.

The central figure of *Concluding* is elderly **Mr. Rock**, who gained fame as a young scientist for a great theory that is never described in the novel. Although he has been granted a cottage on the grounds of the school, his position is tenuous because the fearsome Miss Edge opposes him, and he even has to depend on Maggie Blain remembering to offer him breakfast. Many critics consider Mr. Rock Green's best character; he is not uniformly pitiable, noble, or cranky but all of these things at once. Mr. Rock is both covetous (of his cottage and his granddaughter) and magnanimous (particularly toward Elizabeth), cowardly and occasionally brave, innocent and wily. He is said to represent the last vestiges of an older, liberal civilization giving way to a cold, impersonal totalitarian state, and he feels besieged not only by Edge and what she represents but by the girls, who seem to adore him but whose youth alienates him. Although Mr. Rock is an old man who may be expected to be unconcerned about such things, he is still capable of and hungry for love—the human need that dominates much of Green's writing. With his wife long dead, Mr. Rock focuses his love on Elizabeth, his pets, and his cottage. His feelings for Elizabeth are complex; he treats her with great kindness and solicitude, but he selfishly desires to keep her to himself. The fact that Mr. Rock tells Elizabeth not to worry about what will happen to them, that "everything settles itself in the end," may be interpreted pessimism or a feeble attempt to pacify her. In any case, by the end of the novel Mr. Rock feels calm and satisfied, even though nothing has been resolved. The strange scene in which the intoxicated Miss Edge proposes to Mr. Rock is noteworthy, for here Mr. Rock's greater mental agility and intuitiveness are manifested. He exits in triumph, turns toward the mansion, and intones the Latin version of his name, "Petra," as he basks in his prowess. Some critics consider Mr. Rock an autobiographical character, for he shares with his creator such traits as an obsession with privacy and a penchant for using his deafness to his own advantage. Mr. Rock's age os the same age Green would be at the same point in the future—thus perhaps he is Green's projection of himself as an elderly man.

The novel's primary agent of England's oppressive new government is **Miss Edge**, the institute's director, whose psychic war with Mr. Rock suffers a loss this day. She wants the cottage for the gardener, but mainly she wants Mr. Rock out because he is annoyingly indifferent to her dominance. The two girls' disappearance concerns her as well, not because she is worried for their safety but for her own and the school's reputation. Miss Edge is clearly the selfish, ineffectual bureaucrat that Green considered endemic to a totalitarian system. She is totally devoted to the government she symbolizes, yet her love for the school mansion and grounds counters the rigidity and impersonality of the totalitarianism model. Miss Edge loses one battle in her war with Mr. Rock when she proposes that the two marry as a solution to their conflict, which suggests more complex impulses beneath the surface. In her own mind, Miss Edge considers the proposal a ploy to vanquish Mr. Rock by absorbing him, but in fact it may indicate a deeper need for love or sensual contact with another human being. Like the other state bureaucrats in *Concluding,* Miss Edge always dresses in black—in stark contrast to the white-clad girls—symbolizing the system's flat, impersonal approach.

After suffering a nervous breakdown, **Elizabeth Rock**—in her thirties and unmarried—returns to live with her grandfather in isolation. Her mental instability is attributed to her having failed to subjugate her personality as the system demands. Both gentle and ardent, Elizabeth reveals her interior panic through halting, nervous speech. Although she loves her grandfather, her manner toward him is somewhat selfish and erratic due to her mental instability and her nearly obsessive love for Sebastian, which seems to take up most of her energy and attention. The physical bond the couple share is consistently associated with the institute's wild natural surroundings. Both Elizabeth's emotional condition and Sebastian's uncertainty make their relationship seem tenuous, and one of the novel's unresolved issues is whether they will actually marry. **Sebastian Birt,** the school's rather ineffectual economics teacher and Elizabeth's lover, is one of the novel's few male characters. He is constantly mimicking people in a manner that lacks much comic appeal; along with his sexual escapades with Elizabeth, this role-playing seems an attempt to undermine the oppressive system that employs him. Whether Sebastian actually loves Elizabeth or—as Mr. Rock suspects—simply covets their cottage is never resolved.

Although much of the action in *Concluding* revolves around the 300 girls who attend the school (and particularly the two who have disappeared as the novel opens, they are not individually distinguished. Rather, they are portrayed as a kind of collective character. Each of their names begins with "M"—examples include Mary, Merode, Marion, and Moira—which suggests the murmuring sounds of nature and invokes the moon, which is consistently used to symbolize them. However, the girls embody a rich, unconscious life force, in contrast to the impersonal rigidity of the totalitarian system ruling over them. Though physically mature, they have been confined to an unnatural innocence. Despite eliminating their individuality, the state has not eradicated their instinctive sexuality or their spiritual impulses, as indicated by their secret club with its spontaneous rituals and their hints that some of them slip out at night to meet the groundskeeper, Adams. Mr. Rock thinks of the girls with fondness and some alarm; he regards their attempt to initiate him into their club as neither appropriate nor rational. Nevertheless, many critics consider the girls as personifications of the primal force of nature—or as irrepressibly human, suggesting some hope for the future. **Mary,** the missing girl, distinguishes herself from the others through the very act of escape. Her schoolmates are unable to explain where she has gone, although they hint that she had complained of being overworked; she may have drowned in the pond or escaped with some local boy. The lack of explanation for Mary's disappearance has annoyed some of the novel's readers, but it is consistent with Green's conviction that life is never fully settled and that complete accountings are never possible.

Other characters in *Concluding* include **Miss Baker,** Miss Edge's strangely emotional co-director, who advocates converting the school into a "black and white" farm (in which all of the animals would be either black, white, or black-and-white spotted), a notion that symbolizes systematic reduction of all complexities to simple black and white; **Adams,** the peculiar groundskeeper who is rumored but never proven to have had sexual liaisons with the girls and is rather hostile, particularly toward Mr. Rock; **Maggie Blain,** the cook, who rules over her kitchen with confidence and apparent contentment; the headmistress, **"Ma" Marchbanks,** who (unlike Miss Edge) is genuinely worried about the missing girls; and **Miss Winstanley,** another teacher who harbors a pathetic, unrequited love for Sebastian Birt. Mr. Rock's pets—the widely roaming cat **Alice,** the nervous pig **Daisy,** and the goose **Ted**—are all to some extent characters in the novel. Each is, like Mr. Rock, the only specimen of its particular kind on the estate and thus isolated. The goose Ted is considered pointedly symbolic when it returns after disappearing; the fact that it flies home (even though the goose has never flown before) and returns just as Mr. Rock arrives at the cottage seems to commemorate Mr. Rock's victory over Miss Edge.

Further Reading

Bassoff, Bruce. *Toward Loving: The Poetics of the Novel and the Practice of Henry Green.* Columbia: University of South Carolina Press, 1975.

Contemporary Literary Criticism. Vol. 13. Detroit: Gale Research.

Dictionary of Literary Biography. Vol. 15. Detroit: Gale Research.

Dirda, Michael. "Rediscovering Henry Green." *Chronicle Review* (November 13, 1978): R11-R12.

Engel, Monroe. "Henry Green: Eros and Persistence." *Antaeus* No. 63 (autumn 1989): 97–109.

Facknitz, Mark A. R. "The Edge of Night: Figures of Change in Henry Green's *Concluding.*" *Twentieth Century Literature* Vol. 36 (spring 1990): 10–22.

Holmesland, Oddvar. *A Critical Introduction to Henry Green's Novels: The Living Vision.* London: Macmillan, 1986.

Mengham, Rod. *The Idiom of the Time: The Writings of Henry Green.* Camridge: Cambridge University Press, 1982.

North, Michael. *Henry Green and the Writing of His Generation.* Charlottesville: University Press of Virginia, 1984.

Odom, Keith. *Henry Green.* Boston: Twayne, 1978.

Pritchett, V. S. "Henry Yorke, Henry Green." *London Magazine* Vol. 14 (June–July 1974): 28–32.

Russell, John. *Henry Green: Nine Novels and an Unpacked Bag.* New Brunswick, NJ: Rutgers University Press, 1960.

Stokes, Edward. *The Novels of Henry Green.* London: Hogarth, 1959.

Updike, John. "On Henry Green." *Antaeus* No. 69 (autumn 1992): 146–53.

Welty, Eudora. Foreword to *Concluding,* by Henry Green. Chicago: University of Chicago Press, 1948.

Yagoda, Ben. "Hazards of Language." *New Boston Review* (February–March 1979): 23–4.

Graham Greene
1904–1991

English novelist, essayist, dramatist, short story writer, critic, travel writer, and author of children's books.

Brighton Rock (novel, 1938)

Plot: Set in the English coastal town of Brighton, the novel centers on Pinkie Brown, the teenaged leader of a gang whose territory is the Brighton pier. As the novel opens, a character named Fred Hale is desperate to evade Pinkie and his thugs, who plan to kill him to avenge the murder of their former leader, Kite. Kite was assassinated by the Colleoni gang, of which Hale is a member. After finding temporary sanctuary with Ida Arnold, a Londoner in Brighton for a day's holiday, Hale is killed. Later Pinkie learns that Rose Wilson, a waitress at a nearby restaurant, has potentially incriminating information about the incident. Pinkie plans to silence Rose by marrying her and then convincing her to carry out a suicide pact with him—although Pinkie, of course, has no intention of killing himself. The two marry and move into Pinkie's room together. Meanwhile, Ida hears of Hale's murder and decides to see what she can find out. Returning to Brighton, she learns of Pinkie's involvement and tries to convince Rose to betray him, but Rose loves Pinkie and refuses to comply. At the end of the novel, the suicide pact goes awry and Pinkie alone dies when he falls off a cliff. On the final page Rose, now pregnant, listens to a vituperative message Pinkie recorded for her shortly before his death.

Characters: Green is an important contemporary novelist whose work is marked by moral complexity and religious concerns. His novels are often categorized as either "entertainments" or serious works; the former category comprises his suspense or spy novels, and the latter such critically acclaimed books as *The Power and the Glory* and *The Heart of the Matter*. An early novel recognized as one of Greene's best, *Brighton Rock* is said to blend qualities of both categories: it features both suspenseful action and a concern with the notions of sin and salvation. Through its sympathetically portrayed yet realistic characters, *Brighton Rock* reflects Greene's interest in the influence of early environment on a person's later life and his consistent, particularly Catholic preoccupation with the links between good and evil and with, as articulated by an elderly priest near the end of the novel, "the . . . appalling . . . strangeness of the mercy of God."

The young gangster **Pinkie Brown**—who wears a suit several sizes too large and a weary, cynical expression—is one of the most memorable, tragically warped characters in Greene's fiction. Portrayed as the inevitable product of a dismal environment, Pinkie strikes some critics as an allegorical figure representing Sin. He grew up in a downtrodden area of Brighton ironically called Paradise Piece, witness to his parents' once-weekly copulations in a tiny home that precluded privacy. After being orphaned, Pinkie came under the influence of gang leader Kite, who seems to have been the first person in his life to have shown him any affection; Pinkie proves his loyalty to Kite by being willing to commit murder to avenge Kite's death. Pinkie's worldview is pessimistic; when Rose timidly asserts that life is not so bad, he counters that life is "gaol, it's not knowing where to get some money. Worms and cataracts, cancer. . . . It's dying slowly." At seventeen he is already a murderer, a practiced liar, and a cheat, yet at the same time Pinkie is a professed Catholic. He is perfectly aware of how he deviates from the tenets of his faith, and he considers himself already damned and beyond the hope of salvation. At one time Pinkie considered becoming a priest; indeed, he disdains material possessions, money, and sex and prays in times of need. He considers Catholicism an inherently logical system of belief that gives his actions significance in the wider scheme of things. Thus his life is evil but at least not meaningless, and there is some purpose to his existence even if, as he accepts responsibility for his sins, he believes he will go to hell when he dies. Pinkie's relationship with Rose is complex; he is drawn to her yet repulsed by the sexual aspect of their relationship, attracted to her goodness yet disdainful of it. Ostensibly he marries her only to lure her into suicide to prevent her from exposing his crime, but he has strong feelings for her and he has to admit that they "suit each other down to the ground." The cruel message Pinkie leaves Rose at the end of the novel—"God damn you, you little bitch, why can't you go back home forever and let me be"—depicts Pinkie's warped, desperate life. That Pinkie fathers a child before dying has generated some controversy among critics. Some claim the novel's profundity is undermined by this rather facile symbol of salvation, while others laud Greene for planting amid the story's despair a final seed of hope.

The sixteen-year-old girl who marries Pinkie is **Rose Wilson**, a waiflike waitress and, like Pinkie, a native of Brighton's poorest area. Another similarity is their faith, but while Pinkie focuses on sin and damnation, Rose considers Catholicism a source of hope and salvation. Rose's tender love for Pinkie is her most poignant quality. She finds marriage to him blissful and wonders how she comes to deserve such happiness, and when Ida tries to get Rose to betray Pinkie, she flatly refuses. At the end of the novel, a pregnant Rose claims that she may make her baby "a saint—to pray for his father." Some critics contend that Rose's pregnancy is merely a sentimental device that negates the novel's profound despair. Readers may differ on what Rose makes of Pinkie's cruel recorded message to her.

The worldly **Ida Arnold** provides a stark contrast to the innocent Rose. A resident of London, Ida brings with her a matter-of-factness that seems rooted in her big-city background. Several critics deem Ida—who is modeled at least partially after Mae West— as one of Greene's most memorable characters. She is around forty years old and attractive, a buxom woman who wears cheap perfume and reads dime-store novels. Unlike Rose and Pinkie, she has no traditional religious beliefs, although she follows Spiritualism and consults the Ouija board when she needs guidance. Ida's determination to find Hale's murderer arises partly out of an innate nosiness and partly out of her sense of justice. Whereas Pinkie views the world in terms of good and evil (recognizing his own actions as evil), Ida knows only the blander, shallower concepts of right and wrong. This is in keeping, of course, with her earthiness, for she is concerned always with the present and not with some abstract prospect of heaven or hell. Likewise, in attempting to convince Rose to betray Pinkie, she asserts that people are like the famous Brighton rock candy, which always reads "Brighton" inside no matter where it is bitten—people don't change, and it is necessary to face "the world we got to deal with."

The novel begins with the murder of **Fred Hale**, a member of a gang headed by the criminal tycoon **Colleoni**. Because Hale previously targeted Kite for assassination by his gang, Pinkie and his compatriots are planning to kill him. His failed struggle to evade his killers foreshadows Pinkie's death later in the book. Hale's death is both gruesome and symbolic— he succumbs to a heart attack precipitated when the gangsters shove a stick of Brighton rock candy down his throat. The unsavory middleaged lawyer **Mr. Prewitt** seems to personify disreputability. Although the potential showed during his school days disappeared long ago, he still sprinkles his conversation with (frequently misquoted) literary references; for example, he quotes from Christopher Marlowe's play *Dr. Faustus:* "Why this is hell, nor are we out of it." In fact, this particular quote aptly describes his life and bitterness, for he lives in a miserable location close to a noisy railroad and hates his wife. Other characters in *Brighton Rock* include **Ted Dallow**, who belongs to the same gang as Pinkie, participates in the murder, and seems perfectly content with his life of crime; and **Phil Corkery**, the investigator who works with Ida on solving Hale's murder and is exhausted by the abundant sexual favors she bestows on him. **Kite,** who is already dead by the time the novel begins, is a significant character in that his murder initiates the story's action: Pinkie's loyalty to the man who adopted him on the waterfront after his parents died leads him to help kill Hale.

The Quiet American (novel, 1955)

Plot: The novel is set in Vietnam during the 1950s, when the French colonial government begins its fight against the nationalist Viet Minh forces for control of the country. The central character, Thomas Fowler, is an aloof British journalist with a beautiful Vietnamese lover, Phuong. A young American CIA agent named Alden Pyle arrives in Saigon espousing the formation of a "third force"—that is, an alternative to both colonialism and communism—which he believes will save the country. Fowler considers Pyle dangerously naive and ignorant of the nation and people he himself both knows and admires. Meanwhile, Pyle falls in love with Phuong and wins her away from Fowler with promises to "save" her by marrying her and taking her to America. The Communists inform Fowler that Pyle has supplied material to terrorists to make bombs, one of which has exploded in front of the popular Continental Hotel. Fowler agrees to help arrange his death, and Pyle is killed by the Communists.

Characters: Critics divide Greene's novels into the categories of "entertainments" and serious works, and they may be further subdivided into those with a Catholic or religious focus and those concerned with social or political issues. *The Quiet American,* which may be placed in the latter category, has been lauded for anticipating what was to occur in Vietnam between the late 1950s, when the Communist Viet Minh forces (later called Viet Cong) overthrew the French, and 1975, when the United States finally concluded its unsuccessful intervention in Vietnam's affairs. The novel reflects Greene's journalistic background, for he spent the winters of 1951 through 1955 as a correspondent in Vietnam. The novel's main theme is that innocence can be dangerous, "like a dumb leper who has lost his bell, wandering the world, meaning no harm," and that more harm than good results when the do-gooder lacks a deep understanding of his subject.

Commentators note in several of Greene's works characters who attempt to maintain a detached, observational stance and are defeated by ethical considerations or emotional ties. The world-weary, cynical British journalist **Thomas Fowler,** who narrates *The Quiet American,* is one such protagonist. His resemblance to his creator is striking: Greene too served as a correspondent in what was then called Saigon, and he too developed an appreciation for Vietnam's people and culture. Although Fowler admires the Vietnamese (condescendingly, according to some critics), he claims to subscribe to no ideology or religious stance: "I wrote what I saw: I took no action—even an opinion is a kind of action." By the end of the novel, however, Fowler does take action—against Pyle. Fowler's negative reaction to Pyle operates on several levels. One is sexual jealousy, for Pyle lures Phuong away from him; indeed, Inspector Vigot believes this is Fowler's primary motivation for betraying Pyle. Another factor is his strong distaste for Americans and particularly for America's tendency to try to "save" people in order to protect its own interests—a distaste some critics believe reflects Greene's own feelings. The third and probably most significant impetus is that Fowler recognizes the injustice and potential harm that Pyle could cause. Although Pyle is acting in good faith, he must be eliminated. Therefore Fowler stirs himself from a languor due to both his personality and his opium use (Greene also used opium during his time in Vietnam) and takes the kind of action he has previously shirked. Commentators regard Fowler as an early version of the spy characters in Greene's later novels.

The ambitious do-gooder Alden Pyle is one of several "virtuous" characters in Greene's fiction that cause significant harm. The boyish-looking American CIA agent, a Harvard graduate and the son of a college professor, projects a typically American, puritanical self-assurance. Pyle considers himself politically sophisticated, but the journalist Fowler finds him naive and capable of unleashing lethal political forces that he does not comprehend. Pyle's understanding of Indochina is based on a book written by an "expert" named York Harding, who promotes the implementation of a "third force" as an alternative to both colonialism and communism. Such an approach was, indeed, America's policy in Vietnam, and Pyle is said to have been based on Colonel Edward Lansdale, a CIA agent who went to Vietnam to promote democracy through the "psychological warfare" techniques he had learned during his advertising career. Significantly, Pyle arrives in Vietnam with an established agenda and immediately goes about enacting it, whereas Fowler's values and eventual plan of action only gradually develop. Just as Pyle's understanding of Vietnam is shallow, his love for Phuong is misguided: he plans to take her back to Boston and thus "protect" her from her own country's dangers, but in doing so he would plant her in an alien, probably hostile culture. Some critics detect in Greene's portrayal of Pyle the author's snobbish, disdainful attitude not only toward American policy but toward Americans themselves.

Fowler's beautiful Vietnamese girlfriend, **Phuong,** meets his sexual needs and facilitates his evening opium sessions. Although the charming Phuong seems innocent, she recognizes the limitations of her relationship with her British lover. Because Fowler is already married to a woman who, due to her Catholic faith, refuses to divorce him, he can provide Phuong with little more than their current arrangement. Pyle, on the other hand, offers Phuong marriage and a new, "safe" life in the United States, a place she has idealized. After Pyle's death, Fowler learns that his wife has agreed to a divorce, so Phuong may have a chance for a new life, after all her name means "phoenix" in Vietnamese). Some critics believe that Greene's portrayal of the lovely but shallow Phuong emanates from his condescending attitude toward the Vietnamese.

Another notable character in *The Quiet American* is **Inspector Vigot,** the sympathetically drawn police inspector, who represents the soon-to-be-overthrown French colonial government. Vigot suspects that Fowler has helped to arrange Pyle's assassination but is unable to prove it.

The Human Factor (novel, 1968)

Plot: The novel takes place in contemporary England in the years before the end of the Cold War. For many years Maurice Castle has worked as a spy for his country's Secret Intelligence Service, frequently referred to as the Firm. But he is actually a "double agent" who has delivered information to Russia in payment of an old debt related to the safe escape of his black South African wife, Sarah, from her country. Maurice has a quiet, happy home life with Sarah and Sam (her son from an earlier relationship) and looks forward to his approaching retirement. His relative peace is disturbed, however, when the Firm suspects a leak and targets not Maurice but another agent named Davis as the source. Davis is killed, while Maurice uneasily continues his work. Eventually he learns that the Firm has discovered his treachery, and he must flee England for Russia. Maurice intends to have Sarah and Sam join him later, but the British government foils this plan, and at the end of the novel it appears that Maurice (who has learned that the information he leaked to Russia was without meaning or value) will remain in lonely exile in Moscow for the rest of his life.

Characters: *The Human Factor* is one of the finest examples of those novels in which Greene masterfully blends suspense and intrigue with moral concerns. Considered Greene's most ambitious "spy" novel, the book explores both the possible cost of emotional ties and the mingled absurdity and tragedy to which the practice of espionage may lead. Infused with a sense of weary experience and bleak despair, *The Human Factor* is said to be Greene's most direct indictment of the casual cruelty of spy organizations, which he portrays as lacking any regard for human values.

Greene begins *The Human Factor* with a quote from Joseph Conrad: "I only know that he who forms a tie is lost. The germ of corruption has entered his soul." Thus the reader is prepared to encounter the novel's central character, **Maurice Castle,** who has formed just such a tie with his beloved wife and her son. Castle is a loner who avoids forming relationships outside his own family, and he claims to have "no politics," even though his work as a double agent for Russia is presumably helping South Africa's oppressed black population. Castle is one of several protagonists in Greene's fiction through whom the author considers the concept of "spying"; that is, of gaining advantage over others by gathering information on them while maintaining a detached stance. Both ethical considerations and emotional ties are shown, in several of Greene's novels, to endanger such detachment. Castle recognizes the corruption at the heart of espionage but feels bound to continue his work, due to the debt he owes to a mysterious figure called **Carson** for Sarah's safe escape from South Africa. His commitment is personal, however, not political, and it is only his deep love for Sarah and Sam that keeps him from sinking into complete cynicism. Thus Castle's fate seems particularly cruel, for his treasured ties with others lead to his being cut off from them, probably forever. In addition, he learns that the information he delivered to Russia was part of an intelligence hoax and never benefited anyone. Greene apparently modeled Castle at least partly on Kim Philby, a famous British double agent and friend of the author's who, in Greene's belief, betrayed his country in the service of a higher cause.

It is Castle's strong love for his wife, **Sarah,** a South African black, that both illuminates his life and ensures his dismal fate. When Maurice tells Sarah what he has done, admitting that he has betrayed England, Sarah says, ''Who cares? We have our own country. You and I and Sam. You've never betrayed that country, Maurice.'' This suggests that for Sarah, too, personal connections with others are more important than national interests. Castle deeply loves **Sam,** Sarah's bright, innocent son, even though the boy is not his own.

Other characters in the novel include **Hargreaves**, who embodies the self-righteous cruelty of the Secret Intelligence Service; and **Davis**, the feckless agent who is killed when the Firm mistakenly concludes that he is leaking information to Russia. Before his death, Davis ruefully admits to Castle that the childishly romantic perception of espionage he once held has been shattered by the tedium of his daily work: ''Do you know I came into this outfit for excitement? Excitement, Castle. What a fool I was.''

Further Reading

Allot, Kenneth, and Miriam Farris. *The Art of Graham Greene.* 1951. Reprint, New York: Russell & Russell, 1963.

Atkins, John. *Graham Greene.* Rev. ed. London: Calder & Boyars, 1966.

Contemporary Literary Criticism. Vols. 1, 3, 6, 9, 14, 18, 27, 37, 72. Detroit: Gale Research.

DeVitis, A. A. *Graham Greene.* New York: Twayne, 1964.

Hoskins, Robert. *Graham Greene: A Character Index and Guide.* New York: Garland, 1991.

Johnstone, Richard. ''The Catholic Novelist I: Graham Greene.'' In *The Will to Believe: Novelists of the Nineteen-Thirties.* Oxford University Press, 1982.

Kelly, Richard. *Graham Greene.* New York: Frederick Ungar, 1984.

Kelly, Richard Michael. *Graham Greene: A Study of the Short Fiction.* New York: Twayne, 1992.

Mesnet, Marie-Beatrice. *Graham Greene and the Heart of the Matter.* London: Cresset, 1954.

Miller, R. H. *Understanding Graham Greene.* Columbia: University of South Carolina Press, 1990.

Myers, Jeffrey. *Graham Greene: A Revaluation; New Essays.* New York: St. Martin's Press, 1990.

Pritchett, V. S. ''Graham Greene: 'Disloyalties.''' In *The Tale Bearers: Literary Essays.* New York: Random House, 1980.

Pryce-Jones, David. *Graham Greene.* New York: Barnes & Noble, 1967.

West, Richard. "Graham Greene and *The Quiet American.*" *New York Review of Books* (May 16, 1991): 49–52.

John Guare

1938–

American playwright and screenwriter.

The House of Blue Leaves (play, 1971)

Plot: The play takes place on October 4, 1965, the day the pope is scheduled to travel through Queens en route to the United Nations to speak against war. Artie Shaughnessy is a Queens zookeeper who dreams of success as a Tin Pan Alley–style songwriter but who lacks any talent. His mentally unbalanced wife, whom he calls Bananas, attempted suicide several months earlier and now wanders through the couple's apartment in a fog. Artie is having an affair with his downstairs neighbor, Bunny Flingus, who encourages him to put Bananas in a mental institution and run away with her to Hollywood. Billy Einhorn, who grew up in Artie's neighborhood, has become a wealthy movie producer, and Artie hopes that his old friend will help him get into the movie business. As the play progresses, a number of other characters make appearances in Artie's apartment, including his son, Ronnie, who has deserted from the army and plans to assassinate the pope with a homemade bomb, and a trio of nuns hoping for a better view of the pope. Billy Einhorn also arrives, bringing with him his glamorous girlfriend, Corinne, an actress made deaf by an explosion during the filming of her latest movie. At the play's conclusion, Ronnie has failed to kill the pope and Artie has not only failed to realize his dreams but has lost Bunny to Billy. An utterly abject Bananas clings to him, and he erupts in frustration and kills her. In the audience's final view of Artie, he is standing alone, singing one of his awful songs.

Characters: Originally produced in the early 1970s, *The House of Blue Leaves* received the prestigious Obie and New York Drama Critics Circle awards when it was revived in 1986. The play is a farce that combines black humor with pathos, and Guare has been lauded for his adept shifting from one to the other. Through his often hilarious, mostly deluded characters and their avoidance of reality in favor of grandiose dreams, Guare satirizes the American obsession with celebrities and fame. while he sympathizes with his characters, however, he condemns the superficial culture that both produces and depends on characters like these. Guare has said he is "not interested so much in how people survive as in how they avoid humiliation," which he sees as a key element of tragedy, comedy, and life itself. Through the long, impassioned monologues that are characteristic of Guare's work, his protagonists share their perspectives not just on humiliation but on dreams, desire, and disappointment.

The central figure in *The House of Blue Leaves* is **Artie Shaughnessy**, a middle-aged zookeeper who dreams of a more glamorous life than the one he now lives in his cluttered Queens apartment. Though bereft of talent, he fantasizes about making it big writing songs for the movies. His Tin Pan Alley-type tunes include "Where Is the Devil in Evelyn?" and "I Love You So I Keep Dreaming"—the latter of which, he realizes with dismay, is sung to the tune of "White Christmas." Artie has been compared to Willy Loman, the protagonist of Arthur Miller's 1949 play *Death of a Salesman*; both characters are frustrated, middle-aged men forced to acknowledge that their dreams are unattainable. Like other Guare protagonists, Artie ignores reality as long as he can, and when it finally forces itself upon him, he cannot bear its weight and strikes out. Obsessed with his own desires and oblivious of his wife's, Artie finally turns on her in a violent rage. With Bananas dead and Bunny fled with Billy (who does not offer his old friend a hand up in the movie business), Artie is alone in the spotlight, pathetically crooning a song.

Artie's love-starved wife, **Bananas**, provides a poignant example of how American culture ignores human need and moral values in favor of celebrity worship. In the first act she tells the story of her encounter at a busy intersection with Jacqueline Kennedy, Cardinal Spellman, Bob Hope, and President Johnson, all four of whom were hailing cabs. She says that she gave them all a lift, only to find herself humiliated before millions of viewers as the zany ride was satirized that night on the *Tonight* show. Bananas wonders why celebrities cannot return the love their fans shower on them. Several months before the action in the play, Bananas failed her feeble suicide attempt. Now shabbily dressed and shrinking in manner, Bananas haunts the periphery of the action. She overhears her husband and his mistress discussing their plans to elope and commit her to a mental institution, the place (surrounded by "blue leaves") where the electroshock therapy she dreads is administered. The fact that Bananas is actually the sanest person in the play is a central irony; unable to bear her ability to see the truth, to feel pain deeply, and to express her despair, the others scheme to drug her and lock her up. Bananas claims that she likes animals because they are not famous and because they are free to show the feelings she is forced to stifle. In the end, she resembles a frightened animal as she huddles against Artie, who is unable to forge the human connection she craves and instead kills her.

Bunny Flingus is the Shaughnessys' downstairs neighbor and Artie's mistress. Described by Michael Malone in *Nation* as "deliciously tacky ... a strutting compendium of hackneyed sentiments and Dale Carnegie optimism," Bunny is a brash woman with platinum blonde hair who encourages Artie's musical delusions and prods him to leave with her for stardom in Hollywood. In an absurd reversal of convention, Bunny refuses to cook for Artie until they are married; for now, he will have to settle for sex. Bunny finally runs off with **Billy Einhorn**, a Queens native who has achieved fame and success in the movie business. Typifying the calculated, mercenary approach to art and the consumer flattery that Guare sees in America's mass entertainment industry, Einhorn tells the disappointed Artie that he actually possesses "the greatest talent in the world—to be an audience—anybody can create."

Other characters in *The House of Blue Leaves* include **Corinna**, Billy's starlet girlfriend, who pretends to hear Artie's singing when actually she was made deaf by a movie explosion; Artie's son, **Ronnie**, who deserts the army after serving only twenty-one days and returns to Queens with antiestablishment sentiments and a deranged plot to assassinate the pope; and the **three zany nuns**, who invade the Shaughnessy apartment hoping for a better view of the pope and who are the unintended victims of Ronnie's bomb.

Six Degrees of Separation (play, 1990)

Plot: Set in contemporary New York City, the play begins in the home of Flan and Ouisa Kittredge, a wealthy Manhattan couple with several college-age children. Flan is an art dealer, and he and Ouisa are entertaining a South African billionaire named Geoffrey who they hope will finance their purchase of a Renoir painting, which will then be sold to a Japanese buyer for a high profit. Just as they are about to go out for dinner, a young black man arrives, claiming that he is a Harvard classmate of the Kittredges' children. He explains that he has just been mugged, and that he is the son of the acclaimed black actor Sidney Poitier. The articulate young man, who calls himself Paul Poitier, thoroughly charms the Kittredges and their guest, even cooking dinner for them. Exhilarated by the encounter, Geoffrey agrees to provide the money for the painting. Later, Flan gives Paul fifty dollars to tide him over until the next day, when he is supposed to meet his father (who Paul claims is coming to New York to cast a new film version of the Broadway musical *Cats*), and insists that Paul spend the night with the Kittredges. But in the middle of the night, Flan and Ouisa discover Paul in bed with a male prostitute, and they eject both young men. They later learn that Paul has successfully performed this scam on several of their friends. Some time later, Ouisa receives a phone call from a distressed Paul. Pulling a similar scam on another couple—two would-be actors from Utah—Paul went to bed with the man who then killed himself upon learning that he enjoyed homosexual sex. Though Ouisa is ultimately unable to help Paul, her contact with the strange young man helps her recognize the fraudulence of her life and inspires her to seek deeper connections with those around her.

Characters: The basic plot line of *Six Degrees of Separation*, which was nominated for a Tony Award, is based on an actual confidence scheme, reported in 1983, by which several wealthy New York couples were bilked by a young man posing as a friend of their children and a son of Sidney Poitier. Guare uses this premise as a starting point to explore the social, familial, and cultural divisions between people that he sees as endemic to contemporary American society. As in several of Guare's other plays, his main characters are self-absorbed, easily deluded people who are dazzled by the nearness of fame and dissatisfied with their own relationships. Yet Guare treats his characters with compassion, not contempt, presenting them as multidimensional rather than cartoonish figures.

The young man who convinces the Kittredges that he is both their childrens' friend and the son of a famous actor calls himself **Paul Poitier**, but his real identity is never established. The situation of a black man infiltrating a white household mirrors one of the most popular American films of the 1960s—*Guess Who's Coming to Dinner?*—in which a young white woman brings her black fiance home to meet her supposedly liberal parents. The movie features Sidney Poitier in the role of the fiance. Even though Paul is not really the actor's son, he is himself a good actor, for he convinces the Kittredges that he is a sophisticated college student and a child of privilege. Personable, charming, and articulate, Paul adeptly reads and responds to their moods, becoming what they want him to be and discoursing easily on a wide variety of subjects. The Kittredges' shocked disgust when they learn that Paul is actually a fake—and a homosexual as well—highlights the play's focus on all the possible divisions between people, including those imposed by race, class, and sexual preference. Consistently maintained as a mysterious, enigmatic figure, Paul serves as a catalyst in Ouisa's awakening by providing her with an "experience" that she wants to retain for herself, rather than turning it into an anecdote. Critics often cite Paul's monologue on the imagination as particularly well-crafted and central to the play's message: calling the imagination "God's gift to make the act of self-examination bearable," Paul bemoans its loss in American society and its use as an excuse for violent behavior or as a mere escape mechanism. Through the subplot involving the Utah couple, Paul undergoes a crisis of his own, learning that his clever manipulations can have fatal results.

Ouisa Kittredge is a rich, middle-aged woman who lives on the posh Upper East Side of Manhattan; she is a maker of arch conversation and a sophisticated hostess in an insular realm of privilege. Through her contact with the mysterious Paul, however, Ouisa is moved to try to reach through the many degrees of division between people. In fact, it is she who voices the theory that every human being is connected to every other by a genetic chain of only six links. These "degrees of separation" become the metaphoric obstacles that people who live in a dehumanizing environment such as New York City must break through to reach each other. Despite the many differences between them—racial, social, and sexual—Ouisa forms a meaningful bond with Paul, for she recognizes the truth in what he says even though she eventually learns that he is an impostor. His discourse on the value of the imagination makes Ouisa yearn to connect with her own, deepest self and to revere true experience rather than turning it into material for glib dinner party anecdotes.

Other significant characters in the play include Ouisa's husband, **Flan Kittredge**, an entrepreneurial art dealer who has lost the idealism and passion he once felt for art and who now views it in financial terms. Flan might be seen to represent the grossly inflated, highly mercenary art market of the 1980s. **Geoffrey** is a liberal South African billionaire who finds his contact with the charming, articulate Paul so flattering that he exuberantly agrees to provide the $3 million dollars Flan wants to invest in a Renoir painting.

Further Reading

Barnes, Clive. "Duped to the nth Degree." *New York Post* (June 15, 1990).

Brustein, Robert. "A Shaggy Dog Story." *New Republic* Vol. 194, no. 18 (May 5, 1986): 27–30.

Contemporary Literary Criticism. Vols. 8, 19, 67. Detroit: Gale Research.

Dasgupta, Guatam. *American Playwrights: A Critical Survey.* Vol. I. Drama Book Specialists, 1981.

Dictionary of Literary Biography. Vol. 7. Detroit: Gale Research, 1981.

Kroll, Jack. "The Con Games People Play." *Newsweek* Vol. 115, no. 26 (June 25, 1990): 54.

Major Twentieth-Century Writers. Vol. 2. Detroit: Gale Research, 1991.

Malone, Michael. Review of *The House of Blue Leaves. Nation* (New York) Vol. 242, no. 22 (June 7, 1986): 798–800.

Oliver, Edith. "Old and Improved." *New Yorker* Vol. 62, no. 6 (March 31, 1986): 66, 68.

Rich, Frank. Review of *The House of Blue Leaves. New York Times* (20 March 1986): C21.

———. "Schisms of the City, Comically and Tragically." *New York Times* (June 15, 1990): C1, C3.

———. "Six Degrees Reopens, Larger but Still Intimate." *New York Times* (November 9, 1990): C5.

Rose, Lloyd. "A New American Master." *Atlantic Monthly* Vol. 253, no. 3 (March 1984): 120–22, 124.

Weales, Gerald. "Degrees of Difference." *Commonweal* Vol. 118, no. 1 (January 11, 1991): 17–18.

Wilson, Edwin. "A Smash Revival." *Wall Street Journal* (April 9, 1986): 31.

Allan Gurganus

1947–

American novelist and short story writer.

Oldest Living Confederate Widow Tells All (novel, 1989)

Plot: The novel's central character is ninety-nine-year-old Lucy Marsden, the last surviving widow of a Confederate soldier and a feisty, garrulous storyteller. From her bed in a nursing home, Lucy provides an episodic account of her own experiences and the lives of those around her. She was married at fifteen to middle-aged Captain William Marsden, whose stories of the Civil War gradually became part of her own repertoire. One section of the novel recounts the imagined capture and enslavement of the ancestors of Castalia, the Marsden's African American servant and Lucy's best friend, as well as the burning of the Marsden plantation when General William Sherman's Union soldiers came through the area. In addition, Lucy reflects on her own life as the mother of nine children and wife of a difficult, pompous old man who became something of a tourist attraction toward the end of his life. Lucy also comments on such contemporary matters as the explosion of the space shuttle *Challenger* and the peculiarities of teenage fashion.

Characters: Born and raised in Rocky Mount, North Carolina, Gurganus was inspired to write *Oldest Living Confederate Widow Tells All* partly by his disconcerting discovery that his great-great-grandfather owned thirteen slaves. Structured episodically, the novel focuses on the South's twin legacies of slavery and defeat, exposing both continuities between the nineteenth and the twentieth centuries and some universal human truths that transcend place and time. Although some critics found this seven-hundred-plus-page novel overly sentimental, banal, or self-indulgent, many praised it as an impressive feat marked by witty prose and a deep joy in the art of storytelling.

Gurganus's creation of **Lucy Marsden** was sparked by a newspaper account of women who had married Civil War veterans as teenagers and were, near the end of the twentieth century, still drawing military pensions. Now ninety-nine, half-blind, and confined to a nursing home bed, the garrulous, forthright Lucy pours into her unnamed visitor's tape recorder a voluminous stream of memories and thoughts on such topics as "how it feels to be the last of something, my old man's bad news, what war does." An enthusiastic storyteller who admits that she sometimes embroiders the truth, Lucy claims, "My English may be as ugly as a mud fence but I know what a story is." She speaks in a lively, witty voice and scorns the good grammar that her genteel mother unsuccessfully tried to force on her. This same mother was a party to the arrangement by which fifteen-year-old Lucy was married off to the almost forty-years-older Will Marsden, thus sealing a land merger advantageous to both him and Lucy's parents. Despite this unpromising beginning, Lucy accommodates herself to life with Will, raising his nine children fairly cheerfully and tolerating his quirks. Nevertheless, her determination to reclaim "the boy in him" (lost, she realizes, somewhere in the wreckage of his war experiences) fails, and, according to critic Sterling Watson, the Marsdens' marriage "moves through accommodation to a kind of Victorian positive regard that is never quite love." In Will's declining years, Lucy serves as a kind of docent, offering tours of the old man to visitors eager to see a real Confederate soldier. As the end of her own life approaches, Lucy seems to have retained her mental energy and interest in the world, as well as her amazement at the resilience of human beings: "People recover. Ain't it something, what folks can spring back from?" Gurganus was generally lauded for endowing Lucy with considerable powers of mimicry that allow her to assume other peoples' voices and psyches, thus lending their stories vividness and authenticity. Several critics, however, found Lucy's voice a mannered and ultimately unconvincing blend of folksiness and sophistication. In addition, some commentators took exception to her assertion that "what you call history is really just the luxury of afterwards .... Honey, history ain't so historical. It's just us breaking even, just us trying."

When Lucy meets **Captain William (called Will or Cap) Marsden**, he is already middle-aged. After returning from his service in the Civil War and reestablishing his family's prosperity, he somehow never married. Will was only thirteen when he went off to war and never actually attained any higher rank than private, acquiring the title of "Captain" through his own self-promotional skills and the desire of others to see him as heroic. The reader gradually learns of the seminal event in Will's life: The death of his best friend Ned

Smythe, with whom he had left home and who was killed by a Yankee sniper. Gurganus has said in interviews that he intended to cast Will's lifelong hurt as a manifestation of what became known in the years following the Vietnam War as "post-traumatic syndrome." Gurganus was particularly praised for the sections of the novel that recount Will's war experiences, and especially the scene in which he travels to Boston to visit the family of a Union soldier he himself killed. Some critics found the temperamental, self-centered Will, described by Christopher Lehmann-Haupt as "the image of good-ole-boy masculinity," an unpleasant figure, while others lauded his portrayal as complex and memorable.

One of the novel's most effective passages is the narrative of **Castalia Marsden**, who begins her life as a Marsden family slave and becomes their servant after the Civil War. Approximately the same age as Will, Castalia is for some time his lover, and she initially resents the intrusion of the teenaged Lucy into the household. A self-possessed figure of monumental stature and formidable personality, Castalia eventually grows close to Lucy, who slides into Castalia's voice and African American dialect to envision with energy, humor, and deep pathos the journey of Castalia's African family into slavery in the United States. In addition, Castalia's section recounts the dramatic story of the Marsden plantation's burning by Yankee soldiers, providing a slave's perspective of this event.

Other characters in the novel include Will's beautiful friend **Ned Smythe**, whose sweet disposition and fine soprano voice make him a favorite of the soldiers among whom the two boys serve (he is even said to have sung for General Robert E. Lee) and from whose death Will never recovers; and **Lady More Marsden**, Will's imperious, Southern belle mother, who is tragically toppled from her aristocratic stance when her home is set afire by Union soldiers and she herself is accidentally immolated.

Further Reading

Benedict, Pinckney. "The Endless Story." *Tribune Books* (July 30, 1989): 3.

Bestsellers 90, Issue 1. Detroit: Gale Research.

Burgess, Anthony. "A Glass of the Warm South." *Observer* (November 5, 1989): 54.

Contemporary Literary Criticism Vol. 70. Detroit: Gale Research.

Lehmann-Haupt, Christopher. "A Human Comedy, as Told by a Glib 99-Year-Old." *New York Times* (August 10, 1989): C17.

Watson, Sterling. "A Centarian's Spellbinding Tale of the South." *Los Angeles Times Book Review* (September 24, 1989): 10.

Wilcox, James. "Her Whole Life Passes Before Our Eyes." *New York Times Book Review* (August 13, 1989): 1.

Yardley, Jonathan. "No Thanks for the Memories." *Washington Post Book World* (August 20, 1989): 3.

Barry Hannah
1942–
American novelist and short story writer.

Geronimo Rex (novel, 1972)

Plot: The novel chronicles the life of its narrator, Harriman "Harry" Monroe, from the time he is eight years old and lives in Dream of Pines, Louisiana, to when he is twenty-three and prepares to enter graduate school. In high school, Harry befriends Harley Butte, who plays the French horn in the acclaimed Beta Camina High School (Colored) Marching Band. He dreams of living a more glamorous life and falls in love many times, hopelessly idealizing his very ordinary girlfriends. Harry adopts the rebel Apache chief Geronimo as his hero, admiring the warrior's daring and brutality. In college, Harry's roommate is Bobby Dove Fleece, a self-anointed genius who encourages Harry to study medicine, but Harry says he would rather be a musician. Meanwhile, Harry obsesses over Peter Lepoyster. Called Whitfield Peter after the name of the insane asylum to which he was once committed, Lepoyster is a flaming racist who writes obscene letters to newspaper. His diatribe against Harley's band thoroughly enrages Harry. A gun battle occurs near the end of the novel, in which Harry wounds Lepoyster. Lepoyster has already shot and killed Mrs. Rooney, who is the owner of the boarding house in which Harry lives. For his crime Lepoyster is again sent to a psychiatric institution. Harry becomes engaged to seventeen-year-old Prissy Lombardo and plans to attend graduate school at the University of Arkansas to study literature.

Characters: Praised for his original vision of American life, lyrical language, and memorable characters, Hannah is often said to belong to the southern gothic tradition established by such writers as William Faulkner, Flannery O'Connor, and Eudora Welty. Like these authors, Hannah focuses on the comic, grotesque, or violent elements of southern life, which he renders in rich, exuberant prose. *Geronimo Rex* has been called a picaresque novel due to its episodic structure and depiction of a young man's journey toward adulthood. Considered unusually accomplished for a first novel, *Geronimo Rex* received the Bellaman Foundation and William Faulkner awards for fiction and was nominated for a National Book Award.

The novel, narrated by **Harriman "Harry" Monroe,** who relates his experiences from the ages of eight to twenty-three, is a kind of *bildungsroman* (novel of initiation). The turmoil of contemporary southern society is reflected in Harry's life as he struggles to establish his own identity. In his frequent anger against the establishment, confusion, and his search for meaning and a sense of belonging, Harry resembles other celebrated literary protagonists such as Holden Caulfield (in J. D. Salinger's 1951 novel *A Catcher in the Rye*) and Billy Liar (in Keith Waterhouse's 1959 novel of the same name). Unable to completely dedicate himself to anything, Harry falls in and out of love and frequently changes his career goals. He idolizes the fierce, adversarial Apache chief Geronimo, who periodically advises or admonishes Harry. His identification with Geronimo strikes some commentators as a survival technique of an insecure adolescent convinced that violence is inevitable and at times justified. Some reviewers consider it related to the problem of southern identity, for the southern way of life—like that of the Apache people during the nineteenth century—is threatened. Harry begins to view himself as a kind of warrior, and he takes up the defense of his African American friend Harley, whom he sees as menaced by the obnoxious Whitfield Peter Lepoyster. Unable to understand or walk away from Lepoyster, Harry resorts to the very violence that Lepoyster threatened to perpetrate. Critics acknowledge Harry's many unpleasant qualities—his aggression toward those weaker than himself, his pretensions to nonconformity, his frequent insensitivity—but reviewers praise Hannah for winning for the protagonist the reader's sympathy. Harry is redeemed by his awareness of his own absurdity, his intelligent insights, and his more sensitive moments, including his reaction to the cemetery at the Vicksburg battlefield and his appreciation for the excellence of Harley's art. As the novel concludes, Harry has established an admirable goal: to achieve the same creative integrity in his pursuit of literature that Harley has achieved in music.

The friendship between Harry and the African American **Harley Butte** is significant beyond the fact of the liaison between races, for Harley inspires Harry. Talented, creative, and completely devoted to music—especially the music of John Philip Sousa—Harley serves as a foil to Harry, whose protection he neither particularly needs or wants. Harry is initially jealous of Harley's gifts but moves beyond jealousy to respect and admiration, ready and even eager to defend Harley.

Another significant character is Harry's college roommate **Bobby Dove Fleece.** A sickly, rather effeminate young man from a genteel background, Harry initially assumes Bobby is a "flit." A self-proclaimed genius with a highly romantic view of life, Bobby speaks in an elaborate, Baroque prose which ultimately stirs Harry's latent interest in language and inspires him to pursue a career not in medicine—as Bobby has recommended—but in literature. Bobby is, in turn, influenced by Harry, for his approach to women gradually becomes more reckless and he accepts violence more readily.

One of the book's most memorable characters is **Whitfield Peter Lepoyster**, a mentally unstable racist who writes venomous letters to newspapers. Lepoyster's ardent hatred for anything unfamiliar contrasts strongly with his obsessive love for his wife, Catherine, and his niece (who is renamed Catherine after the death of her aunt). Even after Lepoyster becomes Harry's nemesis, Harry harbors an admiring envy of the old man's capacity for all-consuming love. Although some critics have found Lepoyster a preposterous character, Hannah has claimed that he is modeled after people the author knew during his own Mississippi upbringing. Because he is fascinated with Lepoyster's obsessive devotion to his wife and niece, Harry briefly dates Whitfield Peter's niece **Catherine**, a pretty but poor, unintelligent girl. Eventually, however, Harry realizes that he is using Catherine to fulfil his own, essentially false vision of romance.

Other characters in *Geronimo Rex* include boarding house matron **Mother Rooney**, a humorous figure who blithely ignores her boarders' profanity and who is eventually killed by the insane Lepoyster; and **Dr. Lariat**, the literature professor who agrees with Harry that Harley's marching band is "superb" and suggests that he and Harry should have pursued musical rather than literary careers. Harry's romantic interests include **Ann Mick**, the disreputable mill worker who fills both the high-school-aged Harry and his father with desire; **Sylvia Wyche**, the "technical virgin" Harry meets at summer music camp; and the teenaged **Prissy Lombardo**, a native of Pascagoula, Mississippi who (incongruously, according to several critics) becomes Harry's fiance at the end of the novel.

Ray (novel, 1980)

Plot: Set in Tuscaloosa, Alabama, the novel comprises sixty-two separate, impressionistic segments narrated in both first- and third-person voices by the title character, an alcoholic thirty-three-year-old physician who is trying to make sense of his tangled life. Ray has been passionately pursuing his three main interests: practicing medicines, flying airplanes, and having sex with a wide variety of partners. A jet fighter pilot for two years in Vietnam, Ray also claims to have fought with Confederate general Jeb Stuart during the Civil War. The father of three children from his first marriage and two stepchildren, Ray is now married to the warm, independent Westy, but he finds it impossible to remain faithful. Ray relates such misadventures as his arrangement with the poor white Hooch family, with whom he exchanges drugs for sex with the daughter, Sister; and his hijacking and crashing of a Lear jet. By the end of the novel, Ray's outlook seems to be improving, as he has reconciled with Westy and is able to appreciate life's more mundane pleasures.

Characters: *Ray* shares with much of Hannah's other fiction a focus, according to critic Ruth D. Weston, on "characters . . . searching for the key to the puzzle of themselves." Lauded by many commentators as one of Hannah's most effective, entertaining novels, *Ray* features an experimental, fragmentary structure that mirrors its protagonist's attempt to work his way out of an identity crisis. In this novel, as in his other fiction, Hannah incorporates circumstances from his own life; during the period he was writing *Ray* he was himself suffering the effects of alcoholism and a shattered marriage.

As *Ray* begins, the title character, drying out from alcoholism in a Tuscaloosa hospital, tells himself, "Say what? You want to know who I am?" The rest of the novel may be considered an answer—if fragmented and inevitably incomplete—to this question. Sixty-two fragments flesh out a portrait of **Ray**'s psyche, revealing him, according to critic Michael P. Spikes, to be "a man of monumental extravagances, quirks, and contradictions." Ray narrates his story in a unique voice that critics have generally deemed highly effective: it shifts frequently from first- and third-person and back—sometimes even within the same sentence—Ray both speaks for himself and analyzes his life objectively. A jet fighter pilot during the Vietnam War, Ray (whose last name is never mentioned, though his middle name is Forrest) is now a thirty-three-year-old doctor who loves practicing medicine and flying airplanes. He also writes poetry and cannot keep himself from endangering his marriage through his addiction to random sex. Ray claims to exist in several centuries at once, asserting to have fought not only in Vietnam but in the Civil War. Some critics consider the connection between the two wars (both of which could be said to involve lost causes) distracting and unconvincing, while others maintain that it effectively delineates Ray's view of himself. Ray's many unsavory habits and characteristics include his incessant philandering, his opportunistic bargain with the Hooches, and his tendency to place himself above conventional morality. For example, as a physician, Ray takes it upon himself to cut off the life support systems for an elderly man who has brutally abused his family, which he considers justified. Yet, Ray wins the reader's sympathy through his moments of concern for others, his intelligence, and the noble sentiments that occur to him but which he finds himself unable to enact. Ray does not become a different person by the end of the novel, but he does seem to develop a heightened sense of life's sweetness and the lasting pleasures of commitment to family.

The fact that at the end of *Ray* the title character is still married and apparently newly committed to **Westy,** his feisty but engaging second wife, allows the novel to end on a note of redemption. Ray's behavior toward his strong, unselfish wife is at fault, and, despite his obvious love for her, he endangers their marriage through his weakness for illicit sex. Ray even recognizes his obsession, telling himself, "Ray, the filthy call of random sex is a killer. It kills all you know of the benevolent order of your life." Westy represents that benevolent order and whatever hope there may for Ray's future.

Commentator John Romano has called the memorable Hooch family "the most lovable white trash anyone has dared to portray in any medium," and other critics have also lauded Hannah for his detailed depiction of their sordid yet somehow admirably defiant habits and surroundings. Ray both envies and admires **Mr. Hooch**'s incongruous poetic gift, which far exceeds Ray's ability, and seeing his disreputable friend with a pencil in his hand is part of what, at the end of the novel, heightens Ray's sense of well-being. **Mrs. Hooch** is a morphine addict who obsessively watches movies on cable television, apparently transfixed by the glamour and adventure in such contrast to her own life. Ray carries on a long-term affair with the promiscuous **Sister Hooch,** whose essential honesty and beauty he reveres and who seems to represent for him the possibility of a simple, true love. Sister is eventually murdered by a religious fanatic, **Maynard Castro**. Just as Ray is finally reconciled with Westy, his friend **Charlie DeSoto**, who manages a Tuscaloosa soap factory, eventually resolves his problems with his wife Eileen.

Further Reading

Charney, Mark J. *Barry Hannah*. New York: Twayne, 1992.

Contemporary Literary Criticism. Vols. 23, 38. Detroit: Gale Research.

DeMott, Benjamin. "Rudeness Is Our Only Hope." *New York Times Book Review* (November 16, 1980): 7, 26.

Dictionary of Literary Biography. Vol. 6. Detroit: Gale Research.

Fremont-Smith, Eliot. "Hoo-Ray." *Village Voice* Vol. 25, no. 47 (November 19, 1980): 70, 72.

Lehmann-Haupt, Christopher. "Books of the Times." *New York Times* (November 11, 1980): Sec. III, p. 8.

Spikes, Michael P. "What's in a Name? A Reading of Barry Hannah's *Ray*." *Mississippi Quarterly* Vol. 42 (winter 1988–89): 69–82.

Weston, Ruth D. "'The Whole Lying Opera of It': Dreams, Lies, and Confessions in the Fiction of Barry Hannah." *Mississippi Quarterly* Vol. 44 (fall 1991): 411–28.

Wolff, Geoffrey. "Answering the Odd World." *New Republic* Vol. 183, no. 24 (December 13, 1980): 31–2.

Updike, John. "From Dyna Domes to Turkey-Pressing." *New Yorker* Vol. 48, No. 29 (September 9, 1972): 121–24.

Lorraine Hansberry
1930–1965
American dramatist and essayist.

A Raisin in the Sun (drama, 1959)

Plot: Set in a shabby apartment on Chicago's south side, the play takes place sometime between the end of World War II and the late 1950s. The Youngers are an African American family made up of Lena, the matriarch; her son, Walter Lee, a chauffeur; her daughter, Beneatha, a college student; Walter's wife, Ruth, a part-time domestic worker; and Walter and Ruth's young son, Travis. As the play opens, Walter inquires about a check the family is expecting—the $10,000 payment from Lena's deceased husband, Big Walter's life insurance policy. The family has agreed that Lena should decide what to do with the money, but each member has his or own ideas about it. Walter has dreams of status and getting rich by owning a liquor store, and he pleads with Ruth to convince Lena to give him the money to buy one. Weary Ruth (who is pregnant and considering an abortion) seems unsympathetic with this plan, but after Walter leaves and Lena appears she does repeat his wish. The very commanding, dignified elder woman, however, plans to buy a home, the goal she and her husband worked toward for so many years. Beneatha (who wants to be a doctor and hopes some of the money will help with medical school) receives a visit from her friend Asagai, a

Nigerian student. He brings her some African robes and teases her about her straightened, "mutilated" hair. Later, Beneatha's boyfriend, George Murchison, son of a wealthy black family, arrives to pick her up for their date. He talks down to Walter and scorns Beneatha's interest in her African heritage. When the young couple is gone, Lena returns and announces that she has put a down payment on a house in Clybourne Park, a white neighborhood. Walter is outraged.

Several weeks later, Lena decides to give Walter the $6,500 left after the down payment, but she asks him to put part of it in the bank for Beneatha's medical education. A week later, while the family is packing for their move to the new house, they are visited by one of their neighbors from the new neighborhood, Karl Lindner. Although polite, he ultimately reveals that he and his fellow residents do not want a black family in their neighborhood, and he offers to buy the Youngers' house for a profit. They angrily dismiss Lindner from the apartment. Later, Walter's friend Bobo arrives to inform him that the third partner in the liquor store, Willy, has fled with all their money. Devastated, Walter admits that he never put Beneatha's share of the money aside and that all the money is gone. Convinced she will never be a doctor after all, Beneatha tells Asagai that she will think about his proposal that they marry and return to Nigeria together. Walter believes they have no choice but to accept Lindner's offer to buy the house, until Lena reminds him of their family's hard work and pride and that they have never been so poor that they would accept such money. When Lindner arrives to finalize the deal, Walter informs him that the Youngers have decided to move into the house that their father worked so hard to buy. After Lindner leaves, Ruth says, "Let's get the hell out of here!" and the family finishes their packing and departs.

Characters: Hansberry was the first African American woman (and the youngest American) to win the coveted New York Drama Critics Circle Award, and *A Raisin in the Sun* was the first play by a black woman to be produced on Broadway. The play's title is taken from a poem in Langston Hughes's volume *Montage of a Dream Deferred* ("What happens to a dream deferred?/Does it dry up/Like a raisin in the sun?/ . . . Or does it explode?"), and its central situation is from Hansberry's own biography: when she was eight years old, her family encountered hostility and violence when they moved into a segregated white Chicago neighborhood. In the years since its first performance, the play has generated considerable debate. Early reviewers praised Hansberry's success in creating highly recognizable characters struggling with problems that are both topical and universal. But during the next several decades, some militant critics called the play a cliched melodrama that prettified African American life in order to win approval from white, middle-class audiences and patronizing theater critics. The play's popularity (and that of subsequent film versions) with both black and white audiences has never wavered, however, and most recent commentators have concurred on the scope of Hansberry's accomplishment, agreeing that she incorporated such profound and complex themes as racial integration and tolerance, the desire for freedom and to improve one's life, the dangers of materialism, and the different ways in which human degradation, pride, and courage may be expressed into a naturalistic, highly accessible format. Whether Hansberry scorns or affirms the American dream of "success," as various critics have argued, she offers no easy answers to the Youngers' situation and never suggests that their subsequent lives will be placid; she does, however, affirm the necessity and value of both compassion and self-respect.

Lean, intense **Walter Lee Younger**, whose voice is always charged with a "quality of indictment," is seen by many critics as the play's central character—the pivot around which the action turns. Hansberry has won consistent praise for her characterization of this frustrated, bitter African American male, who has been said to anticipate the black militancy that emerged in the decades following the play's debut. While working as a chauffeur, Walter has witnesses the luxurious lifestyle enjoyed by his affluent employer, Mr. Arnold, in stark contrast to the hardships his own family endures. In a passage critics often cited as encapsulating Walter's self-image, he describes himself: "I'm thirty-five years old; I been married eleven years and I got a boy who sleeps in the living room—and all I can give him is stories about how rich white people live." A complex figure who inspires both sympathy and distaste, Walter struggles with his desire to improve his life, his love for and pride in his family, the frustrations in his marriage, and his feeling of failure and emasculation. Many commentators have noted that Walter, more than any other character in the play, illustrates how elusive is the American dream and how superficial its vision of success, intrinsically tied to material possessions and money. To Lena's deep chagrin, Walter insists that money is all that matters, and this attitude explains his obsession with the insurance check, which he sees as an instant key to affluence. Walter has often been compared to Willy Loman, the protagonist of Arthur Miller's 1949 play *The Death of a Salesman,* who also viewed wealth as the indicator of accomplishment and who eventually experienced the falseness and failure of his dream. Rather than blaming himself or society for his perceived failure, Walter chauvinistically blames the women in his life. He resents Lena for her domination over the family, scorns Beneatha's ambition to be a doctor, and complains that Ruth does not sympathize with him or try to raise his spirits: "Man say: I got to change my life, I'm choking to death, baby! And his woman say—Your eggs is getting cold!" Walter's low point occurs when, after the insurance money has been stolen, he decides they should accept Lindner's offer to buy them out, and he puts on an act of the subservient black man kowtowing to his white master. This behavior provokes Lena's impassioned speech about their family history and pride, which seems to awaken Walter's self-esteem. Critics maintain that when he rejects Lindner's offer, telling him that the Youngers will move into their house because "my father—my father—he earned it," Walter attains manhood, dignity, redemption, or even heroism. Unlike Bigger Thomas—the central figure in Richard Wright's influential 1940 novel, *Native Son,* who resembles Walter in milieu, occupation, and anger—Walter does not "explode" in violence but transcends the despair, hatred, and materialism that previously held him down.

The matriarch of the family, **Lena Younger**, is a commanding presence who seems to radiate moral strength and dignity. Although some critics feel her character is the stereotyped, sentimentalized African American mother often seen in literature—virtuous, long-suffering, and responsible for holding the family together—most find her authentic and effective. Sometimes dictatorial (such as when she slaps Beneatha for denying the existence of God and insists that she repeat the phrase, "In my mother's house there is still God") and occasionally interfering, Lena is a compassionate, loving, presence in their lives. Unlike Walter's affluence, Lena dreams simply of owning a home of their own. This is the goal toward which she and her husband—the late **Big Walter**, who was a railroad porter— worked all their lives. Lena claims that they tried to instill a sense of pride and ambition in their children, and she is dismayed by the materialism and cynicism they express. A survivor of many hardships who is intensely religious and moral, Lena does not understand how Beneatha can deny God's existence or how Walter can value money above all else. "Once upon a time freedom used to be life," she notes, referring to the days of lynchings and Jim Crow laws; "now it's money." Lena views Walter's desire to buy a liquor store and Ruth's wishes to have an abortion as signs of how desperate they have become. Yet Lena also recognizes Walter's pain and the sense of emasculation he feels in his female-dominated home; thus she finally gives him control over the remaining funds. In addition, she urges Beneatha to have more compassion for her brother even after he loses the money and threatens to accept Lindner's demeaning deal; Lena asks her daughter to "measure him right," to try to understand Walter's position. Lena eloquently expresses the play's message of ennobling self-respect when she advises Walter that she comes from "five generations of slaves and sharecroppers" but that no one in her family has "never let anybody pay 'em no money that was a way of telling us we wasn't fit to walk the earth. We ain't never been that poor . . . . that dead inside." Lena's plea for dignity is pivotal in Walter's change of mind and redemption. At the play's conclusion, the iron-strong Lena reveals her softer side one last time when she returns to the apartment to retrieve her houseplant (an apt symbol for her family) in order to carry and nurture it into the future.

Beneatha Younger is an intelligent, energetic college student who intends to become a doctor—if she can get the money for tuition. Somewhat adolescent in her behavior and interests, Beneatha tends to latch onto fads, pursuing such expensive hobbies as horseback riding and guitar playing, which some critics called fan attempt to adopt middle-class white values. Yet Beneatha is also interested in her African heritage, as her friendship with Asagai attests. She wears with delight the African robes he gives her, pretending she is a "Queen of the Nile." Beneatha's conversations with Asagai allow Hansberry to explore some of the key issues African Americans of that period and later years grappled with, such as assimilation versus racial pride, the intellectual's relationship with the masses, and how much Africans and American blacks have in common. Yet Beneatha resists Asagai's chauvinism view of women and—probably—his marriage proposal. She also rejects the "rich snob" George when he tells her he values—not her intelligence—but her good looks and sophistication. Similarly, Beneatha is disgusted by her brother's sexism (he wonders why she doesn't become a nurse or get married instead of pursuing a medical degree) and his selfishness, particularly after he loses the money she needs for her education. Beneatha's commitment to a medical career appears rather shallow when she immediately sinks into despair and admits to Asagai that she is "all mixed up," but the audience may attribute her confusion to her youthful immaturity. Beneatha's response to Walter's behavior—she claims he is "no brother of mine" after he says he will accept Lindner's offer—that provokes Lena's plea for her to "measure him right." Hansberry claimed that she modeled Beneatha after herself at the same age and that she enjoyed poking fun at herself through her portrayal of Beneatha's self-righteousness and faddish interests.

Ruth Younger, Walter's wife, is described as a "settled" woman tired of working as a domestic and of raising a child and maintaining a marriage in a small apartment, which is shared with her husband's mother and sister. Early in the play, we learn that Ruth is pregnant, adding another tension to her life that she may choose to eliminate by having an abortion. Walter complains that Ruth is unsympathetic to his needs; he says that when he cries out for help she just tells him to eat his eggs. The truth, however, seems to be that she is well aware of his pain but unsure how to relieve it. She does, after all, plead Walter's case to her mother-in-law, even though her own views on how the money should be spent are closer to Lena's: she wants a place with a room for her son and its own bathroom (the Youngers share a bathroom with other tenants of their apartment building). It seems that whenever Walter and Ruth try to revive some of the warmth in their relationship, they are constantly interrupted, illustrating how difficult it is to achieve marital harmony in such close quarters. Ruth reveals how important the new house is to her when she claims she will work twenty hours a day with her baby on her back if it will allow the family to move.

Travis Younger, the son of Ruth and Walter, is a well-behaved boy who has caused his family little trouble, although he is somewhat "spoiled" with three adults doting on him. With no room of his own, he sleeps on the living room sofa, a fact that is symbolic of Walter's sense of failure. Yet when Walter rejects Lindner's offer, Walter draws Travis toward him, and the boy seems to serve as the repository of the family's proud heritage and its hope for the future.

Through **Asagai**, a Nigerian student and Beneatha's suitor, Hansberry explores the complex issue of African identity and how it relates to American blacks. An intellectual who plans to return to and serve his own country after finishing school, Asagai encourages Beneatha to explore her racial heritage. He brings her African clothing and music and gently chides her for her artificially straightened hair, which he considers "mutilated." Although Asagai does not believe Beneatha is as emancipated a woman as she likes to believe, he does nickname her *Alaiyo* or "one for whom bread is not enough," an acknowledgement that she yearns for more than the material possessions her brother covets. Asagai is mystified by Beneatha's hopelessness after Walter loses the money that would have paid for her medical education; he feels that she should not allow the course of her life to be determined by such "accidents"—a concept that has been cited as an important theme in the play. Critics feel that Asagai embodies the ebullient pride and optimism that marked the early years of the postcolonial period, when many African countries gained independence. *A Raisin in the Sun* explores the question of how much African Americans had in common with African blacks and whether the latter could be expected to experience the same sense of self-esteem; some commentators, for example, find Asagai an unconvincing character because, unlike Walter, his self-assurance is never tested within the context of the play.

The only white character in the play is **Karl Lindner**, a member of Clybourne Park's New Neighbor Orientation Committee who visits the Youngers in the hope of dissuading them from moving into his community. Described by some critics as a stereotyped white, middle-class suburbanite, Lindner expresses the segregationist ethic. He masks his message of hate and paranoia with polite speech, but the Youngers understand his true message. Ironically, Lindner's description of the residents of Clybourne Park mirrors the Younger family: they are "not rich and fancy people; just hardworking honest people" who harbor "a dream of the kind of community they want to raise their children in." It is to Lindner that Walter makes his moving speech about his pride in his family and their intention to live in the house for which their father worked so hard.

Beneatha's boyfriend, the well-dressed, rather stiff **George Murchison**, is the son of a wealthy black family and the kind of African American, Beneatha tells her mother, who is even more snobbish than the most snobbish white person. George has adopted all the worst aspects of American materialism and thus illustrates the ambiguity of the American dream of success. A complete assimilationist, George scorns Beneatha's interest in her heritage. Having benefited from a success based on trading in racial identity for the trappings of white culture, George cannot understand or relate to Walter's pain and considers him unduly bitter. George also reveals his sexist—when he informs Beneatha that her intelligence is of no consequence to him—an admission that results in Beneatha's rejecting him.

Other characters in *A Raisin in the Sun* include Walter's business partners, **Willy**, who disappears with the money, and **Bobo**, the frightened little man who informs Walter of the theft. In a scene that was cut from the original version of the play but added to later productions, a nosy neighbor named **Mrs. Johnson** appears in the Youngers' apartment to mean-spiritedly predict that there will be bombings in Clybourne Park after they move there.

Further Reading

Abramson, Doris. "The Fifties." In *Negro Playwrights in the American Theatre, 1925–1959*. New York: Columbia University Press, 1969, 165–266.

Baraka, Amiri. "*A Raisin in the Sun*'s Enduring Passion." In *"A Raisin in the Sun" and "The Sign in Sidney Brustein's Window."* Lorraine Hansberry. Edited by Robert Nemiroff. New York: New American Library, 1987, 9–20.

Bigsby, C. W. E. "Lorraine Hansberry." In *Confrontation and Commitment: A Study of Contemporary American Drama, 1959–66*. Columbia: University of Missouri Press, 1968, 156–73.

Black Literature Criticism. Vol. 2. Detroit: Gale Research.

Brown, Lloyd W. "Lorraine Hansberry as Ironist: A Reappraisal of *A Raisin in the Sun*." *Journal of Black Studies* Vol. 4, no. 3 (March 1974): 237–47.

Carter, Steven R. *Hansberry's Drama: Commitment and Complexity.* Champaign-Urbana: University of Illinois Press, 1991.

Cheney, Anne. *Lorraine Hansberry.* Boston: Twayne, 1984.

Contemporary Literary Criticism. Vols. 17, 62. Detroit: Gale Research.

Cruse, Harold. "Lorraine Hansberry." *The Crisis of the Negro Intellectual.* New York: William Morrow, 1967., 267–84.

Freedomways Vol. 19, no. 4 (1979). Special issue devoted to Hansberry.

Hansberry, Lorraine. "Willie Loman, Walter Younger, and He Who Must Live." *Village Voice* Vol. 4, no. 42 (August 12, 1959): 7–8.

Hewes, Henry. "A Plant Grows in Chicago." *Saturday Review* Vol. 42, no. 14 (April 4, 1959): 28.

Keyssar, Helen. "Sounding the Rumble of Dreams Deferred: Lorraine Hansberry's *A Raisin in the Sun.*" In *The Curtain and the Veil: Strategies in Black Drama.* Burt Franklin, 1981, 113–46.

Miller, Jordan Y. "Lorraine Hansberry." In *The Black American Writer: Poetry and Drama. Vol. II.* Edited by C. W. E. Bigsby. Deland, FL: Everett-Edwards, 1969, 157–20.

Nemiroff, Robert. Introduction to *A Raisin in the Sun.* Lorraine Hansberry. New York: New American Library, 1987, ix–xviii.

Washington, J. Charles. "*A Raisin in the Sun* Revisited." *Black American Literature Forum* Vol. 22 (spring 1988): 109–24.

Weales, Gerald. "Thoughts on *A Raisin in the Sun.*" *Commentary* Vol. 27, no. 6 (June 1959): 527–30.

David Hare
1947–

English dramatist, scriptwriter, and filmmaker.

Plenty (drama, 1978)

Plot: Set in France, Belgium, and England, the play chronicles events in the life of Englishwoman Susan Traherne. The first scene takes place in 1962, with Susan walking out on her husband, Raymond Brock, and leaving her house in the care of her friend Alice. Then the action jumps back to 1943, when eighteen-year-old Susan works as a courier for the French Resistance. In St. Benoit, France, she meets British operative Lazar, who has parachuted behind enemy lines. The next scene is set in the British Embassy in Brussels, where Susan goes for help after the death of her lover. There she meets the ambassador, Sir Leonard Darwin, and the third secretary, Brock. Several months later, Brock visits Susan and her bohemian roommate, Alice, in London and tries unsuccessfully to convince Susan—now working in an unfulfilling public relations job—to return to Brussels with him. In a scene set in 1951, Susan convinces Mick, a young merchandiser, to help her conceive a child, promising that she wants only a baby, not a husband and that he will have no further obligations to her. Eighteen months later, Susan is not yet pregnant, but Mick has fallen in love with her. Angered and increasingly unstable, Susan fires her revolver at Mick. She is confined to a sanitarium, where Brock visits her and proposes marriage. Susan finds life as a diplomat's wife stifling, and while hosting a dinner in 1956, she lashes out at Darwin about England's policy during the Suez Canal crisis. Darwin subsequently resigns his post. Susan's erratic behavior affects Brook's career, and he finally leaves diplomatic service to sell insurance. In a scene set at Easter 1962 (just before the action depicted at the beginning of the play), the long-suffering Brook tells Susan she is selfish and insensitive. He threatens to commit her to a psychiatric hospital, but instead Susan manages to sedate him and escape. She then meets Lazar in a French seaside hotel and learns that he shares her disappointment and disillusionment in peacetime life. The play's last scene takes place in St. Benoit, just after the end of the war. A young, jubilant Susan tells a French farmer that the English are going to ''improve the world'' and that ''There will be days and days like this.''

Characters: Hare, a leading English dramatist, first gained renown as one of his country's Fringe Playwrights, who during the 1970s, created dramas highlighting the social and political maladies of contemporary British society. Considered Hare's most important work, *Plenty* received even more critical acclaim in the United States and won the New York Drama Critics Circle Award for Best Foreign Play. The play depicts the disillusionment and declining moral values of postwar England, where illusions of prosperity and abundance gave way to what critic Stanley Kauffman describes as ''a scarcity of convictions.'' Lauded for his incisive, witty dialogue and for the intelligence and moral sense evident in his dramas, Hare describes Plenty as a work ''about the cost of a life spent in dissent . . . of making the past run your life.''

The public maladies of postwar British society contrast with the private turmoil of **Susan Traherne**, the central character in *Plenty*, a technique that earns Hare both praise and criticism. While some critics complain that Hare fails to clarify whether Susan's problems are endemic or personal, others assert that the playwright intends to blur that distinction, which broadens and deepens the play's thematic scope. Susan's work for the French Resistance during the war exposed her at an early age to a passion, danger, and commitment that she would never encounter again, and she later succumbs to boredom and despair, alcohol and drug dependence, and recurring episodes of madness. Susan considers herself above the stifling confines of convention, yet she is also vulnerable. While those around her seem to accept the burden of personal compromise and social decay, Susan resists both. Her work does not satisfy her, her attempt to have a child fails, her marriage proves a mistake, and Susan gradually loses her mind. Commentators note a marked ambiguity in how Hare portrays Susan, who is often an unsympathetic character. As Brock finally tells her, she is selfish, unreasonable, and hurtful and she is so intent on her own suffering that she cannot relate to anyone else. Yet Susan's intelligence and vulnerability make her somewhat appealing, as in the poignant final scene which highlights her youthful expectations for herself and her country. Several commentators compare Susan to the heroine of Henrik Ibsen's 1890 play *Hedda Gabler*: both characters are angry, bored, and self-destructive; both scorn convention; and both characters are highly emotional and have access to firearms.

Susan meets her husband, **Raymond Brock**, when he is a young, ambitious third secretary at the British Embassy in Brussels. Susan seems mainly attracted to him for his financial stability—a state he himself believes to be an indicator of England's inevitable prosperity— a condition that will greatly improve her standard of living. Brock endures Susan's antagonism and bouts of madness for many years before he tells her, ''You claim to be protecting some personal ideal, always at a cost of almost infinite pain to everyone around you.'' To some critics, the long-suffering Brock personifies the stagnant repression of English society. Unlike Susan, Brock accommodates himself to the hypocrisy of diplomatic life, which he defends as keeping ''things pleasant for at least part of the time.''

Susan's friend **Alice** is an aspiring writer and self-styled bohemian who initially sponges off Susan. Spontaneous, adventurous, and independent, Alice shares Susan's disillusionment, but in the end she exhibits a capacity for action that Susan lacks. Alice gives up her solipsism to become a social worker, thus channeling her dissatisfaction into productive work. At the dinner party at which Susan makes a scene, Alice remarks memorably that this behavior is simply part of Susan's "psychiatric cabaret."

Hare explores Britain's economic and moral decline through **Sir Leonard Darwin**. As England's ambassador to Brussels after World War II, Darwin hopes for building a new, egalitarian Europe. Later, however, Darwin loses hope as he witnesses the Suez Canal debacle. Convinced that England intended seize the canal, Darwin resigns from the Foreign Service to protest his governments hypocrisy and duplicity. Critic Joan Fitzpatrick Dean describes another Foreign Service character, personnel director **Sir Andrew Charleson**, as "the paragon of diplomatic language and evasiveness." When Susan visits him in order to convince him to advance her husband's career, Charleson tells her, "Behaviour is all."

Susan never forgets **Lazar**, the British commando she meets when he parachutes into France during the war. Afterward she idealizes their brief encounter, associating it with the romance, danger, and idealism of that period. When the two meet again in 1962, they share mutual disappointment with postwar life, a circumstance that some critics interpret as meaning that Susan's despair is endemic rather than purely personal. As their reunion cannot possibly match her expectations, the scene ends with Susan sinking into a drugged stupor. Another significant secondary character is **Mick**, a young merchandiser from the down-at-the-heels East End of London, who agrees to try to help Susan conceive a child but who breaks the rules of their relationship when he falls in love with her. Like several other of the play's male characters, Mick proves more conventional than Susan, seeking security while she longs for adventure. He is the first to suspect her mental instability, and he receives proof when she fires her revolver at him.

Further Reading

Brustein, Robert. "Good and Plenty." *New Republic* Vol. 187, no. 21 (November 29, 1982): 24–6.

Contemporary Literary Criticism. Vols. 29, 58. Detroit: Gale Research.

Dean, Joan Fitzpatrick. *David Hare.* Boston: Twayne, 1990.

Dictionary of Literary Biography, Vol. 13. Detroit: Gale Research.

Hayman, Ronald. "The Politics of Hatred." In *British Theatre since 1955: A Reassessment.* Oxford: Oxford University Press, 1979, pp. 80–128.

Kauffman, Stanley. Review of *Plenty. Saturday Review* (March 1983).

Levin, Bernard. Review of *Plenty. Sunday Times* (April 16,1978).

Ludlow, Colin. "Hare & Others." *London Magazine* Vol.18, no. 4 (July 1978): 76–81.

Nightingale, Benedict. Interview with David Hare. *New York Times* (October 17, 1982): Sec. II, pp. 1, 6.

Oliva, Judy Lee. *David Hare: Theatricalizing Politics.* Ann Arbor, MI: UMI Research Press, 1990.

Page, Malcolm, ed. *File on Hare.* London: Methuen Drama, 1990.

Rich, Frank. "Drama: From Britain, *Plenty* by David Hare." *New York Times* (October 22, 1982).

Simon, John. "Too Much Heart? Too Much Brain?" *New York Magazine* 15, no. 43 (November 1, 1982): 81–3.

Jim Harrison

1937–

American novelist, poet, essayist, scriptwriter, and critic.

Dalva (novel, 1988)

Plot: The novel is comprised of three sections, all structured as diary entries. The first section is narrated by the title character. Dalva Northridge is a beautiful forty-five-year-old woman who, as the novel begins, has been living in Southern California and working as a social worker, even though her Nebraska family's wealth provides her with ample income. Her diary documents her continuing anguish over the son she gave up for adoption when she was fifteen; the child was born after her affair with a half-Sioux boy named Duane, who turned out to be her half-brother. Dalva also ruminates on her relationships with her mother, Naomi; her long-dead father, Wesley; her beloved grandfather, John Northridge; as well as her sister Ruth and uncle Paul. For many years she had roamed across the United States, South America, and Europe. Dalva then returns to her family's home in Nebraska, intending to teach in a local school. The novel's second section is narrated by one of Dalva's lovers, Michael, a historian at Stanford University. Michael is eager to delve into the Northridge family papers. The diary of Dalva's great-grandfather, J. W. Northridge, promises to offer new insights into the troubled history of Native Americans from the end of the Civil War to the Wounded Knee massacre in 1890. Northridge was a horticulturist who came west to help the Indians adapt to agrarian life, and his sympathy for them and his outrage over the treatment they received from the U.S. government led to his own alienation from society. While reading through Northridge's diaries at Dalva's family's ranch, Michael struggles with his own wayward predilections for alcohol and sex. The novel's final section, narrated again by Dalva, relates her decision to stay in Nebraska even though she loses her schoolteaching job. She is also reunited with her now-thirty-year-old son, who has secretly come to Nebraska to find her.

Characters: A critically acclaimed novelist, Harrison injects into his novels his skill as a poet, his upbringing in northern Michigan, his love of the outdoors, and his appreciation of good food and wine. Because Harrison's earlier novels centered on male characters and concerns, commentators praised Harrison for creating a believable, compelling female protagonist in *Dalva*. The novel combines romance, history, contemplation, and humor in a diary format that allows for rich prose and gradual revelation of character. Harrison states that one of the novel's central purposes is to prick the conscience of the American public about what happened to Native Americans during the last years of the nineteenth century.

Two-thirds of the novel is narrated by the title character, **Dalva Northridge**, who is part-Sioux and was brought up in a wealthy Nebraska ranch family. Beautiful, vigorous, and independent, the tough, worldly, and sensitive forty-five-year-old woman enjoys life and keenly feels the losses she has endured. One is the son she gave up for adoption after his birth when unmarried and fifteen years old, she learns that the father of her child is her half-brother. Dalva saw her half-brother, Duane, only once more, when he returned from fighting in Vietnam, just before he committed suicide. She intends her diary to be a kind of testimony to be read by her son, whom she hopes to locate, despite her misgivings about whether the two should meet. Dalva has spent much of her adult life traveling and has lived, worked, and loved on both coasts of the United States as well as Europe and South America. Though wealthy, she has always worked, favoring jobs that allowed her to express her social conscience. Dalva returns to Nebraska at first to escape from a threatening situation connected with her social work, but she ultimately explores and reconciles herself with her past. Several critics find Dalva unconvincing because she is so perfect: beautiful, intelligent, extremely well-read, and levelheaded, she is also an expert on gourmet food and wine, an accomplished horsewoman, and a free-spirited, generous lover. Nevertheless, most commentators praise Harrison for the eloquent, even lyrical passages in which Dalva contemplates her family, her youthful passion, her losses and triumphs, and her attitude toward life and the world.

The novel's humor is relayed mainly through **Michael**, who narrates the middle chapter. Michael's section is structured as his "workbook," or running commentary, while he is conducting historical research at the Northridge ranch. A professor at Stanford University, Michael is desperate for tenure and pleads with Dalva, who has already been his lover, to allow him access to the family papers, which he suspects are of great academic and social value. In return he promises to help her locate her son, an oath that is never fulfilled. However, Michael arrives in Nebraska a hopeless alcoholic, and Dalva spends much of her time during his stay either administering carefully regulated amounts of alcohol to him or rescuing him from the messes into which his behavior lands him. Despite his self-destructive tendencies, Michael is inherently charming and has real passion for his work. Several of his escapades are humorous, especially his attempts to befriend the resident geese and his disastrous sexual entanglement with a local teenager, whose irate father puts Michael in the hospital with a broken jaw. Michael's chapter features many excerpts from the diary of the Northridge family's nineteenth-century forebear.

Harrison has been lauded for his skillful rendering of the diary of **J. W. Northridge**, Dalva's great-grandfather, who came to Nebraska from the eastern United States to work among the Sioux as a horticulturist and a Methodist minister. The diary entries relate Northridge's marginal successes helping the Indians adapt from a nomadic, hunting-centered life to the agrarian one forced upon them. Meanwhile, Northridge found his own Christian faith waning as he witnessed the physical and spiritual devastation of the Sioux people and their culture. He was briefly married to a lovely young Swedish immigrant girl, **Aase**, who died of tuberculosis, and this loss seems to have haunted him for the rest of his life. Northridge became a kind of doctor to the Sioux and an adviser and friend of

such leaders as He Dog and Kicking Bear. Around the time of the Wounded Knee massacre, which sealed the fate of the Sioux nation and which Northridge witnessed with horror, Northridge took a Sioux wife, who eventually gave birth to Dalva's grandfather. Northridge is portrayed as friend and sympathizer of the Sioux and well as exploiter, since he purchased a large piece of land that once belonged to them. Near the end of the novel, Dalva ventures into the cellar room. There a wide variety of Native American artifacts as well as the skeletons of several Sioux warriors and three U. S. Army officers collected by her great-grandfather have been hidden away for safe keeping.

John Northridge, Dalva's grandfather, who was born in a tipi to the Sioux wife of J. W. Northridge, had a racial inheritance he was always fiercely proud of. Dalva's strong, rugged, independent grandfather instilled in her a strong sense of family heritage and a deep love for her natural surroundings and for the horses and other animals that played such significant roles on the ranch. Always a nurturing, loving force in Dalva's life, her grandfather assured her—after the birth and loss of her son—that she was not wrong to love Duane even if their passion was ill-fated. Dalva's gracious, bird-loving mother, **Naomi,** is another positive influence in her life. Naomi has apparently never fully recovered from the death of her husband, **John Wesley Northridge**, in the Korean war, and admits to Dalva that she has "talked" to him every evening for many years. Dalva's sister, **Ruth,** is a talented pianist but less romantic than her sister. Dalva relates how Ruth's long celibacy is finally broken through an affair with a priest; although this episode is comic, some critics questioned why Dalva would include it in a diary meant for her son. Another significant family member is Dalva's uncle **Paul**, an intellectual, ladies-man, and nature-lover who gave her sanctuary at his Arizona ranch during her pregnancy and again throughout her adulthood.

Dalva's lover and father of her son, **Duane Stone Horse,** disappeared after being told that he and Dalva are half-siblings (Duane was born after an affair between his Sioux mother, Rachel, and Dalva's father). When the teenaged Duane mysteriously appeared at the ranch, he was warmly welcomed by Dalva's grandfather and given a job as a farmhand and a fine buckskin horse that he cherished. The love between beautiful young Dalva and handsome, fiercely independent Duane flowered into a single moment of passion. The two were briefly reunited in 1972, when Duane was dying from a strange ailment possibly caused by his exposure to Agent Orange during the Vietnam war. He summoned Dalva to his home in Florida and, just before committing suicide, married her so that she would receive his veteran's benefits.

A number of minor characters enliven the pages of *Dalva.* Some comic relief is provided through **Lundquist**, who lives near the Northridge ranch and once worked for Dalva's grandfather. He shares Michael's weakness for alcohol, and the two develop a somewhat symbiotic relationship; nevertheless, he is a tender and dignified man who is fiercely loyal to Dalva and her family. Lundquist's feisty but nurturing, never married, fifty-five-year-old daughter **Frieda** is assigned to take care of Michael during his stay. Dalva's remembrances of her girlhood feature her friend **Charlene**, a tough, pretty girl from a deprived background who worked as a waitress in a local cafe; a lesbian, Charlene ultimately moved to Paris. Ruth is separated from her wealthy gay husband, **Ted**, who works in the entertainment industry in southern California. Ted's houseman, **Andrew**, a former policeman, agrees to trace Dalva's son for her. **Sam Creekmouth** is a Sioux of the same generation as Dalva and Duane; Dalva meets him again when, after her return to Nebraska, she goes to buy a puppy from him, and the two begin an affair. **Karen Olafson** is the seductive, sexually canny teenager who, in pursuit of fame as a model, complies with Michael's request that she bring him some revealing photographs of herself. Her father discovers one of the photos and punches Michael so hard that he is hospitalized with a broken jaw.

The Woman Lit by Fireflies (novella, 1990)

Plot: The novella centers on fifty-year-old Clare, a wealthy suburbanite who has been married for nearly thirty years to a boorish, money-obsessed husband. The sensitive Clare has found outlets for her own interests through reading and her friendships with Zilpha and Dr. Roth and her beloved dog, Sammy. As the story opens, Clare has recently lost both Zilpha and Sammy to cancer, while she herself has had to attend an Arizona pain clinic to learn how to deal with her chronic migraine headaches. She and Donald are now driving home to the Detroit suburb of Bloomfield Hills after visiting their veterinarian daughter, Laurel, who lives in Nebraska. On a toilet stall of an Iowa rest stop, Clare leaves a note that reads: "I am in a small red car driving east. My husband has been abusing me. Do not believe anything he says. Call my daughter." Then she walks into the adjacent corn field. There she spends the night, during which she reviews her life in random order, ruminating about her childhood, college experiences, and the early years of her marriage as well as her adventures with Zilpha and Sammy and her talks with Dr. Roth. In the morning Clare is reunited with her daughter and spends an hour with Donald, explaining that for now she must follow her own yearnings. As the novella draws to a close, Clare has fulfilled her dream of traveling to Paris and is even wearing the beret she lacked the courage to don during her earlier, brief interlude in that city.

Characters: Harrison's fiction is laced with metaphor and marked by impressionistic prose and a strong attention to detail, reflecting his skill as a poet. Critics consider *The Woman Lit by Fireflies* one of this underappreciated writer's strongest pieces, particularly praising Harrison's sensitive portrayal of a woman's point of view. Published in a volume that also includes *Brown Dog* and *Sunset Limited,* the novella first appeared in the *New Yorker* magazine and exhibits several qualities often identified as typical of that publication's featured works, including an emphasis on character over plot and on interior reflection over exterior details as well as a digressive structure.

As she nears the age of fifty, the novella's protagonist, **Clare,** has decided that she can no longer live as she has for the last thirty years. Her two children are grown, and she has been profoundly shaken by the deaths of two of the friends who have long sustained her—Zilpha and her beloved dog, Sammy. In addition, she suffers from debilitating headaches that forced her to attend an Arizona pain clinic to learn some techniques for managing the pain. Clare is deeply unhappy, and she believes her unhappiness stems from her husband, who no longer is the socially conscious man she once loved. As her husband lapsed from youthful idealism into the pursuit of money, Clare took refuge in good books, music, food, wine, charity projects, and her love of birds and other animals. But these distractions have failed to fulfill her. When she escapes into a cornfield, where she spends the night alone, reviewing some old dreams and scenes and recognizing some important truths about herself. She recalls her childhood—spent with an alcoholic, distant mother and a beloved father—and her college years, when she began to develop an abiding interest in literature. Clare planned to spend a year in Paris after graduation, but after three weeks her father died, and her then-fiance, Donald, came to take her home. She still yearns for that romantic, aborted idyll, which represents for her—particularly through the symbol of the beret that she was, at that earlier time, too shy to wear—all her lost, youthful yearnings and potential. By the end of the novel, Clare has developed a new appreciation for her own life and abilities; she concludes: "I don't need to change. I'm just this." Some commentators consider the unfailingly smart, sensitive, well-meaning Clare a little too good to be true, while others praise Harrison for his insightful portrayal of a middle-aged woman at an important crossroads in her life.

When the reader first encounters Clare's husband, **Donald,** he is listening on his car's cassette-player to a financial lecture entitled "Tracking the Blues," which, as Clare points out, has nothing to do with black music. While attending college and for a few years thereafter, Donald was a left-wing political science major who favored lumberjack shirts and desired to become either the author of a populist novel or a labor leader. At that time, he shared Clare's interest in books, jazz, and movies and her concern for civil rights. Over the years, however—especially after moving into the grand house bought for the couple by Clare's wealthy mother—his interests turn to making money. He has become politically conservative, and his cultural interests are now apparently limited to Bing Crosby records. Clare describes Donald as someone who "loved the life outside the mind and slept like a rock," someone who, while touring the Cathedral of Notre Dame, whispered "remind me to make a call" in her ear. Nevertheless, Donald loves Clare, and the reader's sympathy is elicited at the end of the novella when he weeps over her announced departure. Some critics find the boorish, conventional, anti-Semitic Donald an unconvincingly negative character; they also doubt that a woman of Clare's intelligence and sensitivity could have stayed with such a character for so long.

Clare's daughter, **Laurel,** is described both in flashbacks to the visit that Clare and her husband have just completed and through imagined conversations during Clare's night in the cornfield. During the previous week, Laurel had encouraged her mother to leave him. A twenty-nine-year-old veterinarian, Laurel has a strong, driven personality and a matter-of-fact approach to life. Unlike her more conventional brother, **Donald, Jr.** (who plays only a small role in Clare's reminiscences and who closely resembles his father), Laurel was a sloppily dressed, beer-drinking college student who excelled at her studies but nevertheless failed to win her father's admiration.

Other characters in *The Woman Lit by Fireflies* include Clare's close friend, **Zilpha**, who at the beginning of the novella has recently died of lung cancer and whose loss in part precipitates Clare's move. Zilpha was an outspoken woman with a strong zest for life, a delightful sense of humor, and a desire for adventure that led her and Clare to many interesting and beautiful places. Yet she was unhappily married to a liberal lawyer. Another important person in Clare's life is her confidant and friend **Dr. Roth**, who was Zilpha's physician. The two have much in common, including similarly liberal social views (they worked together, for example, to fight censorship in local schools), comfortable lifestyles due to inherited wealth, and unhappy marriages (Dr. Roth's wife is manic-depressive). Dr. Roth supports Clare's desire to change her life but does not push her toward any particular solution; although she senses that he may have once harbored a secret love for her, their relationship has always remained platonic.

Minor characters in the novella include **Frank**, a wheat farmer with back spasms who meets Clare at the pain clinic—Clare feels attracted to him but doesn't pursue an affair; and **Michael**, Zilpha's unconventional artist son—Clare once slept with him, to her chagrin, and he propositions her again, through their mutual tears, at Zilpha's funeral.

Further Reading

Clute, John. "Elegaic Heirs." *Times Literary Supplement* No. 4486 (24 March 1990): 299.

Contemporary Literary Criticism Vols. 6, 14, 33, 66. Detroit: Gale Research.

Dictionary of Literary Biography 1982 Yearbook. Detroit: Gale Research.

Erdrich, Louise. Review of *Dalva. Chicago Tribune—Books* (March 20, 1988): 1.

Fergus, Jim. Interview with Jim Harrison. *Paris Review* No. 107 (1988): 53–97.

Freeman, Judith. "Women's Intimations." *Los Angeles Times Book Review* (August 19, 1990): 1, 5.

Houston, Robert. "Love for the Proper Outlaw." *New York Times Book Review* (September 16, 1990): 13.

Huey, Michael C. M. "Writing and Telling in Harrison's Latest." *Christian Science Monitor* (June 13, 1988): 19–20.

Kakutani, Michiko. "The Shapes and Textures of Three Lives." *New York Times* (August 28, 1990): C16.

Krystal, Arthur. "Jim Harrison: Three for the Road." *Book World—The Washington Post* (September 2, 1990): 7.

Roberson, William H. "'A Good Day to Live': The Prose Works of Jim Harrison." *Great Lakes Review* Vol. 8, no. 2 (fall 1982): 29–37.

Yardley, Jonathan. "A Lonely Heart in the Heartland." *Book World—The Washington Post* (March 6, 1988): 3.

Vaclav Havel

1936–

Czechoslovakian dramatist, essayist, and poet.

A Private View (three one-act plays: *Audience*, 1975; *Private View*, 1975; and *Protest*, 1978)

Plot: Set in Czechoslovakia during the 1970s, when that country was still ruled by an oppressive Communist regime, the plays revolve around a common protagonist, dissident playwright Ferdinand Vanek. In *Audience,* Vanek is called in for an interview with the head brewmaster at the brewery where he is employed. The man plies Vanek with beer and eventually reveals that he will secure an easy desk job for the playwright if he will do two things: arrange an assignation with an actress the brewmaster lusts for, and write a report on his own political activities for the brewmaster to turn in to his superiors. Vanek agrees to arrange a meeting with the actress but not to inform on himself. The now very drunk brewmaster falls into a stupor, then begins the interview again as if it had never taken place. Vanek plays along, this time assuming a coarser, more comradely manner.

In *Private View,* Vanek visits his friends Michael and Vera, whose compliance with their oppressive government has earned them a luxurious lifestyle adorned by all the latest American products and music. The couple upbraids the shabbily dressed Vanek for his dissident activities, informing him that he too could enjoy special privileges and benefits if he would loosen his principles. Vanek's impassive response to their entreaty angers Michael and Vera, and he prepares to leave. In the end, however, he joins his friends in listening to American rock records and drinking bourbon.

Protest involves a novelist and television scriptwriter named Stanek, an old friend of Vanek's who has not contacted him in years. Like the couple in *Private View,* Stanek has made concessions to the ruling regime and now enjoys a successful career by writing the kind of material they want. Eventually Stanek reveals why he has invited Vanek to his home: he wants the playwright to write up a petition advocating the release from prison of a young dissident; Stanek's daughter is pregnant with the young man's baby. Vanek immediately pulls just such a petition from his briefcase, already signed by several of his politically active friends. He asks Stanek to sign the petition, but the novelist objects on the grounds that it would be dangerous and unethical for him to do so. Vanek responds calmly to this refusal, which only infuriates the guilt-stricken Stanek. Then they learn that the dissident has already been released from prison, thus making the petition unnecessary. Vanek assures his friend that it was Stanek's "backstage maneuvering" that led to the young man's release.

Characters: Havel is not only a leading Czechoslovakian writer but an important figure in his country's political history. In 1989, after the "Velvet Revolution," which replaced the Communist regime with a more democratic government, Havel was elected president of Czechoslovakia. Twice imprisoned for his political activities, Havel ardently opposed the cultural repression that dominated his country, particularly after the 1968 Soviet invasion that ended the "Prague spring," a brief period of lessened restrictions. During the 1960s, Havel was associated with Prague's avant-garde "Theatre on the Balustrade," but during the 1970s his plays were banned in Czechoslovakia. Thus *A Private View* was initially seen only in private homes or in the West, where Havel garnered critical acclaim not only for his personal courage and dedication but for his accomplished work. His plays are characterized by black humor and—like the writings of his Czech predecessor, Franz Kafka—by an emphasis on the absurdities and hypocrisies rampant in a repressive society. *A Private View* exposes the guilt, cowardice, and erosion of human values that Havel felt prevailed in Communist Czechoslovakia, but it does so entertainingly and without didacticism.

The central figure in the three one-act plays that comprise *A Private View*, **Ferdinand Vanek**, appears in several other dramas as well, including one by Havel's friend Pavel Kahout, who adapted the character to his own purposes. Vanek is at least partially autobiographical and illustrates the importance of the artist as a vital agent of change in a repressive society. Presented as an upholder of decency and truth, Vanek projects a quiet, humble, unprotesting manner. He personifies conscience to those who have cooperated with their repressive government for reasons of cowardice or self-interest (humanly understandable as these responses might be). Because his mild presence reproaches these compromisers and provokes angry reactions, Vanek is an almost pathetically (and sometimes comically) isolated figure. Some critics describe him as overly virtuous, while others claim that his exaggerated agreeableness saves him from being totally self-righteous. Vanek's occupation in *Audience* reflects the time Havel himself spent as a laborer in a brewery; Vanek is portrayed as working there both out of financial necessity and to keep in touch with the working people of his country. Although he would much prefer the desk job that the brewmaster dangles before him, the prospect of informing on himself is too absurd to contemplate. In *Private View*, Vanek's shabby appearance contrasts strongly with the glossy surface of his friends' lives. In this play, Vanek makes a rare personal comment, admitting, "I sometimes have a moment of futility." When *Protest* takes place, Vanek has just been released from a year in prison, reflecting Havel's own incarceration for political activities. The almost Christlike way in which Vanek responds to Stanek's cowardice enrages Stanek, who accuses him of obnoxious self-righteousness. Vanek's behavior toward his friends in both *Private View* and *Protest* and even toward the brewmaster in *Audience* makes it clear that he does sympathize with them and recognize their need for safety and even comfort, but his own principles simply don't allow him to seek the same advantages.

The dull-witted, boorish **head brewmaster** in *Audience* is the personification of the industrial bureaucrat. With his frequent shifts between friendliness and threats, he reminds some critics of the bureaucratic characters found in the fiction of Franz Kafka. Once a common laborer, the brewmaster has been promoted into a managerial position and now spends his time drinking beer, sleeping, and dreaming about his favorite actress. Although undeniably vulgar and self-interested, the brewmaster is neither an automaton nor truly mean. He is just another example of the sad state of affairs in Communist Czechoslovakia, where, Havel asserts, the majority compromise their higher values for their own comfort.

Vanek's friends **Michael and Vera** exemplify the same syndrome. By complying with their country's repressive regime, they earn a luxurious, trendy lifestyle full of the vulgar trappings of material affluence. The couple makes a frantic effort to impress and entertain their friend, but when Vanek appears unmoved by their success, they grow angry. They assert that Vanek can afford to live by rigid principles because he needs no pleasures in life, whereas they want to live life to the fullest. In the end, the always mild-mannered Vanek appeases his friends to some extent by remaining in their apartment, drinking their bourbon, and listening to their records imported from America.

The novelist and television scriptwriter **Stanek** is a former friend of Vanek's from whom he has not heard for several years. Stanek sacrifices his artistic standards—and by extension his personal honor, in Havel's view—by becoming a hack writer for the government. His resulting material prosperity and determination to project a carefree attitude are both evident in the effusive manner in which he greets Vanek, proffering cognac, cigars, and comfortable slippers. Some reviewers consider the blossoming magnolia tree outside Stanek's window—one of few props in the play—a symbol of his success. Critics praise the scene in which Stanek details his reasons for not signing the petition in support of his daughter's dissident boyfriend. Asserting that such an act could endanger his job or his son's schooling or prevent him from performing the "backstage maneuvering" by which he claims he can help people, Stanek practices a form of rationalization that Havel casts as common within repressive societies. Stanek actually convinces himself that it would be unethical to sign the petition because it would lessen what power he has—whereas Vanek has no power of his own to worry about. Vanek's response to Stanek's refusal is to calmly say, "I respect your reasoning," which infuriates Stanek because he senses in it a hidden contempt for compromisers like himself. This reaction, of course, reflects Stanek's own guilt and self-loathing, for he realizes that his conduct is cowardly. Havel's attitude toward Stanek and others like him is essentially sympathetic. "It's sickening the way everybody looks after Number One," says Stanek—yet this is understandable in human terms. The play's tone is not so much angry as regretful that not everyone is strong enough to oppose repression and injustice.

Further Reading

Baranczak, Stanislaw. "All the President's Plays." *New Republic* Vol. 203, no. 4 (July 23, 1990): 27–32.

Brustein, Robert. "Private Views, Public Vistas." *New Republic* Vol. 190, no. 10 (March 12, 1984): 27–29.

Contemporary Literary Criticism. Vols. 25, 58, 65. Detroit: Gale Research.

Goetz-Stankiewicz, Marketa. "Vaclav Havel." In *The Silenced Theatre: Czech Playwrights without a Stage.* University of Toronto Press, 1979.

Gussow, Mel. "Havel's Private View." *New York Times* (November 21, 1983): C16.

Nelson, Don. "'Private View' of Socialist Hell." *New York Daily News* (November 24, 1983).

Sauvage, Leo. "Dramas in Two Worlds." *New Leader* Vol. 66, no. 24 (December 26, 1983): 16–17.

Vladislav, Jan, ed. *Vaclav Havel; or, Living in Truth.* London: Faber & Faber, 1987.

Mark Helprin
1947 -
American short story writer and novelist.

"The Schreuderspitze" (short story, 1981)

Plot: The story's central character is Herr Wallich, a talented but not very successful commercial photographer who lives in Munich, Germany. Wallich's wife and young son were recently killed in a car accident, and his deep grief has led to a decline in his business. Without telling anyone where he has gone, he leaves Munich and travels into the Alps, where he hopes to undergo some "parallel ordeal" that will allow him to overcome his anguish. Wallich decides to climb a nearby mountain peak called the Schreuderspitze, even though he is unathletic and knows nothing about mountain climbing. Taking a room in an inn on the border between Germany and Switzerland, Wallich embarks on a strict regime of exercise and spare diet in order to prepare himself for the ordeal, and he orders an assortment of mountain climbing manuals and equipment. Several months later, he thinks he sees his dead son walking through a meadow. This experience sets off a series of vivid, detailed dreams in which he gradually ascends the Schreuderspitze. When Wallich finally reaches the summit, he is dazzled by a vision of light and beauty that seems infused with the promise of life after death. Convinced he will someday see his wife and child again, Wallich decides to return to Munich and apply himself with renewed vigor to his career.

Characters: Considered one of the best short stories in the critically acclaimed collection *Ellis Island and Other Stories*, "The Schreuderspritze" exhibits the imaginative power, rich texture, and spare yet lyrical prose style that characterize all of Helprin's fiction. Helprin claimed in an interview that everything he writes "is keyed and can be understood as . . . devotional literature," and indeed, this story emphasizes the wonder of life and the illumination that may be derived from nature's beauty. Blending physical reality with metaphysical reflections, Helprin focuses on the human desire for transcendence and healing power that may be found therein.

Through the meanspirited ruminations of **Herr Wallich**'s fellow photographer, the reader learns that the story's central character is a sensitive, talented craftsman who has never been commercially successful. The narrative then shifts to an account of what Wallich has actually been doing while Franzen and others left behind in Munich speculate that he has either gone to South America or thrown himself off a bridge. Devastated by the deaths of his wife and child, Wallich travels into the Alps in search of a "parallel ordeal"—some kind of physical trial that will provide a balance to the grief that threatens to overwhelm him. To illustrate this concept, he recounts a childhood incident in which, when he and his companions were told to carry buckets of water up a hill, he discovered that carrying two buckets instead of one made the job both more agonizing and easier because the load was balanced and the task finished sooner. Wallich is initially mortified to find himself telling someone that he plans to climb the Schreuderspritze, for he is unathletic and has always been afraid of heights. On the other hand, ever since he was a child he has believed in "wonders and wondrous accomplishments," and he decides that this is just the goal he needs. Wallich undertakes a grueling course of physical exercise and near-starvation to prepare himself physically while learning all he can about mountain climbing (a sport at which Helprin, not surprisingly, is an expert). He gradually manages to transform himself into a strong, lean figure with a face that is no longer gentle; he can now run effortlessly for many miles and sleep on a bare wooden floor with no discomfort. Wallich never actually puts his new physique or skills to use, however, except in the vivid dreams in which he carefully and thrillingly climbs the Schreuderspritze. In the last of these dreams, Wallich sees around him not only the dramatically beautiful mountain icescape but a dazzling array of stars that are reflected in the lights shining up from the world below. Through this transcendent vision, in which the divine seems manifest in nature, Wallich comes to see time as "circular and never-ending" so that nothing—including his deceased wife and son—is ever lost. Inspired particularly by the mysteries of light he has witnessed, Wallich resolves to return to his photographic work and commit himself again to ordinary life. Although a few critics complained that Wallich's epiphany was more described than shown or felt, most lauded Helprin for his powerful depiction of a life saved through a nearly ritualistic process of transcendence.

The story's only other character is Wallich's fellow photographer **Franzen**, who appears only at the beginning of the story and is used to relay information about Wallich's circumstances and disappearance. Described as one of those Munich men who "look like weasels"—which affect is heightened by his propensity for wearing tweed—Franzen cannot help but reveal his his glee that Wallich, his competitor, has left Munich. In a pseudosympathetic voice, Franzen calls attention to Wallich's deficiencies of wealth and confidence; he contends that Wallich was never a great photographer because he lacked "that killer instinct." To illustrate this point, Franzen recounts how he and Wallich both competed for an account with a manufacturer of turbines: whereas Franzen studied turbines themselves, Wallich created beautiful photographs that showed how the shape of the mechanism echoes shapes in nature. The client told Wallich that his photographs made the turbines look bad by comparison, and he gave the account to Franzen. Clearly unreliable as a judge of character, Franzen throws into relief Wallich's talent and sensitivity.

Further Reading

Bell, Pearl K. "New Jewish Voices." *Commentary* 71, No. 6 (June 1981): 62-6.

Buckley, Christopher. "A Talk with Mark Helprin: 'I May Be an Anomaly.'" *New York Times Book Review* 89 (25 March 1984): 16.

Butterfield, Isabel. "A Metaphysical Scamp? On Mark Helprin." *Encounter* 72 (January 1989): 48-52.

Contemporary Literary Criticism, Vols. 7, 10, 22, 32. Detroit: Gale Research.

Duchéne, Anne. "Out of the Icebox." *Times Literary Supplement* No. 4067 (13 March 1981): 278.

Koenig, Rhoda. "The Invisible Helping Hand: *Ellis Island and Other Stories*." *New York Magazine* 14, No. 5 (2 February 1981): 52-3.

Price, Reynolds. "The Art of American Short Stories." *New York Times Book Review* (1 March 1981): 1, 20.

Frank Herbert
1920–1986
American novelist.

Dune (novel, 1965)

Plot: As the novel opens, Duke Leto Atriedes, the hereditary leader of Caladan, is about to leave for the desert planet of Arrakis or Dune with his wife, Lady Jessica, and fifteen-year-old son, Paul. In collusion with Baron Vladimir Harkonnen, a sworn enemy of the House of Atriedes, the Emperor Shaddam plans to kill Duke Leto in order to destroy his growing power. Thus the Atriedes have been told to move to Arrakis to supervise the mining of that planet's precious resource, the spice melange, which prolongs life and can also produce prescient visions when used in large quantities. After the family's arrival on Arrakis, Duke Leto is betrayed by a close member of his entourage and killed by the Harkonnens, who then resume their rule of Arrakis. Paul and Jessica, however, escape to the desert, which is the home of the giant sandworms that produce melange and a tough, seminomadic people called the Fremen. Captured by the Fremen, both Paul and Jessica soon prove their worth and are accepted as members of their group. Jessica does so through the extraordinary powers of physical and thought control she learned during her training in the Bene Gesserit. This secret, all-female society has for many generations enacted a breeding program designed to eventually produce the Kwisatz Haderach, a male heir who will combine their own ability to draw on the collective memories of past female generations with the capacity to foresee the future. Jessica's long-held suspicion that Paul is the Kwisatz Haderach is confirmed by the powerful visions Paul experiences after drinking the concentrated form of melange called the "Water of Life." Dismayed to find himself in this unwanted role, Paul initially denies that he is the Kwisatz Haderach. Meanwhile, he takes leadership of the Fremen and leads them in defeating the Harkonnens, while all along he is bitterly aware, through his prescient visions, of the inevitability of a coming jihad (religious war) that he is powerless to avoid. His forces subdued, Baron Harkonnen is killed by Paul's sister, Alia (born after Jessica and Paul join the Fremen), and Paul subsequently deposes the emperor. To ensure his own claim to the throne, Paul contracts a "white" (that is, in name only) marriage with the emperor's daughter, Princess Irulan, who becomes the court historian. Paul's true love and the mother of his children, however, remains the loving, faithful Chani, his Fremen concubine.

Characters: Winner of the two most coveted awards for science fiction, the Hugo (1966) and the Nebula (1965), *Dune* brought Herbert widespread acclaim and continues to be one of the most popular of all science fiction novels. Herbert wrote four sequels (*Dune Messiah,* 1969; *Children of Dune,* 1976; *God Emperor of Dune,* 1981; and *Chapterhouse, Dune,* 1985; the first three in the series are sometimes referred to as "The Dune Trilogy"), but critics generally agree that the first book is the most accomplished. Herbert created a vivid, detailed milieu for his characters to inhabit, thus helping to establish the science fiction tradition of the "invented world" novel, in which all aspects of an imagined world— historical, geological, cultural—are provided. Combining an engaging adventure plot with intellectual, technological, philosophical, and psychological concerns, Herbert explores in *Dune* such themes as the limitations of hero worship and the power of religion both to anesthetize and to lend significance to life. Ecology awareness is central to the book, and Herbert is enthusiastically lauded for his emphasis on the idea of understanding ecological consequences—that actions produce results that affect entire ecosystems. Critics especially praise Herbert for avoiding didacticism in delivering his ideas; instead, *Dune* features an entertaining story that may be enjoyed on several levels.

Paul Atreides is the central character in *Dune* and, by many critics' reckoning, the best drawn protagonist in Herbert's fiction. Fifteen when the novel begins, Paul is both the latest in a long line of hereditary rulers and the beneficiary of his mother's psychological training. He knows how to wield a sword expertly and how to use the thought-control techniques taught to him by Jessica—in defiance of the Bene Gesserit prohibition on sharing knowledge with males. He is also an ecologist who has been raised in a society wary (due to the terrible religious war it once endured) of technology. Commentators identify Paul as *Dune*'s primary illustration of the development of heroes and of people's need for such larger-than-life figures. During the course of the novel, Paul's initiation into maturity involves his having to grapple with his own heroic status; he is forced to play out a mythic role with which he is not entirely comfortable. The first test he faces occurs before he even leaves Caladan, when he submits to the deadly gom jabbar—a poisonous needle that tests the subject's ability to withstand pain—which is administered by a high-ranking member of the Bene Gesserit and which he successfully endures; later the reader learns that Paul had absorbed more pain than any previous human. After his family's arrival on Arrakis and the upheaval that results in his father's death and his escape with his mother into the desert, Paul must prove himself to the Fremen among whom he lands. He does so by returning safely from a ride on a sandworm and by disarming and then killing the arrogant Jamis in a ritual knife fight. Through the latter act, Paul earns the special title of Muad'Dib and the status of a leader among the Fremen. Thus Paul begins a quest that is initially focused on avenging his father, but which develops into the retrieval of Arrakis from Harkonnen rule. A steady diet of melange increases Paul's ability to foresee the future, culminating in the frightening visions he sees after ingesting the highly concentrated Water of Life (which simultaneously allows Paul to tap into both male and female collective memory). To his horror, Paul realizes that he is indeed the Kwisatz Haderach, as his mother had hoped (with the important distinction that the women of the Bene Gesserit have no control over him), but he also realizes the limitations of his power. Although he can perceive and to some extent choose the various paths the future might take, he knows that he is powerless to prevent the jihad that will overtake Arrakis in the years to come. He also knows that he can use his considerable powers only if people are in awe of and obedient to him, and Paul's bitterness about this seems designed to make the reader question the heroic ideal. By the end of the novel, Paul successfully leads the Fremen to victory and becomes emperor, but he remains uneasy about the future. In Herbert's next book, Paul completes his ecological reclamation of Arrakis (a process with unforeseen negative consequences) but also stands by as a bloody religious war rages. At the end of *Dune Messiah,* he withdraws from the society he has created—a decision that displeases many critics and readers, who decry his passivity. A compelling character who struggles with a complex emotional and moral dilemma and illustrates some of the drawbacks of the messianic leader, Paul has been compared to the Homerian figure of Aeneas, who also flees from one dying civilization to establish another.

Although Paul's father, **Duke Leto Atreides,** who dies near the beginning of *Dune,* is not a major figure in the novel, his mother, **Lady Jessica Atriedes,** plays an important role in the action. Considered Herbert's most successfully portrayed and most interesting female character, Jessica is a member of the secretive Bene Gesserit religious order, which carries on a centuries-long breeding program with the goal of producing the Kwisatz Haderach. This male heir will be endowed not only with their own access to the collective memories and knowledge of former generations of females but with the ability to foresee the future. To further this end, the Bene Gesserits provide consort-advisers and even wives to carefully chosen nobles; indeed, Jessica was originally sent to Duke Leto as part of this plan. But Jessica broke her vow of obedience to the Bene Gesserit by falling in love with Leto and producing not the daughter her order had demanded (the choice of her child's sex being her own) but the son Leto desired. Meanwhile, she refused Leto's offer of marriage in order to leave him free for any politically advantageous liaison that might arise. As Paul matures, Jessica inculcates him with her own knowledge and skills, all the while hoping that he is the Kwisatz Haderach. After the death of her husband and her flight with Paul into the desert, Jessica gains esteem among the Fremen by adding the powers of that people's "witch-women," the Sayyadina, to her own. When she successfully converts the potent "Water of Life" to a form usable by all, Jessica is elevated to the status of Reverend Mother. Some critics view Jessica as fulfilling a role that is traditionally or even stereotypically female, for despite her membership in a powerful female organization and her important role as Paul's adviser, Jessica has a decidedly male-oriented outlook. This is best illustrated in her willingness to benefit her son by endangering her unborn daughter, Alia, with whom she is pregnant when she ingests the potentially lethal Water of Life, which negatively affects Alia for the rest of her life. Through Jessica and the intriguing, mysterious Bene Gesserit, Herbert explores the role of the unconscious in human affairs and its potential for manipulation for either benevolent or malicious purposes.

Dune features a fairly extensive, entertaining cast of secondary characters. Among the positive forces in Paul's life is the musician and expert swordsman **Gurney Halleck,** who tutors the young man until—after Leto's death—he is forced to flee from the Harkonnens. Unaware that Paul and Jessica are alive and thriving among the Fremen, Gurney joins a band of smugglers; he unexpectedly meets Paul years later when Paul is leading the Fremen struggle against the Harkonnens, and Gurney is surprised to see how much the young man's experiences have hardened him. Unlike Gurney, the very capable **Duncan Idaho**—Duke Leto's weaponsmaster and another of Paul's teachers—is killed along with his master. Although he is allowed to live, Leto's mentat (a kind of human computer endowed with colossal intelligence), **Thufir Hawat,** is unwillingly pressed into the Harkonnens' service. **Dr. Yueh,** the Atreides' physician, betrays them to the Harkonnens and thus brings about Duke Leto's death.

Most notable of the Fremen characters is **Stilgar,** who embodies many of the prominent attributes of that race. The seminomadic Fremen are independent, fierce, and honest, with a hardiness that reflects their successful adaptation to a harsh environment. Unlike the Harkonnens, who crave security and comfort, the Fremen have a strength borne of their daily confrontations with death, danger, and privation. Following Paul's rise to prominence among the Fremen, Stilgar becomes his trusted battle adviser and helps to imbue Paul with the discipline, skills, and values he needs to become a great leader. **Jamis** is not as benevolent a figure; his anger at being disarmed by a teenaged boy leads to his death in a ritual knife fight with Paul. Another important Fremen character is **Liet Kynes**, a planetologist whose lifelong dream and goal has been to make Arrakis a green, lush planet. Through Liet, Herbert voices the novel's central ecological message: that humanity must understand the consequences of introducing any new element into an ecosystem. Liet is knowledgeable not just about planetary ecology but also about religion, as he demonstrates when, on first meeting Jessica, he senses that she has brought "the shortening of the way" (the Fremen translation of Kwisatz Haderach). Liet's daughter, **Chani**, becomes Paul's beloved concubine, though not his wife; gentle and loving, she responds with fierceness and passion when her loved ones are threatened. Paul's children with Chani are daughter **Ghanima** and son **Leto II**, the latter a prominent character in *Children of Dune,* who transforms himself into a monstrous despot in order to force humanity to adapt survival characteristics.

The novel's central villain is **Baron Vladimir Harkonnen,** who is somewhat cartoonish in his exaggerated evilness but nevertheless memorable. The archrival of the House of Atreides, the baron exhibits the unrestrained self-indulgence typical of his own family. Eventually it is revealed that he is the natural father of Lady Jessica, and in *Dune Messiah* his personality gains access to the world again through the unwilling conduit of Alia. The Bene Gesserit originally planned for the baron's nephew **Feyd-Rautha Harkonnen** to marry the daughter of Duke Leto and Lady Jessica and then produce the boy who would be the Kwisatz Haderach; this plan was thwarted when Jessica defied her order's commands. Paul kills this sole rival for the emperor's throne in a ritual duel. Another somewhat villainous character is the **Reverend Mother Helen Gaius Mohiam,** a high-ranking adviser to **Emperor Shaddum,** who administers the deadly gom jabbar test to Paul. Angry at Jessica's disobedience to the order, she does not disclose that Paul has endured more pain than any other human.

While still in her mother's womb, Paul's sister, **Alia,** is exposed—through Jessica's ingestion of the concentrated melange of the Water of Life—to the collective memories of all of her family's female generations. As chronicled in *Dune Messiah,* Alia struggles all of her life with this legacy as various figures from the past attempt to use her as a means to gain access to life. One who succeeds is her grandfather, Baron Harkonnen; although he is killed by Alia near the end of *Dune,* in the next book he invades her being in order to carry out his own evil purposes. **Princess Irulan,** Emperor Shaddum's daughter, agrees to a "white marriage" (with traditionally female submissiveness, note some critics) to Paul and becomes his court historian, glorifying his image while revealing that she lacks intimate knowledge of him, although she is apparently satisfied with her role. Excerpts from the princess's writings open many chapters of *Dune.*

Further Reading

Contemporary Literary Criticism. Vols. 12, 23, 35, 44. Detroit: Gale Research.

Dictionary of Literary Biography. Vol. 8. Detroit: Gale Research.

DiTommaso, Lorenzo. "History and Historical Effect in Frank Herbert's *Dune.*" *Science-Fiction Studies* Vol. 19 (November 1992): 311–25.

Hand, Jack. "The Traditionalism of Women's Roles in Frank Herbert's *Dune.*" *Extrapolation* Vol. 26 (spring 1985): 24–28.

McLean, Susan. "A Question of Balance: Death and Immortality in Frank Herbert's *Dune* Series." In *Death and the Serpent: Immortality in Science Fiction.* Edited by Carl B. Yoke and Donald M. Hassler. Greenwood Press, 1985.

McNelly, Willis E. "In Memoriam: Frank Herbert, 1920–1986." *Extrapolation* Vol. 27, no. 4 (winter 1986): 352–55.

Miller, David M. *Frank Herbert.* Mercer Island, WA: Starmont House, 1980.

O'Reilly, Timothy. *Frank Herbert.* New York: Frederick Ungar, 1981.

———. "From Concept to Fable: The Evolution of Frank Herbert's *Dune.*" In *Critical Encounters: Writers and Themes in Science Fiction.* Edited by Dick Riley. New York: Frederick Ungar, 1978.

Ower, John. "Idea and Imagery in Herbert's *Dune.*" *Extrapolation* (May 1974): 129–39.

Parkinson, Robert C. "*Dune*—An Unfinished Tetralogy." *Extrapolation* (December 1971): 16–24.

Scigaj, Leonard. "'Prana' and the Presbyterian Fixation: Ecology and Technology in Frank Herbert's 'Dune' Tetralogy." *Extrapolation* Vol. 24, no. 4 (winter 1983): 340–55.

Toupence, William F. *Frank Herbert.* Boston: Twayne, 1988.

Oscar Hijuelos
1951–

American novelist and short story writer.

The Mambo Kings Play Songs of Love (novel, 1989)

Plot: The Mambo Kings of the novel's title are Nestor and Cesar Castillo, brothers who immigrated from Cuba to New York City in 1949 and gained fame as musicians during the Latin dance craze of the 1950s. The novel is narrated primarily by the now-sixty-two-year-old Cesar, who reminisces as he drinks himself to death in the seedy Hotel Splendour, the site of many of his earlier amorous adventures. Before the brothers left Cuba, where they had already begun to perform the distinct Afro-Caribbean music that would propel them to success in America, the quiet, dreamy Nestor fell in love with a girl named Maria. The affair ended unhappily, but Nestor spends the rest of his life pining for the girl, for whom he writes the mournful *bolero* song, "Beautiful Maria of My Soul." At the invitation of fellow Cuban Desi Arnez, the brothers and their band the Mambo Kings, perform Nestor's song on the *I Love Lucy* television program. Nestor eventually marries a Puerto Rican girl named Delores and has a son, Eugenio, who later delights in watching his father's television appearance over and over again. Meanwhile, the sexually rapacious Cesar has affairs with a wide variety of women but (except for being married briefly in Cuba) never settles down. The Mambo Kings achieves a considerable fame and popularity on the local dance hall circuit, makes appearances in several cities, and records an album. One night, however, Nestor is killed when he falls asleep while driving. The Mambo Kings' popularity wanes as the public's enthusiasm for Latin music fades, and Cesar eventually takes a job as the superintendent of his apartment building. As the story returns to the present, Cesar is crippled by heart disease; he decides to die at the Hotel Splendour with a whiskey bottle in his hand.

Characters: Hijuelos has received a Pulitzer Prize for *Mambo Kings*, which critics have praised for its vivid, sensitive evocation of the musical and social atmosphere of New York's Cuban community during the 1950s, when a wave of immigrants from Latin America led to a fascination with such musical forms as the *mamba* and the *rumba*. Hijuelos's knowledge and love of this music is evident, and the author structures the novel like an improvisational musical composition. Although some commentators complain that Hijuelos's prose is overwrought and repetitive, many praise its blend of ordinary language and realistic detail with lyrical, often poignant passages.

In an interview, Hijuelos claimed that the vibrant **Cesar Castillo** is based on an elevator operator in his apartment building who was once a celebrated *bolero* singer. Motivated throughout his life by lust and ambition, Cesar is a garrulous, handsome, vigorous man who practices his music and his amorous conquests with equal enthusiasm. Kind and loving, Cesar never has a lasting relationship with any one woman. He was married a briefly before leaving Cuba, and his later efforts to renew ties with the daughter he left there are unsuccessful. The novel features a number of explicit, exuberant sex scenes between Cesar and his paramours, with whom he radiates pure machismo. A few critics have objected to Cesar's excessive virility, but Hijuelos maintains that it "balances the pain of the book." Like the elevator operator in Hijuelos's apartment building, Cesar must eventually work at a low-status job, yet he displays considerable personal dignity and takes pride in his work as a building superintendent. Indeed, most readers find themselves fond of this the flamboyant but tenderhearted character who, looking vastly older than his sixty-two years, reaches the end of his life at the Hotel Splendour.

Although the book chronicles both Cesar and **Nestor Castillo,** Nestor is less memorably drawn. Thin and broad-shouldered while Cesar is thickset, Nestor is a sensitive introvert who never recovers from the loss of the love of the "Beautiful Maria," for whom he writes (and rewrites twenty-two times) the *bolero* that propels the Mambo Kings to fame. Just as Cesar's machismo is depicted as stereotypically Latin American, so is Nestor's self-destructive pining portrayed as culturally ingrained. As critic Peter Mathews notes, Nestor is "romantically doomed, receding into a world of private loss." Nestor attempts to change his course by reading a self-improvement tome entitled *Forward America!* But changing is hopeless.

Delores Fuentes is a nice, prim Puerto Rican girl who is working as a maid for a rich, unhappy old man when Nestor meets her. Although the two love each other, Nestor continues to ache for his long-lost Maria, in addition to this pain, the serious, independent Delores never realizes her dream of attending college. After Nestor dies she marries the dull but reliable **Pedro**.

Other characters in the novel include **Eugenio**, Nestor's son, who is endlessly fascinated with his father's and uncle's history; the novels open with Eugenio watching the *I Love Lucy* episode on which the Mambo Kings appeared. Actor and singer **Desi Arnaz** appears as a character in the novel; he is portrayed in a nearly heroic light, treating his fellow Cubans with kindness and generosity and even inviting Eugenio, long after Nestor's death, to visit him in Los Angeles. Cesar's long list of romantic conquests includes the blonde, seductive, long-legged **Vanna Vane**, whose photograph appears on the cover of the Mambo Kings' record album and who is elected Miss Mambo of 1954; **Lydia**, much younger than Cesar, appreciates Cesar's kindness toward her and her children, and she cheers him at the end of his life.

Further Reading

Bestsellers 90. Issue 1. Detroit: Gale Research.

Coates, Joseph. "When Cuban Musicians Dream the American Dream." *Book World—Chicago Tribune* (August 13, 1989): 6–7.

Coffey, Michael. Interview with Oscar Hijuelos. *Publishers Weekly* (July 21, 1989): 42, 44.

Contemporary Literary Criticism 1990 Yearbook. Detroit: Gale Research.

Edwards-Yearwood, Grace. "Dancing to the Cuban Beat." *Los Angeles Times Book Review* (September 13, 1989): 1, 10.

Hornby, Nick. "Cuban Heels." *Listener* Vol. 123, no. 3158 (March 29, 1990): 33.

Jefferson, Margo. "Dancing into the Dawn." *New York Times Book Review* (August 27, 1989): 1, 30.

Shacochis, Bob. "The Music of Exile and Regret." *Book World—Washington Post* (August 20, 1989): 1–2.

Tony Hillerman
1925–
American novelist.

Skinwalkers (novel, 1986)

Plot: The novel takes place in the Four Corners region of the American Southwest, at the intersection of the borders of Arizona, Colorado, New Mexico, and Utah. Police detectives Joe Leaphorn and Jim Chee, who investigate crimes on the Navajo and other Indian reservations in this area, collaborate for the first time on the murders of social worker Irma Onesalt and two old men, Dugai Endocheeney and Wilson Sam. The victims seem to have nothing in common except their Navajo heritage. The night before Chee is to arrest a suspect in one of the murders, three shotgun blasts rip through his aluminum-sided trailer home, and Chee narrowly escapes death. The next day, Chee's suspect, the elderly Roosevelt Bistie, admits that he only fired a shot at the murder victim, but because the victim died of stab wounds, Bistie is released. Despite Leaphorn's initial skepticism about Chee's involvement in Navajo shamanism, Leaphorn and Chee grow to respect each other as they work on the case. Chee's suspect, Roosevelt Bistie, is murdered next. Then Chee receives a letter to meet someone to perform a ceremonial singing. Chee is nearly killed. While he is in the hospital recovering from his wounds, Dr. Bahe Yellowheart administers drugs to Chee to kill him. Before he succeeds, Yellowheart, the director of an Indian Health Service clinic offering traditional and modern medicine, is shot dead by the mother of a baby who has recently died. She also turns out to be the assailant who fired the shotgun into Chee's house. The perpetrator behind the murders turns out to be Yellowheart, who was supporting his clinic with money milked from the federal government and who murdered Irma Onesalt when she discovered his crime. He also killed Bistie and conspired in the deaths of the other victims by inciting several desperate people (including the woman who tried to kill Chee) to destroy the skinwalkers (witches or demons) who were tormenting them. Chee was targeted because Yellowheart believed Onesalt had informed on him.

Characters: Hillerman's mystery novels are acclaimed for their authentic, compelling stories about of contemporary Native American culture and the rugged southwestern landscape. Critics and readers alike find Hillerman's books well plotted, and skillfully written, and never condescending. In *Skinwalkers*, aspects of Navajo tradition are naturally woven into the fabric of the story, such as the proper way to approach someone's dwelling, the rudeness of looking directly into a companion's eyes or pointing at him, and the sacredness of water in a desert milieu. Hillerman's detectives mediate between their native community and the white law enforcement agencies, and their techniques blend elements of both worlds, which produce unexpectedly effective results.

Lieutenant Joe Leaphorn is a familiar figure to readers of Hillerman's earlier novels, including *The Blessing Way* (1970), *Dance Hall of the Dead* (1973), and *Listening Woman* (1977). A middle-aged, college-educated Navajo, Leaphorn is a reserved, logical detective who has only partially accommodated himself to the white world. Several aspects of his Navajo culture especially enhance detective work, including the importance of developing strong tracking skills and an excellent memory. Harmony and interconnectedness are also valuable, for these lead to a heightened openness to the irregularities and inconsistencies that may reveal the truth. But Leaphorn does not share Chee's appreciation of shamanism, and he rejects the idea of skinwalkers, which he regards as a harmful superstition. (Indeed, the story's conclusion proves his suspicion.) Throughout the novel, Leaphorn is preoccupied with his beloved wife's mental deterioration, which he fears to be Alzheimer's Disease. He eventually finds out that her symptoms are due to a brain tumor that may or may not be malignant.

Sergeant Jim Chee was introduced in Hillerman's 1978 novel, *The People of Darkness,* and also appears in *The Dark Wind* (1981), *The Ghostway* (1984), and—along with Leaphorn—in *A Thief of Time* (1988) and *Talking God* (1989). A graduate of the University of New Mexico and in his late twenties or early thirties, the intelligent, somewhat reticent Chee is a renowned tracker. Like Leaphorn, Chee uses his Navajo skills in solving crimes. But Chee is more immersed in the spiritual side of his culture than Leaphorn, for he is trained in traditional singing ceremonies (accompanied by expertly rendered sand paintings), including the "Blessing Way," which provide the Navajo people with spiritual healing. Just as Leaphorn is preoccupied throughout the novel with his wife's illness, Chee frequently mulls over his relationship with Mary Landon, a white graduate student he became involved with while she was teaching in the area. Chee's deep connection to his people and to the land make it unlikely that he will answer Mary's call to join her in Wisconsin, and by the end of the novel he seems to have a new love interest, of Navajo lawyer Janet Pete.

The perpetrator of *Skinwalkers* is finally identified as **Dr. Bahe Yellowheart**, the director of a clinic financed partly with his own money and partly by government payments. Inspired to open the clinic when his mother died needlessly—she contracted gangrene after a small cut was left untended—Yellowheart is proud of the advances in medical care his staff has accomplished. He attracts patients, he admits, by posing as a "crystal gazer," then offering his clients modern medicine along with the traditional healing methods they desire. It turns out that he has also been milking the federal government by submitting claims for patients who are either dead or no longer being treated; he claims his fraud is justified by the government's long history of cheating his people. Yellowheart exploits the people's belief in skinwalkers in order to eliminate everyone he thinks may threaten his scheme. When Chee gets too close to the truth, Yellowheart convinces a woman that Chee is responsible for her baby's terminal illness, and she nearly kills the detective.

Secondary characters in *Skinwalkers* include several law enforcement officers who work on the case with Leaphorn and Chee: FBI agents **Jay Kennedy** and **Dilly Streib**, Chee's superior officer **Captain Largo**, and the fat, jolly, but not very cagey **Officer Al Gorman**. **Dr. Randall Jenks** is a pathologist whom Leaphorn categorizes as an "Indian lover": one of the young white doctors who stayed on after paying off their government medical school debts by working for the Indian Health Service for the required two years. Leaphorn finds the headband-wearing Jenks annoying, but the doctor provides the clue about Irma having a list of names Yellowheart was using to fleece the government. **Janet Pete** is the dedicated, tough, Navajo lawyer assigned by the Navajo Nation's equivalent of a public defender's office to represent **Roosevelt Bistie**; Chee finds himself increasingly attracted to her. Characters who play significant roles in the action but never actually appear include Leaphorn's beloved wife, **Emma**, whose increasing memory loss and confusion worry him greatly; **Irma Onesalt**, the cantankerous and unpopular, social worker who becomes Yellowheart's first murder victim when she discovers his scheme against the government; and **Mary Landon**, Chee's *belagana* (white) graduate-student girlfriend, who first appeared in *The People of Darkness*. The apparently insurmountable cultural differences between the two are highlighted for Chee in the incident in which Mary was surprised when he drank the water with which he had just rinsed his coffee cup; for his part, Chee could not understand Mary's disregard for such a precious resource.

Further Reading

Bakerman, Jane S. "Cutting Both Ways: Race, Prejudice, and Motive in Tony Hillerman's Detective Fiction." *MELUS* Vol. 11, no. 3 (fall 1984): 17–25.

Callendar, Newgate. Review of *Skinwalkers*. *New York Times Book Review* (January 18, 1987): 23.

Chapman, G. Clarke. "Crime and Blessing in Tony Hillerman's Fiction." *Christian Century* Vol. 108, no. 33 (November 13, 1991): 1063–65.

Contemporary Literary Criticism. Vol. 62. Detroit: Gale Research.

Pierson, James C. "Mystery Literature and Ethnography: Fictional Detectives as Anthropologists." In *Literature and Anthropology*. Eds. Philip A. Dennis and Wendell Aycock. Lubbock: Texas Tech Press, 1989, pp. 15–30.

Review of *Skinwalkers*. *New Yorker* Vol. 62, no. 50 (February 2, 1987): 102.

Strenski, Ellen, and Robley Evans. "Ritual and Murder in Tony Hillerman's Indian Detective Novels." *Western American Literature* Vol. 16, no. 3 (fall 1981): 205–16.

White, Jean M. "Esprit de Corpse." *Book World—The Washington Post* (February 15, 1987): 4.

John Irving
1942–
American novelist, short story writer, and essayist.

The Cider House Rules (novel, 1985)

Plot: The first half of the novel takes place at an orphanage in St. Cloud, Maine, where obstetrician Dr. Wilbur Larch cares tenderly for unwanted children and also performs illegal abortions. One of the orphans is Homer Wells, who is never adopted and instead becomes an assistant to Dr. Larch. Although he is well-trained in obstetrics, Homer never actually earns a medical degree or diploma; instead, Dr. Larch creates a false identity for him so that he can perform abortions after Dr. Larch dies. Homer, however, refuses to comply with this plan because he is morally opposed to abortion. The novel's second half chronicles Homer's life at a nearby commercial apple orchard run by Candy Kendall and her boyfriend Wally. Candy had been to the orphanage earlier for an abortion when she became inconveniently pregnant. Wally goes off to fight in World War II and is eventually presumed dead, while Homer and Candy fall in love and have a son, Angel. Then it turns out that Wally is not dead, and after he returns, Candy marries him. Several years later, Homer is forced to reevaluate his moral stance when Angel's girlfriend, Rose Rose, is molested by her father and seeks an abortion. Homer ultimately returns to the orphanage and take the place of the now-deceased Dr. Wells.

Characters: Irving is an extremely popular contemporary writer whose works are frequently compared to those of nineteenth-century author Charles Dickens due to their realism, expansive plots, and quirky characters. Although *The Cider House Rules* is, like Irving's earlier novels, a highly entertaining chronicle of several individuals as they move from youth into adulthood, its darker theme renders it something of a departure for Irving, and many commentators feel it evidences a maturing of his considerable talent. They praise Irving for broaching the controversial issue of abortion and for successfully presenting the complex dimensions of both sides of the argument. Benjamin DeMott comments that *The Cider House Rules* shows that "our learned forbearance and cultivated sensibility lie at the root both of acceptance of abortion and repugnance for it."

By the end of the novel, obstetrician **Dr. Wilbur Larch** has attained near sainted status for rescuing both unwanted children and helping desperate women facing unwanted pregnancies. Larch's personal history, related early in the novel, explains how he came to establish the orphanage at St. Cloud. Just before he entered medical school, Larch had a sexual encounter with a prostitute from whom he contracted gonorrhea but who also damaged herself horribly while trying to self-induce an abortion. After witnessing several violent deaths caused by illegal abortions, Larch establishes an orphanage where he would either deliver (and then care for) babies or abort them, according to their mothers' wishes. When Homer—whom Larch has carefully groomed to take his own place—states his moral objection to abortion, Larch responds with understanding, for he too feels a repugnance for this practice. He maintains, however, that because abortion is not yet a legal choice for women, he is morally obligated to provide the medically safe procedures that will at least prevent more suffering. That Larch continues to feel guilty about his work is perhaps evidenced by his addiction to ether, on which he first became dependent during his painful bout of gonorrhea. Larch's inherent compassion is demonstrated not only by his kindness toward the women seeking abortions but by his tender treatment of the orphans under his care. He serves as a father figure to all of them, reading the novels of Charles Dickens to them each night and referring to them as "Princes of Maine" and "Kings of New England"—terms that suggest their potential for future success and happiness.

Homer Wells is one of several orphan or near-orphan characters in Irving's fiction, including T. S. Garp in *The World According to Garp* and John Wheelwright in *A Prayer for Owen Meany*. One significant difference, however, is that Homer never learns who his parents are. He is deemed "unadoptable" after several attempted adoptions fail, including one by the outdoorsy **Winkles**, who Homer watches being crushed in a logjam while boating. Dr. Larch becomes Homer's surrogate father, training him as a gynecological surgeon while carefully preparing a false identity—Dr. Stone—that will help him hide the fact that he is actually an abortionist. But Homer decides that he cannot comply with Larch's plan because he is morally opposed to abortion, and it is this conflict that comprises the thematic center of the novel. Both Larch and Homer have good, solid reasons for their positions; each is presented as an admirable, even noble, figure who adapts his personal code of conduct to his convictions. Near the end of the story, however, Homer finds that rules (like those referred to in the novel's title) and life and one's definitions of morality and duty can shift and change, and he agrees to perform an abortion for Rose Rose, who has become pregnant by her own father. Having made this choice, Homer then returns to St. Cloud to assume the identity of Dr. Stone (who has been carefully constructed as ardently anti-abortion) and take over Larch's work. Although this conclusion seems to favor the pro-choice side of the abortion controversy, most critics agreed that Irving portrays effectively the legitimate claims of both camps.

When they first arrive at the orphanage, the blonde, suntanned, seemingly affluent young couple **Candy Kendall** and Wally Worthington are taken for prospective adoptive parents, although they are actually seeking to abort a pregnancy that has interfered with their carefully laid wedding plans. Like other Irving characters, Candy is a semi-orphan who was raised by her father after her mother's death. She helps to demonstrate the novel's theme of changing rules through her different reactions to her two pregnancies: she chooses to terminate the first one but gives birth to the baby that results from her affair with Homer. Similarly, Candy illustrates some of the shifting permutations and complications of love, for she loves and waits for Wally, then falls in love with Homer, but returns to Wally (whom she still loves) in the end. This conclusion seems particularly life-affirming, borne as it is of the desire of both Candy and Homer to do the right thing. Critics regard Candy as a typical Irving heroine because she combines elements of independence with the qualities of a dutiful, loving wife and mother.

Like the names of many characters in the fiction of Charles Dickens, that of **Wally Worthington** is pointedly symbolic, suggesting his heroic qualities. Blonde and athletic, Wally maintains a jovial, lighthearted, hopeful manner and a loving attitude in spite of his troubles, even joking with Homer about the impotence that befell him after his fighter plane was shot down over Burma. Wally knows all about what happened between Candy and Homer during his absence and remains steadily committed to both of them and willing to wait for their decision; thus he serves as a major stabilizing force in their lives. After Homer returns to the orphanage, Wally and Candy go to work to make a success of their apple orchard.

Like all of Irving's novels, *The Cider House Rules* features a number of quirky secondary characters. One of the most memorable is **Melony**, another orphan under Larch's care who, like Homer, is deemed "unadoptable" after many unsuccessful attempts to establish her with adoptive families. Melony's failures are due primarily to her constant anger; she is a tough, oversized child who talks crudely. Melony harbors a longtime, unrequited love for Homer (whose initiation into sex she undertakes) but finally achieves a measure of domestic bliss with a companion named **Lorna**, with whom she has a turbulent but basically loving relationship.

The product of the love affair between Candy and Homer is their son, **Angel**, who is much loved by both his real parents and Wally, who he thinks is his father until he is finally informed of the truth. A symbol of love and promise—particularly because his birth was chosen, unlike that of Candy's first baby—Angel grows up to be a fiction writer. Like Melony, he is a victim of unrequited love, for the troubled **Rose Rose** does not return his affection. A member of the black migrant community that works in the apple orchard, Rose Rose suffers sexual abuse from her father and, after conceiving his child, kills him and flees. Her desperate need for an abortion catalyzes Homer's change of heart about the subject. **Mr. Rose** is responsible not only for his daughter's pregnancy but for the "cider house rules" mentioned in the novel's title, for his edicts control the illiterate workers, not the written ones posted in the cider house. Mr. Rose apparently accepts his murder at his daughter's hands as just punishment for his sins against her, for he insists that his death be recorded as a suicide.

Other characters in the novel include Wally's devoted mother, **Olive Worthington**, who dies of cancer before his return from Burma; Candy's father, **Ray Kendall**, a self-taught mechanic who owns a dock and lobster pounds; and the four women who help Larch run the orphanage and serve as mother figures to the orphans: **Mrs. Grogan** and nurses **Edna, Angela** (who loves Dr. Larch in vain), and **Caroline**.

A Prayer for Owen Meany (novel, 1989)

Plot: The novel is narrated by the middle-aged John Wheelwright, who recalls some important earlier events and how his friend Owen Meany influenced his life. As the story opens, Owen and John are both eleven years old and in love with John's mother, Tabitha Wheelwright, who has recently married the local drama teacher, Dan Needham. At a Little League baseball game, the unusually tiny Owen hits a foul ball that strikes and kills Tabitha. Both boys are grief-stricken, but the incident convinces Owen—who speaks in a peculiar, high-pitched voice represented in the text by capital letters—that he is "GOD'S INSTRUMENT" and as such is fated to perform some sacrificial deed. Owen and John grow up together, attending the same preparatory school and college. Convinced that he is fated to die in Vietnam, Owen ignores John's attempts to talk him out of joining the army. But Owen only gets as far as the airport before he loses his life by putting himself between a grenade thrown by a psychopath and a group of Vietnamese children. After Owen's death, John moves to Canada and becomes an English teacher. He eventually recovers from his anger over Owen's death and achieves a renewed religious faith that he attributes primarily to Owen's lingering influence.

Characters: A contemporary author whose highly popular work is noted for its sprawling plots, memorable, often comic characters, occasional sentimentality, and emphasis on moral issues, Irving is often compared to nineteenth-century novelist Charles Dickens. *A Prayer for Owen Meany* reflects his customary interest in contemporary concerns, including political corruption, the detrimental influence of television on American society, and particularly the loss of spiritual values. Irving examines such questions as the nature of good and evil, the existence of fate and divinity, and the occurrence of miracles.

When the novel begins, **Owen Meany** is a diminutive eleven-year-old with a peculiar, screeching voice that appears in the text in capital letters. Even as a child, Owen has a strong sense of God's presence in the world and of his own divinity—that he was specifically sent to perform some heroic deed. Although the death of Tabitha Wheelwright at his hands grieves Owen deeply (a sorrow signified by his giving her orphaned son his beloved set of baseball cards), it convinces him that his own life bears some heavenly purpose. Thus he accepts God's presence even in such a terrible circumstance as the death of his best friend's mother, who had served as his own mother as well. In his direct, sometimes brutal manner, Owen frequently dispenses words of wisdom that, despite their platitudinousness, are taken seriously by the people around him; examples include "FAITH TAKES PRACTICE" and "THERE IS NO SUCH THING AS COINCIDENCE." Owen's deep faith contrasts with the prevailing superficiality and brutality of American society and particularly with the Vietnam war, in which Owen nevertheless insists on fighting. He maintains that he must go to Vietnam because he is destined to save the lives of some children there, foreknowledge he first gains while directing a local Christmas pageant. Throughout their adolescence, Owen insists that John help him practice what he calls "the shot," which entails his leaping into John's arms to perform a basketball "slam-dunk." John considers this a ridiculous exercise, but Owen's practicing proves prescient when he uses the maneuver to stop a hand grenade from killing a group of Vietnamese children in an airport restroom. Owen's sacrificial act affects his friends deeply, and results eventually in John's renewal of faith. Therefore it is not surprising that commentators regard Owen as a Christ-figure, even though some critics maintain that his faith is more asserted than demonstrated and that he is more of a curiosity than a full-fledged character.

The novel's now-middle-aged narrator, **John Wheelwright,** tells the story of Owen Meany's life twenty years after it ends. John is a somewhat nondescript, neutral character who serves more as an observer and reporter than a participant. His struggle with faith and his fascination with Owen Meany continue throughout his life, hinging on such momentous events as his mother's death, the Vietnam war, and Owen's fatal sacrifice. Through John, Irving explores some of the novel's central concerns, such as the question of whether fate or chance control life and whether there really is a God who allows tragedies to occur or even decrees them. After Owen's death, an angry and disillusioned John moves to Canada—determined to avoid serving in the war that resulted in his best friend's death—where he lives in isolation and alienation from his own society. In the end, however, John finally attains spiritual healing and reveals that this chronicle has been a prayer of faith for both himself and Owen. A few commentators claim that John rather too easily forgives Owen for killing his mother, while others compare him to Nick Carroway, the narrator of F. Scott Fitzgerald's 1925 *The Great Gatsby* (a novel that John teaches to his Canadian students). Indeed, each tells the story of a more charismatic friend and each comments on contemporary America.

The death of John's beautiful, kind-hearted mother, **Tabitha Wheelwright,** is a central event in the novel, for it profoundly alters the lives of both her son and Owen Meany, a boy she accepts and loves as her own and who, understandably, adores her. Although some critics fault Tabitha's death as too extreme an occurrence simply to prove God's mysterious ways, others feel that Irving effectively conveys its impact on Owen, who interprets it as a sign of his own mission in life. Identified as one of many positively portrayed maternal figures in Irving's fiction, Tabitha is an ideal mother not only to her own son—whose illegitimacy she nobly rose above—but of Owen, and her memory seems to have a healing effect on those she leaves behind.

Another positively drawn parental character is **Dan Needham,** John's tall, gawky stepfather, who marries Tabitha not long before her death but who reacts to the loss by devoting himself even more to his teaching vocation. Dan initially wins John's regard, while courting Tabitha, by bringing him a stuffed armadillo that he later convinces John to give to Owen as a symbol of forgiveness. Dan also offers John emotional support after his mother's death, reminding him, as the adult John remembers, that "there was no way that any or all of this was *acceptable*. What had happened was unacceptable! Yet we still had to live with it." Dan senses Owen's specialness and feels his own faith renewed by Owen's deep spirituality; in addition, he interprets Owen's gift of baseball cards as a sign of how sorry he is about Tabitha's death and of how much he loved her.

The large, bosomy **Hester Eastman** is perhaps the only girl in town unconventional enough to become Owen's girlfriend. Her nickname, "Hester the Molester," refers to her expertise in sexual matters; she is also an accomplished singer and a feminist who rebels against her parents' favoritism toward her brothers. Hester is one of several victims of the Vietnam war in the novel, for she loses Owen to it (he tries to make her fall out of love with him in order to soften the blow he knows is coming). After Owen's death, Hester becomes a hard-rock singer whose songs are full of references to sex, war, and Owen himself.

During the course of *A Prayer for Owen Meany,* John learns that his birth resulted from his mother's liaison with **Reverend Lewis Merrill,** who has never acknowledged his paternity. Merrill's foils are the caring Dan Needham and Tabitha, who never indulged in guilt or self-pity and who raised John lovingly. Merrill loses his faith when Tabitha dies just after he has casually wished that she would drop dead; his faith is restored, however, by Owen, who persuades him to confront and atone for his past. Accordingly, Merrill speaks with renewed and moving spirituality at Owen's funeral.

Other characters in the novel include **Aunt Martha** and **Uncle Alfred Eastman**, Hester's parents, who provide a model of a happy marriage and strong family structure; **Randy White**, the cloying headmaster of Gravesend Academy, whom Owen criticizes in his editorials for the academy's newspaper; and **Dick Jarvits**, who becomes obsessed with the war after the death of his soldier brother and who goes berserk at the airport and throws a grenade at some Vietnamese children but kills Owen instead. Jarvits is killed, in turn, by **Major Rawls**, who describes him as the "chief wacko" in an unstable, destructive family.

Further Reading

Bausch, Richard. "'What We Thought Not God Contrives.'" *Los Angeles Times Book Review* (March 26, 1989): 1, 5.

Bestsellers 89. Issue 3. Detroit: Gale Research.

Burgess, Anthony. "A Novel of Obstetrics." *Atlantic* Vol. 256, no. 1 (July 1985): 98–100.

Contemporary Literary Criticism. Vols. 13, 23, 38. Detroit: Gale Research.

DeMott, Benjamin. "Guilt and Compassion." *New York Times Book Review* Vol. 124, no. 46,421 (May 26, 1985): 1, 25.

Dictionary of Literary Biography. Vol. 6, 1982 Yearbook. Detroit: Gale Research.

Harter, Carol C. *John Irving.* New York: Twayne, 1986.

James, Caryn. "John Irving's Owen Meany: Life with Booby Traps." *New York Times* Vol. 138, no. 47,803 (March 8, 1989): C22.

Kazin, Alfred. "God's Own Little Squirt." *New York Times Book Review* (March 12, 1989): 1, 30–31.

King, Stephen. "The Gospel According to John Irving." *Book World—Washington Post* Vol. 19, no. 10 (March 5, 1989): 1, 14.

Lehmann-Haupt, Christopher. Review of *The Cider House Rules. New York Times* Vol. 134, no. 46,415 (May 20, 1985): C20.

Miller, Gabriel. *John Irving.* New York: Frederick Ungar, 1982.

Reilly, Edward C. *Understanding John Irving.* Columbia: University of South Carolina Press, 1991.

Wall, James M. "Owen Meany and the Presence of God." *Christian Century* (March 23–29, 1989): 299–300.

Kazuo Ishiguro

1954–

English novelist and critic.

The Remains of the Day (novel, 1988)

Plot: The novel centers on Stevens, a butler of about sixty who has worked at Darlington Hall (located near Oxford, England) since he was a young man. Initially employed by the deceased Lord Darlington, Stevens now works for an American businessman, Mr. Farraday, who owns the estate. The novel opens in July 1956 with Stevens contemplating a journey to Cornwall on England's west coast; Mr. Farraday suggests that he take a vacation and offers the use of his vintage Ford. Stevens agrees to the plan only when he decides that he can use the opportunity to visit Miss Kenyon, the hall's former housekeeper, whom he hopes to persuade to rejoin the staff. Miss Kenyon left the estate in 1936 when she married. Stevens has recently received a letter from her revealing that she is separated from her husband. The novel chronicles Stevens's journey west, which gives ample opportunity to contemplate his past. He particularly focuses on the 1920s and 1930s, when Lord Darlington entertained a number of famous, powerful politicians at the hall. Convinced that the Germans had not been treated fairly by the Versailles Treaty, Darlington arranged informal meetings to try to bring about greater leniency toward them. Although well intentioned, Darlington allowed himself to be manipulated by the Nazis, and by the end of World War II he was in disgrace for collaborating with them.

Stevens ruminates extensively on what makes a great butler, and he settles on two requirements: an honorable employer, for serving such an employer thus enables the butler to contribute to the world's betterment; and dignity, which resides in never abandoning one's professional demeanor. Although Stevens has always held himself to the high professional standard set by his butler father and other role models, he gradually realizes that his employer's moral stature was not as sterling as he always pretended. This brings the value of his own life of service into question. In addition, Stevens has a bittersweet reunion with Miss Kenyon, who, declining to return to Darlington Hall, reminds him that the two might once have married if he had not made his rigid professionalism a barrier. Standing on a pier that evening, Stevens gives way to tears. A stranger he confides in advises him to forget the past and make the best of the "remains of the day." As the novel closes, Stevens has decided to try to please his new employer by learning to banter.

Characters: Critics praised *The Remains of the Day*—which received England's prestigious Booker Prize—for its finely crafted, subtle prose and complex central character, who reveals more than he intends about his years at Darlington Hall. Ishiguro moved to England from Japan at the age of six, and many commentators have noted distinctly Japanese qualities in his writing, including his indirect style and his preoccupation with such concepts as dignity, tradition, ritual, duty, and stoicism. The novel provides an illuminating portrait not only of its memorable protagonist but of England in the years following World War II, when its anachronistic social system began to crumble. Ishiguro effectively blends pathos, humor, irony, and compassion in a story that explores such themes as the difficulty of communication and the problem of personal responsibility.

Ishiguro has been uniformly lauded for his impeccable portrait of **Stevens**, the English butler who narrates *The Remains of the Day*. Now in his sixties, Stevens has always worked at Darlington Hall, initially serving the aristocrat Lord Darlington and now employed by an American, Mr. Farraday. Stevens's stiff, formal, laboriously cautious speech is perhaps his most noticeable trait; it reflects his reserved, prim nature and mimics the conversation of the upper-class English for whom Stevens has long toiled. During his journey to Cornwall, Stevens reminisces about the past and ruminates on the values by which he has ordered his life. But as many commentators have noted, Stevens is an unreliable narrator who reveals more about himself and the history of Darlington Hall than he intends. It becomes clear to the reader, for example, that the emotional restraint Stevens has so carefully cultivated precludes the ordinary warmth and companionship that human beings crave. Modeling himself after such legendary butlers as Mr. Marshall, Mr. Lane, and his own father, Stevens Senior (with whom he apparently had a respectful but rather cold relationship), Stevens has always dedicated himself wholeheartedly to the painstakingly efficient performance of his duties. As he drives, admiring the English countryside for its "very *lack* of drama or spectacle," Stevens muses on what makes a great butler. One requirement is an upstanding employer like Lord Darlington—Stevens describes him as "a gentleman of great moral stature"—for by serving such an employer a butler may contribute to improving the world; another is dignity, or the "ability not to abandon the professional being he inhabits." Thus Stevens carefully hid his grief when, his father died so as not to interrupt his duties supervising an important occasion at the hall likewise, he appeared not to notice Miss Kenton's feelings for him, so that she finally married someone else. In addition, Stevens lived many years in deliberate denial about the true nature of Darlington's activities during the years before World War II, when his employer collaborated with the Nazis. Stevens must now come to terms with his extravagant dedication to an ideal. He admits his heart was breaking when Miss Kenton reminded him they might have married and avoided the loveless lives they both endured. He also admits that he recently denied ever working for Lord Darlington, knowing he dedicated his life to a man who was morally weak. Even so, Stevens envies Darlington for having made his own choices, at least: "I can't even say I made my own mistakes. Really—one has to ask—where is the dignity in that?"

Beneath Stevens's restraint and propriety, the reader gradually detects Ishiguro's compassion for him. Most reviewers found profoundly the scene on the pier where Stevens sheds tears of regret. Encouraged by the stranger he meets there not to dwell in the past but to enjoy "the remains of the day," Stevens decides to develop his bantering skills, which will please Mr. Farraday and may possibly even add some human warmth in his life. Critics see Stevens as a more complex version of the classic butler character appearing often in works of English literature (such as the lovably imperturbable Jeeves in P. G. Wodehouse's stories and novels). Stevens is also often compared to the protagonist of Ishiguro's 1986 novel, *An Artist of the Floating World,* a Japanese artist who must deal with the consequences of the misguided choices he made during World War II.

Stevens initially describes his former employer, **Lord Darlington**, as a shy, modest man with a "deep sense of moral duty." Through the butler's subsequent ruminations, however, the reader discovers that this characterization does not tell the whole story. Darlington was a member of the landed gentry who believed the Germans had been mistreated by the Versailles Treaty, so he used his political influence to hold "unofficial" conferences at his home, which were attended by politicians from various countries. His sincere though misguided idealism ultimately led to collaborating with the Nazis, who manipulated him for their own ends. Stevens tells of the time Lord Darlington ordered him to fire two maids solely because they were Jewish. A year later Darlington admitted to Stevens that he was wrong to have them fired and asked whether the two young women could be rehired (Stevens considered his employer's change of heart "redemptive"). After the war, reviled as a Nazi dupe, Darlington died in disgrace. By the end of the novel, Stevens acknowledges Darlington's shortcomings, which, by Stevens's own definition of a butler's worth, devalue his years of service and devotion to his employer. Nevertheless Stevens envies Lord Darlington for having been able, unlike himself, to make his own choices, even if they were the wrong ones.

Miss Kenton worked as Darlington Hall's housekeeper during the eventful 1920s and 1930s. Although she was as competent and committed to her work as Stevens, she was much more high spirited and open about her own feelings. During the many evenings of cocoa-drinking and conversation the two shared, Miss Kenton often playfully challenged the reticent, rather stuffy Stevens. Through his reminiscences, Stevens unintentionally reveals that he knew Miss Kenton loved him and would have married him, but he never broke through the walls of professionalism he had built around himself. Instead, she married another man who apparently failed to make her happy, although she finally decides to stay with him. Ishiguro has been praised for infusing Stevens's reunion with Miss Kenyon (now Mrs. Benn) with a subtle poignancy; she breaks Stevens's heart by confessing that she wishes they had married. Significantly, Miss Kenton had opposed the firing of the Jewish maids while Stevens quietly carried out his orders, and when he later implied that he too had been outraged by the incident she challenged him, asking ''Why, why, why do you always have to *pretend*?''

Stevens's butler father, **Stevens Senior**, served as his son's ideal (along with the other ''legendary great butlers'' Mr. Marshall and Mr. Lane). Supremely self-possessed, Stevens Senior, cultivated a severe appearance and scrupulously formal manners and speech, even in talking to his own son. In fact, there are indications that their relationship was chilly and uncommunicative. As an example of his father's professionalism, Stevens tells how he once calmly served a general whose incompetence led to his own son's death in battle; he even passed the tip he received from the man along to a charity. In his old age, Stevens Senior, was finally unable to maintain his former efficiency and was brought to Darlington Hall to work as his own son's subordinate. Stevens refused to see the signs of mental and physical deterioration that were obvious to the rest of the staff, but eventually Stevens Senior, suffered a stroke that left him nearly helpless. Stevens's obligation to keep the hall running smoothly kept him from his father's deathbed, a lapse he claims Stevens Senior, would have understood and approved.

The new owner of Darlington Hall is **Mr. John Farraday**, an American businessman from Boston with a more egalitarian approach than his titled predecessor. Farraday is happy to employ an English butler as authentic and distinguished as Stevens, and he is consequently dismayed when Stevens denies to a guest that he ever worked for Lord Darlington. Stevens initially finds Farraday's jovial banter disconcerting, but by the end of the novel he has decided to try to adapt himself to this unfamiliar manner. Other characters in the novel include **Sir Oswald Mosley**, the head of the British Union of Fascists, who makes several visits to the hall in the years preceding World War II; **Joachim von Ribbentrop**, Hitler's ambassador to England, who also arrives at Darlington Hall to meet with various politicians; and working-class **Mr. and Mrs. Taylor**, Stevens's overnight hosts during his journey, who assume (along with their neighbors) that Stevens is an aristocrat and who seem to represent the influence of more democratic ideals on modern English society.

Further Reading

Annan, Gabriele. ''On the High Wire.'' *New York Review of Books* Vol. 36, no. 19 (December 7, 1989): 3–4.

Contemporary Literary Criticism. Vols. 27, 56, and 1989 Yearbook. Detroit: Gale Research.

Graver, Lawrence. ''What the Butler Saw.'' *New York Times Book Review* (October 8, 1989): 3, 33.

Gurewich, David. ''Upstairs, Downstairs.'' *New Criterion* Vol. 8, no. 4 (December 1989): 77–80.

Hassan, Ihab. ''An Extravagant Reticence.'' *The World and I* Vol. 5, no. 2 (February 1990): 369–74.

Kamine, Mark. ''A Servant of Self-Deceit.'' *New Leader* Vol., no. 17 (November 13, 1989): 21–22.

Rushdie, Salman. ''What the Butler Didn't See.'' *Observer* (May 21, 1989): 53.

Strawson, Galen. ''Tragically Disciplined and Dignified.'' *Times Literary Supplement* No. 4494 (May 19–25, 1989): 535.

Thwaite, Anthony. "In Service." *London Review of Books* Vol. 11, no. 10 (May 18, 1989): 17–18.

Ruth Prawer Jhabvala

1927–

British novelist, short story writer, and screenwriter.

Heat and Dust (novel, 1975)

Plot: The novel interweaves the stories of two Englishwomen, Olivia Rivers and the unnamed narrator. Olivia goes to India in 1923 with her husband Douglas, who is a British colonial administrator in the town of Satipur. Happily married at first, Olivia gradually finds her husband to be dull and rigid. She dislikes the colonial ambiance of the Anglo-Indian community and spends most of her time shut up in her house. Then she meets an Englishman named Harry who is living with the local Indian Nawab, or prince, whom Olivia also befriends. Olivia is increasingly attracted to the Nawab, and he seduces her during an excursion to a nearby temple. She conceives a child, probably by the Nawab but possibly by her husband. Olivia's subsequent abortion is discovered by an English doctor, and the secret of her affair with the Nawab becomes widely known. Olivia flees Satipur for a remote region of the Himalayas, where she lives (visited infrequently by the Nawab), for the rest of her life, in voluntary exile.

The modern narrator, the granddaughter of Douglas Rivers and his second wife, is a writer who becomes interested in Olivia's story. She travels to India around 1973, arriving in the now-dilapidated Satipur, where she rents a small, plain room from a civil servant named Inder Lal, who guides her around the city. The narrator meets several other westerners during her sojourn, including a young Englishman who, in thrall to Indian spiritualism, has renamed himself Chidananda. She has sexual encounters with both Inder Lal and Chid and, like Olivia, becomes pregnant. Although the narrator considers an abortion, she decides to have her baby. She too finally seeks refuge in the Himalayas.

Characters: Most of Jhabvala's novels are written from the perspective of a woman born and raised in the West but resident in India for many years. *Heat and Dust,* for which Jhabvala received England's coveted Booker-McConnell Prize for Fiction, is widely recognized as her most accomplished work. The novel exhibits the "splicing," or frequent time shifts, that reflect Jhabvala's acclaimed style in the screenwriting genre. The story-within-a-story structure of *Heat and Dust* has led some critics to liken it to works by Joseph Conrad and E. M. Forster, who employed similar techniques; the latter author is, in fact, almost always mentioned in reviews of the novel. There are many parallels between Forster's *A Passage to India* (1924) and *Heat and Dust,* and Jhabvala is thought to have deliberately modeled her tale after Forster's book. While both chronicle the devastating effect of India on westerners, Jhabvala seems to hold out more hope of survival.

Some reviewers find **Olivia Rivers**, whose story comprises the sections of *Heat and Dust* set in 1923, the more interesting of the novel's two female protagonists; indeed, the narrator stresses that it is Olivia's experiences, not her own, on which she means to concentrate. An imaginative young woman with a humane sensibility, Olivia brings to India both an inclination to be captivated by its fascinating culture and a naivete that prevents her from recognizing its dangers. Thus she may be compared to such literary heroines as Dorothea Brooke in George Eliot's *Middlemarch* or Isabel Archer in Henry James's *The Portrait of a*

Lady, who also made poor choices despite their intelligence and sensitivity. Olivia exhibits naivete and romanticism when, soon after her arrival in India, she shockingly defends the Indian tradition of *suttee* or *sati,* by which widows are immolated on their husbands' funeral pyres. Olivia suggests that the desire to accompany one's beloved out of life is noble but overlooks the fact that many of the women subject to this practice are not willing participants. When her more cynical husband questions her enthusiasm for her new home, Olivia insists that "people can still be friends, can't they, even if it is in India?" Disenchanted with the banal and racist English community and bored by her circumscribed life, Olivia eagerly embraces the entertainment offered by her new friends, Harry and the Nawab. She finds herself attracted to the authoritative and flatteringly courteous Indian prince while becoming increasingly disenchanted with the stuffy husband with whom she had once thought herself in love. Olivia seems completely unaware of the Nawab's darker activities—some of which result in the deaths of innocent people in riots—and she understands only afterward that seducing her enables him to avenge himself on the hated British authorities. If her role in Douglas's life has been mainly decorative, she is also exploited by the Nawab. The course on which Olivia decides represents a rejection, in a sense, of both men: she aborts the baby that is probably the Nawab's, thus preventing him from achieving his revenge, and she leaves Douglas for exile in the Himalayas. The narrator offers no answers about whether Olivia ever achieves happiness and why she never returns to England. The fact that at the end of her life she requests a Hindu-style cremation rather than Christian burial suggests that Olivia merges more deeply with the Indian culture about which she was once so naive. Olivia is frequently compared to Adele Quested, the character in *A Passage to India* who also is fascinated by India and repulsed by the behavior of the British colonials; Forster's book also contains a sexually charged experience with an Indian man, but Adele's encounter is only imagined.

Just as Olivia may be compared to Adele Quested, her husband, **Douglas Rivers**, bears some resemblance to Adele's fiance, Ronny Heaslop. Both work for the British colonial government in India as magistrates who are well regarded by their countrymen and who treat the Indians as children in need of supervision. A highly competent administrator with a calm, controlled manner, Douglas takes seriously his role as upholder of the British code of honor and justice. Unlike Olivia, he is not entranced by India; rather, he longs for the earlier and more heroic days of English colonialism. Olivia gradually recognizes that Douglas's paternalistic focus on the Indians is also trained on her; thus to her he epitomizes the arrogant superiority not only of westerners in India in particular but of males in patriarchal societies in general. Several critics note the similarities in name, character, and relationship to the heroine between Douglas and St. John Rivers, the gentlemanly, upright, but overly rigid missionary who wants to marry the protagonist of Charlotte Brontë's 1847 novel, *Jane Eyre.*

Whereas Douglas embodies Western attitudes, the **Nawab** personifies the attraction and danger that the East represents to many westerners. A wealthy but powerless minor prince, the Nawab lives in a labyrinthine house that symbolizes his own shadowy background. Attracted by his good looks, charm, and commanding manner, Olivia is either ignorant or tolerant of his ties to local bandits and his role in the yearly riots by Muslims against Hindus. Harry describes the Nawab as "very manly and strong. When he wants something, nothing must stand in his way. Never, ever." His seduction of the sympathetic Olivia is no doubt motivated by his desire to avenge himself on the English, whom he resents, and when she becomes pregnant, he scoffs at the suggestion that Douglas might be the father. The Nawab may have inherited a certain degree of ruthlessness from his ancestors, with whom he is fascinated and in whose violent deeds he seems to take comfort whenever he encounters frustrations. His story of his relative Amanullah Khan, who slaughtered a tent full of dinner guests because of a minor slight, precedes his successful seduction of Olivia, demonstrating the erotic allure of power. Critics vary on how to interpret the Nawab and on how Jhabvala judges him: some maintain that he is a thorough scoundrel, while others note that despite his untrustworthiness, his charisma, vitality, and intelligence make him a welcome alternative to the novel's hypocritical or dull colonials. Indeed, when the Nawab visits Harry many years later in London, there is something endearing about him, even though he has become soft, fat, and effeminate. The Nawab may be compared to the similarly attractive (though much more upstanding) character of Aziz in *A Passage to India*, and if Douglas Rivers resembles Charlotte Brontë's St. John Rivers, then the Nawab may be likened to the dark, mysterious, worldly Rochester in *Jane Eyre*, particularly since both characters have demented wives.

Olivia never questions the role that the Englishman **Harry** plays in the Nawab's palace or life, overlooking the obvious homosexual tone of their relationship. Harry and Olivia are, in fact, rivals for the Nawab's attention, and both are probably being used by him for a similar purpose: to embarrass the British. Like Olivia, Harry rejects the insulated, racist viewpoint shared by the English community and is fascinated by the complex—and sexually powerful—culture in general and the Nawab in particular. Many reviewers compare Harry to the character of Fielding in *A Passage to India*, who also idealizes what he interprets as the maharajahs' admirable elevation of friendship over politics. Fielding is considered an autobiographical character, and Harry too seems Forsterian, particularly in his homosexuality.

Most significant of the minor characters in the novel's 1923 sections is **Major Minnies**, a former English official so enamored of India that he retires there. While admitting his own infatuation with India's culture, he publishes a monograph warning others that it is "dangerous for the European who allows himself to love too much. India always finds the weak spot and presses on it." Thus the major holds a view balanced somewhere between those of Olivia and Douglas, and some critics feel that Jhabvala herself endorses their contention. Other members of Satipur's English community include the straitlaced **Dr. Saunders**, who discovers Olivia's abortion, and **Mrs. Saunders**, who expresses the sexual paranoia of many European women in India when she says that Indian men have "only one thought in their heads and that's to you-know-what with a white woman." At the beginning of the novel, Douglas tells Olivia that her fellow Englishwoman **Beth Crawford** is sure that Olivia will come to view India in the correct way (that is, as the other English people do); after Olivia's departure, Beth's sister **Tessie** marries Douglas and becomes the modern narrator's grandmother. The Nawab's mother, the **Begum**, exerts behind-the-scenes power, the only kind available to women in that society. She constantly plots to advance her son's interests and thus arranges for Olivia to terminate the pregnancy, knowing that the birth will not benefit the Nawab.

Fifty years after Olivia's arrival in India, the novel's **narrator** goes there to explore what happened to her grandfather's first wife. Although her own experiences closely parallel Olivia's—she conceives a child with an Indian lover and finally retreats into the Himalayas—there are some significant differences in their milieus and personalities. The narrator is never named, and the reader never learns much about her previous life; furthermore, she speaks in a flat, detached voice that reinforces her stance as an observer. The narrator admits that her personal life is emotionally empty, which may explain her interest in Olivia's engrossing story. However, Olivia is a romantic idealist, and the narrator is antiromantic and eschews the traditional feminine qualities that Olivia exhibits. In fact, the narrator describes Olivia as "everything I'm not." One of the most important of this narrator's functions is to illustrate the changes in women's lives since Olivia's time in colonial India. Unlike her restricted predecessor, the narrator goes where she wishes when she wishes, pursues her writing career, and indulges in casual sex. Nevertheless, some aspects of the two women's experiences remain unchanged over the fifty-year gap between them. Both face unplanned pregnancies. The narrator nearly chooses the same route as Olivia, but the humane, mystical Magi helps her recognize her wish to carry the pregnancy to term. Although her final decision to retreat into the Himalayas parallels Olivia's, the narrator seems to be embracing India more consciously. Some critics contend that the narrator successfully adapts to India, while others are not convinced and even predict that India can never fill the emptiness of the narrator's life.

Most of the secondary characters in the 1970s sections of *Heat and Dust* closely parallel characters in the 1923 parts. Like the Nawab, the young Indian civil servant **Inder Lal** becomes intimate with an Englishwoman, who conceives a child; in addition, both characters are burdened with "mad" wives whom they neglect. Whereas the Nawab participates in various intrigues involving local bandits, Inder Lal suffers the annoyances of petty office politics. The Nawab and Inder Lal make love to their respective Englishwomen in the same grove near the shrine, but in the modern story, it is the narrator who seduces Inder Lal, whose childish charm and playfulness she finds attractive. The narrator's other lover is **Chidanandra,** or **Chid**, one of many contemporary Britons who have come to India seeking spiritual enlightenment. Chid shaves his head and adopts Indian clothing and a Hindu name (which means—ironically, in view of his mental instability—"Bliss of Mind"), but he never loses his English-midlands accent, which may foreshadow his eventual departure. Some critics regard the narrator's attraction to (or at least her willingness to have sex with) this character as unconvincing.

The most positively portrayed Indian character in the novel is **Maji**, the earthy peasant woman who plays an important role in the narrator's decision to keep her baby. Maji massages the narrator, which will supposedly induce a spontaneous abortion but instead initiates an awareness of the "rapture" she actually feels in her pregnancy. Another notable Indian character is **Inder Lal's mother**, who is nearly as domineering as the Nawab's Begum. She and her friends form a group the narrator calls the "merry widows," who are conspicuous in their vigor, enjoyment, and freedom of widowhood. Illustrating more negative aspects of Indian life are the beggar-woman **Leelavati**, who, after being driven from her dead husband's home and enduring terrible privation, is dying when Maji tenderly ministers to her; and Inder Lal's wife, **Ritu**, whose madness is portrayed as the logical result of the often slave-like role of Indian wives in traditional marriages. At the Bombay hostel in which the narrator spends her first night in India, she meets an elderly **Christian missionary** who warns her of the dangers that await her in this alien place. Described by the narrator as "a ghost with a backbone," the missionary has lived in India for thirty years in the service of Christ; although her system of values bears little relevance for the narrator, she reinforces the novel's emphasis on the risks involved when East meets West.

Further Reading

Agarwal, Ramlal G. *Ruth Prawer Jhabvala: A Study of Her Fiction.* New York: Envoy Press, 1990.

Contemporary Literary Criticism. Vols. 4, 8, 29. Detroit: Gale Research.

Crane, Ralph J. *Ruth Prawer Jhabvala.* New York: Twayne, 1992.

Gooneratne, Yasmine. "Film into Fiction: The Influence upon Ruth Prawer Jhabvala's Fiction of Her Work for the Cinema, 1960–1976." *World Literature Written in English* Vol. 18, no. 2 (November 1979): 368–86.

Newman, Judie. "The Untold Story and the Retold Story: Intertextuality in Post-Colonial Women's Fiction." In *Motherlands: Black Women's Writing from Africa, the Caribbean, and South Asia.* Edited by Susheila Nasta.

Rubin, David. "Ruth Jhabvala in India." *Modern Fiction Studies* Vol. 30, no. 4 (winter 1984): 669–82.

Sucher, Laurie. *The Fiction of Ruth Prawer Jhabvala: The Politics of Passion.* New York: St. Martin's Press, 1989.

Summerfield, H. "Holy Women and Unholy Men: Ruth Prawer Jhabvala Confronts the Non-Rational." *Ariel* Vol. 17, no. 3 (July 1986): 85–101.

Charles Johnson
1948–
American novelist, essayist, short story writer, and scriptwriter.

Middle Passage (novel, 1990)

Plot: The novel begins in 1829 in New Orleans. Rutherford Calhoun, a twenty-two-year-old African American, is a former slave from southern Illinois who was set free by his master, Reverend Chandler. A Protestant minister who disapproved of slavery, Chandler gave the orphaned Rutherford and his brother Jackson a broad, liberal education. While living in New Orleans, the adventurous, rebellious Rutherford occupies himself drinking, gambling, and carousing with the city's underworld inhabitants. He also comes to know Isadora Bailey, a well-educated, proper young black woman whose Boston family has been free for about fifty years. Although he appreciates Isadora's gentleness and cultivation, Rutherford resists her attempts to reform him. Isadora tries to force his hand by arranging to pay off his considerable debts to a sleazy black gangster, "Papa" Zeringue, contingent on their marriage. Faced with marriage or death, Rutherford stows away on the *Republic,* a poorly maintained ship bound for Africa to pick up a load of illegal slaves. Soon discovered by the first mate, Peter Cringle, Rutherford is assigned to serve as an assistant to Josiah Squibb, the ship's cook. The *Republic*'s captain, Ebenezer Falcon, is an eccentric, highly ambitious mariner of dwarflike stature, perverse sexual tastes, and a propensity for philosophical pondering. Arriving on the Guinea coast, Falcon takes aboard a group of Allmuseri tribespeople (considered particularly desirable as slaves) and a mysterious crate said to contain their part-creature, part-spirit god. The captain intends to use this curiosity to earn fame and fortune for himself, but instead it seems to exert a strong and destructive power over all who approach it.

During the voyage back to America, Rutherford finds his loyalties divided between the Allmuseri, with whom he sympathizes and whose culture interests him, and his white fellow crew members, who want to mutiny and set Falcon adrift. Eventually, Rutherford helps the Allmuseri escape from their chains, and after the resulting bloodbath only Rutherford, Squibb, Cringle, and Falcon are left alive to guide the ship back. Falcon subsequently kills himself. Venturing below decks to "feed" the Allmuseri's god, Rutherford encounters a revealing vision of his own past. The self-knowledge he gains seems likely to be wasted, however, as he (and nearly everyone else on board) languishes near death from disease. When an overzealous Allmuseri attempts to fire a cannon at a passing ship, the *Republic* is instead blown apart. Squibb, Rutherford, and Baleka (an eight-year-old Allmuseri girl Rutherford has befriended) survive and are taken aboard the *Juno,* a pleasure ship cruising the West Indies. Learning that "Papa" Zeringue and Isadora are aboard and are, in fact, about to be married, Rutherford uses his knowledge of Zeringue's financial investment in the *Republic*'s illegal cargo to blackmail him and prevent the marriage. By now Rutherford has come to appreciate the benefits of a stable domestic life, and he reconciles with Isadora, who agrees to marry him and make a home for him and Baleka.

Characters: Johnson won the 1990 National Book Award for *Middle Passage*, the first book by an African American writer to attain this honor since Ralph Ellison's *Invisible Man* in 1953. The award generated something of a controversy when one of the judges claimed that the other judges chose *Middle Passage* because of "politically correct" ideology rather than true merit. Johnson strenuously disputed this allegation, asserting that his book actually constitutes a *denial* of rigid ideology. Johnson resists the expectation that a black writer be a spokesperson for his race; he claims to have no interest in writing "protest" novels and believes that African American writers ought to infuse their work with intellectual and philosophical concerns and thus "move from narrow complaint to broad celebration." Johnson intended *Middle Passage* as a "serious entertainment" combining adventure, humor, and philosophical discourse, and most critics—regardless of their overall opinions of the novel's merit—have found it highly readable. In creating a story that is at once picaresque, romantic, historically informative, and thematically resonant, Johnson juxta-posed such twentieth-century terms as "hung over" and concepts such as affirmative action with nineteenth-century maritime jargon and well-researched descriptions of slave conditions. Some reviewers faulted Johnson for this approach (said to have been based on a technique often used by eighteenth-century author Samuel Johnson), claiming that it deprives the work of individual authenticity, while others claimed that it lends the novel both accessibility and deeper meaning.

In his review of *Middle Passage,* George F. Will praised Johnson for showing "that black experiences have been various," a reference to the protagonist's refusal to conform to the stereotype of a nineteenth-century African American man. **Rutherford Calhoun** speaks in a jocular tone that reflects his adventurous spirit and (at least initially) carefree approach to life. Born a slave, Rutherford and his brother are raised—after the death of their mother and disappearance of their father—by a Protestant minister who disapproves of slavery and gives both boys a broad, humanist education. Unlike his well-behaved, considerate brother, Rutherford is unruly and rebellious. When he reaches adulthood, he moves to New Orleans and immerses himself in the city's sordid underground, indulging in gambling, drinking, and prostitutes. Although he disdains the snobbishness of New Orleans' Creole citizens, Rutherford is somewhat drawn to prim Isadora Bailey, with whom he shares the more learned, cultured side of his personality. Nevertheless, the prospect of marriage to Isadora holds no appeal for the wild, roguish young man. Faced with either matrimony or possible murder by Zeringue's thugs, Rutherford chooses escape aboard the *Republic.* Like Ishmael, the protagonist of Herman Melville's *Moby-Dick; or, The White Whale* (to which *Middle Passage* is often compared), Rutherford encounters a colorful variety of people during his journey, but his self-knowledge expands as well. Rutherford finds his loyalties divided between his white crewmates, who resist Captain Falcon's tyranny and the Allmuseri, whom he comes to admire and sympathize with. Rutherford sees something of himself in Falcon and his Allmuseri friend Ngonyama: like Falcon he is hungry for new experiences, and like Ngonyama he is altered forever by his time aboard the *Republic.* Descending below ship's deck to "feed" the Allmuseri's god, Rutherford encounters a vision of his father, whose abandonment he has always resented. He learns about his father's rebelliousness and resistance to captivity—qualities he realizes he has inherited—and that his father died while trying to escape to freedom. This experience seems to help Rutherford develop a sense of his own identity. Remembering how Reverend Chandler, the former master who freed him, complained that he would never be of any help to anyone, Rutherford now makes himself useful by comforting the people suffering aboard the *Republic,* an activity that brings him purpose and satisfaction. His relationship with Baleka is also important, for, as he explains to Isadora after their reunion, he considers the child's needs more important than his own and he finally understands what it means to take responsibility for another person's well-being. Thus he is now ready to commit himself to Isadora, whose memory has been enhanced by his perilous adventures.

Near the end of his journey, Rutherford realizes that he has no wish to go to Africa, that "this weird, upside-down caricature of a country called America" is his true home. Critics praised Johnson for his success in creating a character who is a patriot, despite being a former slave who will face countless hardships and humiliations in the future. Rutherford has also been compared to another important literary figure who takes a quintessential American journey of self-discovery: Mark Twain's Huckleberry Finn.

Critics often consider nineteenth-century American author Herman Melville as a strong influence on Johnson, and indeed *Middle Passage*'s **Captain Ebenezer Falcon** bears some resemblance to Captain Ahab in *Moby-Dick*. Both are eccentric, ruthless, and tormented seamen seeking victory over intangible forces. However, Falcon's grotesque, dwarfish exterior has been said to reflect his stunted humanity. He is paranoid, calculating, and cruel not only in his treatment of his crew and human cargo but of young **Tommy O'Toole**, with whom he satisfies his sexual proclivities. He considers the black race inherently unintelligent, so he does not really expect Rutherford to understand his musings during their long conversations. Prone to philosophizing, Falcon makes such statements as "slavery . . . is the social correlate of a deeper, ontic wound," which some critics have found strained and unconvincing. Rutherford describes the captain as "a Faustian man of powerful loves, passions, hatreds, a creature of preposterous, volatile contradictions." Greedy for fame and fortune, Falcon plunders his human cargo for his own gain—he sees the mysterious Allmuseri god as a potential treasure. Falcon suffers defeat when his own excesses prompt his crew to turn against him. Wounded during the slave mutiny, Falcon kills himself, leaving no one to pilot the ship.

The *Republic*'s first mate and quartermaster is **Peter Cringle**, a product of "New England gentility" with a stiff, ministerial manner. Cringle's precise speech, sensitivity, and firm principles set him apart from his shipmates. The son of a wealthy man, Cringle has failed at every previous employment, and his assignment to the *Republic* is his last-ditch attempt to succeed. In the end, Cringle attains—albeit in a bizarre way—a kind of nobility; after enduring various catastrophes with the rest of the crew and already close to death, he instructs Squibb to kill him so that those remaining aboard the *Republic* can eat him and thus avoid starvation. **Josiah Squibb** is the ship's fat, good-natured, alcoholic cook. Rutherford meets Squibb in a New Orleans pub, steals his papers, and stows away aboard the *Republic*, planning to impersonate the cook. After the ship's departure he is discovered, but Squibb is also aboard and has reported the theft of his papers. Assigned to work as Squibb's assistant, Rutherford comes to admire the cook, whose sole distinction is having married five wives who all resembled the first, Maud (whom he truly loved). Near the novel's conclusion, Squibb helps Rutherford and Baleka escape from the sinking ship and is rescued with them aboard the *Juno*.

Rutherford's love interest is **Isadora Bailey**, an educated, cultured young black woman with a quiet, gentle (though sometimes sententious) manner and an understated prettiness. The product of a Boston family that has been free since the Revolutionary War, Isadora has come south to teach, but she seems out of place in rough, rowdy New Orleans. She is a sympathetic friend to any wounded dog, cat, or bird she encounters, taking them into her home, and she would also like to undertake supervision of Rutherford. When he proves resistant to her wish to reform him, Isadora concocts a plan of her own, arranging with Zeringue to pay off Rutherford's debts if he will marry her. This plan backfires when Rutherford flees aboard the *Republic*, leaving Isadora—as she tells him when they are reunited—feeling rejected and humiliated. So she agrees to marry Zeringue but regrets her agreement when she learns more about her fiance. Then Rutherford blackmails Zeringue, preventing Isadora from marrying him, and—now appreciative of Isadora—gets her to agree to marry him.

The forty Allmuseri tribespeople taken aboard the *Republic* as chattel to be transported back to America are part of an ancient African tribe of magicians or wizards. Rutherford, who calls them "the Ur-tribe of humanity itself," is fascinated with their view of life as a quest for the "Unity of Being." This essentially Buddhist outlook runs counter to the Western philosophy of dualism or opposites (e.g., light/dark, good/evil). Prominent among the Allmuseri are the cool, intelligent **Ngonyama**, to whom Falcon assigns leadership status and from whom Rutherford learns about the culture and history of the tribe; bloodthirsty, hate-obsessed **Diamelo**, who takes control of the slave mutiny and ultimately causes the destruction of the *Republic;* and **Baleka**, an eight-year-old girl who adopts Rutherford as her father and through whom he learns the satisfaction of putting another person's well-being before one's own.

Several characters appear in the novel only in Rutherford's recollections of his past. **Reverend Peleg Chandler**, Rutherford's former master, was a slaveholder who disapproved of slavery and who gave Rutherford and his brother an excellent education. Rutherford describes his brother, **Jackson Calhoun**, as a negative of himself, for Jackson is obedient, patient, and responsible. Rutherford has always scorned his brother for aspiring to be a "gentleman of color," a status Rutherford considers demeaning, and especially for suggesting to the dying Reverend Chandler that the old man's estate be divided between all of its slaves rather than just the Calhoun brothers. During his journey, Rutherford develops an appreciation for his brother's compassion, which he previously considered a weakness. **Riley "Da" Calhoun**, Rutherford's father, was an irresponsible ne'er-do-well who infuriated other slaves by sleeping with their wives but also inspired them to feel pride in themselves and their people. He continually resisted the constraints imposed on him and was finally killed trying to escape.

Other characters in the novel include **Phillipe "Papa" Zeringue**, the wealthy, wicked Creole gangster who so values money (which he equates with power) that he is willing to betray other blacks by owning slaves himself; and his henchman **Santos**, a huge former slave—described by Rutherford as a "walking wrecking crew"—who is enraged to learn that his employer is a slave-owner. **Nathaniel Meadows** is a native of Liverpool who serves as the *Republic*'s barber-surgeon; despite his meek manner and scrawny appearance, he is reputed to have murdered his wife and children with an ax. **Tommy O'Toole** is a handsome cabin boy forced to endure Captain Falcon's sexual attentions; Tommy is also the first to encounter the creature below-decks, and emerges half-insane.

Further Reading

Coates, Joseph. "Uncharted Waters." *Chicago Tribune—Books* (July 8, 1990): 6–7.

Contemporary Literary Criticism. Vols. 7, 51, 65. Detroit: Gale Research.

Dictionary of Literary Biography. Vol. 33. Detroit: Gale Research.

Dixon, Melvin. "Mutiny on the Republic." *Book World—Washington Post* (July 15, 1990): 6.

Flick, Arend. "Stowaway on a Slave Ship to Africa." *Los Angeles Times Book Review* (June 24, 1990): 1, 7.

Iannone, Carol. "Literature by Quota." *Commentary* Vol. 91, no. 3 (March 1991): 50–53.

Keneally, Thomas. "Misadventures in the Slave Trade." *New York Times Book Review* (July 1, 1990): 8–9.

Ross, Michael E. "*Passage* Author Detects New Currents in Modern Black Fiction." *San Francisco Chronicle* (August 12, 1990): 1, 12.

Will, George F. "Beyond the Literature of Protest." *Washington Post* (December 13, 1990): A23.

Wills, Garry. "The Long Voyage Home." *New York Review of Books* Vol. 38, nos. 1 & 2 (January 17, 1991): 3.

William Kennedy

1928–

American novelist, journalist, editor, scriptwriter, critic, and nonfiction writer.

Ironweed (novel, 1983)

Plot: The novel takes place in Albany, New York, over the course of a twenty-four-hour period in 1938. Francis Phelan, a homeless alcoholic, returns to Albany on Halloween Day after twenty-two years of wandering. His first flight from responsibility dates back to 1901 when, during the city's trolley strike, Francis throws a rock that kills one of the strikebreakers. Although he eventually returns to Albany (becoming a professional baseball player), Francis leaves again in 1916 after his youngest child, Gerald, dies of a broken neck when Francis accidentally drops him. Francis wrongly assumes that his wife, Annie, can never forgive him. He returns now after years of hard living and violence, and in order to earn some quick money he hires himself out to the powerful McCoy family to stuff ballot boxes for their candidate in a local election. He is arrested before he can collect all the money. Broke again, Francis works one day filling graves at the cemetery in which Gerald is buried. There he communes with Gerald's spirit, who tells him he is about to undergo a process of "expiation." The next day, Francis works for a junk dealer to earn enough money to buy a turkey, which he takes to his family's home. Along the way, Francis encounters the ghosts of several significant figures from his past. When he reaches the house, Annie welcomes him warmly, expresses compassion for his years of exile and suffering, and assures him that she has never blamed him for the baby's death. Francis's children, Billy and Peg, join Annie in asking him to stay, but Francis spends the night in a "hobo jungle." That night, when a band of American Legionnaires raids their camp, Francis attacks and kills the man who kills his hobo friend Rudy. He then goes to the derelict hotel in which his beloved female companion of nine years, another homeless wanderer named Helen Archer, is staying, and learns that she has died of cancer. Francis considers leaving Albany for good but decides to stay. He returns to the Phelan home, where he takes refuge in the attic and plans eventually to move downstairs to the cozier room of his grandson Danny.

Characters: Kennedy is winner of the Pulitzer Prize for Fiction and the National Book Critics Circle Award for *Ironweed,* the third and most acclaimed work in what is called his "Albany cycle." Although all of these novels reflect Kennedy's upbringing in Albany's Irish Catholic community, *Ironweed* most successfully portrays a harsh Depression-era setting by means of the lyrical language and metaphysical musings that are hallmarks of his style. Like William Faulkner and James Joyce, his literary forebears, Kennedy is a regional writer who explores universal themes. Critics trace connections between Dante's *Purgatorio,* Homer's *Odyssey,* and *Ironweed*—which expresses concerns of guilt, expiation of sins, and salvation and chronicles the events of one full day. Kennedy renders with compassion, wit, and vigor a group of characters whose dignity and humanity shine through their tattered clothing and wounded psyches.

The novel's title refers to the resilience of its protagonist, whose toughness resembles that of the stem of the ironweed plant. **Francis Phelan** first appears in the second book in the Albany series, *Billy Phelan's Greatest Game,* as the just-returned father of the title character; *Ironweed* begins only weeks after the action in the previous novel ends. A former third baseman with a self-described talent for running (around a baseball diamond as well as away from trouble), Francis is a fifty-eight-year-old hard-drinking wanderer who stays away from his family for twenty years. Kennedy's portrayal of Francis's privation is unsentimentally realistic, showing the hardships faced by those whose goal is merely to get through "the next twenty minutes." Critics applaud the author's success in creating characters who inhabit the lowest strata of society but are nevertheless complex, and Francis is cited as the best example of this feat. Though frequently violent, Francis is capable of great tenderness and compassion; though a victim of unlucky circumstances, he chooses his course of action. Though cowardly in leaving his family, he later exhibits courage and integrity. The novel chronicles Francis's journey toward redemption, on which he is guided by a number of ghosts who lead him on a Dantean tour of his past and prompt him to ask himself what he is and how he became what he is. The overpowering guilt Francis feels after he causes his baby's death and kills a strikebreaker is compounded by other unfortunate incidents. Although Francis performs acts of kindness that should expiate his sins—such as his tender care of Helen and his compassionate treatment of Rudy and Sandra—he does not let go of his guilt, for he says, "If I lose it, I have stood for nothing, done nothing, been nothing." A few critics find *Ironweed's* conclusion ambiguous (particularly in view of Francis's dreaming that he has resumed his old pattern of violence and flight), but most contend that he does finally achieve redemption. Two characters aid this process: Helen, who accelerates her own dying in order to free him, and Annie, who welcomes him back into the family with great tenderness and compassion. As several commentators note, Francis may be likened to the mythological figures of Odysseus, who also traveled among the dead, endured many dangers, and finally returned to an ever-faithful wife, and Aeneas, whose struggles with fate are recounted in Virgil's epic poem, *The Aeneid.*

Critic Edward C. Reilly describes wise, magnanimous **Annie Phelan** as a "hearth goddess who symbolizes stability and eventual redemption for Francis." Like Penelope, who faithfully waits for her husband, Odysseus, to return from his long journey, Annie remains loyal to her husband even though he abandons her and their children. Whereas their family tragedy causes Francis to mire himself in guilt, it deepens Annie's compassion. Far from blaming Francis for Gerald's death, she feels responsible herself, because she initially pins the diaper that comes loose when Francis picks up the baby; in any case, she assures Francis, the accident is "nobody's fault." She never tells Billy and Peg (or anyone else) about Francis's role in Gerald's death, and she encourages them to pity and forgive their father. Annie resembles Helen in her Catholicism and love for Francis, but with her red hands, stained apron, and stellar position as wife and mother, she is much more a figure of domestic happiness than Helen.

While unlike Annie in background and personality, **Helen Archer** plays a similar role in Francis's redemption. Her own life courses on a downward spiral like Francis's, due to a mixture of bad luck, circumstance, and personal weakness. As a young girl, Helen is considered a promising singer by her adoring father. After he commits suicide, Helen's greedy mother withholds money from Helen, and she is unable to finish her education at Vassar. After she has a degrading affair with a married man, Helen realizes that she will never marry or have her musical career, and thus begins her descent into alcoholism and destitution. When *Ironweed* begins, Helen has become a grotesque, continually drunken figure with spindly legs and a stomach swollen with a tumor. She has been Francis's lover and companion for nine years, and he has shown his tenderness and love by caring for her— finding food for her and warm places to sleep and once, when she was sick, even begging for her (something he never does for himself). Unlike Francis, Helen practices her Catholic faith to the end and attends mass even on the last day of her life, thus highlighting the novel's emphasis on sin and salvation. Kennedy's success in creating characters whose humanity and dignity are evident despite their lowly stature and appearance is exemplified by Helen, who accepts responsibility for her own life and expects no pity from anyone. She dies peacefully, accelerating her death in order to free Francis to return to his family.

Other important figures in Francis's Albany world include his children, **Billy**, who is portrayed in *Billy Phelan's Greatest Game* as a bookmaker and pool shark who combines hustler's instincts with integrity, and **Peg**, who is initially angry at her father for abandoning the family but eventually forgives and accepts him. Francis's grandson **Danny** welcomes the return of the grandfather he already idolizes, and Francis anticipates moving into Danny's "mighty nice little room" as soon as he readjusts to family life. Francis sees the ghosts of his parents while working at the cemetery; **Katherine Phelan** is a life-denying Irish Catholic who disapproves of most human pleasures, particularly non-procreative sex. Francis's sensuous neighbor **Katrina Daugherty** (the mother of Martin Daugherty from *Billy Phelan*), is the lover of his teenaged years, a goddess who called him her "beautiful Adonis."

Commentators praise Kennedy for his depiction of the down-and-out characters in *Ironweed,* who are all just trying to "survive the next twenty minutes." Although Francis's simple-minded, alcoholic friend **Rudy Newton** suffers from stomach cancer, he dies when Legionnaires attack the hobo encampment; Francis carries Rudy on his back to the hospital but fails to save him. Drunken **Sandra**, whose face is partially eaten away by dogs after she freezes to death just outside of the rescue mission, also illustrates the cruel realities of homeless life, as does the consumptive, antagonistic **Clara**. Among the ghosts who visit Francis are **Rowdy Dick Doolan**—Francis kills him under a Chicago bridge after he goes insane and attacks Francis with a meat cleaver; **Aldo Campione**, who is shot when Francis fails to pull him aboard a moving boxcar; **Harold Allen**, the strikebreaker Francis kills with a rock; and **Strawberry Bill Benson**, who encourages Francis to return to the sanctuary of the Phelan attic. Other minor characters in *Ironweed* include **Rosskam**, the junk dealer Francis works for who tries to cheat him out of some of his pay; and **Michigan Mac**, a bum with a wife and baby to whom Francis gives some food.

Further Reading

Clarke, Peter P. "Classical Myth in William Kennedy's *Ironweed.*" *Critique: Studies in Modern Fiction* Vol. 27, no. 3 (spring 1986): 167–76.

Contemporary Literary Criticism. Vols. 6, 28, 34, 53. Detroit: Gale Research.

Dictionary of Literary Biography. 1985 Yearbook. Detroit: Gale Research.

Hunt, George W. "William Kennedy's Albany Trilogy." *America.* Vol. 150, no. 19 (May 19, 1984): 373–75.

Lehmann-Haupt, Christopher. Review of *Ironweed. New York Times* (January 10, 1983): C18.

Nichols, Loxley F. "William Kennedy Comes of Age." *National Review* (New York) Vol. 37 (August 9, 1985): 46–48.

Pritchard, William H. "The Spirits of Albany." *New Republic* Vol. 188, no. 6 (February 14, 1983): 37–38.

Reilly, Edward C. *William Kennedy.* Boston: Twayne, 1991.

Schott, Webster. Review of *Ironweed. Book World–Washington Post* (January 16, 1983): 1, 6.

Stade, George. "Life on the Lam." *New York Times Book Review* (January 23, 1983): 1, 14–15.

Towers, Robert. "Violent Places." *New York Review of Books* Vol. 30, no. 5 (March 31, 1983): 11–12.

Van Dover, J. Kenneth. *Understanding William Kennedy.* Columbia: University of South Carolina, 1991.

Winch, Terence. "The Albany Novels." *American Book Review* Vol. 7, no. 4 (May–June 1985): 19.

Jamaica Kincaid
1949(?)–
West Indian-born American short story writer and novelist.

Annie John (novel, 1985)

Plot: Set on the Caribbean island of Antigua during the late 1950s or early 1960s, the novel compromises of eight sections that chronicle the title character's passage from childhood to young adulthood. In "Figures in the Distance," Annie describes her first encounters with death, first through the funerals in a nearby cemetery that she watches from afar, then through the successive deaths of the child of her mother's friend, her neighbor Miss Charlotte, and a humpbacked girl her own age. Annie's close relationship with her mother is featured in "The Circling Hand," in which she relates her daily routine during school holidays, when she and her mother would share fragrant herbal baths, breakfast, and shopping excursions, followed by lunch with Annie's carpenter father and a series of pleasant domestic tasks during the afternoon. Annie especially enjoyed cleaning out the trunk in which her mother stored her baby clothes, which would inevitably provoke stories about Annie's babyhood. When Annie turns twelve, however, her mother begins to withdraw their earlier closeness. "Gwen" tells of Annie's experiences at her new school, where she dazzles her teachers and classmates with an accomplished essay about her mother and establishes a passionate friendship with a neat, serious girl named Gwen. Annie excels at academics and sports, and she starts to menstruate.

In "The Red Girl," Annie spends more and more time with a dirty, unkempt, tomboyish girl who appeals to a different side of her than the always proper Gwen. It is through the Red Girl's influence that Annie starts playing marbles, in direct defiance of her mother's wishes. Annie's denial about taking up this pastime leads to a serious rift with her mother. Annie's school experiences are the focus of "Columbus in Chains," in which she incites a teacher's wrath by writing a mildly insolent caption underneath the picture of Christopher Columbus in her history book. In "Somewhere, Belgium," Annie is in her fifteenth year and deeply unhappy about the antagonism between herself and her mother; she imagines moving far away and receiving letters addressed to herself in "Somewhere, Belgium." "The Long Rain" chronicles Annie's mysterious, three-and-a-half-month illness, which coincides with a period of relentless rain. Annie's bewildered and worried parents consult a medical doctor and a traditional obeah woman, and Annie's grandmother Ma Chess also arrives from the island of Dominica to treat her. Just as the rain stops, Annie recovers and has grown several inches during her illness. The book closes with "A Walk to the Jetty," in which the now-seventeen-year-old Annie prepares to leave Antigua for England, where she will train to be a nurse. After saying goodbye to several friends and neighbors, she walks down the road to the jetty with her parents. She boards her ship, bids her parents a strained but emotional goodbye, and waves wildly to them as the ship pulls away and they fade from view. Finally she turns back into her cabin and lies down on her berth.

Characters: *Annie John* first appeared as a series of short stories in the *New Yorker* magazine. Praised for its poetic but sharp, precise language and it's sensitivity in portraying a young woman's coming of age, the novel reflects Kincaid's childhood on Antigua. Critics lauded Kincaid for her lush, lucid prose and her insights into the intensity and ambivalence of mother/daughter relationships and the development of the artistic sensibility.

The novel's narrator and central character is **Annie Victoria John**, the only child of adoring parents who call her "Little Miss" and who give her an idyllic childhood. Sensitive and curious, Annie is initially as proud of her beautiful, efficient mother as her mother is of her unusually bright little girl. When Annie is a child, her mother makes her dresses from the same fabric as her own; she takes Annie shopping, bathes her in special, protective herbs, and lovingly relates stories about her own and Annie's early lives. But as Annie reaches adolescence, her relationship with her mother changes. She tells Annie that she is now too old to wear a dress that matches her mother's, and she is no longer willing to sort through Annie's baby clothes with her. Annie reacts to this change with bewilderment, alarm, and finally resentment. She starts to feel intensely angry toward her mother, yet cannot imagine a life without her, as her account—in an autobiographical essay—of nearly losing her mother in the ocean illustrates. Other relationships supplant Annie's intimacy with her mother: first she befriends the very proper Gwen, whom her mother likes, then she carries on a more illicit and secret friendship with the Red Girl, knowing her mother would disapprove. Annie has always been a dutiful daughter, excellent student, and a good girl whose teachers love her, but her marble playing and friendship with the Red Girl manifest a new desire to explore other facets of her personality. Annie's mysterious ailment, from which she emerges several inches taller, symbolizes that she has undergone initiation and come out a different person. By the end of the novel, Annie leaves her familiar island home and the parents who have both nurtured and stifled her. She plans to study nursing, the main attraction of which seems to be the opportunity it offers for escape. Some critics have interpreted Annie's departing coldness as evidence of her continuing antagonism against her mother's influence; others maintain that it is merely a protective facade, while still others contend that it reflects both love and resistance. In any case, Kincaid is credited with an effective, poignant portrayal of a young woman's struggle to assert her own identity and emerge from the shadow of the mother she both loves and hates.

Annie and her mother share the same name, **Annie Victoria John**, and the younger Annie becomes known as Little Miss. Some critics find Annie's mother an even stronger presence than the daughter, and these reviewers describe the mother in vivid terms that relay both her positive and her negative qualities. Annie's childhood is lovingly dominated by this beautiful, efficient, woman who is apparently revered by all her neighbors and was chosen by Annie's father as the one of his many lovers with whom he wanted to settle down and raise a child. Annie's mother conveys her tender devotion until Annie reaches adolescence. It seems that her mother is pushing her away, that she has become unresponsive and even suspicious. Despite Annie's growing antagonism against her mother, however, their bond remains deep, as proven in the book's final scene. At their parting, both mother and daughter cry, but at the same time Annie feels smothered by the embrace. Likewise, her mother's reminder, "It doesn't matter what you do or where you go, I'll always be your mother and this will always be your home," seems both a comfort and a curse.

Annie's father, **Alexander John**, is thirty-five years older than his wife, a benevolent character who provides well for his family through his apparently thriving carpentry business. He has known many, many paramours, who are all jealous of Annie and her mother, which both exposes the two Annies to danger and makes them feel specially chosen. Annie's father does not approve of consulting an obeah during Annie's illness, but he does not prevent her mother from calling in a practitioner; first, however, he carries Annie on his own back to a conventional medical doctor.

Other characters in *Annie John* include the title character's beloved friend **Gwen**, with whom she experiences an intensity of feeling that is markedly romantic in nature. Conventional, prim Gwen, whose personality is very similar to Annie's eventually bores Annie, who then pursues a relationship with the wild, unkempt **Red Girl**. The two obeah women called in to help Annie when she is sick are **Ma Jolie** and Annie's own grandmother, **Ma Chess**, an impressive tall figure whose appearances and departures are always mysterious. Annie's predominantly British teachers are perhaps best represented by **Miss Moore**, the school's headmistress, who looks "like a prune left out of its jar a long time" and who sounds "as if she had borrowed her voice from an owl." Another English person who does not fare well in Antigua is Annie's fellow student **Ruth**, a timid, embarrassed blonde girl who looks as if she would rather be in England "where no one would remind her constantly of the terrible things her ancestors had done."

Further Reading

Austin, Jacqueline. "Up from Eden." *VLS* No. 34 (1985): 6–7.

Bemrose, John. "Growing Pains of Girlhood." *Maclean's* Magazine Vol. 98, no. 20 (May 20, 1985): 61.

Black Literature Criticism. Vol. 2. Detroit: Gale Research.

Bonnell, Paula. "'Annie' Travels to Second Childhood." *Boston Herald* (March 31, 1985): 126.

Contemporary Literary Criticism. Vol. 43. Detroit: Gale Research.

Cudjoe, Selwyn R. Interview with Jamaica Kincaid. *Callaloo* Vol. 12, no. 2 (spring 1989): 396–411.

Dutton, Wendy. "Merge and Separate: Jamaica Kincaid's Fiction." *World Literature Today* Vol. 63, no. 3 (summer 1989): 406–10.

Morris, Ann R., and Margaret M. Dunn. "'The Bloodstream of Our Inheritance': Female Identity and the Caribbean Mothers'-Land." In *Motherlands: Black Women's Writing from Africa, the Caribbean and South Asia.* Ed. Susheila Nasta. New Brunswick, NJ: Rutgers University Press, 1992, pp. 219–37.

Murdoch, H. Adlai. "Severing the (M)other Connection: The Representation of Cultural Identity in Jamaica Kincaid's *Annie John.*" *Callaloo* Vol. 13, no. 2 (spring 1990): 325–40.

Onwordi, Ike. "Wising Up." *Times Literary Supplement* No. 4313 (November 29, 1985): 1374.

Stephen King
1947–

American novelist, short story writer, scriptwriter, nonfiction writer, autobiographer, and author of children's books.

The Shining (novel, 1977)

Plot: Most of the novel's action takes place at a mountain resort hotel in Colorado. Jack Torrance, an alcoholic writer who has recently been fired from his university job, agrees to serve as the winter caretaker for the Overlook Hotel, which is closed until spring. Jack takes his wife, Wendy, and five-year-old son, Danny—both of whom he has in the past physically abused—with him to the isolated hotel, hoping that, because the job requires only that he perform routine repairs and furnace maintenance, he will have time to work on the play he has long planned to write. When the family arrives at the hotel, its staff is preparing to leave for the winter. The cook, Dick Hallorann, shows Wendy and Danny around the kitchen and discovers that Danny has a psychic gift, or "shining," like his own. He tells Danny to contact him telepathically if he needs help. As the family settles into life at the hotel, Jack becomes aware of a lurking evil manifested in such strange sights as the garden's topiary animals, which come to life and move toward him. He becomes increasingly drawn to alcohol—which mysteriously appears in the hotel—and unable to write. Instead of working on his play, he obsesses over a scrapbook he finds in the basement that relates the Overlook's history. He learns that many bizarre and sinister things have happened in the hotel, the malevolent spirit of which now seems to be trying to take control of him. Tensions rise between Jack and Wendy, and Wendy fears for her own and her son's safety. Meanwhile, Danny too senses the hotel's evil and is tormented by gruesome images and ghostly attacks that try to overwhelm him. Jack is finally completely possessed by the Overlook's malevolent spirits and tries to kill his family with a mallet; when Danny appeals to Jack's fatherly instinct, however, Jack kills himself instead. Aided by Dick Hallorann, who answers Danny's psychic call for help, Wendy and Danny escape from the hotel just before its furnace explodes.

Characters: Sometimes cited as the best-selling author of his time, King is a remarkably prolific and popular writer who is critically acclaimed for accurately rendering both physical detail and emotional states. King's work blends elements of several genres, including the traditional gothic horror tale, the psychological thriller, and science fiction. He often explores the inexplicable intrusion of evil into otherwise ordinary lives and conveys the varied responses of his often tragically flawed characters. Like other King novels, *The Shining* provides a riveting story of supernatural evil underlaid with a concern for the interrelationships between the conscious and unconscious and between the past and the present. In addition, the novel touches on the contemporary issues of child abuse (particularly the idea that such behavior may recur in successive generations of families) and alcoholism.

The central figure in *The Shining* is **Jack Torrance**, whose life, as the novel begins, is rapidly collapsing around him. An alcoholic whose frustrations have in the past erupted into violence against his wife and child, Torrance has recently lost his university teaching job. In accepting the caretaker's position at the Overlook Hotel, Jack hopes to reestablish his credibility as an employee and work on the play he has been wanting to write. (He is portrayed as a genuinely talented writer who has not yet achieved success.) In addition to his other problems, Jack has not yet come to terms with the legacy of his own alcoholic, abusive father and is haunted by unpleasant images from the past; this continuing denial contributes to Jack's instability and threatens Danny, with whom Jack seems bound to repeat old patterns. Soon after arriving at the Overlook, Jack senses the ineffable danger that lurks there, but he refuses to endanger his job—and by extension his pride—by leaving. The evil spirit of the hotel (which almost becomes a character in its own right) exploits Jack's emotional frailty and his weakness for alcohol, factors that are compounded by his inability to write. Instead of working on his play, he becomes obsessed with the Overlook's scrapbook and spends more and more time poring over it in the basement. Thus he might be said to lose the command of language through which he could have gained control of his own life. The process by which he loses his mind and soul to the dark forces concentrated at the Overlook parallels the loss of his craft. (King also explores the connection between writing and survival in his 1987 novel, *Misery*.) The hotel's malevolence possesses Jack and is expelled only when, in response to Danny's appeal to his fatherly instincts, he kills himself instead of his wife and child. Jack is a fundamentally decent man done in not only by the supernatural forces of evil but by his own human weaknesses.

Critics fault King for failing to create strong, multidimensional female characters, a weakness he readily confesses to in interviews. Like many of the women in King's fiction, **Wendy Torrance** is a traditional wife and mother whose energies focus on the safety of her child. Although she is primarily concerned about the physical damage Jack might do to Danny, she knows that certain elements in her own upbringing may affect her performance as a mother—notably the influence of her own resentful, highly critical mother. Wendy tries to treat Jack with patience and understanding but succumbs to reminding him of his failures and allows him to see that she does not trust him with their son. Wendy's complete dependence on men is illustrated at the end of *The Shining,* when she and Danny must be rescued by Dick Hallorann.

Danny Torrance is a likable five-year-old with a powerful psychic gift that he neither fully understands nor fully controls. In the past his "shining" has been either a slight annoyance or an instrument of fun, but the evil circumstances at the Overlook Hotel prove too powerful for Danny, who is both physically and emotionally endangered by what happens there. Some critics complain that Danny displays an improbable maturity for a child his age. **Dick Hallorann**, the Overlook's cook, also has psychic abilities and immediately recognizes the same gift in Danny. Alerted by Danny's telepathic call for help, Dick arrives at the Overlook in time to rescue Wendy and Danny. Moments before the explosion that destroys the hotel, Dick sees a looming black shape emerge from the Presidential Suite, which suggests that the Overlook's malevolence has survived and perhaps can never be destroyed.

The Stand (novel, 1978)

Plot: This apocalyptic novel begins in July 1985 on an air force base in California where government research on biological weapons is being conducted. A panicked employee allows the release of a germ that causes a deadly "super-flu," which quickly spreads from the Southwest across the country. For some unknown reason, a small percentage of people is immune to the disease. All of the survivors have dreams that result in their choosing to join either the benevolent forces, headed by a saintly old black woman named Mother Abagail, or the "Dark Side," ruled by the evil Randall Flagg, whose forces are moving westward. Beginning a similar trip are two young New Englanders, Fran Goldsmith (who is pregnant) and the highly intelligent but socially awkward Harold Lauder, who is in love with Fran. Through their dreams, they are called west by Mother Abagail. Along the way they meet Texas factory worker Stuart Redman. Harold's jealousy of Stuart begins to draw him toward the Dark Side. Another westward traveler is Larry Underwood, a popular rock star who becomes disenchanted with success just before the onslaught of the plague. Arkansan deaf-mute Nick Andros also answers Mother Abagail's call to the west, and he is eventually joined by a mentally disabled man named Tom Cullen. Eventually Mother Abagail's followers gather in Boulder, Colorado, while Flagg's group masses in Las Vegas, Nevada.

While Flagg begins to organize a military force, the Boulder survivors establish a democratic community called the Free Zone with Andros and Redman as its main leaders. Mother Abagail commands them to send a group to Las Vegas to confront Flagg, and Redman, Underwood, sociologist Glen Bateman, and a man named Ralph Brentner strike out for Nevada. Meanwhile, Harold is drawn over to the Dark Side by Nadine Cross, a vindictive young woman, and he plans to assassinate the Boulder leaders; the resulting bomb explosion kills Andros. In the Nevada desert, Redman breaks his leg and must be left behind by the others. They continue to Las Vegas where they face Flagg, who proves to be only an inept shadow of the powerful image he has projected. All are subsequently killed in a massive nuclear explosion accidentally set off by one of Flagg's sidekicks. Stuart Redman and Tom Cullen, the sole survivor of three spies sent to Las Vegas earlier in the novel, return to Boulder. Stuart and Fran, who is now pregnant with a second child, decide to leave the fledgling society at Boulder and establish a rural home in Maine.

Characters: According to critic Edwin F. Casebeer, in *The Stand,* King "uses the horror novel as a literary metaphor to explore dark contemporary psychological and social realities," including the sinister prospect of potentially destructive, secret governmental research and the horrors of modern warfare. The novel features a skillful blend of elements of the horror, science fiction, and fantasy genres. Because it is an apocalyptic epic structured as a heroic quest and peopled by a cast of characters who range from good to flawed to malevolent to monstrous, *The Stand* is frequently compared to J. R. R. Tolkien's classic fantasy saga, *The Lord of the Rings.* The novel provides a mythic portrayal of a conflict between good and evil that takes place in a distinctly American setting, with the cities of Boulder, Colorado, and Las Vegas, Nevada, serving as centers of these two forces. The peace that is achieved at the end of *The Stand* is notably tentative, and the dark forces are not definitively destroyed.

Protagonists Stuart Redman and Fran Goldsmith are sometimes characterized as Adam and Eve figures who will be the progenitors of the new age. (One critic even casts Redman as Native American, especially in view of his name.) A widower who once worked as a manual laborer at a calculator factory in a depressed Texas town, **Stuart Redman** is unemployed when the plague begins. His recounting of how his rural community deteriorates in the aftermath of the disease is one of several regional accounts offered by various characters. Critics cite Redman's leadership role and his softspoken, stoic manner and reliability to identify him with the kind of classic heroes played by actors like Gary Cooper in films set in the American West. Like them, he makes his "stand" against evil bravely after being left in the desert with a broken leg, and returns to Boulder with Tom Cullen and Bateman's dog, Kojak, after the others have been killed. Redman's decision to leave for Maine and establish a rural homestead seems to affirm the notion that the traditional family structure is preferable to any organized society for human survival.

Described by critic Mary Pharr as a "model madonna and helpmate," **Fran Goldsmith** is one of the most positively portrayed female characters in King's fiction. In fact, some critics see her as the quintessential nurturing female that King seems to favor—as opposed, for example, to destructive characters like Nadine Cross. At the beginning of *The Stand,* she is a pregnant college student who decides to bear her child despite the immaturity and indifference of its father. Fran has inherited her gentle, loving nature from her compassionate father, whose influence is stronger than that of her uncaring mother. Fran manifests a strong maternal instinct and makes heroic efforts to protect her unborn child during the long and arduous cross-country journey. Her special nurturing ability is also demonstrated when she senses that Harold's bomb is about to explode and manages to save most of the Free Zone Committee members. The new society at Boulder apparently features the collapse of feminism, for Fran acknowledges that she "needs a man" in order to survive. In any case,

Fran aligns with Redman, a worthy mate for her and surrogate father for her first child, Peter. Fran and Redman leave for Maine to carve out a safe niche for their family.

Mother Abagail, the spiritual leader of the "good" people in *The Stand,* has been called a Christ figure who rallies her forces against the evil embodied by Randall Flagg and his followers. A 108-year old black woman, she lives alone in a house in rural Hemingford Home, Nebraska. A guitarist and singer in her youth, she inherits some land that she eventually loses; but through everything she maintains her faith in God. Mother Abagail represents the positive forces of music, intuition, and vision that oppose the violence and despair of Flagg, whose attempts to destroy her (including a harrowing attack by weasels under his control) are ultimately unsuccessful. Significantly, Mother Abagail does not seek to establish a new society at Boulder—that is the idea of the people gathered there—but to bring about a final, cataclysmic confrontation with and victory over Flagg.

Described as the "walkin' dude" or the "creeping Judas," **Randall Flagg** is indistinct in appearance: neither black nor white, his expressions are malleable and masklike. A pointedly satanic figure, he takes the form of a drifter, an outdated castoff from the counterculture of the 1960s. He claims to have been present at or involved in many of the past decades' most flagrant manifestations of evil, including activities of the Ku Klux Klan, Lee Harvey Oswald's assassination of President John F. Kennedy, and the killing of policemen by gang members in New York City. Flagg is often compared to the sinister Sauron in *Lord of the Rings,* who also collapses when confronted. Even though the characters find that Flagg is less formidable than they thought, the novel in no way guarantees that the evil he manifests is destroyed.

Most of the novel's characters are divided into the "good" or the "bad" camps, although a few drift from the former to the latter during the course of events. The "Free Zone" established at Boulder is led by **Nick Andros**, a deaf-mute of solid integrity. During his journey west, Andros befriends **Tom Cullen**, who has the intelligence of a six-year-old child but also a deep innocence and instinctive wisdom. **Larry Underwood** is a rock star who struggles against poverty and anonymity for many years before finally achieving success. Disillusioned with his nihilistic lifestyle of drinking, sex, and drugs, Larry returns to his mother's home in New York City just as the super-flu strikes. Initially immature (he abandons the body of his female traveling companion), by the end of the novel he proves himself responsible and firmly aligned with the forces of good. Another positively portrayed figure is **Glen Bateman**, an aging sociologist accompanied by his dog, **Kojak** (who, near the end of the novel, helps Tom Cullen and the injured Redman return to Boulder). An eccentric professor who is ridiculed by his professional colleagues, Bateman becomes the Free Zone's principal philosopher, voicing the theme that the formation of human society leads to a need for order that can prove disastrous, and that the family is thus a more workable social structure.

Straddling the line between good and evil are **Harold Lauder** and **Nadine Cross**, both of whom eventually join Flagg's forces. Harold is an overweight, awkward teenaged genius who is frustrated in his love for Fran by her alliance with Redman. His jealousy corrupts his nature, and he becomes a Judas figure when he plants the bomb that kills Andros and other Free Zone committee members. Schoolteacher Nadine Cross joins Flagg's forces because she is frustrated with her spinster status and because her former lover rejects her; she is instrumental in tempting Harold over to the Dark Side. Other notable followers of Flagg include his right-hand man, **Lloyd Henreid**, a convicted murderer devoted to Flagg after the "walkin' dude" rescues him from a prison full of corpses. The **Trashcan Man** serves as the evil version of Tom Cullen; he is a once-innocent but emotionally damaged, mentally deficient car-wash attendant whom Flagg uses as an instrument of evil (whereas Cullen becomes "God's Tom" during his journeys). The Trashcan Man is not portrayed as inherently evil so much as wounded and confused. It is he who accidently sets off the novel's final conflagration at Las Vegas.

Misery (novel, 1987)

Plot: The novel focuses on Paul Sheldon, a highly successful author of popular romance novels that feature an aristocratic nineteenth-century heroine named Misery Chastain. Paul finally writes what he considers a "serious" novel, and he concludes his "Misery" series with a book in which this protagonist dies. After a bad car accident on a snowy Colorado road, Paul wakes to find himself in the house of former nurse (and serial killer) Annie Wilkes. His badly damaged, unusable legs cause excruciating pain, and he is dependent on Annie's care for survival. He soon learns that Annie is a frighteningly psychotic but ardent fan of his Misery novels who is enraged by his killing off her beloved heroine. In addition, she is offended by the profane language and complex themes of his new novel. She punishes Paul by amputating his foot (he later also loses his thumb to Annie's rage) and burning the manuscript. Bringing Paul an old manual typewriter, she orders him to write another Misery novel. Paul realizes that he will only be allowed to live as long as he is still in the process of writing this book. Despite his physical pain and the psychic pressure exerted by the deranged woman, Paul manages to produce the best work of his career, entitled *Misery's Return*. Finally, Paul makes Annie think that he has burned the manuscript, and in her panic she trips over his strategically placed typewriter and hits her head on the mantel. She dies, and Paul escapes.

Characters: Although *Misery* features only two characters, critics cite it as one of King's most compelling works, particularly for what it reveals about the author's attitude toward his own craft. On one level, the novel functions as a highly entertaining psychological thriller, but it also explores the nature of creation, suggesting that, through the artistic process, the artist becomes a captive of his craft and that access to "misery" may actually bring about a higher form of art. Many commentators detect in *Misery* an explication of King's feelings about his own phenomenal success in an often-maligned genre, about the demands and power of his audience, and about the satisfactions and dangers of the writing process itself.

Paul Sheldon is a twice-divorced, best-selling author of historical romances who feels that, despite his fame and wealth, he has wasted his talents on second-rate writing. But like other King protagonists, he gets a chance to renew himself through adversity. Forced to take on the role of Scheherazade (the narrator of the "Arabian Nights" tales, who postpones her execution through the riveting stories she tells her husband each night) in order to stay alive, Paul finds within himself the self-discipline and creative inspiration he desperately needs. His survival depends not only on being able to write but on not provoking his volatile captor. He has to constantly read her moods, subdue his own fear and panic, and think of a way to outsmart her. The old manual typewriter Annie gives Paul becomes a symbol of his power when it plays a crucial role in Annie's defeat, while Annie herself becomes, ironically, Paul's muse or the instrument of his self-discovery. She gives Paul the opportunity to explore and affirm his commitment to his craft; remembering the "Can You?" game he played as a child, Paul finds that indeed he can. He is surprised to realize that this new Misery novel is his best ever, with its richer plot and livelier characters—that it is, in fact, a fine example of the gothic novel. Usually viewed as an autobiographical character, Paul works in a genre that is often disparaged by critics and readers of "serious" literature. His experience renews his sense that if he writes well enough he need not be ashamed of what he does. In addition to developing artistically, Paul's humanity is expanded by his encounter with Annie, with whom he sympathizes even after she brutalizes him; seeing Annie's tears, he reflects on the woman she might have been with a different upbringing or body chemistry. Although Paul is missing two body parts when he emerges from Annie's house, he is a more complete person.

Critics often note the similarities between *Misery* and John Fowles's acclaimed 1958 novel, *The Collector,* which also features a deranged character who holds another captive. A significant difference between the two novels is that Fowles's villain is male and King's **Annie Wilkes** is female. Critic Kim Newman describes Annie as King's "most monstrous of monsters: Ultimate Evil as Ultimate Banality." Grotesque in appearance—huge and hulking with a chillingly blank gaze—Annie is a former nurse who, as Paul learns by looking through her scrapbook, achieves some professional success before she develops her penchant for disposing of her patients. Some critics detect in her behavior some of the classic symptoms of manic depression, such as alternating periods of glee and rage, while most label her a psychotic with a twisted view of the world and her own role in it. She divides people into three categories, "brats, poor things, and Annie," and considers it her responsibility to punish the brats and put the poor things out of their misery. Annie's adulation of Misery Chastain, who is her polar opposite in most ways but especially in terms of femininity, also illustrates her instability; she is the most extreme example of what Paul calls "radical reader involvement." Having "rescued" Paul, Annie quickly establishes dominance over him by getting him addicted to painkillers, and later increasing his dependence by amputating his foot. She adopts the role of the ultimate critic or editor as she chastises him for the profanity and complexity of his new novel, *Fast Cars,* and punishes him by forcing him to drink the water she has used to clean his room and by burning his only copy of the manuscript. Then she propels Paul into the role of Scheherazade, insisting that he bring Misery back to life. Yet it is Annie's very interest in Misery that brings about her downfall, for she is so eager to learn what happens next in *Misery's Return* that she loses control of the situation and allows herself to be tricked. Paul makes her think that he has burned the book, and in the ensuing calamity, she trips over his typewriter and receives a fatal blow to her head. Although Annie might be seen as an unconventional character in that she is a woman who wields considerable power, most commentators label her a misogynistic creation. Some even claim that Annie represents the potentially castrating nature of women, their inability to handle power effectively, and their need for dominance. Annie might also embody the forces against which popular writers like King struggle, such as the expectations of the audience and the scorn of their critics.

One other figure in Misery might be considered a character: **Misery Chastain**, the protagonist of Paul's highly popular historical romances. A nineteenth-century aristocrat, Misery is beautiful, indomitable, and ideally feminine, unlike the psychotic nurse who adopts her as a personal heroine. Nevertheless, her name is ominous, evoking such words as "misery," "chastise," "chain," and "stain." Although Paul has long claimed to hate Misery, he finds it remarkably easy to return to her world, and in fact, bringing her back to life results not only in his physical survival but his artistic renewal.

Further Reading

Banks, Carolyn. Review of *Misery. Book World–Washington Post* (June 14, 1987): 1, 14.

Collings, Michael R. *The Annotated Guide to Stephen King: A Primary and Secondary Bibliography of the Works of America's Premier Horror Writer.* Mercer Island, WA: Starmont House, 1986.

Collings, Michael R., and David A. Engebretson. *The Shorter Works of Stephen King.* Mercer Island, WA: Starmont House, 1985.

Contemporary Literary Criticism. Vols. 12, 26, 37, 61. Detroit: Gale Research.

Hanson, Clare. "Stephen King: Powers of Horror." In *American Horror Fiction: From Brockden Brown to Stephen King.* Edited by Brian Docherty. New York: St. Martin's Press, 1990.

Katzenbach, John. "Sheldon Gets the Ax." *New York Times Book Review* (May 31, 1987): 20.

Lehmann-Haupt, Christopher. Review of *Misery. New York Times* (June 8, 1987): C17.

Magistrale, Tony. *The Dark Descent: Essays Defining Stephen King's Horrorscape.* New York: Greenwood Press, 1992.

———. *Landscape of Fear: Stephen King's American Gothic.* Bowling Green University Press, 1988.

———. *Stephen King: The Second Decade; "Danse Macabre" to "The Dark Half."* Boston: Twayne, 1992.

Newman, Kim. "Body Snatcher." *New Statesman* Vol. 114, no. 2947 (September 18, 1987): 30–31.

Underwood, Tim. *Kingdom of Fear: The World of Stephen King.* New York: New American Library/Signet, 1987.

———, and Chuck Miller, eds. *Fear Itself: The Horror Fiction of Stephen King.* New York: New American Library/Signet, 1982.

Winter, Douglas E. *Stephen King.* Mercer Island, WA: Starmont House, 1982.

———. *Stephen King: The Art of Darkness.* New York: New American Library, 1984.

Milan Kundera

1929–

Czechoslovakian novelist, short story writer, essayist, playwright, and poet.

Immortality (novel, 1990)

Plot: Set primarily in contemporary France, the novel comprises two loosely structured plot lines, one involving modern characters whom the author (who himself appears in the novel) both creates and interacts with, and one centering on the great nineteenth-century German writer Johann Wolfgang von Goethe. In Part One, "The Face," the author is waiting for his friend Professor Avenarius in a Paris health spa when he is struck by the unselfconscious gesture of an older woman as she turns to wave goodbye to her swimming instructor. The experience gives rise to his invention of a character named Agnes for his new book. He describes Agnes' past, personality, and family, which includes her husband, Paul, and grown daughter, Brigitte. Part Two, "Immortality," features twenty-six-year-old Bettina von Arnim, who, while staying with her husband at Goethe's home in Weimar, has a confrontation with the writer's wife, Christiane, which leads to the younger woman's banishment. After Goethe's death, Bettina publishes *Goethe's Correspondence with a Child,* detailing her relationship with the author and, in Kundera's view, evidencing her desire to achieve her own measure of immortality. During a celestial conversation between Goethe and Ernest Hemingway, the latter complains about an unflattering biography that has just been published about him. Back in contemporary Paris, Agnes' sister, Laura, falls in love with a radio broadcaster named Bertrand Bernard, but the affair ends unhappily. About to be fired from his job as the host of a radio program on legal affairs, Paul—Agnes' husband—talks to his boss, the Bear, about advertising and the validity of "high culture." Agnes and her sister have an argument about which of them knows more about love.

Part Three, "Homo Sentimentalis," begins with three celebrated literary figures—Rainer Maria Rilke, Romain Rolland, and Paul Eduard—testifying at Goethe's "eternal trial," at which all three side with Bettina. The author ruminates on the sentimental, romantic concept of "love" and its use as an excuse for all kinds of reprehensible behavior. A scene between Laura and Paul, set in the future, refers to the "terrible death of Agnes." Laura and the widowed Paul begin an affair. Meanwhile, Goethe and Hemingway meet again in heaven and discuss the tenuous relationship between a person and his image. In Part Four, "Chance," Agnes is still alive and staying in a hotel in Switzerland, her childhood home, where she has decided to move. While sitting in a jacuzzi with the author, Professor Avenarius relates his struggles with "Diabolum," his term for the stupidity in the world; he is eventually arrested for tire-slashing, his primary gesture against this force. The author claims that most novels are "too obedient to the rules of unity of action." In Switzerland, a suicidal young girl sits down in the middle of a busy road, causing an accident that kills several other people—one of them Agnes—though the young girl herself is unharmed. Because Avenarius has slashed his tires, Paul is delayed in reaching Agnes' bedside, and she dies fifteen minutes before his arrival.

In Part Six, "The Dial," the reader encounters for the first time a character named Rubens, an ardent womanizer and failed artist. Having earned his nickname because of his clever caricatures of his schoolmates, the young Rubens is not admitted to art school and decides to study law instead. Despite his sexual promiscuity, he marries a beautiful woman whom he soon divorces. Then follow several encounters between Rubens and a woman he describes only as "the lute player," as well as one with an unattractively dressed, matter-of-fact Australian student. Eventually the reader learns that Agnes is the lute player; after her death, Rubens' days as a voracious lover come to an end. The novel's final chapter, "The Celebration," returns to the Paris health club, where the author is drinking wine with Avenarius. They are joined by an already drunk Paul, who declares that perfection in art is unimportant because it can never be fully appreciated by the audience. Laura arrives and begins swimming, and Paul—who appears much aged to the author—relates that the couple now has a three-month-old daughter and that Brigitte too has had a baby. As Laura leaves, she turns to wave, repeating the gesture that Agnes made at the beginning of the novel. The author and Avenarius embrace and part.

Characters: Kundera is one of Europe's most acclaimed novelists. He was forced to leave his native Czechoslovakia in 1975, when that country's then-Communist government deemed his work counter-revolutionary, and he has since lived in Paris. *Immortality* is the first of his novels to be set in the city of his exile. It shares with its predecessors, however, a nontraditional structure featuring a disjointed time frame, multiple perspectives, juxtapositions of fantasy and realism, and frequent authorial commentary. *Immortality* is itself an illustration of the theory voiced within it by Kundera (who appears among the other characters) that "a novel shouldn't be a bicycle race but a feast of many courses." The novel's major concerns include society's increasing dependence on the "imagology" reinforced through advertising, political campaigns, designer fads, and celebrity worship and the concurrent obsession with individual "rights." While some reviewers claimed that the novel's characters are subordinate to its ideas, most found it an inventive, compelling use of the novel form to explore personal, social, and philosophical questions.

Kundera takes an unusual approach to several of the characters in *Immortality*, first describing how he came to create them and then allowing their personalities and lives to expand seemingly without his direct intervention. The central example of this technique is

Agnes, who originated, Kundera tells us, from the gesture of a sixty-year-old woman at a swimming pool. The author says that he was entranced by her graceful wave to her swimming instructor, which intimated that she had forgotten for a moment that she was no longer beautiful. He was moved to imagine Agnes's life, and much of the novel is devoted to recounting its last stage. Agnes is an attractive (though rarely erotic) and sensitive woman who finds much of the modern world unbearable. She yearns for escape from its noise, bustle, and lack of privacy and often thinks nostalgically of her peaceful childhood in Switzerland. Agnes feels cut off from others and craves solitude more than anything else. In fact, she even admits to herself that if she had the choice of spending eternity either with or without her husband, Paul, she would choose to spend it alone. Some critics have viewed Agnes as a purely symbolic character who embodies, according to Jonathan Yardley, "the deep longing to transcend time." Others, however, find Agnes believable and sympathetic. The enigmatic smile that appears on Agnes' face at her death—which so troubles her husband—suggests that she has finally found the escape she sought.

Agnes' husband, **Paul**, is a lawyer who broadcasts a radio commentary program called "Rights and the Law," which is finally deemed too dull and is cancelled. Just before he is fired, Paul has a long conversation with his employer during which he defends the concept of frivolity against that of "high culture." Paul sincerely loves his wife, and his grief is intensified when, arriving fifteen minutes after her death, he finds a baffling smile her face. By the end of the novel, Paul has married his wife's sister and is the father of a baby girl, but he seems to the author (with whom he interacts, thus merging the fictional and "real" worlds of the novel) much older and sadder.

Laura differs from her sister, Agnes, in several significant ways: whereas Agnes' focus is primarily ascetic and she is rarely erotic, Laura is a sensualist who is always aware of her body and its responses; in addition, she does not share Agnes' craving for oblivion but instead asserts that everyone wants "to leave something behind." In this latter characteristic, Laura resembles Bettina von Arnim, who sought immortality through her relationship with Goethe. Laura is described as perpetually imitating her sister—in trivial matters like wearing dark glasses as well as the more serious issue of deciding that she loves Agnes' husband. After Laura's relationship with the much younger Bertrand Bernard fails and she threatens to commit suicide, the sisters have a heated argument in which Laura maintains that Agnes knows nothing about love and Agnes calls Laura self-dramatizing and egocentric. After Agnes' death, Laura pursues her long-harbored love for Paul, and the two eventually marry. The scene in which Laura is terrorized by a group of drunkards while she is collecting money in the Paris Metro for African lepers has been cited as one of many instance in Kundera's fiction in which women are humiliated.

The author discusses a variety of philosophical and other matters with his friend **Professor Avenarius**, who provides a link between the world of the fictional characters and that of their creator because he sleeps with Laura (after rescuing her from her drunken tormentors) and invites Paul to join him and the author for a drink. The portly, eccentric Avenarius has made it his life's mission to battle "Diabolum," his name for the limitless stupidity of the world. His main action toward this end is to sneak around wearing a coat to hide a large knife, which he uses to slash the tires of offensively polluting cars. Some commentators consider Avenarius a mouthpiece for Kundera's own bleak view who transforms life's horror into a joke, a trait of Eastern Europeans.

Episodes featuring the great nineteenth-century German author **Johann Wolfgang von Goethe** appear throughout the novel, some recounting his relations with Bettina von Arnim and some his conversations with **Ernest Hemingway** in heaven. The triangle involving Goethe, his wife, Christiane, and the flirtatious young Bettina parallels in some ways the modern situation between Paul, Agnes, and Laura. Just as Hemingway is powerless to alter the public's changing image of him after the publication of an unflattering biography,

Goethe can do nothing, after his own death, about Bettina's exploitation and inflation of their relationship for her own benefit. Indeed, even before his death he apparently recognized Bettina's motives but mostly went along with her. Goethe tells Hemingway that they are "condemned to immortality for the sin of writing books," and that they will only be free when they stop worrying about immortality.

Goethe's admirer **Bettina von Arnim** is a silly but ambitious young woman who published Goethe's *Conversations with a Child* (1835), a work that was later discredited as largely invented. In her attempt to achieve immortality by commandeering Goethe's image for her own purposes, Bettina is presented as one of the first "groupies" and also as an incarnation of romanticism, which Kundera casts as reprehensible self-absorption. In direct contrast to Bettina is **Christiane**, who became Goethe's mistress when she was a twenty-three-year-old peasant and then his wife. Unlike Bettina, Christiane does not "yearn to exhibit herself on the great stage of history." Although she is not an intellectual, she loves her husband and is irritated by Bettina's flirting; the tension between the two women escalates until Christiane knocks Bettina's glasses to the ground; Bettina describes her rival as a "fat sausage" when recounting the story. Goethe, however, takes Christiane's side, and Bettina is banished from their home for many years.

Kundera does not introduce the character of **Rubens** until almost the end of the novel. A veteran of innumerable sexual encounters with women, Rubens divides his sexual life into five distinct stages or periods: athletic muteness, metaphors, obscene truth, telephone, and mystical. The reader learns that Rubens earned his nickname through his skillful caricatures of his schoolmates and that he failed to gain entry into the School of Fine Arts. Instead he studied law and married a beautiful woman, whom he soon divorced. Rubens ruminates on the relationship between talent and fame and on his encounters with a woman he refers to only as "the lute player" her identity as Agnes is only revealed when he calls her house and learns that she has died in a car accident). A womanizer unable to recall the names of most of his lovers, Rubens has been seen as misogynistic, a trait shared by other characters in Kundera's fiction, particularly Tomas in Kundera's 1984 novel, *The Unbearable Lightness of Being.* At the end of *Immortality,* however, Rubens has decided to take a permanent rest from women.

Another character in *Immortality* whose creation Kundera describes is **Bertrand Bernard,** who originated in the voice of a radio broadcaster Kundera heard every morning on waking. The fashionable but insecure son of a famous, conservative politician, Bertrand once studied law but chose journalism because it gave him "the right to demand an answer." His affair with Laura deteriorates after he is severely upset by an incident in which a man (later revealed to be Professor Avenarius) delivers to his office a diploma declaring him a Complete Ass. Other characters in the novel include Paul and Agnes' grown daughter, **Brigitte**, whose assertion of her "right" to park on a sidewalk when she cannot find a parking place helps to illustrate the theme of the modern confusion between self-indulgence and entitlement; and **the Bear**, Paul's employer, who, during their discussion about imagology, asserts that "we are only what other people consider us to be."

Further Reading

Aji, Aron, ed. *Kundera and the Art of Fiction: Critical Essays.* New York: Garland, 1992.

Annan, Gabriele. "Selective Affinities." *New York Review of Books* Vol. 38, no. 10 (May 30, 1991): 3–4.

Coates, Joseph. "Amid the Din of Images." *Chicago Tribune* (May 12, 1991): 1, 4.

Contemporary Literary Criticism Vols. 4, 9, 19, 32, 68. Detroit: Gale Research.

Leonard, John. "Morte d'Auteur." *Nation* Vol. 252, no. 22 (June 10, 1991): 770–75.

Mars-Jones, Adam. "A Lecture from the Philosopher of Carnality." *Times Literary Supplement* No. 4598 (May 17, 1991): 17.

Thomas, D. M. "The Woman of His Dreams." *New York Times Book Review* (April 28, 1991): 7.

Wolcott, James. "The Unbearable Lightness of Reason." *Vanity Fair* Vol. 54, no. 5 (May 1991): 54, 58.

Wood, Michael. "Kundera's Man of Feeling." *London Review of Books* 13, No. 11 (June 13, 1991): 13–14.

Woolf, David. "A Radically Different Sort of Novel." *Books* (London) No. 3 (July–August 1991): 6.

Yardley, Jonathan. "Talking about the Big Questions." *Book World—Washington Post* (May 5, 1991): 3.

Camara Laye
1928-1980
Guinean novelist, autobiographer, and short story writer.

The Radiance of the King (*Le regard du roi*; novel, 1954)

Plot: The novel begins in Adramé, a city in the northern part of a fictional African country. The central character is Clarence, a white man who came to Africa for unexplained reasons and subsequently lost all his money gambling. Rejected by his fellow Europeans, Clarence is about to be ejected from his hotel. He joins the crowd awaiting the arrival of the King, with whom he hopes to receive an audience so that he can request employment. Clarence meets an elderly beggar who tells him the King will never consent to see him but who agrees to plead his case with the young monarch. The beggar is unable to gain Clarence an audience but offers to take him to the South, where the King is next scheduled to appear. At Clarence's hotel, he and the beggar drink a great deal of palm wine, and Clarence's confusion grows. Unable to pay his hotel bill, Clarence gives the innkeeper his suit coat. He is subsequently arrested for theft, and a nonsensical trial ensues. Clarence finally escapes and begins the journey South with the beggar. Although it seems to Clarence that they are traveling in circles, they eventually reach the village of Aziana, which is ruled by the elderly Naba. Clarence is given a hut in which to live while he waits for the King's appearance, as well as an African wife. What Clarence does not know is that the beggar has traded him to the Naba and that he is to serve as stud to the old man's harem. Each night, drugged by the flowers brought to his bedside, Clarence has sex with a different woman. He gradually adapts to life in Aziana, but when he learns the true nature of his role in the village, Clarence is disgusted and feels unworthy to appear before the king. Thus when the king finally arrives, Clarence hides in his hut. Finally, however, he senses that the king is seeking him, and Clarence goes forth and embraces him in all his radiance.

Characters: Considered the most important work of this highly respected West African writer, *The Radiance of the King* blends elements of traditional African culture with such modern dilemmas as alienation and the search for identity. Reversing the conventional literary situation of a black character adrift in an unfamiliar European culture, the novel dramatizes the contrast between the African emphasis on the natural world, emotion, and sensuality and western European rationalism. Many commentators have compared *The Radiance of the King* to the works of early twentieth-century existentialist author Franz Kafka, whose fiction depicts a nightmarish modern bureaucracy and features enigmatic characters and an atmosphere of moral oppression. Others detect in the novel elements of the *négritude* movement, which sought in African literature the celebration of a noble, untainted African culture; others, however, contend that *The Radiance of the King* actually parodies this movement in that it seems to propose a transcendence of these very values.

The novel chronicles the struggles of its protagonist, **Clarence** (whose name may refer to the search for clarity), to find meaning and identity in a confusing world. The reader never learns why Clarence, a middleaged white man, initially came to Africa, though he frequently refers to his dangerous passage across a reef to reach its shore. Clarence has separated himself from other Europeans through his weakness for gambling, which has resulted in his impoverishment. He must now make his way in an alien culture, the traditions and ways of which are incomprehensible to him. Initially, Clarence asserts his difference from and superiority to those around him, telling the Beggar, ''I am not 'just anybody' . . . . I am a white man.'' But Clarence undergoes a kind of disintegration of personality that begins with the absurd, notably Kafkaesque trial—during which his attempts at rational persuasion fail—and continues with the bewildering journey to the South and his life in Aziana. There, Clarence gradually adapts to his surroundings, shedding his western clothes and learning to weave in the native manner. Although he is quite comfortable and surrounded by pleasant companions, Clarence is shocked by his heightened sexual drive and ashamed of his apparent purposelessness. When he discovers that his true role has been that of stud to the Naba's harem, Clarence is overcome with self-revulsion and feels unworthy to see the King, whose arrival he has previously anticipated so eagerly. Through his encounters and discussions with those around him, however, Clarence perceives that his sexual role is accepted as a positive contribution to community life. The vision he sees during his visit to Dioki also helps Clarence feel more tied to this natural African world, where dreams are more significant than logic. In the novel's final, surreal scene, the walls of Clarence's hut (which perhaps symbolize his shame) fall away and he goes forward to embrace the King, thus transcending both the physical and the psychological barriers that had previously bound him. Some commentators interpret Clarence's journey as a reversal of the familiar story of the African sold into slavery, for he is a representative of the European colonizers who is sold into slavery by Africans (who, significantly, treat him with kindness and respect) and forced to assimilate into an alien society. Other critics emphasize the importance of Clarence's sexuality and his eventual discovery of its worth as a means of perpetuating life; still others have suggested that Clarence is not a white man but rather a ''been-to''—an African who has left the continent and returned full of European influences and values.

One of the qualities that has led critics to compare *The Radiance of the King* with the work of Kafka is its predominance of surreal, even symbolic characters. One such figure is the elderly **Beggar**, who frequently scoffs at Clarence's naivete and presumptions and whose apparently benevolent promise to take Clarence to the South to see the King turns out to have selfish motives. Some commentators have identified the Beggar as a manifestation of the ''trickster'' character so common in the folk tradition of African and other cultures. Clarence meets the energetic, unruly young brothers **Nagoa** and **Noaga** in Adramé during his first attempt to see the King. Clarence is unable to distinguish between these mischievous characters—who accompany Clarence and the Beggar on their journey and who turn out to be the grandsons of Aziana's Naga—which some commentators have interpreted as a comment on the idea that all blacks look the same to whites.

In Aziana, Clarence is given an attractive, accommodating young wife named **Akissi**, whom he later learns has been facilitating his nightly liaisons with the women of the Naba's harem.

The harem is supervised by the jovial eunuch **Samba Baloum**, who also provides Clarence with a great deal of companionship. The stern, highly legalistic **Master of Ceremonies** serves as a mediator between the King and his people, administering the society's laws. Even the Master of Ceremonies does not approve when Clarence stops the whipping he is receiving for having revealed to Clarence the fact that he is a stud to the harem; this disruption of custom actually prevents the Master of Ceremonies from purging his shame. Another of Clarence's frequent companions is the blacksmith **Diallo**, who embraces his own social role (and thus provides a good example for Clarence) by vowing to make the best axe he has ever produced in honor of the King's arrival, even though the King may never see it. **Dioki** is a frightening old woman with the power to induce and interpret visions; she lives and even copulates with a large number of snakes. The young, frail **King** makes only two appearances in the novel, at the beginning and the end. Ethereal in aspect, the white-robed King wears numerous gold bracelets that allow him to radiate with "the purest kind of love;" he has been interpreted as both a Christian savior figure and the unknowable Allah of the Islamic religion.

Further Reading

Cook, David. "The Relevance of the King in Camara Laye's *Le Regard du Roi*." In *Perspectives on African Literature*, edited by Christopher Heywood, pp. 138-47. Africana, 1971.

Contemporary Literary Criticism, Vols. 4, 38. Detroit: Gale Research.

Deduck, Patricia. "Kafka's Influence on Camara Laye's *Le Regard due Roi*". *Studies in Twentieth-century Literature* IV (Spring 1980): 239-55.

Irele, Abiola. "Camara Laye: An Imagination Attuned to the Spiritual." *West Africa* No. 3272 (April 7, 1980: 617-18.

King, Adele. *The Writings of Camara Laye*. London: Heinemann Educational Books Ltd., 1980.

Larson, Charles R. "Assimilated Négritude: Camara Laye's *Le regard du roi*". In *The Emergence of African Fiction*, pp. 167-226. Indiana University Press, 1971.

Moore, Gerald. "The Aesthetic Vision." In *Twelve African Writers*, pp. 84-103. Indiana University Press, 1980): 84-103.

Naipaul, Shiva. "Black and Ethereal." *Books & Bookmen* (February 1971): 41, 57.

David Leavitt

1961–

American short story writer and novelist

"Territory" (short story, 1982)

Plot: The story chronicles Neil Campbell, a twenty-three-year-old homosexual who lives on the East Coast, and the visit he makes to his mother in California. Neil, has not been home for two years, and he wonders how his mother will react to his current lover, Wayne, who has accompanied him. Flashbacks reveal Mrs. Campbell's apparent acceptance of her son's sexual preference; she even becomes involved with the Coalition of Parents of Lesbians and Gays and attends a gay rights rally. Yet Neil resents his mother, for her activism, because even though well intentioned, it intrudes too much into his private life. Similarly, the supposedly liberal Mrs. Campbell feels that her son's visit is an intrusion. Although she likes Wayne, the physical relationship between her son and his companion disconcerts her. In a final confrontation, Mrs. Campbell tells Neil that she can "only take so much," while Neil reminds his mother that they are no longer responsible for each other's lives. With relief and clasped hands, Neil and Wayne return to New York City, and Mrs. Campbell resumes her orderly life.

Characters: Considered one of the most promising young writers in America, Leavitt published his first story in *New Yorker* magazine at the age of twenty-one. The stories in his highly regarded collection *Family Dancing* have been said to exhibit a degree of empathy and insight unusual in someone of Leavitt's age. Writing in an elegant, ironic style, Leavitt explores the dilemmas experienced by families caught in the social and personal upheaval that characterizes life in the contemporary United States. In "Territory," frequently cited as one of the collections most successful stories, Leavitt focuses on the intricacies of love and hidden anger between parent and child and the need for each to establish a separate, autonomous existence.

The central character in "Territory" is **Neil Campbell,** a twenty-three-year-old gay man who feels insecure about his sexuality when he is around his mother, despite her efforts to be supportive. He stirs up old resentments when he visits his mother in California after moving to New York and establishing an entirely separate life. Neil regards Mrs. Campbell's involvement with the Coalition of Parents of Lesbians and Gays as an intrusion into his sexual life. He feels jealous when she welcomes Wayne and seems genuinely to like him; thus he is happy to note how uncomfortable she is when he and Wayne are openly affectionate. He is "glad his mother knows that he is desired, glad it makes her flinch." Although the visit is marked by pain, it seems to propel Neil toward establishing a firmer, more confident identity—even if, as he tells Wayne, "Guilt goes with the territory."

Mrs. Barbara Campbell is an attractive, sophisticated woman with a well-appointed home, a husband who is seldom present, and three female Airedale terriers. When her son announced his homosexuality, the politically liberal woman assured him, "That's okay, honey," then she became active in the gay rights movement. When Neil visits her accompanied by his lover, she seems to welcome them warmly, but the presence of the couple gradually seems to fray her nerves; it is obvious that she is not comfortable with their physical relationship. Neil remembers how dismayed she was, several years ago, when she encountered a garishly made-up man at a gay rights rally. Despite her intellectual willingness to accept her son's sexual orientation, Mrs. Campbell is uncomfortable with the physical reality of homosexuality. Some critics suggest that she subconsciously resents both her husband and her son, which is expressed by her owning three female dogs (as opposed to the family's first dog, a male named Rasputin, whose licking helped awaken Neil's sexuality).

Neil explains that he has settled down with his likable, twenty-eight-year-old lover, **Wayne,** after the short and regrettable period of promiscuity that followed his coming out as a gay man. Wayne seems more comfortable with his sexuality than Neil, due to being older and more distanced from the family tensions explored in the story. Wayne behaves naturally toward his lover, reaching for Neil's hand in the presence of Mrs. Campbell, whose regard he has already won. Similarly, Wayne laughs when he and Neil are discovered on the verge of making love in Mrs. Campbell's garden. However, it is Wayne on whom one of the Airedales later urinates, eliciting from Mrs. Campbell the apparently double-edged remark, "I'm sorry, Wayne . . . It goes with the territory." Nevertheless at the end of the story, Wayne tells Neil that he has a "great mom" about whom he shouldn't complain.

Further Reading

Boatwright, James. "*Family Dancing:* Rich and Touching." *USA Today* (October 5, 1984): 3D.

Contemporary Literary Criticism. Vol. 34. Detroit: Gale Research.

Iannone, Carol. "Post-Counterculture Tristesse." *Commentary* Vol. 83 (February 1987): 57–61.

Klarer, Mario. "David Leavitt's 'Territory': René Girard Homoerotic 'Trigonometry' and Julia Kristeva's 'Semiotic Chora.'" *Studies in Short Fiction* Vol. 28 (winter 1991): 63–76.

Lesser, Wendy. "Domestic Disclosures." *New York Times Book Review* (September 2, 1984): 7–8.

Harper Lee
1926–
American novelist.

To Kill a Mockingbird (novel, 1960)

Plot: Set in the fictional Alabama town of Maycomb in the mid-1930s, the novel centers on Jean Louise "Scout" Finch and her brother Jem, who are being raised by their widowed lawyer father, Atticus, with the help of their African American housekeeper Calpurnia. The novel is narrated by the adult voice of Scout, who recalls events that occurred over a period of several years, beginning when Scout and Jem were, respectively, six and nine. In the novel's opening pages, the brother and sister befriend Dill Harris, the young nephew of their neighbor, who has come to Maycomb for the summer. The three children spend much of their time speculating about mysterious Arthur "Boo" Radley, a recluse who has not emerged from his house since his involvement, fifteen years earlier, in an adolescent prank. After Dill has returned to his parents' home and the school year has begun, Jem and Scout begin to find small gifts hidden in a tree on the Radley's property, which they must pass on their way to their own house. Later in the year, Atticus agrees to defend a black man, Tom Robinson, who has been accused of raping a white woman. During the months before the trial is to begin, Jem and Scout endure taunts from classmates whose parents disapprove of their father's defending a black man. The next summer, Dill returns to Maycomb in time to accompany Scout and Jem as they observe the trial of Tom Robinson. The alleged victim, a poor young woman named Mayella Ewell, claims that Tom raped her after she asked him to perform a manual task for her. Her notoriously shiftless father, Bob Ewell, testifies that he saw Tom in the act of assaulting his daughter. Atticus, however, proves conclusively that events could not possibly have occurred as the Ewells describe them and that Tom is innocent. Nevertheless, the all-white jury returns a guilty verdict, deeply dismaying and bewildering Jem and Scout. Some time later, Tom is killed while attempting to escape from prison. The next Halloween, Jem and Scout are walking home from a school pageant when they are attacked by an unknown person. Another shadowy figure assists them, repelling their assailant and carrying Jem—whose arm is broken—home in his arms. The children later learn that their rescuer was Boo Radley, and that he had killed their attacker, Bob Ewell. In order to spare Boo the turmoil of publicity and exposure, Atticus and the sheriff agree not to identify him as Ewell's killer. That night, Scout accompanies Boo back to his house; the adult Scout reports that she never saw him again.

Characters: Lee won a Pulitzer Prize for *To Kill a Mockingbird* (her first and only novel), which was both critically acclaimed and widely popular. In addition, the 1962 filmed version of the novel earned an Academy Award. Lee was praised for her faithful depiction of a regional setting, within which she focuses on such universal themes as the loss of childhood innocence, the difference between appearance and reality, and particularly the damaging effects of racism. Casting prejudice as the product of fear and lack of knowledge, Lee portrays the turbulence of Southern society in the mid-twentieth century but also suggests that its maladies may be overcome through increased understanding.

The novel's narrator, **Jean Louise "Scout" Finch**, is clearly an autobiographical character, for Lee too was the daughter of a Southern lawyer and was about Scout's age in the mid-1930s. Several early reviewers complained that Lee was attributing to her narrator observations that someone so young could not be expected to make; however, it is the adult Scout who recalls these events from her childhood. Most commentators, however, praised Lee for her sensitive portrayal of Scout and the other children in the novel. An intelligent, perceptive, tomboyish little girl perpetually clad in overalls, Scout struggles mightily to assert her equality with her brother and otherwise establish her independence. She is forthright, sometimes to the point of inappropriate outspokenness—as when she chides young Walter Cunningham for his odd eating habits when he is a guest at the Finch table. Scout's critical faculties and innate sense of truth (which Lee portrays as inherent in children) have been nurtured by her loving father, although his sister maintains that he has neglected to inculcate in Scout the ladylike manners her social standing necessitates. In one of the novel's most significant scenes, Scout interrupts the would-be lynching party that has gathered near the jail cell occupied by Tom Robinson and guarded by Atticus. Recognizing the father of one of her classmates, Scout politely inquires after his son, and her unself-conscious innocence shames the men into leaving. Although Scout does not always fully comprehend what is happening around her, by the end of the novel she has gained deeper insight into at least one aspect of life, for she knows more about the reclusive Boo Radley and of what she and her brother must have meant to him. The adult Scout reports that she would later come to fuller understanding of the portentous events of the few years the novel recounts.

Although the widowed lawyer **Atticus Finch** (who also serves in the state legislature) is a member of one of the area's oldest families, he is an individualist who reveres the values of equality, tolerance, and understanding. One critic identified Atticus as a southern version of the ideal man envisioned by nineteenth-century American philosopher Ralph Waldo Emerson: he is guided not by societal dictates but by his own inherent sense of justice, his own conscience. An affectionate father who is also a firm disciplinarian, Atticus has always encouraged his children to treat others with tolerance and respect; he asserts that "you never really understand a person until you consider things from his point of view . . . until you climb into his skin and walk around in it." Atticus defies the expectations of his predominantly racist community by defending Tom Robinson with as much commitment and legal expertise as he would any other client. When his children, who are being harassed by their classmates about their father's role in the case, question this decision, Atticus tells them that if he had refused to defend Tom he would not be able to hold his head up in town or even to tell Jem and Scout what to do. This stance is in keeping with the definition of true courage Atticus gives Jem during the incident with Mrs. Dubose: "It's when you know you're licked before you begin but you see it through no matter what." And despite Atticus's seemingly inevitable defeat in the courtroom, he does win a small victory in that he keeps the jury out longer (two hours) than any previous jury in a case involving a black defendant. An idealized character in his dignity, integrity, strength, and tenderness, Atticus was described by critic William T. Going as "the most memorable portrait in recent fiction of a just and equitable Southern liberal."

Scout's constant companion in her adventures and in the process of maturation chronicled in the novel is her brother **Jem Finch**, who is nine years old when it begins. Because Jem is older than Scout (indeed, he is nearly a teenager by the novel's conclusion) he might be expected to understand more about their experiences than she does, and his stronger emotional reaction to them suggests that this is so. Initially an intelligent but playful, lighthearted young boy, Jem grows more thoughtful and distraught during and after the trial. He reacts angrily to Mrs. Dubose's abuse of his father and cuts off the blooms of her beloved camellias, an act that Atticus turns into a lesson about how courage has more to do with stoicism than with aggression. Bewildered when the jury convicts the obviously innocent Tom Robinson, Jem asks Atticus, "How could they do it, how could they?" Atticus replies that they always have and always will, and that "when they do, it seems that only children will weep." Another important child character in the novel is the diminutive, mischievous, highly imaginative **Dill Harris**, who loves spending his summers in Maycomb and even runs away from his parents (who are apparently rather indifferent to him) to do so. Lee said that she based Dill on the Southern-born writer Truman Capote, who was a childhood friend.

Although he does not appear until late in the action, **Arthur "Boo" Radley** is a central presence in the novel—particularly in the imaginations of Jem, Scout, and Dill as they speculate whether he really does roam the neighborhood at night, dining on squirrels, and how they can get him to come out of his house. After committing a relatively harmless childhood prank for which he was arrested, Boo became a recluse who once supposedly attacked his father with a pair of scissors. His confinement to his own dark house has led to the popular belief that he is a kind of monster, but his successive acts of kindness toward the children (including sewing up Jem's torn pants, leaving gifts in the tree, putting a blanket around Scout the night of the fire, and finally saving their lives by attacking Bob Ewell) attest to his true nature. Like Tom Robinson, Boo is victimized by prejudice that is based on ignorance and fear, and both characters are connected with the image of the harmless mockingbird that it would be a sin to kill.

Several female characters play strong roles in the lives of the motherless Finch children. Foremost among them is **Calpurnia**, the family's black housekeeper, who has helped their father raise Jem and Scout. Like Atticus, she is strict but loving; for example, she sternly scolds Scout for her rudeness toward Walter Cunningham, but later offers to make Scout's favorite food, crackling bread. In a memorable scene, she takes Jem and Scout with her to her church, where they are greeted with general warmth but with resentment from one member of the congregation. Sometimes likened to the similarly endowed character of Dilsey in William Faulkner's classic novel *The Sound and the Fury*, Calpurnia exhibits an admirable blend of compassion and moral courage. Another positive force in the children's lives is their neighbor **Miss Maudie**, who treats them with great kindness and always speaks to them in a forthright manner. She affirms their father's admonition that it is a sin to kill a mockingbird, explaining that "they don't do one thing but sing their hearts out for us." Miss Maudie manifests her courage and stoicism when, after her house burns down, she tells Jem that she is looking forward to building a smaller house and having more room for her azaleas.

In contrast to Calpurnia and Miss Maudie, **Aunt Alexandria** (Atticus's sister) is a formidable conservative who seeks to uphold traditional Southern mores and who tries to counteract her brother's liberal influence on his children. Concerned with such superficial distinctions as class and family background, Aunt Alexandria bemoans Scout's lack of ladylike attributes. She and her female friends (referred to as her "missionary circle") expend their energies worrying about the plight of the people of Africa, even as those closer to them are in need. The adult Scout describes her tall, imposing aunt as "analogous to Mount Everest . . . cold and there." Another female character who lacks tolerance and insight is **Miss Caroline Fisher**, Scout's first-grade teacher, a recent graduate from northern Alabama who believes she will revolutionize Maycomb by introducing it to the Dewey Decimal System. Miss Caroline advises Scout to discontinue her nightly reading sessions with Atticus, as this does not accord with her own views on education; this episode underlines the novel's support the value of learning through contact with and understanding of others rather than through institutionalized education.

The Finch's ornery, elderly neighbor **Mrs. Henry Lafayette Dubose** spends much of her time sitting on her front porch haranguing those who pass by. To punish Jem for reacting angrily to Mrs. Dubose's calling his father "no better than the trash and niggers he works for," Atticus makes Jem spend many hours reading to Mrs. Dubose. After her death, Atticus explains that Mrs. Dubose was, during that same period, valiantly fighting a hopeless morphine addiction and thus exhibiting true courage.

Mild-mannered, hardworking **Tom Robinson** is the black man accused of raping Mayella Ewing. He testifies that he felt sorry for the isolated, impoverished young woman and thus agreed to break up an old piece of furniture for her. She then tried to seduce him and, while he was trying to escape, Bob Ewell came upon the scene. Proven innocent by Atticus, Tom is nevertheless convicted, thus dramatically evidencing the stubborn influence of racism in Southern society. Tom's alleged victim, **Mayella Ewell**, is apparently herself the victim of her father's abuse, and it is probably fear of him that has prompted her to accuse Tom of raping her. The fact that Mayella's word would be credited over that of a respectable black man—whose innocence, moreover, has been demonstrated—simply because she is white attests to the continuing power not only of racism in general but of the sexual taboo between blacks and whites that dominated the South at that time. The shiftless **Bob Ewell**, who is a rather one-dimensional character in his cruelty and vulgarity, resides on the second-to-the-bottom rung of the Maycomb society, just above the blacks upon whom he lavishes his contempt. Humiliated and enraged by Atticus's exposure of him on the witness stand, Ewell vows revenge and carries out his threat by attacking Jem and Scout, during which episode he is himself killed by Boo Radley.

Other characters in the novel include **Walter Cunningham**, who represents those poor but basically respectable whites in the area who "hadn't taken anything from or off anybody since they migrated to the New World;" **Judge Taylor**, who demonstrates his own sense of fairness by appointing a distinguished lawyer to Tom Robinson's case, knowing that Atticus will defend Tom to the best of his abilities; and **Braxton Underwood**, the owner-editor of Maycomb's newspapers, who decries the idiocy and inhumanity that led to Tom's death and compares it to the murder of a songbird.

Further Reading

Contemporary Literary Criticism Vols. 12, 60. Detroit: Gale Research.

Erisman, Fred. "The Romantic Regionalism of Harper Lee." *Alabama Review* Vol. 26, no. 2 (April 1973): 122–36.

Going, William T. "Store and Mockingbird: Two Pulitzer Novels about Alabama." In *Essays on Alabama Literature*, Tuscaloosa, AL: University of Alabama Press, 1975, 9–31.

LeMay, Harding. "Children Play; Adults Betray." *New York Herald Tribune Book Review* (July 10, 1960): 5.

Schuster, Edgar H. "Discovering Theme and Structure in the Novel." *English Journal* (October 1963): 506–11.

Sullivan, Richard. "Engrossing First Novel of Rare Excellence." *Chicago Sunday Tribune* (July 17, 1960): 1.

Ursula K. Le Guin
1929–

American novelist, short story writer, nonfiction writer, critic, editor, poet, dramatist, and author of books for children.

The Left Hand of Darkness (novel, 1969)

Plot: Set in a future time when it is possible to travel between planets, the novel chronicles the experiences of Genly Ai, an envoy from an organization of planets called the Ekumen. Ai travels to the planet Gethen in order to convince its inhabitants to join the Ekumen, which is based on the principals of cooperation and harmony. He struggles both with Gethen's harsh, wintry climate and its unfamiliar culture—particularly the fact that the Gethens are androgynous and take on male or female characteristics only during their monthly fertile periods. Ai initially mistrusts Estraven, the Prime Minister of Karhide (the first Gethen country he visits), but Estraven is drawn to the Ekumen concept of peaceful coexistence and thus develops a liking for Ai. Because of political opposition in Karhide, Estraven is unable to accept Ai's offer of membership in the Ekumen. Ai then travels to another Gethen country, Orgoreyn, which is better organized and more efficient than Karhide and which, consequently, he initially prefers. When Ai is suspected of being a spy and imprisoned by what he now realizes is an oppressive system, Estraven rescues him and the two begin an eight-hundred-mile journey across Gethen's frozen wasteland. During this trip, Ai comes to trust Estraven, and they forge a strong friendship. On their return to Karhide, Estraven explains that Ai must call down an Ekumen starship to prove his authenticity, and that he must do so in a way that allows the Karhide leaders to retain their dignity. This means that Ai must violate Ekumen procedure, which requires that a starship may only land on a planet if it has received guarantees of its welcome. Ai does complete his mission, but in the process Estraven is killed by his political opponents.

Characters: A highly respected writer of science fiction and fantasy, Le Guin is lauded for having raised the genre's literary standard through her elegant prose and richly inventive plots. Le Guin received the Hugo and Nebula awards for *The Left Hand of Darkness*, which is widely considered one of her best works. Her work is infused with ethical concerns and focuses more on philosophical, anthropological, and psychological issues than on the technical sciences. Composed not only of standard narrative but of native legends and myths, descriptions of religious ceremonies, and diary entries, *The Left Hand of Darkness* (like many of Le Guin's novels and short stories) centers on the precept that unity may be achieved through the interaction and tension between opposites. The novel's central metaphor for this theme is the androgynous Gethenian culture, within which identity and status are not related to gender. In an interview, Le Guin explained that with the advent of the women's movement in the mid-1960s, "I began . . . to want to define and understand the meaning of sexuality and the meaning of gender, in my life and in our society."

Le Guin's fiction often features a questing hero or heroine who undergoes difficulties and challenges and emerges with a stronger sense of identity. Such a character is **Genly Ai**, who during the course of his mission to Gethen develops a deeper perception of the meaning of the principals he has, as an envoy of the Ekumen, been charged with promoting. And like other Le Guin protagonists, Ai is an outsider, a visitor who serves primarily as an observer and who sometimes must reconcile his public duty with his private values. During the first half of the novel, Ai travels around Karhide and then into Orgoreyn, learning about the cultures of these two Gethenian countries. He is bewildered by Karhide's political intricacies and by its culture as a whole—particularly its inhabitants' androgynous sexuality. Whereas Karhide is a loosely organized, perhaps illogical, but generally humane tribal society, Orgoreyn is a centralized, highly efficient but repressive bureaucracy (some commentators have identified the two countries as representing, respectively, the United States and the Soviet Union). Ai is presented as a young, compassionate, dedicated but rather conventional and occasionally pompous character whose fallibility leads him to make mistaken judgments. Indeed, it is this very fallibility that Le Guin uses to explore the concept of cultural relativism. Having been rescued by Estraven, whom he mistrusts, Ai must travel with him across eight hundred miles of frozen tundra. During this journey, the two are united against a common foe—the mindless, devastating power of their harsh environment—and Ai comes not only to trust Estraven but to love him. Le Guin has been praised for her sensitive portrayal of the developing relationship between Ai and Estraven, who communicate telepathically. Although they never completely comprehend the differences between them, their surmounting of these differences to form a friendship demonstrates the meaning of the Ekumen.

Whereas Ai initially mistrusts **Therem Harth Rem Ir Estraven**, the Prime Minister of Karhide, the latter recognizes Ai as a proponent of worthy values and thus attempts to befriend him. Unlike other members of his society, Estraven has rejected ethnocentrism and favors unity between peoples, no matter what their cultural differences. Ai is a visitor whose role is to observe what happens around him, but Estraven is a visionary who struggles against great odds to bring about change. He tries to do so through his knowledge of Karhide's political intrigues, and his efforts lead ultimately not only to Gethen's inclusion in the Ekumen but in his own death. During the long trek across the ice with Ai, Estraven succeeds in breaking through the other's mistrust by emphasizing the positive values of his own culture, such as its focus on harmony with nature, continuity with the past, social graces, and inner tranquility. The thorny issue of Gethenian sexuality is only uneasily transcended by the two friends, for Estraven once bore a child by his own brother, and Ai's telepathic voice is that of this now-dead lover. For a while it appears that the relationship between Ai and Estraven may be sexually consummated, when Estraven enters his fertile period and takes female form, but this never occurs. Estraven provides a fitting metaphor for his friendship with Ai when he points out that in the ice-covered landscape they are crossing it is necessary to see shadows in order to know where one is; likewise, unity may be achieved through a balancing of opposites. The fact that at the end of the novel Estraven is killed and that Ai is not even able to clear his name, as he had promised, provides a concluding emphasis on, according to critic George Edgar Slusser, "the imperfection of human friendship in the inconclusive world of man's affairs."

Further Reading

Bittner, James W. *Approaches to the Fiction of Ursula K. Le Guin*. Ann Arbor: UMI Research Press, 1984.

Bucknall, Barbara J. *Ursula K. Le Guin*. New York: Ungar, 1981.

Contemporary Literary Criticism, Vols. 8, 13, 22, 45, 71. Detroit: Gale Research.

Cummins, Elizabeth. *Understanding Ursula K. Le Guin*. Columbia: University of South Carolina Press, 1990.

DeBolt, Joe, ed. *Ursula K. Le Guin: Voyage to Inner Lands and Outer Space*. Kennikat, 1979.

Dictionary of Literary Biography, Vols. 8, 52. Detroit: Gale Research.

Ketterer, David. *"The Left Hand of Darkness*: Ursula K. Le Guin's Archetypal 'Winter Journey.'"* In *New Worlds for Old: The Apocalyptic Imagination, Science Fiction, and American Literature*, pp. 76-91. New York: Anchor Press, 1974.

Olander, Joseph D. and Greenberg, Martin Harry, eds. *Ursula K. Le Guin.* New York: Taplinger, 1979.

Slusser, George Edgar. *The Farthest Shores of Ursula K. Le Guin.* Borgo Press, 1976.

Doris Lessing
1919–

English novelist, short story writer, essayist, dramatist, poet, nonfiction writer, journalist, and travel writer.

The Good Terrorist (novel, 1986)

Plot: The novel centers on a group of disaffected young people living in contemporary London. They consider themselves political revolutionaries but lack any ideology beyond a generalized hatred of Prime Minister Margaret Thatcher and her policies. Into their midst comes thirty-six-year-old Alice Mellings, who shares both their disgust with society and their lack of cohesive ideas about how to change it. Alice takes charge of the dilapidated house in which the group is "squatting" (living illegally) and—through a combination of hard work and trading on her middle-class respectability—soon transforms it into a comfortable, orderly haven in which the group can plan the act of terrorism that has previously been beyond their ability. Meanwhile, Alice's hysterical rages and memory lapses hint at her mental imbalance. Finally one of the group members succeeds in making a car bomb, setting in motion a sequence of events that ends in an explosion that kills the bomb's courier as well as four innocent passersby. At the end of the novel, it appears that Alice will soon arrested for her role in the incident.

Characters: One of the world's most respected novelists, Lessing broaches a wide range of topics and concerns in her fiction, including racism, communism, feminism, psychology, mysticism, and the connections among them. Such early, acclaimed works as the *Children of Violence* series (1952–69) and *The Golden Notebook* (1962) are noted for a realism that Lessing abandons in her science or speculative fiction, producing the five *Canopus in Argus: Archives* novels to mixed reviews. Many critics see *The Good Terrorist* as a positive return to Lessing's former strengths. Although the novel provides a disheartening vision of contemporary British society, Lessing avoids political analysis, focusing instead on a group of feckless, young, would-be revolutionaries. Because of the negative portrayal of radicalism found in *The Good Terrorist*, some commentators suggest that Lessing, who was once a communist, has become politically conservative. Others, however, assert that she is still committed to liberal ideals but wary of extremists.

The "good terrorist" of the novel's title is thirty-six-year-old **Alice Mellings**, whose best qualities ultimately make possible an act of terrorism. Raised by liberal parents, Alice develops a strong disgust for the "bloody filthy *accumulating* middle class creeps" whose most prominent representative is Prime Minister Margaret Thatcher. Sympathizing with England's downtrodden, Alice harbors vague dreams of a revolution that will cleanse her society of its ugliness, of police brutality and overcrowded housing, and generally alleviate the suffering of the underclass. To this end she takes charge of a loose, fractious band of self-styled revolutionaries who have previously been unable to agree on any course of action. Warmhearted, generous, and efficient, Alice pours all her energy into refurbishing the squatters' house and tending to their needs, behaving curiously domestic. Despite her radical leanings, Alice creates a respectable haven full of middle-class comforts, an atmosphere that allows the group to plan and carry out their act of terrorism. Alice slides into participation partly through sheer naivete, but she may also be mentally unbalanced, a suggestion many critics agree with. Her uncontrollable rages, memory lapses, and strong aversion to sexual contact contribute to this impression, as do her frequent retreats into her memories of an idyllic childhood and her antagonism toward her parents since their divorce. Alice seems to connect madness and terrorism. One critic notes the similarity between Alice's name and Lessing's, suggesting that the character may be an exaggerated version of her creator. Another critic compares Alice to the protagonist of Lewis Carroll's *Alice's Adventures in Wonderland* (1865)—a sensible, innocent, curious child perplexed by the absurd and often cruel adult world. Indeed, at the end of the book, Alice seems childlike, happily sipping a big cup of sweet tea before meeting the British agent who will probably arrest her.

Whereas some critics see in Alice at least a few qualities in common with her creator, others hear in the dry, sensible, middle-aged voice of Alice's mother, **Dorothy Mellings**, possible echoes of Lessing's own viewpoint. Dorothy (who does not actually appear until almost the end of the novel but with whom Alice is constantly sparring) reconsiders the liberal ideals she previously endorsed even as her daughter becomes more dangerously radical. Perhaps because of her daughter's extremism, Dorothy questions what she once held to be true and even admits that she may one day be forced to side with Margaret Thatcher and the Conservative party. Loving, supportive parents, Dorothy and her husband have given Alice a comfortable childhood, but their eventual divorce leads Alice to blame Dorothy for the loss of that Eden. For her part, Dorothy is disappointed that Alice adopts the conventional woman's role, for Alice performs the same function—that of the ''all-purpose female drudge''—for her revolutionary friends that Dorothy performed for her own family. An alcoholic, Dorothy now rents a shabby flat, the only accommodations she can afford supporting her daughter and then having to sell her house. Her future seems bleak and promises only isolation, detachment, and cynicism. Again, critics question whether this stance is also Lessing's or whether it represents only disappointed hopes.

Through the members of the Communist Centre Union, the group of would-be revolutionaries for which Alice becomes a sort of den mother, Lessing creates an unflattering portrait of political extremism. At the group's center is the repellent **Jasper**, who is Alice's cohort and mentor for about fifteen years. A homosexual who exploits Alice's strong feelings for him, Jasper is self-important, dishonest, and sulky. He is also mean-spirited and sometimes violent. Alice's friends have long warned her against Jasper, yet she remains completely devoted to him. Two other activists in the group are the lesbian couple **Roberta and Faye**, whose feigned Cockney accents hide their own middle-class origins in Northern England. Motherly Roberta faithfully looks after Faye, who is prone to weeping and fits of rage and must take antipsychotic drugs. Faye is killed when the car bomb she is carrying explodes.

Several critics note that most of the terrorists featured in the novel are women and point out how this counters the notion that a revolution launched by women would be somehow gentler and more enlightened. A notable example is **Jocelin**, who uses her considerable manual dexterity to construct the bomb that ultimately kills five people. Jocelin lives in a state of perpetual anger against the world. **Muriel and Pat**, who live next door to the group, are also political activists but their relative cheerfulness and efficiency are in stark contrast to the CCU members; not surprisingly, they are recruited by the KGB, who would never consider asking any of Alice's friends to join their ranks. Alice exploits **Philip**, an unemployed carpenter, but never pays him for the labor he good-naturedly provides to refurbish the house. Philip points out that the self-styled revolutionaries are social "parasites" who "never lift a finger."

Further Reading

Bell, Pearl K. "Bad Housekeeping." *New Republic* Vol. 193, no. 18 (October 28, 1985): 47–50.

Contemporary Literary Criticism. Vols. 1, 2, 3, 6, 10, 15, 22, 40. Detroit: Gale Research.

Donoghue, Denis. "Alice, the Radical Homemaker." *New York Times Book Review.* (September 22, 1985): 3, 29.

Lurie, Alison. "Bad Housekeeping." *New York Review of Books* Vol. 32, no. 20 (December 19, 1985): 8–10.

Major Twentieth-Century Writers. Vol. 3. Detroit: Gale Research.

Pickering, Jean. *Understanding Doris Lessing.* Columbia: University of South Carolina Press, 1990.

Robinson, Marilynne. "Doris Lessing's Gentrified Revolutionaries." *Book World—The Washington Post.* (September 22, 1985): 4.

Scanlan, Margaret. "Language and the Politics of Despair in Doris Lessing's *The Good Terrorist.*" *Novel* Vol. 23, no. 2 (winter 1990): 182–98.

Snitow, Ann. "We Are Overcome: A Vindication of Doris Lessing." *VLS* No. 39 (October 1985): 1, 6–9.

Sprague, Claire, ed. *In Pursuit of Doris Lessing: Nine Nations Reading.* New York: St. Martin's, 1990.

Waugh, Harriet. "An Entertaining Pongy Belch." *Spectator* Vol. 255, no. 8203 (September 28, 1985): 31.

Whittaker, Ruth. *Doris Lessing.* New York: St. Martin's Press, 1988.

Penelope Lively

1933–

English novelist, short story writer, and writer of books for children.

Moon Tiger (novel, 1987)

Plot: The novel centers on Claudia Hampton, an elderly English historian who is dying of cancer. From her hospital bed, she proposes to offer a history of her era by focusing on the events of her own life. Shifting frequently from past to present, Claudia relates her childhood as a precocious, independent child and young girl, her education at Oxford University, and her career as a war correspondent in Cairo during World War II. Along the way, the reader encounters her brilliant brother Gordon, with whom she had an extremely close relationship, and her daughter Lisa, who disappointed Claudia with her normality and average intellect. Lisa is the daughter of Claudia's former lover Jasper, a half-Russian television producer. As the novel progresses, Claudia reveals that the most important event in her life was her short love affair with Tom Southern, an English tank commander whom she met in Egypt. The two spent several idyllic interludes together before Tom was killed in the Western Desert campaign. The book concludes with Claudia's peaceful death, just before which she seems to have experienced a sense of—if not resolution—wellbeing.

Characters: Previously known primarily as an author of children's books, Lively won the prestigious Booker-McConnell Prize for Fiction for *Moon Tiger*, which exhibits her characteristic preoccupation with time and with the relationship between collective memory or history and private recollection. Structured as an impressionistic series of episodes, the novel features a shifting narrative voice that, according to critic Julie J. Nichols, explores and affirms "the twin powers of love and memory to give value to the present."

The novel's central character is **Claudia Hampton**, an English historian in her late seventies who has achieved great popular success with her vivid, unconventional books (which some scornful critics have labeled "technicolor history") and who now lies dying in a hospital. To her kindly nurses and to the reader she states her intention to write a history of her era that will include "the whole triumphant murderous unstoppable chute—from the mud to the stars, universal and poetic, your story and mine." She plans to accomplish this feat by reassessing her own life, a task that has been prompted both by her impending death and by the arrival of a diary that chronicles her longlost lover's last days. Claudia does not promise that this history will be chronological, because she is "composed of a myriad Claudias" and because she sees history as random or kaleidoscopic and life as inherently transitory. In addition, other views of Claudia will be offered through the voices and perspectives of those around her, including her brother, daughter, and former lover.

Claudia was a bright, spirited, impetuous child and young girl who, cherished and encouraged by her family, grew up rebellious and questioning and with a very high opinion of herself. She was beautiful but intimidated many men with her archness, vigorous intellect, and sometimes abrasive manner. Feisty and willful, she followed her own ambitions and desires and could be said to have lived a self-centered life, with the possible exception of the period in which she was involved with Tom Southern. Captured for Claudia in the image of the moon tiger, which burns brightly through the night and is finally transformed into a coil of ash, this relationship was something of a revelation, for she found herself making someone else happy for the first time in her life. Several critics particularly lauded Lively for her portrayal of Claudia's affair with Tom and especially her reaction to his death, when the imperviousness that might previously have rendered her a pompous bore somehow deepens the poignancy of her profound grief. An important part of Claudia's struggle to make sense of her life has to do with the human need for love—a need she has previously overlooked in others, whose feelings she now tries to imagine. At the end of the novel, Claudia does not appear to have reached any concrete conclusions about her life, and some critics faulted her for lacking a self-critical capacity. Nevertheless, she has proved herself, in the words of reviewer J. K. L. Walker, "a formidable and articulate protagonist" who may be admired for having lived a joyful life on her own terms and for facing her death without self-pity.

One of the most important people in Claudia's life is her brother **Gordon**, with whom she had a loving but intense relationship until his death about five years before she begins her reminiscences. A brilliant economist who taught at both Harvard and Oxford universities, Gordon also lent his expertise to various third-world governments. Claudia describes the young Gordon as having "that lank, casual attenuated look of those who go through life with their hands in their pockets, whistling. A golden lad, Gordon. Winning prizes and making friends." Gordon was the standard by which Claudia (who considered her brother one of very few people of either sex who were her intellectual equals) measured all other men, most of whom fell short; he was "my sense of identity, my mirror, my critic, judge and ally," and perhaps a version of herself if she had been born a man. At one point during their adolescence, the relationship between Claudia and Gordon veered toward the incestuous, which some critics have viewed as an expression of their narcissism.

The other significant man in Claudia's life is **Tom Southern**, an earnest Englishman and former journalist whom she meant when he was fighting in the Egyptian desert and she was serving as a war correspondent. Claudia remembers their brief but passionate love affair as the central core of her life which, like the coil of the "moon tiger" mosquito repellent, seemed to burn intensely for one night and then turned to ash. What Claudia most mourns is the fact that if she met Tom now the two would be strangers—that he is frozen forever in youth, while she has gone on into middle and old age without him. Lively has been praised for her poignant rendering of their romance as well as the authentic accounts of the 1942 desert campaign contained in Tom's diary, which she receives from his sister.

Claudia has a strained relationship with her daughter **Lisa**, who was fathered by Claudia's former lover, Jasper, and raised primarily by her grandmothers. The dowdy adult Lisa is a disappointment to her brilliant mother, despite Claudia's claim that insists that she sees intelligence as a handicap and that it is preferable to be of only average intellect. Claudia remembers Lisa as an aloof child, but Lisa's own reflections reveal that she always felt "too pallid" for and thus rejected by her mother. Ironically, her normality is a form of rebellion against unconventional Claudia, and she hides her illicit lover from her mother because she knows Claudia would actually approve of such a daring act.

Other characters in the novel include Lisa's sophisticated, glamourous father **Jasper**, a half-Russian graduate of Cambridge University who is a very successful television producer; **Sylvia Hampton**, Gordon's pretty but vacant, tedious wife, against whom Gordon and Claudia are rather cruelly allied; and **Lazlo**, a surly, homosexual refugee from Russia's 1956 invasion of Hungary and a would-be artist whom Claudia (ignoring the advice of her family and friends) allows to live in her flat.

Further Reading

Contemporary Literary Criticism, Vols. 32, 50. Detroit: Gale Research.

Dictionary of Literary Biography, Vol. 14. Detroit: Gale Research.

Eder, Richard. "Lived and Lost and Never Lived at All." *Los Angeles Times Book Review* (8 May 1988): 3, 9.

King, Francis. "Death on the Wartime Nile." *Spectator* 258, No. 8289 (23 May 1987): 48-9.

Maitland, Sara. "The History Woman." *New Statesman* 113, No. 2928 (8 may 1987): 23-4.

Martin, Carolyn. "Nurturing the Lifelong Afterglow of a Youthful Love Affair." *Tribune Books* (15 May 1988): 6.

Nichols, Julie J. "Retrospective: Penelope Lively." *Belles Lettres* (Spring 1992): 26-9.

Tyler, Anne. "Life Moves Too Fast for the Picture." *New York Times Book Review* (17 April 1988): 9.

Walker, J. K. L. "In Time of War." *Times Literary Supplement* No. 4389 (15 May 1987): 515.

Alison Lurie
1926–
American novelist, nonfiction writer, children's writer, and critic.

Foreign Affairs (novel, 1984)

Plot: The novel's central character is Virginia "Vinnie" Miner, a fifty-four-year-old professor of children's literature at an Ivy League university. An admitted Anglophile, Vinnie is to spend a six-month sabbatical in London. On the airplane to England, she meets a retired waste disposal engineer named Chuck Mumpson whom she views as an embodiment of everything that is tasteless and uncouth about America. But Chuck pursues Vinnie's companionship, and she eventually finds herself in love with him. Vinnie's experiences are juxtaposed to those of a younger professor, Fred Turner, who teaches eighteenth century literature at the same university and who is in London to research Restoration poet John Gay. Fred has an affair with a beautiful television actress, Rosemary Radley, who introduces him to the world of the English aristocracy. Meanwhile, his work at the British Museum proves futile. After a comic interlude at a country manor exposes Rosemary's true colors, Fred returns with relief to America and a possible reunion with his estranged wife. Vinnie too will resume her life much as it was before, for Chuck dies of a heart attack.

Characters: Lurie won the Pulitzer Prize for *Foreign Affairs*, which exhibits her characteristic satirical wit, solid structuring, and emphasis on human fallibility. Commentators noted the novel's fairy tale aspects, such as the suggestion that the ordinary or ugly may be transformed by love, and its many references to children's literature. In addition, critics detected the influence of nineteenth-century authors Henry James (in the novel's "innocents abroad" theme) and Jane Austen (in its omniscient, sometimes sardonic authorial voice and its examination of manners).

As several commentators pointed out, **Virginia "Vinnie" Miner** resembles her creator in several significant ways: both are professors of children's literature (Vinnie at the fictional Corinth University and Lurie at Cornell University) and both are Anglophiles; in fact, Lurie spends a month of every year in England. The unmarried Vinnie is tiny, dowdy, and not particularly attractive, "the sort of person no one ever notices." Prone to self-pity, she has even invented an imaginary dog called Fido to embody this quality. Significantly, however, Fido appears only at the beginning and end of the novel, disappearing while Vinnie is involved—initially against her will but finally with enjoyment—in her love affair with Chuck Mumpson. When Vinnie first meets Chuck, she snobbishly labels him a veritable personification of everything cheap and tacky about American society. Vinnie's life, however, is intellectually rich but emotionally barren. After one short, failed marriage, she has had a series of relationships but has always withdrawn before love could transpire. Vinnie prefers the experience she finds in literature over real personal commitment. Thus she is chagrined to find herself drawn to Chuck, who is certainly the most real of any of her previous suitors. Vinnie wonders if, at fifty-four, she is too old for love; indeed, she has noticed that her beloved English literature contains no one of interest who is over fifty years old. Why, she asks, must she "become a minor character in her own life? Why shouldn't she imagine herself as an explorer standing on the edge of some landscape as yet unmapped by literature, interested, even excited—ready to be surprised?" So Vinnie does succumb to love, however briefly. As she returns to America, she muses on the London life she and Chuck might have created if he had lived, but she finally concludes that it never would have happened, that "her fate is to be always single, unloved, alone."

Plump, balding, tackily dressed **Chuck Mumpson** is a retired waste disposal engineer from Tulsa, Oklahoma, whom Vinnie initially dismisses as "of no particular education or distinction; the sort of person who goes on package tours to Europe." Chuck speaks in an exaggerated Southern twang and is frequently attired in a green plastic raincoat that becomes a metaphor for his Americanness. Commentators have labeled Chuck a kind of frog prince in the fairy tale that *Foreign Affairs* resembles: He seems repulsive at first but grows increasingly charming as he exhibits his underlying capacity for love. He is the first of Vinnie's lovers who truly loves her, and this realization jars her from her pretentiousness and disdain. Although Chuck is initially an embodiment of everything ugly about America, he finally comes to represent its openness and essential decency; he also affirms the validity of the real world that exists outside of the literary and academic realm to which Vinnie has previously confined herself. However, Chuck dies of a heart attack, ending the possibility of future happiness for the couple, perhaps in keeping with the novel's fairy tale quality, for this frog prince cannot survive outside the magical context of the fairy tale.

Several commentators found the alternative plot involving literature professor **Fred Turner** inferior to the main story, maintaining that Fred and his lover were not as convincingly portrayed as Vinnie and Chuck. Fred is presented as Vinnie's opposite in a variety of ways: whereas she is female, plain, middle-aged, and knowing, he is male, good-looking, young, and naive. Recently separated from his wife Roo (who appears in an earlier Lurie novel), Fred arrives in London to gather research on the eighteenth-century poet John Gay, but his visits to the British Museum (which he dubs the Bowel Movement) prove tedious and unfruitful. Almost immediately, Fred becomes involved with Rosemary Radley, and his erroneous perception of her as a Jamesian heroine—lovely, delicate, and too trusting—matches with his general impression that he has landed in a James short story. Initially dazzled by the aristocratic world to which Rosemary introduces him, Fred discovers its more sordid underside during a weekend at a country estate. He returns to America with his academic aims still unfulfilled and his soul not much more enlightened than before he came to London, although it appears he may return to his wife.

Several critics faulted Lurie for her flat portrayal of flighty, giggly **Rosemary Radley**, the well-known television actress and daughter of an earl, with whom Fred has an affair. Rosemary's beauty and aristocratic aura initially dazzle Fred, but he eventually comes to see her as the embodiment of a self-indulgent, decadent society. The country weekend, during which she and Fred participate in a sex-tinged game of charades, exposes Rosemary as, according to critic Charles Champlin, "scandalous and untidy, spiderlike at the center of a salon that is insubstantial as a web."

Further Reading

Bernays, Anne. "What to Think About Chuck and Vinnie." *New York Times Book Review* (September 16, 1984): 9.

Boston, Richard. "Minerva in London." *Punch* Vol. 288, no. 7520 (January 23, 1985): 52.

Bradbury, Malcolm. "The Paleface Professor." *London Times* (January 19, 1985): 6.

Butler, Marilyn. "Amor Vincit Vinnie." *London Review of Books* (February, 21, 1985): 5–6.

Champlin, Charles. Review of *Foreign Affairs*. *Los Angeles Times Book Review* (October 21, 1984): 1, 12.

Clemons, Walter. "Lovers and Other Strangers." *Newsweek* CIV, no. 13 (September 24, 1984): 80.

Conarroe, Joel. "Footnotes to Lovenotes." *Book World—Washington Post* (September 30, 1984): 6.

Contemporary Literary Criticism Vols. 4, 5, 18, 39. Detroit: Gale Research.

Corrigan, Maureen. Review of *Foreign Affairs. VLS* no. 29 (October 1984): 5.

Costa, Richard Hauer. *Alison Lurie.* New York: Twayne, 1992.

Dictionary of Literary Biography Vol. 2. Detroit: Gale Research.

Lehmann-Haupt, Christopher. Review of *Foreign Affairs. New York Times* (September 13, 1984): C21.

Sage, Lorna. "Adventures in the Old World." *Times Literary Supplement* no. 4270 (February 1, 1985): 109.

Wickenden, Dorothy. "Love in London." *New Republic* Vol. 191, no. 15 (October 8, 1984): 34–6.

Naguib Mahfouz

1912–

Egyptian novelist, short story writer, dramatist, and scriptwriter.

The Cairo Trilogy (*Al-Thulathiyya;* novels, 1956–57: *Palace Walk* [*Bayn al-qasrayn,* 1956], *Palace of Desire* [*Qasr al-shawq,* 1957], and *Sugar Street* [*Al-Sukkariyya,* 1957])

Plot: Set in Cairo, Egypt, from 1917 to 1944, the novel chronicles several generations of the middle-class al-Jawad family as it adapts to the social, cultural, and political changes sweeping the country during those years. In *Palace Walk,* the reader learns about the family's daily lives, the personalities of the individual members, and some of their joys, doubts, pleasures, conflicts, and sorrows. Al-Sayyid Ahmad Abd al-Jawad, the family's patriarch, maintains a stern, dictatorial manner with his wife and five children, who fear and obey him. Yet Abd al-Jawad leads a double life, going out at night to drink and carouse with his friends, who consider him a spectacular wit, singer, and ladies man. His wife, Amina, is meek and submissive, greeting her returning husband each night with a lantern at the top of the stairs, running her household efficiently, and, in the Muslim tradition, never venturing outside her home. The gentle, religious, and tolerant Amina is much loved by her three sons, lusty Yasin (Abd al-Jawad's son by a previous marriage), studious Fahmi, and bright, happy, ten-year-old Kamal; and two daughters, outspoken Khadija and beautiful Aisha. Each day the al-Jawad children join their mother for a pleasant hour of coffee-drinking and conversation. But their placid life changes as revolutionary movement seeks to supplant the English colonial government and modern influences infiltrate Egypt's closed society. Gradually the composition of the al-Jawad family also begins to change, as Aisha and Khadija marry two brothers, Khalil and Ibrahim Shawkat, and start their own families. The ever-lustful Yasin also marries, but his union with a woman accustomed to more freedom than her new father-in-law allows proves a failure; she ultimately divorces Yasin. Fahmi, meanwhile, becomes active in the revolutionary movement, despite his father's disapproval. While participating in a peaceful demonstration, Fahmi is killed, causing terrible heartbreak to his parents and siblings.

Palace of Desire begins in the early 1920s, about five years after the end of *Palace Walk.* During the intervening years, while grieving his dead son, Ahmad Abd al-Jawad also has avoided the nightly partying with his friends. But when he learns that they now congregate on houseboats to cavort with several famous singers and musicians, Abd al-Jawad is drawn back into his former habits. He becomes involved with a seductive lute player named Zanuba who manipulates him into buying her a houseboat. Much of the book, however, is devoted to Kamal, now a pensive, troubled, and passionate high school student who suffers a futile infatuation with aristocratic Aida Shaddad, the beautiful older sister of a friend. Kamal also struggles with religious doubts when he learns about nineteenth-century English naturalist Charles Darwin's evolutionary theory. Yasin, meanwhile, contracts another disastrous marriage, this time with Maryam, the family's longtime-neighbor; while engaged to Maryam, Yasin has an affair with her widowed mother, Bahija. After his eventual divorce from Maryam, Yasin marries his father's former lover, Zanuba. As this volume ends, Kamal prepares for a career as a teacher, while several of his friends plan to leave Egypt travel abroad. Having rejected Kamal, Aida marries another of her brother's friends, and Kamal attends her wedding.

Sugar Street finds the Abd al-Jawad family tragically altered in a number of ways. Aisha's husband and two sons have died of typhoid, leaving her grief-stricken and dependent on her only surviving child, lovely Naima. The previously vigorous Ahmad Abd al-Jawad grows increasingly frail, until he is finally confined to the house; meanwhile, Amina ventures outside to visit various religious sites. Kamal is now a middle-aged teacher who struggles with the conflicting strains of intellect and physicality within himself, writing philosophical articles but also visiting bars and brothels. He has remained single, rejecting a chance to marry the youngest daughter of the now-impoverished Shaddad family. The grandchildren of Ahmad and Amina are now grown and pursuing their very different interests: Khadija's sons, Ahmad becomes a socialist and Abd al-Munim is an Islamic fundamentalist; Yasin's son, Ridwan, uses his homosexuality to gain political favor and good jobs for various family members. After Aisha's daughter, Naima, marries her cousin Abd al-Munim, Naima dies in childbirth, pushing Aisha into insanity. Khadija's sons are both sent to jail for their radical beliefs. During World War II Cairo is bombed. After one air raid, Ahmad Abd al-Jawad must be carried home from a shelter by Kamal. His heart too weak for this experience, the family patriarch dies. Amina soon follows him, her death coinciding with the birth of Yasin's grandchild.

Characters: In 1988, Mahfouz became the first Arabic-language author to receive the Nobel Prize in Literature, confirming his stature not only as Egypt's leading literary figure but as one of the most revered writers in the Arab world. Employing a style that combines social and political issues with convincing characterizations and engaging, often lyrical prose, Mahfouz is credited with bringing the Arab novel to maturity. Although not widely known to English-language readers until the early 1990s, the monumental *Cairo Trilogy*—which totals about 1,500 pages—is one of Mahfouz's most acclaimed works. It provides a detailed portrait of life in Egypt from 1917 to 1944, when the country was struggling to shed some of its more medieval customs, emerge from foreign dominance, and enter the modern age. Frequently compared to the works of such nineteenth- and early twentieth-century realists as Honoré de Balzac, Emile Zola, and Leo Tolstoy—but particularly to Thomas Mann's multigenerational family saga, *Buddenbrooks*—the *Cairo Trilogy* goes beyond the chronicling of a specific time and place to invoke universal issues and truths. Its themes include political change and freedom; the loss of faith; religious and humanistic values; the effects of modernization on attitudes toward women, education, and science; the role of the writer in society; and the eternal joys and sorrows inherent in love and family relationships.

Although he plays a fairly minor role in the first volume, in which he is a carefree child, **Kamal Abd al-Jawad**, the family's youngest son, is a central character in the trilogy. Often identified as an autobiographical figure, Kamal reflects many of his creator's experiences and attributes. Among their differences, however, is that Kamal apparently never finds the outlet for his thoughts and feelings that Mahfouz found in writing fiction. Mahfouz has been lauded for avoiding the subjectivism with which many writers imbue their autobiographical characters; instead, he maintains a fond but detached, balanced approach to Kamal. In *Palace Walk*, Kamal is a curious, imaginative, happy child who loves his parents (especially his adoring mother, who tells him enthralling stories of the spirit world and shapes his religious values) and siblings. He misses his sisters after they marry and leave their parents' home and naively wonders why their bellies swell up so soon after their marriages. He is upset to learn that the head of the prophet Muhammed's grandson Husayn is not actually present in the neighborhood mosque, foreshadowing his later religious disillusionment (and mirror a similar discovery by Mahfouz when he was a child). Unlike the rest of his family, Kamal easily befriends the English soldiers in the camp near his home, finding their presence thrilling, not ominous, and they in turn give him treats to eat and sing for him. Kamal hopes for harmony between his people and the English, but as *Palace Walk* draws to a close and his brother Fahmi is killed in a demonstration, the prospect of harmony seems dim.

Kamal's perspective is central in *Palace of Desire* and *Sugar Street*. As the trilogy's second volume begins, Kamal is an intelligent, inquisitive high school student painfully self-conscious about his big head and big nose. His adolescent ardor and insecurity are both prominent in the sections chronicling his hopeless infatuation with Aida Shaddad, the beautiful sister of his aristocratic friend Husayn. Unlike his own sisters, Aida mingles freely with her brother's friends, and by the end of the novel she has selected her future husband from among them. Many pages of *Palace of Desire* are devoted to Kamal's excited, anguished musings over his unrequited passion, and critics praised these passages as well as those describing his intellectual and religious soul-searching for their intensity, immediacy, and poetic quality. In the second volume Kamal rejects his father's wish that he study something prestigious like law or finance, and he enrolls in Teacher's College, where he is exposed to modern scientific theory and Western modes of thought, shaking his foundation to its core. By the end of *Palace of Desire,* Kamal begins to turn away from the religion and customs of his parents, and he has also said goodbye to the now-married Aida and to his beloved schoolmates as they leave Egypt to pursue their own interests abroad.

The adult Kamal's doubts and interior struggles dominate *Sugar Street,* during which his society's traditions have crumbled yet the future remains uncertain. Teaching English and writing trite articles on modern philosophy for literary magazines, Kamal becomes an introverted intellectual who indulges in alcohol and prostitutes but avoids the responsibilities inherent in legitimate love and marriage. No longer strongly religious as his pious, superstitious mother was and as his stern father claimed to be (Kamal has learned about his father's debauchery), Kamal is still reluctant to take on the Western values to which he has been exposed. Instead, like the protagonist of Shakespeare's *Hamlet,* he retreats into continual self-questioning and inaction. Kamal sees turmoil everywhere. He learns that the Shaddads have lost their wealth and that haughty Aida has even been divorced by her aristocratic husband and has had to become the second wife of a much older man. Kamal becomes reacquainted with **Budur**, Aida's younger sister—ho had been his special pet when she was a toddler—but finds himself unable to commit to the marriage her family hopes for. Mahfouz has said that Kamal's bewilderment and misgivings reflect not only his own but those of a whole generation of Egyptian intellectuals who came of age at this time in history, when the old was lost but the new had not yet taken shape.

The trilogy's primary agent of the older Egyptian ways is **Al-Sayyid** (a title of respect meaning "Lord" or "Master") **Ahmad Abd al-Jawad**, a prosperous merchant and the stereotypical autocratic Muslim patriarch: stern and unbending, he demands complete obedience from his wife and children. In accordance with Islamic tradition, Abd al-Jawad's sons attend school and may come and go as they please, while his wife and daughters are confined within their home according to Muslim tradition—their father disapproves even of hearing their names spoken in public. Despite his piety displayed at home, however, Abd al-

Jawad shows another behavior at night, when he indulgences in wine, women, and merrymaking with his friends. A large, vital, handsome man, he is a talented singer, storyteller, and wit, a prodigious drinker, a wise adviser, and an accomplished lover. Every night he is greeted on his return by the meek, submissive mother of his children, who is indulgent of his drunkenness and oblivious to his infidelity. Abd al-Jawad's double standard (he trusts that God will excuse his sins based on his devoutness at home) is apparent when he learns that, after twenty-five years of scrupulous obedience and service, his wife, Amina, has left the house on a religious pilgrimage (Amina's only transgression). For this Abd al-Jawad banishes Amina; soon missing her attentiveness and efficiency, however, he decides to forgive her. The fact that Abd al-Jawad is able to successively sustain these contradictions shows the basic stability of the older way of life he represents—but, through the course of the *Cairo Trilogy,* it gradually deteriorates.

This deterioration begins near the end of *Palace Walk,* with Fahmi's death. Though Abd al-Jawad gave the revolution his philosophical and financial support, it never occurred to him that it might ever touch his family. His first inkling comes on his way home one night, when he is arrested and forced to help fill in a trench dug by the revolutionaries. Fahmi's death so unhinges Abd al-Jawad that he suspends his usual nightly activities for five years. Although he eventually goes back to them, merrymaking, he never quite recovers his former jollity. The aging Abd al-Jawad is at the mercy of a scheming, much younger lute player, Zanuba, who later marries his son. Abd al-Jawad is also bewildered by his children's (especially Kamal's) religious rejection. By the end of *Sugar Street* Abd al-Jawad is confined to his bed, dependent on the radio (which he had once held in contempt), while his wife ventures outside the house's enclosure every day. He endures the deaths of companions and family members. The extent of his deterioration is notable in the scene in which Kamal carries Abd al-Jawad home from an air raid shelter: once a large, vigorous figure in full command of his world, Abd al-Jawad is now frail and dependent. Unable to withstand this experience, the old man dies, succumbing to nature and to modernity.

Through Abd al-Jawad's submissive, obedient wife, **Amina,** Mahfouz portrays the traditional role of the Muslim woman and the effects of modernization on Egyptian women's lives. Married at thirteen and a mother within a year, Amina has lived since then entirely within the walls of her husband's house; she sees the outside world only through the slats of her balcony. Gentle, compassionate, and uncomplaining, Amina is utterly devoted to her family and her household. Every night she greets her returning husband pleasantly, standing at the top of the stairs with a lantern and making him comfortable as he prepares for bed. Accepting of his drunkenness and seemingly oblivious to his infidelity, Amina prides in her tyrannical, arrogant husband and indulges her children, who repay her tenderness with warm, familiar affection. Amina knows little about the political world and thinks naively that it would be impolite to ask the English to leave because they are Egypt's guests, and she suggests that those who seek independence ask for the help of Queen Victoria (dead twenty years by this time), who will, as a woman, surely sympathize with them. Devoutly religious, Amina believes in the *jinn* (spirits) and continually worries about appeasing them. She transmits the colorful images and stories of her faith to her youngest son, Kamal, who will later reject them as ignorant superstition. Throughout the course of the *Cairo Trilogy* Amina earns not only her children's love and neighbors' respect but the reader's regard, attesting to Mahfouz's skill in creating female characters who are substantial and multilayered. Amina models the gradual loosening of restrictions on women as the twentieth century progressed. In *Palace Walk* she is punished with banishment the first time she ventured out of the house in twenty-five years, but by the end of *Sugar Street* Amina visits her beloved religious sites daily. She is the last person to die but in the trilogy, but because she dies just when her great-grandchild is being born suggests that life will continue, albeit much different than her own.

Although Amina's eldest child, **Fahmi,** is physically present only in the trilogy's first volume, his memory is often invoked in the second and third volumes. Early in *Palace Walk,* Fahmi's primary concern is his love for **Maryam**, the family's next-door neighbor whom his father forbids him to marry. Initially heartbroken, Fahmi later learns of Maryam's shameless flirtation with a British soldier. An intelligent, idealistic law student, Fahmi joins the political movement to oust the British, and put in place a constitutional Egyptian government. Fahmi's death in a peaceful demonstration during the 1919 rebellion represents the convergence of political and private that is a strong theme in the trilogy. The loss of their son and brother to the nationalist cause brings home the point that they cannot exist independent of history.

Yasin Abd al-Jawad, the son of his father's first marriage to the morally weak **Haniyya,** exemplifies Mahfouz's belief that behavior is genetically determined: from his father comes his good looks and lustful nature (though Yasin missed the piety and discipline), and from his mother supposedly came vulgarity and lack of self-control. Employed as a clerk in a school and lacking self-discipline, Yasin spends his free time in coffee houses and on various sexual conquests. Divorced by his first wife, **Zaynab** (a union arranged by his father in an attempt to curb the young man's sexual excesses after he is caught raping a black servant on the roof of his family's home), Yasin then marries Maryam, the girl his brother Fahmi once loved, and this marriage fails—as well. Having carried on an affair with Maryam's mother, **Bahija**, during their engagement, Yasin is later caught dallying with Zanuba, his father's former lover. Although it is initially scandalous, Yasin's marriage to Zanuba proves relatively stable.

Like their mother, the Abd al-Jawad daughters are initially confined inside their home until their father arranges marriages for them. As the trilogy progresses, however, these younger women experience fewer restrictions than their mother knew. **Khadija** (who inherited a large nose from her father) is endowed with a strong, domineering personality and quick wit. Despite Khadija's sharp-tongued retorts to family members, she is fiercely loyal to them and adds, as Yasin notes after her departure, a welcome spice to their gatherings. After marrying the good-natured but indolent Ibrahim Shawkat, Khadija quickly asserts her dominance over her new family, fighting epic battles with her widowed mother-in-law and emerging as the stronger partner in her marriage. Unlike her sister and her brother Yasin, Khadija manifests her parents' energy and efficiency, qualities her own sons will also reflect.

In contrast to Khadija, the golden-haired **Aisha** is portrayed as beautiful but useless and vain and interested only in singing. She resembles her husband, Khalil Shawkat, in her carefree indolence, an approach to life that is shattered by the deaths of her husband, sons, and beloved daughter. Aisha's grief leaves her mentally ill, and her deterioration into complete insanity by the end of *Sugar Street* is one of the trilogy's most poignant tragedies.

The wealthy, lazy brothers who marry the Abd al-Jawad sisters are **Khalil and Ibrahim Shawkat**, who regard work with contempt and have no interest in public affairs. The events in the trilogy prove that what Mahfouz refers to as "Shawkatism"—the attempt to stand outside the current of history—is ultimately ill-fated. While Ibrahim is just as useless as his brother, he is redeemed by his energetic, committed wife, but Khalil and Aisha see their indolence punished by the destruction of their family. Khadija and Ibrahim's children include **Abd al-Munim**, who believes traditionalism is the answer to Egypt's problems and thereby joins the Muslim Brethren, and **Ahmad**, who thinks his country should embrace the progressive values of science and socialism. Critics consider Ahmad to be the reincarnation of Fahmi, as well as an example of what Kamal might have become if he had not been crippled by self-doubt. Together the brothers reflect the division between traditionalism and modernism that dominated their society. As the trilogy closes, both have been imprisoned for their beliefs, a circumstance that may reflect Mahfouz's moralistic view of social life—that people should be willing to make personal sacrifices to benefit the whole of humanity.

The other Abd al-Jawad grandchildren include Yasin's son, Ridwan, an attractive, ambitious young man who uses his homosexuality to gain political privileges; and **Naima**, Aisha's beautiful, lighthearted, music-loving daughter, who dies in childbirth after marrying her cousin Abd al-Munim. Between the end of *Palace of Desire* and the beginning of *Sugar Street*, Aisha's sons Muhammed and Uthman die in the typhoid epidemic that also kills their father.

Many pages of *Palace Walk* are devoted to Kamal's unrequited passion for **Aida Shaddad**, the beautiful sister of Kamal's wealthy, aristocratic friend **Husayn Shaddad**. Educated in Paris, Aida belongs to Egypt's Westernized, more secular upper class, and Kamal is put off by her ignorance about Islam (whereas she is well versed in Christianity) and the ease with which she breaks traditional sanctions. At the same time Kamal is dazzled by Aida's glamour and sophistication, and her modern habits and qualities figure in the gradual secularization he undergoes. But Kamal recognizes all along that he will never win her regard for she is three years older and separated by great cultural and social differences. Allowed to mingle freely with her brother's friends, who share their social status and gather at the Shaddad home for intellectual discussions, Aida chooses a handsome mate for herself. Rejecting Kamal, Aida also mocks his appearance, which has already caused him much worry. By the end of *Sugar Street,* however, Aida's fortunes—like those of so many characters in the trilogy—have been reversed: divorced by her first husband, she dies the second wife of a much older man; Kamal even stumbles unwittingly into her funeral procession. Mahfouz patterned Kamal's infatuation for Aida after his own adolescent experience with an upper-class young woman a few years older than he.

Another notable female character in the trilogy is **Sawsan Hammad,** who in *Sugar Street* becomes the wife of Khadija's son, Ahmad Shawkat. The product of a poor background— of which she seems unashamed—Sawsan is a journalist who shares her husband's progressive views. An independent woman, Sawsan holds a job and illustrates the modernization of women's lives, in contrast to the traditional roles played by Amina, Khadija, and Aisha. Sawsan agrees to marry Ahmad only if he promises to abandon his conventional ideas about marriage; she intends to be an equal partner to her husband.

The *Cairo Trilogy* features a broad spectrum of minor characters who help illuminate the authentic portrait of Egyptian life that the three volumes provide. Some of the most notable include such members of Cairo's forbidden after-dark scene as the physically impressive and musically gifted singer **Jalila** (who ends her life as a drunken, deranged beggar) and the lovely lute player, **Zanuba**, who has an affair with the patriarch of the Ahmad Abd al-Jawad family but eventually marries his son. The patriarch attends nightly galas with a number of longtime friends, including the prominent **Muhammed Iffat**, whose daughter Zaynab is briefly married to Yasin. **Fu'ad al-Hamzawi** is the son of Abd al-Jawad's assistant in his store and Kamal's schoolmate and friend. Once pointedly inferior to Kamal in social status, the intelligent and ambitious Fu'ad earns a law degree and becomes a prominent prosecutor; he insults the Abd al-Jawad family when he declines to marry Naima, whom he apparently considers beneath him. Kamal shares many intellectual debates with his friend **Qaldas Riyad**, an adherent of the Coptic faith (Egypt's native Christian church). **Umm Hanafi**, the family's loyal servant, is present throughout the trilogy, contributing to the smooth operation of their daily lives and sharing their joys and sorrows.

Further Reading

Allen, Roger. ''Arabic Literature and the Nobel Prize.'' *World Literature Today* Vol. 62, no. 2 (spring 1988): 201–3.

Badawi, M. M. "Microcosms of Old Cairo." *Times Literary Supplement* No. 4095 (September 25, 1981): 1104.

Bestsellers, Vol. 89, issue 2. Detroit: Gale Research.

Contemporary Literary Criticism, Vols. 52, 55. Detroit: Gale Research.

Dictionary of Literary Biography, 1988 Yearbook. Detroit: Gale Research.

El-Enany, Rasheed. *Naghib Mahfouz: The Pursuit of Meaning, A Critical Study.* London: Routledge, 1993.

Gordon, Hayim. *Naguib Mahfouz's Egypt: Existential Themes in His Writings.* New York: Greenwood Press, 1990.

Honan, William H. "From 'Balzac of Europe,' Energy and Nuance." *New York Times* (October 14, 1988): C32.

Le Gassick, Trevor, ed. *Critical Perspectives on Naguib Mahfouz.* Washington, DC: Three Continents Press, 1991.

Milson, Menahem. "A Great 20th-Century Novelist." *Commentary* Vol. 91, no. 6 (June 1991): 34–8.

————. "Reality, Allegory, and Myth in the Work of Najib Mahfouz." *Asian and African Studies* Vol. 11, no. 2 (autumn 1976): 157–79.

Shammas, Anton. "The Shroud of Mahfouz." *New York Review of Books* Vol. 36, no. 1 (February 2, 1989): 19–21.

Somekh, Sasson. *The Changing Rhythm: A Study of Najib Mahfouz's Novels.* E. J. Brill, 1973.

Norman Mailer

1923–

American novelist, short story writer, nonfiction writer, screenwriter, and journalist.

Harlot's Ghost (novel, 1991)

Plot: Narrated by Hedrick "Harry" Hubbard, a ghostwriter for the Central Intelligence Agency (CIA), the novel begins with a prologue in which Harry relates some of his family's and his own history. The son of CIA veteran Cal Hubbard, Harry is much influenced by his father's colleague Hugh Montague, whose agency code name is Harlot. The urbane, intellectualizing Hugh shepherds Harry through his CIA career, and Harry serves as godfather to Hugh's son with his beautiful wife, Hadley Kittredge Gardiner (known as Kittredge). Harry harbors a long-simmering passion for Kittredge, however, and the two finally become lovers. When Hugh is paralyzed in a rock-climbing accident that kills his son, Kittredge divorces him and marries Harry. An ominous series of events leads to the fiery destruction of Harry's old ancestral home, the Keep, and Kittredge's disappearance in the company of Dix Butler, an animalistic former CIA agent.

The rest of the book is structured as Harry's memoir—disguised as a history of the KGB—of the years leading up to these events. He reads the manuscript on microfilm in Moscow, where he goes expecting to find Hugh. The memoir chronicles Harry's education at exclusive St. Matthew's preparatory school and Yale University, his apprenticeship with Hugh, and his CIA assignments in Berlin, where he meets the wild, perverse Dix Butler, and Uruguay, where he works with E. Howard Hunt (later one of the central players in the Watergate scandal). During this period Harry corresponds with his mentor, Hugh, and with Kittredge, with whom he exchanges long letters discussing, among other topics, her theory that human nature is divided into the masculine, rational Alpha principle and the feminine, intuitive Omega. Transferred to Miami, Harry takes part in CIA operations connected with such events as the Cuban missile crisis and attempts to assassinate Fidel Castro. Harry's account ends at the time of the assassination of President John F. Kennedy, concluding with the words "To be continued."

Characters: Mailer is an important, often controversial American literary figure noted for the scope and diversity of his work. *Harlot's Ghost* (which Mailer claims is the first installment of a longer work) focuses on the inner workings of the Central Intelligence Agency (CIA), portraying it as a haven for Ivy-League elitists whose work has little or no real value or significance. Some critics contend that Mailer is offering the CIA as a symbol of America's moral ambiguity or of the importance of the covert in the American imagination. Others discern in the novel such familiar Mailerian themes as the ruthless pursuit of power and sex, paranoia, and perversity. While several commentators fault *Harlot's Ghost* for excessive length, others assert that its world is vividly imagined and the action riveting enough to hold the reader's attention.

The "ghost" referred to in the title is **Hedrick "Harry" Hubbard**, who works as a ghostwriter of planted spy novels that portray the CIA in a positive light; in addition, Harry admits at one point that he has become his mentor's "shade" to the point where he may actually supersede him. Harry is the son of a member of the OSS (the predecessor to the CIA), but his own career seems driven by a desire neither to please his father nor to rid the world of communism; rather, he explains, "I like the work." He seems to derive a vicarious thrill from working for and among such ruthless characters as Dix Butler and William King Harvey. Harry's memoirs comprise the bulk of the novel, and he serves as an inside witness to such events as the death of Marilyn Monroe, the rift between Robert Kennedy and CIA director J. Edgar Hoover, and John F. Kennedy's assassination. Nevertheless, several critics note that he never becomes a full-fleshed character himself, so that the reader wonders, for instance, why Kittredge is so infatuated with him. Because Harry is cast as a half-Jewish writer, critics consider him as Mailer's attempt to imagine himself as a CIA agent.

Urbane, cool **Hugh Tremont Montague** is a top-level CIA official whose code name is Harlot. He is Harry's mentor and surrogate father, watching over his career and imparting to the younger man his own vision of their agency's role and meaning. In fact, he is something of a philosopher of the CIA, asserting that the agency's duty is "to become the mind of America." Hugh's lectures to other CIA personnel on espionage and counter-espionage give Mailer an opportunity to display his prodigious knowledge of the CIA, although some commentators claim that Mailer's observations are inaccurate. Hugh is said to be based on James Angleton, the CIA "mole hunter" whose near religious dedication to ferreting out the communists he felt were rife throughout the agency made him one of the most notorious figures in CIA history. Hugh exhibits the same fervor to his work, so that Harry says of him, "What a man of the cloth he would have been!" Hugh is unaccounted for at the end of *Harlot's Ghost,* suggesting that he may reappear in the promised sequel. Mailer claims in an interview that Hugh is a contemporary version of Dr. Huer, a villainous character in a novel called *The Martian Invasion* that Mailer wrote when he was ten years old.

Hadley Kittredge Gardiner, Hugh's much younger wife, is a beautiful Radcliffe graduate from a family of academics. Although she remains faithful for most her marriage to Hugh, Kittredge flirts often with Harry, eventually has an affair with him, marries him, and then later abandons him for the brutal Dix Butler. Employed as a psychologist for the CIA, Kittredge devises the theory central to *Harlot's Ghost* and that may be characterized as typically Mailerian: each human psyche comprises both the rational, masculine Alpha and the instinctual, feminine Omega, making for different selves that fight for dominance within the same person. A significant portion of the novel is composed of the long, confessional letters that Kittredge and Harry exchange while Harry is working in Uruguay, which some commentators find unconvincingly arch.

Most reviewers applaud Mailer's successful incorporation of a number of actual historical figures—who are fictionalized to varying degrees—into *Harlot's Ghost.* **William King Harvey**, the chief of the CIA's Berlin station, is portrayed as a dangerous fanatic; Wilfrid Sheed describes him as "both grandiose and seedy." The formidable **E. Howard Hunt**, shown in his pre-Watergate days, runs the CIA operation in Uruguay, conducting such vacuous projects as taping an adulterous encounter between two Russian diplomats. Other real people who appear in *Harlot's Ghost* include former CIA director **Allen Dulles**, who comments from the audience at one of Hugh's lectures, and **General Edward Lansdale**, the dangerously dedicated CIA official on whom Graham Greene based one of the main characters in his 1955 novel, *The Quiet American.* Mailer created the flaky flight attendant **Modene Murphy**, who has affairs with a number of famous figures, as an amalgam of Marilyn Monroe and Judith Exner. Harry too has a brief sexual liaison with her.

Perhaps the most colorful of the novel's CIA characters is **Dix Butler**, who becomes extremely wealthy through questionable means after leaving the agency. Classically handsome but ruthless and bestial, Butler is known for torturing the spies who work for him, and he leads a wild, unscrupulous life. Harry's friend, the Jewish homosexual **Arnie Rosen**, is intelligent and shrewd but never becomes comfortable in the WASP enclave of the CIA. Harry's father, **Cal Hubbard**, a "leathery old warrior WASP," according to critic Christopher Hitchens, is straightforward, hard-drinking, and not an easy man for his son to please. Other characters in *Harlot's Ghost* include **Ingrid**, Harry's first sexual partner; **Sally Porringer**, the wife of one of Harry's CIA colleagues in Uruguay, with whom he has an affair; and **Chevi Fuertes**, a philosophizing Cuban double agent.

Further Reading

Bawer, Bruce. "Big & Bad." *New Criterion* Vol. 10, no. 5 (January 1992): 58–63.

Begiebing, Robert J. *Acts of Regeneration: Allegory and Archetype in the Works of Norman Mailer.* Columbia: University of Missouri Press, 1980.

Contemporary Literary Criticism. Vols. 1, 2, 3, 4, 5, 8, 11, 14, 28, 39, 74. Detroit: Gale Research.

Hitchens, Christopher. "On the Imagining of Conspiracy." *London Review of Books* Vol. 13, no. 21 (November 7, 1991): 6–8, 10.

Leigh, Nigel. *Radical Fictions and the Novels of Norman Mailer.* New York: St. Martin's Press, 1990.

Major Twentieth-Century Writers. Vol. 3. Detroit: Gale Research.

Merrill, Robert. *Norman Mailer Revisited.* New York: Twayne, 1992.

Sheed, Wilfrid. "Armageddon Now?" *New York Review of Books* Vol. 38, no. 20 (December 5, 1991): 41–48.

Simon, John. "The Company They Keep." *New York Times Book Review* (September 29, 1991): 1, 24–26.

Thompson, Toby. "Mailer's Alpha and Omega." *Vanity Fair* Vol. 54, no. 10 (October 1991): 150–62.

David Mamet

1947–

American dramatist.

Speed-the-Plow (drama, 1988)

Plot: The play takes place in the Hollywood office of Bobby Gould, who has just been promoted to a high-level job at a major film studio. His old friend Charlie Fox, a would-be producer, arrives to congratulate him and to propose a film deal he predicts will make them both wealthy. He has acquired a twenty-four-hour option on a highly commercial action film that will feature a popular male movie star. Bobby agrees to pitch the deal to his superior, Ross the Boss, the following morning. Meanwhile, Bobby's temporary secretary arrives for her first day of work. Attractive but shy, Karen is new to Hollywood and exhibits her naivete in various ways. Charlie bets Bobby that he will not succeed in luring Karen into sleeping with him. In pursuit of this goal, Bobby gives Karen the task of reading an idealistic novel about nuclear apocalypse that has been suggested as a film possibility but that Bobby has already described to Charlie as written by some "Eastern sissy writer." Bobby tells Karen to come to his house that night to discuss the novel. By the next morning, in addition to sleeping with Bobby, Karen has convinced him of the book's worth, and he has decided to pursue it instead of Charlie's project. Enraged, Charlie sets about to undermine Bobby's new idealism and eventually convinces him that Karen has manipulated him to her own advantage. At the end of the play, Bobby and Charlie go off together, newly committed to producing a morally bankrupt but commercially promising film.

Characters: One of America's leading playwrights, Mamet is renowned for his energetic, overlapping, often vulgar dialogue and his bleak view of contemporary life. As in his other works, in *Speed-the-Plow* American business (in this case, the film industry, with which Mamet has had some experience due to his various screenwriting ventures) reflects the corruption and decadence of the larger society. Some critics interpret the play as affirming the importance of male friendship within this context; others view it as a satire of Hollywood that exposes the moral shallowness of both those who make movies and those who watch them.

Fledgling movie mogul **Bobby Gould** has been identified as an embodiment of Hollywood's greed and immorality: his job is not to create films (for which, in fact, he has no particular appreciation) but to arrange for their production and ensure that they will be as financially lucrative as possible. Bobby's revelation to Charlie that his goal is to "make the thing everyone made last year" reveals his lack of creative integrity, as does his comment that there is no such thing as a successful movie that didn't bring in a profit. Karen's success in making Bobby swerve, however briefly, off his usual course suggests that at one time he harbored some idealism that he has since succeeded in stifling. Indeed, he tells Charlie that he has wasted his life, that it is "a sham." After a thorough dressing-down from Charlie, however, Bobby admits that he "wanted to do Good," but "became foolish" and returns with apparent relief and pleasure to his former dealmaking.

Bobby has known his friend **Charlie Fox** since both worked in a film-studio mailroom nearly twenty years earlier. Whereas Bobby has finally achieved a high-level studio position, Charlie seems to have been less successful and is still scrambling to make a lucrative film deal. Although one might more charitably describe Charlie as pragmatic, he is by his own admission a shameless huckster who cares only for commercial success and not at all about the moral content of the films he produces. Yet some commentators have focused on Charlie's honesty about himself and reverence for the ties of friendship (which he feels Bobby has violated through his alliance with Karen) as positive qualities. Critic Robert Brustein particularly admired the "primal energy and colloquial fluency" with which Charlie, enraged and frightened by the prospect of losing a lucrative deal, attacks Bobby's newfound idealism. Gerald Weales concurred, asserting that Mamet invests these characters with "so much energy, so much *chutzpah*, so much tacky charm that we find ourselves rooting for Bobby's return to chicanery."

The play's third character is perhaps its most enigmatic. Bobby's temporary secretary **Karen** initially strikes the audience as shy, inexperienced, and even slightly inept, and she projects an innocence that contrasts strongly with the two men's greed and cynicism. Given an opportunity to read the novel that Bobby has already dismissed, Karen feels inspired by its idealistic message and encourages Bobby to pursue it; her acquiescence to Bobby's sexual overture is apparently motivated by her commitment to the book. Confronted by Charlie the next day, Karen admits that she hoped to cement the deal by sleeping with Bobby. This admission, along with her earlier, proprietary comment to Bobby that "We have a meeting!," suggests to some critics that Karen is a manipulator, a con artist bent on her own advancement in the film industry. Others, however, contend that Karen is as innocent and sincere as she initially seems. Still other commentators complain that, like other female figures in Mamet's dramas, Karen is a flat character whose purpose is to serve as the traditional female intruder in the intense "buddy" relationship of two men. The Broadway premier of *Speed-the-Plow* featured pop star Madonna in the role of Karen, prompting accusations that Mamet was cynically practicing the same calculated commercialism he had satirized in the play.

Further Reading

Brustein, Robert. "The Last Refuge of Scoundrels." *New Republic* 198, No. 23 (June 6, 1988): 29–32.

Henry, William A., III. "Madonna Comes to Broadway." *Time* (May 16, 1988): 98–9.

Hodgson, Moira. Review of *Speed-the-Plow*. *Nation* Vol. 246, no. 24 (June 18, 1988): 874–75.

Jones, Nesta Wyn, ed. *File on Mamet*. London: Methuen Drama, 1991.

Kroll, Jack. "The Terrors of Tinseltown: Mamet's Black Comedy." *Newsweek* (May 16, 1988).

Rich, Frank. Review of *Speed-the-Plow*. *New York Times* (May 4, 1988): 17.

Simon, John. "Word Power." *New York* (May 16, 1988): 106.

Weales, Gerald. "Rough Diamonds: Mamet's *Speed-the-Plow*." *Commonweal* Vol. 115, no. 12 (June 17, 1988): 371.

Katherine Mansfield
1888–1923
New Zealand short story writer, critic, and poet.

"Prelude" (short story, 1917)

Plot: The story takes place in New Zealand during the first quarter of the twentieth century. It provides an impressionistic portrait of the Burnell family's move from one house to another and their first week in their new home. As "Prelude" opens, the mother, Linda Burnell, the grandmother, Mrs. Fairfield, and the oldest daughter, Isabel, are settled in a buggy packed tightly with the family's possessions. There is no room for the two younger girls, Lottie and Kezia, so Mrs. Fairfield decides that they should stay with a neighbor until the grocery man can bring them home in his wagon. When Lottie and Kezia arrive it is night and the new setting appears to Kezia especially ominous and mysterious. The various rooms of the house are meticulously described. As the days pass, Mrs. Fairfield and her other daughter, Beryl, put the household in order while Linda—who is ill or possibly pregnant— hovers on the edge of the action, wrapped in a shawl. Kezia and her sisters gradually settle into their new home, and Kezia explores her surroundings. The family's days are framed by the departure of the father, Stanley, for work and his return in the evening.

Characters: Mansfield is a central figure in the development of the modern short story, and "Prelude" (highly praised and singled out for publication by Virginia Woolf) is considered one of her best stories. Although she spent most of her adult life in England, Mansfield was born and raised in New Zealand, and she mined material from her New Zealand childhood after the death of her brother in World War I. Early on Mansfield made use of such modern techniques as stream-of-consciousness narration, flashbacks, and interior monologues. Like the musical form for which it is named, "Prelude" features an imaginative structure freed from conventional dictates. The story exemplifies Mansfield's impressionistic art: its purpose is not so much to tell a story as to create an atmosphere, accomplished by shifting the narrative perspective from one character to another. Basically plotless, "Prelude" explores the individual's struggle to impose meaning and order on a chaotic world, family and love relationships, the mysteries of childhood, and the special plight of women in their roles as wives and mothers.

Lovely, melancholy **Linda Burnell** is often identified as the central figure in "Prelude." Detached from the care of her children and house, which is undertaken by her mother and sister, Linda hovers somewhat mysteriously on the edge of the action, usually wrapped in a shawl or blanket. She is apparently either pregnant or soon to be pregnant, and her character is closely associated with the natural force of procreation. Yet Linda's thoughts reveal her ambiguity about this traditional female role: she seems to have borne her children unwillingly and does not have strong maternal feelings for them. Her attitude toward her energetic, devoted husband are also complex, for she admits to herself with characteristic honesty that she both loves and hates him. Linda compares Stanley to a Newfoundland dog who bounds toward her unpleasantly and gazes at her too eagerly. At the same time, she appreciates his loyalty and willingness to support her mother and sister. The large aloe plant found growing on their new property has sexual overtones: Notably phallic, it may represent the sexuality that forces Linda into the role of breeding machine as she bears child after child, but it may also signify the durability and mysterious beauty of nature. Despite Linda's ambivalence, by the end of the story she seems to have resigned herself—despite her earlier wish to escape—to a circumscribed destiny. Some critics conclude that Linda's relationship with her husband and children is basically satisfactory, while others focus on its oppressive nature. Many note that Mansfield never portrayed a marriage in which the partners were equal or the woman truly happy with her lot, suggesting that she viewed relations between men and women as almost invariably problematic.

Mansfield has been praised for her skill in portraying children, and **Kezia Burnell** is one of her most successful creations. Featured in several other stories about the Burnell family, including "At the Bay" and "A Doll's House," Kezia seems to be modeled after her creator—both in the New Zealand setting and in personality. As a character Kezia is a composition of impressions as she leaves one home and adjusts to a new one. This impressionistic technique is similar to the method James Joyce used in his influential 1916 novel, *A Portrait of the Artist as a Young Man.* Kezia has her mother's sensitivity, her fears (particularly of animals rushing toward her), and her reluctance to accept things as they are. Imaginative and inquisitive, she explores her new environment with mingled excitement and anxiety and with an awareness deeper and more complex than her sisters', which marks her as an embryonic artist. The scene in which Kezia witnesses the decapitation of a duck and begs the servant, **Pat**, to put the creature's head back on is often cited as significant; quickly distracted by Pat's earring, Kezia accepts the security of his embrace, a sign of the resignation to life's realities that adulthood requires.

Warm, stoic **Mrs. Fairfield**, on whom both her daughter Linda and her granddaughter Kezia are highly dependent, is the family's most stable female figure. Practical, hard-working, and calm, she takes responsibility for a wide range of necessary tasks, from making jam and organizing the kitchen to waiting on and placating her son-in-law. Unlike Linda, Mrs. Fairfield seems content with the nurturer's role, and she accepts the circumstances of her life—made possible by her age, wisdom, tolerance, and awareness of her dependence. Mrs. Fairfield intuits that the aloe, which Linda claims blooms only once every century, will bloom this year. Like the plant, Mrs. Fairfield is upright, deeply rooted, and dependable.

The family's patriarch, **Stanley Burnell**, is a big, ebullient man whose devotion to his wife makes her feel stifled; admitting that she both loves and hates him, Linda compares him to a large, overeager dog. Stanley, a conventional person who observes routine in his well-ordered life, appears content with things as they are (except for his lack of a male heir). However, he experiences moments of panic, usually just before he leaves home for work or just before he reaches home in the evening, which are only dispelled by the sound of Linda's voice. These lapses in self-assurance suggest that Stanley's happiness may be superficial. Stanley is an example of what Mansfield called a "pa man," who (like her own father and paternal grandfather) is domineering, blustering, and practical but also somewhat vulnerable and insecure. Demanding and insistent on service from the women around him, Stanley typifies the oppressive male figure Mansfield claimed was a cause for women's unhappiness. In addition, Stanley exhibits a sexual eagerness that he imposes on Linda by casting her into the physically dangerous, emotionally demanding, and circumscribed arena of childbearing. Frequently associated with the sun, Stanley's departures and arrivals to and from work at sunrise and sunset set the boundaries of the Burnell family's days.

Beryl Fairfield is Linda's younger, unmarried sister, who lives with the family and is dependent on Stanley's largesse for material support. Pretty, flirtatious, and idealistic, Beryl yearns to be married, a condition she romanticizes despite Linda's ambivalent experience with it. Beryl frets about her isolation, worrying that she will lose her youth and beauty while exiled in the country. Her unexpended sexual energies emerge when she flirts with her brother-in-law; she even considers having an affair with Stanley, though she later chides herself for such thoughts. Unlike Linda, Beryl believes that she has a better, "real self" still to be discovered; meanwhile, she concludes that "life is mysterious and good."

Kezia's sisters are **Isabel**, the oldest, a conventional child preoccupied with dolls; and **Lottie**, who is ordinary and unimaginative compared to Kezia.

"Bliss" (short story, 1918)

Plot: Set in a European city (probably London), "Bliss" opens with the thirty-year-old Bertha Young arriving home after a short trip. Pleased with everything about her life— plenty of money, a baby, interesting friends, and a handsome, successful husband who is her "good pal"—Bertha is overcome with bliss. She prepares for her evening dinner party and visits her baby daughter in her nursery, where the child's nurse seems to resent her interference. Bertha speaks with her husband, Harry, on the phone but represses her urge to share her happiness with him. She thinks about the party to come, especially anticipating the lovely, enigmatic Pearl Fulton. Bertha admires a blooming pear tree in her yard, viewing it as a symbol of her own rich life. The dinner party guests include Mr. Norman Knight, who wants to produce plays, and his interior decorator wife; Eddie Warren, the author of a popular book of poems; and Pearl Fulton, who arrives just ahead of the energetic Harry. During the evening the guests trade witty and fashionable remarks, and Bertha waits for an opportunity to share her bliss with Pearl. Finally alone with Pearl, she shows her the beautiful pear tree, and Pearl's murmured response makes Bertha feel they have made a deep connection. Bertha also feels an unexpected surge of desire for her husband, for whom she has previously experienced no physical passion. As the guests are leaving, Bertha glances into the front hall and sees her husband embracing Pearl. She runs to the window, crying "What is going to happen now?" The little pear tree, however, remains unchanged.

Characters: Mansfield was an influential short story writer who used the modern methods of stream-of-consciousness narration and interior monologues even before such celebrated authors as James Joyce and Virginia Woolf. She often centered her stories on a single moment or epiphany in her characters' lives. Like nineteenth-century Russian author Anton Chekhov, whose work she admired, Mansfield emphasized character over plot and sought the kernel of significance in an outwardly trivial event. In "Bliss," one of Mansfield's most celebrated stories, she establishes a mood of joyful expectation that is startlingly reversed when the protagonist discovers what appears to be evidence of her husband's infidelity. As several critics have noted, however, the story's conclusion is ambiguous; Bertha's closing cry is open to interpretation. The unaltered beauty of the pear tree, considered an effective symbol, suggests that nature will continue on its course.

Mansfield seems to have considered marriage a mostly negative state for women. Many critics have pointed out that none of the marriages portrayed in her work are equal partnerships. In "Bliss," thirty-year-old **Bertha Young** prides herself on her "modern" relationship with her husband; though devoid of sexual passion, they are "such good pals." Bertha achieves bliss from having a handsome, successful husband, her delightful baby (with whom she is allowed very little interaction by the child's jealous nanny), her fine house, her sophisticated friends, and even her new cook, an adept preparer of omelettes. The woman Bertha sees in the mirror is "radiant, with smiling, trembling lips, with big dark eyes and an air of listening, waiting for something . . . divine to happen." This description adds an element of mystery to Bertha's bliss that is shattered when the "something" that happens is not the profound sympathy she believes she has established with Pearl but the discovery of Pearl's liaison with her husband. A few critics have viewed Bertha as a female stereotype in her childishness, frigidity, sentimentality, and self-delusion, concluding that she deserves to be shaken out of her naive "bliss" (some even suggest that she misinterprets the embrace between Harry and Pearl). Others, however, noting that Mansfield intended her fiction as a "cry against corruption," contend that she wants her readers to take Bertha seriously—to interpret her heightened awareness as genuine. Bertha's rather breathless, exclamatory speech differs markedly from the other characters, and whereas she fails to perceive her friends' shallowness and her husband's insensitivity, she succeeds in being open to true feeling and desiring to connect deeply with others. The story provides no answer to Bertha's final question, which expresses her powerlessness and awareness of the future.

Bertha's husband, **Harry Young,** is an energetic, ambitious businessman who likes to operate at "high pressure," a trait apparent when he answers Mrs. Knight's inquiry about his daughter: "My dear Mrs. Knight, don't ask me about my baby. I never see her. I shan't feel the slightest interest in her until she has a lover." This comment seems sinister when the reader learns that Harry has a lover. The story's ending also exposes his insincerity to Bertha, for he has pretended to dislike Pearl, describing her as having "anaemia of the brain."

Bertha anticipates seeing lovely, enigmatic **Pearl Fulton,** believing that only this female friend can understand her bliss. Bertha interprets Pearl's request to see the garden as a sign of communion and she thinks she hears Pearl say "Yes. Just *that*" in response to the blooming pear tree. Nothing in the story actually confirms that a deep connection has been made except Bertha's belief that it has, and she realizes this when she sees Pearl and Harry embracing. That Pearl is sexually linked to Harry seems to make Pearl into Bertha's double—a kind of mirror character who is both similar to Bertha and her opposite. Unlike Bertha, Pearl lives "by listening rather than by seeing," suggesting her subjugation to desire.

The guests at the Youngs' dinner party are humorous caricatures of fashionable but shallow upper-class society. **Mr. Norman Knight,** a would-be theatrical producer, makes pretentious use of a monocle, while **Mrs. Norman Knight** wears a ridiculous orange coat with monkeys along its hem. The popular young poet **Eddie Warren** italicizes every other word of his conversation, describing as "incredibly beautiful" such a mundane line of poetry as "Why must it always be tomato soup?"

"Miss Brill" (short story, 1920)

Plot: The title character is an aging woman who lives alone in Paris, eking out a meager existence by teaching English and reading to an elderly invalid each afternoon. As the story begins, Miss Brill is preparing for her usual Sunday outing to a nearby park. Despite the pleasure she takes in going out and in wearing her fox-fur collar, she has an unexplainably ominous feeling. Taking her usual seat in the park, Miss Brill focuses on the people around her, speculating and fantasizing about them. She sees an elderly couple who prove uninteresting, followed by several noisy children, a beggar selling flowers, and some pairs of laughing girls and soldier boys. Miss Brill feels uncomfortable when she sees a woman wearing a fur hat who looks like herself and who is being rebuffed by a man. Nevertheless, Miss Brill thinks about how much she enjoys observing the passersby and imagines herself an "actress" rather than a mere spectator. Now she notices a well-dressed young couple who she fantasizes are just returning from the young man's father's yacht. But then she realizes that the two are talking about her disparagingly, calling her a "stupid old thing" and ridiculing her beloved fur collar. Miss Brill returns to her cupboard-like room, foregoing her usual stop at a bakery for a piece of cake. As she hurriedly returns her fur to its box, she thinks she hears it crying.

Characters: Mansfield's innovations in point of view, manipulation of time, and use of the epiphany (isolating a single significant moment in a character's life) made her an influential figure in the development of the modern short story. One of several portraits of isolated, aging women in Mansfield's fiction, "Miss Brill" is an understated story with no authorial commentary—the narrative perspective is controlled from within the central character. Some early critics consider Mansfield's portrayal of Miss Brill and other similar characters cruel and snobbish, but most believe her stance to be sympathetic; acclaimed short story writer and novelist Katherine Anne Porter wrote of Mansfield that "beyond all she had a burning, indignant heart that was capable of great compassion."

Through the story's title character, Mansfield explores the loneliness of exile, the human need to belong, and the pain of aging in a hostile world. **Miss Brill** lives an apparently friendless life of shabby gentility in Paris, where she teaches English and reads to a cadaverous old man until he falls asleep. She sustains her spirits through the routine of her Sunday outings, enjoying the humble luxury of a bakery cake and the pleasure of wearing a fur collar she calls a "dear little thing," and pretending that she is a necessary part of the scene at the park rather than a mere spectator. Miss Brill uses her fantasies about the strangers around her to escape for a few moments from loneliness and insignificance. She tries to ignore the warning signs that some unpleasant revelation is coming, which include her vaguely ominous feelings and the disturbing scene in which a man rebuffs the fur-hatted woman who resembles her. Instead, Miss Brill imagines herself an actress and even fantasizes about describing herself this way to her elderly employer. She is shocked by the young couple's cruel remarks about her, and Miss Brill returns to her dreary room without stopping at the bakery for her usual treat. She misperceives the secondhand nature of her life just as she misperceives her own crying as coming from the fox fur. Mansfield drew her title character's name from her own background, for the "brill" is a common New Zealand fish that lacks any monetary or food value.

The **young man and woman** responsible for Miss Brill's cruel awakening are lovers sitting near her in the park. The girl has refused some unexplained entreaty by the boy, who, assuming she must feel inhibited by Miss Brill's presence, says, "Why does she come here at all—who wants her? Why doesn't she keep her silly old mug at home?" The girl responds with derisive laughter, comparing Miss Brill's beloved fur collar to a "fried whiting."

"The Daughters of the Late Colonel" (short story, 1921)

Plot: Divided into eight segments, the story recounts the activities of two middle-aged sisters, Josephine and Constantia Pinner, in the week following their father's death. The sisters were badly cowed by their tyrannical father when he was alive, and they are still in bonds. Most of the story is set on Saturday, one week after the colonel's death, and there are flashbacks to the death and to a visit by his grandson Cyril. The Pinner sisters are browbeaten by several outsiders, including the impertinent maid, Kate, whom they are afraid to dismiss; Nurse Andrew, who dominated their father's death scene and now seems in no hurry to leave; and the local vicar, Mr. Farolles, who alarms them with his offer to bring communion to their home. Josephine and Constantia can hardly believe their father is dead and fear they will be punished for burying him, for the expense of the funeral, or for entering his room without permission. Just as he died, their father opened one eye at them, a sight that continues to haunt them. The sisters debate whether the colonel's watch should go to their brother Benny, who lives in far-off Ceylon, or to Cyril, whose last visit to his grandfather is chronicled in the story. The sisters do not remember that Cyril refused the treats they pinched pennies to buy or that he invented an excuse to leave— they only remember that he needs a watch. Toward the end of the story, both sisters feel the stirrings of the freedom in their future, but by the end the reader knows that neither will ever realize it.

Characters: Sometimes described as a black comedy (combining elements of both humor and tragedy), "The Daughters of the Late Colonel" features the shifting narrative perspective that was one of Mansfield's most important innovations. The story is told from multiple points of view, from that of a traditionally omniscient narrator to those of the sisters themselves. Another influential technique employed here is the flashback—a return to a moment or event in the past that helps illuminate the present. A few early reviewers claimed that Mansfield was ridiculing her aging protagonists, whose lives (like those of many women in her fiction) have been permanently blighted by the tyranny of an insensitive man. But Manfield was angered by this accusation, and subsequent critics have attested to the story's underlying tone of compassion.

The story focuses on middle-aged sisters **Josephine or "Jug" Pinner** and **Constantia or "Con" Pinner** as they adjust to their father's absence and confront the future. For all of the sisters' adult lives they have been devoted to the colonel's care, always striving to appease his whims and careful to avoid his anger. His death leaves them feeling unmoored, and their mundane "busyness" in the days after his death shows their displacement. Mansfield won praise for her skill in portraying Josephine and Constantia as silly, childish, and ineffectual and at the same time generating sympathy for them and establishing the real tragedy of their situation. Their father so terrorized them during his lifetime that they still fear him; after they have, with great trepidation, buried him, Constantia blurts that "Father will never forgive us for this—never!" The elder of the two, Josephine is shorter than her sister but more authoritative and also somewhat irascible; she is described as having small, beady eyes. Reportedly modeled after Mansfield's friend Ida Constance Baker, Constantia has a long, pale face and a soft, wavering manner. She considers her decision to lock up the colonel's wardrobe and thus put off sorting through his possessions one of the boldest of her life, but in fact it represents denial and lack of will.

Near the end of the story, an organ grinder's music drifts in through a window, a sound they would formerly have had to shut out to avoid annoying their father. The sudden realization that they are free to enjoy the music if they wish sets both sisters to musing about their lives. They look at their deceased mother's picture and wonder what might have happened if she had been alive to care for their father. Constantia gazes at a favorite knickknack, a Buddha statue that has always given her a kind of "pleasant pain"; she remembers some solitary moments of passion when, many years ago, she laid in the moonlight or stood singing by the sea. These memories confirm Constantia's emotional capacity; she asks, "Now? Now?" but it is too late. Each of the sisters starts to make a statement, but in deferring to each other they forget what they wanted to say. The sun slides behind a cloud, a symbol that nothing will change in the stifled lives of Josephine and Constantia.

The otherwise unnamed **Colonel** is physically present in only a few of the eight segments, but his negative influence permeates the story. Irascible, overbearing, and bullying, he demands servility from his daughters yet disdains them for being servile. At the moment of his death, the colonel opens one eye to stare accusingly at them, and thus he disables them even from the grave. Critic James H. Justus describes the colonel as Mansfield's "most extreme statement on the assertive male who subordinates and shapes to his own ends the lives around him."

The Colonel's grandson **Cyril** manages to escape–his ornery grandfather's influence, unlike his aunts, by living far away and visiting only rarely. One such visit, recounted in a flashback, establishes that Cyril is handsome but irresponsible and insensitive to his indulgent aunts, who sacrifice to buy him special cakes that he does not eat; he later declines to attend the funeral. A humorous episode occurs when the sisters discuss with Cyril the important question of whether his father enjoys meringues (an airy kind of cake), then labor mightily to relay the content of their conversation to the nearly deaf colonel. When he finally understands that they have been talking about his son's fondness for meringues, the colonel looks at Cyril in mystification and blusters, "What an esstrordinary [sic] thing to come all this way here to tell me!" Cyril's father, **Benny**, also escapes the colonel's tyranny by moving to Ceylon (now Sri Lanka). Their brother is never on their minds at all for a long time after their father's death, highlighting that they have always viewed the colonel as their own responsibility. When the sisters discuss whether to give their father's watch to Benny or Cyril, they both picture a black man running through a field to deliver their brown-paper-wrapped parcel to Benny.

Among the story's other characters is **Kate**, the insolent and impertinent young maid. Despite their suspicion that she snoops through their drawers, the sisters cannot bring themselves to dismiss her. Critics especially relished the sentence "And proud young Kate, the enchanted princess, came in to see what the old tabbies wanted now" for capturing Kate's brash self-possession and its intimidating effect on the envious sisters. The imperious Nurse Andrew, with a laugh "like a spoon tinkling against a medicine glass," is another presence that Josephine and Constantia are unsure how to dispel. Unable to say so, they resent Nurse Andrew for usurping their place at their father's side as he dies. The sisters acquiesce to **Mr. Farolles**, the vicar of St. John's church, when he asks if their father's death was peaceful, but the memory of his opening one accusatory eye haunts them with the possibility that he was actually angry at them when he died. Their panic at Mr. Farolles's suggestion to offer communion in their living room may either indicate their fear of new situations or subconscious unwillingness to offer the divine to the man who so profanely blighted their lives.

"A Doll's House" (short story, 1922)

Plot: "A Doll's House" takes place at the New Zealand home of the Burnell family, who are featured in several Mansfield stories. The gift from a family friend of a wonderful doll's house has made the Burnell daughters—Isabel, Lottie, and Kezia—instant celebrities among their friends. Kezia is enchanted by a miniature lamp that sits on the tiny dining room table. The Burnells have allowed their daughters to invite their schoolmates to view the doll's house, but only under a set of very strict rules: only two are to come at one time, they will not be served tea, and they must stand quietly in the outside courtyard where the doll's house has been placed. Kezia and her sisters attend a school in which, much to the disapproval of their parents, children of different social classes are mixed together. At the bottom rung are the Kelvey girls, Lil and "our Else," whose mother is a washerwoman and whose father is supposedly in jail. The Kelveys are shunned and cruelly taunted by the other children. One day Kezia sees Lil and our Else walking down the street near her home and decides to show them the doll's house. Lil hesitates, but her younger sister pleads with her eyes, so the two venture into the courtyard with Kezia. They have been looking at the enchanting structure for only a moment when Kezia's Aunt Beryl arrives and shoos them away. Aunt Beryl scorns the Kelveys and scolds Kezia for granting them the inappropriate privilege. In the story's final scene, the Kelvey girls have scampered away from the Burnell house and now sit down to rest. With a "rare smile," our Else tells her sister, "I seen the little lamp."

Characters: Like many of Mansfield's most accomplished stories, "A Doll's House" is set in New Zealand, where the author was born and raised and where she turned for inspiration after the death of her brother in World War I. Given the same name as Henrik Ibsen's 1879 play, which evokes a similar sense of domestic oppression and revolt against social rules, the story features the Burnell family, who also appear in such stories as "Prelude" and "At the Bay." Critics have seen the doll's house itself as both a central symbol of conventional domesticity and materialism and a spur to the imagination. The story's concerns include class prejudice, resistance to stereotypical female roles, and the plight of the outsider or artist.

While in the other Burnell stories the narrative focus shifts among the various family members, this one centers on **Kezia**, the middle daughter. Often viewed as an autobiographical character, Kezia is a sensitive, imaginative child who exhibits signs of an artistic vocation. Her fascination with the tiny lamp in the doll's house may be considered such a sign, as the lamp is traditionally associated with the dawning of knowledge and insight. In addition, Kezia's rebellion against the rules of her society, as when she invites the socially outcast Kelvey girls to view the doll's house, marks her as an outsider. Kezia does undergo a moment of indecision that commentators have compared to that of the protagonist of Mark Twain's 1884 novel, *The Adventures of Huckleberry Finn,* when he must decide whether to help the runaway slave, Jim, escape. Kezia's swinging back and forth on the gate as she watches the Kelveys approaching indicates her vacillation. Like Huck Finn, Kezia acts without regard to cultural dictates. She alone in her family (or, indeed, in her community) understands and shares the light of understanding and compassion.

Lil and **"our Else"** Kelvey are the children of a washerwoman who dresses them in the cast-off clothing of her employers; their father is reportedly in jail. The girls are mistreated by their schoolmates (one of whom hisses at Lil, "Yah, yer father's in prison!"), and are considered unfit to view the doll's house. Lil's caution to enter Kezia's yard proves the children know about their status. Although passive and inarticulate, Lil and our Else are devoted to each other, an attribute the other children (most notably Kezia and her sisters) lack. The story's spare but powerful conclusion, when our Else's "rare" smile illuminates her face as she confides to Lil that "I seen the little lamp," signifies a link between our Else and Kezia. Despite the differences in their circumstances and prospects, both have the insight (and, many critics contend, the artistic imagination) to appreciate the miniature lamp.

Kezia's parents, **Linda** and **Stanley Burnell**, are hardly present in "A Doll's House"; rather, her aunt **Beryl Fairfield** personifies class rigidity and exclusivity. She is described as shooing the Kelvey girls away from the Burnells' yard "as if they were chickens" and later thinks of them as rats, never as human beings. Beryl has some troubles of her own, for earlier in the day she had received a threatening letter from a Willie Brent, demanding that she meet him or expect a visit from him. The nature of Beryl's relationship with this man is not explained—only that her anxiety is relieved after she frightens the Kelveys and scolds Kezia.

Unlike Kezia, **Isabel** and **Lottie Burnell** accept dictates about social status. As the eldest sister, Isabel claims the right to be the first to tell about the doll's house at school, and Kezia and Lottie must defer. While Kezia appreciates the little lamp, Isabel prefers the miniature carpets and beds that symbolize conventional domesticity and feminine interests. Lottie is also more conventional than Kezia, gladly changing into a clean dress in anticipation of visitors while Kezia slips out of the house.

Further Reading

Alpers, Antony. *The Life of Katherine Mansfield.* Rev. ed. London: Viking Penguin, 1980.

Banks, Joanne Trautmann. "Virginia Woolf and Katherine Mansfield." In *The English Short Story, 1880–1945: A Critical History.* Edited by Joseph M. Flora. Boston: Twayne, 1985, 57–82.

Berkman, Sylvia. *Katherine Mansfield: A Critical Study.* New Haven: Yale University Press, 1951.

Boddy, Gillian. *Katherine Mansfield: The Woman and the Writer.* Penguin Books, 1988.

Bowen, Elizabeth. Introduction to *Stories by Katherine Mansfield.* Katherine Mansfield. Edited by Elizabeth Bowen. New York: Vintage Books, 1956, pp. v–xxiv.

Delany, Paul. "Short and Simple Annals for the Poor: Katherine Mansfield's 'A Doll's House.'" *MOSAIC: A Journal for the Comparative Study of Literature and Ideas* Vol. 10, no. 1 (fall 1976): 7–17.

Fullbrook, Kate. *Katherine Mansfield.* Sussex: Harvester Press, 1986.

Gordon, Ian A. Introduction to *Undiscovered Country: The New Zealand Stories of Katherine Mansfield,* by Katherine Mansfield. Edited by Ian A. Gordon. London: Longman Group, 1974, pp. ix–xxi.

Gurr, Andrew, and Clare Hanson. *Katherine Mansfield.* New York: St. Martin's Press, 1981.

Hankin, C. A. *Katherine Mansfield and Her Confessional Stories.* New York: St. Martin's Press, 1983.

Justus, James H. "Katherine Mansfield: The Triumph of Egoism." *MOSAIC: A Journal for the Comparative Study of Literature and Ideas* Vol. 6, no. 3 (spring 1973): 13–22.

Kaplan, Sydney Janet. *Katherine Mansfield and the Origins of Modernist Fiction.* Ithaca, NY: Cornell University Press, 1991.

Kobler, J. F. *Katherine Mansfield: A Study of the Short Fiction.* Boston: Twayne, 1990.

Magalaner, Marvin. *The Fiction of Katherine Mansfield.* Carbondale and Edwardsville: Southern Illinois University Press, 1971.

Modern Fiction Studies Special Issue: Katherine Mansfield. Vol. 24, no. 3 (autumn 1978): 337–479.

Murry, John Middleton. "Katherine Mansfield." In *Katherine Mansfield and Other Literary Portraits.* N.p.: Peter Nevill, 1949, 7–31.

Nathan, Rhoda B. *Katherine Mansfield.* New York: Continuum, 1988.

Porter, Katherine Anne. "The Art of Katherine Mansfield." 1937. In *The Collected Essays and Occasional Writings of Katherine Anne Porter,* Repr. New York: Delacorte Press, 1970, 47–52.

Twentieth-Century Literary Criticism Vols. 2, 8, 39. Detroit: Gale Research.

Zorn, Marilyn. "Visionary Flowers: Another Study of Katherine Mansfield's 'Bliss.'" *Studies in Short Fiction* Vol. 17, no. 2 (spring 1980): 141–47.

Paule Marshall

1929–

American novelist and short story writer.

Brown Girl, Brownstones (novel, 1959)

Plot: The novel chronicles six years in the adolescence of Selina Doyle, whose parents immigrated to Brooklyn, New York, from Barbados before her birth. Selina's ambitious mother, Silla, wants to buy the family's rented brownstone, while her charming but impecunious father, Deighton, dreams of returning to his homeland. Deighton unexpectedly inherits some land on Barbados and plans to build a house there, but Silla schemes to sell this land and use the money to buy the family's house. Eventually Silla manages to have Deighton deported to Barbados, and he commits suicide en route. Meanwhile, Selina struggles not only with the rift between her parents but with her own search for identity. Attracted by some aspects of her Barbadian heritage but repelled by others, Selina rebels against her mother's world through an affair with an artist whose immaturity she eventually recognizes. She also plans to finance her university education by bilking the Association of Barbadian Homeowners and Businessmen but has a change of heart and turns down their offer of a scholarship. As the novel ends, Selina is planning to explore her heritage further by visiting Barbados.

Characters: Marshall is recognized as one of the first writers to chronicle the psychological struggles of intelligent, sensitive African American women as they make their way in a racist, sexist society. Yet the universality of Marshall's themes—notably the individual's search for identity—lends her fiction appeal to a wide audience. Although a commercial failure, *Brown Girl, Brownstones* (Marshall's first book) is critically acclaimed for its compelling characters and powerfully descriptive, often lyrical language. Critics especially admire Marshall's effective use of Barbadian dialect and exploration of the effect of American materialism on Barbadian-American culture.

Many critics feel that with **Selina Boyce**, Marshall ushered in a new era in African American literature by writing about an intelligent, complex young woman within the context of a black community rather than in conflict with a hostile white society. Recounting a six-year period in which Selina grows from girlhood to maturity, *Brown Girl* portrays her search for identity and thus is a *bildungsroman* (a novel of initiation into adulthood). As a child who loved poetry and adventure, Selina always identifies more with her dreamy, charming father than with her ambitious mother. For her part, Silla sees Selina as a stubborn child who deliberately aligns herself with her irresponsible father. Selina's complex feelings toward her mother are a central concern in the novel. She admires the verbal eloquence and dexterity Silla and her friends exhibit as they talk around the kitchen table, but she is completely indifferent to her mother's housebuying plan and feels constrained by the materialism of the Barbadian community. Sensitive to the conflict between her parents, Selina also struggles to discover who she is and what she wants. Her affair with Clive is an act of defiance as well as sexual exploration; she demonstrates her growing maturity by recognizing Clive's faults and ending the relationship. Selina's plan to bilk the Barbadian association into giving her a scholarship is also an act of defiance, but she eventually apologizes to the group and refuses the money. By the end of the novel, Selina achieves a balance within herself; though she respects her Barbadian heritage, Selina knows she must determine her own personality and shape her life accordingly. She comes to admire her mother and other Barbadians for their "sources of endurance . . . their purposefulness—charging the air like a strong current," and Selina recognizes her similarity to her mother, particularly in her yearning for independence. Near the end of the novel, she tells Silla: "Remember how you used to talk about how you left home and came here alone as a girl of eighteen and was your own woman? I used to love hearing that." *Brown Girl* ends on a hopeful note, with Selina planning to explore her heritage through a trip to Barbados. Before leaving Brooklyn, she tosses one of her silver bracelets into a community cemetery and keeps its twin, either a gesture of challenge or solidarity with the people she leaves behind.

Selina's gaunt, strong mother, **Silla Boyce**, contends that "in this white man's world you got to take yah mouth and make a gun." Indeed, one of Silla's most powerful qualities is her verbal facility, displayed as she and her friends carry on an easy, lyrical flow of "Bajan" dialect around the kitchen table. Silla is modeled after Marshall's own mother, whose Barbadian discussions with her "talking women" friends instilled in her admiring daughter an early awareness of language as a distinct art form. Silla's determination to buy a house and her materialism (as well as the fact that she virtually drives her husband to suicide) arise from a childhood of extreme poverty. Despite her solidarity with other Barbadians and her recognition of the beauty of her island home, Barbados represents deprivation to Silla. A house of her own, on the other hand, symbolizes victory over that deprivation.

Selina's charming, handsome father, **Deighton Boyce**, is a spendthrift, dandy, and incorrigible dreamer who is, according to the perceptive Silla, "always looking for something big and praying hard not to find it." Thus he enrolls in and then abandons a variety of correspondence courses that will supposedly transform him into a radio mechanic, jazz trumpeter, or accountant. Like Silla, Deighton is a complex character. He wants more from life than material acquisitions, is more in touch than Silla with the poetry of his Barbados heritage, and passes his imaginative qualities along to his daughter. Yet he is also irresponsible and hurts his family when he joins the cult of Father Divine, whose tenets include the renunciation of family ties. Like Marshall's own father, Deighton insists that his daughters call him not Daddy but "Brother Deighton." His frustration with racism and his subsequent powerlessness set him up for tragedy by the end of the novel. Rejected by his community and deported back to the home he claims to long for but now dreads, Deighton ends his life by plunging into the sea.

The novel's secondary characters help to illustrate and reinforce its central concerns. **Mrs. Benton** is a white acquaintance of Silla who expresses stereotypes about African Americans—she praises the "natural talent for dancing and music" of Selina's race—while imagining herself a "liberal," which heightens Selina's awareness of racism and the subtle forms it takes. Most notable among Silla's "talking women" friends is **Miss Thompson**, who operates a local beauty salon and demonstrates her nurturing capacity through the advice she dispenses and through her care of some abandoned children. Whereas Miss Thompson is, like Silla, devoted to the work ethic, Selina's friend **Suggie** resembles Deighton in her emphasis on pleasure. She works as a maid in a white suburb during the week, then returns to her apartment to dance to calypso music and indulge in drinking and sex with a variety of men. Like Selina, her Jewish friend **Rachel** resents her community's expectations of her; she defiantly cuts and dyes her light-colored hair, which they perceive as a status symbol because it allows her to pass for a gentile. Rachel helps Selina arrange her trip to Barbados. Selina's lover, **Clive**, is an unsuccessful artist who also fails in his relationship with her. She discovers his immaturity partly through his scathing indictment of mothers as clinging and manipulative—a judgment that, she senses, he extends to all women. **Miss Mary** is a senile old Irish lodger whose identity is totally submerged in her devotion to her former employers. She glorifies their qualities and activities but berates her own daughter, **Maritze**, who drowns her frustrations in fanatic Catholicism. Unlike Selina, her older sister, **Ina Boyce**, responds to their mother's dominance with meek submissiveness.

Praisesong for the Widow (novel, 1983)

Plot: The novel's central character is sixty-four-year-old Avey Johnson, whose husband, Jerome (formerly called Jay), has recently died. In an effort to ease her grief, Avey joins two friends on a Caribbean cruise. Two of her three daughters, Sis and Annawilda, support her plan, while the third, Marion, feels she should do something more interesting. During the cruise, Avey is tormented by recurring dreams about her great aunt Cuney, who was a fixture of the childhood summers she spent on Tatem Island off the coast of South Carolina. Avey is so disturbed by these dreams that she decides to leave the cruise and return to New York. She disembarks in Grenada, where she meets an old man named Lebert Joseph, who convinces her to accompany him and other Grenadians to the island of Carriacou for the annual Big Drum ritual through which they honor their ancestors. During the arduous sea voyage and her subsequent participation in the ritual, Avey undergoes a process of emotional healing as she relives her past. She reviews her childhood under the firm tutelage of her wise aunt Cuney and her marriage to Jay, a carefree, life-affirming young man who gradually becomes hardened by his desire for material success. By the end of the novel, Avey reconnects with her true self, affirms her heritage by reclaiming her childhood name, Avatara, and resolves to adopt the role of the griot (who transmits to young people their people's history and values), once the function of her aunt Cuney. Although she will return to New York, she plans to move to Carriacou for part of every year.

Characters: Marshall is the recipient of the Before Columbus American Book Award for *Praisesong,* which evidences her consistent emphasis on the importance of understanding and accepting one's past in order to achieve self-fulfillment. Critics applaud this author's insightful portrayals of African American women establishing their identities, and *Praisesong* explores this theme as well as the more universal issue of upward mobility and the materialism of American society.

The protagonist of *Praisesong for the Widow* is **Avatara "Avey" Johnson**, who undergoes a process of self-discovery during a journey she takes. As the novel opens, the decorous, always tastefully dressed Avey seems emphatically middle class. Through her recollections, the reader learns that she and her husband, Jay, begin their married life as an impoverished but happy young couple who dance to jazz records and recite poetry to each other in their tiny apartment. Over the years their struggle for material affluence cost them their ties with their younger selves. Avey also loses her connection to her childhood and the wise aunt who tells her about her people's heritage. The dreams she experiences while on the cruise indicate that it is time to attend to her spiritually barren lifestyle. Although Avey initially resists this process, planning to abandon the cruise and return home, she eventually joins the excursion to Carriacou. When she becomes seasick en route to the island, she undergoes a nearly ritualistic cleansing or purging, during which she is ministered to by a group of Carriacou women. Like many protagonists in African American literature, Avey thinks of the suffering of her ancestors on "the Middle Passage" (their forced, brutal journey from Africa), which seems to dwarf her own pain, while the women who care for her remind her of the nurturing mothers of her childhood Baptist church. Avey's participation in the Big Drum ritual completes her healing process. She reclaims her full name, Avatara, and accepts the role of passing along her people's traditions to the future generations represented by her grandsons. Thus she will retell the same stories told to her by her great aunt Cuney, especially the tale of how the Ibo people walk back across the ocean to Africa. Through Avey and the spiritual transformation she achieves, Marshall affirms the necessity of forging deeper connections with one's heritage.

Although Avey's husband, **Jerome "Jay" Johnson**, is already dead when the novel begins, he is an important figure in her recollections and represents the cost of abandoning one's true self to shallow values. Avey recalls Jay's once fun-loving and spontaneous side, sharing with her a love of music and poetry. Jay grows more somber and conservative as he struggles to achieve the American Dream; he even criticizes other African Americans who do not share his ambitions. The pressure to succeed makes Jay a different person, and eventually he is called only Jerome; his personality dulls as he shirks his ethnic sensibility. Although one critic faults Marshall for treating Jay somewhat condescendingly, most feel she portrays his desire to provide for his family with compassion. An important part of Avey's healing process is mourning not just her loss of Jay but the loss of self that he suffers when he loses touch with his heritage.

Provided as a contrast to Jay is **Lebert Joseph**, the old man Avey meets in a Grenada bar who arranges the excursion to Carriacou. Unlike Jay, Lebert maintains close ties to his ethnic tradition, as he demonstrates through his participation in the Big Drum ritual; he tells Avey that it is essential to thank one's ancestors for any success one achieves. Mysteriously associated with a local divinity called Legba, Joseph has a kind of psychic gift or clairvoyance that allows him to understand things about people without being told. He recognizes Avey's need for healing, and he affirms his knowledge of her problem when he claims to have met many visitors to Grenada "who can't call their own nation"—that is, who know nothing about their heritage and thus little about themselves. By encouraging her to go to Carriacou, Joseph plays an important role in Avey's rejuvenation.

Other characters in *Praisesong* include Avey's daughters **Sis**, **Annawilda**, and **Marion**. Sis and Annawilda lead lives as conventionally middle class as their mother and thus see nothing wrong with her plan to take a Caribbean cruise. But the political, Afrocentric Marion calls the trip "a meaningless cruise with a bunch of white folks" and suggests that her mother do something more instructive. Significantly, when Avey was pregnant with Marion, she tried to abort the baby, and this daughter has since become a troublesome reminder of the part of herself she has long denied. Avey's traveling companions on the cruise are overbearing, shallow **Thomasina Moore** and meek, staid **Clarice**, whose lack of self-esteem leads her to overeat. Joseph's daughter **Rosalie Parvay**, who bathes Avey after her bout of seasickness, is the most prominent among the Carriacou women. Rosalie's maid, **Milda**, explains to Avey the stages of the Big Drum ritual.

Further Reading

Black Literature Criticism. Vol. 2. Detroit: Gale Research.

Brown, Lloyd W. "The Rhythms of Power in Paule Marshall's Fiction." *Novel: A Forum on Fiction* Vol. 7, no. 2 (winter 1974): 159–67.

Contemporary Literary Criticism. Vol. 27. Detroit: Gale Research.

Dance, Daryl Cumber. Interview with Paule Marshall. *Southern Review* Vol. 28 (winter 1992): 1–20.

Dictionary of Literary Biography. Vol. 33. Detroit: Gale Research.

Eko, Ebele. "Beyond the Myth of Confrontation: A Comparative Study of African and African-American Female Protagonists." *Ariel* Vol. 17, no. 4 (October 1986): 139–52.

Field, Carol. "Fresh, Fierce and 'First.'" *New York Herald Tribune Book Review* (August 16, 1959): 5.

Kapai, Leela. "Dominant Themes and Technique in Paule Marshall's Fiction." *CLA Journal* Vol. 16, no. 1 (September 1972): 49–59.

Kubitschek, Missy Dehn. "Paule Marshall's Witness to History." In *Claiming the Heritage: African-American Women Novelists and History.* Jackson: University of Mississippi Press, 1991, pp. 69–89.

———. "Paule Marshall's Women on Quest." *Black American Literature Forum* Vol. 21, nos. 1–2 (spring–summer 1987): 43–60.

McCluskey, John, Jr. "And Called Every Generation Blessed: Theme, Setting, and Ritual in the Works of Paule Marshall." In *Black Women Writers (1950-1980): A New Critical Evaluation.* Edited by Mari Evans. New York: Anchor Press/Doubleday, 1984.

Pinckney, Darryl. "Roots." *New York Review of Books* Vol. 30, no. 7 (April 28, 1983): 26–30.

Short Story Criticism. Vol. 3. Detroit: Gale Research.

Tyler, Anne. "A Widow's Tale." *New York Times Book Review* (February 20, 1983): 7, 34.

Bobbie Ann Mason
1940–

American short story writer, novelist, and critic.

"Shiloh" (short story, 1982)

Plot: The story takes places in western Kentucky, which is the setting for all of Mason's fiction. Leroy Moffitt is a truckdriver who has been at home for four months recuperating from an accident. He is reluctant to look for a new job and instead spends his time working on craft kits, including a popsicle-stick model of the log cabin he would like to build. Meanwhile, his wife, Norma Jean, has been lifting weights, taking adult education classes, and learning to cook "unusual" foods like tacos and lasagna. Concerned about the apparent disintegration of his marriage, Leroy tries to please Norma Jean by buying her an electric organ; briefly obsessed with learning all the songs in the "Sixties Songbook," Norma then loses interest in the organ. Norma Jean's mother, Mabel, suggests that the couple take a trip to the Civil War battlefield at Shiloh, Tennessee, where she and her husband spent their honeymoon. Arriving at the site, Leroy and Norma Jean find it does not meet up to their expectations. As they are walking through the battlefield cemetery, Norma Jean works up the courage to tell Leroy that she plans to leave him. Leroy realizes that he knows no more about the "inner workings of marriage" than he does about the true content of history.

Characters: Mason is a critically acclaimed contemporary author whose fiction is set in the changing landscape of western Kentucky, where farms and small towns are giving way to shopping malls and subdivisions. Most of her characters are grappling in some way with the shift from rural traditions to a culture centered on television, junk food, and popular music. They are unremarkable, working-class people who usually lack money and education but who are sensitive enough to realize that something is missing in their lives. Mason writes in a plain, laconic prose style that some reviewers fault as monotonous and flat, but most praise her for her compassionate, unsentimental depictions of contemporary American lives. Critics identify two routes that Mason's characters take to deal with their confusion: they either stay put and rely on the comfort of the familiar, or they strike out and try to establish a new identity elsewhere. Both types appear in "Shiloh," often cited as one of the most accomplished stories in the collection.

During the four months that precede the story's action, while recovering from an injury, **Leroy** maintains a sedentary routine at home, collecting disability pension, smoking marijuana, and working on craft kits (such as a needlepointed *Star Trek* pillow). Meanwhile, his wife pursues an entirely different course leading her away from him. Leroy's desire to build a log cabin to replace the couple's current home evidences his wish to return to a time he imagines is simpler and more certain, even though his mother-in-law points out that actually living in a log cabin falls far short of the idyllic. When he sees the little bullet-riddled cabin at Shiloh Battlefield, Leroy realizes he has failed to learn not just about history, which he acknowledges is not merely names and dates, but of his own relationship: "the inner workings of marriage, like most of history, have escaped him." While the reader might conclude that the always forward-looking Norma Jean is better equipped to handle the future than Leroy, Mason has stated in an interview that Leroy too may eventually find a positive way to adapt to the changes occurring around him.

Married when she was only eighteen, the now thirty-four year old **Norma Jean Moffitt** is aware that something important has passed her by. She articulates this sense of loss when she connects her obsession with the "Sixties Songbook" to a feeling that she was somehow not a part of this era when it was occurring. Norma Jean's efforts to improve herself through weight-lifting and composition classes and to spice up her life with such exotic dishes as lasagna and tacos indicate that, unlike Leroy, she is looking beyond the familiar for what she needs. Thus she is one of Mason's "transients," who strike out on their own to forge new identities. In fact, several female characters in Mason's fiction are tougher and more independent than their men (who are, consequently, left behind). Norma Jean faces the fact that she and Leroy will not be able to achieve the fresh start he imagines; referring to their efforts to rebuild their relationship after the death of their baby years ago, Norma Jean notes: "We have started all over again. And this is how it turned out."

The only other significant character in "Shiloh" is **Mabel**, Norma Jean's mother, who gives her daughter a great deal of unrequested advice. Having enjoyed her own honeymoon at

Shiloh Battlefield, Mabel suggests that Norma Jean and Leroy take a trip there, hardly aware that the park will not hold the same meaning for them or that their marriage is not salvageable. Mabel is an agent of reality in another way, however; she tells Leroy that as a child she lived in a log cabin out of necessity, not choice, and that she hated it.

In Country (novel, 1985)

Plot: The novel takes place in summer 1984. Eighteen-year-old Samantha "Sam" Hughes has just graduated from high school in Hopewell, Kentucky, a small town where she lives with her uncle Emmet Smith. Sam's father, Dwayne, was killed in Vietnam in 1966 without ever seeing his daughter; Emmet also served in Vietnam and bears emotional—and possibly physical—scars from the experience. Sam's mother, Irene, has remarried and moved to Lexington, where she lives with her successful husband and baby daughter. The novel chronicles Sam's struggles to establish a link with her past as well as to plan her future, processes complicated by her boyfriend, Lonnie, and her ailing, unemployed uncle, who she fears may be suffering from Agent Orange contamination. Sam tries to learn more about her father and the Vietnam War by asking questions of the older people around her, but they seem unwilling or unable to answer her questions. By reading her father's war journal, Sam develops a somewhat more realistic view of what he experienced in Vietnam, and she gains further insight by visiting her grandparents, Grandma and Granddad Smith and Mamaw and Pap Hughes. Sam decides to try to recreate her father's experience "in country" (the name by which many veterans refer to Vietnam) by spending a night alone at Cawood's Pond. The next morning, Emmet comes looking for Sam and finally shares with her his true feelings about the war. As the novel draws to a close, Sam, Emmet, and Mamaw travel in Sam's old Volkswagen to visit the Vietnam Memorial in Washington, D. C., where all three reconcile with the past.

Characters: Mason claims that she did not set out to write a novel about the lingering effects of the Vietnam War; she had the characters in mind for a long time before her own visit to the Vietnam Memorial, during which she realized that the book would center on this subject. *In Country* features the unadorned, straightforward prose and working-class characters of Mason's short fiction, as well as her customary use of the present tense, realistic description, ironic humor, and interweaving of product brand names, references to television programs, and rock lyrics. Although a few critics feel that the novel's characters are stereotypes who lack the depth to make them interesting, most praise Mason for her sensitive yet undidactic approach to the tragic legacy of America's involvement in the Vietnam War.

The novel relates the events of an important summer in the life of **Samantha "Sam" Hughes**, a spirited, somewhat stubborn eighteen-year-old who has just graduated from high school and is unsure whether she wants to attend college in the fall or take a job at the local Burger Boy. Critics pay tribute to Mason for her depiction of Sam's speech; its references to rock lyrics and television and its frequent sarcasm strike commentators as an authentic viewpoint of a typical American teenager. *In Country* is considered a novel of initiation because it chronicles Sam's maturation as she gropes with both the past and the present and attempts to establish a deeper sense of herself and her place in the world. A variety of strong feelings are percolating within Sam, including confusion about her future and whether it includes Lonnie or even the town of Hopewell, jealousy toward and longing for her absent mother, anxiety about her uncle's physical and emotional health, and resentment toward the Vietnam War for taking her father away before she had a chance to get to know him. Sam grows almost obsessively interested in the war, partly due to her concern about her uncle and his veteran friends and partly because of its impact on her own life. She finds the adults around her reluctant to discuss those years, and history books provide no answers. Sam turns to her father's war journal to learn about him and about his experiences in Vietnam; she emerges shocked by the realities of war and her father's casual attitude toward killing "gooks." Although Sam's overnight interlude at Cawood's Pond is far too tame to reveal much about the lives of American soldiers in Vietnam, she gains some new insights through her subsequent talk with Emmet, during which his grief surfaces that nothing he could do now would be meaningful after having been "in country." Sam reaches a new level of love and understanding toward her uncle, and her sympathy for her naive, frightened young father also grows. The trip to Washington, D. C., resolves the summer's quest and uncertainty, for Sam finds her father's name on the black wall of the Vietnam Memorial. By sharing this experience with her uncle and grandmother, she forges a strong connection with the past. Sam also faces the future squarely and with excitement, planning to leave Hopewell for college and further exploration of the wider world.

Unlike his friend (and Samantha's father) Dwayne Hughes, thirty-five-year-old **Emmet Smith** survived the Vietnam War and went home, only to experience the same bewilderment felt by many returning Vietnam veterans when they encountered hostility or indifference. Emmet also resembles other veterans of this era in his inertia and his feeling that conventional work is meaningless after the mingled horror and excitement of his war experiences. He also finds relationships difficult and spends most of his time home alone watching television. Emmet rarely discusses the war, except to decry it as a waste or to complain about the Veterans Administration's neglect of those who fought in Vietnam. Sam knows that despite his silence, Emmet is deeply scarred; she also worries that he may suffer from exposure to Agent Orange, which supposedly produces physical symptoms like those Emmet has experienced. It is not until their encounter at Cawood's Pond, however, that Emmet shares with Sam his true feelings about Vietnam, an experience that seems to set in motion a healing process. He tells Sam that he knows something is wrong with him, that "[it's] like something in the center of my heart is gone and I can't get it back." Yet, as Sam points out, he demonstrates his capacity for love in his concern for her, adopting the protective role usually assumed by Sam and coming to rescue her. Sam now learns that Emmet's longtime interest in birds and search for one bird in particular results from in his Vietnam experience: while fighting there he saw a white egret, which became his only positive memory of that time: "That beautiful bird just going about its business with all that crazy stuff going on." Thus the egret serves as a symbol of the possibility of rising above horror to reach love and beauty. Although Emmet tells Sam that "you can't learn from the past," he does seem to achieve peace when he visits the Vietnam Memorial. Emmet sits crosslegged and absorbs the deaths of his friends through seeing their names etched on the wall, and his final, radiant smile indicates the beneficial effect of the visit.

Through Sam's grandmother, **Mamaw**, Mason explores the effect of the Vietnam War on the generation of parents whose children fought in it. After a two-year lapse, Sam visits her father's family in the hope of discovering some clues to her own past. There she learns more about her parents' relationship, which she has previously idealized but now sees as a conventional relationship between two very young people. She also learns her grandparents' view of the war when Mamaw maintains that her son died for a noble cause. She visits the memorial with Emmet and Sam. The journey is to Washington is difficult for this heavy, unsophisticated woman, who is amazed by many of the trappings of contemporary life (such as credit cards and plastic coffee-creamer dispensers). Mason portrays with both comedy and pathos Mamaw's physical struggle to reach her son's name, located high on the black wall. Her tears when she does touch the name indicate that this experience liberates her as well; finally, her great loss has been publicly acknowledged.

Sam is frustrated because her mother, **Irene**, is unable to remember much about the Vietnam War, when she was a very young bride, mother, and then widow. Apparently as independent and spirited as Sam is, Irene has remarried and moved to Lexington with her prosperous husband and baby daughter, while Sam stays in Hopewell with Emmet. Mildly jealous of her half sister, Sam longs for the old days when she and Irene would watch television and eat popcorn together, and she plays records from the 1960s as a way of connecting with her mother. Irene voices the view that some critics say is actually Mason's that it is primarily country boys who paid the ultimate price for Vietnam.

Other members of Sam's family include **Pap Hughes**, Mamaw's husband, and **Grandma and Granddad Smith**, whose conversation reveals the conflicting opinions that existed within their generation about whether American boys should be fighting in Vietnam. Granddad Smith reminds his wife that Emmet was eager to go to Vietnam, while Grandma Smith talks with regret about the changes that occurred during the 1960s, when traditional values were tarnished or lost. Other characters in the novel include Emmet's fellow veteran **Tom**, with whom Sam nearly has a love affair and who sells her his dilapidated but serviceable Volkswagen; Sam's best friend **Dawn**, who exemplifies for Sam the constricting nature of some women's roles because her pregnancy seems likely to tie her permanently to Hopewell; and **Lonnie**, Sam's boyfriend, who has just lost his job but nevertheless wants to marry her, a prospect she instinctively resists.

Further Reading

Becker, Robin. "Fear-of-Success Stories?" *Women's Review of Books* Vol. 1, no. 7 (April 1984): 5–6.

Boston, Anne. "With the Vets in Hopewell." *Times Literary Supplement* no. 4333 (April 18, 1986): 416.

Broyard, Anatole. Review of *Shiloh and Other Stories*. *New York Times* (November 23, 1982): C14.

Conarroe, Joel. "Winning Her Father's War." *New York Times Book Review* (September 15, 1985): 7.

Contemporary Literary Criticism. Vols. 28, 43. Detroit: Gale Research.

Dictionary of Literary Biography. 1987 Yearbook. Detroit: Gale Research.

Durham, Sandra Bonilla. "Women and War: Bobbie Ann Mason's *In Country*." *Southern Literary Journal* Vol. 22, no. 2 (spring 1990): 45–52.

Kakutani, Michiko. Review of *In Country*. *New York Times* (September 4, 1985): C20.

Newman, Robert. Review of *Shiloh and Other Stories*. *Carolina Quarterly* Vol. 35, no. 3 (spring 1983): 92–3.

Pietro, Thomas de. "In Quest of the Bloody Truth." *Commonweal* Vol, no. 19 (November 1, 1985): 620–22.

Quammen, David. "Plain Folk and Puzzling Changes." *New York Times Book Review* (November 21, 1982): 7, 33.

Ryan, Maureen. "Stopping Places: Bobbie Ann Mason's Short Stories." *Women Writers of the Contemporary South*. Ed. Peggy Whitman Prenshaw. Oxford: University Press of Mississippi, 1984, pp. 283–94.

Short Story Criticism. Vol. 4. Detroit: Gale Research.

Towers, Robert. "American Graffiti." *New York Review of Books* Vol. 29, no. 20 (December 16, 1982): 38–40.

Tyler, Anne. "Kentucky Cameos." *New Republic* Vol. 187, no. 17 (November 1, 1982): 36, 38.

Vigderman, Patricia. "K-Marts and Failing Farms." *Nation* Vol. 236, no. 11 (March 19, 1983): 345–47.

Wilhelm, Albert E. "Making Over or Making Off: The Problem of Identity in Bobbie Ann Mason's Short Fiction." *Southern Literary Journal* Vol. 18, no. 2 (spring 1986): 76–82.

Peter Matthiessen
1927–

American novelist, nonfiction writer, short story writer, and editor.

At Play in the Fields of the Lord (novel, 1965)

Plot: The novel takes place in the early 1960s in a fictional South American province called Oriente State, located somewhere in the Amazon jungle. A group of American missionaries arrives in the remote area inhabited by the Niaruna people, whom they hope to convert to Christianity. Martin Quarrier, the leader of the missionaries, is accompanied by his wife, Hazel, and young son, Billy, as well as an assistant, Les Huben, and Les's wife, Andy. At about the same time, Lewis Moon—a disenchanted, part-Cheyenne mercenary who has been working for the unscrupulous local military leader, Commandante Guzman—parachutes into a Niaruna encampment. Accepted as a near-god descended from heaven, he plans to help the Niaruna resist the threats to their spiritual and natural environments. Moon befriends the Niaruna's chief, Boronai, but arouses the ire of the suspicious young Aeore, who waits for a chance to discredit Moon. Meanwhile, Quarrier establishes a base on the river but finds the Niaruna impervious to his teachings, while his wife grows increasingly distraught and immobilized by fear. When Billy dies of a tropical fever, Huben insensitively characterizes the loss as a gift from God that will produce more Niaruna conversions. After an encounter with Andy, Moon contracts influenza and unintentionally brings the disease into the Niaruna community. No longer a part of either the white or Niaruna worlds, Moon drifts off in Boronai's funeral canoe to an unknown place.

Characters: Matthiessen is a respected nonfiction writer whose novels reflect his background as an anthropologist and naturalist. He writes with compassion and intensity about threatened cultures, peoples, wildlife, and environments in many different parts of the world. Considered one of his most accomplished works, *At Play in the Fields of the Lord* combines a riveting plot with interesting characters and vivid, sometimes lyrical prose. The novel has been likened to those of early-twentieth-century writer Joseph Conrad because of its dark, gloomy atmosphere and depiction of a tragic encounter between Europeans and a less developed society. Matthiessen inverts the stereotype of savage Indians who are "civilized" by the whites entering their world and portrays instead how a traditional culture and ecological system are damaged by the arrival of outsiders.

The novel's two most prominent figures, Martin Quarrier and Lewis Moon, are contrasting characters who both attempt to help the Niaruna—each according to his convictions—and who both are unsuccessful. **Martin Quarrier** is a Protestant missionary who does not foresee the challenges and sacrifices he will encounter among the Niaruna. He discovers that his physical clumsiness, weak eyesight, and lack of stamina are greater defects in this harsh jungle than in other settings, and that he was naive about how easy it would be to convert the area's inhabitants. The Niaruna prove indifferent to his teachings, his wife gradually loses her sanity, and his son dies, while all along the way Quarrier exhibits, according to critic Thomas Curley, a "steady, stupid honesty" that is "at first ridiculous, becomes exasperating and then, despite oneself . . . admirable.'' Indeed, Quarrier is an essentially good person who, under other circumstances, might have acted on his deepening insight. Instead, Quarrier dies at the hands of a supposed Christian convert employed by Guzman.

Although the half-Cheyenne **Lewis Moon** differs from Quarrier in most ways, he too has to abandon his original goals among the Niaruna. Moon's unhappy childhood on an Indian reservation has left him with a strong dislike for missionaries and the hypocrisy of white culture, a distaste not altered by his college education. As *At Play in the Fields of the Lord* begins, the thoroughly disenchanted Moon has accepted a job helping Commandante Guzman subdue the Niaruna. But Moon finds himself admiring these people (one of whom has the audacity to shoot an arrow at his airplane) and decides to help them resist the forces that threaten their way of life. An Indian himself, Moon adapts well to life with the Niaruna. Interpreted as an emissary from the gods, he is renamed Kisu-Mu and even given a Niaruna woman. Thus Moon seems to bridge the white society of the north and the indigenous culture of the south; for example, Moon achieves a harmony with nature that aligns him with the Niaruna, yet his plan to organize a military resistance evidences the exploitative north. Despite his desire to help the Niaruna, Moon is responsible for many of their deaths when he introduces influenza among them, and he must flee from them as well as from the world of whites. His retreat into the jungle and an unknown destiny may signify either immersion into a Conradian ''heart of darkness'' or a more positive union with nature.

The pastoral efforts of Quarrier's assistant missionary, **Les Huben**, are also rejected, but he is less honest in his reaction to that rejection. He demonstrates how out of touch he is with reality when he interprets the death of Billy as God's method for converting the Niaruna. Among the novel's missionary characters, Huben's attractive, sensitive wife, **Andy**, is perhaps the one least negatively affected by her environment. Warm and nurturing, she consoles the others on their losses and also expresses sympathy for the Niaruna. Ironically, however, the well-meaning Andy also introduces influenza among the Niaruna—after an unexpected encounter with Moon—further dramatizing the apparently unbridgeable gap between white and indigenous cultures. After arriving at the isolated mission, Quarrier's wife, **Hazel**, grows increasingly passive, sullen, and fearful, then nearly catatonic. Living among an unfamiliar people in a harsh environment, she feels oppressed by the immediacy of both sex and death around her, and after the death of her son, she retreats completely into her own mind. Unlike the other members of the missionary community, nine-year-old **Billy** is interested in the Niaruna's language and culture.

Critics praise Matthiessen for portraying the novel's Indian characters as neither particularly brutal nor completely noble, although they are notably adaptable and stoic in their relationship with their environment and responses to what happens to them. The Niaruna's chief, **Boronai**, befriends Moon, helps him understand his people's ways, and even shares his own woman with his new friend. The influenza that kills Boronai could be interpreted as a symbol of the gulf between the two cultures whose encounter is depicted in the novel. It was Boronai's rival, **Aeore**, who impressed Moon by shooting an arrow at his airplane. Aeore refuses to accept Moon's godly status among the other Niaruna and waits for a chance to discredit or hurt him; after Boronai's death he persuades the others to attack the mission. **Pindi**, Moon's lover, kills her female infant in order to enhance its male twin's chances for survival; Uyuyu, a Niaruna convert to Christianity, kills Quarrier during Guzman's military intervention.

Commandante Guzman, the imperious, ruthless military governor of Oriente, rules tyrannically over the people of the town of Madre de Dios while plotting to overcome the Niaruna and exploit the land they inhabit. The town's other leading citizen, the Dominican priest **Father Xantes**, is not as corrupt as Guzman but assumes no responsibility to his flock, preferring instead to silently witness their suffering. Xantes is much more realistic about the slim chances for true conversions among the Niaruna than Quarrier. Commentators laud Matthiessen for his portrayal of **Wolfie**, Moon's lusty, boozing fellow mercenary. Though slovenly and uncouth, Wolfie is honest and essentially likable.

Further Reading

Bawer, Bruce. "Nature Boy: The Novels of Peter Matthiessen." *New Criterion* Vol. 6, no. 10 (June 1988): 32–40.

Contemporary Literary Criticism. Vols. 5, 7, 11, 32. Detroit: Gale Research.

Curley, Thomas. Review of *At Play in the Fields of the Lord. Commonweal* Vol. 83, no. 13 (January 7, 1966): 413–14.

Dictionary of Literary Biography. Vol. 6. Detroit: Gale Research.

Patteson, Richard F. "*At Play in the Fields of the Lord*: The Imperialist Idea and the Discovery of the Self." *Critique* Vol 21, no. 2 (1979): 5–14.

Trachtenberg, Stanley. "Accommodation and Protest." *Yale Review* Vol. 55, no. 3 (March 1966): 444–50.

Cormac McCarthy
1933–
American novelist.

Outer Dark (novel, 1968)

Plot: The novel takes place at an unspecified time in a mountainous area designated only as Johnson County. Culla and Rinthy Holme are a brother and sister who live together in an isolated cabin. Their incestuous relationship results in the birth of a baby that Culla, in shame and fright, abandons in the woods. He tells Rinthy the baby has died, but she does not believe him and goes out to find her child. She suspects that Culla has given the baby to a wandering tinker who visited the cabin before the baby's birth. Culla later sets out after Rinthy, although he makes no real effort to find her. The novel recounts the different experiences of these two travelers: seemingly protected by her inherent innocence and maternal grace, Rinthy is treated kindly by those she meets, while Culla encounters only suspicion and threats. Culla frequently interacts with a gruesome trio of men whose identities are never revealed but who range over the countryside wreaking death and destruction, while Culla is invariably blamed for their deeds. These dark men eventually kill the tinker and take Rinthy's baby, for whom the tinker has been caring. Culla stumbles upon the trio at their campsite and tries to convince them to give the baby back to his sister. But when he refuses to admit that he is the baby's father, the trio's leader slits its throat. Rinthy later arrives at the site and discovers the bones of the tinker and her baby; not knowing what to make of this sight, she falls asleep. Culla, meanwhile, seems doomed to perpetual wandering. At the end of the novel, which takes place years later, he meets a blind man in whose sightless journeying he fails to recognize his own image.

Characters: Long recognized as an important contemporary novelist, McCarthy has only recently gained widespread recognition. Due to his skillful blending of Appalachian dialect with archaic diction and a polysyllabic vocabulary, along with his creation of a highly regionalized world in which universal themes are explored, McCarthy is placed within the southern Gothic literary tradition that features such writers as William Faulkner and Flannery O'Connor. Some critics claim that McCarthy blatantly imitates Faulkner, although most point out that his concerns and perspective differ from Faulkner's. McCarthy's work (like O'Connor's) reveals his Catholic background in its frequent emphasis on evil, sin, morality, and retribution. Structured as a kind of allegory or folk tale, *Outer Dark* is marked by both an abundance of violence and horror and a focus on the notion of redemption. It exhibits some of the strongest elements of McCarthy's writing, including his dark humor, intense characterizations, and interweaving of the mythic and the naturalistic.

Culla Holme and his sister live in complete isolation, far from the influence of any civic or moral authority. Both embark on journeys through a landscape that is notably mythical—a spiritual wasteland in which horrific things happen. The seemingly innocent Rinthy is treated kindly by the strangers she meets on the way, but Culla encounters only suspicion and distaste. He is repeatedly mistaken for being a suspect and fugitive, and the harsher treatment Culla receives suggests that his sin is not merely incest but faithlessness; he does not achieve the same redemption as his sister because he lacks her simple faith. Unlike Rinthy, Culla recognizes the sinful nature of their relationship as well as his subsequent actions, and his guilt follows him wherever he goes. Although Culla is ostensibly trying to find his sister, his failure to ever inquire after her indicates that he is fleeing rather than searching. The three evil men he continually meets victimize him, yet he is the only person they encounter whom they do not kill. They are forces of darkness, yet they finally serve as judges when they question Culla if he is the father of Rinthy's baby and punish him for his denial. At one point Culla tells another character that his father once said that a man makes his own luck; the novel suggests that the evil in which Culla is submerged is his own choosing. At the end of *Outer Dark,* he is still without faith or hope and has taken the tinker's place (or that of the blind old man he encounters) as an eternal wanderer through a barren landscape.

Critic Vereen M. Bell asserts that **Rinthy Holme** represents ''a fragile human beauty'' amid the violence and spiritual devastation of *Outer Dark.* Although she is an equal participant with her brother in the sin of incest, she loves her child and feels no shame or regret about its birth, and she exhibits an admirable willingness to take responsibility for it. Her self-image is epitomized by her claim that ''I don't live nowheres no more. . . . I never did much. I just go around huntin my chap.'' Despite her sexual experience, Rinthy is essentially innocent, perhaps because she responds to the world with simple faith rather than with any attempt to understand events; thus she has been compared to Lena Grove, an important character in William Faulkner's *Light in August.* Throughout her search for her baby, Rinthy's breasts continue to produce milk, which signifies to her that the child is still alive and to the reader her maternal grace and natural quality. Whereas people immediately recognize Culla's sinfulness, they sense Rinthy's honesty and faith and treat her kindly. Some critics interpret the scene in which an uncomprehending Rinthy falls asleep near the site of her baby's death as infused with a sense of salvation, while others contend that it represents the inevitable victory of evil over innocence.

The tinker, who visits the Holmeses shortly before the baby's birth and who later finds and saves the child, is an ambiguous figure in the novel. He straps his cart loaded with pots, food, soap, gadgets, and other items to his back and pulls it along, suggesting his animalistic nature. In his constant wandering through a hostile environment, he invites comparison to the archetypal Wandering Jew. Although he is closely associated with evil (for example, he sells Culla liquor and pornographic materials), he succumbs to evil when the three dark men hang him.

Often characterized as an evil version of the Magi (the three kings who visited the infant Jesus Christ), **the three dark men** dress in clothing stolen from graves and constantly commit atrocities. The novel never explains who they are or even whether they are actual human beings; they may be escaped murderers or some supernatural manifestation of Satan himself. These evil characters kill everyone they meet except Culla, who is invariably blamed for their crimes. They suggest that they are in league with him by offering him some grisly, blackened meat at their campsite, foreshadowing the cannibalistic meal in which one of them will later partake. The black-clothed, bearded leader of the trio, who refers to himself as a minister, is perhaps the most foreboding. He acts as prosecutor during Culla's "trial" and then as the baby's executioner when Culla fails to acknowledge his paternity; the minister is at once evil and retribution for evil. Only one of the men, the psychopathic Harmon, is given a name. The third is a monstrous, mentally disabled creature who appears to feast on the dead baby after his leader cuts its throat.

Another notable character in *Outer Dark* is the elderly **blind man** Culla meets at the end of the novel, who claims that he is "at the Lord's work," looking for a man that "nobody knowed what's wrong with''—a description that might well fit Culla. But Culla turns away from the man, failing to recognize either his connection or his resemblance to this sightless wanderer.

Suttree (novel, 1978)

Plot: *Suttree* takes place in and around Knoxville, Tennessee, in the early 1950s. The son of a prominent family, Cornelius Suttree was educated in Catholic schools and at the University of Tennessee. He then married a mountain girl and fathered a son, but later abandoned his family and moved to Knoxville. He occupied a houseboat on the Tennessee River, living as a fisherman and drinking and carousing with the other residents of the tawdry McAnally Flats area. As the novel opens, Suttree is finishing his sentence in the penitentiary, where he has met a conniving but foolish country boy named Gene Harrogate who follows him back to Knoxville after both are released from prison. The novel is structured episodically, relating Suttree's experiences with the various characters who inhabit his seamy world. Already burdened with guilt and obsessed with death because his twin brother died at birth, Suttree must deal with death again when he learns that his son has died. He tries to attend the funeral but is attacked by his grief-maddened mother-in-law and is sent out of town by a sheriff. After returning to Knoxville, Suttree is forced to travel through the city's sewer tunnels to save Harrogate, who nearly drowns in sewage after blowing up a retaining wall in a crazy scheme to reach a bank vault. Suttree later moves in with a prostitute who employs him to hold the money she earns; frustrated with Suttree's unresponsiveness, she finally kicks him out. Finally, Suttree contracts typhoid fever, and during his resulting delirium he attains a kind of redemption by reviewing his life and concluding that he must renounce his old ways. Returning to McAnally Flats, he discovers in his houseboat the corpse of a man who assumed Suttree's identity during his absence, then died. Suttree decides to hitchhike out of town. He is offered first a drink by a smiling boy and then a ride from a passing car, even though he has asked for neither.

Characters: The novel *Suttree* exhibits many qualities of McCarthy's previous works— including rich descriptive detail, a predominance of violence and perversity, and an effective interweaving of vernacular with archaic dictionary and polysyllabic words. It differs from them, however, in its realistic rather than mythical setting, reflecting McCarthy's upbringing in Knoxville. Critics detect in the novel echoes of both William Faulkner's lyrical prose (to which McCarthy's is often compared) and the broad southwestern humor of George Washington Harris's *Sut Lovingood's Yarns* (1867).

The novel's title character resembles other McCarthy protagonists in his outcast, spiritually bereft status, but he exhibits a greater degree of intelligence and experience than, for example, Culla Holme in *Outer Dark*. **Cornelius Suttree** is regarded as a somewhat autobiographical character, because, like his creator, he is a Knoxville native who attended

Catholic schools and the University of Tennessee. In addition, as McCarthy has described in interviews about his own rift with his parents, whose expectations for him did not coincide with his own desires, Suttree has broken with his family over differences that are not clearly delineated. Suttree describes himself as the "reprobate" descendant of "doomed Saxon clans." Rejecting traditional values of family and work and what he sees as the corruption of American society, he instead chooses a debauched, economically precarious life on the Tennessee River. Commentators point out that although the novel is set in the 1950s, Suttree resembles the kind of social dropout who appears in much of American literature written or set during the 1960s. Affected all his life by the death of his twin brother at birth, he is burdened by guilt and obsessed with death. In the course of the novel, death again visits him when his own son dies, which reinforces the father-son motif that is prevalent in all of McCarthy's work. Despite his drinking, fighting, and carousing and his desire to remain aloof from others, Suttree emerges as a sympathetic character. He reveals his essentially humane instincts through his interactions with the other residents of McAnally Flats, into whose lives and problems he is consistently drawn. The episode in which Suttree descends into Knoxville's sewer system to rescue Gene Harrogate best illustrates this; some critics see the journey as Suttree's symbolic search for his lost brother and his own soul. Most critics consider the novel's conclusion essentially hopeful: during his bout with typhoid, Suttree achieves spiritual rejuvenation; newly aware that he has been wasting his life, he renounces his corrupt ways. His recognition of the dark forces that dominated and still threaten him is evident in his description of the ominous "huntsman" whose "work lies all wheres and [whose] hounds tire not." Suttree's discovery of a corpse in his houseboat and his subsequent departure from Knoxville signify his abandonment of his old life, while the young boy he meets (who smilingly offers him a drink of water) and the car that stops for him before he has even begun to hitchhike serve as hopeful omens for his future and for the prospect of his salvation.

Suttree meets his "country mouse" friend **Gene Harrogate** in prison, where this character's comic perversity is immediately established by the fact that he was arrested for sexually molesting some watermelons. Harrogate is a foil to the more reflective Suttree; both sly and foolish, he devises a number of ridiculous schemes that allow McCarthy to infuse a considerable degree of humor into the novel. Critic Walter Sullivan describes Harrogate as a "scrawny outrageous blunderer who steals and begs and connives most shamelessly but somehow elicits the help of those around him and a grudging acceptance from the reader." Thus Suttree risks his own safety to venture into the Knoxville sewers to rescue Harrogate, who has blown up a sewage retaining wall with dynamite in a mad scheme to break into a bank vault. At the end of the novel, Harrogate is arrested again and taken back to prison by train, and the scene in which this captured rascal contemplates the scenery from which he will soon be locked away is quite poignant.

A number of other colorful characters populate the pages of *Suttree,* many of them based on people McCarthy knew during his own days in Knoxville. **Abednego "Ab" Jones** is a huge black tavern owner who is constantly fighting with the police, and they eventually kill him. **Leonard** is a "pale and pimpled part-time catamite" (male prostitute) who manages to draw Suttree into his scheme to bury his dead father, whose corpse he has kept in a refrigerator for six months in order to continue receiving his welfare checks. **Harvey** is a nihilistic, drunken junkman whose tirades against God and life Suttree considers wise; he dies just before Suttree contracts typhoid. **Michael** is a quiet Indian fisherman with whom Suttree enjoys a relatively dignified friendship. **Reese** is a shellfisherman who convinces Suttree to join him and his large, comic family on the French Broad River for a short period of scavenging. There Suttree has a surprisingly sweet (if wanton) love affair with Reese's daughter **Wanda**, who is eventually killed in a freak avalanche. Suttree is taken in by **a prostitute** who employs him as her money holder; she eventually becomes annoyed by Suttree's immaturity and unresponsiveness and—after he destroys the car and money she has given him—she ejects him from her home. The pleasantly smiling **blonde boy** who, at the end of the novel, offers Suttree a glass of water, seems to critics to be not only a symbol of hope for Suttree's salvation but a possible manifestation of his own dead son, offering forgiveness for Suttree's past sins.

Further Reading

Charyn, Jerome. "Doomed Huck." *New York Times Book Review* (February 18, 1979): 14–15.

Coles, Robert. "The Empty Road." In *Farewell to the South*. Boston, MA: Atlantic-Little Brown, 1972, pp. 119–26.

Contemporary Literary Criticism. Vols. 4, 57. Detroit: Gale Research.

Davenport, Guy. "Appalachian Gothic." *New York Times Book Review* (September 29, 1968): 4.

Ditsky, John. "Further into Darkness: The Novels of Cormac McCarthy." Hollins Critic Vol. 18, no. 2 (April 1981): 1–11.

Lask, Thomas. "Southern Gothic." *New York Times* (September 23, 1968): 33.

Schafer, William J. "Cormac McCarthy: The Hard Wages of Original Sin." *Appalachian Journal* Vol. 4 (winter 1977): 105–19.

Sullivan, Walter. "Model Citizens and Marginal Cases: Heroes of the Day." *Sewanee Review* Vol. 87, no. 2 (spring 1979): 337–44.

Wickenden, Dorothy. Review of *Suttree*. *New Republic* Vol. 180, no. 10 (March 10, 1979): 46.

Winchell, Mark Royden. "Inner Dark; or, The Place of Cormac McCarthy." *Southern Review* Vol. 26 (spring 1990): 293–309.

Jay McInerney
1955–

American novelist.

Bright Lights, Big City (novel, 1984)

Plot: Set in contemporary New York City, the novel begins in a nightclub where the protagonist-narrator, whose name is never revealed, ingests cocaine and talks to a girl with a shaved head before stumbling home. On Monday morning he arrives late at the offices of the famous magazine where he works in the Department of Factual Verification. He is assigned to check the facts in an article on the French elections, an especially difficult task that requires him to work late. At this point we learn that the narrator is an aspiring writer whose wife Amanda, a high-paid model, recently left him and now lives in Paris. Later that night, he accompanies his friend Tad Allagash and two young women to the Odeon nightclub, where the four use cocaine that makes the narrator feel "omnipotent." The next day, he learns that Amanda has returned to New York. (He relates that he met his former wife in Kansas City and lived with her for two years before they moved to New York and married. Amanda's escalating success in modeling led to a fast-paced, glamorous lifestyle. While in

Paris for a modeling job, Amanda called the narrator to say she was leaving him. He has not yet informed his coworkers or family about the break-up.)

Maneuvered into taking Allagash's visiting cousin Vicky to dinner, the narrator is surprised to find her attractive, intelligent, and warm. The next day, the narrator is fired because of his sloppy work on the French elections article. That night he returns to the office with Tad to wreak revenge, a plan that ends with a ferret running loose and an alcoholic veteran writer passed out on the floor. The narrator's mishaps continue when he makes a scene at a fashion show in which Amanda is modeling. His brother Michael arrives at his apartment and explains that their father is worried about him and wants him to come home for the weekend so that the family can commemorate the first anniversary of the mother's death. The two young men argue and Michael punches the narrator, who, when he revives, admits that Amanda has left him and that he misses his mother. He now recounts his intimate conversations with his mother three days before her death. Much later that night, the narrator again accompanies Tad to Odeon, where he sees Amanda with her "Mediterranean hulk" fiance. He calls Vicky from the club to tell her about his mother's death. As dawn arrives, the narrator is walking home when he sees a bakery truck being loaded; he trades his sunglasses for bread and eats it there in the street.

Characters: *Bright Lights, Big City* is a tragicomic novel that blends satirical accounts of the protagonist's misadventures in the New York City magazine publishing and nightclub scenes with revelations of his true emotional distress. McInerney was lauded for his spare, polished prose, his skillful handling of a second-person narrative voice, his ear for dialogue, and his authentic evocation of his characters' environment.

The novel chronicles the unnamed **narrator**'s struggles to come to terms with himself as his marriage and job disintegrate and he depends on drugs and nightclubbing for distraction. Most critics praised McInerney's handling of the unusual second-person narrative voice, which highlights the narrator's sense of detachment and isolation. Although some commentators have found his frequently flippant tone overly sarcastic and self-pitying, others identify it as a cover for the narrator's deep anguish. The narrator is a well-educated, twenty-four-year-old aspiring writer whose situation reflects his creator's, for McInerney worked as a fact-checker at the *New Yorker* magazine, which the narrator's fictional employer closely resembles. During the one year of his marriage, the narrator devoted more and more time to the glittery, druggy social world to which his wife's and his own success had allowed him access, while his writing receded into the background. The narrator describes himself as "the kind of guy who appreciates a quiet night at home with a good book," listening to Mozart and drinking cocoa, but he never actually pursues these activities. Nor does he ever read the volumes of Faulkner, Tolstoy, and Dostoyevsky on his bookshelves. With his wife gone and his job in danger, the narrator now finds that he can neither write nor resist the lure of the nightclub scene and the comforts of Bolivian Marching Powder (his euphemism for cocaine). Admitting that he has always felt like an outsider and a fraud, the narrator remarks sardonically that he could start an organization called the Brotherhood of Unfulfilled Early Promise. The reader is made increasingly aware of the causes and depth of the narrator's distress, which is particularly illuminated by the revelation of his mother's death a year earlier. Obviously, he has reached the point at which he must confront simultaneously this loss, the collapse of his marriage, and his failure to live up to his own and others' expectations. The narrator's encounter with his generally supportive brother, which spurs memories of his mother, and his blossoming relationship with Vicky (who promises to be a healthy influence on him) suggest that he may yet recover his equilibrium. After one more exhausting night of partying, the narrator stops on the street to eat bread that reminds him of his mother's love and concludes that he "will have to learn everything all over again."

The narrator's wife **Amanda** appears in person only once in the novel, when she encounters him at a nightclub and her "How's it going?" sends him into a fit of hysterical laughter. The narrator met Amanda when he was working, soon after graduating from college, as a reporter in Kansas City. Attracted by her unpretentious beauty, her naivete, and the pathos of her childhood, he did not stop to consider the differences in their backgrounds and interests as possible impediments to a successful marriage. Raised by an embittered, impoverished single mother who resented her daughter's broader prospects, Amanda longed for escape and thus was eager to move to New York City and marry the narrator. Surprised by her success in modeling, which she initially claimed not to like, Amanda gradually adapted to the money and glamorous connections it brought her. McInerney portrays Amanda as both innocent and vacuous, and some critics have suggested that he is unsure whether to satirize or sympathize with her. At the end of the novel Amanda's engagement to an employee of a male escort service implies that the narrator, despite his own troubles, emerges victorious.

Tad Allagash is more pragmatic and cynical than the narrator, embracing his life of nightclubbing, drugs, and casual sex without remorse or anxiety, like "a figure skater who never considers the sharks under the ice." Tad advises the narrator that telling women that his wife died tragically will win him sexual favors. The narrator agrees to a blind date with Tad's visiting cousin, **Vicky Allagash**, whom he envisions as a dowdy intellectual. He is surprised and pleased when Vicky, a graduate student at Princeton University, proves to be attractive, intelligent, and sensitive; her arrival in his life seems to signal the possibility of redemption. Another generally positive force in the narrator's life is his brother **Michael**, who arrives in New York from the family's home town in Bucks County, Pennsylvania. Although Michael claims that he has come only at their father's bequest, his own concern for the narrator's welfare is evident. More practical and down-to-earth than his brother, Michael offers the narrator not only sympathy but a job helping him restore old houses. Michael's visit spurs the narrator's memories of his mother's last days, when he cared for her as she was dying of cancer and shared intimate conversations with her. Some critics have found her stated envy of her son's lifestyle of drugs and sex unconvincing.

Many of the narrator's coworkers at the unnamed, venerable magazine are portrayed sympathetically; the narrator appreciates their concern and spirit of camaraderie but realizes he cannot live up to their regard for him. His friends there include **Rittenhouse**, a highly scrupulous, bowtie-wearing, fourteen-year veteran of the magazine; the half-Japanese, ever-irreverent, homosexual **Yasu Wade**; and the somewhat older, considerate, sensible **Megan Avery**, who invites the narrator over for dinner and in whose bathroom he (after taking drugs) passes out. Less positively depicted is the rigid, schoolteacherish head of the Department of Factual Verification, **Clara Tillinghast**, whose reverence for facts overrides all other considerations. A graduate of Vassar College who resembles the subject of a Walker Evans Depression-era photograph, Clara has "a mind like a steel mousetrap and a heart like a twelve-minute egg."

Several other members of the magazine staff help provide comic relief: the **Druid**, the magazine's reticent, quietly dictatorial chief editor, looks like a "Victorian clerk"; and the **Ghost,** a reclusive writer who has supposedly been working on the same article for seven years. The narrator shares a boozy lunch with **Alex Hardy**, a bitter, alcoholic editor who has worked at the magazine for many years and whose influence has steadily declined. A drunken Alex interrupts the narrator and Tad while they are attempting to deposit a ferret in Clara's office, and he ends up passed out on the floor but not seriously hurt.

Further Reading

Blum, David. "Slave of New York." *New York* (September 5, 1988): 40–45.

Contemporary Literary Criticism Vol. 34. Detroit: Gale Research.

Hendin, Josephine. "Fictions of Acquisition." *Culture in an Age of Money: The Legacy of the 1980s in America*, edited by Nicolaus Mills. Chicago: Ivan R. Dee, Inc., 1990.

Kotzwinkle, William. "You're Fired, So You Buy a Ferret." *New York Times Book Review* (November 25, 1984): 9.

Moran, Terrence. Review of *Bright Lights, Big City. New Republic* Vol. 191, no. 23 (December 3, 1984): 41–2.

Pinckney, Darryl. "The Fast Lane." *New York Review of Books* Vol. 31, no. 17 (December 8, 1984): 12–14.

Terry McMillan
1951–
American novelist and short story writer.

Waiting to Exhale (novel, 1992)

Plot: The novel focuses on four African-American women who are all in their thirties, financially comfortable, professionally successful, but struggling with a number of dilemmas. Savannah Jackson has a good job in media relations, owns a condo and a car, and has money in the bank, but she has not yet met a man she wants to marry. Dissatisfied with her life in Denver, she decides to move to Phoenix, where her college roommate Bernadine Harris lives. Although Bernadine's life as the wife of a wealthy businessman and mother of two children seems ideal, she has problems of her own: her husband suddenly informs her that he is leaving her for his pretty blonde secretary. After arriving in Phoenix, Savannah meets two more of Bernadine's friends (and fellow members of Black Women on the Move), Robin Stokes and Gloria Matthews. Robin is a highly competent insurance executive with terrible taste in men; she returns repeatedly, for instance, to the womanizing, lazy Russell and also has a brief affair with Troy, a crack cocaine addict. Gloria is the owner of the Oasis Salon, where the other women congregate, and the mother of a teenaged son, Tarik. She channels all her energy into worrying about Tarik and overeating to the point of endangering her health. The novel charts these women's lives over the course of about a year, chronicling such events as Savannah's dates with men who are flawed in various ways, Bernadine's nasty divorce and struggle to establish a new, single life, and Robin's concern over her Alzheimer's-afflicted father. Near the end of the book, Gloria—who has recently met a considerate, supportive man—suffers a mild heart attack. Savannah acquires a new, more interesting job, while Robin becomes pregnant and decides to keep the baby. Bernadine wins a huge divorce settlement from her ex-husband and makes plans to treat her friends to some well-deserved rewards.

Characters: Lauded for her realistic, raunchily humorous evocations of the lives of contemporary women, McMillan is one of America's most popular novelists. Like her previous novels, *Mama* (1987) and *Disappearing Acts* (1989), the bestselling *Waiting to Exhale* chronicles its female characters' efforts to achieve fulfillment in a modern world rife with such problems as AIDS, drugs, Alzheimer's disease, and unsuitable men. Although McMillan was faulted for her negative portrayal of black males and her sometimes too polemical tone, she received kudos for creating a story with which many readers, African American or not, could identify.

Of the four friends featured in *Waiting to Exhale*, McMillan has identified **Savannah Jackson** as the one who most resembles her. Narrated in a first-person voice, Savannah's chapters record her search for fulfillment in both work and love. Cool and competent, she relates her experiences with honesty and a risque humor that is particularly effective when describing her ill-fated sexual encounters. Savannah is a successful media relations executive in her mid-thirties with a solid savings account, a car, and a condo, but she is not yet satisfied with her life. Her professional goal is to become a television producer, and she would like to find a man who will value her, although she claims that she is not yet desperate. Whereas Savannah's ideal man would be mature, tender, and self-assured but not arrogant, the men she meets always turn out to be irresponsible, selfish, married, unattractive, or otherwise flawed. During the course of the novel, Savannah receives occasional phone calls from her mother, who lives in financially strapped circumstances in Pittsburgh and whom Savannah helps to support. As *Waiting to Exhale* draws to a close, Savannah has realized one of her aspirations by landing a production job, and she also reveals that—having broken off definitively with the married **Kenneth**—she is dating a promising artist.

Savannah's college roommate, **Bernadine Harris**, appears to be living an ideal life in suburban Scottsdale, Arizona, where her husband is a highly successful business executive who has provided his family with a luxurious home and expensive clothing. Bernadine feels that her husband is too materialistic, however, and senses a hollowness at the center of their lives. Having scarified her own interests to serve as the kind of devoted, traditional wife and mother that her husband desired, Bernadine finds herself in a particularly precarious position when he leaves her. The book chronicles her struggles to recover her self esteem and to handle the practical concerns of the newly single mother—especially how to support herself while waiting for the divorce settlement to come through. At the end of the book, Bernadine learns that she will receive nearly a million dollars from her husband, allowing her to realize her long-harbored dream of opening a catering business. In addition, after a period when she had little interest in men, Bernadine is dating a socially conscious lawyer.

Robin Stokes is effective in her job as an insurance company executive but apparently incapable of choosing an appropriate male partner. She admits that she likes men who are handsome and sexually well-endowed, but these qualities rarely seem to ensure a satisfying relationship. Yet Robin, who claims she wants a husband and children, remains eternally optimistic, or perhaps perpetually blind, returning again and again to the irresponsible Russell and rejecting considerate, devoted Michael because he does not excite her. In the midst of her troubles with men, Robin must deal with family problems, for her beloved father has Alzheimer's disease and is becoming an increasingly heavy burden for her mother. By the end of the novel, Robin's father has died in a nursing home and she is pregnant and determined to raise her child alone, with or without Russell's help.

Gloria Matthews is a beauty salon owner and hair stylist who takes good care of her son and friends but neglects her own health, responding to the abundant stress in her life by overeating. She maintains an honest, solid, if occasionally strained relationship with her son, whose sullenness worries her but who ultimately seems destined for success. Gloria's friends worry that she has made herself fat as a protection against the possibility of romance with its concurrent risk of pain. Indeed, Gloria's only sexual relationship seems to be her sporadic encounters with David, her son's father, who finally tells her that he is homosexual. Just before her heart attack (which serves as an effective warning that she must change her habits), Gloria has begun a relationship with her sweet, helpful neighbor, Marvin.

Many critics noted that the male characters in *Waiting to Exhale* are one-dimensional, and that one dimension is negative: They are all downright dangerous, unresponsive, irresponsible, or sexually inadequate. McMillan defended herself against this charge by pointing out that "the men are on the periphery, they're not the focus of the story, therefore they don't get the three-dimensionality that the women do." Perhaps the least flattering depiction is of **John Harris,** Bernadine's husband, a wealthy computer engineer who leaves her for his blonde secretary, **Kathleen.** John is indifferent to his wife's feelings and aspirations, shallow, and highly acquisitive; he chases what Bernadine considers the white ideal of the American dream or models himself, perhaps, after the television character Cliff Huxtable. Tall, handsome **Lionel,** whom Savannah meets on a blind date, initially seems successful and sensitive, but when he starts to ask to borrow money from her she loses her initial enthusiasm. Robin's boyfriend **Russell** is good-looking but indolent and incapable of remaining faithful to her; nevertheless, Russell seems relatively harmless compared with the initially charming **Troy,** whom Robin meets in a supermarket and who turns out to be a drug addict. Robin would be much better off with nice, understanding **Michael,** but his only average looks, pudginess, and lack of sexual finesse prevent her from committing herself to him. The book's few admirable male characters include Gloria's smart, talented, if somewhat troubled son **Tarik** and her new boyfriend, the slightly older **Marvin,** one of whose best qualities appears to be his skill at home repairs.

Further Reading

Barnes, Paula C. Review of *Waiting to Exhale. Belles Lettres* Vol. 8, no. 1 (Fall 1992): 56–7.

Contemporary Literary Criticism Vols. 50, 61. Detroit: Gale Research.

Edwards, Audrey. "Terry McMillan: Waiting to Inhale." *Essence* Vol. 23, no. 6 (October 1992): 77–8, 82, 118.

Isaacs, Susan. "Chilling Out in Phoenix." *New York Times Book Review* (May 31, 1992): 12.

Mansour, Carol. "Ugly, Short, Stupid Men." *Observer* no. 10486 (October 4, 1992): 61.

Pinckney, Darryl. "The Best of Everything." *New York Review of Books* Vol. 40, no. 18 (November 4, 1993): 33–7.

Sellers, Frances Stead. Review of *Waiting to Exhale. Times Literary Supplement* no. 4675 (November 6, 1992): 20.

Smith, Wendy. Interview with Terry McMillan. *Publisher's Weekly* Vol. 239, no. 22 (May 11, 1992): 50–1.

Williams, Dana Brunvand. Review of *Waiting to Exhale. Western American Literature,* Vol. 28, no. 1 (May, 1993): 90–1.

Larry McMurtry

1936–

American novelist, essayist, critic, and screenwriter.

Anything for Billy (novel, 1988)

Plot: Set in the southwestern United States (primarily New Mexico) in the late nineteenth century, the novel is narrated by middle-aged Ben Sippy, an upper-class Philadelphian whose attraction to frontier lore and western fiction led him to become a writer of "dime novels.'' The unhappily married Sippy decides to flee his dull urban life, and he travels to the Southwest. After an unsuccessful attempt to become a train robber, Sippy meets the notorious outlaw Billy Bone, whose reputation for bloodthirstiness proves ill-founded. Sippy accompanies Billy and his cowboy sidekick Joe Lovelady as they tangle with various opponents, including other gunfighters, Indians, and the cattle baron Will Isinglass. Along the way, Billy has an affair with Isinglass's sophisticated stepdaughter, Lady Cecily Snow, and hankers after a half-Mexican *bandita* named Katie Garza. He also begins to live up to his vicious reputation, remorselessly killing a number of people for little or no reason. Finally, Isinglass's desire to protect his three-million-acre ranch leads to a bloody confrontation called the Whiskey Glass War. Billy is ultimately killed not by any of Isinglass's men but by Katie, who knows he is going to die and wants his killer to be someone who loves him. The only one of Billy's followers to survive, Sippy goes on to become a Hollywood screenwriter. He explains that it was he who gave his friend the nickname ''Billy the Kid'' when he wrote a little-known biography of him.

Characters: McMurtry has achieved the rare status of a contemporary author whose work is both critically acclaimed and immensely popular with a wide spectrum of readers. His novels depict the landscape, characters, and themes of the American southwest—particularly his native Texas—in both the nineteenth and the twentieth centuries. Like his earlier, Pulitzer Prize-winning novel *Lonesome Dove, Anything for Billy* is a highly readable, engaging adventure story that also attempts to demythologize America's frontier past. Composed of short, episodic chapters, the novel centers on the question of how and why ordinary or even reprehensible people become heroes, comments on the American tolerance for casually committed violence, and, according to Clay Reynolds, explores ''the folly of frontier myth and the futility of its continued application.''

Several critics have called narrator **Ben Sippy** the real hero of *Anything for Billy*. In an ironic, laconic voice, he tells the story of his adventures with the legendary outlaw ''Billy the Kid'' from a vantage point of several decades later. At the time of the novel's action, Ben is a fifty-year-old native of Philadelphia, a cultured, intelligent member of that city's highest social stratum who is married to an unpleasant woman and the father of eight obnoxious daughters. A self-described sufferer from ''dime novel mania,'' Ben has relieved his frustrations by reading Western fiction, an interest that eventually leads him to try his hand in this genre. He is, in fact, the successful author of sixty-five novels, some of whose titles include *Solemn Sam, the Sad Man from San Saba* and *Sandycraw, Man of Grit.* Ben leaves Philadelphia to escape his bleak domestic situation and guilt over the death of his long-neglected butler and to fulfill his long-term infatuation with the West and validate his vision of the frontier validated. In his first confrontation with the reality of the world he has entered, Ben's attempt to rob a train elicits only laughter from the train conductor. Attaching himself to Billy Bone leads to further disillusionment as Ben learns about the dismal lives and brutal pursuits of the gunfighters he has previously romanticized. Despite his attraction to the strangely vulnerable Billy, Ben comes to recognize the futility and waste of his friend's existence, which is centered on trying to live up to his own nasty reputation. Ben notes that whereas gunfighters are traditionally portrayed as ''a confident, satisfied lot . . . the truth is they were mainly disappointed men.'' After escaping with his own life from the melee in which Billy is killed, Ben writes a biography called *Billy the Kid; or, the Wandering Boy's Doom*; only one of many books written about Billy, Ben's never received much notice. Sadder but wiser, Ben goes on to become a Hollywood screenwriter and reports that he is the author of ''the biggest hit of 1908,'' *Sweethearts of Greasy Corners*. Critics have identified Ben as an autobiographical character, for like his creator he is a writer enthralled with the landscape and lore of the West but aware of its harsher, darker realities. Ben has also been compared with Sancho Panza, sidekick to the title character of Cervantes' seventeenth-century novel *Don Quixote*: both ride mules, and both try to warn their friends about the danger of their romantic delusions.

McMurtry spun his story of **Billy Bone** out of the real-life legend of Billy the Kid, whose full name was William Bonney (or, according to some historians, Henry McCarthy). McMurtry's character resembles the actual Billy the Kid in some ways—both are born in New York, taken west as children, and make their careers in crime in New Mexico—but Billy Bone meets a somewhat different end, killed not by Sheriff Pat Garrett but by his own lover. He is cast as "an untried boy who had acquired a big reputation from doing little or nothing, and now no one could persuade him he didn't deserve the reputation." When Billy first becomes known as a ruthless killer, he has actually killed only one man, almost by accident. A runty, bucktoothed hypochondriac prone to sick headaches and fits of moodiness and fear, Billy is superstitious and uneducated. For all his faults, however, he attracts a circle of loyal friends who want to protect him, who would, as Ben says, do "anything for Billy." Ben is apparently won by the aura of vulnerability that surrounds Billy, whom he describes as "just a little Western waif, with such a lonely look stuck on his ugly young face." As the novel progresses, Billy progresses from a frightened boy and novice outlaw to an experienced killer who, despite his lack of skill with a gun, commits many murders without remorse. Ben contends that he does not, in fact, acknowledge the right of anyone else to exist. In showing how Billy is, in the words of Clay Reynolds, "driven by the image of himself others—such as Sippy—have created," McMurtry highlights the hollow brutality of the frontier myth, the image of the daring, independent gunfighter whose vicious acts are glorified in popular culture.

Perhaps the most loyal and unquestioning of Billy's followers is his sidekick **Joe Lovelady**, who is as determined to live up to the image of the noble cowboy as Billy is to that of the ruthless gunslinger. Joe turned down the considerable honor of a job as foreman of Will Isinglass's ranch to ride instead with Billy, for whom he ultimately sacrifices his life. Other gunfighter characters in the novel include **Vivian Maldonado**, who is rendered nearly immobile by his love for a fourteen-year-old Apache girl, **Hill Coe**, who is astonished when Katie Garza outshoots him, and **Barbecue Campbell**, who is shot and killed one morning when he steps outside to relieve himself.

The cowboys who work for rancher **Will Isinglass** call him "Old Whiskey" due to his reported habit of strapping a whiskey jar to his saddle every morning, then replenishing it at noon. McMurtry seems to have based Isinglass on cattleman John Chisum, for whom the real Billy the Kid once worked and who was his opponent in the Lincoln County War (in which Billy was killed). Described as "a remorseless old reprobate" by critic Jack Butler, Isinglass is trying desperately to protect his three-million-acre spread from encroachment by buffalo hunters and gunfighters. Taciturn and stoic, he has carefully established a reputation for hardness and will tolerate no challenge to his authority, yet his effort to hold on to such a huge amount of land at a time when so many Americans were setting their sights on western expansion was doomed. Thus Isinglass's eventual death seems fitting: he dies in a car wreck caused by his own failure to learn how to stop the modern contraption that will ultimately replace the horse. Isinglass's memorable sidekick is **Mesty-Woolah**, a tracker and hired assassin of Islamic African heritage. Seven feet tall, Mesty-Woolah is a frighteningly adept swordsman and rides a camel.

Several critics have noted that the West portrayed by McMurtry is heavily dominated by men. Nevertheless, the two featured female characters in *Anything for Billy* do play significant roles. The half-Mexican bandita **Katie Garza** is one of several exotic children fathered by Will Isinglass. Blackhaired, dark-eyed, an expert markswoman, and possessed of a fiery temperament, Katie captivates—and is captivated by—the physically unattractive yet somehow appealing Billy, and the two become lovers. When she knows that Billy will surely be killed by one of his many enemies, however, Katie decides that she herself should shoot him, so that he will meet his end at the hands of someone who loves him. Critics have compared Katie with other willful but lovestruck female characters in McMurtry's fiction, particularly Lorena Wood in *Lonesome Dove*. The cool, seductive **Lady Cecily Snow** provides a contrast to hot-tempered Katie. Elegant, sophisticated, and extremely promiscuous, Cecily lives in a turreted, well-appointed mansion complete with butler. After the death of her English father, who had been Isinglass's business partner, Cecily's mother married Isinglass, whom Cecily claims subsequently ruined her entire family. Predatory and coldhearted, Cecily seduces men in order to use them for her own purposes. Her lovers include Billy, Ben, and her own stepfather, whom she tries to kill by putting a ground-up wine glass in his daily bowl of chili.

Other characters in *Anything for Billy* include the Apache chief **Bloody Feathers**, who is one of Isinglass's children; and **Tully Roebuck**, who seems closely modeled on Sheriff Pat Garrett in that he overcomes a shady past to become a lawman, pursues Billy the Kid (although unlike Garrett he does not kill him), and later writes a fabricated version of the outlaw's life.

Texasville (novel, 1987)

Plot: *Texasville* takes place in the small town of Thalia, Texas, during the 1980s. Like other Texas communities during this period, Thalia is suffering the effects of the decline in the oil industry that followed the decade of great prosperity set in motion by the Arab oil embargo of the early 1970s. Middle-aged businessman Duane Moore made a fortune during that period but—despite his luxuriously appointed home and other possessions—is now millions of dollars in debt. Duane's personal life is also in disarray, for his marriage to beautiful, outspoken Karla has become tedious and he has had a series of extramarital affairs; his two older children lead disreputable lives; and his eleven-year-old twins are hellions. Nevertheless, Duane's fellow Thalians consider him one of their most upstanding citizens, and he is appointed to the chairmanship of a committee to plan the celebration of the town's centennial. Meanwhile, Duane's old friend Sonny Crawford, who has been moderately successful in real estate, seems to be slowly losing his mind. Duane's life is further complicated by the arrival in Thalia of Jacy Farrow, with whom he was in love some thirty years ago. Since then, Jacy has been married twice and forged a career as a model and as an actress in second-rate, Italian Tarzan movies; she has apparently returned to Thalia in order to reconnect with her past. Jacy befriends Karla, who leaves Duane and moves into Jacy's rented mansion. Thalia's centennial celebration, which features the appearance of Duane and Jacy playing Adam and Eve in a ludicrous pageant, turns into a fiasco when the town's children stage a massive egg fight after they find an unguarded truck loaded with sixty thousand eggs. The novel ends the next morning on a slightly more optimistic note than it began, even though no one's problems have been definitively resolved.

Characters: Marked by the same exuberance, loose-jointed style, and focus on life in the American Southwest as McMurtry's previous works, *Texasville* is a sequel to his Pulitzer Prize-winning *The Last Picture Show* (1966). The novel depicts the lives of many of the previous work's characters as, thirty years later, they grapple with mid-life crises of various stripes and face the loss of their youthful aspirations and dreams. Although some commentators found *Texasville* inferior to its predecessor because of its more lighthearted, tolerant tone, many lauded it as an insightful portrait of life in Reagan-era America that suggests that materialism and the pursuit of money had replaced the traditional regard for family and community.

At the end of *The Last Picture Show*, high school jock **Duane Moore** went off to fight in the Korean War, telling his friend Sonny (who had just lost his eye in a fight with Duane over Jacy Farrow), "See you in a year or two, if I don't get shot." In the intervening years, the now forty-eight-year-old Duane has made and lost a fortune in the oil business; he reports that he is now twelve million dollars in debt and has only 850 dollars in the bank, and during the course of the novel an attempt to revive his foundering business fails. As *Texasville* opens, Duane is shooting at an elaborate, custom-made doghouse (never actually occupied by his beloved dog Shorty) with a .44 Magnum and bemoaning the general disarray of his life. His marriage to the attractive, feisty Karla has ceased to satisfy either partner, and both have engaged in extramarital affairs. Duane's relationships with various women, however, have only led to more confusion and messiness and have failed to alleviate his anxiety over the loss of his youth and self-respect. Duane suffers from perpetual fatigue and frequent headaches that seem to be outward signs of his spiritual malaise, and he notices that his fellow Thalians (whose insistence on seeing him as the town's most successful citizen baffles him) are suffering from the same disease. Duane articulates a central concern of the novel when he comments that everyone around him speaks only "utter nonsense" and seems to have "lost all balance" as the "old model" of a life based on devotion to family and neighbors has been sacrificed to money. *Texasville* offers only a mild hint that Duane will eventually be redeemed, for at the end of the novel he has reconciled with Karla (telling her "I miss the comedy") and is somewhat more self-aware.

Critic and novelist Louise Erdrich called **Karla Moore** *Texasville*'s "most outrageous, vulnerable, exasperating and vibrant character." Forty-six years old and still beautiful, Karla is unpredictable and earthy, expressing herself by wearing T-shirts imprinted with such slightly risque slogans as "Lead Me Not Into Temptation, I'll Find It for Myself," "Party Til You Puke," and "Life's Too Short to Dance with Ugly Men." Karla admits to having drawn many of her ideas about life from such mass-market publications as *USA Today* and *Cosmopolitan* magazine, including the "open marriage" arrangement that does not seem to have brought either her or Duane much happiness. Karla is an ardent consumer and a believer in dramatic gestures; for example, depressed over having missed seeing her hero, country singer Willie Nelson, when he supposedly came through Thalia, Karla drives her pick-up over her collection of nearly one hundred Willie Nelson cassettes. During the course of the novel, Karla starts wearing blank T-shirts, a sure sign that she has caught the prevailing spiritual malaise, and she leaves Duane and moves in with Jacy. Near the end of the novel, however, the couple reconciles; Karla tells Duane that her initial attraction and subsequent loyalty to him were rooted in his appreciation of her being *both* attractive and intelligent.

In *The Last Picture Show*, **Sonny Crawford** was a sensitive teenager who yearned after the beautiful Jacy Farrow and had an affair with the middle-aged wife of the local football coach. In *Texasville*, Sonny seems to serve as an embodiment of that past or, in any case, as someone who has failed to sever himself from it. He has attained moderate success not though the pursuit of oil riches in which many other Thalians (to their current sorrow) indulged but through the judicious purchase of real estate. He now owns a car wash, laundry, and Kwik-Sack convenience store, yet the perpetually sad, lonely Sonny considers himself a failure. The combined pressures of his wife's abandonment and the approaching centennial celebration and thirty-year high school reunion contribute to Sonny's mental decline. He claims that his head plays videos of the past; Jacy says, "His timing gear's broken, or something. He thinks it's 1954." Described by critic Jonathan Yardley as "an honorable yet forlorn figure," Sonny has by the end of the novel shown no sign of emerging from his fog of loneliness and bewilderment.

Another important recurring character from *The Last Picture Show* is **Jacy Farrow**, who in the previous novel was the beautiful but self-centered tease who won the hearts of both Duane and Sonny. (McMurtry dedicated *Texasville* to Cybil Shepard, the actress who played Jacy in the film version of the novel.) Jacy has returned to Thalia after a career as a B-movie starlet: She played a character named "Jungla" in some Italian-made Tarzan movies. Ensconced in a secluded adobe mansion full of books she does not read, Jacy seems to be seeking some kind of refuge in Thalia. None of the old sparks between Duane and Jacy re-ignite (not even when they play Adam and Eve in the centennial pageant), and Jacy even facilitates the reconciliation between Duane and Karla when she kidnaps Duane's dog so that he will feel Karla's absence more keenly. At the end of the novel, Jacy tearfully admits to Duane that she was devastated by the death of her six-year-old son, who was accidentally electrocuted on the set of one of her movies. Several critics faulted McMurtry for his portrayal of Jacy, whose essential vacancy, they claim, makes her an unsympathetic character.

Duane's four children all contribute to his feeling that his life has spun out of control. Lazy, nineteen-year-old **Nellie** has already been married several times and is the mother of two small children; twenty-one-year-old **Dickie** is a womanizer and occasional drug dealer who is always in trouble with the police and wrecks several cars a year; and the twins **Jack and Julie** are foulmouthed terrors who Duane considers "as uninfluenceable as wild animals." It is Jack who, having just orchestrated the egg-throwing melee that caps Thalia's one-hundredth birthday celebration, utters the memorable line, "These centennials are awesome . . . I think we should have one every year." Other characters in the novel include **Ruth Popper**, the beleaguered wife of the high school football coach who, in *The Last Picture Show*, had a doomed affair with Sonny and who is now a sensible, spry, seventy-two-year-old jogger and Duane's secretary; and **Lester Marlow**, a gloomy banker who is under indictment for seventy-three counts of bank fraud. Duane's girlfriends include **Janine Wells**, who, after becoming bored with Duane, takes Lester Marlow as her lover; and **Suzie Nolan**, the wife of Duane's employee **Junior Nolan**, who eventually runs away with Duane's son Dickie.

Further Reading

Adams, Robert M. "The Bard of Wichita Falls." *New York Review of Books* (August 13, 1987): 39–41.

Bestsellers Vol. 89, issue 2. Detroit: Gale Research.

Butler, Jack. "The Irresistible Gunfighter." *New York Times Book Review* (October 16, 1988): 3.

Cox, Diana H. "*Anything for Billy*: A Fiction Stranger than Truth." *Journal of Popular American Culture* 14 (Summer 1991): 75–81.

Erdrich, Louise. "Why Is that Man Tired?" *New York Times Book Review* (April 19, 1987): 6.

Gish, Robert. "Anything for Larry." *Los Angeles Times Book Review* (October 30, 1988): 1, 13.

Hansen, Ron. "The New Adventures of Billy the Kid." *Washington Post—Book World* (October 9, 1988): 1, 13.

Rafferty, Terrence. Review of *Texasville*. *New Yorker* (June 15, 1987): 92–4.

Reynolds, Clay. *Taking Stock: A Larry McMurtry Casebook*. Dallas: Southern Methodist University Press, 1989.

Reynolds, R. C. Review of *Texasville*. *Southern Humanities Review* (Winter 1989): 92–4.

Sigal, Clancy. "The Old West McMurtry-Style." *Chicago Tribune–Books* (October 9, 1988): 1, 5.

Woodward, Daniel. "Larry McMurtry's *Texasville*: A Comic Pastoral of the Oilpatch." *Huntington Library Quarterly* Vol. 56, no. 2 (Spring 1993): 167–80.

Yardley, Jonathan. "Deep in the Heart of Larry McMurtry." *Washington Post—Book World* (April 12, 1987): 3.

Sue Miller
194(?)–
American novelist and short story writer.

The Good Mother (novel, 1986)

Plot: The novel takes place in contemporary Cambridge, Massachusetts. As it opens, Anna Dunlap is married to Brian, a stodgy lawyer, and has a four-year-old daughter named Molly. Anna and Brian divorce, and Anna gets custody of Molly. Anna gradually builds a new life, supporting herself and her daughter by giving piano lessons and working part-time in a research laboratory, while fending off her interfering family's attempts to control her. She meets an independent, passionate artist, Leo Cutter, who becomes her lover, and for the first time in her life experiences sexual fulfillment. Molly seems to like Leo very much, and Anna feels that the three make an ideal family group. Their happiness is shattered, however, when Brian sues for custody of Molly, accusing Leo of "sexual irregularities" in his relationship with the little girl. The allegation is based on an incident in which Molly had encountered Leo naked in the bathroom and asked if she could touch him; unsure how to react and aware of Anna's belief in openness, Leo said yes. In addition, Anna and Leo had once made love while Molly slept with them in their bed. As the trial proceeds, Anna questions her own attitudes and responsibilities and finds herself unable to defend Leo or fight very rigorously for custody of her daughter. At the novel's conclusion, Anna has lost Leo and is adapting to seeing her daughter only during limited visits.

Characters: *The Good Mother*, Miller's first and most highly praised novel, evidences a skillful blending of physical detail with psychological realism and a sure grasp of such topical issues as divorce, child custody, and child sexual abuse. Informed by a moral perspective but avoiding any easy answers, the novel examines the tension between passion and responsibility and suggests that the sexual revolution has not significantly reduced the price that women may pay for sexual fulfillment.

Many critics have placed **Anna Dunlap** within the literary tradition of female protagonists whose pursuit of sexual passion leads to punishment. Her predecessors include Flaubert's Emma Bovary, Edna Pontellier in Kate Chopin's *The Awakening*, and especially the title character in Tolstoy's *Anna Karenina*, who is generally thought to be Anna Dunlap's namesake. Through Anna, Miller explores the complications that evolve when a modern woman attempts to accommodate both her individual sexuality and her role as a mother. Newly divorced from a husband who failed to satisfy her needs, Anna is enjoying her new, more precarious but also more interesting life as a single mother. Through flashbacks, the reader learns about her childhood in a family that valued decorum above all else and that, she now feels, was injuriously secretive about sex. It is Anna's desire not to perpetuate this tradition with her own daughter that leads her to promote an atmosphere of openness in her home when she begins a relationship with Leo Cutter. Ironically, though, this openness results in her forced separation from Molly when Brian accuses her and Leo of sexual "irregularities." Anna reacts to this catastrophe with a passivity that mystifies some commentators, making little effort to defend either herself or Leo. Yet Miller establishes the roots of this passivity in Anna's childhood; for example, she declined to pursue the musical career her mother had planned for her, and her later claim that she simply lacked the required talent does not necessarily ring true. Near the end of the novel, Anna does express her rage when she runs out of her house with Leo's gun and the wild intention, perhaps, of kidnapping Molly, but she finally fires the gun into a sand dune. This act seems to signify her acceptance of her situation; she concludes that she was wrong to succumb to the "euphoric forgetfulness of all the rules" that her passion for Leo had produced. Anna is left with a sadly diminished life bereft of both Molly, whom she sees only at scheduled interludes, and Leo. Although some critics found the novel's conclusion infused with despair and resignation, Miller asserted that *The Good Mother* demonstrates her interest "in the meaning of the heroic in domestic life . . . a life that's constrained by ties to other people . . . To me Anna is heroic."

Anna is passionately devoted to her precocious, energetic, somewhat demanding daughter **Molly**. Critics differed in their assessments of Miller's portrayal of Molly: some agreed with Mary Pinard, who wrote that Molly is "so real, so true to the integrity and independent life of a four-year-old, [that] I don't remember when I've met such an accurately drawn child in fiction," whereas others would side with Joanne Kaufman, who called Molly "a wispy-haired whiner." Anna's ex-husband **Brian Dunlap**, the son of a minister (Miller is the daughter of a minister), is a stiff, moralistic, humorless lawyer. Commentators who align Anna with Emma Bovary and Anna Karenina call attention to Brian's similarities to those characters' similarly inadequate husbands, Charles Bovary and Alexei Karenin. Anna comments that Brian was as "stern" and "judgmental" with himself as she was with herself, and that this likeness between them prevented them from making each other happy.

Anna's lover **Leo Cutter** is a poor but self-sufficient artist who is intensely committed to his work. Impetuous and sensual, he introduces an unprecedented and much-appreciated passion into Anna's life; she notes that life "seemed to reach in and touch" him as "it never did me." Anna's abandonment of Leo by declining to defend him against the allegations raised against him may be interpreted as either weak or courageous—as an expression of her inherent passivity or as an acknowledgment that her relationship with her child is foremost in her life. Other characters in the novel include Anna's **grandfather**, a wealthy, retired New England businessman who continues to exert an autocratic power over his family; her friend **Ursula**, who admonishes her for not fighting Brian's allegations and defending her lover; and her lawyer **Muth**, on whose soothing voice she becomes dependent. A character who never appears but whose memory plays a significant role in Anna's psyche is **Aunt Babe**, who gave birth to and relinquished an illegitimate baby in Switzerland and returned home, only to drown while drunk. Anna regards her story as a "cautionary tale" about a woman whose free spirit was ultimately crushed by her family's excessive decorum.

Further Reading

Contemporary Literary Criticism Vol. 44. Detroit: Gale Research.

Humphreys, Josephine. "Private Matters." *Nation* Vol. 242, no. 18 (May 10, 1986): 648–50.

Johnston, Darcie Conner. "Blinded by the Light." *Belles Lettres* Vol. 2, no. 2 (November–December 1986): 13.

Kakutani, Michiko. Review of *The Good Mother*. *New York Times* (April 23, 1986): C20.

Lehmann-Haupt, Christopher. "How a Good Mother Expresses Rage." *New York Times* (September 15, 1986): C12.

Navas, Deborah. "Home Deliveries: Cautionary Sex & Violence." *New Letters* Vol. 1, no. 1 (Spring 1987): 9–10.

Pinard, Mary. "Caught between Motherlove and Passion." *New Directions for Women* Vol. 15, no. 4 (July–August 1986): 10.

Wolfe, Linda. "Men, Women and Children First." *New York Times Book Review* April 27, 1986): 1, 40.

Zinman, Tony Silverman. "The Good Old Days in *The Good Mother.*" *Modern Fiction Studies* Vol. 34, no. 3 (Autumn 1988): 405–12.

N. Scott Momaday

1934 –

American novelist, memoirist, and poet.

House Made of Dawn (novel, 1969)

Plot: The novel centers on a Native American named Abel, the illegitimate son of a Tanoan mother and a father of unknown (but probably Navajo) origin. Born in Walatowa, a New Mexico pueblo village, Abel is raised by his grandfather, Francisco, after the deaths of his mother and brother. As the novel opens, Abel has returned to the village after serving in the army during World War II. Although he was anxious to get back home, Abel feels displaced and lost after his return, and he begins using alcohol. At the Feast of Santiago, he participates in a ceremonial game which Fragua, an albino Tanoan, wins. Fragua chooses Abel to receive the beating prescribed by the ritual, and later Abel kills Fragua in a knife fight, for which he is sentenced to seven years in jail.

After serving his sentence, Abel is relocated to Los Angeles. There he encounters a hostile policeman named Martinez and a Kiowa Indian, John Big Bluff Tosamah, who taunts him for behaving like a "savage." Troubled and inarticulate, Abel again turns to alcohol and eventually loses his job. After nearly dying from a beating by Martinez, Abel returns to Walatowa, where his grandfather is dying. At Francisco's death, Abel performs the traditional Tanoan burial ritual and also runs in a ceremonial race to evoke good hunting and harvests. As he runs, Abel sings a Navajo prayer called "House Made of Dawn," and he seems to have achieved a measure of peace.

Characters: Momaday is a highly acclaimed Native American writer. *House Made of Dawn,* his first novel, met enthusiastic praise and won the Pulitzer Prize for literature in 1969. The novel is set in the fictional village of Walatowa, which is closely modeled after the Jemez pueblo in New Mexico, where Momaday was born and raised. Momaday (a Kiowa) asserts that Native Americans must continuously examine their identities in order to survive, and *House Made of Dawn* tells of one such struggle for self-definition. Richly laced with fantastic imagery and Native American mythology, the novel also is infused with strains of confusion, violence, and loss. Although some critics deem it a protest novel illuminating the plight of Indians in white America, others believe *House Made of Dawn* has universal appeal and laud its hopeful conclusion.

The novel's protagonist is **Abel,** a Native American raised in a small pueblo village in New Mexico. Abel's last name is never mentioned, for he is the son of a Tanoan Indian mother and an unknown father. The only other members of Abel's immediate family, his mother and brother Vidal, die during his childhood, and even though he lives with his medicine man grandfather, Francisco, he feels isolated by his lack of family. As Abel approaches manhood, he balks under his grandfather's demands that he observe tribal culture, so he leaves the sheltered reservation environment to flight in World War II. Yet he soon finds himself caught between two cultures: that of his ancestors (which he had never wholeheartedly adopted even when it surrounded him) and that of the dominant culture. Both the dehumanizing nature of war and the way he is treated by his fellow soldiers (they nickname him "Chief") heighten his sense of loss and lack of cultural or personal identity. After the war, Abel returns to Walatowa and soon realizes he is hardly more at home in Walatowa than outside it. His relationship with his grandfather is strained, and, incapable of expressing his feelings, he begins to drink heavily. Abel's ill-fated reaction to his beating after the ceremonial game on the Feast of Santiago typifies his alienation: he feels humiliated by something that is culturally prescribed. Murdering Fragua results not only from this disgrace but from a belief that Fragua is evil and must be destroyed. Completely demoralized, Abel lacks interest in his murder trial. His despair continues through his jail term and relocation to Los Angeles, where Tosamah's taunting sends him back to alcohol for solace. After a vicious beating by Martinez, Abel lies on the beach, nearly dead and "reeling on the edge of the void." During this powerfully conveyed scene, Abel finally begins his recovery. Through his fragmented remembrances of childhood and reflections on the natural world around him, Abel reconnects with all creation and realizes that he must return to his Native American ways if he is to survive. Abel returns to Walatowa and finds his grandfather dying. During their time together, the old medicine man conveys his knowledge and belief to his grandson. Francisco's death proves liberating for Abel, and he confidently performs the Tanoan burial ritual and later joins in the ceremonial run to oppose evil and ensure a good harvest. Abel's participation in the run has been interpreted to show his successful reintegration into Indian life and his spiritual and emotional well-being, which bode well for the future. His singing of a Navajo chant also seems to heal his painful inarticulateness.

Those who interpret *House Made of Dawn* as a protest novel consider Abel a victim of white anti-Indian racism. Some liken him to Ira Hayes, the World War II hero who became an alcoholic and died in ignominy after returning to the reservation. Other critics claim Abel to be a complex character defying cliche or easy categorization. Momaday said in interviews that he modeled Abel after Indians he knew at Jemez; he also conceded the significance of his central character's name: in the Bible, Abel is the son of Adam and Eve who is victimized by his own brother, and many of Abel's troubles arise from his own people and not specifically from whites. Abel's personality crisis provides insight into the plight of many Indian men in the years following World War II, while at the same time the story is universal and hopeful.

Abel's grandfather, **Francisco**, is a farmer and medicine man who, after the deaths of Abel's mother and brother, raises the boy in the traditional Tanoan way of life. He instructs Abel in the Native American relationship with the natural environment and in various rituals and customs, but he also prohibits his grandson from close contact with other members of the community. This isolates Abel and he eventually rejects his grandfather's teachings as he leaves Walatowa for the army and, later, for jail and life in Los Angeles. Their very different reactions to the albino underscore the differences between Francisco and Abel: both regard the opponent as evil, but while Abel strikes out in violence against him, Francisco accepts evil as a natural force to be circumvented in other, nonviolent ways. One way is the ceremonial race, in which Francisco ran as a young man and in which Abel, too, will run, after he returns to the ways of his people. Together with Francisco's deathbed advice to Abel, the running ritual links the generations and gives the younger man the strength to face the future.

Fragua, the huge, albino Tanoan, chooses Abel for the beating after the ceremonial game and then dies outside a bar in a knife fight with Abel. He is considered an evil force: Everyone in Walatowa believes the albino is a witch, highlighting the Native American belief in evil as a natural force in the universe. That Fragua is an albino prompted some commentators to conclude that he represents white America, while others assert that the albinoism is more complex. Many critics see the influence of nineteenth-century American author Herman Melville—whose work Momaday regards highly—and particularly his epic novel *Moby-Dick; or, The White Whale,* in which the title creature embodies a strange malevolence. In his novel Melville claims that whiteness intensifies whatever is horrible and that albinos are thus particularly repellent. The scene in which Abel struggles with Fragua and finally stabs him to death is often cited for its sexual overtones, which reviewers take to mean that Abel is resisting rape by the albino or, by extension, the assault of white American culture. Other critics propose that Abel fears Fragua, because Fragua reflects the destructive elements of Abel's own personality and of the white and Indian cultures between which he struggles.

Significant characters from the Walatowa sections of the novel include **Father Olguin**, a Catholic priest assigned to minister to the Native American community—a reminder of the role Christianity has played in the history of Indians in America. Though he lives every day among the Tanoan people and is interested in their ceremonial dances and rituals, Father Olguin has not succeeded in converting many of them to his own faith. During Abel's trial for murder, he attempts to illuminate the young man's action by explaining its cultural context. The novel includes entries from the diary of **Fray Nicolas**, a priest who served in Walatowa in the late nineteenth century and who expresses shock and disgust over the traditional ceremonies performed by the Indians. **Angela St. John** is a white social worker with whom Abel has a brief affair after failing to reconnect with his own people. This relationship fails, too, due to Abel's inarticulateness and unwillingness to expose himself to humiliation.

In Los Angeles, Abel meets a self-styled holy man named **John Big Bluff Tosamah**, a Kiowa Indian with an extensive knowledge of his people's history. Several critics claim that Tosamah is Momaday's mouthpiece in the novel; indeed, the two are similar in tribal heritage, appearance (both are big and lithe with narrow eyes), and their belief in the sacred power of language. Tosamah is something of a comic figure, however—a religious con man who never speaks the whole truth, true to his middle name. Yet Tosamah too is isolated from others for unsuccessfully mixing elements of native religion with Christianity and for his arrogant superiority toward other Indians. For example, he calls Abel an ignorant savage, claiming he is embarrassed by Abel's violent, superstitious, and inarticulate—Indian—behavior. This taunting so disturbs Abel that he turns to alcohol again. Other Los Angeles characters include **Martinez**, the violent, corrupt police officer of either Hispanic or Indian—not caucasian—descent who eventually beats Abel nearly to death; and Abel's friend **Ben Benally**, a Navajo who performs a healing Night Chant ceremony that seems to help Abel achieve the harmony between body and spirit that he needs to recover. Benally also teaches Abel the "House Made of Dawn" song he sings at the end of the novel; Momaday commented that he particularly identified with this character and his confidence in the power of language.

Further Reading

Contemporary Literary Criticism, Vols. 2, 19. Detroit: Gale Research.

Kerr, Baine. "The Novel as Sacred Text: N. Scott Momaday's Myth-Making Ethic." *Southwest Review* Vol. 63, no. 2 (spring 1978): 172–9.

Lattin, Vernon E. "The Quest for Mythic Vision in Contemporary Native American and Chicano Fiction." *American Literature* Vol. 50, no. 4 (January 1979): 625–40.

Scarberry-García, Susan. *Landmarks of Healing: A Study of House Made of Dawn.* Albuquerque: University of New Mexico Press, 1990.

Schubnell, Matthias. *N. Scott Momaday: The Cultural and Literary Background.* Norman: University of Oklahoma Press, 1985.

Velie, Alan R. "Momaday: Nobody's Protest Novel." In *Four Indian Literary Masters.* Norman: University of Oklahoma Press, 1982, 52–64.

Weiler, Dagmar. "N. Scott Momaday: Story Teller." *Journal of Ethnic Studies* Vol. 16, no. 1 (spring 1988): 118–26.

Toni Morrison
1931–
American novelist, dramatist, essayist, and editor.

Jazz (novel, 1992)

Plot: The main action of the novel takes place in the African American community of New York City in 1926, twenty years after Joe and Violet Trace have moved north from rural Virginia. For a long time they were happy together in their new life, but eventually their relationship staled. Violet experiences strange "cracks" in her consciousness when she does and says surprising things. Meanwhile, Joe falls in love with eighteen-year-old Dorcas Manfred. When Dorcas spurns Joe in favor of a younger lover, he follows her to a party and shoots her; since no one has seen him commit the crime, however, he is not suspected when Dorcas later dies. At Dorcas's funeral, Violet creates a scene by slashing the dead girl's face with a knife. During the next few months, both Joe and Violet are tormented by thoughts of Dorcas, and Violet begins visiting the girl's aunt, Alice Manfred, in order to understand what has happened. Eventually both Violet and Joe achieve peace with themselves and with each other and return to a state of comfortable, ordinary love. Throughout the central narrative, anecdotes recount the Traces' early lives and tell about the mulatto son of Violet's grandmother's employer, who returned to Virginia from his home in Baltimore to find his black father.

Characters: Winner of the 1993 Nobel Prize in Literature, Morrison is acclaimed for fiction that focuses on the sorrow, joy, and complexity of African American experience. Her works are populated predominantly by troubled characters who seek identity and meaning in an oppressive society and who often derive strength from their rich, resilient cultural heritage. The structure of *Jazz* imitates the musical form that is an important element of black culture, and critics identify various parts of the story as the melody, riffs, and improvisation that make up a jazz composition. Concerned in all her novels with African American history, in this one Morrison examines black culture in New York City during the 1920s—the decade of the Harlem Renaissance in literature, the emergence of jazz, and the "Great Migration" of rural southern blacks to the northern cities. In her usual elegant, fluid prose and with careful attention to detail, Morrison shows how African Americans responded to, and in many cases overcame, both harsh political realities and personal hardships.

Although the novel's **narrator** never actually appears as a character, her voice has a strong presence and shaping role that might be compared to that of a bandleader at a jazz performance. The narrator speaks as if she lives in the characters' neighborhood and knows them personally; her manner is garrulous and chatty as well as intelligent and insightful. It is partly through the narrator's lyrical, affectionate ruminations about New York that Morrison creates a sense of the city's hypnotic and rejuvenative atmosphere in the 1920s. Near the end of the novel, the narrator admits that she is surprised at the direction the characters' lives have taken, for they seem to have conquered the pain she thought was insurmountable and achieved the forgiveness and happiness she assumed would evade them. Thus she highlights the idea that happy endings may be possible even in lives filled with pain.

Violet Trace, at fifty, is an attractive hairdresser in a state of emotional crisis after the death of her husband's teenaged lover. As the novel opens, she has discovered Joe's infidelity and responds first by releasing her beloved pet birds (thus reminding some commentators of the half-mad Miss Flite in Charles Dickens' 1852–53 novel *Bleak House,* whose pet birds also bore a connection to her psychic state) and then by taking a knife to the face of the dead girl. For the past twenty years, since before her move to New York, Violet was a hardworking, determined woman who had recovered admirably from the early loss of her parents and had forged a strong, sustaining love with her husband. She and Joe had not been able to have children but didn't much miss them. In recent years, however, the couple's relationship has gone dull, and Violet has begun to experience "cracks" in her consciousness, during which she does and says unexplainable things. During one episode, Violet nearly kidnaps a baby she has been asked to watch, thus acting out some deep, unanswered need within her. Violet's anger and despair over Joe's affair with her lover, Dorcas, push Violet closer to madness, but her visits to the girl's aunt help her gain equilibrium as she learns more about Dorcas and shares observations on love and life with Alice. Finally Violet achieves a kind of self-acceptance, asserting that "now I want to be the woman my mother didn't stay around long enough to see. . . . The one she would have liked."

Violet's husband, **Joe Trace**, is middle-aged and still attractive to women, with his different-colored eyes and gentle manner. A salesman of beauty products, he knows how to cajole and flirt with his customers; Dorcas's friend Felice observes that he seems to genuinely like women, who immediately sense this about him. Like Violet, Joe is the survivor of a difficult childhood: raised by the kindly Williams family, he was an orphan whose mother was probably the deranged, rarely seen woman known in the community as "Wild." Joe suspects that he sees in the wild-spirited, teenaged Dorcas some shadow of the mother he never knew, and he confides to Dorcas about the one time—when he was fourteen—that he ever encountered the strange, hidden figure he suspected was his mother. The narrator explains that Joe loves Dorcas with "one of those deepdown, spooky loves that made him so sad and happy he shot her just to keep the feeling going." Joe claims that he has undergone seven transformations during his lifetime—beginning with the one in which he gave himself the name "Trace" to signify his parents' disappearance without him—and that his interlude with Dorcas is another such change. She has a rejuvenating power over him that he cannot bear to relinquish. For months after her death, Joe spends all of his days and nights grieving and even loses his job. But just as Violet finally attains self-acceptance, Joe overcomes his sorrow and guilt, perhaps partially through the couple's conversations with Felice, who reveals that Dorcas had hurried along her own death, which was not otherwise inevitable. By the end of the novel, Joe and Violet settle into a "whispering, old-time love" that, while different from either their early relationship or Joe's passion with Dorcas, promises to sustain them through the rest of their lives.

The central plot line of *Jazz* is based on an actual event, described in Camille Billop's *The Harlem Book of the Dead*, in which a dying lover refused to name her attacker. Morrison imagines that dying lover as eighteen-year-old **Dorcas Manfred**, who has long, wavy hair and a light complexion slightly marred by pimples along her cheeks. After losing her parents in the East St. Louis race riots of 1917, Dorcas lives with her strict, proper aunt Alice

Manfred. A stubborn, bold girl who relishes secrets, Dorcas resists her aunt's efforts to shelter her from the world of sexual license and inevitable ruin, which the older woman connects closely with jazz music. With her friend Felice, Dorcas attends parties where slickly dressed boys appraise her critically and she absorbs some of the glamour of dancing and fancy clothing. She responds eagerly to Joe's interest in her, and he introduces her into sex and love, but she eventually grows restless in her knowledge of her own power over him and of all that he cannot give her. Thus Dorcas acquires a new lover, the self-centered, aloof **Acton,** who is impossible to please and whose main response to her shooting is annoyance that his jacket has been stained with blood. Although Felice characterizes Dorcas as selfish and suicidal (because she might have prevented her own death but insisted on not being taken to the hospital), Dorcas refuses to reveal that her killer is her kind, much-older former lover. Morrison portrays Dorcas as a troubled, somewhat mysterious girl eager for thrills and risk and perhaps also drawn to death, which took her parents from her so tragically.

Alice Manfred is the dignified, always decorous seamstress who raised the orphaned Dorcas after the death of her parents. She tries to instill in her niece the self-respect and modesty she hopes would help her resist the lure of sex, which she identifies as the essence of the new music being played in 1920s Harlem. Alice senses in jazz the concurrent and equally dangerous forces of "anger and appetite" and a call to "do wrong" that promises only "Imminent Demise." After Dorcas's death, however, Alice muses that the roots of her obsession with not allowing an unwed pregnancy to mar her niece's life lie in her own early experience with that catastrophe, which filled her with the self-loathing she tried to pass on to Dorcas. With Dorcas's death, anger supplants Alice's usual fearfulness—anger against Joe and Violet, who both chose violence as a refuge from their problems just as others choose religion. Yet the friendship that develops between Alice and Violet proves to benefit them both. For perhaps the first time in her life, Alice feels perfectly free to say what she thinks, and in abandoning her customary politeness she gains an unexpected clarity. Thus Alice finally advises Violet to let go of her anger and hold on to what love already exists in her life.

Other characters in the New York sections of the novel include Dorcas's friend **Felice,** who befriends the Traces after the girl's death and helps them understand how Dorcas "liked to push people" and even hastened along her own death; and **Malvonne,** the observant or even nosy single woman who allows Joe and Dorcas to use her apartment while she works evenings cleaning offices. The parts of *Jazz* that take place in rural, early-twentieth-century Virginia are populated by such characters as Violet's mother, **Rose Dear,** who committed suicide in despair over her poverty and her absent husband, and her grandmother **True Belle,** who arrived in time to rescue and raise her daughter's children. Before her return to Virginia, True Belle had worked in Baltimore for **Miss Vera Louise Gray,** a former southern belle banished from the family plantation after becoming pregnant by a black boy. When her son, **Golden Gray** (whose name commemorates his beautiful, creamy skin and yellow curls), learned that his father was black, he went to Virginia to kill the man. There he found not only his father, the renowned woodsman **Henry Lestory,** but a pregnant black girl—later to be called **Wild**—who was probably Joe's mother.

Further Reading

Contemporary Literary Criticism. Vols. 4, 10, 22, 55. Detroit: Gale Research.

Dictionary of Literary Biography. Vols. 6, 33, 1981 Yearbook. Detroit: Gale Research.

Major Twentieth-Century Writers. Vol. 3. Detroit: Gale Research.

Mayer, Elsie F. Review of *Jazz. America* 167, No. 10 (10 October 1992): 257–58.

Mbalia, Doreatha D. *Toni Morrison's Developing Class Consciousness*. Selinsgrove, PA: Susquehanna University Press, 1991.

Mobley, Marilyn Sanders. "The Mellow Moods and Difficult Truths of Toni Morrison." *Southern Review* Vol. 29, no. 3 (July 1993): 614–28.

O'Brien, Edna. Review of *Jazz. New York Times Book Review* (April 5, 1992): 1, 29–30.

Otten, Terri. *The Crime of Innocence in the Fiction of Toni Morrison*. Columbia: University of Missouri Press, 1989.

Rigney, Barbara Hill. *The Voices of Toni Morrison*. Columbus: Ohio State University Press, 1991.

Seligman, Craig. "Toni Morrison." *Threepenny Review* 52 (Winter 1993): 7–9.

Wood, Michael. "Life Studies." *New York Review of Books* (November 19, 1992): 7–11.

Alice Munro
1931–
Canadian short story writer and novelist.

"Dance of the Happy Shades" (short story, 1968)

Plot: The story takes place in a small Canadian town where Miss Marsalles, an elderly woman who never married, lives with her stroke-ridden sister. Miss Marsalles has given piano lessons to many generations of children, and the narrator (who is telling the story as an adult remembering an incident from her childhood) is one of Miss Marsalles's pupils. The narrator's mother would rather not attend the teacher's annual piano recital but finally agrees to go. As Miss Marsalles's has grown older and her finances more pinched, her once-tolerable—though never enjoyable—yearly parties have become more embarrassing and unpleasant for the women accompanying their children. Arriving for the recital, the narrator and her mother see that the teacher's new house is even more cramped than her former home, that only a few of her students are participating, and that the food and punch have been sitting out for far too long. The recital begins. While the narrator is playing her piece, a group of about eight children is led in by a uniformed woman. The mothers in the audience are alarmed and even irritated to realize that these children are students from a nearby school for the mentally disabled. The women's discomfort grows when one of the children, Delores Boyle, delivers a stunningly accomplished performance. Pleased but not triumphant, Miss Marsalles informs the audience that Delores's piece is entitled "Dance of the Happy Shades."

Characters: Celebrated as one of Canada's most accomplished writers, Munro won that country's prestigious Governor's Award for Fiction for the short story volume to which "Dance of the Happy Shades" lends its name. Munro's juxtapositions of the mundane and the exotic and her strict attention to detail have led critics to compare her work to that of such "magic realist" painters as Edward Hopper. She has also been identified as a regional writer in the tradition of Flannery O'Connor, Carson McCullers, and Eudora Welty—authors whose fiction rooted in the American South Munro particularly admires. Munro frequently employs irony and paradox to explore the inconsistencies and contradictions in human behavior. "Dance of the Happy Shades" typifies Munro's portrayal of a small-town milieu in which nonconformity is viewed with hostility, and because it is structured as a recollected episode significant in the emotional development of its central female character.

Through the story's **narrator**, Munro presents a kind of double narrative perspective, allowing the reader simultaneously insight into the naive though sensitive and observant young girl who participated in the event described and the older, wiser woman who recounts it. Thus the narrator both takes part in and stands apart from the action, serving as a moral critic and elucidating the theme at the story's heart. The adult narrator describes her younger self as somewhat petulant—and embarrassed at being the oldest child at the recital—but aware of the tension in the air and the impending crisis, even if she does not, at the time, understand what has caused it.

The central character in "Dance of the Happy Shades" is the aging piano teacher, **Miss Marsalles**, whose pinched finances (aggravated, surely, by her sister's debilitating illness) force her to move into a smaller house in a shabbier, though still tidy, neighborhood. She and her sister are described as "sexless, wild and gentle creatures, bizarre yet domestic"; Miss Marsalles's face—with tiny, shortsighted red eyes—is grotesque yet kind, revealing her naivete and tenderheartedness. She has given many generations of the town's children piano lessons and feels that children need and love music, even if unconsciously. Miss Marsalles's outlook makes her radically different from those around her, who find not only her temperament but her material circumstances unacceptable, and as the story takes place she is almost entirely a social outcast. Yet during the recital, Miss Marsalles "announces each child's name as if it were cause for celebration," and she greets the retarded children warmly, unaware that she has broken any social taboo by introducing them into such staid company. The old lady's reaction to Delores's magnificent performance is particularly revealing. While she might justifiably consider it a moral victory over the conformity required local custom, she treats it as a simple and—most important—not unexpected cause for enjoyment. While the others react to this moment of unpredictable beauty with anxiety and embarrassment, Miss Marsalles accepts it with calm gladness and no sense of triumph.

The narrator's unnamed **mother** represents the forces of social conformity that dominate this rural Ontario town. Like the other mothers, she would rather reject Miss Marsalles's invitation, for the old lady has diminished in social stature along with her finances, her sister's health, and her own appearance. In the weeks before the recital, the narrator's mother commiserates with another mother, Marg French, who shares her view that "things are getting out of hand [with Miss Marsalles's annual parties], anything may happen" and who, despite her promise to attend, never appears at the event. Also in the audience is **Mrs. Clegg**, a garishly dressed woman with a brick-red face and many gaps in her teeth who lives in the other side of Miss Marsalles's house and treats her elderly neighbors with sympathy. The narrator's mother views Mrs. Clegg with distaste and considers her presence further evidence that the piano recitals have become intolerable. **Delores Boyle** is the mentally disabled young girl whose inspired piano playing disturbs the audience's sense of superiority. She plays her piece in a "fragile, courtly, gay" manner and imbues it with "the freedom of a great unemotional happiness," suggesting that her overly cautious, socially rigid audience is more handicapped than she.

"Lichen" (short story, 1986)

Plot: Stella is a short, fat, middle-aged woman who lives fairly contentedly in a weatherbeaten house on the Canadian shore of Lake Huron. As the story opens, her ex-husband, David, to whom she was married for twenty-one years, arrives with his current lover, Catherine. David comes every year to visit Stella's father-in-law, who lives in a nearby nursing home. After Stella and David return from the nursing home, David tells her that he has grown tired of Catherine and has been carrying on a secret affair with a much younger woman named Dina. He shows Stella a photograph of Dina's nude body, her legs open to reveal what Stella identifies as "lichen." David tells Stella he wants her to keep the photo because he is afraid he will be tempted to show it to Catherine, but she refuses. After dinner, Stella talks to a drunk or drugged Catherine while David sneaks out to phone Dina, whom he is unable to reach. A flashback to the nursing home relates that Stella's father seemed pleased to see David and that, in an unexpected moment of warmth, David and Stella embraced. Stella recognized and called attention to David's embarrassment when a young nurse saw him hugging such an unattractive older woman. A week after David's visit, Stella discovers that he has left the photograph behind, hidden behind a curtain. The sun has caused it to fade so that what Stella initially identified as lichen—even though she knew very well what it really was—has come to match that description.

Characters: "Lichen" is one of the most acclaimed stories in the volume entitled *The Progress of Love,* which earned for Munro her third Governor General's Award for Fiction. As opposed to Munro's earlier work with its focus on young, sensitive female protagonists, the stories in this collection feature mature characters who grapple with adult themes, such as the ways in which human beings deceive themselves about love and in which love changes, endures, or "progresses" over time.

The central female character in "Lichen" is **Stella**, a middle-aged, divorced woman with two grown children who lives alone in an old house in Ontario on the shore of Lake Huron. Although she is short, fat, and already white-haired, Stella's healthy tan, wide brown eyes, and general cheerfulness lend her attractiveness. She occupies herself with tending her plants, making jam and wine, participating in community drama and church choir, and writing historical articles. David remembers her as a generous, sociable, and charming wife who was unable to satisfy his longing for risk and excitement. Since their break-up, Stella has fashioned a new and fairly satisfying (if solitary) life for herself, while David still wanders from affair to ill-fated affair. As the story progresses, Stella's moral ascendancy over David becomes clear when, ever immature, he shows Stella the photograph of his new girlfriend. Stella reacts coolly, commenting that the photograph looks like lichen, but she later admits that she "felt the old cavity opening up in her." Critics note that Stella typifies Munro's older female characters in her knowing tolerance for this flawed man she once loved.

Munro's portrayal of Stella's former husband, **David**, is unflattering but somewhat sympathetic. A civil servant who works, claims Stella, quite diligently for the Department of Education, David is an aging but still immature man whose yearning for youthfulness manifests physically in his dying his hair and emotionally in his involvement with younger and younger women, none of whom hold his interest for long. At the nursing home, David observes that with Stella he "could never feel any lightness, any secret and victorious expansion" as he could with someone like Dina, because Stella knows so much about him and is, in fact, "bloated with all she knew." David's self-indulgence and cruelty are evident in his scornful comments about Catherine, whom he intends to leave for Dina, as well as his carrying around an intimate photo of his new girlfriend, which he shows to Stella. Despite his fatuous self-indulgence, David does seem to recognize the futility and potential for humiliation in his own behavior, but he feels powerless to change it.

Tall, frail, always tentative, **Catherine** is David's current but doomed lover, whose very vulnerability, he claims, makes him want to hurt her. A part-time art teacher with long hair and a penchant for filmy dresses, the nearly-forty-year-old Catherine is a sometime vegetarian interested in horoscopes; David ridicules her as a "hippy survivor" who doesn't realize that the 1960s have ended. Catherine tells Stella that she feels a change approaching in her life—a change that will, though she does not realize it, be brought on by David's incapacity for true intimacy and commitment. David's new, twenty-two-year-old girlfriend, **Dina**, has dramatically dyed black hair and a wildness that David claims to savor, even though he realizes that in a few years she will have abandoned her superficial unconventionality for marriage and children. David's shallow approach to relationships is symbolized by the photo of Dina he carries, which utterly depersonalizes her; indeed, Stella sees in it a resemblance not only to lichen but to an animal's pelt. Other characters in the story include Stella's elderly **father**, who dimly seems to appreciate the visit from his once-alarming former son-in-law; and Stella's cheerful, trim, boring neighbor **Ron**, who provokes David into shocking him by revealing his photo of Dina.

Further Reading

Blodgett, E. D. *Alice Munro*. Boston: Twayne, 1988.

Byatt, A. S. "Vanishing Time." *Listener* Vol. 117, no. 2996 (January 29, 1987): 22–23.

Contemporary Literary Criticism Vols. 6, 10, 19, 50. Detroit: Gale Research.

Dahlie, H. "Unconsummated Relationships: Isolation and Rejection in Alice Munro's Stories." *World Literature Written in English* Vol. 11, no. 1 (April 1972): 42–48.

Dictionary of Literary Biography Vol. 53. Detroit: Gale Research.

Hoy, Helen. "(Dull, Simple, Amazing and Unfathomable): Paradox and Double Vision in Alice Munro's Fiction." *Studies in Canadian Literature* Vol. 5 (1980): 100–15.

Jones, D. A. N. "What Women Think about Men." *London Review of Books* Vol. 9, no. 3 (February 5, 1987): 23.

Kakutani, Michiko. Review of *The Progress of Love*. New York Times (September 3, 1986): C22.

MacDonald, Rae McCarthy. "A Madman Loose in the World: The Vision of Alice Munro." *Modern Fiction Studies* Vol. 22, no. 3 (autumn 1976): 364–74.

Oates, Joyce Carol. "Characters Dangerously Like Us." *New York Times Book Review* (September 14, 1986): 7, 9.

Rasporich, Beverly Jean. *Dance of the Sexes: Art and Gender in the Fiction of Alice Munro*. Edmonton: University of Alberta Press, 1990.

Redekop, Magdalene. *Mothers and Other Clowns: The Stories of Alice Munro*. London: Routledge, 1992.

Short Story Criticism Vol. 3. Detroit: Gale Research.

Tyler, Anne. "Canadian Club." *New Republic* Vol. 195, nos. 11 & 12 (September 15 & 22, 1986): 54–55.

Woodcock, George. "The Plots of Life: The Realism of Alice Munro." *Queen's Quarterly* Vol. 93, no. 2 (summer 1986): 235–50.

Gloria Naylor

1950–

American novelist, short story writer, and critic.

The Women of Brewster Place (novel, 1982)

Plot: Brewster Place is a run-down, dead-end street in an unnamed northern city that resembles Boston; the dying neighborhood is sealed off from the rest of the city by a brick wall. The novel's central character is Mattie Michael, who moves to Brewster Place from the South in her middle age. Years earlier, as a young woman in the South, Mattie was thrown out of her home by her strict father when she became pregnant by an attractive but irresponsible young man. She thereafter devoted herself to her son, Basil, and they eventually moved in with a generous older woman named Miss Eva Turner, who was raising her granddaughter Lucielia (usually called Ciel). After Miss Eva's death, Mattie inherited the house. Meanwhile, Basil, much-indulged and near adulthood, displayed increasingly reckless behavior and in the end was arrested for murder. Mattie mortgaged the house to raise bail for her son, and when he skipped town before his trial she was not only emotionally devastated but financially ruined. After that Mattie moved north to Brewster Place, where the now-grown Ciel is also living. Then her old friend Etta Mae Johnson arrives. Etta Mae has spent her adult life wandering from city to city and from man to man. Her desire for stability and a respectable marriage lead to a one-night stand with a visiting preacher, who proves no more dependable than her previous lovers.

Another resident of Brewster Place is young Kiswana Browne, who has renounced her middle-class background in favor of political activism. Kiswana befriends the childlike Cora Lee, who keeps having babies by a succession of unnamed men but loses interest in them as they grow older. Kiswana invites Cora Lee and her children to an African-American version of Shakespeare's *Midsummer Night's Dream*, an experience that seems to increase Cora Lee's self-esteem and awareness of the importance of education. Meanwhile, Ciel is struggling to raise her daughter, Serena, without much help from her irresponsible husband, Eugene, whose anger at her second pregnancy leads her to have an abortion. When Serena dies in a freak household accident, Ciel nearly succumbs to heartbreak but is coaxed back to life by Mattie.

Many of the residents of Brewster Place shun the newcomers Theresa and Lorraine when they realize the women are lesbians. This unfriendly reception leads to tension between the two; Theresa makes no apologies for her sexual orientation, but Lorraine longs for acceptance. Lorraine befriends the gentle, alcoholic handyman, Ben, who sees in her a reflection of his own beloved and long-lost daughter. Ironically, however, Lorraine kills Ben when, hysterical after being brutally gang raped, she mistakes him for an attacker. A week after Lorraine's rape and Ben's death, the Block Association organized by Kiswana plans a block party to raise money to improve Brewster Place. In what is later revealed to be Mattie's dream, the block party is ruined by rain, but the neighborhood women find an outlet for their anger and frustration by destroying the brick wall that symbolizes all that oppresses them. Finally, Mattie wakes to find that preparations for the block party are progressing.

Characters: *The Women of Brewster Place* earned Naylor the 1982 American Book Award for best first novel. Acclaimed for her realistic yet poetically rendered portrayals of the lives of contemporary African American women, Naylor focuses both on the broad issues of political and social oppression and the everyday, personal traumas that confront her characters. *The Women of Brewster Place* presents in seven chapters the stories of seven women who differ in personality and background but share similar problems and offer each other emotional support. While a few critics fault Naylor for not delving deeply into either the deep-rooted causes of or possible solutions to the women's troubles, all agree that the novel celebrates their courage and resilience.

Middle-aged **Mattie Michael** is usually identified as the emotional center of *The Women of Brewster Place;* critic Jill L. Matus calls her "the community's best voice and sharpest eye." Strong, truthful, and morally upright, she is respected by all the other characters for the undaunted spirit that has helped her survive abuse, loss, and betrayal. A native of the South, the young Mattie rejected the dull suitor favored by her father, succumbing instead to the lure of a handsome but shiftless young man who had no intention of marrying her. Mattie's father beat her when she refused to name her lover then banished her. She poured all of her love and energy into raising her son. Isolated from others—especially from men and the possibility of sex—Mattie began to define herself only as a mother. Despite her selflessness and devotion, however, her son never learned to accept responsibility for his own behavior. After Basil disappears from her life, Mattie accomplishes what critic Larry R. Andrews calls an "act of primal mothering" when she coaxes the grief-stricken Ciel back to life. The bond that then exists between the two women is not only maternal but one of equality, for each has suffered the loss of a child. The novel ends with Mattie's vision of the Brewster Place women destroying the wall that symbolizes the oppression they've endured at the hands of their men (as evidenced by the blood left on the wall after Lorraine's rape) and society.

Mattie's attractive, flamboyant friend **Etta Mae Johnson** has lived an unsettled life, traveling to various cities in search of good times and attaching herself to a succession of worthless men. Proud, independent, and irreverent, she nevertheless finds the prospect of life as the respectable wife of a minister attractive and hopes that Preacher Woods will be her route to such a life. Woods, however, views Etta Mae as a sexual diversion, not a potential mate. Her dream of redemption vanishes after a night in a hotel with Woods, and Etta Mae returns to Mattie with relief, knowing that her sometimes judgmental friend will offer her solace and love.

Twenty-three-year-old **Kiswana Browne** has recently dropped out of college, traded in her birth-given name, Melanie, for an African name, and moved into Brewster Place with her boyfriend. An idealist who is proud of her African heritage, Kiswana has pointedly denounced her parents' comfortable, middle-class lifestyle and pours her own energies into social activism, such as organizing a Brewster Place Block Association to fight for better conditions. Kiswana's character may derive from the Black Power Movement of the 1960s, for its adherents advocated both political activism and cultural awareness; one critic notes that Kiswana is the only one of the novel's characters who envisions a better future. Another significant difference between Kiswana and the others is that she deliberately seeks a path of downward mobility, whereas the others have always been financially deprived. Initially somewhat condescending in her attitude toward the childish Cora Lee, Kiswana eventually develops a sisterly, nurturing relationship with her that results in Cora Lee's apparent change for the better. The visit of Kiswana's prim mother to her daughter's ghetto apartment is a particularly effective scene: Kiswana accuses her mother of lacking pride in her race and Mrs. Brown forcefully contradicts her, reminding Kiswana of the strong, positive heritage the two women share. In addition, Kiswana discovers that both she and her mother wear toenail polish—a seemingly minor similarity that symbolizes, for Kiswana, their deeper likeness and helps to heal the rift between them.

Soon after giving birth to her son, Mattie finds a home with the strong, nurturing **Miss Eva Turner,** who ultimately leaves Mattie her house. Although she is always generous and supportive (Mattie considers her a surrogate mother), Miss Eva finds Mattie's excessive attentions to her son and her sexual abstinence unnatural. While Mattie is raising Basil, Miss Eva is raising her granddaughter, **Lucielia "Ciel" Louise Turner.** As an adult, Ciel experiences the misery of loving a man unable to support her and their child, emotionally or financially. After having an abortion because Eugene was so against the pregnancy, Ciel also loses her toddler, **Serena**, whom she has previously described as "the only thing I have ever loved without pain." Devastated by this loss, Ciel seems determined to die, but she is rocked back to life in the arms of Mattie, with whom she shares a bond of suffering and who is determined to keep her alive.

Cora Lee is a character who seems to be based on the stereotype of the "welfare mother": despite her financially strapped circumstances and the disorder of her household, she continues to have babies by different fathers, with whom relationships are only temporary. Yet Naylor's depiction affords the reader insight into Cora Lee's background and motivations, thus making her a more sympathetic—if not quite admirable—character. As a child, Cora Lee loved baby dolls and shirked all other toys. When she reached the age of thirteen, her parents decided that she was too old for dolls and cut off her supply. Cora Lee reacted by channeling her overactive mothering instinct into having real babies, when she loves and fusses over until they lose their infant charm. Cora Lee has a houseful of older children whom she neglects in favor of her current baby, whose needs are so much simpler, and she seems more interested in the lives of the characters on her favorite soap opera than in her own offspring. Encouraged by Kiswana to attend the performance of *Midsummer Night's Dream,* Cora Lee happily prepares the family for the excursion, and she is delighted with the play and with the children's responses to it. Cora Lee begins to plan for their futures, promising herself that she will pay more attention to their education and welfare from now on. Yet when Cora Lee returns to her home, she climbs into bed with her current "shadow" (her name for her current lover), and in Mattie's dream she is pregnant again; thus Naylor suggests that Cora Lee's redemption is not guaranteed.

A chapter entitled "The Two" chronicles the arrival of a pair of lesbians in Brewster Place and their negative reception by many of the neighborhood's residents. The two women have very different personalities: **Theresa** is tough and somewhat cynical, and she doesn't care what anyone thinks of their sexual preference, while **Lorraine** is more vulnerable and longs for acceptance. Despite her own independence, however, Theresa resents Lorraine's friendship with Ben, because she feels that the two outcasts should depend only on each other for support. In Mattie's dream, Theresa joins the other women in dismantling the wall, thus venting her pain and frustration over her lover's ordeal. Lorraine, a teacher, does not share Theresa's enjoyment of gay bars and the companionship of other homosexual men and women; rather, she craves normalcy and also fears for the security of her job if her sexual preference becomes known. Lorraine is glad for Ben's kindness and seems to see in him the father who, on learning she was a lesbian, banished her from his life. Described by critic Annie Gottlieb as "a blood sacrifice brutally proving the sisterhood of all women," Lorraine's gang rape unites the female residents of Brewster Place (in Mattie's dream, anyway) and sparks the act of defiance with which the book concludes.

Building superintendent **Ben**, who was one of Brewster Place's earliest residents, is one of only two positively portrayed men in the novel. He is a gentle, caring alcoholic. Helping to set his handicapped daughter up as the mistress of a rich white man has filled Ben with guilt, which he drowns with drink, and he is now isolated from his family. Ben forms a mutually sympathetic friendship with Lorraine: he is a father who betrayed and lost his daughter, while she is a daughter banished by an unaccepting father. Ben's murder by the wounded, delirious Lorraine illustrates the tragic reality of violence begetting more violence. The novel's other admirable male character is **Abshu Ben-Jamal**, Kiswana's lover, who is supportive of Kiswana and sincerely devoted to helping other African Americans improve their lives. Abshu has received a grant from the city to produce a black version of *Midsummer Night's Dream.*

Several critics note that most male characters in *The Women of Brewster Place* are undependable and reckless. Naylor herself has worried that readers would find her portrayals of men overly negative, but most critics regard them more incidental than despicable, marginal figures who are subordinate to the more interesting female characters. **Butch Fuller**, Mattie's seducer, is charming but shiftless and has no intention of marrying her. Mattie's much indulged son, **Basil**, is a trouble-prone young man who refuses to take responsibility for his actions; he betrays his mother when he disappears before his murder trial. Ciel's irresponsible husband, **Eugene**, blames her for their poverty, claiming that, with a wife and child to provide for, he will never be able to improve his lot. The **Reverend Moreland T. Woods**, a visiting minister who electrifies the congregation at Mattie's church with his inspired preaching, is more than willing to exploit Etta Mae's interest in him and use her as a sexual vehicle. **C. C. Baker** is the leader of the gang which brutally rapes Lorraine, embodying a menacing form a masculinity that expresses itself in violence against women.

Other characters in *The Women of Brewster Place* include Kiswana's mother, **Mrs. Browne**, the very image of middle-class propriety, who, after Kiswana accuses her of being a ''white man's nigger who's ashamed of being black!'' reminds her daughter that ''black isn't beautiful and black isn't ugly—black is!''; and **Sophie**, the neighborhood busybody, who vehemently disapproves of Theresa and Lorraine's lesbian relationship.

Further Reading

Andrews, Larry R. ''Black Sisterhood in Gloria Naylor's Novels.'' *CLA Journal* Vol. 33, no. 1 (September 1989): 1–25.

Black Literature Criticism. Vol. 2. Detroit: Gale Research.

Branzburg, Judith B. ''Seven Women and a Wall.'' *Callaloo* Vol. 7, no. 2 (spring–summer 1984): 116–19.

Contemporary Literary Criticism. Vols. 28, 52. Detroit: Gale Research.

Eko, Ebele. ''Beyond the Myth of Confrontation: A Comparative Study of African and African-American Female Protagonists.'' *Ariel* Vol. 17, no. 4 (October 1986): 139–52.

Gottlieb, Annie. ''Women Together.'' *New York Times Book Review* (August 22, 1982): 11, 25.

Hairston, Loyle. Review of *The Women of Brewster Place. Freedomways* Vol. 23, no. 4 (1983): 282–85.

Matus, Jill L. ''Dream, Deferral, and Closure in *The Women of Brewster Place.*'' *Black American Literature Forum* Vol. 24, no. 1 (spring 1990): 49–64.

Russell, Sandi. '''The Unblinking Eye.''' In *Render Me My Song: African-American Women Writers from Slavery to the Present.* New York: St. Martin's Press, 1990, pp. 143–61.

John Nichols
1940–
American novelist, nonfiction writer, and essayist.

The Milagro Beanfield War (novel, 1974)

Plot: The novel takes place in and around the impoverished rural town of Milagro, New Mexico, a community of predominantly Chicano and Pueblo Indian inhabitants. The action is precipitated by the spontaneous decision of itinerant handyman Joe Mondragón to irrigate his family's long-dormant bean field. This sparks a water-rights dispute between wealthy rancher Ladd Divine, who intends to exploit the area's potential as a resort, and the townfolk of Milagro, whom Divine has long conned out of their irrigation rights. Inspired by Joe's impetuous act, the community tries to present an organized opposition to Divine, but they lack a committed leader. Meanwhile, Joe shoots a neighbor whose pig has trampled his bean field. He is arrested, but his friends eventually succeed in getting him released from jail. The "beanfield war" comes to a (perhaps temporary) close when the governor tells Divine to end his dispute with Milagro.

Characters: Nichols's novels are admired for their skillful blend of humor and pathos and their exuberant prose. *The Milagro Beanfield War* is considered the best of a trilogy of novels set in New Mexico, where Nichols has lived for several decades. Centered on the land and water rights that are a source of great controversy and concern in the western United States, the novel reveals Nichols's personal commitment to the region's history and culture and to social justice, which he considers threatened by those with selfish economic interests. Although some reviewers faulted the novel's characters as stereotypical, most found it highly entertaining and compelling.

Several critics noted that *The Milagro Beanfield War* contains no central character, and one even suggested that all of the characters contribute to the creation of the town of Milagro as a protagonist. In any case, the initiator of the novel's action is handy man and sometime migrant worker **Joe Mondragón**, a small but fierce figure who is often in jail for fighting, drinking, or antagonizing the police. One day, Joe decides to reclaim his ancestors' land in defiance of the powerful economic interests that now control it; his impetuous act, however, is not motivated by any conscious political intent or desire to create a community conflict. And he is certainly not prepared to lead Milagro in its effort to defy Ladd Divine and his cronies. He is only a temporary hero, as evidenced by his shooting (albeit in self-defense) of his longtime neighbor and flight into the hills.

One of the most inspiring characters in *The Milagro Beanfield War* is ninety-three-year-old **Amaranto Cordova**, called "the human zipper" because he has had surgery so many times. Perpetually near death, Amaranto continues to survive, thus serving as a symbol of endurance and the possibility of vitality in the face of adversity. Amaranto believes (wrongly, as it turns out) that Joe Mondragón has been sent by God to lead Milagro in a revolution. Like Amaranto, **Cloefes Apodaca** plays a symbolic role in the novel. All of Milagro's inhabitants know the story of how Cloefes, an outcast nineteenth-century sheepherder said to possess the evil eye, was so fanatically devoted to his dog that when the beast disappeared he neglected his work and health to search for him. This selfless love for other creatures seems to the townfolk both crazy and admirable. Similarly, Nichols casts the novel's Chicano-Indian community as somewhat irrationally but also nobly devoted to its own, old ways, while the dominant Anglo culture watches its disintegration with scorn.

Another colorful, near-mythical figure is the highly independent, one-armed **Onofre Martinez**, who drives a dilapidated pickup truck with a three-legged dog perched on the roof of its cab. Onofre claims that his arm simply fell off one day, releasing a cloud of bright red butterflies, and many strange occurrences in Milagro are attributed to the supernatural presence of "el brazo Onofre." Other characters in *The Milagro Beanfield War* include the liberal, Jewish lawyer and East Coast drop-out **Charlie Bloom**, who tries to help the Milagrans in their struggle; the robust, sexy widow **Ruby**; **Benny Maestas**, who sums up Milagro's history of organized action with the phrase, "United we flounder, divided we flounder;" and **Seferino Pacheco**, Joe's gentle neighbor, whom Joe shoots in self-defense when the old man attacks him after he has shot Seferino's beloved pig.

Most of the novel's white characters are unflatteringly portrayed. Principal among them is wealthy rancher **Ladd Divine**, described by critic Peter Wild as "an empire builder out of the Old West." Ambitious and unsentimental, Divine has no intention of allowing what he views as a bunch of good-for-nothing Chicanos and Indians (who in turn call him "Zopilote," or buzzard) to threaten his power. Divine serves as a symbol of white economic dominance, individual and corporate greed, and the seemingly unstoppable encroachment of development. Although in the end Divine is told by the state's governor—a personal crony of his—to leave the Milagrans alone, it is suggested that this is only a temporary reprieve. Like Divine, **Kyril Montana**, the clean-cut undercover agent sent by the government to investigate the situation in Milagro (in the words of commentator John Loftis), "exemplifies the faceless, ruthless, manipulative Anglo establishment that knows what it wants and (it thinks) how to get it."

Further Reading

Busch, Frederick. Review of *The Milagro Beanfield War*. *New York Times Book Review* (October 27, 1974): 53–4.

Contemporary Literary Criticism Vol. 38. Detroit: Gale Research.

Deakin, Motley. Review of *The Milagro Beanfield War*. *Western American Literature* Vol. 10, no. 3 (November 1975): 249–50.

Dictionary of Literary Biography, 1982 Yearbook. Detroit: Gale Research.

King, Larry L. "Few Shots in a 'Beanfield War.'" *National Observer* (November 16, 1974): 27.

Loftis, John E. "Community as Protagonist in John Nichols' *The Milagro Beanfield War*. *Rocky Mountain Review of Language and Literature* Vol. 38, no. 4 (1984): 201–13.

Pfeil, Fred. "Down the Beanstalk." *Nation* (June 20, 1987): 857–60.

Wild, Peter. *John Nichols*. Boise, ID: Boise State University Press, 1986.

Anais Nin
1903–1977
French-born American novelist, diarist, short story writer, and critic.

A Spy in the House of Love (novel, 1954)

Plot: The novel's plot is minimal, centering on the efforts of the protagonist, a would-be actress named Sabina, to find fulfillment and self-knowledge through a series of love affairs. She is married to the stable, complaisant, but insensitive Alan, who tolerates her liaisons with other men. Sabina's lovers include the handsome opera singer, Philip, and the former aviator, John. She also has encounters with an African American drummer named Mambo and a homosexual named Donald. Sabina's former lover Jay, a painter, now serves as her confident, as does her female friend Djuna, a dancer. In addition to seeking guilt-free, meaningful sexual expression, Sabina attempts to define her identity as an actress, a process complicated by her stage fright. By the end of the novel, Sabina returns to her husband. Although she fails to achieve the deep fulfillment she sought, she develops a stronger awareness of her true complexity. The novel's prologue and epilogue feature a mysterious figure called the Lie Detector who helps Sabina see the truth about herself.

Characters: One of the earliest practitioners of the psychological novel, Nïn shared with such modernist writers as D.H. Lawrence, James Joyce, and Virginia Woolf a belief in the importance of the subconscious. Nïn's interest and background in psychology (she consulted with the celebrated psychoanalysts Rene Allendy and Otto Rank in Paris in the 1930s and later practiced with the latter in New York) is evident in all of her work, which is written in a poetic, often structurally experimental style. Nïn is probably best known for her diaries, which she began keeping when she was eleven years old and supplied many of the experiences and impressions found in her fiction. *A Spy in the House of Love* is the fourth in a series of five impressionistic novels that includes *Ladders to Fire* (1946), *Children of the Albatross* (1947), *The Four-Chambered Heart* (1950), and *Seduction of the Minotaur*. These novels focus on various aspects of the feminine psyche through three characters—pianist Lillian, actress Sabina, and dancer Djuna—one of whom takes center stage in each novel. *A Spy in the House of Love* centers on a women's need for both passion and artifice: to achieve fulfillment through love but also to conceal her true nature from her lover.

Nïn is praised for the intense exploration of the female psyche found in both her diaries and her fiction, and in *A Spy in the House of Love* this exploration occurs through **Sabina.** Critics note that the novel's other characters are shadowy figures who function primarily to elucidate Sabina's personality. Sabina shares several important characteristics with her creator: she is sensitive and artistic, associates with sophisticated, creative people, and is married to a conventional but tolerant man who apparently allows her unlimited freedom to act on her desires. Sabina wishes to be a free spirit and challenge the sexual restraints imposed on women, a "Dona Juana" who, like the classic male figure Don Juan, enjoys sexual passion without guilt or anxiety. Similarly, Sabina disguises her stage fright by substituting actual stage work with appearances in a flowing black cape, suggesting freedom from inhibition, and through acting the sexual temptress. Sabina's succession of lovers prove unsatisfying, however, and she finally faces (with the Lie Detector's help) the truth about herself: that although she has defined herself as "a spy in the house of love"—an aloof observer and recorder—she is actually frightened, repressed, and incapable of unconstrained passion. Yet Sabina also realizes that her nature is multi-layered, like the multiple outlines of female figure featured in a painting by Marcel Duchamps, *Nude Descending a Staircase*. She recognizes that her personality comprises complex and sometimes contradictory elements. Thus her journey of self-discovery is not completely fruitless.

A mysterious figure who appears only in the novel's prologue and epilogue, the **Lie Detector** provides a less subjective view on Sabina's perspective. Either as Sabina's alter ego or as an omniscient "spy" capable of discerning the truth, the Lie Detector grounds an otherwise completely subjective narration. Some critics interpret this character as the kind of father figure found in much of Nïn's work (Nïn's own father abandoned the family when she was a child)—in this case, the good father who helps her face her guilt and recognize that, in choosing "divided" loves over commitment to one lover, she is seeking safety from the traumas that she has experienced in the past.

Sabina's complaisant, forgiving husband, **Alan**, cares deeply about her but is insensitive to her deepest needs. Nevertheless he seems to be aware that he should not try to dominate her, and he allows her to freely explore erotic liaisons with other men. Presumably modeled after Nïn's husband Hugh Guiler (also known as Ian Hugo), the stable Alan is the refuge to which Sabina returns at the end of her adventures. Sabina has a brief affair with **Philip**, a handsome Wagnerian tenor whose appreciation for music and nature pleases her. Virile and assertive, Philip seems to be an authentic Don Juan figure (whereas Sabina is a failed Dona Juana). Sabina's liaison with former airplane pilot **John** is also brief, despite the erotic pleasure he affords her. John suffers from malaria and perhaps battle fatigue; he is nearly mad, and Sabina often associates him with the image of the moon. Sabina's friend **Jay** is said to have been based on Nïn's close friend, the acclaimed novelist Henry Miller. Like Miller, Jay is an artist (although he is a painter rather than a writer), a native of Brooklyn, New York, and serves as Sabina's confidant and critic. It is Jay who introduces Sabina to the concept of the self multi-layered.

Other characters in the novel include **Mambo,** an African American political exile and musician who desires Sabina but finally decides she is too timid and self-involved for an affair with him; in addition, he resents her condescending characterization of him as "primitive." The homosexual **Donald** shares some caresses with Sabina that prove calming rather than passionate; her feelings for him are maternal, not erotic. Sabina's friend **Djuna** (who figures more prominently in other novels) helps her achieve serenity after her return from her sexual adventures, partly by introducing her to Beethoven's *Quartets*, which embody for Sabina the concept of harmony drawn from complexity. **Lillian,** another of Sabina's friend, plays only a minor role in the novel; in other works by Nïn, she defines herself through conventional domesticity.

Further Reading

Baljakian, Anna. " . . . and the Pursuit of Happiness': *The Scarlet Letter* and *A Spy in the House of Love*." *Mosaic* Vol. 11, no. 2 (Winter 1978): 163–70.

Contemporary Literary Criticism. Vols. 1, 4, 8, 11, 14. Detroit: Gale Research.

Cutting, Rose Marie. *Anais Nïn: A Reference Guide.* Boston: G.K. Hall, 1978.

Dictionary of Literary Biography. Vols. 2, 4. Detroit: Gale Research.

Hinz, Evelyn J. *The Mirror and the Garden: Realism and Reality in the Writings of Anais Nïn.* Columbus: Ohio University Press, 1971.

Major Twentieth-Century Writers. Vols. 3. Detroit Gale Research.

Molyneux, Maxine, and Julia Casterton. "Looking Again at Anais Nïn." *Minnesota Review* n.s., no. 18 (spring 1982): 86–101.

Miller, Henry. "Un Etre Etoilique." *Criterion* Vol. 17, no. 66 (October 1973): 33–52.

Spencer, Sharon. *Collage of Dreams: The Writings of Anais Nïn.* Swallow, 1977.

Lewis Nkosi
1936–
South African novelist, critic, dramatist, scriptwriter, and short story writer.

Mating Birds (novel, 1986)

Plot: The novel takes place in the seacoast town of Durban, South Africa during the period when that country was under the rigid *apartheid* system, which sought to separate blacks and whites and severely limited the rights of blacks. A central precept of apartheid—and a central concern of the novel—was the law prohibiting sexual relations between members of different races. The main character in *Mating Birds* is Ndi Sibiya, a former college student in his mid-twenties who informs the reader that he is in prison awaiting execution for the rape of a white woman. Shifting frequently between the past and present, Sibiya describes how he first noticed a beautiful white woman lying on the "Whites Only" beach close to the small stream that divides that section of the sand from the part open to blacks. Returning to the beach day after day, Sibiya becomes obsessed with the woman, who he learns is a nightclub stripper named Veronica Slater. For her part, the woman appears to flirt silently with Sibiya, and the two develop a kind of relationship despite the fact that they do not know or speak to each other. One day, the two young people manage to make love while each lies on his or her separate part of the beach, facing each other. The next day, Sibiya follows Veronica to her bungalow. Seeing him watching her, Veronica leaves her door open while she slowly undresses and lies down naked on her bed. Sibiya enters the house and has sex with Veronica, apparently with her consent, but when the two are discovered by passersby she claims that he has raped her. The novel recounts Sibiya's subsequent trial, which he knows can have no other outcome than to convict him. He is duly convicted and sentenced to be executed, and as the novel ends he is facing his death with resignation and appreciation for the freedom songs he hears his fellow prisoners singing.

Characters: Known primarily as an exiled South African scholar of contemporary African literature, Nkosi garnered widespread praise for *Mating Birds*, which is his first novel. Because it is an exploration of a crime (or alleged crime) committed by a protagonist who is indifferent both to his own impending death and to his society's moral strictures, *Mating Birds* has been compared to Albert Camus' renowned existentialist novel *The Stranger*. Some critics faulted Nkosi for weakening his rebuttal of the fantasy of the sex-crazed African male by employing a stereotypical female character; Rob Nixon commented that the novel is marked by "bold psychological insight, but . . . marred by vexing sexual politics."

The novel's narrator and central character is sensitive, articulate, twenty-five-year-old **Ndi Sibiya**, who hopes to record his experiences in an unemotional, unsentimental manner and thus perhaps understand what has happened to him. Sibiya reminisces about his childhood in a Zulu village, where he was cherished by a large extended family and sheltered from many of the realities of the wider South African society. The son of a conservative, traditional elderly man and a young, spirited mother eager for her son to achieve great things, Sibiya was allowed to attend a nearby Lutheran school. After the death of his father, he and his mother moved to Durban, and he eventually entered the university. An aspiring writer of some promise, Sibiya was expelled after he became active in opposing the university's discrimination against black students. He then began to spend his days idly, during which period he noticed and became increasingly obsessed with Veronica Slater. During the first glance exchanged between the two, Sibiya defies his society's rigid social strictures by not looking away, thus asserting his right to be viewed as a whole human being. In his efforts to understand his subsequent behavior, Sibiya remembers an incident from his childhood in which a lovely young white girl treated him with kindness; he feels that this experience permanently "marked" him and led eventually to his obsession with a white woman. From the beginning of the novel, Sibiya admits that he is not sure that he is blameless, for in the weeks before his physical encounter with Veronica he had been consumed by a dangerous, escalating combination of lust and anger that destroyed his autonomy and self-worth. Critics praised Nkosi for his skillful portrayal of the ambiguity of Sibiya's motivation, which remains an unresolved mystery. Sibiya's feeling of isolation and alienation during the trial may be attributed both to his inherent confusion about whether he has actually committed a crime and to his belief that a black person cannot attain justice in South Africa. He manifests his feeling that he is simply a goat being prepared for a ritual slaughter through his obvious boredom with the proceedings—he even falls asleep at one point. The novel ends on a slight note of hope, however, as Sibiya listens to the freedom songs that may possibly herald a coming time when people, like the birds he sees mating outside his prison window, may come together in freedom and joy.

Perhaps the most controversial aspect of the *Mating Birds* is Nkosi's portrayal of **Veronica Slater**, the white woman with whom Sibiya develops an ambiguous, unspoken, and obsessive connection. Early in his life, Sibiya's father had warned him against involvement with white women, terming them a kind of seductive "bait" by which black men are inevitably drawn toward destruction. But on the day that he first notices Veronica, Sibiya sees in her expression "the offer of a familiarity for which nothing had prepared me," an apparent acknowledgment of him as a person and man. From that point on, Veronica seems to communicate with Sibiya through her eyes and body (a skill he claims she has honed in her work as a nightclub stripper) and appears aware of and eager to manipulate the power that both her race and her sex give her over him. Although he is not sure exactly what happened during the alleged rape, Sibiya is convinced that his obsession was reciprocated by Veronica and that there was a kind of pact between them. During the trial, however, Veronica makes no acknowledgment of this relationship and in fact tries to cast herself as the pale, vulnerable, virtuous victim of a sex-crazed monster. In the end, Sibiya asserts that Veronica is only marginally responsible for his fate, for she is merely the instrument of an inhumane society. Many critics considered Nkosi's one-dimensional depiction of Veronica—who is presented only through Sibiya's eyes—as the stereotypical evil seductress a serious flaw in the novel. Further, some were offended by the implicit suggestion that Veronica actually invited the rape.

Sibiya calls the criminal psychiatrist **Dr. Emile Dufré**—a Swiss Jew who wants to record Sibiya's story for the "augmentation of scientific knowledge"—"my persistent suitor, my solemn inquisitor, the wrecker of my peace, my inquisitor." A large man with a hooked nose and rimless spectacles, Dufré questions Sibiya in a calm, patient, methodical manner that gradually reveals that he shares the prevailing view of the prisoner as a compulsive rapist. He delves into Sibiya's childhood but is disappointed when he does not uncover the kind of dramatic evidence that would allow a Freudian analysis of his behavior; meanwhile, he overlooks or fails to probe more meaningful memories. In fact, the doctor seeks not so much the truth as verification of his own preconceived notions. Reflecting that he and Dufré are separated by an unbreachable gulf of race and culture, Sibiya notes that the doctor will at least benefit from this debacle when his report earns accolades from his colleagues.

A dominant figure in Sibiya's early life is his beautiful, proud, restless mother **Nonkanyezi**, who was the youngest and apparent favorite of his father's four wives. Uneducated herself but ambitious and shrewd, she managed to persuade her husband to let their son attend school, which the old man feared would plant unreasonable ambition and dissatisfaction in the boy's consciousness. After her husband's death, Nonkanyezi takes her son to live in the black slum of Durban, where she eventually succumbs to the degradation of selling bootleg liquor. She briefly converts to an evangelical church, but gradually grows more cynical and promiscuous, and adopts an exaggeratedly gay manner. Commentators have noted that

Sibiya's portrayal of Nonkanyezi, who is repeatedly described in such terms as "provocative" and "coquettish," resembles his notably one-dimensional, sexualized depictions of other female characters.

The novel's courtroom scenes highlight the hypocrisy of South Africa's criminal justice system during the apartheid period, when civil rights were systematically denied to blacks even as the grandiose pomp of "empty ritual" continued. Presiding at Sibiya's trial is **Chief Justice Milne,** in whose solicitousness toward the prisoner Sibiya sees proof that he will be convicted. The flagrantly racist prosecutor, **Kakmekaar,** casts Sibiya as a depraved monster and urges the judge to make an example of this prisoner and thus defend the sanctity of white South African womanhood. Although Sibiya's defense attorney, dapper, white-haired **Max Siegfried Muller** (a refugee from Nazi Germany who routinely defends the oppressed people of his adopted country) is considered "the scourge of the Establishment," he is powerless to protect Sibiya from their society's thirst for vengeance. Other characters include the notoriously brutal prison commander, **Colonel A. C. Van Rooyen,** whom Sibiya recognizes as a miserable man with an unhappy home life; and **Professor Van Niekerk,** a racist history professor at Sibiya's university who maintains that African history begins with the arrival of white men on the continent.

Further Reading

Black Literature Criticism, Vol. 2. Detroit: Gale Research.

Contemporary Literary Criticism, Vol. 45. Detroit: Gale Research.

Gates, Henry Louis, Jr. "The Power of Her Sex, the Power of Her Race." *New York Times Book Review* (May 18, 1986): 3.

Hanley, Lynne. "Writing Across the Color Bar: Apartheid and Desire." *Massachusetts Review* 32 (Winter 1991/1992): 495-506.

Lazarus, Neil. "Measure and Unmeasure: The Antimonies of Lewis Nkosi." *Southern Review* 23, No. 1 (January 1987): 106-18.

Maitland, Sara. "Small Worlds." *New Statesman* 112, No. 2892 (August 29, 1986): 25-6.

Maja-Pearce, Adewale. "Compensatory Acts." *Times Literary Supplement* No. 4349 (August 8, 1986): 863.

Nixon, Rob. "Race Case." *Village Voice* XXXI, No. 30 (July 19, 1986): 46.

Packer, George. "Reports from the Inside." *Nation* 243, No. 17 (November 22, 1986): 570-74.

Joyce Carol Oates
1938–

American novelist, short story writer, poet, dramatist, essayist, critic, and editor.

You Must Remember This (novel, 1987)

Plot: The novel chronicles the years 1953–56 in the lives of the middle-class Stevick family, who live in the small town of Port Oriskany, New York. The family consists of the father, Lyle, who owns a used furniture store, his wife, Hannah, and children Warren (a

Korean War veteran), Geraldine, Lizzie, and Enid Maria, who is the central character of the novel. A bright and outwardly obedient fifteen-year-old, Enid is secretly having an affair with her father's half-brother Felix, a former boxer. When Felix tries to end the relationship, Enid swallows a bottle of aspirin in a suicide attempt that ultimately gives her more leverage with Felix. The affair continues. Meanwhile, Felix acquires a young protege named Jo-Jo through whom he experiences vicariously the thrill of his lost vocation until Jo-Jo is killed in the ring. For some time Enid's passion for her uncle seems to balance all the other areas of her life, but gradually their liaison grows more sordid and Enid more disillusioned. The affair ends when Enid becomes pregnant and has an abortion. The novel's conclusion reveals that Felix finally marries and leaves Port Oriskany, while Enid receives a scholarship to study at a prestigious music school.

Characters: A master of many genres, Oates is lauded as one of America's most prolific and talented contemporary writers. She employs dense, elliptical prose in her fiction, often delving into the dark, even violent corners of the human psyche. The observation that Oates's characters nevertheless tend to be survivors is particularly true of *You Must Remember This,* which is considered one of her finest novels for its expert storytelling, richly detailed description, and complex main characters. Like much of Oates's fiction, the novel takes place in fictional Eden County, New York, which is closely modeled after the author's native Erie County. Oates has been praised for her convincing portrayal of American life in the 1950s; *You Must Remember This* contains references to such current events as the "Red scare," the Rosenberg executions, the growing popularity of television, and the national obsession with civil defense. Critics note that the novel concludes more optimistically than most of Oates's previous works, for the characters navigate safely through the storms of obsessive love, lust, jealousy, and hate that rage through their lives.

Teenaged **Enid Maria Stevick** and her uncle-lover Felix are the central characters in *You Must Remember This,* and their love affair provides the novel's primary tension. Many commentators view Enid as another example of Oates's skill in portraying the crises and confusions of adolescence. Enid presents herself as an obedient, dutiful Catholic girl, and she is talented musically and intellectually, yet she also possesses what she calls her "Angel-face" persona, which is cynical, sly, watchful, and sexually precocious. It is Angel-face who tempts Enid to jaywalk, shoplift, and pursue the sexual relationship with her half-uncle. Enid also suffers from what she terms her "death-panic"—an attraction to death closely tied to her wish to control: she does not want to die like the dove she once saw set afire. Suicide would be better, because it would mean she had chosen her own death (indeed, her actual suicide attempt does increase her control over her lover). Several critics note that in this novel Oates devotes an unusual amount of attention to sex, through which her characters achieve obliteration of personality. Indeed, Enid finds that sex with Felix affords her a closer connection with physical, instinctual life, and gives her whole life deeper meaning. Nevertheless, their passion ebbs as Enid learns more about her uncle's character, and her harrowing abortion provides the final blow. Oates has been lauded for so effectively describing this experience, during which Enid's mind keeps replaying the image of the enflamed dove frantically trying to escape death. Enid eventually recovers from her affair with Felix. Unlike other heroines in Oates's work (such as Maureen Wendall in *Them*), Enid has not suffered serious damage. In fact, she has a bright future because of her music school scholarship, which could indicate a trend in Oates's recent work to emphasize survival and the resilience of the human spirit.

Through Enid's half-uncle and lover **Felix Stevick**, Oates manifests her interest in boxing, which she characterizes (particularly in her nonfiction book *On Boxing*, 1987) as a regulated expression of the violence that lurks just beneath the surface of ordinary existence. Felix's promising career is cut short when he mistakenly lets himself act out of anger. With his invulnerability thus destroyed comes the realization that he could actually die. Now he can only feel the thrill of boxing through his protege, Jo-Jo, and Felix finds vicarious experience a poor substitute for the real thing. All his life Felix "thrived on opposition, resistance." He appreciates the clear-cut simplicity of the sport—that if a boxer is hit by his opponent, he deserves the blow—nothing is accidental. Felix lives simplistically as well, and after his initial, frenzied sexual encounter with his teenaged niece, Felix tries to resist having anything more to do with her, explaining that he is not the kind of man who would take advantage of his half-brother's young daughter. But Enid's suicide attempt enables her to control him—he admits they are now on equal footing—and he gives in to the same passion she feels for him. Although Oates portrays the affair as a sordid one, she does not seem to judge either partner too harshly. Both go on to brighter futures, with Enid studying music and Felix marrying and leaving Port Oriskany.

The seemingly placid middle-class Stevick family shows signs of being affected by the same currents of disorder and bewilderment seen in American society as a whole during the 1950s. **Lyle Stevick**, the often foolish, generally failed proprietor of a second-hand furniture store, is nevertheless affectionately rendered by Oates. In an episode that underlines the ridiculous excesses of the "Red scare," Lyle is arrested as a suspected traitor when he points out to a customer that the Soviet Union and China have more land mass than the United States. Lyle's wife, **Hannah**, is a typical overwhelmed mother and homemaker; several critics have been moved by the scene in which this aging, overweight couple has sex in a bomb shelter and affirm their love for each other. **Warren Stevick**, the family's only son, has been badly disfigured while fighting in the Korean War; a complex, interesting character, he manifests the same resilience shown by Enid when, maintaining his idealism despite his hardships, he becomes an antinuclear protester. Enid's sisters illustrate two possible routes open to American women in the 1950s: **Geraldine** marries early and begins a life of domestic drudgery, while **Lizzie** becomes a singer (and possibly a prostitute) in a sleazy New York City establishment.

Other characters in the novel include the dying **Grandfather Stevick**, who commits suicide in a hospital bed, which Enid claims is his way to assert control over his own life and death; and Felix's young boxing protege, **Jo-Jo**, who reminds him of the "joy of the body" that the sport epitomizes but who is battered to death during a match.

Further Reading

Contemporary Literary Criticism. Vols. 1, 2, 3, 6, 9, 11, 15, 19, 33, 52. Detroit: Gale Research.

Creighton, Joanne V. *Joyce Carol Oates: Novels of the Middle Years.* New York: Twayne, 1992.

Dictionary of Literary Biography. Vols. 2, 5, 1981 Yearbook. Detroit: Gale Research.

Johnson, Greg. *Understanding Joyce Carol Oates.* Columbia: University of South Carolina Press, 1987.

Kakutani, Michiko. Review of *You Must Remember This. New York Times* (August 10, 1987): C20.

Major twentieth-Century Writers. Vol. 3. Detroit: Gale Research.

Phillips, Robert. Review of *You Must Remember This. America* Vol. 157, no. 14 (November 14, 1987): 360, 362.

Updike, John. "What You Deserve Is What You Get." *New Yorker* Vol. 63, no. 45 (December 28, 1987): 119–23.

Edna O'Brien

1932–

Irish novelist, short story writer, dramatist, scriptwriter, autobiographer, and editor.

"Storm" (short story, 1990)

Plot: The story's narrator is Eileen, a middleaged woman who is vacationing with her grown son Mark and his girlfriend Penny in what appears to be an island village off the coast of Italy. Depressed over the end of her relationship with a married lover, Eileen feels isolated and alienated from the two passionate young people. This irritation leads to her bursting out with a barrage of complaints, which her son answers with an angry tirade of his own. Mortified, Eileen tries to apologize, but the atmosphere among the three remains tense. The morning after the argument, Eileen suggests that Mark and Penny leave her alone for the day, and they decide to go sailing. During the late afternoon, a big storm blows in, and when the two young people fail to appear Eileen begins to worry. Her anxiety grows as the evening passes, and she attempts to prepare herself for the worst. Finally, however, Mark and Penny arrive and happily relate the events of their day, most of which was spent safely off the sea. They promise to take Eileen, the next night, to a restaurant they have discovered. As the story closes, Eileen's relationship with her son and his girlfriend has—at least on the surface—returned to normal.

Characters: O'Brien won the Los Angeles Times Book Award for *Lantern Slides*, the short story collection in which "Storm" appears. A highly respected contemporary writer praised as both an accomplished storyteller and a consummate prose writer, O'Brien focuses more on evoking feelings than on experimenting with form. Although some commentators contend that the often heavily melancholy tone of her fiction lessens its overall impact, most praise her ability to render with elegance and compassion the complexities of relationships and of human emotions.

O'Brien's fiction is dominated by female protagonists who are grieving over lost love or otherwise struggling to overcome their pasts; although they are essentially romantics, these characters have lost many of their illusions and feel lonely and isolated. Recently been abandoned by her married lover, middleaged **Eileen** has like other O'Brien protagonists experienced passion, marriage, and raising children but is essentially alone now. She has been left with a feeling that the best part of her life is now past and that she is irreparably separate from her traveling companions. Intensely aware of the youth and fresh, burgeoning love of Mark and Penny, Eileen reflects with annoyance that she was never as young or carefree as these two. Her resentment finally erupts in her angrily accusing them of excluding her while taking advantage of her generosity. Eileen is immediately appalled by her own tirade, which provokes a shockingly savage response from her son and alienates her further from the young couple. She spends a miserable day alone, during which she has an embarrassing encounter with a mentally defective youth when she tries to go swimming. O'Brien's evocation of Eileen's thoughts and fears during and after the storm is detailed and highly effective: her mind careens from imagining how Penny's parents will react to their daughter's drowning to assuming the two are safe to remembering incidents from Mark's childhood. At the end of the story, she and Mark have silently agreed to act as if nothing troubling has occurred between them, the narrator notes that "They have each looked into the abyss and drawn back, frightened of the primitive forces that lurk there."

The tender but mysterious link between mothers and children is a dominant concern in O'Brien's fiction and a central theme of "Storms." During the bleak day she spends alone,

Eileen observes someone flying a kite, an image that "suggests to her the thin thread between mother and child"—the fragility of which her recent rift with her college-student son **Mark** has reminded her. Having always been a mild, gentle person, Mark shocks Eileen with the intensity of his rage after she has let loose her string of complaints. Eileen interprets this outburst as a sign that Mark is aligning himself with Penny, not her, and the memory of it causes her special pain during the agonizing period she spends worrying about the fate of the young couple. But Eileen also remembers happier moments from her shared past with Mark, such as the time he wanted to pluck his long eyelashes and give them to her. After Mark's return, Eileen recognizes—and seems to accept—that Mark is aware of but unable or unwilling to deal with her pain.

The story's other significant character is Mark's tall, blonde, pretty girlfriend, **Penny**, whose self-assurance, frequent moodiness, and untidy habits all grate on Eileen's nerves and contribute to her feeling of alienation. Interestingly, however, it is Penny who pleads with Mark not to be so angry and vicious when he is berating his mother. After the couple's return from their day away from her, Eileen senses that Penny has forgiven her for her outburst, and she feels, strangely, younger and more insecure than twenty-year-old Penny.

Further Reading

Annan, Gabrielle. "Bitterness Is Her Theme." *Spectator* 264, No. 8448 (June 9, 1990): 40-1.

Cahill, Thomas. "On Edna O'Brien's *Lantern Slides*." *Los Angeles Times Book Review* (4 November 1990): 11.

Contemporary Literary Criticism, Vols. 3, 5, 8, 13, 36, 65. Detroit: Gale Research.

Doughty, Louise. "Restless Dreaming Souls." *Times Literary Supplement* No. 4549 (June 8, 1990): 616.

Fuller, Jack. "Wryly Irish." *Chicago Tribune—Books* (May 27, 1990): 1, 3.

Leavitt, David. "Small Tragedies and Ordinary Passions." *New York Times Book Review* (June 24, 1990): 9.

O'Hara, Kiera. "Love Objects: Love and Obsession in the Stories of Edna O'Brien." *Studies in Short Fiction* 30 (1993): 317-25.

Tremain, Rose. "Walking Wounded." *Listener* 123, No. 3168 (June 7, 1990): 27.

Tim O'Brien
1946–
American novelist and journalist.

Going After Cacciato (novel, 1978)

Plot: The novel features three interwoven narrative strands that relate both actual and dreamed events in the lives of Paul Berlin, a young American soldier fighting in the Vietnam War, and some of the other members of the Third Squad, First Platoon of Alpha Company in the 46th Infantry. After a period in which several members of the squad have been killed, an apparently simpleminded soldier named Cacciato walks away with the stated intention of eventually reaching freedom in Paris. The rest of the squad is charged with following Cacciato, but their efforts are fruitless and they return to camp. While standing guard in an observation tower near the sea, however, Paul imagines the squad traveling over 8000 miles from Vietnam to France in search of Cacciato and having many adventures along the way. When they finally reach Paris, they locate Cacciato but soon lose him again and return on foot to Vietnam. Paul's account of this fantastic journey alternates with his ruminations, during his six hours of guard duty, about his childhood and his views on courage, duty, and his own role in the war.

Characters: O'Brien won the National Book Award for *Going After Cacciato*, which reflects his own experiences as a foot soldier in the Vietnam War and has been called one of the most accomplished works to emerge from that conflict. The complex narrative structure blends realistic descriptions of the soldiers' daily lives with well-rendered accounts of their imagined adventures and of Paul's philosophical explorations while standing guard. Although a few critics faulted this structure as confusing, most found it an effective approach to the fragmentation and complexity of the Vietnam War. In crisp prose that is alternately gritty and lyrical, O'Brien explores such themes as the power and limits of imagination; the nature of courage, duty, and responsibility; the absurdity of war; and the persistence of compassion in the face of the irrational.

The events related in *Going After Cacciato* are viewed primarily through the perspective of **Paul Berlin**, who is obviously the most reflecting and imaginative member of his squad even if he is also essentially ordinary. Paul remembers that before he came to Vietnam, his father—with whom he seems to have a warm relationship—told him that he would surely see many bad things during the war but that he should try to look for good things, too. This advice has proved futile in the face of the reality of Vietnam, and Paul's confusion about the purpose of the conflict and his own role in it echoes that of many American soldiers. Both Paul's long, elaborate fantasy of a transcontinental search for Cacciato and his observation-post meditations constitute a "way of asking questions" and of "exploring possibilities." They allow him to expand his self-knowledge and face the fear and confusion that are natural to a soldier in any war but particularly characteristic of this bewildering conflict. The task of chasing a soldier who may or may not have made a conscious decision to escape the war prompts Paul to consider the option of desertion himself, and he initially views it as a "happy thing." The attractive Vietnamese woman Sarkin Aung Wan, whom Paul has invented as a companion during the imagined journey, tries to persuade him to join her in a life of love and freedom far from the brutality of Vietnam. But by the end of their discussion in the Majestic Hotel in Paris (where, significantly, the Paris Peace Talks are being held at the same time), Paul rejects this possibility. He admits that he does not know exactly what he is fighting for but that he is doing it for "reasons beyond knowledge. Because he believed in law, and law told him to go." It is not just civil law that binds Paul however, but also his sense of obligation to others. "I am afraid of running away," he says, " . . . I fear what might be thought of me by those I love." Paul explains that "Even in imagination, obligation cannot be outrun." Although Paul's understanding is not necessarily yet complete nor his courage well-developed (as demonstrated by his account of losing control of his bowels during a confrontation), he seems to have established at least a small measure of control over his *response* to his circumstances, if not the circumstances themselves. Paul is sometimes compared with Frederick Henry in Ernest Hemingway's *A Farewell to Arms* (1929) and Captain Yossarian in Joseph Heller's *Catch-22* (1961), for all three characters yearn for escape from terrifying, absurd conflicts. Yet Paul differs significantly from these protagonists in his rejection of the "separate peace" they seek and his acceptance of his role in the war, despite its possible illogic.

Pleasant, childlike **Private Cacciato** is depicted in the novel's realistic segments as a goofy young man with "no purchase on life's slippery runway." He eats too much and engages in pointless games, such as fishing in bomb craters that could not possibly contain fish. Described as "openfaced and naive and plump," Cacciato lacks the normal refinements men acquire as they mature, so that he is as "blurred and uncolored and bland" as the traditional concepts of courage and duty have become in the context of the Vietnam War. Cacciato is something of an enigmatic figure, for his fellow soldiers do not understand his motives for going AWOL (absent without leave). Cacciato had not taken part in the recent "fragging" (Vietnam-era term for incidents in which officers were killed by their own men) of a lieutenant whose orders had led to the deaths of several squad members, and his departure could be a conscious rejection of such brutality. Cacciato has previously exhibited considerable bravery, but most of his fellow soldiers have attributed this to ignorance or accident and they are similarly inclined to dismiss his departure as an innocent whim. Paul seems to view Cacciato as exhibiting a form of moral courage, although he himself chooses a different route in the end. In any case, Cacciato—whose name means "hunted" or "caught" in Italian—evades capture in both the actual course of events and Paul's fantasy, and the reader never learns what happens to him.

O'Brien has been praised for his gritty, sometimes lurid account of the daily life of ordinary soldiers in Vietnam, his sensitive articulation of their confrontation with an unfamiliar, often hostile landscape and culture, and his riveting depiction of the squad's imaginary adventures as they cross the 8000 miles between Vietnam and Paris. Some of the most prominent members of Paul's squad are **Oscar Johnson**; **Stink Harris**, who jumps ship near Greece in order to avoid capture; and **Doc Peret**, a medic who, during one of the novel's realistic sections, administers M&Ms to a dying soldier in place of medicine. Other soldiers include **Frenchie Tucker** and **Bernie Lynn**, who die in a mined Viet Cong tunnel; and **Billy Boy Watkins**, who is said to have died of fright. **Lieutenant Sidney Martin** is an extremely proper officer who always closely follows regulations and thus ignores his mens' pleas that they be excused from crawling into a Viet Cong tunnel. When the incident leads to the deaths of several soldiers, the men silently agree to kill Martin with a hand grenade.

Paul invents a beautiful young Vietnamese woman, **Sarkin Aung Wan**, to accompany them on their journey to Paris. A refugee from Cholon whose restaurateur father was executed by the Viet Cong, she tries to persuade Paul to flee the war with her; like Catherine Barkley in *A Farewell to Arms*, she encourages him to seek a "separate peace." Several critics found Sarkin Aung Wan a one-dimensional character present primarily to facilitate the plot. Another significant Vietnamese character is **Major Li Van Hgoc**, an urbane Viet Cong officer whom the American soldiers encounter when, during their journey to Paris, they accidentally fall into the tunnel he inhabits. A representative, according to critic Milton J. Bates, of "every enemy soldier the Americans have ever encountered," Van (as he prefers to be called) is trapped underground by his own set of obligations.

While trekking through Yugoslavia, the squad meets a young **American woman** who gives them a ride in her van. She tells the men she admires them because they "saw evil and walked away," and she claims that she did something similar when she dropped out of San Diego State University. Outraged and incredulous at this comparison, the men throw her out of the van and continue on their way. The woman's attitude and failure to comprehend the true complexities of the soldiers' situation may reflect the popular perception, in many segments of American society, that the Vietnam War was evil and its participants tainted.

Further Reading

Bell, Pearl K. "Writing About Vietnam." *Commentary* (October 1978): 74–7.

Bates, Milton J. "Tim O'Brien's Myth of Courage." *Modern Fiction Studies* Vol. 33, no. 2 (Summer 1987): 263–79.

Contemporary Literary Criticism Vols. 7, 19, 40. Detroit: Gale Research.

Edwards, Thomas R. "Feeding on Fantasy." *New York Review of Books* Vol. 26, no. 12 (July 19, 1979): 41–2.

Freedman, Richard. "A Separate Peace." *New York Times Book Review* (February 12, 1978): 1, 21.

Herzog, Toby C. "*Going After Cacciato*: The Soldier-Author-Character Seeking Control." *Critique* (Winter 1983): 88–96.

Ludington, Townsend. "Comprehending the American Experience in Vietnam–A Review Essay." *Southern Humanities Review* (Fall 1984): 339–49.

Palm, Edward F. "The Search for a Usable Past: Vietnam Literature and the Separate Peace Syndrome." *South Atlantic Quarterly* (Spring 1983): 115–28.

Pochoda, Elizabeth. "Vietnam, We've All Been There." *Nation* Vol. 226, no. 11 (March 25, 1978): 344–46.

Raymond, Michael W. "Imagined Responses to Vietnam: Tim O'Brien's *Going After Cacciato*." *Critique* (Winter 1983): 97–104.

Updike, John. Review of *Going After Cacciato*. *New Yorker* Vol. 54, no. 6 (March 27, 1978): 128–30, 133.

Clifford Odets
1906-1963
American dramatist and scriptwriter.

Awake and Sing! (play, 1935)

Plot: Set in the mid-1930s in the Bronx, New York, the play centers on working-class Jewish family, the Bergers, whose members include its domineering matriarch, Bessie, her ineffectual husband Myron and businessman brother Morty, and her son Ralph and daughter Hennie, who are in their twenties. Bessie's father Jacob, an embittered old Socialist, also lives with the family, and a small-time racketeer named Moe Alexander rents a room in the house. With the exception of prosperous Morty, the family has struggled for years with poverty and disappointed aspirations, always goaded onward by Bessie's materialism and yearning for respectability. When Hennie becomes pregnant by an unnamed man, Bessie forces her to marry naive, hapless Sam Feinschreiber so that the family can avoid the shame of an illegitimate birth. Idealistic Ralph is disgusted by this development and stunned that his grandfather, who shares his feelings about the matter, did nothing to stop it. Soon after exhorting Ralph to pursue his dream of helping to create a better society, Jacob commits suicide. Although Ralph had previously been downcast about his limited opportunities and his broken romance with a working-class girl, he is inspired by his grandfather's act to do what he can to follow Jacob's advice. Meanwhile, Moe encourages Hennie to abandon her husband and child and run away with him. Hennie finally decides that she will leave with Moe, and in the play's final scene Ralph encourages her in this plan.

Characters: The son of Russian-Jewish emigrés, Odets was one of the most prominent American playwrights of the 1930s, and his plays are still respected for the compelling chronicle of the hardships and thwarted dreams of the Depression period that they provide. Despite the rather propagandistic nature of its themes, many commentators consider *Awake* *and Sing!* Odets's best play due to its authentic characterizations and vibrant, wisecracking, yet revealing dialogue. The play exposes the falsity behind the American dream of success—what Odets termed the "general fraud" of a capitalistic system that could not possibly deliver to all what it seemed to promise. *Awake and Sing!* ends on a note of hope so muted that some critics have suggested the play's title is ironic.

If any character in the play is autobiographical it is probably **Ralph Berger**, a sensitive, intelligent, idealistic twenty-two-year-old who still lives with his parents. His life has always been threadbare, and he feels stymied by a lack of opportunities to improve his lot; Ralph claims that he is "just looking for a chance to get to first base." His yearning to go somewhere, to achieve something, and to believe that life has meaning is symbolized by the sound of the mail plane he often hears flying overhead. Meanwhile, Ralph is surrounded by figures either of failure, like his father and grandfather, cynicism, like Moe, or spiritually bankrupt success, like his Uncle Morty. Meanwhile, Ralph's mother attempts to dictate who his friends should be and belittles his working-class girlfriend Blanche. What changes Ralph's course is Jacob's suicide, which occurs soon after the old man has advised Ralph not to abandon his hope of a better society. Ralph declares that his grandfather's example has rejuventated his own hope and his sparked his determination that "My days won't be for nothing." Odets does not specify just what it is that Ralph will now do, since he apparently intends to keep living with his parents, and the audience is left wondering if he will ever achieve his vague ambitions. Several commentators have faulted this character for the ease with which he gives up his sweetheart (especially after the money he inherits from Jacob should have allowed him to marry her) and for encouraging Hennie to abandon her responsibilities. These troubling aspects of Ralph's character give the play's final message an ambiguity that may or may not be intentional.

Family matriarch **Bessie Berger** is a domineering figure who tries to dictate what her children do and with whom they associate. Bessie's fear both that others are judging her and that she may lose the stability and relative security she values lead her into nagging, manipulative, and finally unscrupulous behavior. Bessie's insistence that the pregnant Hennie marry a man she does not love simply to maintain the family's good name evidences her concern with respectability above all. She keeps a spotless house that symbolizes the essential shallowness of her values, and yet Bessie also represents an admirable strength and continuity; her daughter predicts that she will "go on forever."

Bessie's husband **Myron Berger** has abdicated control of the family to her. A clerk for thirty years, Myron once studied law but has resigned himself to an impoverished existence and is, according to Odets's stage directions, "heartbroken without being aware of it." He takes refuge in the past, idolizing someone—President Theodore Roosevelt—whose personality was the exact opposite of his own. Although Myron has not yet achieved success in any endeavor, neither has he completely lost hope; in fact, he is extremely gullible and perpetually enters sweepstakes and bets on horse races and other contests. Challenged on the wisdom of this activity, Myron naively insists that "Someone's got to win. The government isn't gonna allow everything to be a fake." Ralph is disheartened by his father's example and even says, "Let me die like a dog, if I can't get more from life."

As opposed to Myron's hope for individual betterment some fine day, Bessie's father **Jacob** is an old Socialist with long-harbored utopian fantasies about a society in which all will thrive. Embittered by the collapse of his Marxist dreams, Jacob does nothing to prevent his granddaughter's forced marriage even though he knows it is wrong. He lacks the fortitude to act, but he hopes for better behavior from Ralph, whom he advises to "DO! Do what is in your heart and carry in yourself a revolution . . . . Not like me. A man who had a golden opportunity but drank instead a glass of tea." The despair and shame engendered by so many years of poverty and powerlessness drive Jacob to suicide, but this event has the at least marginally positive result of inspiring Ralph to pursue his dreams.

Ralph's twenty-six-year-old sister **Hennie** is an unmarried woman whose boredom led her into an affair that has resulted in pregnancy. Forced into marriage with a man she does not love, Hennie dreams of escape, her fantasies fuelled by Hollywood movies. Whereas her brother and grandfather dream of a future in which everyone lives happier, more fulfilling lives, Hennie envisions only her own material comfort. Unable to face life realistically, she is susceptible to Moe's description of an easy, sumptuous existence in the land of sunshine and orange trees. Yet Hennie's decision to accompany Moe seems at least as much a capitulation to his aggression as a freely made choice. Her abandonment of her husband and child is one of the play's most controversial aspects, for many critics question why Ralph seems to sanction what they view as an irresponsible act. Others contend that Odets uses Hennie to illustrate how circumstances can kill a person's morality and capacity for love.

Bessie's brother **Morty**, a wealthy clothing manufacturer, is the play's primary representive of capitalism. Smug and self-aggrandizing, Morty is devoted only to making money and ensuring his own comfort. Indifferent to the feelings or aspirations of others, he has successfully insulated himself against any emotion that might compromise or weaken his position. He claims to elevate common sense over love and comments that "to raise a family nowadays you must be a damn fool." Critics have lauded Odets for effectively dramatizing how capitalism has actually victimized its own proponent, Morty, by depriving him of his humanity. Similarly, small-time gangster Moe Alexander is damaged not only physically (he lost a leg in World War I) but spiritually, for he claims that all of life as "a racket." Moe assures Hennie that paradise lies neither heavenward nor in Marxism but in the pursuit of individual pleasures. His philosophy involves using "one thing to get another;" i.e., Hennie can and should exchange her family for freedom and material comfort.

Other characters in the play include Hennie's naive, self-loathing husband **Sam Feinschreiber**, whose shame, humiliation, and desire for anonymity make him a strong contrast to Morty; and the overworked **Schlosser**, whose wife left him and whose daughter later ran away to become a chorus girl, thus providing an example of the fate that may await the husband and child that Hennie leaves behind.

Further Reading

Contemporary Literary Criticism, Vols. 2, 28. Detroit: Gale Research.

Gassner, John. "The Long Journey of a Talent." *Theatre Arts* XXXIII, No. 6 (July 1949): 25-30.

Lahr, John. "Waiting for Odets." *New Yorker* (October 26, 1992): 119.

Murray, Edward. *Clifford Odets: The Thirties and After*. New York: Ungar, 1968.

Shuman, R. Baird. *Clifford Odets*. Boston: Twayne, 1962.

Sembene Ousmane

1923–

Senegalese novelist, screenwriter, short story writer, and editor.

Xala (novel, 1973)

Plot: Set in Senegal some time after the West African country's independence from colonial rule, *Xala* relates events in the life of a successful businessman named Abdou Kader Beye, who is called El Hadji. His prosperity is so great that he is about to marry his third wife, pretty young N'Gone. Each of his first two wives, Adja Awa Astou and Oumi N'Doye, has her own house where she lives with her children by El Hadji. At the wedding party, the aunt of El Hadji's new wife advises him to perform a traditional ritual that ensures potency, but he scornfully dismisses her warning. That night, however, El Hadji is unable to complete the sexual act with N'Gone. Learning that someone has put a xala (a cure of impotence) on him, El Hadji is extremely distressed and visits a number of marabouts (holy men, or healers) to get the xala lifted. Meanwhile, he neglects his financial affairs, which have already begun to decline due to his extravagant lifestyle. El Hadji finally locates a marabout who agrees to lift the curse for a very high fee. After writing the marabout a check, El Hadji feels his potency returning. When he finds out that his new wife is having her menstrual period, he spends a night of lovemaking with his second wife. But when El Hadji emerges from this sexual success, he discovers that his financial situation is completely collapsing. His friends desert him and the bank won't lend him money. The check El Hadji wrote to the marabout bounces, so the marabout restores the xala. His second and third wives return to their families. Only his first wife remains loyal to him, and El Hadji goes to her house to evade his creditors. The next morning, the same beggar who has long haunted his office building is waiting for him outside the house. The beggar tells him that it was he who placed the curse on El Hadji, because El Hadji ruined him financially and personally many years before. He explains that El Hadji can reverse the xala only by standing naked before the beggar and his companions and allowing them to spit on him. As the desperate El Hadji agrees, armed police wait outside, apparently expecting a riot to ensue.

Characters: Ousmane's novels and films address social concerns from a markedly Marxist-Leninist perspective. He frequently denounces the Western-influenced elite in Senegal, contending that their greed and consumerism have further oppressed the Senegalese majority. In *Xala,* Ousmane attacks the elitism of these "New Africans" and the long-standing practice of polygamy. The novel ends on what some critics term is an inescapably pessimistic note. Ousmane is one of Africa's most renowned filmmakers, a role he considers the contemporary version of the traditional *griot* (storyteller) because film has the potential to reach a much wider audience than either printed or oral communication. *Xala* was adapted as a film in 1974.

Ousmane uses the protagonist of *Xala,* **Abdou Kader Beye,** called El Hadji, to satirize the shallow, greedy Senegalese elite class. The fifty-year-old El Hadji has become very prosperous since independence and is the envy of all his friends; the fact that he can afford to marry a third wife is a bold statement of his success. Yet Ousmane points out that even though El Hadji defines himself as a "businessman," he is actually just a middleman for the big, foreign-owned trading companies that have conducted their business in post-independence Senegal much as they did during the colonial period. El Hadji's finances are never as secure as he pretends—he has grievously overextended himself—and he also overestimates the loyalty of his friends and his second and third wives. A self-involved, foolish man, El Hadji responds with horror and panic to the loss of his sexual prowess. His impotence completely obsesses him, and—even though he has previously denounced such superstition as backward—he turns immediately to the traditional marabout. Likewise, at the end of the novel El Hadji is willing to accept complete humiliation in order to get his sexual powers back. Some critics questioned the meaning of this final ritual, which is neither a true act of religious faith (for despite his title of El Hadji, which indicates that he has made a pilgrimage to Mecca, his concerns are entirely secular) nor an act of contrition for his former excesses. In addition, this punishment and the novel's dreary conclusion seem rather jarring to those commentators who find the rest of the novel more directly satirical. In any case, the ending exemplifies the moral indignation Ousmane directs at his country's elite, and it emphasizes a particularly African sense of community responsibility and retribution.

The theme of polygamy as an ultimately injurious practice is enacted through El Hadji's three wives, each of whom maintains her own household and family of children, who have little contact with their father and mainly serve as a drain on his finances. **Adja Awa Astou** is his first wife and the only one who stands by him during his crisis. The title Awa is Arabic for "first woman on earth," implying that she holds special status as her husband's first— and perhaps most deliberate—choice. Adja is a devout Muslim, and Ousmane alludes to the Marxist dictum that "religion is the opiate of the people" when he comments that she drugs herself with piety. El Hadji's second, younger wife **Oumi N'Doye** is a sharp-tongued woman with extravagant, Westernized tastes. She enjoys the status of sexual favorite until her husband selects a third, even younger wife, and when N'Gone is unavailable to El Hadji after his xala has been removed, Oumi steps in as the recipient of his newfound prowess. **N'Gone**, El Hadji's third wife, is a pretty young woman; thus he is chagrined when he cannot fulfil his desire for her.

The officious **Yay Bineta,** N'Gone's paternal aunt, or *badyen,* is matchmaker to the couple; she also advises El Hadji to observe the traditional potency ritual and later informs him that someone has put a xala on him. Critics consider Yay Bineta as illustrating one route open to African women: a traditional figure in Senegalese society, her control centers in the home, where she has influence over men (such as El Hadji) over whom she would otherwise have no control. By contrast, **Rama**—the eldest daughter of El Hadji and his first wife— illustrates the modern African woman. An advocate of nationalism, education, and sexual freedom for women, Rama nevertheless overlooks her disapproval of her father's polygamy and accepts his financial support. Although Rama's beliefs are more in line with Ousmane's than those of any of the other characters, she is portrayed as an essentially self-interested character with a telling lack of understanding about why the beggars harassing her father at the end of the novel are so angry. Through Rama, Ousmane portrays the children of Senegal's elite class as both well-intentioned and limited.

Sereen Mada is the marabout (an extremely pious Islamic hermit who serves as a kind of healer) who cures El Hadji of his xala. He proves that his interests are worldly, however, when he restores the curse after El Hadji's check bounces; thus Ousmane extends his satire from contemporary consumerism to the world of traditional religion.

Further Reading

Bayo, Ogunjimi. "Ritual Archetypes—Sembene's Aesthetic Medium in *Xala.*" *Ufahamu: Journal of the African Activist Association* No. 3 (1985): 128–38.

Black Literature Criticism. Vol. 3. Detroit: Gale Research.

Iyam, David Uru. "The Silent Revolutionaries: Ousmane Sembene's 'Emitai,' 'Xala,' and 'Ceddo.'" *African Studies Review* Vol. 29, no. 4 (December 1986): 79–87.

Lyons, Harriet D. "The Uses of Ritual in Sembene's *Xala.*" *Canadian Review of African Studies* Vol. 18, no. 2 (1984): 319–28.

Pfaff, Francoise. *The Cinema of Ousmane Sembene, A Pioneer of African Film.* Westport, Conn.: Greenwood Press, 1984.

Updike, John. "The World Called Third." In *Hugging the Shore: Essays and Criticism,* New York: Knopf, 1983, pp. 676–86.

Contemporary Literary Criticism, Vol. 66. Detroit: Gale Research.

Cynthia Ozick

1928–

American short story writer, novelist, essayist, poet, and translator.

"The Pagan Rabbi" (short story, 1971)

Plot: As the story opens, the narrator reveals that his old friend Rabbi Isaac Kornfeld has committed suicide by hanging himself from an oak tree. The narrator wants to know what led the rabbi to this act. The two men attended rabbinical school together but subsequently chose different paths. While the narrator abandoned his Jewish faith for atheism, Rabbi Kornfeld adopted pantheism—viewing God as manifest in all things—and appreciated the pleasures and beauties of the natural world in opposition to Jewish law. From the rabbi's widow, Scheindel—an Orthodox Jew who condemns her dead husband for his belief and suicide—and from Kornfeld's diary, the narrator learns that his friend continually struggled with the conflicting demands of religion and nature, or Judaism and paganism. A surrealistic passage relates how Rabbi Kornfeld, having severed himself from his real soul (represented by the figure of a weary, book-burdened old man), finally attempts to couple with the nymph who inhabits the oak tree. Abandoned by her, the devastated rabbi takes his own life. As the story closes, the narrator admits that he had been attracted to Scheindel and considered marrying her, but that her pitiless attitude toward Rabbi Kornfeld finally repels him.

Characters: Ozick employs rich, complex prose to chronicle with intellectual rigor the efforts of her Jewish characters to maintain and understand their heritage in a contemporary and predominantly gentile world. In "The Pagan Rabbi," the title story of an acclaimed collection, Ozick explores the opposing claims of nature and God, of the profane and the sacred. Most critics conclude that Ozick means to affirm the importance of adhering to tradition while also acknowledging the attractions of a greater imaginative and sensual freedom.

Through the story's central character, **Rabbi Isaac Kornfeld**, Ozick illustrates the devastating effects of the interior conflict between Judaism and paganism. Indeed, even the rabbi's name embodies this conflict: "Isaac" is the biblical son who demonstrated supreme trust in his father, and "Kornfeld" alludes to Demeter, the Greek goddess of fertility. The story begins with an epigraph in which a scholar neglects his studies to admire the scenery as he walks along a path; the epigraph concludes, "Scripture regards such a one as having hurt his being." A serious scholar and model rabbinical student, Rabbi Kornfeld becomes interested not only in sacred texts but in profane literature, particularly the pantheistic philosophy of Spinoza. He develops a deep appreciation for nature that leads him to read books on agronomy and horticulture, join a hiking club, and write fairy tales full of sprites and nymphs. Kornfeld recognizes that these activities run counter to his religion, which demands exclusive allegiance to holy law, and he struggles to reconcile the opposing forces represented in his mind by the mythical figure of Pan and the prophet Moses. The rabbi's wife, Scheindel, disapproves of his behavior, which she sees as an "abomination," and her rejection turns him to the oak tree's nymph for succor. Just before his death, Rabbi Kornfeld learns that he has lost not only his soul, or Judaism—which limps away from him in the form of an old man, but his paganism, because his confusion causes the nymph to abandon him. From the tree in which the nymph dwells, the rabbi hangs himself by his prayer shawl (symbolizing his loss of religious faith). Critics consider Rabbi Kornfeld to represent the Talmudic or traditional, highly rational Jewish culture torn apart and destroyed by the attractions of the outside world. Many interpret the rabbi's fate as evidence that he distorts and denies his essential nature when he embraces paganism; others, however, assert that Ozick also exposes the emptiness of life without imagination.

The narrator's attempt to discover the truth behind his old friend's suicide leads him to reappraise his own life, particularly his affinities with Rabbi Kornfeld. Once Kornfeld's fellow rabbinical student, the narrator abandoned his Jewish faith and even married a gentile woman, thereby permanently alienating his strict, orthodox father. Whereas Kornfeld's philosophical waywardness led him to pantheism, or seeing God everywhere, the narrator's led to atheism; nevertheless, he seems to identify with the guilt and internal conflict his friend experienced. His lingering affinity for the religion of his youth seems to surface when the narrator admits to being attracted to Scheindel and thinking about marrying her, and his destroying some plants after his return to his apartment indicates that he may share Scheindel's aversion to nature and disapproval of the rabbi's paganism. But the narrator eventually rejects Scheindel, who lacks any pity or forgiveness for her dead husband, which may signify either that the narrator is still too weak to re-embrace his faith or that Ozick does not sanction Scheindel's heartlessness.

Kornfeld's wife, **Scheindel**, is universally regarded as the traditionally pious, strict adherent to Jewish law. A survivor of the Holocaust who was born in a concentration camp and miraculously survived a guard's attempt to kill her by hurling her against the electrified fence, Scheindel is the quintessential Jewish wife and the opposite of the nymph with whom her husband tries to couple. Described by the narrator as "one of those born to dread imagination," Scheindel considers Kornfeld's interest in nature an "abomination." His suicide provokes only her contempt, for she claims that according to Jewish law, a person who kills himself deserves no pity. Scheindel seem to some critics to be an essentially negative figure who appalls the narrator (and the reader) with her attitude toward her husband; others, however, claim that Ozick means to affirm Scheindel's elevation of religious values over natural beauty.

Ozick introduces a mythical aspect to "The Pagan Rabbi" with the two symbolic characters, the **nymph** and the **old man**. The polar opposite of the pious Scheindel, the nymph manifests the seductive pleasures and moral pitfalls of nature and, by extension, of imagination. After beguiling the rabbi into wanting sexual union with her, the nymph rejects him, claiming, "You have spoiled yourself, spoiled yourself with confusions." Thus he plunges into a despair that leads to suicide. Just before she disappears, Kornfeld cries out to her, "For pity of me, come, come." The fact that she rejects him may mean either that Moses has defeated Pan or that Kornfeld loses everything when he loses his soul. The nymph cites as her enemy the **old man**, who—taking the form of an ugly, pious, scholarly Jew trudging along with a great burden of books—symbolizes Kornfeld's soul. Representing orthodox Judaism, the old man enacts the story's epigram when he rejects natural beauty; admonishing Kornfeld for having abandoned him, he claims that Jewish law sounds "more beautiful than crickets," smells "more radiant than moss," and tastes better than "clear water." Just as the figures as Scheindel and the nymph, the old man is subject to different interpretations: the story may affirm his elevation of Judaism over nature or illustrate the ugliness that results from a life completely bereft of beauty and imagination.

The Shawl (novel, 1990)

Plot: *The Shawl* has two sections: "The Shawl," set in a concentration camp during World War II, and "Rosa," which takes place in contemporary Miami. The first section tells about Rosa Lublin, a Polish Jew living in the camp with her fourteen-year-old niece, Stella, and her infant daughter, Magda. Rosa has successfully kept the baby's existence a secret from the German guards, but when Stella snatches away the shawl in which Magda is hidden, the baby cries and is discovered. Rosa watches in helpless shock as the guard hurls the baby against the electrified fence and kills her. In "Rosa," the same central character is now fifty years old and has become "a madwoman and a scavenger." After burning down her New York City antique store, Rosa has moved to Miami, where she wanders aimlessly and eats whatever she can find. Convinced that her life has been stolen from her, Rosa ruminates on the past and ignores the present. She writes letters to her dead daughter (whose death she alternately mourns and denies) and to Stella (who still lives in New York and who has tried to persuade Rosa to reclaim her life); the letters explain her tragic past and her present state. In a laundromat Rosa meets an elderly Jew named Persky who also comes from Warsaw. Although she is briefly obsessed with the idea that Persky has stolen a pair of her underpants, Rosa eventually seems more inclined to accept his friendship. By the end of the story, the shawl she has turned into an object of worship since Magda's death loses some of its power over her.

Characters: Ozick has received widespread praise for *The Shawl,* which critics have hailed as a sensitive, imaginatively wrought portrayal of the difficulties experienced by post-Holocaust Jews in contemporary America. Marked by intense, poetic prose and intellectual depth, the novel is Ozick's first attempt to depict the horror of the Nazi concentration camps. She has stated in interviews that she fears the trivialization of the Holocaust in literature but believes strongly in bearing witness to those who endured it. Focusing on such themes as survival, victimization, motherhood, and loss, Ozick conveys the sorrow and the courage experienced in the camps.

Through the protagonist of *The Shawl,* **Rosa Lublin,** Ozick examines the impact of history on an individual psyche, showing how Rosa's identity is shaped—like those of many Holocaust survivors—by life in the concentration camp. For Rosa, the central event of her past was the murder of her child, which she witnessed but could do nothing about. Even her own survival instinct seemed horrifying to Rosa; at the moment of her baby's death, she knew that if she cried out or ran to Magda's body she herself would be killed, so Rosa stood still and stuffed the shawl into her mouth so that her scream would not escape. Although Rosa eventually moved to New York and established an antique store, she maintained that her "real life" was stolen by thieves. Thus she eventually destroyed her business and moved to Miami, where she wanders among its predominantly elderly residents as "a madwoman and a scavenger" as if interned in a death camp. Uninterested in the present, Rosa dwells in the past, hanging on to her shawl. Possessed of some mythic quality, the shawl that hid her baby, warmed her niece Stella, and saved Rosa's life by muffling her scream, it becomes for Rosa a kind of relic. Through her letters to the dead Magda and to Stella, Rosa recounts her history and vacillates between acknowledging and denying reality. Rosa was born in Warsaw, Poland, to a nonreligious Jewish family that assimilated with the country's predominantly gentile lifestyle and culture. When the Nazis began to persecute Polish Jews, however, the assimilated Jews were as vulnerable as the devout. Rosa has always believed that it was only through "a case of mistaken identity" that she ended up in the camps with the others. Ozick has suggested that Jews like Rosa may be more pitiable than those who went to their deaths during the Holocaust with a clear sense of their Jewish identity. Rosa so denies her heritage that she disdains the Yiddish language and prefers the elegant Polish of her youth. She also fails to learn English well. Rosa initially claims that she and Persky have nothing in common, and she even transfers some of her anger to him when she accuses him of stealing her underpants (which may symbolize her stolen life). Gradually, however, Rosa appears to accept Persky's friendship, recognizing their common Jewish heritage they share and become willing to reclaim her life. At the end of "Rosa" her behavior indicates that she does not need the shawl so much anymore.

Rosa's infant daughter **Magda** appears only briefly in *The Shawl,* but she plays a continuing role in Rosa's life. Rosa's letters reveal that the baby had blue eyes and blonde hair and that she was fathered not by the upstanding young Polish father Rosa has invented but by a

German guard who raped Rosa. Rosa claims that Magda stayed alive for three days after her milk dried up by suckling on the shawl, an image that some critics maintain is connected with that of the infant Christ. After Magda's murder, Rosa turns the baby into a kind of saint, and the shawl that protected her becomes a kind of holy relic; thus she manages to evade her truly horrible reality. At different points during the course of her letters, Rosa imagines Magda as the wife of a wealthy Long Island doctor, a professor of Greek philosophy, or a blooming sixteen-year-old girl, while at other points she acknowledges that Magda is dead.

Rosa's relationship with her niece, **Stella**, is affected by the role Stella played in Magda's death. A starving fourteen-year-old imprisoned with her aunt and cousin in the concentration camp, Stella was freezing when she snatched the shawl away from Magda. When the baby cried, she was discovered, then killed, and Rosa has since considered her niece a hostile or even cannibalistic force opposed to her own beloved daughter. The adult Stella seems well adjusted, refuses to dwell in the past, speaks English well, and urges her aunt start living again. Stella disapproves of Rosa's obsession with the shawl, comparing her to "those people in the Middle Ages who worshipped a piece of the True Cross, a splinter from some old outhouse as far as anybody knew."

The elderly **Persky**, who meets Rosa in a laundromat, recognizes their affinity and makes an effort to befriend Rosa. He too has experienced tragedy; he once owned a button factory that his son forced him to sell, and his wife is confined to an insane asylum. And like Rosa, he is a Jew and a native of Warsaw. Rosa initially claims that his Warsaw—that is, the Jewish ghetto and the Yiddish-speaking Jews—was not her Warsaw, but she eventually acknowledges their common background, which seems to signify her readiness to reclaim her stolen life.

Although he does not actually appear in the novel, **Dr. Tree**, a clinical sociologist who writes to Rosa to ask her to participate in his study of concentration camp survivors, signifies the trivialization of the Holocaust that Ozick fears: his letter reduces Rosa's deep, complex anguish to sterile sociological jargon.

Further Reading

Bestsellers 90. Issue 1. Detroit: Gale Research.

Burstein, Janet Handler. "Cynthia Ozick and the Transgressions of Art." *American Literature* Vol. 59, no. 1 (March 1987): 85–101.

Contemporary Literary Criticism. Vols. 3, 7, 28, 62. Detroit: Gale Research.

Dictionary of Literary Biography. Vol. 28, 1982 Yearbook. Detroit: Gale Research.

Friedman, Lawrence S. *Understanding Cynthia Ozick*. Columbia, SC: University of South Carolina Press, 1991.

Gitenstein, R. Barbara. "The Temptation of Apollo and the Loss of Yiddish in Cynthia Ozick's Fiction." *Studies in American Jewish Literature* No. 3 (1983): 194–201.

Kakutani, Michiko. "Cynthia Ozick on the Holocaust, Idolatry and Loss." *New York Times* (September 5, 1989): C17.

Kauvar, Elaine M. *Cynthia Ozick's Fiction: Tradition and Invention*. Bloomington: Indiana University Press, 1993.

Prose, Francine. "Idolatry in Miami." *New York Times Book Review* (September 10, 1989): 1, 39.

Scrafford, Barbara. "Nature's Silent Scream: A Commentary on Cynthia Ozick's 'The Shawl.'" *Critique* Vol. 31, no. 1 (fall 1989): 11–15.

Wiesel, Elie. "Ozick Asks Whether There Can Be Life After Auschwitz." *Chicago Tribune Books* (September 17, 1989): 6.

Dorothy Parker
1893–1967
American short story writer, poet, critic, playwright, and screenwriter.

"Big Blonde" (short story, 1930)

Plot: Set in New York City in the 1920s, the story centers on well-endowed, fair-haired Hazel Morse, who learns, in her twenties, the advantages of being a "good sport" with men. After about ten years of this life, she is relieved to marry Herbie Morse and settle into a comfortable, if dull, domestic life with him. Eventually, however, Herbie tires of this arrangement and of Hazel's indulgence in periods of melancholy, and he takes to drink. Left alone too much, Hazel starts to drink too in order to have something in common with Herbie. During her husband's frequent absences, Hazel attends the congenial gatherings of middle-aged men hosted by her neighbor, Mrs. Martin. There Hazel meets Ed, a married man who pays her particular attention. When Herbie finally leaves her, Hazel becomes Ed's mistress. She grows increasingly dependent on alcohol to maintain her high spirits, for Ed and her other friends are annoyed by any display of sadness. Ed's eventual departure from her life is followed by liaisons with a number of similar men. Meanwhile, Hazel sinks so deep into depression that she begins to contemplate suicide, but her attempt to overdose on sleeping pills is unsuccessful. The story ends with Hazel calling for a drink, while silently praying that God will "keep her always drunk."

Characters: Parker was a literary celebrity of the 1920s and 1930s who was particularly renowned for her witticisms and for her membership in New York's "Algonquin Round Table," which comprised such writers as Robert Benchley, Alexander Woolcott, and George S. Kaufman. Written in spare, ironic prose and marked by both satire and compassion, many of Parker's stories portray the domestic unhappiness of middle-class characters who are both victimized and lacking in the power to rescue themselves. Regarded as the most accomplished of the stories collected in *Lament for the Living*, the frequently anthologized "Big Blonde" evidences Parker's particular interest in the problems of women who are pathetically dependent on men.

Asked in an interview on whom she modeled **Hazel Morse**, Parker said, "I knew a lady—a friend of mine who went through holy hell. Just say I knew a woman once." Some commentators contend that Hazel's drinking, numerous liaisons with men, and suicidal impulse reflect similar aspects of her creator's life. A large, fair-haired, fair-skinned woman, with small feet she nevertheless stuffs into shoes a size too small, Hazel is decent enough, though unreflecting. She learned early in life that men liked her, and she took it for granted that "the liking of men was a desirable thing." Thus she strives to be the kind of "good sport" whose physical attractiveness and accommodating personality will earn her material advantages. Although Hazel is successful in this effort, it grows tiring, and she is relieved to settle into the dull routines of marriage. She makes the mistake of assuming, however, that she will now be able to express the rather agreeable melancholy she sometimes feels. Herbie derides her for "crabbing" and begins to spend more and more time away from home. Confused by the sour turn her marriage has taken, Hazel turns to alcohol and develops an addiction that gradually erodes her mental and physical health even as it give her temporary relief from loneliness and despair. As she makes her way through a series of relationships with progressively less desirable men, Hazel notices that neither they nor the other men and women she considers her friends will tolerate even her slightest expression of unhappiness. The effort of maintaining the facade of the "good sport" exhausts her and the thought of death becomes increasingly attractive. Her almost tragically unsuccessful suicide attempt is spurred by the sight of a horse being beaten in the street, which causes her to envision life as "a long parade of weary horses and shivering beggars and all beaten, driven, stumbling things." Critics commend Parker for creating in Hazel Morse a genuinely tragic figure whose weaknesses do not justify her dismal fate. Perhaps the most memorable character in Parker's fiction, she is an effective embodiment of one of her creator's persistent themes: the vulnerability of women who trade their beauty or sexuality for security.

None of the characters who surround Hazel are portrayed in a flattering light; in fact, all the men help to dramatize the exploitation of women like Hazel. She meets her thin, fast-talking husband, **Herbie Morse**, while she is working as a model in a dress shop. Initially charmed by Hazel's domesticity, Herbie tires of the marriage and begins to drink heavily, finally leaving Hazel with the explanation that he has landed a job in Detroit. Hazel's next liaison is with **Ed**, one of the jovial middle-aged men who congregate at the apartment of **Mrs. Martin** (Hazel's neighbor and fellow "big blonde"). Married to a rigidly domestic woman, Ed is proud of his ability to support an idle mistress; he is intolerant of Hazel's melancholy and insists on constant gaiety during his periodic visits to New York. Ed is eventually replaced by **Charley**, whom Hazel describes as "not so bad" and who is himself replaced by the clever, Jewish **Sydney**. At the time of her suicide attempt, Hazel is involved with short, fat **Art**, who is difficult to handle when he is drunk and who displays a particularly repellent insensitivity to her unhappiness.

Further Reading

Capron, Marion. Interview with Dorothy Parker. In *Writers at Work: The "Paris Review" Interviews*, edited by Malcolm Cowley. New York: Viking, 1958, pp. 69–85.

Contemporary Literary Criticism Vols. 15, 68. Detroit: Gale Research.

Dictionary of Literary Biography Vols. 11, 45, 86. Detroit: Gale Research.

Hellman, Lillian. "Dorothy Parker." In *An Unfinished Woman*. Boston, MA: Little, Brown, 1969, pp. 212–28.

Kinney, Arthur F. *Dorothy Parker*. Boston, MA: Twayne, 1978.

Labrie, Ross. "Dorothy Parker Revisited." *Canadian Review of American Studies* Vol. 7, no. 1 (Spring 1976): 48–56.

Maugham, W. Somerset. "Variations on a Theme." In *Dorothy Parker*. New York: Viking, 1944, pp. 11–18.

Short Story Criticism Vol. 2. Detroit: Gale Research.

Toth, Emily. "A Laughter of Their Own: Women's Humor in the United States." In *Critical Essays on American Humor*, edited by William Bedford Clark and W. Craig Turner. Boston, MA: G. K. Hall, 1984, pp. 199–215.

Yates, Norris W. "Dorothy Parker's Idle Men and Women." In *The American Humorist: Conscience of the Twentieth Century*. Ames: Iowa State University Press, 1964, pp. 262–73.

Walker Percy

1916–1990

American novelist and essayist.

The Last Gentleman (novel, 1966)

Plot: The novel centers on Williston "Will" Bibb Barrett, a twenty-five-year-old native of Mississippi now living in New York City, where he works as a humidification engineer at Macy's Department Store. Subject to frequent "fugue" states (periods of disorientation and malaise), Will quits the psychoanalysis he has been undergoing for five years; instead, he buys an expensive telescope with the intention of observing rather than being observed. While looking through his telescope one day in Central Park, Will spots pretty Kitty Vaught. He follows her to the hospital where she and her family attend her dying brother Jamie. Will ingratiates himself with the Vaughts and is hired to help them take Jamie home to Georgia in the family's Trav-L-Aire trailer. While staying at the Vaught mansion near Atlanta, Will meets Kitty's sister, Valentine, a nun who works with poor black children; she wants Will to help her convert Jamie before he dies. Will also encounters the oldest Vaught sibling, Sutter, an eccentric assistant coroner who seems deeply troubled.

When Sutter disappears with Jamie, Will is asked to locate the two brothers. Guided by a map he finds in Sutter's apartment, Will heads toward New Mexico, and along the way he reads Sutter's journal entries, containing bleak views on modern life. Will visits his own home town of Ithaca, Mississippi, where he confronts his memories of his suicidal father. When he finally reaches Sante Fe, Will learns that Sutter is working on a ranch and that Jamie is in a hospital close to death. Will and Jamie reaffirm and deepen their friendship. Meanwhile, Will reads in Sutter's journal that a year ago Sutter tried to kill himself, and Will realizes that Sutter will try again. Jamie is baptized moments before his death. Sutter then leaves the hospital for the ranch to end his own life, but Will chases after him. The novel ends as Will gets into Sutter's car, evidently determined to help his friend.

Characters: Percy is a highly respected contemporary American author whose work frequently depicts his protagonists searching for meaning and direction amid the alienation and malaise of modern life. Although he is often identified as a Southern writer–particularly because he uses Southern settings and focuses on how the South has changed over the last century—Percy has claimed to identify more with the French existential novelist Albert Camus than with William Faulkner. Indeed, Percy blends an existential preoccupation with life's apparent meaninglessness with distinctly Christian values reflecting his Catholicism. In *The Last Gentleman,* as in all his novels, Percy rejects the idea of human perfectibility in favor of waiting for the God-given grace to accept life as it is.

The novel's title refers to its protagonist, **Williston "Will" Bibb Barrett**, a twenty-five-year-old engineer from Mississippi whose "amiable Southern radar" allows him to perceive and adapt to those around him. Despite this keen insight and the added advantages of good looks and intelligence, however, Will is unable to act decisively and is subject to fugue states (periods of gloom and amnesia) during which he wanders with little awareness of what he is doing. (One such episode saw him spending long hours pointlessly ruminating on various Civil War battlefields in northern Virginia.) Will is portrayed as typically Southern in his extreme openness to possibility, which keeps him from acting until he is acted upon. At the beginning of the novel, Will has decided to live by the kind of scientific principles that govern his profession as well as the self-knowledge he feels he must have acquired after five years of psychoanalysis. But Will must first come to terms with his memories of his father, who committed suicide when Will was a boy and who, he believes, once tried to kill him in a supposed hunting accident. Through his relationships with Jamie and Sutter Vaught and his visit to his home town of Ithaca, Mississippi, Will seems to achieve a measure of maturity and balance. He moves from pure observer (complete with telescope) to comforting friend for the dying Jamie and a potential agent of help to Sutter. Will's efforts to facilitate Jamie's baptism before his death suggest that he has acquired an appreciation of faith—of the possibility of heaven-sent grace—as does his later action with Sutter. Shocked into action by the threat of Sutter's suicide, Will calls out "Wait!" to his friend, for he now understands the need to wait for truth and to trust in its existence. Although most critics deem the novel's conclusion optimistic, some question Will's intention to marry the vacuous and immature Kitty Vaught, who seems to be a poor match for him. Indeed, the novel's sequel, *The Second Coming*, reveals that Will does not marry her.

Some of the novel's concerns come into focus through the diary entries of **Sutter Vaught**, which Will reads as he travels toward New Mexico. Despite his stellar performance at Harvard Medical School, thirty-four-year-old Sutter works as an assistant coroner, writing the autopsy reports that are intermingled with his journal entries. Sutter believes that sex is all-powerful in "post-Christian America"; an article he writes shows how sex is used to transcend the stifling "everydayness" of life, although malaise (or even suicide) is its eventual result. Sutter conquers his own malaise by embracing extremes of emotion and choice and extolling lewdness over courtesy. Percy's disapproval of Sutter's philosophy is evidenced by this character's intention to kill himself and by Will's efforts to prevent it. Instead, Percy affirms the kind of communication between fellow sufferers that Will and Sutter share at the novel's conclusion.

The fact that Will first spots **Kitty Vaught** through the lens of his telescope prompts some commentators to predict that he will never make a true connection with her, despite his apparent intention to marry her. Kitty is twenty-one and pretty, a would-be ballet dancer who continually performs the role of the proper Southern girl. Will finds her approach to lovemaking "too dutiful and athletic," and their failed sexual encounter in Central Park points to her true immaturity. Several critics dismiss the prospect of a marriage between Kitty and Will as unconvincing; they contend that Will would quickly tire of such a vacuous mate.

All of the novel's characters seem to revolve around Kitty's sixteen-year-old brother **Jamie**, who is dying of leukemia. Jamie reminds some critics of Lonnie in Percy's 1961 novel, *The Moviegoer,* another dying child who teaches the protagonist a valuable lesson in living. **Chandler Vaught**, the family's patriarch, is a wealthy, self-made Alabamian who owns the world's second-largest Chevrolet dealership. Personifying the attributes of the Old South, Chandler likes Will, whose gentlemanliness and affability he considers quintessentially Southern, whereas he is bewildered by Sutter's attitudes and behavior. **Valentine "Val" Vaught** is a Catholic nun who devotes her energies to helping poor, neglected black children. Inspired by how the children respond to her attention, she forges a deep bond with them. The strength of Val's faith surprises even her, and she actually lives out her spiritual values, which may make her Percy's mouthpiece in the book. Less flatteringly depicted is Sutter's former wife, **Rita**, a meddlesome, domineering woman who claims to love poetry and the Zuni Indians and who obviously enjoys the adulation she receives from Kitty. Through Rita, who quotes from such works as Erich Fromm's *The Art of Loving,* Percy satirizes the secular humanists, whose humane values are detached from religion.

The Second Coming (novel, 1980)

Plot: Set in and around affluent Linwood, North Carolina, the novel features Will Barrett—the protagonist of Percy's earlier novel *The Last Gentleman*—who is now a wealthy, widowed, forty-nine-year-old retired lawyer. Despite his material success, Will suffers from extreme malaise, and he is still greatly troubled over his father's suicide when he was twelve years old. The other protagonist of *The Second Coming,* Allison "Allie" Huger, is a young patient of a mental institution who escapes to make a new life for herself. Remembering that she owns some land in North Carolina, Allie arrives to find only a dilapidated greenhouse, which she goes about making habitable. Meanwhile, Will decides to test God by living in a cave until God gives him a sign. If he receives a sign, he will come out and repudiate his father's hold on him; otherwise he will stay in the cave until he starves to death. But Will develops a toothache, and its pain and nausea make him desperate to locate a dentist. Losing his way, he falls through a shaft that leads into Allie's greenhouse on the other side of the mountain. Allie nurses Will back to health and the two fall in love. Will's family temporarily confine him to a nursing home, but he returns to Allie, whom he intends to marry. During a night the couple spends in a hotel, Will disposes of his father's guns, including the one his father used to kill himself. Along with some other lost souls they have befriended, Will and Allie make plans to live contentedly, improving her land and greenhouse.

Characters: Percy incorporates elements of allegory and satire into this tale of two mentally troubled people who find in each other strength to overcome their problems. Infused with psychological, philosophical, and religious overtones as well as humor, *The Second Coming* chronicles a search for sanity and renewal found elsewhere in Percy's work, which frequently focuses on modern alienation and rootlessness. Here, as in his other novels, Percy suggests that love and Christian values are key to conquering apathy and boredom and taking control of one's own life.

At the end of *The Last Gentleman,* **Will Barrett** seemed about to achieve a state of grace. In *The Second Coming*, he is a middle-aged, successful, retired lawyer who has performed many good works and won respect in his community. He has not, however, managed to overcome a sense of meaningless. Burdened by despair, melancholy, and an excess of memory, he begins falling inexplicably while playing golf. An important element in Will's malaise is the still unresolved issue of his father's death, for in killing himself Ed Barrett not only abandoned his son but left him fearful that he is doomed to come to the same end. Unlike most of the people around him, Will professes no belief in God; although he has lived ethically, he has never been comforted by faith and has never transcended the great pain in his life. Now Will decides to test God by waiting in a cave until God sends him a sign or he dies. But as great as his spiritual anguish might be, it is no match for what reality can dish up in the form of a raging toothache. As he seeks relief from the pain, Will is symbolically reborn when he accidentally falls through the cave into Allie's greenhouse. Having passed through a kind of dark night of the soul, he now comes to life through his relationship with Allie. She seems to represent a life force that conquers the death wish that Will believes he has inherited from his father. Will's recovery is symbolized by his journey out of the hotel in the middle of the night, carrying his father's guns: instead of killing himself, Will throws the guns into a gully, thus rejecting his father's specter.

Will's co-protagonist in *The Second Coming* is **Allison "Allie" Huger**, a bright young woman who escapes from a psychiatric institution, which has diagnosed her as a schizophrenic and wiped clean much of her memory with electroshock treatments. Although the causes or circumstances of her mental condition are not described, Allie is judged by her parents and others to be a passive, static person unequipped for normal life. Allie demonstrates her essential sanity, however, by successfully escaping from the institution and reaching the land she owns in North Carolina. By reclaiming the greenhouse and particularly the stove (both a source and a symbol of warmth), she demonstrates her self-reliance. Another important aspect of Allie's character is the way she restructures language. In the notebook she entitles "Instructions from Myself to Myself," Allie records her experiences and her understanding of herself in precise and often poetic language. Percy does not usually feature *female* questers in his fiction, and Allie is an quester. She finds strength in joining forces with Will, her fellow seeker after truth, who tells her he needs her "for hoisting" while she needs him "for interpretation." The love and hope she gives will enable him to overcome his morbid outlook.

Will's friend **Lewis Peckham,** also an unbeliever, is an intellectual type who favors classical music and good books. Peckham's lack of convictions appalls even Will, who may see in his friend's aridity an aspect of his own personality. Peckham's profession is significant; author Percy portrays golf as symbolizing a pinnacle of achievement for American men. But as even Peckham admits, golf is not enough, and Will's quest takes him farther and farther away from the golf course.

Throughout *The Second Coming,* Will is haunted by the voice of his dead father, **Ed Barrett.** Like Percy's own father, Ed killed himself when his son was twelve years old, bequeathing his cynicism to his son, as well as his propensity toward suicide. At the other end of the spiritual spectrum is Will's daughter, **Leslie,** a born-again Christian who perplexes her father by proclaiming her joy in Jesus but constantly frowning. Critics claim that Leslie personifies what Percy has termed "the tremendous re-Christianization of the South—high-powered evangelical Christianity."

Other characters in *The Second Coming* include **Ewell McBee,** a vulgar, bullying smalltown businessman who wants Will to join him in a pornographic-filmmaking venture; and **Jack Curl,** the chaplain of the nursing home in which Will is briefly confined, who gives Will evasive answers about God's existence.

The Thanatos Syndrome (novel, 1987)

Plot: The novel takes place in 1997 in Feliciana, Louisiana. Dr. Tom More—who is also the protagonist of Percy's 1971 novel, *Love in the Ruins*—is a psychiatrist who has recently returned from a two-year prison term for selling drugs. He immediately notices significant personality changes in two of his patients, Mickey Lafaye and Donna Stubbs, as well as his own wife, Ellen. All three have become distracted and unself-consciously erotic, while Ellen has also devoted herself increasingly to bridge competitions and is rarely at home. Meanwhile, one of the doctors on Tom's probationary committee, Bob Comeaux, wants him to come to work at the Federal Complex where he serves as the director of the Quality of Life Division and supervises euthanasia cases. Suspicious of this offer, Tom says he prefers to return to private practice.

Tom's old friend, Father Rinaldo Smith, who has operated a nearly bankrupt hospice, appears to have become mentally unbalanced, for he has shut himself up in an old firetower in the woods and refuses to come down. Tom is sent to reason with Father Smith, who declares that he is disgusted with the world's evil and with people's arrogant attempts to improve on God's creation. When Father Smith warns that tenderness always leads "to the gas chamber," Tom is confused and suspects that the old priest is insane. With the help of his scientist cousin Dr. Lucy Lipscomb, Tom investigates the strange behavior of the people around him. Their research leads them to theorize that Feliciana's water supply has been poisoned with a substance called Heavy Sodium that causes docility and lack of self-consciousness. Tom eventually arrives at the Belle Ame Academy, run by Comeaux's cohort, John Van Dorn. There Tom exposes the scheme behind their supposedly enlightened social engineering program and finds photos incriminating its leaders of child molestation and other sexual perversions. The novel ends with Tom and a partially recovered Ellen vacationing in Florida with their children, still immersed in a difficult period in their marriage but apparently committed to seeing it through.

Characters: Percy's work features a skillful, compelling blend of existentialism and religious values. Focusing on characters who struggle to overcome malaise and despair, Percy ultimately affirms the benefits of spiritual and interpersonal commitment. Although his fiction takes place in the South, Percy resists being labeled a "Southern novelist" and claims to have been influenced more by existentialists like Albert Camus than by William Faulkner or Flannery O'Connor. Indeed, the modern South Percy depicts in *The Thanatos Syndrome* is as crass and despairing as the rest of American society. The novel is a kind of morality tale that casts the twentieth century as one dominated by death—thus the title of the book—which renders people soulless. Within the framework of a riveting, fast-moving plot, Percy condemns those who would "improve" God's creation through science and social engineering as morally bankrupt.

The novel's central character is **Dr. Tom More**, a middle-aged psychiatrist who is also the protagonist of Percy's earlier novel, *Love in the Ruins,* in which he struggled with alcoholism, career failure, and marital infidelity. As *The Thanatos Syndrome* begins, Tom is returning home after two years in jail. Despite his troubled history, however, Tom is, according to critic Linda Whitney Hobson, "the least mentally ill of all the Percy heroes." This allows Percy to focus not so much on Tom's problems but on the novel's larger themes, while Tom serves as the detective or seeker who unearths the solution to the central mystery. Tom's jail term has sharpened his powers of observation; his heightened perception, or "radar," is similar to another renowned Percy character, Will Barrett. With his radar, which he describes as the capacity "to sense the connection between small discoveries," Tom knows that something is amiss in his home town. In addition to being the detective, Tom also upholds the moral values affirmed in the novel, including a commitment to his patients and family, a sense of responsibility toward the rest of creation, and an acceptance of life's imperfection. Several critics have noted the similarities between Tom and his namesake, the Tudor-era martyr Sir Thomas More, who was executed for refusing to swear allegiance to King Henry VIII above God. Similarly, Tom acknowledges no authority higher than God. Unlike such characters as Bob Comeaux and John Van Dorn, Tom rejects the notion that mere humans can improve creation.

The main voice against the social engineering is **Father Rinaldo Smith**, an old friend of Tom's and a Catholic priest who operated a financially troubled hospice. However, disgusted with humanity, Father Rinaldo shuts himself up in an old firetower as a passive religious protest against the evil and arrogance he perceives around him. The priest tells Tom that he can no longer preach because the meanings of words are, in this century of death and artificiality, no longer clear. Tom does not initially understand Father Rinaldo's warning that tenderness always leads "to the gas chamber," but in the chapter entitled "Father Rinaldo's Confession" the priest explains what he means. Described as "Percy's most direct fictional warning that contemporary American culture is moving toward an open expression of the death wish," this "small cautionary tale" relates Father Rinaldo's visits to Germany in the 1930s and 1945. During the first visit, he found himself attracted by the Nazi's seemingly noble dreams of human perfection, and he was impressed by the dedication of their recruits. But when he saw how they tried to achieve their goals by "killing Jews," he became a priest. Although Tom initially suspects that Father Rinaldo is mentally unbalanced, he eventually changes his mind.

Bob Comeaux, the director of the Quality of Life Division at the Federal Complex, is the primary villain in *The Thanatos Syndrome.* As supervisor of euthanasia cases—deciding which handicapped children and old people will be disposed of—he is the would-be do-gooder who has taken the right to determine life or death into his own hands. And as it turns out, Comeaux's arrogance extends even further, for he is involved in a conspiracy to create a perfect world, a dystopia inhabited by docile, soulless people. Comeaux tries to engage Tom in the work by explaining that widespread use of Heavy Sodium will result in a lower incidence of crime, violence, suicide, sexual promiscuity, depression, and chemical dependency. But Tom discovers the darker side of Comeaux's vision, which resurrects the racist social hierarchy of the Old South. Tom also discovers that Comeaux and his colleagues are child molesters who lower their own and their victims' self-consciousness with Heavy Sodium.

Another of the novel's villains is **John Van Dorn**, who heads the computer division at a nearby nuclear plant and who is also the founder of the Belle Ame Academy, where children are educated according to Comeaux's visions of social engineering. Van Dorn allows the conspirators to inject Heavy Sodium into the town's water supply through the nuclear reactor. Both Van Dorn and his seemingly decorous wife engage in child molestation and other sexual perversions, proving that Comeaux's vision entails a complete loss of conscience and indulgence in harmful excess.

Before Tom's incarceration, his wife, **Ellen**, was a moralistic but warm, maternal nurse. After he returns, Tom finds Ellen materialistic, acquisitive, distracted, and argumentative. She is also increasingly devoted to her bridge competitions and is rarely at home. Tom eventually learns that her behavioral changes are side effects of ingesting Heavy Sodium. Critics praise Percy for his perceptive portrayal of the troubled relationship between Tom and Ellen, who undergo a serious rift but seem, as the novel closes, determined to stay together. Their continuing commitment to each other even in a time of misunderstanding evidences Percy's belief that marriage is both difficult and necessary. Conversely, Tom rejects the less troubled but ultimately less valuable alternative offered by his beautiful cousin, **Lucy Lipscomb**. The owner of a plantation that combines the most gracious elements of the Old South with the benefits of the modern age, Lucy is a charming hostess and a competent scientist whose computer expertise helps Tom identify the possibility of Heavy Sodium poisoning.

Tom is first alerted to the strange goings-on in Feliciana by the altered behavior of two of his patients. Before Tom's incarceration, **Mickey Lafaye** was a refined, cautious New Englander who suffered from generalized anxiety. Tom is bewildered by her sudden lack of self-consciousness. By the end of the novel, however, Mickey has recovered from the effects of Heavy Sodium and again comes to Tom for psychiatric help, suggesting that the best way to overcome despair is to communicate with other ordinary, suffering human beings. Donna Stubbs has also changed during Tom's absence: once fat and jolly, she is now slimmer and unself-consciously erotic, and even tries to seduce Tom. Donna's behavior exemplifies Comeaux's plan to neutralize the influence of conscience in sexuality and render sex a mere biological function; the result, however, is a regression to animality.

Other characters in *The Thanatos Syndrome* include **Chandra**, the independent, spirited, but irascible and outspoken young African American woman who looks after Tom's children and who is the only member of his household who is not embarrassed by his prison sentence; and **Max Gottlieb**, a teaching psychiatrist on Tom's probation committee who supports his plan to return to practice but suspects that Tom has become paranoid when he hears about his concerns about patients.

Further Reading

Brooks, Cleanth. "Walker Percy, 1916-1990." *New Criterion* Vol. 9, no. 1 (September 1990): 82–5.

Ciuba, Gary M. *Walker Percy: Books of Revelations.* Athens: University of Georgia Press, 1991.

Coles, Robert. *Walker Percy: An American Search.* Boston: Atlantic-Little, Brown, 1978.

Contemporary Literary Criticism. Vols. 2, 3, 6, 8, 14, 18, 47, 65. Detroit: Gale Research.

Dictionary of Literary Biography. Vol. 2 and 1980 Yearbook. Detroit: Gale Research.

Gretlund, Jan Nordby, and Karl-Heinz Westarp, eds. *Walker Percy: Novelist and Philosopher.* Oxford: University Press of Mississippi, 1991.

Hobson, Linda Whitney. *Understanding Walker Percy.* Columbia: University of South Carolina Press, 1988.

Luschei, Martin. *The Sovereign Wayfarer: Walker Percy's Diagnosis of the Malaise.* Baton Rouge: Louisiana State University Press, 1972.

Simpson, Louis P. "Walker Percy, 1916–1990." *Southern Review* Vol. 26, no. 4 (October 1990): 924–28.

Tremonte, Colleen M. "The Poet-Prophet and Feminine Capability in Walker Percy's *The Second Coming.*" *Mississippi Quarterly* Vol. 43, no. 2 (spring 1990): 172–81.

Georges Perec
1936–1982

French novelist, dramatist, poet, scriptwriter, translator, and nonfiction writer.

Life: A User's Manual (*La vie mode d'emploi;* novel, 1978)

Plot: The novel's setting is a nine-story Parisian apartment building. Each chapter of the novel focuses on one of the ninety-nine rooms, detailing the inhabitant's surroundings and providing a narrative about his or her life. The three central characters are Percival Bartlebooth, an eccentric Englishman; Serge Valène, a dying painter; and Gaspard Winckler, an expert puzzlemaker. In 1925 the wealthy but supremely bored Bartlebooth devised an elaborate, essentially pointless plan to fill the next fifty years: for ten years he would study painting with Valène; he would spend twenty years traveling to 500 ports around the world and painting a watercolor view of each, which he would then send to Winckler to be made into jigsaw puzzles; for the last twenty years he would solve the puzzles, then return them to their various ports and immerse them in the sea so nothing would be left but blank pieces of paper. As the novel opens, the plan is nearing its completion, with Bartlebooth working on the 439th puzzle. Winckler has died, disillusioned and heartbroken. Valène, meanwhile, envisions a grand fresco painting that will illuminate the stories of the apartment building's residents, whom he has come to know well during his fifty-five years there. He proposes to capture an image of each character at a particular moment: eight o'clock on the evening of June 23, 1975. These stories provide many details about the characters, most of whom are faithful to some obsession. At the novel's conclusion, Bartlebooth dies with his project uncompleted, the last piece of 439 in his hand; two months later, Winckler also dies, and the reader learns that his canvas is blank.

Characters: Perec was a respected, innovative writer of experimental fiction that is both intriguing and entertaining. He was a dedicated member of Oulipo (*Ouvoir de Littérature Potentialle,* or Workshop of Potential Literature), a French literary society founded in 1960 by novelist Raymond Queneau and mathematician François LeLionnais to promote the use of constrictive prose forms and procedures as spurs to the imagination. Perec's works reflect his passion for such puzzles and word games as anagrams, acrostics, palindromes, and crosswords. Considered his masterpiece, *Life: A User's Manual* is structured around three formal concepts: a mathematical formula (the Greco-Roman square of ten) that determines the number of rooms in the apartment house and chapters in the book; a chess move called the Knight's Tour, in which the knight piece visits each square on the chessboard once and none twice; and a mathematical algorithm that establishes a predetermined list of forty-two elements to be included in each chapter. Within this framework, Perec offers a dazzling array of stories, cataloguing in encyclopedic detail his characters' surroundings and histories. Critics consider the novel an allegory of the human need to impose order on life and nature's continual frustration of that need. Beneath the novel's elegant structure is Perec's awareness of the entropy as well as his understanding and compassion for those who work fruitlessly to achieve perfect order.

Life: A User's Manual features a wide array of characters, many of whom are artists or dreamers driven by some obsession. Three characters are particularly featured: Percival Bartlebooth, Serge Valène, and Gaspard Winckler. Since the age of thirty, the very wealthy **Percival Bartlebooth** had no need to work for a living and he was apparently uninterested in power or women, so he fought boredom with a notably Oulipean plan for the next fifty years. He devoted himself to an enterprise both logical and intentionally pointless. Whereas much of Perec's work is concerned with the idea of leaving a "trace" behind through such an endeavor as writing, Bartlebooth plans to leave no trace at all—his paintings will purposely be destroyed. Perhaps more than any of the novel's other characters, Bartlebooth exemplifies the human desire for order; but like all such desires, Perec suggests, this one is doomed to failure. Bartlebooth does not anticipate the glitches that life will put in the way of his completing his project, such as the frustrated Winckler's sabotaging the puzzles by making them extremely difficult to solve. In addition, Bartlebooth finds himself unexpectedly slowed by the very emptiness of his endeavor, which is prematurely ended, in any case, by his death. When he dies holding the last piece of the 439th puzzle in hand, the reader knows that life has triumphed over the passionless, gratuitous process he tried to impose on it.

As the novel opens, **Serge Valène** has lived in the Paris apartment building for fifty-five years and is now close to death. He has a unique perspective on the lives of the building's residents and a heightened sensitivity to its sights, sounds, smells, and particularly the continual changes it has endured over the years. Valène imagines a vast fresco that will capture, from one vantage point and at one moment in time, the stories of all the inhabitants, composing the disparate fragments into one unified vision. This vision holds the narrative together, and some commentators believe Valène is Perec's alter ego: both are artists who seek to tell a story or, in this case, a dazzling array of stories. When Valène dies, the reader learns that his canvas is blank, or nearly blank; it contains only the outline or grid of the apartment building. Although it is now clear that the stories just told in so much detail were in fact a mental revery that Valène never committed to canvas, there is a sense in which, for the reader, the canvas *has* been filled by the artist's engaged, skillful storytelling.

Though some critics think Valène is Perec's other self, Perec identifies with **Gaspard Winckler**, the expert puzzlemaker assigned to transform Bartlebooth's watercolors into jigsaw puzzles. In an interview, Perec stated that he makes books in the same spirit as Winckler makes puzzles. A talented artisan, Winckler was a young man when he was chosen from among several competitors to transform Bartlebooth's paintings into jigsaw puzzles. Eight years after he began his task, Winckler's beloved wife died in childbirth, which caused him to abandon the puzzles for five or six months. When Winckler resumed work on them, he became increasingly consumed with bitterness. He began to sabotage the jigsaw puzzles, incorporating complications that stymied Bartlebooth's progress. Some critics consider the inventor's rebellious struggle with the formalized, meaningless project to manifest the triumph of the artistic imagination over passionless order.

The diverse, detailed stories of the minor characters in *Life: A User's Manual* fill out the novel's narrative. One of the most notable is **Cinoc** (Perec suggests twenty different ways to pronounce this character's name), who works as a "word killer" for a publisher, eliminating obsolete words from a dictionary; he becomes obsessed with these deleted words and devises his own dictionary listing them. **Anna Breidel** is an overweight teenager whose list of the caloric values of the foods she eats is included in her chapter; for five years she is obsessed with building the world's largest and most powerful radio beacon, but she abruptly abandons the project to study for her college entrance examinations. **Henri Fresnel** is a would-be actor who deserts his family in order to pursue his dream, while his vengeful wife waits many years for his return in order to throw him out again. **James Sherwood** (Bartlebooth's uncle) collects such one-of-a-kind items as a huge double bass that can only be played by two musicians, one of them standing on a ladder. **Maximilien and Berthe Danglars** are a respected judge and his wife who find sexual gratification in crime and are ultimately arrested. **Lino Margay** is a bicyclist whose face is disfigured in an accident caused when he follows the bad advice of his trainer, Massy; Massy's sister marries Margay out of pity and then leaves him; then Margay goes to South America, is imprisoned for involvement in a drug deal, and develops a minute knowledge of underworld methods, which allows him to become a millionaire, repair his face, and reclaim his wife.

Further Reading

Auster, Paul. "The Bartlebooth Follies." *New York Times Book Review* (November 15, 1987): 7.

Birkerts, Sven. "House of Games." *New Republic* Vol. 198, no. 6 (February 8, 1988): 38–40.

Burgelin, Claude. *Georges Perec*. Paris: Seuil, 1988.

Contemporary Literary Criticism, Vol. 56. Detroit: Gale Research.

Dictionary of Literary Biography, Vol. 83. Detroit: Gale Research.

Goodman, Lanie. "Fiction at Play: Welcome to the Fun House." *Washington Post Book World* (December 20, 1987): 1, 14.

Matthews, Harry. "That Ephemeral Thing." *New York Review of Books* Vol. 35, no. 10 (June 16, 1988): 34–7.

Mobilio, Albert. "Perpetual Motion Machines." *VLS* No. 60 (November 1987): 11–12.

Motte, Warren F. Jr. *The Poetics of Experiment: A Study of the Work of Georges Perec.* French Forum, 1984.

Parrinder, Patrick. "Tall Storeys." *London Review of Books* Vol. 9, no. 22 (December 10, 1987): 26.

Schwartz, Paul. *Georges Perec: Traces of His Passage*. Birmingham, AL: Summa Publications, 1988.

Slater, Maya. "The Game of Life: On Georges Perec." *Encounter* Vol. 73, no. 2 (July/ August 1989): 50–5.

Marge Piercy

1936–

American novelist, poet, and essayist.

Fly Away Home (novel, 1984)

Plot: The novel centers on forty-three-year-old Daria Walker, a successful cookbook writer who lives with her lawyer husband Ross and two daughters, Robin and Tracy, in suburban Boston. Long a complacent person, Daria is forced to face reality when Ross, after initially moving into another bedroom and then leaving mysterious notes around the house, leaves her for another woman. Then a group of inner-city residents called Save Our Neighborhood (SON) arrives on her doorstep and informs her that she and Ross are slum landlords whose negligence has led to a series of arson incidents—and the consequent death of a child—in their building. Daria's investigation of this claim and of Ross's financial status lead to her discovery of her husband's misdeeds. At the same time, she becomes romantically involved with one of the SON members, a sensitive and politically committed carpenter named Tom. One day, Ross arrives at Daria's beloved 140-year-old home and carts away the couple's valuable antiques; the next day, he attempts to burn down the house when Daria is inside. Together Daria and Tom expose Ross's villainy and he is convicted of conspiracy to commit arson and manslaughter. Daria finds new domestic happiness with Tom in an apartment in the working-class, East Boston neighborhood of Allston.

Characters: Often characterized as a feminist writer, Piercy is praised for her ability to successfully weave political commentary into her highly readable novels. Her interest in such social concerns as poverty, the environment, and civil and women's rights shows in all of her work, which illustrates the maxim that "the personal is the political." Like her other work, *Fly Away Home* reflects not only her political commitment but her belief in the redemptive power of love and her appreciation for the sensual pleasures of food, sex, pets, and gardening. Although several critics faulted the novel's secondary characters as wooden, most viewed it as a kind of counterculture romance that manages to avoid polemicism.

Even those commentators who found fault with Piercy's other characterizations praised her portrayal of **Daria Porfirio Walker**, the protagonist of *Fly Away Home*. The novel chronicles Daria's awakening to the illusions of her marriage and her progression from a willful naivete to a sense of social responsibility. *Fly Away Home* opens on Daria's forty-third birthday, when she is still living a privileged life as an accomplished writer and the wife of a successful businessman. Born into an Italian family in rough-edged East Boston, Daria has left her working class roots behind her, although the progress of the novel shows that she has never quite abandoned her core values. Daria married Ross Walker when she was so young that she was "not fully human, a fish-girl, half jelly and half bones," and she has since allowed herself immunity from such realities as her personal and family financial status and the changes in her once-idealistic husband. Daria is profoundly shaken by, in rapid succession, her mother's death, husband's infidelity, divorce, older daughter's betrayal, and discovery that Ross has been carrying on shady real estate dealings in her name. Pondering her earlier, long-harbored naivete, Daria asks whether "innocent [was] the opposite of guilt or the opposite of wise?" A typically resilient Piercy heroine, Daria rallies through her involvement with the tenant's association, her relationship with liberated Tom, and her thwarting of Ross's evil intents. Her move from her big house in the suburbs to a humble inner-city apartment suggests that she has replaced insulated materialism with a new commitment to communal values and social justice. While a few critics found Daria unconvincingly virtuous and naive, others appreciated her warmth, sensuality, and basic decency. Characterizing Daria as good but not perfect, perceptive but not wise, critic

Elizabeth Wheeler found her "extraordinary enough to be interesting yet average enough to be representative."

Reviewers were uniform in faulting Piercy's portrayal of Daria's husband **Ross Walker**, a handsome, prosperous lawyer with extensive real estate holdings. Once an idealist who vowed to help the poor, Ross gradually metamorphosed into a selfish, greedy snob and bully who masterminds not only the fires at inner-city property but the house fire that endangers his ex-wife, all for his own gain. Chauvinistic and insensitive, Ross considers Daria grossly overweight and demeans her cookbooks as "fat books," then leaves her for a woman who is predictably thinner and younger. Critics found Ross a one-dimensional character who serves primarily as an embodiment of an insensitive, patriarchal, capitalistic system. Carol Sternhell noted that Ross resembles "the star of a vaudeville melodrama who has wandered by mistake into contemporary Boston."

Although a few commentators asserted that the virtuous carpenter **Tom** is also a caricature, most found him an effective foil to the brutish Ross. Eight years younger than Daria, Tom is physically big and strong but emotionally tender and vulnerable, a sexy and generous man who nurtures not only Daria's political commitment but her sensuality. The two have in common a tendency to plumpness, former spouses who were obsessed with thinness and upward mobility, and a capacity for good cooking and good sex. Those who identified *Fly Away Home* as a counterculture romance found Tom an ideal working-class hero who both performs manual labor and has done "power structure research."

Most commentators found Daria's daughters **Robin** and **Walker** convincingly portrayed. Daria is deeply hurt by Robin's siding with her father, whose ambitiousness and obsession with thinness she shares. Other characters in the novel include Ross's lover, the extremely rich, skinny **Gail Abbott Wisby**; the Puerto Rican single mother, **Sandra Maria**, who shares an Allston apartment with Daria and Tom after she is burned out of her own home; her six-year-old daughter **Mariela**; and Daria's more worldly friend **Gretta**.

Further Reading

Contemporary Literary Criticism Vols. 3, 6, 14, 18, 27, 62. Detroit: Gale Research.

O'Reilly, Jane. "Utopians and Firebugs." *New York Times Book Review* February 5, 1984): 7.

Sweet, Ellen. Review of *Fly Away Home*. *Ms*. Vol. 12, No. 9 (March 1984): 32.

Clute, John. "Seeing the Light." *Times Literary Supplement* no. 4237 (June 15, 1984): 658.

Mernit, Susan. "Suburban Housewife Makes Good." *Women's Review of Books* Vol. 1, no. 11 (August 1984): 18.

Wheeler, Elizabeth. "It's Her Life and Welcome to It." *Los Angeles Times Book Review* (August 12, 1984): 7.

Miner, Valerie. "Marge Piercy and the Candor of Our Fictions." *Christian Science Monitor* (May 4, 1984): B3.

Sternhell, Carol. "Sex, Politics, Vegetables." *Nation* (March 24, 1984): 363–64.

Reynolds Price
1933–

American novelist, short story writer, poet, playwright, essayist, memoirist, translator, and critic.

A Long and Happy Life (novel, 1962)

Plot: Set in rural Afton, North Carolina, the novel centers on the passionate but unhappy love of Rosacoke Mustian for Wesley Beavers, a womanizing, motorcycle-riding Navy veteran with a tendency to roam. Rosacoke decides to take the advice of her more worldly brother, Miles, and capture Wesley through sex. She becomes pregnant, but by this time Wesley has gone off to the more exciting town of Norfolk, Virginia. He finally hears of Rosa's condition and returns, intending to marry her, but she turns down his proposal. While portraying the mother of Jesus in a church Christmas pageant, however, Rosacoke is moved by the occasion and determines that she will, after all, accept Wesley. As the novel draws to a close, it appears that Rosacoke and Wesley will indeed marry and try to achieve the "long and happy life" mentioned in the title.

Characters: Recognized as one of the most accomplished contemporary writers of the American South, Price frequently depicts the struggles of young protagonists as they encounter for the first time such overwhelming forces as love, sex, death, and marriage. His fiction is distinguished by his rich, lyrical prose style and use of symbolism and irony. Critics laud Price's authentic rendering not only of his characters' North Carolina dialect but of their natural surroundings. In *A Long and Happy Life*, Price explores the tension between marriage and autonomy, and most commentators feel that he casts the former as a mixed blessing—a natural enough choice, but one that does not ensure happiness.

Readers and critics have found **Rosacoke Mustian** one of the most appealing and memorable characters in Price's fiction. She is a simple country girl who nevertheless possesses a subtle intelligence; sensitive, generous, and warmhearted, she is endowed with a strong sense both of herself and of her connections and duties to others. Rosacoke's love for Wesley is almost obsessive, but at the same time she fears that in loving him she will lose herself and that he will never fully recognize or acknowledge her value. This may explain why Rosacoke initially turns down Wesley's marriage proposal, an act that gives her an unfamiliar and welcome feeling of freedom. In the end Rosacoke, while holding the infant who is portraying Jesus to her breast, changes her mind about marrying Wesley; this shift has been interpreted differently by various critics. Some critics consider it an instance of an extraordinary young girl making an unfortunate concession to social pressure, whereas others contend that Price intends this scene as an affirmation of the value of marriage and motherhood. Although most early commentators assumed that Price's sympathy was with Rosacoke rather than with the freewheeling Wesley, several later works in which the couple appears (including the 1977 play *Early Dark* and the 1988 novel *Good Hearts*) suggest that his attitude toward her is not entirely approving and that in fact he sympathizes more with Wesley. In any case, Rosacoke's wish that she and Wesley will have "a long life together" in which they will be "happy sometimes" clearly carries with it no guarantee of success.

Despite his womanizing, recklessness, and callous behavior, free-spirited **Wesley Beavers** is a compelling character whose sexual magnetism is very well conveyed. Wesley's motorcycle has been interpreted as a symbol of his virility; in addition, he is very closely associated with the natural world. Whereas Rosacoke has both a strong sense of duty to others and expectations for the future, Wesley exists firmly in the present and acts according to the demands of his own nature, telling Rosacoke, for instance, that he has done something "because I am Wesley." Even some early critics detected in Price's portrayal of Wesley a measure of sympathy for the loss of freedom that seems inevitable as he plans to marry Rosacoke, and this view was confirmed in the later novel about the couple, *Good Hearts*, in which Wesley flees his too-circumscribed life and marriage.

Many of the secondary characters in *A Long and Happy Life* help to illustrate the theme of love, marriage, and reproduction by providing examples of the various choices available. **Isaac Alston**, for example, has chosen to remain single, and the fact that he is paralyzed on one side of his body may imply that his bachelorhood has crippled him. The richest man in town, Alston is a much-respected but nevertheless isolated figure. His caretaker, the mysterious **Sammy Ransom**, is the unacknowledged father of the baby **Sledge**, whose mother **Mildred Sutton** dies in childbirth. Sammy embodies the possibility of evading responsibility for parenthood, while Mildred fate shows that one's reproductive decisions may have fatal results. Rosacoke's sister, **Sissie**, illustrates another side of the same issue when she gives birth to a stillborn son. Rosacoke's brother **Milo Mustian**, who grows from a sensitive boy to a young man with a coarse approach to sexuality, advises Rosacoke to have sex with Wesley if she wants to keep him.

Kate Vaiden (novel, 1986)

Plot: Narrated by the title character, the novel is a chronicle of her essentially solitary, wandering life that focuses particularly on the period from 1938, when eleven-year-old Kate is left an orphan, to 1948, when she abandons her infant son. She is the beloved daughter of Dan and Frances Vaiden, who both die at Dan's hand when he discovers Frances' infidelity. At the time, Frances and Kate are in the small town of Macon, North Carolina, visiting Kate's Aunt Caroline and Uncle Walter Porter, with whom Kate lives for the next five years. At thirteen, Kate falls in love with a neighbor, Gaston Stegall, who is inexplicably killed three years later while training to fight in World War II. Kate soon leaves Macon to live with her cousin Walter Porter and his housemate Douglas Lee in Norfolk, Virginia. When Kate becomes pregnant by Douglas, the two initially plan to move together to Raleigh, but instead Kate returns to her aunt and uncle in Macon. She gives birth to her baby and names him Lee, but eventually decides that he will be better off without her. Leaving Lee with Caroline and Holt, Kates goes to Raleigh to work for Douglas's former employer, a blind man named Whitfield Eller, in whose home Douglas commits suicide. Although Eller has offered to marry her, Kate leaves and, with the help of a former teacher, establishes a home and job in Greensboro. For the next forty years she lives alone, supporting herself and enjoying the company of lovers and friends but never marrying and never attempting to contact her family or see her son. In the middle of her sixth decade, Kate contracts cervical cancer, and the experience motivates her to find Lee. She returns to Macon to discover that Holt and Caroline have died and that Lee is now living in Norfolk in the home of Walter Porter (also recently dead). Kate leaves a message on his telephone answering machine, and it seems likely that she will be reunited with him. She reveals that the preceding narrative has been composed for her son's benefit.

Characters: Price's work reflects his knowledge of and affection for the people, speech, and natural environment of his native North Carolina. Written in a fluid, lyrical style that some commentators find overwrought, Price's novels often chronicle their young protagonist's quests for maturity and self-knowledge. Price won the National Book Critics Circle Award for *Kate Vaiden*, which explores such themes as the long-term damage endured by orphans, the pressure to conform to traditional roles, and the simultaneous love and harm incurred in human relationships.

Price has said that he based **Kate Vaiden** partially on his own mother, Elizabeth Rodwell Price, a vibrant, independent woman and an orphan whose nature, he claims, was always mysterious to him (unlike Kate, however, she never abandoned her family). Kate describes herself as "a real middlesized white woman that has kept on going with strong eyes and teeth for fifty-seven years." Hers is the story—told, she finally reveals, for the edification of her son—of a woman who endures many heartaches and somehow survives, even if irreparably damaged in some ways. Although the early years of Kate Vaiden's childhood were idyllic, her life was permanently altered by what happened when she was eleven: her father chose to end both her mother's life and his own, leaving Kate an orphan who would thereafter wonder if she had somehow caused her parents' deaths. The loss of her first and perhaps most meaningful love, Gaston Stegall, in what appears to be a suicide further compounds her anguish. Kate explains her subsequent, repeated abandonments of those who love her as rooted in her conviction that she must leave people before they have a chance to leave her; she is both strongly attracted to the notion of permanence and unable to accept it when it seems within her reach. Most critics have praised Price for his portrayal of this engaging, self-assured, witty character, who speaks in an authentically rendered North Carolina dialect that is both informal and laced with metaphor and cogent images. Kate has been viewed as a picaresque figure with many similarities to the heroine of Daniel Defoe's 1722 novel *Moll Flanders*; in fact, at one point Kate herself mentions this work and her own resemblance to its protagonist. Both Moll and Kate are orphaned at an early age, both are unconventional, resourceful, resilient, and courageous, and both have adventures with a series of men. Perhaps the most controversial aspect of Kate's story is her leaving her baby to be raised by her aunt and uncle and then making no attempt to see or contact him for the next forty years. Some critics accept Kate's explanation—that she felt her son would be better off without her—while others find her behavior heartless and unconvincing.

The key figures in Kate's early life are her parents, **Frances and Daniel Vaiden**. A warm, attractive woman devoted to her husband and daughter, Frances herself could be said to have been abandoned at an early age, for her mother died in childbirth. Another significant similarity between her and Kate is her early initiation into sex with her nephew Swift (a liaison that continued until the day of her death and that fatally enraged her husband). Kate is relieved when Walter Porter advises her to forgive her dead father, a passionately jealous man who cannot bear the thought of his wife's infidelity, for killing her mother and himself. She prefers to remember him as the handsome, loving father he was during her childhood; indeed, Dan states his devotion to Kate in the letter he writes her before leaving for what he well knows may be a fatal encounter with Frances.

The orphaned Kate is taken in by her patient, loving **Aunt Caroline Porter**, whose saintliness some commentators have labeled unbelievable. Kate repays her aunt's kindness by running away twice, finally leaving her son to be raised by a couple whose childbearing years should have been over long before. **Uncle Holt** is characterized as weak and alcoholic, with the potential for violent behavior when angry. Nevertheless he is consistently kind to Kate and expresses a deep love for her. The Porters' youngest son, **Swift**, is described as dangerously "hungry" and disreputable. Although he was Frances' nephew, he was only two years younger than her, and the two apparently had a sexual relationship from the time they were children until Frances' death. In fact, when Kate visits the elderly Swift in a nursing home, he tells her that he and Frances had made love not long before Dan's arrival on that tragic day. Swift is at least partly responsible for Kate's first departure from Macon, for she feels sexually menaced by his claim that he witnessed her encounters with Gaston in their forest hiding place and his suggestion that he will use this knowledge to his own benefit.

One of the most memorable characters from the sections of the novel set in Macon is the Porters' black cook, **Noony Patrick**, a strong, very tall woman who is nineteen when Kate first meets her. Initially married to an ailing eighty-year-old man, Noony indulges in sexual liaisons with younger men and seems to share with the adult Kate a frank pleasure in her own sexuality. Although Noony serves as a friend to Kate during the early years, giving her advice and shelter on various occasions, at the end of the book the reader learns that she has not forgiven Kate for abandoning her baby and family; when Kate asks her forgiveness, she says only, "Too late." Some critics have seen Noon as one of several idealized African American characters in Price's fiction. Other Macon characters include **Gaston Stegall**, the strange, ardent boy who is Kate's first lover and whose death, which appears to be a suicide, contributes to her feeling of guilt; **Fob Foster**, Kate's distant cousin, a wealthy but simple-living bachelor in his fifties who befriends Kate and encourages her to make something of herself; and **Tot**, the young black man who tends Fob's household and to whom Fob leaves his land when he dies.

Walter Porter, the oldest child of Caroline and Holt, has lived in Norfolk since his departure from Macon many years earlier. It gradually becomes evident that it was Walter's homosexuality that caused his rift with his family—a rift that is at least partially healed after Kate comes to live with her aunt and uncle and helps facilitate Walter's return visit. After her frightening encounter with Swift, Kate decides to accept Walter's earlier offer to live with him in Norfolk. Witty, tenderhearted, and effeminate, Walter seems to some reviewers another of Price's unconvincingly saintly characters. For example, he reacts to Kate's pregnancy (which constitutes a betrayal of sorts in view of the very close relationship between him and Douglas Lee) by envisioning a cozy family comprising himself, Douglas, Kate, and the baby.

The enigmatic, attractive **Douglas Lee** is a native of Macon who was, like Kate, orphaned at an early age and apparently permanently damaged by the experience. He was informally adopted by Walter, with whom he eventually left Macon for Norfolk when he was thirteen. It is suggested that he and Walter were or subsequently became lovers, although he later has a sexual relationship with Kate. The attraction between Douglas and Kate seems to be based on a common conviction that they are "not good enough magnets to hold even parents." Douglas reveals the violence seething beneath the surface of his personality when he stabs Walter and later kills himself, an act attributed to his intense self-hatred but which Kate can't help but attribute to her own lethal effect on those who love her. For her part, Kate admits that she never really loves Douglas, who offers to marry her after the birth of their baby, Daniel Lee Vaiden (called Lee). After forty years, Kate learns that Lee has grown up to be a successful, well-liked Navy commander who, like her, is not particularly happy in love.

Kate's other male admirers include taxi driver **Tim Slaughter**, a kind, fifty-six-year-old bachelor she meets during her first trip to Norfolk and with whom she later stays for several weeks; and the handsome, considerate, blind **Whitfield Eller**, who allows Kate to take over Douglas' former position as his assistant and who eventually asks her to marry him. Kate is reunited with her beloved fifth-grade teacher, **Rosalind Limer**, in Greensboro; she helps Kate finish high school and establish herself there. Kate meets **Daphne and Cliff Baxter** on the train to Norfolk and spends a night with them when she is unable to locate Walter; the three become long-term friends.

Further Reading

Brown, Rosellen. "Travels with a Dangerous Woman." *New York Times Book Review* (June 29, 1986): 1, 40–1.

Contemporary Literary Criticism Vols. 3, 6, 13, 43, 50, 63. Detroit: Gale Research.

Core, George. "Reynolds Price's Ballad of the South." *Book World—The Washington Post* (July 6, 1986): 1, 14.

Dictionary of Literary Biography Vol. 2. Detroit: Gale Research.

Eichenberger, Clayton. "Reynolds Price: *A Banner in Defeat. Journal of Popular Culture* Vol. 1, no. 4 (Spring 1968): 410–17.

Humphries, Jefferson. "*A Vast Common Room*: Twenty-five Years of Essays and Fiction by Reynolds Price." *Southern Review* Vol. 24, no. 3 (Summer 1988): 686–95.

Keates, Jonathan. "Southern Discomfort." *Observer* (February 22, 1987): 29.

Kimball, Sue Leslie, and Lynn Veach Sadler, eds. *Reynolds Price: From 'A Long and Happy Life' to 'Good Hearts.'* Fayetteville, NC: Methodist College Press, 1989.

Rooke, Constance. *Reynolds Price*. Boston, MA: Twayne, 1983.

Shepherd, Allen. "Love (and Marriage) in *A Long and Happy Life.*" *Twentieth Century Literature* (January 1971): 29–35.

Solotaroff, Theodore. "The Reynolds Price Who Outgrew the Southern Pastoral." *Saturday Review* Vol. 53, no. 39 (September 26, 1970): 27–9, 46.

Towers, Robert. "Ways Down South." *New York Review of Books* Vol. 33, no. 14 (September 25, 1986): 55–7.

Wilson, Robert. "Confessions of a Country Girl." *New Republic* Vol. 195, no. 13 (September 29, 1986): 40–2.

V.S. Pritchett
1900–

English short story writer, novelist, critic, travel writer, and autobiographer.

"It May Never Happen" (short story, 1945)

Plot: The seventeen-year-old narrator, Vincent, is sent to work as an assistant to his Uncle Belton, who is a partner in a furniture factory. Belton describes the other partner, Mr. Phillimore, in the most admiring terms and encourages his nephew to treat him with great respect. Thus Vincent is surprised to find that Mr. Phillimore is an effeminate man who constantly professes his own inadequacy and pessimism. Temperamentally the opposite of Belton, who is a dreamy optimist, Phillimore has an almost marital relationship with his partner. Eventually, however, their partnership deteriorates as rumors about alliances with competitors and possible new partners begin to circulate. Phillimore's behavior grows increasingly strange, until one day he makes a clumsy pass at the company's secretary, Miss Croft. He leaves and never returns, and Belton and Vincent eventually learn that he has joined their company's main competitor, Salter. Many months later, Vincent sees Phillimore in a crowd that has gathered to watch a window washer on a tall building. Phillimore gives Vincent a contemptuous glance, then disappears.

Characters: One of England's most celebrated "men of letters," Pritchett is best known for his short fiction, which emphasizes not plot or social issues but character revelation. He has said that he is more interested in the human drama of "unconscious self-revelation" than in events. Characterized by lean, uncluttered prose and wry humor, Pritchett's stories feature characters who are often ridiculous but always recognizably human. Although he exposes their weaknesses, delusions, and anxieties, Pritchett's satire is essentially warmhearted. Often cited as a particularly successful story, "It May Never Happen" typifies Pritchett's work with its eccentric characters and unresolved conclusion.

The story's narrator is seventeen-year-old **Vincent**, a naive young man making his first foray into the world of adults and business. Critics often note that Pritchett's experience as an apprentice in the London leather trade when he was sixteen undoubtedly influenced his portrayal of Vincent. Although the story may be interpreted as chronicling Vincent's initiation into the moral ambiguity and mysteries of adult life, he may also be seen as a neutral observer through whose eyes the reader is afforded a view into an unexpectedly eccentric realm.

Vincent's **Uncle Belton**, who offers him an apprentice position, is a partner and salesman in a London furniture factory. Dapper, earnest, and essentially idle, Belton is a kind man who maintains a stern, pompous exterior. Like the author's father, Walter Pritchett (after whom he apparently modeled several notable characters in his fiction), Belton is a relentless optimist who avoids responsibility by spending more time daydreaming than working and who purchases innumerable luxuries for himself. The difference in personality between Belton and Phillimore—whose relationship is likened to a marriage—is exemplified by their reactions to the framed needlepoint Belton brings to the office, which reads, "It May Never Happen." Belton considers the phrase a reassuring affirmation of his tendency not to worry about things that probably won't occur, whereas Phillimore thinks it warns of life's futility in the absence of materialized fears. Critics regard Belton and Phillimore as nearly Dickensian in their eccentricity, although Pritchett's characters are generally considered more three-dimensional than Dicken's.

Belton's partner, **Mr. Phillimore**, brought the necessary capital to their furniture business, although Belton contends that he rescued Phillimore from his mother's dominance. Having been assured by his uncle of Phillimore's nearly godlike status, Vincent is surprised to find that Phillimore is effeminate, clumsy, and fretful and has an overwhelmingly pessimistic view of life, as he himself frequently proclaims. To Phillimore, Belton's needlepointed slogan, "It May Never Happen," refers to the bareness of a life without fear; indeed, it seems to be Phillimore's theatricality that protects him from pain and tedium. Despite his dithering and self-dramatization, Phillimore is an enigmatic figure whom Vincent gradually begins to see as "cunning and obstinate, and longsighted." That Phillimore is a homosexual is suggested but never confirmed; his attempted seduction of Miss Croft may comprise an expression of genuine desire, an attempt to mock Miss Croft, or a transference of his true feelings for Vincent, whom he has continually encouraged to pursue the secretary. Ultimately, the reader knows Phillimore only through Vincent's eyes, and the final image offered of him—telling someone "I should die!" as he watches a window washer on a high building, then giving Vincent a contemptuous look—is inconclusive.

Other characters in the story include **Miss Croft**, the company secretary, who is slightly older than Vincent and mildly disdainful of him, typical of young women toward younger adolescent males. For his part, Vincent considers Miss Croft exotic and unattainable, while Phillimore's encounter with her may express either real desire or a transference of his attraction to Vincent. Belton describes **Mr. Salter**, who was once his partner and is now

his competitor, as a veritable monster, so Vincent is astonished to learn that Salter's personality is as weak and worried as Phillimore's.

"The Camberwell Beauty" (short story, 1974)

Plot: The story's narrator, who once worked in the London antique trade, relates his experiences among such fellow dealers as August, a collector of ivory, and Pliny, whose passion was for porcelain. August's mistress, Mrs. Price, had a teenaged niece, Isabel, whom she once accused August of trying to seduce. The narrator himself felt drawn to the girl, but he lost track of her and the others when poor business forced him to become a real estate auctioneer. Several years later, the narrator passes Pliny's shop and stops to visit but finds it closed. He returns several times and is eventually shocked to learn that the beautiful Isabel has married the elderly, eccentric Pliny. The narrator becomes obsessed with Isabel and plots to win her away from Pliny. He goes to the shop often, but Isabel rarely lets him in. Then she confesses that her husband insists that she wear a helmet, bang on a drum, and play a bugle when she is alone in order to frighten away intruders. The narrator finally professes his feelings for Isabel, but she rejects him, claiming against his objections that what she shares with Pliny is love. Pliny never has sex with Isabel but makes her come to his room every night and undress so that he can admire her beauty. The narrator is forced to leave when Pliny returns unexpectedly.

Characters: A versatile writer, Pritchett is most acclaimed for his short stories, which feature characters who are eccentric but authentically human. Frequently cited as one of his most accomplished stories, ''The Camberwell Beauty'' exhibits Pritchett's knowledge of the London antique trade, which he portrays as a strange subculture inhabited by individuals whose acquisitiveness has led to a loss of their humanity. With his usual eye for both physical detail and the quirks of human nature, Pritchett exposes the materialism of a society in which sex is a commodity and people are objects to be collected and possessed.

The story unfolds through the reminiscences of the unnamed **narrator**, who seems to be in his twenties when it takes place. He is portrayed as more normal than his colleagues in the antique trade, whose ''stored up lust'' for the objects they covet repels him. At the beginning of the story, the narrator is new to the antique business and has not yet developed a passion for any particular type of item, as August and Pliny have. The fact that he finally changes his profession suggests that the narrator differs fundamentally from the other dealers, yet his secret passion for Isabel seems dangerously close to the acquisitive lust they exhibit.

The narrator's fellow antique dealers are **August**, an ivory collector who is eventually imprisoned for his involvement in petty crime and who once attempted to seduce the teenaged Isabel, and **Pliny**, August's archrival, who specializes in Meissen ware porcelain. Tall and thin with big ears, Pliny, as a fiftyish bachelor, once promised his domineering mother he would give up sex, but according to his colleagues, persisted in visiting his mistress once a month. The narrator later learns that lovely Isabel has married the unattractive, eccentric Pliny, and he is shocked to discover how Pliny has reduced his young wife to an object he has been clever enough to acquire.

The story's title refers to the pale, childlike **Isabel**, a beauty who is ultimately collected by one of the story's antique dealers. It is through Isabel that Pritchett illustrates the theme of possession and dehumanization—particularly of women by men.

She is a rather enigmatic character whose motivations are never revealed, though she does insist that Pliny's bizarre attentions to her do constitute love. Her loyalty to her elderly husband may be related to her earlier near-molestation by August, whose mistress was her aunt, **Mrs. Price**; perhaps Isabel finds Pliny a safe alternative. The ritual Isabel must enact to scare away intruders turns her into a kind of mechanized doll, thus underlining her status as an object rather than a human being.

Further Reading

Baldwin, Dean R. *V. S. Pritchett*. Boston: G. K. Hall, 1987.

Contemporary Literary Criticism. Vols. 5, 13, 15, 41. Detroit: Gale Research.

Cunningham, Valentine. ''Coping with the Bigger Words.'' *Times Literary Supplement* No. 4134 (June 25, 1982): 687.

Davies, Robertson. ''V. S. Pritchett: Storyteller Supreme.'' *Book World—The Washington Post* (April 25, 1982): 1–2, 15.

Dictionary of Literary Biography. Vol. 15. Detroit: Gale Research.

Stinson, John J. *V. S. Pritchett: A Study of the Short Fiction.* New York: Twayne, 1992.

Trevor, William. "Child of the Century." *New York Review of Books* (June 13, 1991): 8–10.

Welty, Eudora. "A Family of Emotions." *New York Times Book Review* (June 25, 1978): 1, 39–40.

E. Annie Proulx

1935–

American novelist, short story writer, and journalist.

The Shipping News (novel, 1993)

Plot: The novel's central character is Quoyle, a physically unattractive resident of upstate New York whose unhappy childhood was followed by an adulthood marked by failure. Quoyle marries pretty, coldhearted Petal Bear, who spends the next six years sleeping with other men while Quoyle continues to love her and their two daughters, Bunny and Sunshine. Meanwhile, Quoyle's friend Partridge helps him get a job as a newspaper reporter, a position he performs indifferently. Then Petal (after running away with a lover and selling her daughters to a child pornographer, from whom they are later rescued) dies in a car accident, and Quoyle's parents commit a double suicide. The latter event sparks the arrival of Quoyle's aunt, Agnis Hamm, who encourages her devastated nephew to start a new life and suggests he accompany her to Newfoundland, where their family originated. Partridge finds Quoyle a job at the *Gammy Bird* newspaper in the town of Killick-Claw, and Quoyle, his aunt, Bunny, and Sunshine drive to Newfoundland and start to establish themselves. They try to rehabilitate the old Quoyle house but are forced by the prospect of harsh winter weather to move into town. Quoyle gradually gains confidence in his work at the *Gammy Bird*, which is staffed by a variety of eccentric characters and headed by lobster fisherman Jack Buggit. Quoyle also slowly develops a relationship with Wavey Prowse, the widowed mother of a child with Down's syndrome. Meanwhile, the Aunt opens a yacht upholstering business and Bunny and Sunshine make new friends while still struggling with the loss of their mother. Following the disappearance into the sea of the old Quoyle house and the rejuvenation of a supposedly dead Jack Buggit, the novel ends on a hopeful note, with Quoyle suspecting that "perhaps love sometimes occurs without pain or misery."

Characters: *The Shipping News* was perhaps the most acclaimed book in America in 1993, winning the National Book Award, the Pulitzer Prize, and the PEN/Faulkner Award. Proulx was praised for her affectionate portrait of a set of memorable, eccentric characters and the harshly beautiful Newfoundland setting, her skillful incorporation of local dialect and folklore, and her highly inventive language, which features detailed inventories, arcane words, and an often surreal wit. The novel suggests that it is possible to escape the burdens of the past and also that change, while inevitable, is not necessarily to be feared.

The reader never learns the first name of the novel's protagonist, **Quoyle**, whose surname calls to mind a "coil" of rope designed—as the first chapter's epigraph explains—"so that it may be walked on if necessary." Thirty-six years old when the story begins, Quoyle has a "great damp loaf of a body," no neck, reddish hair, bunched features, and a huge chin that he constantly tries to hide by bringing his hand up to his face. Quoyle endured a miserable childhood in which he was tormented by other children and unloved by his family, particularly his cruel, favored brother. After an undistinguished college career he holds a number of menial positions (such as convenience store clerk), but finally befriends a kindhearted copy editor named Partridge who gets him a job as a reporter. There Quoyle exhibits a "fatal flair for the false passive" and an aversion to "all but twelve to fifteen verbs;" he also starts to mentally narrate his own life in headlines: "Stupid Man Does Wrong Thing Once More." Quoyle falls helplessly in love with Petal, who appreciates only his unusually large penis and proceeds to treat him cruelly and to neglect the two daughters that are born to the couple. Nevertheless, tenderhearted, ever-loyal Quoyle is devastated by Petal's death. His move to Newfoundland is rooted in a desire to escape his unhappy past, and the novel chronicles his eventual success in this endeavor. He recovers his sense of self-worth as he turns his unpromising newspaper assignment (keeping track of the ships that visit Killick-Claw) into an interesting, well-respected column, builds a promisingly healthy relationship with Wavey and a network of other friendships, and expresses his deep love for and delight in his daughters.

Usually referred to as "the Aunt," **Agnis Hamm** is a stouthearted, highly efficient, resourceful woman who sometimes grows a little impatient with her nephew's helplessness. Regaling him with stories of Newfoundland and their ancestors' exploits, Agnis persuades Quoyle to move there with her, reclaim the old family house, and start a new life. The reader gradually learns that Agnis is an expert upholsterer who still grieves for her dead female lover, **Irene Warren**, after whom she names her dog Warren in order to hear that name every day. Agnis provides one of the novel's strongest illustrations of the theme of recovering from the past, for she flushes down the toilet the ashes of the brother (Quoyle's father) who raped her repeatedly when she was a child. Near the end of the novel—somewhat to Agnis's dismay—Quoyle learns this secret.

Quoyle's wife **Petal Bear** is a lovely, petite, but heartless sex-addict whom he loves through "six kinked years of suffering," the births of two daughters, and countless humiliations as she sleeps with every man, apparently, who comes near her. According to Nicci Gerrard, Petal "tramples with sharp shoes over his besotted emotions" even after she dies in a car crash. Quoyle's daughters are six-year-old **Bunny**, a homely but intelligent child, and **Sunshine**, four-and-a-half, who has her "wee beauty in her frowst of orange curls." Bunny is particularly troubled by her mother's absence and remains convinced that Petal will eventually wake up again; meanwhile, Bunny expresses her anguish through her hot temper and her nightmares about a vicious white dog.

Quoyle's new friend (and eventually his lover) **Wavey Prowse** compassionately tries to help Bunny understand death, just as she has tenderly cared for her own sweet-tempered son, **Herry**, who has Down's syndrome. One of Quoyle's friends suggests to him that the usually silent Wavey may be the "Tall and Quiet Woman" his father sometimes mentioned, evoking the image of a partner who provides both strength and refuge from a chaotic world. As Wavey and Quoyle move gradually toward each other, they learn that they have in common the pain caused by an unfaithful spouse, for Wavey's dead husband was a notorious philanderer who treated her with scorn.

Proulx creates in the staff of the *Gammy Bird* a cast of highly unusual but somehow plausible characters. The weekly newspaper is run by blunt, loud-voiced **Jack Buggit**, who tells Quoyle, "I know what my readers wants and expects and I give 'em that." Buggit insists on running a photograph of a car wreck on the newspaper's front page (whether there was a car wreck that week or not), and he has an uncanny ability to match each reporter with the beat that plays on his greatest fear. Jack has lost one son to the sea and once rescued his son **Dennis** from a floundering boat that was thought already sunk. He forbids Dennis to work on the sea and insists that he become a carpenter instead, a circumstance that has led to estrangement between the two. Near the end of the novel, Jack falls off his boat while fishing and is thought drowned, but in the middle of his wake he suddenly recovers from a kind of coma and sits up in his coffin; some commentators found this occurrence unconvincing and gratuitous. Reporter **B. Beaufield Nutbeem** is an Englishman who was stranded in Killick-Claw while sailing around the world on his boat, the *Borogove*. Molested by a teacher and older students when he was in boarding school, Nutbeem is assigned to write stories on the region's many sexual abuse cases. His plan to leave Newfoundland is thwarted by his drunken friends who, reluctant to part with him, destroy his boat during a raucous party. Small, seventy-year-old **Billy Pretty**, a bachelor and former fisherman, writes the *Gammy Bird*'s homemaking column. Sarcastic, bitter **Tert Card**, the newspaper's acne-scarred managing editor, finally decides to leave Killick-Claw for a job with an oil company in the larger city of St. John.

Contributing much to the Quoyle family's comfort in Killick-Claw is warm, domestic **Beety Buggit**, Dennis's wife, whose children are the same ages as Bunny and Sunshine. At the community's annual Christmas show, Beety exhibits a considerable gift for comedic mimicry. All are much relieved when the Buggit's imminent departure from Killick-Claw is made unnecessary by Jack's handing his lobster-fishing license over to his son. Another positive influence in Quoyle's life is his friend **Partridge**, a copy editor and gourmet cook who moves to California with his truck-driver wife but keeps in touch with Quoyle and gets him a job at the *Gammy Bird*. **Diddy Shovel**, the town's grizzled harbormaster, shares his knowledge of ships and sea lore with Quoyle. **Mrs. Mavis Bangs** and **Dawn Budgel** are assistants in Agnis's upholstery shop; the former eventually moves in with Agnis (suggesting that the two have become lovers) while the latter moves to St. John's in search of a more eventful life. Two unusual visitors to Killick-Claw are the rich, dissipated, and unhappily married **Bayonet** and **Silver Melville**, residents of Long Island, New York who hire Agnis to reupholster their glamorous yacht. Later, Bayonet's headless corpse is found floating offshore, and it is eventually revealed that Silver murdered him. Quoyle's weird old relative **Nolan Quoyle**, whom he commits to a psychiatric asylum in order to save his life, tells him the story of how Agnis was made pregnant by her own brother, whose baby she aborted.

Further Reading

Contemporary Literary Criticism Vol. 81. Detroit: Gale Research.

Garner, Dwight. "Northeastern Exposure." *VLS* no. 114 (April 1993): 29.

Gerrard, Nicci. "A Gale Force Winner." *Observer* (November 14, 1993): 18.

Kaveney, Roz. "Local Hero." *New Statesmen & Society* Vol. 6, no. 281 (December 3, 1993): 39.

Kendrick, Walter. Review of *The Shipping News*. *Yale Review* Vol. 81, no. 4 (October 1993): 133–35.

Klinkenborg, Verlyn. "The Princess of Tides." *New Republic* Vol. 210, no. 22, issue 4141 (May 30, 1994): 35–7.

Norman, Howard. Review of *The Shipping News*. *New York Times Book Review* (April 4, 1993): 13.

Rompkey, Ronald. "Island Pastoral." *Canadian Forum* Vol. 73, no. 832 (September 1994): 36–7.

Thomas Pynchon
1937–
American novelist and short story writer.

Vineland (novel, 1990)

Plot: The novel takes place in the fictional northern California community of Vineland in 1984. Zoyd Wheeler is a fortyish former hippy and part-time handyman who lives with his teenaged daughter, Prairie. His former wife, Frenesi Gates, disappeared when Prairie was two to enter the FBI's Witness Protection Program under the stewardship of her lover, federal prosecutor Brock Vond. In the local bar in which Zoyd performs the yearly stunt that assures him mental disability checks, Zoyd meets Hector Zuniga, a Drug Enforcement Agency agent he had often encountered during the 1960s. Hector tells Zoyd that Frenesi's source of funding has dried up due to Reagan administration budget cuts and that she has disappeared. Most ominously, Brock Vond is desperate to find Frenesi and may try to reach Prairie in order to force her mother out of hiding. Zoyd sends Prairie to the retreat of the Kunoichi Attentives for safe keeping. There she is under the care of D. L. Chastain, an old friend of Frenesi's and a "ninjette" skilled in the martial arts. DL and her partner, Takeshi Fumimota, use computer records and film archives to tell Prairie about her mother, who was a founding member of a radical documentary film collective in the 1960s. After coming under Vond's influence, Frenesi became an FBI informer and betrayed campus political leader Weed Atman, contributing directly to his murder. She later married Zoyd and gave birth to Prairie but found she could escape neither the weight of the past nor Vond's attraction; thus she joined the Witness Protection Program, eventually marrying another informer. Meanwhile, Vond has marshaled a huge strike force and plans to invade Vineland, where he believes Frenesi is hiding. At the last moment, however, he too is a victim of federal budget cuts and must cancel the attack. The novel ends with a large, idyllic family reunion at which Prairie finally meets her mother.

Characters: Recognized as one of America's most eminent novelists, Pynchon writes encyclopedic, labyrinthian novels that reveal his wide knowledge of the natural and social sciences and blend sophisticated ideas with verbal play, black humor, and parody. Seventeen years elapsed between the publication of Pynchon's previous novel, *Gravity's Rainbow,* and *Vineland,* and during this period his admirers speculated on what form his genius would take. Although some reviewers deem *Vineland* a worthy successor to Pynchon's other works, most find it less ambitious in scope and complexity; a few commentators even speculate that the novel is a mere diversion and that Pynchon is still working on a *true* masterpiece. In any case, *Vineland* features some of the same concerns as Pynchon's earlier novels, including corporate greed, political paranoia, and particularly the influence of television on American culture. Characterized as both a nostalgic meditation on the 1960s and a condemnation of the delusions and shallowness of that decade, *Vineland* ends with a hint of redemption that is unusual for Pynchon and which, consequently, some critics consider ironic.

Described by critic Edward Mendelson as "the latest of Pynchon's passive and bewildered representatives," fortyish, amiable **Zoyd Wheeler** is a "gypsy roofer" who subsists on income from odd jobs and the mental disability checks he receives from the state due to his yearly stunt of crashing through the window of a local bar. A veteran of the drug-taking, free-loving sixties, Zoyd has also farmed marijuana and played keyboard in a rock band, all the while raising his daughter, Prairie, without the involvement of her mother. Zoyd still loves and misses the beautiful, enigmatic Frenesi (who married him primarily because he knew nothing about her past) and has never fully recovered from her disappearance. His deep love for Prairie, however, has given him "his belated moment of welcome to planet Earth." Pynchon's fond portrayal of Zoyd has been cited by some critics as evidence that despite his intellectual sophistication, Pynchon sides with the lovable schlemiels of the world, who would no doubt find his books unfathomable.

Some commentators see **Prairie Wheeler** as the central character of *Vineland,* for much of the novel chronicles her quest to uncover the truth about her family and thus illuminate her own identity. Sharp, cool, and inquisitive, Prairie seems more aware than her father that something is missing from their lives, and despite her love for Zoyd, she privately admits to longing for an ordinary family life. Prairie has been motherless for twelve of her fourteen years and is eager for any information about Frenesi, whose story she finally learns when she is in hiding from Brock Vond at the Retreat of the Kunoichi Attentives. Prairie's reunion with her mother near the end of the novel strikes some reviewers as anticlimactic; in addition, the final scene—in which Prairie's lost dog (a direct descendent of her mother's old dog) reappears and licks her face—is subject to varying interpretations. Some critics claim that Pynchon (with uncharacteristic sentimentality) is casting Prairie as a redemptive character whose future is hopeful despite the disorder of her society, while others find this happy ending parodic.

Frenesi Gates is nearly a mythical figure in *Vineland,* although several critics assert that she never actually fulfills the reader's expectations. A beauty with arresting blue eyes and a gaze of invincible innocence that Pynchon characterizes as typifying the youth of the 1960s, Frenesi was a founding member of the Death to the Pig Nihilist Film Kollective, a radical group dedicated to the art of "guerilla" documentary filmmaking. The daughter of a Hollywood gaffer (sound technician), Frenesi had a family history of both film and political activism, for both her parents were active members of the labor movement. Frenesi met Brock Vond when she was imprisoned in his "re-education camp" for campus revolutionaries. Her helpless desire for this man who embodies everything she supposedly despises illustrates the idea that beneath the antagonism between hippies and authority figures in the 1960s was an underlying attraction to what the other represented—either freedom or order. In any case, Vond succeeds in "turning" Frenesi, who eventually delivers to his murderer the gun that kills Weed Atman (her former lover) and even films his death. Appalled by what she has done, Frenesi marries Zoyd and has a child but is eventually overwhelmed by her past. Her reappearance at the family reunion seems anticlimactic to commentators, who find her a disappointingly shallow character who never earns the adoration she receives from everyone around her.

According to critic Rhoda Koenig, federal prosecutor **Brock Vond** is a "dark genius of political control," a calculating, malevolent representative of institutionalized repression and intolerance. Vond began his career during the Nixon administration and first encountered Frenesi when she was rounded up with other counter-culture types into the secret "re-education" camp he had established. Pynchon uses Vond to articulate the concept that the political rebellion and activism of the 1960s was actually rooted in a desire for order and discipline, a "need only to stay children forever, safe inside some extended national family." In fact, Vond's success in "re-educating" radicals had much to do with the promise that those who agreed to become FBI informers could continue to attend college indefinitely. A threatening embodiment of the resistance to change and of "the State law enforcement apparatus . . . calling itself 'America,'" Vond is finally defeated by the same budget cuts that forced Frenesi out of the Witness Protection Program.

Some commentators find **Darryl Louise "DL" Chastain** a more admirable character than her old friend Frenesi. A biker and "ninjette," or woman warrior, and a resident of the Retreat of the Kunoichi Attentives, DL is well versed in Eastern martial arts and related philosophy practiced by the Kunoichi Sisterhood, which is headed by **Sister Rochelle**. DL's relationship with her partner (and eventual lover) **Takeshi Fumimota** began when she was assigned to assassinate Brock Vond. DL accidentally applied the Vibrating Palm (or Ninja Death Touch)—which kills its victim one year later—to Takeshi, who was disguised as Vond. After the death sentence reversed, DL and Takeshi form a partnership through which DL will balance her "karmic account" and work off the harm she has done him. Critics believe that Takeshi, a stereotypically inscrutable amphetamine addict who runs a "karmic adjustment" service, is actually a refugee from the novel, about a Japanese insurance adjuster, that Pynchon is rumored to be writing. The romance between DL and Takeshi may be a positive version of the ultimately destructive union of opposites that Frenesi and Brock comprise. Together DL and Takeshi protect Prairie from her ominous pursuer and also initiate her into her mother's history through a high-tech film and computer presentation.

Through Drug Enforcement Agency field representative **Hector Zuniga**, Pynchon satirizes America's dependence on television. A "Tube" addict, Hector once arrested his wife when, frustrated with his obsession, she threw a pot roast at the television set. He has recently escaped from a Tubaldetox program and is being pursued by an organization called NEVER—National Endowment for Video Education and Rehabilitation. Also providing a perspective on television and American culture is Prairie's boyfriend, **Isaiah Two-Four**, whose hippy parents named him after the swords-into-plowshares passage in the Bible. A heavy-metal musician in a group called **Billy Barf and the Vomitones**, Isaiah Two-Four points out that the sixties generation failed to recognize the power of television to separate people from actual experience and make them vulnerable to manipulation. Another group of characters who combine comic relief with serious themes are the **Thanatoids**, a kind of "living dead" race who, as victims of unavenged, unconfessed sins, are doomed to sleepless, powerless wandering. Inhabitants of the aptly named suburb of Shade Creek, the Thanatoids are described as "not living but persisting, on the skimpiest of hopes."

Frenesi's socialist-minded parents are **Hubbell Gates**, who worked as a Hollywood gaffer until the blacklisting during the Red Scare of the 1950s, and **Sasha Gates**, who herself came from a strong union family and through whom Pynchon introduces some interesting ruminations on the labor movement of the American West. Sasha's father **Jess Traverse**, an even more ardent radical than his daughter, attempts to comfort the attendees at the family reunion held near the end of the novel by quoting from Ralph Waldo Emerson: "Secret retributions are always restoring the level of the divine justice." Other characters in *Vineland* include mathematics professor Weed Altman, a former lover of Frenesi's and a rather unlikely campus political hero who is betrayed by her and, after his death, becomes a Thanatoid; **Flash Fletcher**, another former radical, who marries Frenesi and shares her exile in the Witness Protection Program; and the "legally ambiguous tow-truck team" of **Eusebio "Vato" Gomez** and **Cleveland "Blood" Bonnifoy**, who play the role of Charon on the mythical River Styx as they shepherd people to Shade Creek to visit the Thanatoids.

Further Reading

Chambers, Judith. *Thomas Pynchon.* New York: Twayne, 1992.

Contemporary Literary Criticism. Vols. 2, 3, 6, 9, 11, 18, 33, 62. Detroit: Gale Research.

Dictionary of Literary Biography. Vol. 2. Detroit: Gale Research.

Dugdale, John. *Thomas Pynchon: Allusive Parables of Power.* New York: St. Martin's Press, 1990.

Eddins, Dwight. *The Gnostic Pynchon.* Bloomington: Indiana University Press, 1990.

Koenig, Rhoda. "Worth Its Wait." *New York Magazine* Vol. 23, no. 4 (January 29, 1990): 66–7.

Lehmann-Haupt, Christopher. "Vineland: Pynchon's First Novel in 17 Years." *New York Times* (December 26, 1989): C21.

Leithauser, Brad. "Any Place You Want." *New York Review of Books* Vol. 37, no. 4 (March 15, 1990): 7–10.

Leonard, John. "The Styxties." *Nation* Vol. 250, no. 8 (February 26, 1990): 281–86.

Madsen, Deborah L. *The Postmodernist Allegories of Thomas Pynchon.* New York: St. Martin's Press, 1991.

McManus, James. "Pynchon's Return." *Chicago Tribune—Books* (January 14, 1990): 3.

Mendelson, Edward. "Levity's Rainbow." *New Republic* Vol. 203, nos. 2 & 3 (July 9 & 16, 1990): 40–6.

Rafferty, Terrence. "Long Last." *New Yorker* Vol. 66, no. 1 (February 19, 1990): 108–12.

Rushdie, Salman. "Thomas Pynchon." In *Imaginary Homelands: Essays and Criticism 1981–1991.* London: Granta Books, 1991, pp. 352–57.

Wilde, Alan. "Love and Death in and around Vineland, U.S.A." *boundary 2* (summer 1991): 166–80.

Joao Ubaldo Ribeiro

1941–

Brazilian novelist, short story writer, and journalist.

Sergeant Getúlio (novel, 1971)

Plot: Set in contemporary Brazil, the novel is structured as the long, rambling narrative of the title character, a state militia deserter hired as a killer by an ambitious politician. Speaking either to himself or to his silent driver, Getúlio recalls his violent past as he carries out his assignment to capture and deliver a political prisoner. When the political situation changes, however, Getúlio's boss denies ordering the prisoner's capture. He sends a group of soldiers to release the prisoner, but Getúlio's self-styled mission does not allow him to comply, and he kills their lieutenant. Getúlio survives several subsequent ambushes until he is finally killed by government troops.

Characters: Ribeiro received international acclaim with the publication of *Sergeant Getúlio.* Jorge Amada, famous Brazilian novelist, lauded Ribeiro for his "persistent concern with exposing both individual and social problems." Commentators have characterized *Sergeant Getúlio* as a testament to the mindless cruelty that lies beneath a thin veneer of order in Latin American society, as well as the tension between civilization and barbarism in contemporary Brazil.

The novel is structured as the stream-of-consciousness narrative of a hired gunman, **Sergeant Getúlio,** into whose mind and brutal existence the reader is offered entry. Getúlio takes twenty lives–including those, he eventually reveals, of his own wife and unborn child after he discovers his wife's infidelity. Ribeiro quickly establishes that Getúlio is a crude, savage brute indifferent to the suffering and torture of his captive, referring to him as a "creature" and a "pox." Sergeant Getúlio thrives on the fear he inspires in others. Yet there is a certain insecurity behind the exaggerated confidence displayed in such claims as "my equal has not yet been born,'' for he also admits that ''the worst thing is to be nobody.'' Despite Getúlio's savagery, The Sergeant is portrayed the author succeeds in making Getúlio both repellent and heroic as adhering to his own code of morality and integrity–his killing is never gratuitous. When Getúlio refuses to comply to his employer's change of orders, his motives include not only his conception of courage and manliness but his devotion to the profession that has given him his identity. Ribeiro's skillful portrayal of this complex characters voice blends madness and poignancy, and the monstrous and the lyrical. Although some critics condemned the novel's graphically portrayed violence, most found Getúlio a tragic figure whose death is redemptive in that it concludes his quest to carry out his own will. In his brutality, alienation, and dedication to a personal code of behavior, Getúlio has been compared to such renowned literary characters as Camilo José Cela's Pascual Duarte, Fyodor Dostoyevsky's Underground Man, and Albert Camus's Meersault.

The novel's other characters are portrayed entirely through the consciousness of Sergeant Getúlio. **Senhor Antunes**, Getúlio's employer, is a local political boss who orders his henchman to capture and deliver one of his enemies, then bows to political pressure and reverses the order. Much of Getúlio's narrative is spoken aloud to his driver **Amaro**, who serves as a silent witness to Getúlio's confessions and brutal treatment of his prisoner. Although Amaro is a mysterious figure within the action of the novel, Getúlio describes him as highly religious and playful. Indeed, Amaro seems to be one of very few people for whom Getúlio feels any affection; nevertheless, he shows little concern when Amaro is finally killed. Nor does Getúlio mourn the death of his lover, **Luzinete**, a strong woman who shares his taste for violence and urges him to continue his mission. Through Getúlio's unnamed **captive**, Ribeiro highlights the pitiless brutality of twentieth-century politics in Latin America. The captive undergoes a Kafkaesque nightmare of dehumanizing victimization through Getúlio's anger and aggression. The reader learns little about the captive except that he is a high school graduate (which anti-intellectual Getúlio resents) innocent symbolizing the persecuted by a ruthless, oppressive political system.

Further Reading

Adams, Phoebe-Lou. Review of *Sergeant Getúlio. Atlantic Monthly* (February 1978): 977.

Contemporary Literary Criticism. Vols. 10, 67. Detroit: Gale Research.

DiAntonio, Robert. ''Chthonian Visions and Mythic Redemption in Joao Ubaldo Ribeiro's *Sergeant Getúlio. Modern Fiction Studies* Vol. 32, no. 3 (autumn 1986): 449–58.

Feinstein, Adam. ''No Nobody He.'' *Times Literary Supplement* No. 4029 (June 13, 1980): 674.

Hollinghurst, Alan. ''Heroic Integrity.'' *New Statesman* Vol. 99, no. 2556 (March 14, 1980): 402.

Kemp, Peter. ''Messy Pasts.'' *Listener* Vol. 103, no. 2653 (March 13, 1980): 350–51.

Larios, Luis. Review of *Sergeant Getúlio. World Literature Today* Vol, 53, no. 1 (winter 1979): 94.

Prescott, Peter S. ''A Good Barbarian.'' *Newsweek* Vol. 91, no. 5 (January 30, 1978): 68.

Solomon, Barbara Probst. Review of *Sergeant Getúlio. New York Times Book Review* (April 9, 1978): 11, 30.

Anne Rice

1941–

American novelist and critic.

Interview With the Vampire (novel, 1976)

Plot: The novel chronicles the life of the vampire Louis, who tells his story to a young interviewer, from the late eighteenth century to about the middle of the nineteenth. Louis is initiated by another vampire, Lestat, whom he meets soon after the tragic death of his brother, for which he feels responsible. Louis initiates a child named Claudia into vampirehood, after which she retains a perpetually five-year-old body. After sixty years with Louis and Lestat, Claudia tries to kill Lestat so that she and Louis can escape his domination. Lestat returns to life, however, and attacks Louis and Claudia. When they flee to Europe in search of the origin and nature of vampires, they encounter a whole community of their fellow creatures at the Théâtre des Vampires in Paris. Claudia forms a liaison with an adult woman vampire named Madeleine, while Louis comes under the influence of Armand, an extremely old and knowledgeable vampire. Lestat suddenly appears and kills Claudia and Madeleine while Louis flees from Armand.

Characters: A unique blend of elements of the classic gothic horror story and contemporary philosophical concerns, *Interview With a Vampire* has attracted a wide audience. While some commentators criticize Rice's ornate prose style, others find her story spellbinding and original and her writing polished. Rice explores such issues as alienation and the struggle for identity, the nature of good and evil, and the ambiguities inherent in human nature and morality.

Rice considers the legendary figure of the vampire as "a powerful metaphor for the outcast—and the monster in all of us." This perception is evidenced in her characterization of **Louis.** The novel's central figure, Louis is unique among other vampires in that he experiences guilt and remorse about his own murderousness, feels alienated from both human beings and other vampires, and struggles to achieve a more meaningful life. Louis does not share the traditional vampire's powerful aversion to churches and crucifixes and even visits a church in the hope of finding some comfort. Indeed, Louis' brother Paul was a religious devotee whose beliefs Louis came to respect only after Paul's death, and he regrets not following the same path. Louis accepts responsibility for and condemns his behavior, but he must finally accept the constraints of his own nature and the eternal solitude. Louis tells his story to the young interviewer in order to warn others who might want to be a vampire; however, Louis seems to produce a different result altogether when the interviewer tells Louis he would like to become a vampire.

The older, charismatic vampire, **Lestat**, initiates Louis as a vampire after a long period struggling with his brother's death. The ruthless Lestat exerts a power that overcomes Louis's considerable ego. Lestat makes the case for vampirism in language that blurs the distinction between good and evil, so that Louis finds it difficult to discern or choose between the two. In Paris, Louis meets the novel's other central vampire character, the ancient **Armand**. Louis develops a deep love (both physical and spiritual) and admiration for this profoundly cynical vampire, who serves as his instructor in the ways and complexities of evil. Armand denies the existence of both God and the devil, asserting that the self is the only authority and promoting the concept of evil without guilt. Louis' relationship with Armand verifies for Louis the emptiness of life and the impossibility of his ever finding love or meaning.

The female vampire **Claudia** is a tragic figure in that she gains perpetual life at the age of five, but she is doomed to retain the physical form she had at that age. Thus she embodies the particularly frightening image of a bloodthirsty adventuress inside the body of a child. Claudia's anger and resentment of her predicament are evidenced in her attempt to kill Lestat. She symbolizes the restraints of traditional femininity, which demands from women the childish qualities of dependence and obedience; in addition, Claudia represents the female as an object of both desire and horror. Claudia finally convinces Louis (whose hesitation evidences his moral conflict) to turn **Madeleine**—a dollmaker who became insane following the death of her daughter—into a vampire. Although Claudia envisions Madeleine as a possible companion for Louis, she may also seek in Madeleine a surrogate mother for herself.

The novel takes the form of Louis telling his story over one long night to a young, unnamed **interviewer** armed with a tape recorder. This format encourages the reader to identify with Louis as if he were a human being. If Louis intends this interview to accomplish something meaningful in his life by warning others away from vampirehood, he apparently fails, for the interviewer ultimately asks to be initiated and join Louis' search for Lestat.

Further Reading

Braudy, Leo. "Queer Monsters." *New York Times Book Review* (May 2, 1976): 7, 14.

Contemporary Literary Criticism. Vol. 41. Detroit: Gale Research Co.

Heldman, Irma Pascal. "The Fangs Have It." *Village Voice* Vol. 21, no. 19 (May 10, 1976): 50.

Hodges, Devon, and Janice L. Doane. "Undoing Feminism in Anne Rice's Vampire Chronicles." In *Modernity and Mass Culture*, Eds. James Naremore and Patrick Brantlinger. Bloomington: Indiana University Press, 1991, pp. 158–75.

Johnson, Brian D. "Queen of the Night." *Maclean's* Vol. 105, no. 46 (November 16, 1992): 68.

Milton, Edith. Review of *Interview with the Vampire. New Republic* Vol. 174, no. 19 (May 8, 1976): 29–30.

Ramsland, Katherine M. *Prism of the Night: A Biography of Anne Rice.* New York: Dutton, 1991.

Mordecai Richler
1931–

Canadian novelist, essayist, scriptwriter, short story writer, critic, and author of books for children.

Solomon Gursky Was Here (novel, 1989)

Plot: Structured episodically, the novel covers a period of about one hundred years in the history of a Canadian family whose progenitor is Russian-Jewish immigrant Ephraim Gursky. A one-time London pickpocket, Ephraim stows away with the Franklin expedition and is the only survivor of this illfated attempt to locate a Northwest Passage to the Arctic.

His later adventures include gunrunning during the American Civil War and posing as a shaman to a band of Canadian Inuits, whom he converts to Judaism. Ephraim recognizes a kindred spirit in his grandson Solomon, whom he kidnaps and takes into the woods to initiate him into his own lore and viewpoint. Later Solomon and his two brothers, Bernard and Morrie, use Solomon's poker winnings to establish a bootlegging enterprise that eventually becomes a hugely profitable liquor empire. The crude but savvy Bernard operates the family business after the disappearance of the enigmatic, charismatic Solomon, who is thought dead after his small airplane is lost in a snowstorm.

The sections of the novel set in the 1980s center on Moses Berger, a failed, alcoholic writer who has spent thirty years working on a history of the Gurskys. Berger is convinced that Solomon did not die in the plane crash but was, in fact, not only the wealthy Sir Hyman Kaplansky he met in London during the 1950s but the unidentified Jewish gentleman spotted at such disparate historical events as Mao Zedong's Long March, the Israeli raid on Entebbe, and the Watergate hearings. Finally, however, Berger concludes that Solomon is now dead and that he will never be able to publish his chronicle, which is so fantastic that no one would believe it.

Characters: Written by one of Canada's most respected contemporary novelists, *Solomon Gursky Was Here* chronicles the rise to power and wealth of a family that resembles the Bronfmans, founders of the Seagram's liquor dynasty. Richly textured and savagely funny, the novel combines elements of satire, myth, realism, and mystery. As in his other novels, Richler explores here the question of Jewish identity in a New World context as well as the Canadian national character in general and the inferiority complex that he and other Canadian writers portray as endemic in their country.

Some critics identify fifty-two-year-old **Moses Berger**, the self-appointed biographer of the Gurskys, as Richler's alter ego in the novel. He has also been identified as one of several chronicler characters in Richler's fiction, such as Jake Hersh in *St. Urbain's Horseman* (1971), who also takes on a larger-than-life subject. Moses' first exposure to the family occurred when he was eleven years old and his father took him to a birthday party for one of the Gursky children. He later became a friend of Solomon's son Henry and, briefly, a lover of his daughter Lucy, and he has remained obsessed by the Gursky legacy; he even calls himself a "Gurskyologist." Described by Henry as "an enormous failure, a tragic waste," Moses was a literary prodigy who never realized his early promise. He turned down a Rhodes scholarship in order to begin the thirty-year project of recording the lives of the Gurskys, meanwhile slipping into alcoholism and emotional isolation. Although Moses claims that he wants to expose the Gurskys' inherent crookedness and thus spite his father, who both failed to support his son's aspirations and compromised himself to become Bernard's toady, Moses finally admits to some grudging admiration for them, and particularly for the enigmatic Solomon. Unlike his subject, Moses is consumed with the self-doubt that marks him as the kind of insecure Canadian artist portrayed by many of the country's writers. In the end, he abandons his project because he is convinced that if it was published he would be "carted off in a straitjacket."

The first Gursky to arrive in the new world is **Ephraim**, who lived from 1817 to 1910. Supposedly the illegitimate son of a Minsk cantor and a baroness who fled to England to escape the persecution of Jews in Russia, Ephraim was a teenaged pickpocket in London who spent some time in the famous Newgate Prison. He managed to stow away on Sir John Franklin's 1845 polar expedition, which ended disastrously with the members not only failing to locate a Northwest Passage but forced to resort to cannibalism. Having miraculously survived this experience, Ephraim subsequently turned up in a variety of locations and guises: he smuggled guns to New Orleans during the American Civil War, played the piano in Alaska's Klondike region, fathered twenty-seven children, and served as the opportunistic head of the "Church of the Millenarian," converting a band of Inuit to

Judaism. Along with his grandson Solomon, Ephraim is presented as a trickster figure like those (including the raven with which both are closely associated) in the mythology of indigenous Canadians and other peoples, who are part God and part animal, have the ability to change shape, and frequently meddle in the affairs of human beings.

Like his grandfather, the charismatic **Solomon Gursky** seems to have the ability to reinvent himself at will; in fact, he comments that "living twice, maybe three times is the best revenge." Born in 1899, Solomon is taken by Ephraim (who recognizes the boy's affinities with himself) to the Canadian wilds for initiation into the Gursky legacy. When his grandfather dies, Solomon is led to safety by a raven, the animal he later claims to resemble in his "unquenchable itch to meddle and provoke things, to play tricks on the world and its creatures." Distinguished as the most intelligent, bold, and decent of Ephraim's three grandsons, Solomon grows into adulthood with a broader view of life and history than any of them–even if he is similarly unscrupulous. It is his poker winnings that provide the basis of the Gursky fortune, and in addition to becoming a bootlegger of whiskey he becomes, according to John Leonard, a "bootlegger of ideas." Sometimes deceitful but always charming, Solomon conspires with the famous (his friends range from George Bernard Shaw to Dutch Schultz) and has a Gatsby-like affair with the beautiful, Gentile Diane McClure. Some time after his scheme to provide a Canadian refuge for European Jews is scuttled, Solomon takes off in a Gypsy Moth plane that crashes in a snowstorm; although his body is never found, he is thought dead. Nevertheless, throughout the next four decades or so, a figure who closely resembles Solomon keeps reappearing at key historical moments: he accompanies Mao Zedong on the Long March, makes the last telephone call to Marilyn Monroe, sits next to Maureen Dean at the Watergate hearings, and participates in the Israeli raid on Entebbe. His last communication is a letter to his biographer, Moses Berger, that is mailed from Saigon in 1978.

In London in the 1950s, Moses meets **Sir Herman Kaplansky**, a wealthy Jew who serves as his benefactor during the writing of the Gursky family history and whom he eventually learns is actually Solomon Gursky. Described by critic John Clute as a "shadowy financier, crow-faced philanderer, mocker and celebrant," Kaplansky is, despite his religion, a well-connected denizen of London's elite and is often mentioned in the diaries of such famous people of the period as novelist Evelyn Waugh. In one much-cited passage, Kaplansky invites many of London's most flagrant anti-Semites to a Passover Seder at which he serves them matzoh filled with a blood-like fluid that sends them fleeing in horror, leaving Kaplansky to cackle with delight. In addition to his support of Moses, Kaplansky secretly provides for an air force for the new state of Israel.

At one point in the novel, Solomon says, "Dig deep enough into the past of any noble family and there is a Bernard at the root. The founder with the dirty fingernails." The early career of the powerful, self-aggrandizing **Bernard Gursky**—who boasts that "I don't get ulcers, I give them"—was reportedly based on that of Samuel Bronfman, the founder of the Seagram's whiskey dynasty, whose fortune also originated during the Prohibition era. Although he is jealous of his charismatic brother, Bernard uses his considerable business acumen to parlay Solomon's poker earnings into a bootlegging empire. He serves as the novel's primary representative of the capitalistic greed for money and power, but the respectability he also craves proves elusive, for he remains unalterably grubby.

Several critics have noted the predominance of negatively portrayed father-son relationships in *Solomon Gursky Was Here*, and a prime example is that of Moses Berger and his father, **L. B. Berger**. Reportedly modeled after Canadian Jewish poet and socialist A. M. Klein, the vain, highly erudite Berger is a former liberal who changed his politics and sold out his art in order to become a speechwriter and advisor to Bernard Gursky, whose praises he sings in cheap verse recited at parties. Although he frequently professes a boundless love for Moses, Berger is apparently jealous of his talented son and tries to foil him by, for example, destroying the letter informing Moses that the *New Yorker* has accepted one of his short stories, and demeaning the Rhodes scholarship that Moses wins. Ironically, it is to spite his father that Moses gives up a promising literary career to pursue the biography that he believes will expose his father's employers as corrupt.

Not all of the Gurskys are as memorable as the aforementioned. **Aaron Gursky**, Ephraim's son, is an inept shopkeeper, and **Morrie Gursky**, the brother of Bernard and Solomon, is a mildmannered *nebbish* (Yiddish for an ineffective, dull person) who writes his own, notably sanitized memoir of the Gursky family. The contemporary generation of Gurskys include the eccentric **Henry**, Solomon's son and Moses' best friend, who becomes a strictly observant Hasidic Jew and moves to the Arctic to await the Messiah in the company of his Inuit wife **Nialie** (a skillful kosher cook) and son **Isaac**. Henry's faith and rejection of materialism make him the polar opposite of the other Gurskys. His sister **Lucy**, with whom Moses has an affair, is a dizzy character who puts on an appalling vanity production of *The Diary of Anne Frank* that reveals her own spectacular lack of acting talent. Through Bernard's son **Lionel**, Richler provides another example of a harmful father-son relationship: when the seven-year-old Lionel runs away from a fight, Bernard announces that he is going to call the hospital to try to exchange his son for a girl; he later tells the boy, "I'm stuck with you. They don't take cowards."

Several commentators faulted Richler for the novel's weakly drawn female characters, including Moses' lover **Beatrice**, who finally finds his drinking intolerable, and **Diane McClure**, the beautiful Gentile who plays Daisy to Solomon's Gatsby. Diane forever regrets her decision to turn down Solomon's marriage proposal, and she later contracts not one but two debilitating diseases, polio and cancer. Other secondary characters include the bigoted (though honest) and decidedly Anglo-Saxon customs inspector **Bert Smith**, whose fears for Canada's racial purity lead him to thwart Solomon's plan to provide refuge for European Jews during World War II. Solomon says of this character, "This country had no tap root. Instead there's Bert Smith. The very essence." The Gursky's employer Tim Callaghan delivers the much-quoted observation that "Canada is not so much a country as a holding tank filled with the disgruntled progeny of defeated peoples." Gitel Kugelmass is a disheartened former socialist who asks Moses, "Does anybody care about our stories now? Who will wing our songs, Moishe?" Bernard's disreputable sidekick, Harvey Schwartz, "never met a rich man he didn't like."

Further Reading

Bell, Pearl K. "Canada Wry." *New Republic* 202, No. 19 (7 May 1990): 42-4.

Clute, John. "Tricksters from the Heart of the North." *Times Literary Supplement* no. 4550 (15-21 June 1990): 653.

Contemporary Literary Criticism, Vols. 3, 5, 9, 13, 18, 46, 70. Detroit: Gale Research.

Dictionary of Literary Biography, Vol. 53. Detroit: Gale Research.

Kirsch, Jonathan. "Next Door to the Promised Land." *Los Angeles Times Book Review* (17 June 1990): 4.

Koenig, Rhoda. "Canadian Club." *New York* 23, No. 15 (16 April 1990): 95-6.

Lavery, John. "Ravening." *Canadian Literature* No. 129 (Summer 1991): 198-200.

Leonard, John. "Sermon on the Mountie." *Nation* 250, no. 22 (4 June 1990): 785-86, 788-91.

Prose, Francine. "Hopping Mad in Montreal." *New York Times Book Review* (8 April 1990): 7.

Ritts, Morton. "Witness to His Time." *Maclean's* 102, No. 46 (13 November 1989): 64-7.

Rooke, Leon. "Tales from the Caboose." *Books in Canada* 18, No. 8 (November 1989): 11-13.

Yanofsky, Joel. "Funny, You Don't Look Canadian." *Village Voice* XXXV, No. 18 (1 May 1990): 86.

Tom Robbins

1936–

American novelist and short story writer.

Even Cowgirls Get the Blues (novel, 1976)

Plot: The novel centers on Sissy Hankshaw, a native of South Richmond, Virginia, whose nine-inch thumbs are considered a deformity by her family and neighbors. Sissy makes the best of her condition, however, by becoming America's greatest hitchhiker. Between journeys, she works as a model for the Countess, who owns a feminine hygiene company as well as the Rubber Rose Ranch, a weight reduction spa in South Dakota. In New York, Sissy meets and marries Julian Gitche, an artist who spurns his Mohawk Indian heritage and considers Sissy's acceptance of her oversized thumbs neurotic. Sissy agrees to go to the Rubber Rose Ranch to be photographed with the whooping cranes who congregate there. The ranch has by now been taken over by Bonanza Jellybean and her cowgirls, who have transformed it into a feminist community oriented toward personal fulfillment. Sissy has a brief affair with Bonanza and also meets a Japanese-American named the Chink, who becomes her lover and mentor. A refugee from conventional society, the Chink has been influenced by the kindness, humility, and fluid view of time practiced by a group of Indians called the Clock People, who believe in pantheistic values and individual freedom. Sissy returns to New York but finds city life stifling and longs to go back to hitchhiking. Her husband sends her to a psychiatrist, Dr. Goldman, who tells her she is neurotic. This diagnosis is countered, however, by another psychiatrist—Dr. Tom Robbins, who finds her self-esteem and yearning for freedom healthy.

Worried about the Rubber Rose Ranch, Sissy starts to hitchhike, but a rape attempt sends her back to New York. At Julian's urging, she agrees to have her thumbs amputated by a defrocked plastic surgeon, Dr. Dreyfus. Sissy has had only one thumb surgically altered when she is called back to the Rubber Rose, which is about to be attacked by the FBI. Several of the cowgirls—including Bonanza—are killed as well as many of the FBI agents. Afterward, some surviving cowgirls remain on the ranch while others return to other places to spread their message of self-fulfillment. Meanwhile, Sissy has become pregnant through her dalliance with the Chink. Dr. Robbins, who has fallen in love with Sissy, foresees a contented life raising big-thumbed children with her. The Chink predicts Sissy's offspring will be unable to manipulate tools or weapons, and they will generate a way of life more in harmony with nature.

Characters: The readers of Robbins's novels identify with his advocacy of personal fulfillment rather than social transformation. Like such authors as Thomas Pynchon, John Barth, and Kurt Vonnegut—who are often identified as his literary forebears—Robbins focuses on the absurdity of modern life, rejects conformity, and incorporates elements of metafiction (fiction concerned with the act of writing or creating fiction) into his writing. Considered more focused and disciplined than his first novel (*Another Roadside Attraction*), *Even Cowgirls Get the Blues* features Robbins's elaborate, energetic style and underlying optimism. According to critic Mark Siegel, the novel "posits the abandonment of outworn mainstream social roles that are destructive in their rigidity" in favor of a more self-aware, pantheistic mode of being.

A significant portion of the novel is devoted to the education and maturation of **Sissy Hankshaw**, a part-Indian native of South Richmond, Virginia. Her identifying features are her nine-inch thumbs which she manipulates like baseball bats. Sissy struggles to retain a positive self-image in spite of the disapproval she encounters over her deformity. However, Sissy transforms her defect into an asset by becoming America's greatest hitchhiker. Her obsessive journeys back and forth across the country have been interpreted as both a parody and a celebration of the American preoccupation with the road; Sissy claims that she once had a sexual dalliance with Jack Kerouac, the author of the "beat" novels *On the Road* and *Dharma Bums*. Sissy is presented as a highly appealing character in her physical attractiveness, essential innocence, healthy sexuality, and ability to overcome what others interpret as a major handicap and make her own, joyful way through the world. Her consistent yearning for freedom of movement and her openness to others make her, according to some commentators, a quintessentially American heroine. Sissy's sacrifice of one of her enlarged thumbs might seem to be a partial loss of her individuality. But her different-sized thumbs symbolize a balance between the confines of society and alienation from civilization.

Some critics have seen Sissy's teacher and lover **the Chink** as a parody of the kind of guru, mystic, or sage figure often found in the counterculture literature of the 1960s; most, however, agree that his philosophy is presented in a positive light. Interned with other Japanese-Americans during World War II, the Chink has adopted the Clock people's view of life which revolves around individual freedom and closeness to nature. Sissy describes the Chink as an ideal lover (despite his advanced age) because of his sincere, non-possessive appreciation of women; and an ideal father of her child-to-be, whom he predicts will be the vanguard of a more liberated generation. He predicts a brighter future for Sissy's big-thumbed children because their inability to use tools or weapons will result in a more harmonious relationship with their environment. The Chink advises Sissy to "Be your own master! . . . Rescue yourself. Be your own valentine!" The Chink does not advocate a simpleminded retreat into some mythical, rustic past. Rather, he advocates adapting the longlost pantheism (i.e., seeing the divine in all creation).

Sissy's husband, **Julian Gitche**, is the novel's primary representative of social conformity or of shallow "Establishment" values. Sissy is initially attracted to Julian because of his inherent kindness, but she feels stifled by her life with him, she finally leaves him for Dr. Robbins. Although he is a full-blooded Mohawk Indian, Julian is entirely oriented toward Western European standards and considers his own heritage hopelessly backward. Thus he has been identified as a comic reversal of the "natural man" after which many Native American characters in literature are modeled. Julian is an effete, Yale-educated watercolorist with chronic asthma squandering his artistic talent into socially acceptable but dull forms.

At the middle point of male characters (between Julian and the Chink) is the author's self-reflexive character, **Dr. Tom Robbins**, an example of Robbins's use of metafictional techniques. Dr. Robbins is a psychiatrist and truth-seeker who finds Sissy's self-esteem admirable and who falls in love with her, anticipating a blissful future raising big-thumbed children. He also comes under the influence of the Chink, whose teachings inspire him to quit his job, calling in "well" instead of sick. At the end of the book, the reader learns that Dr. Robbins has been the story's narrator all along.

The leader of the cowgirls is **Bonanza Jellybean**, a dynamic figure who embodies the kind of affirmative feminism Robbins advocates. Born into an ordinary middle-class family, Bonanza yearned all her life for the active, heroic western lifestyle available only to men depicted in movies. Repelled by the brain washing of the Rubber Rose Ranch clients, Bonanza instigated a feminist take-over that allowed the female residents to explore new roles and routes to self-fulfillment. The ranch also began to provide sanctuary for the threatened whooping cranes, the novel's strong symbol of freedom. Although Bonanza is ultimately killed by the FBI agents during their attack on the ranch, her legacy lives on as her cowgirls travel across the country to spread their message of female self-esteem.

Other characters in the novel include **Delores del Ruby**, one of Bonanza's cowgirls, who eventually overcomes her aversion to men; **the Countess**, the good-natured male eunuch who heads the feminine hygiene products company that owns Rubber Rose Ranch; and **Billy West**, a fat, jolly, life-affirming goat-seller who aids the cowgirls during the FBI raid. Sissy is persecuted by two members of the medical establishment: the psychiatrist **Dr. Goldman**, who finds her positive attitude toward her oversized thumbs a sign of neurosis; and **Dr. Dreyfus**, a talented but unscrupulous plastic surgeon who allows his devotion to his art overcome his moral reservations about altering Sissy's unique thumbs.

Further Reading

Cameron, Ann. "A Nose Thumb at Normality." *Nation* (August 28, 1976): 152–53.

Cloonan, William. "Tom Robbins' Culture: The Brain Takes Its Lumps." *New Boston Review* Vol., no. 3 (December 1977): 5–6.

Contemporary Literary Criticism. Vols. 9, 32, 64. Detroit: Gale Research.

Dictionary of Literary Biography. 1980 Yearbook. Detroit: Gale Research.

Karl, Frederick R. "Growing Up in America: The 1940s and Thereafter." In *American Fictions, 1940/1980: A Comprehensive History and Critical Evaluation.* New York: Harper & Row, 1983, pp. 129–75.

LeClair, Thomas. Review of *Even Cowgirls Get the Blues. New York Times Book Review* (May 23, 1976): 5.

Nadeau, Robert. "Tom Robbins." In *Readings from the New Book on Nature: Physics and Metaphysics in the Modern Novel.* University of Massachusetts Press, 1981, pp. 149-61.

Nelson, William. "Unlikely Heroes: The Central Figures in *The World According to Garp, Even Cowgirls Get the Blues*, and *A Confederacy of Dunces.*" In *The Hero in Transition.* Eds. Ray B. Browne and Marshall W. Fishwick. Bowling Green, KY: Bowling Green University Popular Press, 1983, pp. 163–70.

Siegel, Mark. *Tom Robbins.* Boise: Boise State University, 1980.

Philip Roth

1933–

American novelist and short story writer.

The Counterlife (novel, 1987)

Plot: The novel comprises five sections, each presenting a "counterlife" (Roth's term for imagined other selves) of one or more of the main characters. The central figure is Nathan Zuckerman, the middle-aged, Jewish-American novelist who was featured in an earlier trilogy of novels by Roth (*The Ghost Writer*, 1979; *Zuckerman Unbound*, 1981; and *The Anatomy Lesson*, 1983). The first section of *The Counterlife*, entitled "Basel," centers on Nathan's brother Henry, a New Jersey dentist who finds that his heart medication makes him impotent. He must decide whether to have a very dangerous operation that could restore his sexual powers or adapt to life without sex. Henry goes ahead with the surgery, but he dies. Before this, however, he confessed to his estranged brother Nathan about affairs with his current dental assistant, Wendy, and ten years previously with a beautiful Swiss woman named Maria. At Henry's funeral, Nathan is unable to deliver his prepared eulogy. As he is saying goodbye to Henry's devoted wife Carol, he imagines her revealing her husband's infidelities, but in reality she merely thanks Nathan for being present.

"Judea" chronicles Henry's counterlife—a version of the story in which he has survived the heart surgery. After a period of depression, he decides to move to Israel and live in a West Bank community headed by right-wing Jewish extremist Mordecai Lippman. At Carol's urging, Nathan goes to Israel to try to persuade Henry to return to the United States. There Nathan sees his old friend of twenty years, liberal journalist Shuki Elchanan. At a Sabbath dinner, Lippman articulates his conception of Jewish nationalism. When Nathan confronts Henry about his defection to Israel the brothers part in anger. In "Aloft," Nathan travels back to the United States on an airliner, and he begins a letter to Henry, disagreeing with his brother's viewpoint. The man sitting next to Nathan turns out to be Jimmy Ben-Joseph of New Jersey, now disguised as a rabbi. He reveals to Nathan that he intends to hijack the airplane to promote that Jews should "Forget Remembering" and shed their masochism. But Israeli security agents overhear Jimmy and take both him and Nathan into custody and interrogate them roughly.

The section entitled "Gloucestershire" presents a counterlife in which Nathan, not Henry, suffers from a heart ailment. Nathan falls in love with his upstairs neighbor, the unhappily married Maria, and he finally decides to have the operation so that the two can consummate their passion. Nathan subsequently dies in surgery, and this time it is Henry who is unable to deliver the eulogy at his brother's funeral. In Nathan's apartment, Henry discovers a draft of a novel entitled *The Counterlife*; he is enraged to learn that his brother attributed elements of his own life to Henry, thus "disguising himself as a reasonable man while I am revealed as the absolute dope." Henry takes most of the manuscript away with him and throws it in a garbage can, but later Maria arrives at the apartment and reads the final section, "Christendom." In this counterlife, Maria and Nathan are married and expecting their first child. While living in England, Nathan encounters a great deal of anti-semitism from Maria's family. Maria accuses Nathan of being hypersensitive and departs in anger, leaving him to speculate on whether he is paranoid about his own Jewishness. He imagines Maria writing that she is leaving not only him but this novel because she finds Nathan's "preoccupation with irresolvable conflict" too trying. In an imaginary letter, Nathan reminds Maria that everyone impersonates a number of selves and urges her to return to the counterlife that comprises Nathan, Maria, and their child as a family. In this version of Nathan's story, Maria does return.

Characters: Novelist William Gass termed *The Counterlife* "a triumph," claiming that it "constitutes a fulfillment of tendencies, a successful integration of themes, and the final working through of obsessions that have previously troubled if not marred [Roth's] work." This complex, skillfully structured novel features a variety of characters who present their own stories, or versions of reality, which are presented as "counterselves." Roth uses this self-reflexive, comic work to confront his own preoccupations with what it means to be an artist, a Jew, and a human being. While exploring the author's power to alter, exaggerate, and fictionalize events and character, Roth simultaneously celebrates the power of imagination and questions the ordinary reality and experience.

Often identified as an autobiographical character or as Roth's alter ego, **Nathan Zuckerman** is, like his creator, a Jewish-American novelist who devotes much of his energy to critical self-examination. In *Zuckerman Unbound*, Nathan authors a controversial novel called *Carnovsky* that bears a close resemblance to Roth's novel *Portnoy's Complaint*. Throughout *The Counterlife*, Nathan grapples with such issues as the relationship between impotence and self-image, the complexities of Jewish identity, and the artist's moral responsibilities. In "Basel," Nathan is unable to deliver the eulogy for his estranged brother who had confessed to Nathan his marital infidelity. Nathan finds that he views his brother's life and death only with his novelist's eye, and that the only words are "morally inappropriate" for the occasion. Thus Roth explores the question of whether an artist's deepest loyalties lie with his art or his loved ones. Nathan confronts his Jewish-American heritage in "Judea" when he visits Israel after an absence of twenty years. During his first visit (which coincides with Roth's 1960 trip to Israel), Nathan had tried to convince his friend Shuki that although he considered himself a committed Jew he felt more American than Jewish, unable to adapt well to life in Israel. During this second trip, Nathan feels cowed by Lippman's diatribe and curious about Henry's reasons for his defection. In the letter to Henry featured in "Aloft," Nathan makes observations on the novelist's reality versus the actual, lived life and the concept of Zionism as a remarkable instance of human transformation.

Nathan's characteristic self-questioning continues in "Gloucestershire," which casts him as having to choose between impotence and potentially fatal heart surgery. Although unsure about his own motives—which seem to be closely connected to his desire for the beautiful *shiksa* (the Yiddish word for a Gentile woman) Maria—Nathan goes ahead with the operation. After his death, Maria reads the section entitled "Christendom," in which Nathan struggles with his Jewishness as he detects signs of anti-semitism all around him and particularly within his wife's English family. He wonders if, as Maria asserts, he is being paranoid, or even inventing conflicts. Nathan concludes, however, that every individual plays many roles and tries out many counterselves before settling on one. The novel ends on this fairly upbeat note, in favor of a pluralistic view of life.

Parallels are drawn between Nathan's solidly middle-class, dentist brother **Henry Zuckerman** and Roth's own brother, Sandy. The novel is viewed as a meditation on the counterlives that many brothers enact for each other. In "Basel," Nathan and Henry are estranged because Henry is unable to forgive Nathan for publishing his controversial, reportedly autobiographical novel *Carnovsky*, which he feels caused their father enough shame and heartache to hasten his death. The brothers have a reconciliation before Henry's death when he confesses his two infidelities. Henry's fantasy about running away with Maria to become an expatriate dentist in Basel, Switzerland, gives this chapter its title. Significantly, both Henry and Nathan choose to risk death in order to regain their sexual potency, suggesting that for both sexuality is an important part of a meaningful life. Yet in "Judea," the reader learns that regaining his sexual powers has only left Henry depressed, precipitating his flight to Israel and renewed establishment of his Jewish identity. He tells Nathan he has escaped the "intellectual games" played by American Jews like his brother and is in a place where people are concerned not with petty personal neuroses but with politics and the "larger world." He obviously finds his Israeli counterlife empowering and invigorating. Henry's long speech to Nathan includes central themes such as the individual's desire to radically transform his life and novelistic reality as opposed to lived reality. "Gloucestershire" presents Henry in the same position Nathan occupied at the beginning of the novel: his brother has died during heart surgery, and he is unable to deliver the eulogy. In Henry's case, it is his resentment of his brother's novelistic approach to life that interferes with his sorrow. This resentment increases when he discovers the manuscript of *The Counterlife* and sees that Nathan has appropriated elements of Henry's life as his own and vice versa. Henry views Nathan's art—beginning with *Carnovsky* and culminating in the current novel—as exploitative and morally damaging.

Maria first enters *The Counterlife* when she is mentioned by Henry as his beautiful Swiss lover of ten years earlier, a former patient with whom he fantasized about running away. In "Judea" Maria is Nathan's English wife, living with him in London and pregnant with their first child; she occupies the same position in "Christendom," which focuses directly on her life with Nathan. In "Gloucestershire," however, Maria is Nathan's upstairs neighbor, with whom he forms a relationship that must, due to his heart condition, remain platonic. Married to an insensitive English diplomat, Maria is a writer who disparages her own writing as "hack" work for "silly magazines." A strong (and, to Nathan, welcome) contrast to Nathan in her delicacy and passivity, Maria worries that her conventional, English upbringing make her an inappropriate partner for Nathan. Nevertheless, she agrees to his plan to have heart surgery and overcome his impotence so that she can leave her husband to marry Nathan. After Nathan's death, the grief-stricken Maria enters his apartment and finds the section of *The Counterlife* called "Christendom," which Henry left behind. Upon reading it, she sympathizes with Nathan's need to create a counterlife in which the two are married. "Christendom" features Maria's long monologue expressing her weariness with Nathan's hypersensitivity about his Jewishness; she claims he played the role of the loyal Jewish child long enough. She also criticizes Nathan's tendency to fictionalize the people around him and asserts that if he puts her into a novel he will be "inventing a woman who does not exist." Nathan imagines a letter from Maria announcing she is leaving both him and the novel because he has always expected her to go along with his plans for her. Certainly one of very few literary characters who rebel against the author who has created them, Maria is described by commentator Jay L. Halio as "one of the most spirited and intellectually attractive women in [Roth's] novels." Her incisive critique of Nathan has been interpreted as evidence of Roth's capacity for self-criticism.

The important chapter of *The Counterlife* entitled "Judea" is inhabited by two characters who represent different poles of Israeli thought and experience. **Shuki Elchanan** is a liberal but world-weary journalist whom Nathan befriended on his first trip to Israel. Twenty years earlier, Shuki is more disillusioned with his country (a refuge for social misfits and religious fanatics) but still supports the same ideals, including compromise with the Arab world and a conviction that extremists like Lippman pervert the intent of the Jewish state. Shuki articulates some interesting and pertinent points in the novel, such as the fact that despite Nathan's claim of detachment from his Jewish heritage, all of his novels are centered around the question, "What is a Jew?" He also criticizes Nathan for exploiting the comic possibilities of serious subjects, and he worries that Nathan's novelist bent will cause him to dramatize not the forces of calm reason in Israel but such explosive figures as Lippman. During Nathan's first visit to Israel, he met Shuki's father, **Mr. Elchanan**, a welder and member of the Knesset (Israel's parliament) who does not understand why a Jew would want to live anywhere other than Israel.

At the other end of the political spectrum from Shuki is **Mordecai Lippman**, the leader of the West Bank settlement of Agor that Henry joins after his defection to Israel. An American exile, Lippman is a representative of Israel's extreme right wing. At the Sabbath dinner Nathan attends, Lippman delivers his defense of Israeli nationalism, which is based on the assumption that anti-Semitism is a constant threat to Jews. Although he professes an ability to live in peace with Arabs, he fiercely opposes the idea of an Arab state within Israel's boundaries.

The comic character of **Jimmy Ben-Joseph** (born Lustig) embodies a perversion of both Jewish perspectives, the conciliatory and the aggressive. Convinced that Jews need to shirk their masochism, he urges them to "Forget Remembering" by closing down the memorial to the Holocaust in Jerusalem. Another significant minor character in *The Counterlife* is **Carol Zuckerman**, Henry's devoted wife, who in "Basel" is opposed to his having heart surgery because she claims their marriage is comfortable enough without sex. Carol is unaware that her husband has been having oral sex daily with his adoring dental assistant, **Wendy Casselman**, a shiksa who critic Debra Shostak describes as representing "escape as the forbidden erotic object."

Further Reading

Baumgarten, Murray. *Understanding Philip Roth*. Columbia: University of South Carolina Press, 1990.

Contemporary Literary Criticism. Vols. 1–4, 6, 9, 15, 22, 31. Detroit: Gale Research.

Dictionary of Literary Biography. Vols. 2, 28, 1982 Yearbook. Detroit: Gale Research.

Halio, Jay L. *Philip Roth Revisited*. New York: Twayne, 1992.

Kamenetz, Rodger. "'The Hocker, Misnomer . . . Love/Dad': Philip Roth's Patrimony." *Southern Review* Vol. 27, no. 4 (autumn 1991): 937–45.

Major Twentieth-Century Writers. Vol. 4. Detroit: Gale Research, 1991.

McDaniel, John. *The Fiction of Philip Roth*. Haddonfield House, 1974.

Shostak, Debra. "'This Obsessive Reinvention of the Real': Speculative Narrative in Philip Roth's *The Counterlife*." *Modern Fiction Studies* Vol. 37, no. 2 (summer 1991): 197–215.

Salman Rushdie
1947–
Indian-born English novelist and critic.

Midnight's Children (novel, 1981)

Plot: The novel takes place in India and Pakistan between 1947, when India became independent of its British colonizers, and about 1975, when Indian prime minister Indira Gandhi declared a State of Emergency in the troubled country. Protagonist and narrator Saleem Sinai is one of 1,001 "midnight's children"—those born within India's first hour of independence; in addition, he is one of two males born at the strike of midnight. As the novel begins, Saleem is past thirty years old and working as a supervisor in a pickle factory. Prematurely aged and apparently soon to die, Saleem reads the story of his life to a devoted, sometimes impatient chutney stirrer named Padma. The illegitimate son of a departing Englishman and the wife of a Hindu street singer, Saleem was switched at birth with Shiva, the offspring of a prosperous Muslim family. The error was not discovered until much later, when Saleem's family decided it was too late to correct it. At nine, Saleem discovered that he had incredible telepathic powers that allowed him to communicate with the other surviving midnight's children, each of whom was also endowed with a special gift of some kind. Saleem's midnight twin Shiva, for example, possessed the "gifts of war" that would eventually make him a great military hero. Saleem organizes an entirely telepathic "Midnight Children's Conference" of the surviving 580 that ends in near chaos.

As the novel progresses, Saleem witnesses and participates in the major events of modern Indian history. The most significant of these is the war over the partition of Pakistan, where

Saleem moves with his Muslim family. After most of his relatives are killed and he loses his memory, Saleem is spirited back into India by another of the midnight's children. When "the Widow," the novel's fictional version of Indira Gandhi, decrees that due to the State of Emergency all the midnight's children must be sterilized, Saleem is castrated. His troubles having dispirited him profoundly and depleted his physical strength, Saleem ends up working at the pickly factory and waiting for death.

Characters: Until the international controversy that erupted over the publication of Rushdie's 1988 novel *The Satanic Verses*, which enraged Muslims and forced Rushdie into hiding, he was best known for *Midnight's Children*, for which he earned England's prestigious Booker McConnell Prize for fiction. Distinguished by its stylistic brilliance and often comic exuberance, the novel is ranked by some critics among the most astute chronicles of modern India. It is often compared to Laurence Sterne's eighteenth-century novel *Tristram Shandy* due to its self-reflective narrative stance and to Gabriel Garcia Marquez's *One Hundred Years of Solitude* (1967) for its skillful blending of the mundane and the fantastic. *Midnight's Children* explores not only political, social, and cultural events in modern India but such universal issues as the nature of literature and the relationship between individual and collective history.

The novel's protagonist and narrator, **Saleem Sinai**, describes himself as "mysteriously handcuffed to history," and it is through his life story that Rushdie chronicles events in India over the important thirty-year period when the country's hopes and aspirations gradually gave way to disorder and despair. When the reader first encounters Saleem, he is prematurely old, mutilated, and close to death but still determined to explore—following the dictum that "what you are is forever who you were"—the events of his life. An unreliable, highly self-conscious narrator, Saleem is alternately aggressive, subtle, coy, flippant, and grave, tormenting his uneducated, much more practical listener with his digressions and musings (many of them focused on the nature of his own narrative task). It is evident quite early in Saleem's account that he has played a primarily passive role in his own life, that he has been more acted on than active. Born at the stroke of midnight on India's independence day and mistakenly accepted into a respectable Muslim family, the infant Saleem received a letter of welcome and congratulations from then-prime minister Jawarhal Nehru, who promised that the nation would be following his development with great interest since his life would be "in a sense, the mirror of our own." Saleem's account of his fairly happy childhood evidences the harmonious blend of western and Indian traditions achieved in his grandfather's household, but eventually he had to enter the turbulent stream of social change that overtook India when the tension between an essentially rural past and a technological present erupted into the violent war over Pakistan's partition. Critics have identified Saleem as a representative of the post-Independence generation of Indians, in whom was embodied all of the nation's hopes for a better future, and whom, in turn, had to endure the disappointment of those hopes and the frustrations of reality. Some commentators have interpreted Saleem's impotence and impending death at the end of *Midnight's Children* as symbolizing India's hopelessness, but others have seen his creation of this exuberant, profuse narrative as a sign that even in the face of human fallibility and despair meaningful works of art are possible.

Critics have identified **Padma**, an illiterate chutney stirrer at the pickle factory and Saleem's caretaker and would-be wife, as a kind of artistic conscience who acts as both audience and critic. She initially provides a frame for the novel by insisting that he read aloud to her the narrative he is writing, and she frequently becomes annoyed with his digressions and pretentions. A figure of great common sense and stability, she provides a counterweight to his educated, middle-class point of view, both calling attention to his selfconscious, metafictional tendencies and keeping them in check.

Saleem is one of two male babies born at the exact stroke of midnight on the first day of India's independence from Great Britain. The other is **Shiva**, who is handed over to the Hindu street singer who—since not only were the babies switched at birth but his now-dead wife had had an English lover—is doubly not the child's father. Raised on the rough streets of Bombay, Shiva manifests the magical power with which each of the midnight's children is endowed through his incredibly strong knees. Eventually this strength is channelled into the "gifts of war" that result in his becoming India's most decorated war hero and the leader of a crude, violent, and effective army. The fact that Shiva, a Muslim by birth, is raised as a Hindu while Saleem, offspring of a union between a Hindu and an Englishman, becomes a Muslim provides a metaphor for the stratification and complexity of Indian society.

The most significant of the other midnight's children in the novel is **Parvati**, whose magical powers allow her to smuggle Saleem back into India after most of his family is killed in Pakistan. Although Saleem is attracted to Parvati, his forbidden passion for his sister (who is not, of course, his biological relative) prevents him from making love to her. Parvati manages to get Shiva to impregnate her, and when she later marries Saleem, her son **Aadam** becomes part of the Sinai family and thus rights the wrong done years earlier when the two babies were exchanged.

Other notable characters in the novel include Saleem's sister **Jamila**, who becomes a national sensation in Pakistan as a chaste singer (she performs behind a sheet) of uplifting patriotic songs; Saleem's friend **Cyrus Dubash**, who is transformed by his religious fanatic mother into a guru named **Lord Khusro Khusrovand** and becomes very wealthy; and **Mary Pereira**, the nurse who, as a revolutionary political act, switches Saleem and Shiva. Actual historical figures who are fictionalized by Rushdie include the Pakistani Commander in Chief **Ayub Khan**, whom Saleem meets at his uncle's home and who outlines there his plan of attack for a coup d'etat; and **the Widow**, who represents Indira Gandhi.

Further Reading

Blaise, Clarke. "A Novel of India's Coming of Age." *New York Times Book Review* (April 19, 1981): 1, 18-19.

Contemporary Literary Criticism, Vols. 23, 31, 55. Detroit: Gale Research.

Couto, Maria. *"Midnight's Children* & Parents." *Encounter* LVIII, No. 2 (February 1982): 61-6.

Cunningham, Valentine. "Nosing Out the Indian Reality." *Times Literary Supplement* No. 4076 (May 15, 1981): 535.

Desai, Anita. "Where Cultures Clash by Night." *Book World—Washington Post* (March 15, 1981): 1, 13.

Harrison, James. *Salman Rushdie*. New York: Twayne, 1992.

Major 20th-Century Writers, Vol. 4. Detroit: Gale Research, 1991.

Taneja, G. R. and Dhawan, R. K., eds. *The Novels of Salman Rushdie*. New Delhi: Indian Society for Commonwealth Studies, 1992.

Anatoli Rybakov

1911–

Russian novelist and author of children's books.

Children of the Arbat (*Deti arbata*; novel, 1987)

Plot: The novel comprises two major plot strands. The first centers on Sasha Pankratov, a student in his early twenties who lives in Moscow's bohemian Arbati neighborhood. Although an idealist and enthusiastic supporter of the Communist Party, Sasha commits a gaffe when, in his capacity as editor of his college's newspaper, he publishes a joke about an official. This would normally warrant only a mild admonition, but it is used to help bring a larger case against an old Bolshevik (i.e., participant in Russia's 1917 Bolshevist Revolution). Convicted of treason and sentenced to three years in Siberia, Sasha works on a collectivist farm. Sasha undergoes a series of trials and hardships, while at home his friends prove unwilling or unable to support him. Through his Siberian experiences, Sasha concludes that the human capacity for sacrifice and good can never be stifled. The novel's other plot strand involves Russian political leader Joseph Stalin, who succeeded Vladimir Lenin and ruled until his own death in 1953. In the novel, Stalin is a ruthless, power-hungry, paranoid figure who carefully consolidates his power and crushes those he perceives as threatening his reign. The novel ends just before the assassination of popular (and relatively liberal) party leader Sergei Kirov, strongly suggesting that Stalin was implicated in Kirov's murder. In a short epilogue set in 1944, Sasha, a major in the Russian army, meets his old friend Maxim, a general. They reminisce about their Arbati friends, and Sasha tells Maxim that his personal record still carries his sentence for treason.

Characters: Written during the 1960s, *Children of the Arbat* was not published until 1987, when Soviet premier Gorbachev's *glasnost* policies allowed greater freedom of expression. The novel features a traditional, realistic prose style similar to that employed by the great Russian novelists of the nineteenth century. It is lauded not so much for its literary merit as for its political significance, for *Children of the Arbat* comprises a serious indictment of past Soviet policies, particularly of Joseph Stalin. However, many commentators said Rybakov, with his Marxist-Leninist perspective, attributes the tragic excesses of the Stalin period to true analysis of Stalin's power and personality rather than to weakness in the Communist system.

The younger of the two protagonists of *Children of the Arbat* is twenty-two-year-old **Sasha Pankratov**, a handsome, fairly intelligent though naive engineering student who enthusiastically upholds his government's Communist ideals. Sasha is clearly an autobiographical character, for Rybakov too lived in the Moscow's Arbat district as a college student and was also exiled to Siberia; some critics complain that Rybakov's kindly portrayal renders Sasha overly virtuous and colorless. The novel has been identified as a *bildungsroman* (novel of initiation) in that it chronicles Sasha's progress toward maturity as he endures hardship, danger, and loneliness in isolated Siberia. Sasha is tested by prison interrogations to wrest admissions of guilt, pressure to sign incriminating statements, and being offered false identification papers and freedom if he will spy on his friends. Sasha not only resists temptation but learns patience and flexibility, emerging from his prison sentence with his spirit still intact. Along the way, he has to shed his blind obedience to the party, for he sees that the current regime has perverted the original motives of the Russian revolution. His own steadfastly Marxist-Leninist orientation, in contrast to Stalin's practice, is essentially humanistic. In the novel's epilogue, the reader learns that Sasha's troubles are not over: his record of treason leaves him vulnerable to persecution.

Rybakov has been praised for his highly detailed characterization of **Joseph Stalin**, who presided over a "Reign of Terror" in which many Soviets lost their lives for alleged crimes against the state. *Children of the Arbat* is considered the first novel to feature Stalin as a central character and to depict his steady consolidation of power until he became one of the most feared leaders in history. Blending internal monologues with facts and interpretation, Rybakov creates an unflattering portrait that casts Stalin as a ruthless, paranoid autocrat who treated nearly everyone around him with contempt and cruelty. Rybakov effectively renders Stalin's speech patterns, including his tendency to frequently ask and then answer rhetorical questions and to refer to himself in the third person. Rybakov roots Stalin's strong distrust of people and general mental instability in childhood, when he often felt alienated and humiliated. Resentful and fearful of his country's intelligentsia, Stalin takes a Machiavellian approach to power: he believes that human beings are inherently deceptive, and that amassing power means taking advantage of whatever means will further that goal. Although a few critics noted that Rybakov endows Stalin with some humanizing traits (such as his fondness for vocal music and his troublesome teeth), others felt that his excessive evilness makes him unconvincing. Commentators noted that Rybakov seems to attribute the regime's terror to Stalin's pathological personality, thus deflecting blame away from communism.

Other historically-based characters in the novel include **Sergei Kirov**, the popular Leningrad party leader whose assassination, Rybakov strongly implies, was masterminded by Stalin. Kirov is portrayed as a decent, relatively liberal figure whose loyalty to Stalin and the Communist Party conflict with his disapproval of Stalin's purges. His struggle is typical of many loyal Soviets overlooking what they recognized as Stalin's excesses. A similar character is **Alferov**, the administrator to whom Sasha reports in Siberia, whose commitment to the ideals of the revolution requires him to defend the system he represents. He does so despite the fact Alferov has been treated unjustly, sentenced to Siberia only because he supposedly lived too long outside of the Soviet Union. Alferov maintains that concepts such as justice, law, and fairness are relative, and that, for example, harshly punishing someone who has disabled a tractor will teach that person to be more careful in the future. Even more self-deluding is **Mark Riazanov**, Sasha's uncle, an old Bolshevik whose devotion to the Communist Party has blinded him to reality. Riazanov does not want to compromise his own precious power by defending his nephew.

Sasha's Arbat friends and fellow members of the Komsomol or Young Communists League present a cross-section of Moscow youth and serve as foils to the more positively rendered protagonist. Typical of the others in her cowardly reaction to Sasha's arrest is **Nina**, who initially pledges her support but finally withdraws it in order to protect her own interests. Even more reprehensible is the behavior of the ambitious, cunning **Yuri Sharok**, a working-class, boy who resents his more intellectual and better-connected neighbors and so joins Stalin's Secret Police. With his lack of conscience, craving for power, and dislike for the intelligentsia, Yuri is the type to carry out Stalin's repressive policies.

While most of his friends let him down, the two most important women in Sasha's life remain loyal to him. Brave, supportive, and self-sacrificing, **Sasha's mother** is willing to confront the regime about its mistreatment of her son; she tells Sasha's uncle, a party official, that if the tsars had treated their subjects as harshly as the Communists they would still be in power. Seventeen-year-old **Varya** is a vivacious young girl who is initially only concerned with trying to carve out a typical teenager's life amid the political upheaval of her country. After Sasha's arrest, she gains independence and maturity and comes to an awareness of her feelings for Sasha as he falls in love with her.

Other characters in the novel include **Beriozin**, the local head of the secret police who helps Sasha evade serious trouble during his time in Siberia; and Stalin's dentist, **Lipman**, who is flown in from Moscow in a comic scene requiring a dentist whose hands don't shake; and

Interrogator Kiakov, who extracts from each prisoner not the truth but an admission of whatever transgression he is charged with. In Siberia, Sasha meets **Lydia Grigoryevna,** a former high official whose current devotion to her adopted child is part of what inspires Sasha to proclaim that human beings are capable of self-sacrifice even in the most trying circumstances.

Further Reading

Bayley, John. "The Shock of the Old." *New Republic* Vol. 198, no. 21 (May 23, 1988): 40–2.

Conquest, Robert. "Skeletons from the Closets of the Kremlin." *Mother Jones* Vol. 13, no. 5 (June 1988): 40–1.

Contemporary Literary Criticism. Vols. 23, 53. Detroit: Gale Research.

Goodman, Walter. "Stalin's Evil Shadow in a Long-Suppressed Novel." *New York Times* (May 10, 1988): C17.

Howe, Irving. "At the Mercy of Apparatchiks." *New York Times Book Review* (May 22, 1988): 7, 9.

Laqueur, Walter. "Beyond Glasnost." *Commentary* Vol. 84, no. 4 (October 1987): 63–5.

McLaughlin, Sigrid. "Rybakov's *Deti Arbata*: Reintegrating Stalin into Soviet History." *Slavic Review* Vol. 50 (spring 1990): 90–9.

Updike, John. "Doubt and Difficulty in Leningrad and Moscow." *New Yorker* Vol. 64, no. 30 (September 12, 1988): 108–10, 112–14.

Woll, Josephine. "Stalin's Ghost." *Atlantic Monthly* Vol. 261, no. 6 (June 1988): 102–05.

Isaac Bashevis Singer
1904–1991
Polish-born American novelist, short story writer, author of children's books, memoirist, playwright, journalist, editor, and translator.

Scum (novel, 1991)

Plot: The novel takes place in 1906 in the Jewish quarter of Warsaw, Poland. The central character, Max Barabander, is a wealthy, middle-aged businessman who left Warsaw—where he had been a petty thief—twenty years before for a new life in Buenos Aires, Argentina. Max has returned to Warsaw, he claims, to visit his parents' graves, but he is actually fleeing from the despair and sexual impotence he has experienced in the wake of his seventeen-year-old son's death. Max's grief-stricken wife, Rochelle, has lost all interest in sex, and Max's doctors have recommended that he seek new sights and companionship. Max quickly finds himself drawn back into the seedy underworld he inhabited before he left Warsaw. After a failed sexual encounter with the eager wife of a baker, Max sets his sights on Tsirele, the beautiful and politically radical daughter of a poor rabbi. Casting himself as a widower, Max ingratiates himself with both the girl and the rabbi and eventually asks to marry her. Despite his lack of religious faith, Max agrees to the rabbi's demand that he live an exemplary, pious life in order to win Tsirele's hand. Meanwhile, however, Max has also become involved with the lusty, scheming Reyzl, a gangster's girlfriend who proposes that he join her in a scheme to sell Polish women into sexual slavery in South America. Their first victim is to be a servant girl named Basha, whom Max seduces. He also sleeps with an unhappy psychic medium, Theresa, with whom he plots to escape from Warsaw. Finally, Max's unscrupulous and impetuous behavior leads to his downfall. He is angrily cursed by Tsirele when she learns he is already married, and he accidentally shoots Reyzl to death. Feeling that his life has come full circle, Max finds himself in prison.

Characters: Although *Scum* was not published until just before the death of Singer, who is one of the twentieth century's most renowned and beloved writers, it was probably written about twenty years earlier and was serialized in a Yiddish periodical. The novel exhibits Singer's persistent concern with the conflict between tradition and modernism, religion and faithlessness, morality and temptation. Both the epigraph and title come from the title story of Singer's short story collection *The Death of Methuselah* (1971), in which he states, "Flesh and corruption always will remain the scum of creation, the very opposite of God's wisdom, mercy and splendor. . . ." Indeed, *Scum* presents a bleak, sometimes poignant portrait of a world and people in transition. Though critics generally agree that the novel is not Singer's finest, it evidences his prodigious storytelling skills and is praised for its richly rendered descriptions and vivid characters.

The name of the novel's protagonist, **Max Barabander**, has been linked to the Yiddish word *barabeven*, which means "robber" or "looter". Indeed, Max is a former thief who left Warsaw's sordid underworld for a new life in Argentina, where he achieved financial success and established a family. The forty-seven-year-old Max is a tall, broad-shouldered, square-chinned man with blue eyes and blonde hair who was once a prodigious womanizer but who now finds himself sexually impotent. Distraught over his son's inexplicable death, his wife's withdrawal, and his own resulting loss of virility, Max has come to Warsaw in search of rejuvenation. Returning to the scene of his youthful misadventures, Max feels both comfortable and spiritually empty. He is not religious and has long lived among non-Jews, but he recognizes Warsaw's Krochmalna Street as the heart of a Jewish culture that also resides somewhere deep inside himself. Max is both attracted and repulsed by the Jewish faith. He lacks any true religious convictions but does believe in sin and damnation, so that even as he succumbs over and over again to his own base impulses, he experiences relentless feelings of guilt. At one point he even comments that a *dybbuk* (malicious spirit) must have possessed him. Max acts with no regard for consequences; always a glib persuader, he relies "completely on his tongue, which was his ruler and his destiny." In his faithlessness and corruption, Max seems to represent the modern world, which Singer depicts as spiritually and morally desolate. The novel's conclusion reveals that its protagonist has completed a kind of circle: having made a bad beginning, he comes to a bad end, and he himself feels that this was ordained all along. Although some critics have found Max a repellent character with no redeeming qualities, others agree with Francis King that Singer invests him with a "tragic grandeur" that makes him at least partly sympathetic. He may be viewed as an autobiographical figure in that both he and his creator once lived on Warsaw's Krochmalna Street and, after leaving and achieving success in the outside world, are drawn back to it and all that it represents.

The novel's most notable secondary characters are the women with whom Max interacts. Once a dynamic personality, his wife **Rochelle** was made bitter and half-insane by her son's death, and she has lost all interest in sex and even recommended that Max seek satisfaction with other women. Max's first attempt to overcome his impotence is with **Esther**, the plump baker's wife who immediately lets Max know she is willing and that her husband is easily fooled; as Esther is undressing, however, Max loses his nerve and flees the scene. He is more successful with **Reyzl**, a flamboyant former prostitute and the girlfriend of a gangster. She possesses "great sparkling eyes [that] looked at a man with appetite and experience and without a trace of shame." Reyzl cures Max's impotence, but she also figures in his downfall when he accidentally shoots her to death. Even as he is carrying on with a number of other women, Max is courting **Tsirele**, a rabbi's daughter with advanced political ideas who longs for escape to the modern world. Beautiful and neurotic, Tsirele supposedly once tried to kill herself when faced with an arranged marriage. Despite her radical views, she refuses to sleep with Max—whom she believes is an aggrieved widower—until they are married, and she curses him bitterly when she learns the truth about him.

Max's other lovers include **Theresa**, the unhappy medium who longs to flee from her too-possessive boyfriend and who defends her art to Max by claiming that ''either the dead live, or the living are dead;'' and **Basha**, the naive, innocent servant girl whom Max and Reyzl intend to make the first victim of their white slavery scheme. Other characters in *Scum* include **Shmuel Smetana**, the aging small-time gangster whose mistress is Reyzl, and **Blind Mayer**, a comic figure who serves as a kind of rabbi to the denizens of Warsaw's criminal underworld.

Further Reading

Alexander, Edward. *Isaac Bashevis Singer*. Boston, MA: Twayne, 1980.

———. *Isaac Bashevis Singer: A Study of the Short Fiction*. Boston, MA: Twayne, 1990.

Bayley, John. ''Singer's Last Word.'' *London Review of Books* (October 24, 1991): 17–18.

Kakutani, Michiko. ''Trapped in a Somber Dialectic of Faith and Flesh.'' *New York Times* (April 9, 1991): C14.

King, Francis. ''Wresting Tragic Grandeur from the Ordinary.'' *Spectator* (October 13, 1991): 39–40.

Kirsch, Jonathan. ''The Dybbuk Made Him Do It.'' *Los Angeles Times Book Review* (April 14, 1991): 12.

Leonard, George J. ''Betraying Israel?'' *San Francisco Review of Books* (Summer 1991): 15–16.

Malin, Irving, ed. *Critical Views of Isaac Bashevis Singer*. New York: New York University Press, 1969.

Pesetsky, Bette. ''Looking for Love on Krochmalna Street.'' *New York Times Book Review* (March 24, 1991): 7.

Sinclair, Clive. ''Singer's Sweetened Poison.'' *Times Literary Supplement* (October 4, 1991): 25.

Yardley, Jonathan. ''The Ills of the Flesh.'' *Book World—Washington Post* (March 3, 1991): 3.

Josef Skvorecky
1924–

Czechoslovakian-born Canadian novelist, short story writer, essayist, poet, scriptwriter, critic, translator, and editor.

The Engineer of Human Souls (novel, 1977)

Plot: The book's narrator and central character is Daniel Smiricky, a writer whose controversial work led to his 1968 escape from Czechoslovakia during the Soviet invasion. He is now a rather melancholy professor of American and English literature at Edenvale College in Toronto, Canada. The narrative shifts from present-day accounts of Smiricky's life in 1976 to his memories of the past–particularly of the World War II period when Czechoslovakia was under German rule—and also includes letters from several of Smiricky's old friends. Each chapter, named for a celebrated writer, is delivered through Smiricky's lectures to and dialogues with his students. Smiricky finds these young Canadians naive about politics and ignorant of history and art, and his vocation as a writer is stymied due to the limited audience for books written in Czech. Like other Czech emigres, he feels torn between nostalgia for home and distaste for his country's oppressive political system, while finding the culture around him shallow and materialistic. Smiricky fondly remembers his youth, occupied with playing jazz and chasing girls even while the horrors of the war were going on around him. At that time he had worked in a German-run factory in his home town of Kostelec, where he met and fell in love with a simple, working-class girl named Nadia Jirouskova who married someone else and died of tuberculosis in 1946. Letters from Smiricky's other friends from that time reveal their various fates: poet Jan Prouza stayed in Czechoslovakia but eventually committed suicide; activist Prema Skocopole was forced to spend much of his later life in Australia where he died; Rebecca survived the Auschwitz concentration camp only to lose her family to a terrorist's bomb in 1970s Israel; and opportunistic Lojza adapted himself to prevailing conditions in his homeland and thrived there. As the book ends, Smiricky's emigre friends Dotty and Veronika choose different routes, with Dotty settling into marriage, Veronika returning to Czechoslovakia, and Smiricky leaving for a trip to Paris with his student and lover, the beautiful Irene Svensson.

Characters: One of the Czech Republic's most acclaimed writers before his 1968 defection, Skvorecky is best known to English-speaking audiences for this novel, which won Canada's prestigious Governor General's Award for Literature in 1985. The title is an ironic reference to Communist leader Joseph Stalin's reported dictum that "as an engineer constructs a machine, so must a writer construct the mind of the New Man." Blending an examination of political oppression and personal tragedy with humor and farce, Skvorecky condemns both the oppressiveness of totalitarian states and the naivete of many Westerners. Although some critics found the novel's fragmented, episodic structure confusing or unwieldy, most praised *The Engineer of Human Souls* for its underlying celebration of such ordinary values as youth, friendship, and love.

The novel's central character, forty-eight-year-old Czech emigre writer and professor **Daniel Smiricky**, appeared in several of Skvorecky's earlier novels, including *The Cowards* (1958) and *The Swell Season* (1975). His career closely mimics that of his creator, who also defected from his homeland in 1968, taught at the University of Toronto's Erindale College, and has a love of jazz and a broad appreciation of literature. Smiricky is portrayed as caught between the Eastern European culture of his youth and living in the Western world. The dilemma of the expatriate writer. Smiricky's life is a complex, multifaceted blend of thoughts, feelings, experiences, and memories but it offers no concrete solutions to his troubles or answers to his questions. Finding himself aging in a country not his own, the sentimental, often mournful, Smiricky is increasingly drawn to the past. Skvorecky's lightheartedness portrays Smiricky, exuberantly pursuing his interests in jazz and girls despite the World War II tragedies. Ironically, the older Smiricky is much more troubled and world-weary in calm, tedious, democratic Canada. Smiricky's discussions with his students allow Skvorecky to reflect not only on literature but on political systems, particularly totalitarianism. Oriented much more to the writing life than to academia, Smiricky is a rather uninspiring teacher who finds it difficult to stir his students' interest in either literature or politics. Indeed, he considers them naive and shallow, leading some commentators to fault him for his condescending attitude and pompous sermonizing. Others, however, noted that Smiricky does appreciate the basic decency and hopefulness of the young Canadians around him and seems to like them. Their apparent indifference to his insights, however, helps bring into focus the question of the writer's role in the world and his or her struggle to relay the universal truths revealed within individual experience.

Perhaps the most memorable figure from Danny's youth is his teenaged lover, **Nadia Jirouskova**, who some critics deemed the novel's finest character. Although already engaged to a young man named **Fanta**, while working at the Kostelec factory, she meets Danny, Nadia enters wholeheartedly into an affair and initiates him into the world of sex. Skvorecky portrays this embracing of sensuality as pure and natural. Indeed, Nadia attains a nearly mythical status during the course of the novel as a symbol of Smiricky's lost youth. Unlike Danny, Nadia comes from a poor family, and her lower-status background is manifest in her ungrammatical language, her mismatched, oversized clothing, and persistent hunger. Danny does not seem to consider himself superior to Nadia, however, and in fact admires her natural self-assurance and practicality, which contrast with his own fears and doubts. The fact that Nadia died of tuberculosis at the age of twenty-one, only a year after her marriage to Fanta and without ever bearing the children she so wanted, dramatically illustrates the irrevocable losses that Danny and others of his generation have suffered.

Thirty years after his affair with Nadia, Smiricky is involved with his nineteen-year-old student **Irene Svensson**, who is presented as a strong contrast to Nadia in personality and appearance. Whereas Nadia was poor and unassuming, Irene is the beautiful, carefully coiffed, polished daughter of a wealthy family. Smiricky often refers to her as "Nicole" in reference to one of the protagonists of F. Scott Fitzgerald's 1934 novel *Tender Is the Night*, who came from a similar background. Whereas Nadia introduced Smiricky to love and sex, it is he—now the jaded veteran of many affairs—who initiates her, but he does not commit himself to her emotionally. (In fact, a few critics faulted Smiricky for happily taking advantage of sexual opportunities that arise through his position as a teacher.) Irene may be identified as the novel's primary representative of the young people Smiricky encounters in Canada, whose impressions have been formed by television and movies and whose understanding of literature, politics, or any of the truly profound issues of modern life is minimal. In an interview, however, Skvorecky claimed that he felt the Canadian students are "rather likeable" if politically innocent.

Many critics particularly praised Skvorecky for his portrayal, through both Smiricky's narrative and the letters he receives, of the characters with whom he shared his youth. Several of them help to illustrate both the passion of those days and the disappointment and even tragedies that were to later occur. **Prema Skocdopole** was a young underground leader during Germany's occupation of Czechoslovakia who blew up a German fuel depot. This heroism was followed by a life of wandering that finally led Prema to Australia where he eventually died in a hurricane. Prema provides a poignant example of how youthful idealism may be crushed by the realities of twentieth-century history.

Smiricky's poet friend **Jan Prouza** illustrates a different but equally tragic fate: he chose to stay in Czechoslovakia, but his despair over censorship and having to fashion his work in the manner of state-prescribed "Social Realism," results in his suicide in 1972. A tortured, left-wing intellectual, Jan had hoped that Marxism and humanism would prove compatible. Presented as a kind of foil to Jan is **Vrata**, a playwright (reportedly modeled after Skvorecky's friend Vratislav Blazek) whose extroverted, vivacious manner contrast with Jan's melancholy brooding. Other figures from Smiricky's youth include **Uipelt**, the much-feared Nazi overseer at the Kostelec factory who turns out to be a resistance leader (suppressing Danny's role in a sabotage attempt) and who is ultimately killed by other Czechs after the war; **Rebecca Silbernaglova**, who survives the Nazi concentration camps and emigrates to Israel, only to lose her son and daughter-in-law to a terrorist's bomb in Tel Aviv in 1972; and **Lojza**, a jovial materialist described by critic Paul I. Trensky as a "caricature of the modern happy man," who adapts first to the German occupation and then to Communism in order to further his own interests. The experiences of **Dr. Toth**, a decent, mild-mannered electrical engineer, help to depict the absurdities of life in a totalitarian society: Czech newspapers report his defection while he is still living in Czechoslovakia, but eventually he does emigrate.

Several notable characters animate the sections of the novel set in 1970s Toronto. Smiricky is both part of and somewhat distanced from the Czech emigre community, whose nostalgia he shares while also perceiving the futility of such an attitude. **Veronika Prst** is an intelligent, attractive student who was a successful rock star in Czechoslovakia, is unable to find similar work in Canada due to her strongly accented English. Accustomed to a life of danger, she does not adapt well to the safety and freedom of her new life, and she is always sad and bitter. She expresses the plight of the emigre when she comments that "We need them both, Prague and freedom, but the way things are, we can't have both. It's either/or." Ultimately Veronika chooses to return to Czechoslovakia and face an uncertain and probably dismal future; in a final telegram to Smiricky, she admits that she is "a fool." Although he is sensitive, generous, and forthright, Irene's brother **Percy Svensson**, who has a love affair with Veronika, has too little in common culturally with her to be able to help her. Other emigres include Smiricky's publisher, **Mrs. Santner**; and **Milena "Dotty" Cabricarova**, whom,—unlike Veronika—makes a smooth transition after emigrating from Czechoslovakia, marrying a Canadian businessman and settling comfortably into her new life.

Further Reading

Burgess, Anthony. "Laughing It Off." *Observer* (March 3, 1985): 26.

Contemporary Literary Criticism. Vols. 15, 39, 69. Detroit: Gale Research.

Eder, Richard. "'Exiles' Epic as an Entertainment." *Los Angeles Times Book Review* (July 1, 1984): 1, 10.

Heim, Michael Henry. "Dangerously Wonderful." *Nation* Vol. 239, no. 3 (August 4 & 11, 1984): 86–8.

Kott, John. "The Emigrant as Hero." *New Republic* Vol. 191, no. 9 (August 27, 1984): 34–7.

Lasdun, James. "The Great or the Good?" *Encounter* Vol. 65, no. 2 (July-August 1985): 47–51.

Major Twentieth-Century Writers. Vol. 4. Detroit: Gale Research.

Solecki, Sam. "The Laughter and Pain of Remembering." *Canadian Forum* Vol. 64, no. 741 (August-September 1984): 39–41.

Towers, Robert. "Pursuer of Lost Maidens." *New York Times Book Review* (August 19, 1984): 9.

Trensky, Paul I. *The Fiction of Josef Skvorecky*. New York: St. Martin's Press, 1991.

West, Paul. "Last Tango in Toronto." *Book World—The Washington Post* (July 29, 1984): 10.

Jane Smiley
1949–

American novelist, short story writer, and nonfiction writer.

A Thousand Acres (novel, 1991)

Plot: Most of the novel takes place in the spring and summer of 1979. Larry Cook is the most prosperous farmer in Zebulon County, Iowa, where, with his daughters Ginny and Rose and their husbands Tyler and Pete, he farms one thousand acres of highly fertile land. Narrated by thirty-six-year-old Ginny, the novel chronicles what happens after Larry decides to turn the farm over to his daughters, who also include the youngest, Caroline a lawyer who lives in Des Moines. When Caroline expresses doubt about the arrangement, Larry angrily cuts her out of the deal. The others, however, are eager to take over and expand the farm. All are enlivened by the arrival of Jess Smith, the son of Larry's best friend Harold Smith, who has recently returned to the community after an absence of thirteen years. Despite her happy marriage, Ginny finds herself drawn to Jess and eventually sleeps with him. Meanwhile, the newly idle Larry slowly becomes mentally unhinged. Convinced that his daughters and their husbands are conspiring against him, he storms out into a rainy night, eventually taking refuge with Harold. Hoping to revoke the farm transfer, Larry files a suit against Ginny, Rose, Ty, and Pete; he is joined in this action by Caroline. Tensions rise among the formerly harmonious sisters and their husbands, particularly when Rose informs Ginny that they were both sexually abused by their father when they were teenagers and Ginny denies remembering this. Pete commits suicide by driving his truck into a pond, and afterward Rose tells Ginny that she has fallen in love with Jess and plans to make a life with him. Jealous and resentful, Ginny—who now remembers her father's nocturnal visits—plots revenge against Rose. At the trial to decide whether the farm transfer should be revoked, Larry acts erratically and the judge finds for the defendants. In the wake of the trial, Ginny decides to leave the farm and her husband. She becomes a waitress in St. Paul, Minnesota and does not see any of her family members until three years later, when she learns that Rose is dying of cancer. Ginny returns to Iowa in time to reconcile with Rose, and after her death she takes Rose's two daughters, Pammy and Linda, back to St. Paul with her.

Characters: Smiley is a respected contemporary novelist whose work is lauded for its insight, moral complexity, and tight, effective prose. Most reviewers deemed successful Smiley's attempt to fashion *A Thousand Acres* as a contemporary version of Shakespeare's classic tragedy, *King Lear*. Awarded a Pulitzer Prize, the novel blends a suspenseful story with social and moral concerns, exploring such themes as sibling rivalry, the debilitating consequences of incest, the psychological burdens and complexities of family relationships, and the relationship between nature and human behavior.

Whereas most commentators on *King Lear* focus on the anguish of the title character and the pure villainy of his two older daughters, Goneril and Regan, Smiley tells the story from a different perspective. Shakespeare casts Goneril and Regan as selfish hypocrites who proclaim their love for their father in order to attain his riches; the negative attitude of Smiley's counterparts toward their father, by contrast, is related to *his* past misbehavior. In an interview, Smiley explained that her interest in writing an adaptation of *King Lear* grew out of her feeling that "there must be some explanation" for the behavior of Goneril and Regan, "not 'pure evil' perhaps, but a desperate anger." In *A Thousand Acres*, that anger is rooted in incest, a topic of much contemporary interest but one that Smiley incorporates with minimal polemicism. The novel's Goneril figure and narrator is **Ginny Smith**, who has always played a conciliatory role in her family and whose role as caretaker has recently been intensified by her sister's breast cancer. Meanwhile, Ginny stifles the anguish caused by her own inability to carry a pregnancy to term. She has had five miscarriages, the last two kept secret from her husband because she had agreed after the third not to attempt pregnancy again. As critic Richard Eder notes, Ginny "has lived all her life placating, holding things together, denying her pain." That denial has included her memories of her father's sexual abuse when she was a teenager. Through the course of the novel, Ginny's formerly placid relationships with her father, sister, and husband are all dislocated. Her discovery of Rose's vengefulness as well as her affair with the same man with whom Ginny herself had imagined herself in love result in an unsuccessful attempt to poison her sister, followed by several years of alienation. (In *King Lear*, Goneril poisons Regan when she discovers the latter's affair with the treacherous Edmond, whom she also loves.) Ginny's relationship with Ty is also soured by everything that takes place over the summer, and she finally drives away from her home and marriage, telling him that the farm is now his. By the end of *A Thousand Acres*, Ginny has emerged from her former denial and passivity, but at the cost of what had been a placid, reasonably satisfying life. The reader must decide for him- or herself how to interpret this conclusion.

In *A Thousand Acres*, the role of Shakespeare's Regan is played by thirty-four-year-old **Rose**, who has recently undergone the trauma of breast cancer treatment and a mastectomy. Rose's personality is much different from her sister's, for she is as determined and indomitable as Ginny is pliant and placating. It is thus not surprising that Rose, ever the realist, is the first of the sisters to confront her memories of their father's sexual abuse of both during their teenaged years. Although she has long kept silent about this abuse, Rose's deeply held resentment has contributed to her irascibility and disruptiveness. She keeps close score of the wrongs done against her—for example, when a drunken Pete broke her arm, she wrote on the cast "PETE DID THIS" to remind him and others of his bad behavior. Ginny is increasingly dismayed by Rose's thirst for vengeance, which—along with their love for the same man—results in their estrangement. Near the end of the novel, the dying Rose summons Ginny in order to ask her to care for her two daughters, and the sisters reconcile before Rose's death.

The third and youngest of the Cook sisters, twenty-eight-year-old **Caroline**, has the most minor role in the novel. A lawyer who has escaped the confines of the farm for the relative excitement of Des Moines, Caroline appears only a few times, each time making the division between her and her sisters evident. Caroline was a small child when the girls' mother died and she was raised primarily by Ginny and Rose, who were determined that she have more freedom and wider prospects than they had. The unexpected result was that an unbroachable chasm developed between Caroline and her sisters. When Larry first proposes to turn his farm over to his daughters, only Caroline questions the move, and he initially rejects her. This follows the model of King Lear and his daughter Cordelia, who refused to flatter him with undue devotion but claimed to love him according to her bond and "no more, no less." And like King Lear, Larry later values Caroline's initial resistance to his plan, and he enlists her aid in suing her sisters and their husbands. Despite her apparent devotion to her father, however, Caroline exhibits a marked emotional coldness. Significantly, she declines to hear about the painful memories that have tormented Rose and Ginny when, after Rose's death, she and Ginny meet at the farm to divide the family's belongings between them.

Through the prosperous, autocratic farmer **Larry Cook**, Smiley explores the theme of men's domination of women, connecting it symbolically with a similar domination of nature. Sullen, laconic, and short-tempered, Larry grows increasingly irascible after relinquishing his farm to his daughters and their husbands. Accustomed to a daily routine of hard work—a routine in which he has long expected the rest of the family to join—Larry's life is disrupted by his new idleness, and he turns to heavy drinking, wandering around in his pickup truck, and foolish spending sprees to occupy his time. He also becomes more and more paranoid about the motives and intentions of those around him, and in a shocking confrontation one stormy night curses them and goes out alone into the rain. This is the scene that perhaps most strongly underlines Larry's role as the King Lear figure in *A Thousand Acres*, for Shakespeare's character undergoes a similar experience. Eventually it is revealed that Larry's tyranny over his daughters has, in the past, included sexual abuse, an offense that he never acknowledges or seeks atonement for. Several critics noted that Larry's uniform monstrousness and utter lack of remorse is a major weakness in the novel and constitutes a point of departure from the model of King Lear, who ultimately gains insight into his own behavior.

The part of Shakespeare's Albany, the husband of Goneril, is played by **Tyler Smith**, a polite, conscientious man and competent farmer. When he was twenty-two, Ty inherited his father's farm after his father died, and several years later he married Ginny. Both hardworking and conciliatory, Ty has always been popular with Larry. His happy marriage disintegrates through the course of the novel, as his feeling that the sisters should "let things slide" with their father—that their resentment is out of proportion—as well as Ginny's emotional upheaval drive wedges between the couple. By contrast to Ty, Rose's husband **Pete** has a volatile personality and has often been in conflict with his father-in-law. As a young man he was good-looking and a spectacularly talented musician, but he gave up his musical aspirations to farm and start a family with Rose. When his enthusiastic plans for the farm met with silence or derision from Larry, Pete turned increasingly to drink and even began to physically abuse Rose (until the incident in which he broke her arm). Pete is perhaps the most tragic character in *A Thousand Acres*, for his frustration and despair lead to suicide.

The arrival of thirty-one-year-old **Jess Clark** in Zebulon County is anticipated with interest in the community, for everyone wonders how he has spent the last thirteen years. Jess relates that after being drafted to serve in the Vietnam War, he fled to Canada and stayed there until only a few years ago, when he moved to Seattle. He reveals to Ginny that he was once engaged to a young woman who, three years earlier, died in a car accident. Good-looking and physically fit, Jess is a vegetarian whose interest in organic farming (a special concern of Smiley's) leads him to consider moving back to Iowa to start a farm run according to his ideas about agriculture. Initially welcomed by Ginny, Rose, and their husbands, Jess proves a disruptive force as he becomes involved with both women (though not, apparently, at exactly the same time); he is also accused by his father of having designs on the family farm. Charming and sensitive on the surface but calculating underneath, Jess is the novel's counterpart of Shakespeare's Edmund.

The part of King Lear's faithful friend Gloucester is played in the novel by **Harold Clark**, a neighboring farmer who is not as foolish as he likes to appear. Like Gloucester, Harold has two sons—one a charming prodigal and one more virtuous—and shifts his favor between the two during the course of the novel. Smiley underlines her environmental concerns through Harold's blinding by anhydrous ammonia, a dangerous chemical used in contemporary farming. Harold's other son, the easygoing, responsible **Loren**, resembles Shakespeare's Edgar in that his father is blinded to his virtues by the calculating Jess (Edmund).

Other characters in the novel include the rather eccentric, nutrition-obsessed **Marv Carson**, Larry's banker, who encourages Larry to transfer his farm to his children; and Rose and Pete's daughters **Pammy** and **Linda**. Ginny is devoted to conscientious, thirteen-year-old Pammy and the more carefree, twelve-year-old Linda, and she is initially dismayed by Rose's decision to send the girls away to boarding school; as it turns out, this move was prompted by Rose's fear that her father would try to subject her daughters to the same abuse she had endured.

Further Reading

Berne, Suzanne. Interview with Jane Smiley. *Belles Lettres* (Summer 1992): 36–8.

Carlson, Ron. "King Lear in Zebulon County." *New York Times Book Review* (November 3, 1991): 12.

Christiansen, Rupert. "Sharper Than the Serpent's Tooth." *Observer* (October 25, 1992): 63.

———. "Speaking Less than She Knowest." *Spectator* (October 10, 1992): 38-9.

Contemporary Literary Criticism Vol. 53. Detroit: Gale Research.

Duffy, Martha. "The Case for Goneril and Regan." *Time* (November 11, 1991): GB4, GT8, GT12.

Eder, Richard. "Sharper Than a Serpent's Tooth." *Los Angeles Times Book Review* (November 10, 1991): 3, 13.

Rifkind, Donna. "A Man Had Three Daughters . . . " *Washington Post—Book World* (October 27, 1991): 1, 13.

Wole Soyinka
1934–

Nigerian dramatist, poet, novelist, critic, translator, editor, autobiographer, and short story writer.

The Interpreters (novel, 1965)

Plot: The novel takes place in Lagos, Nigeria, a short time after that country achieved independence in 1960 from British colonial rule. The title characters are five young intellectuals, each of whom has been living and studying abroad and has returned to Nigeria with the intention of making a contribution to the country's development. "The Interpreters" include Egbo, a worker in the government's foreign office as well as the inheritor of a traditional chieftaincy; Sekoni, an idealistic engineer; Sagoe, a journalist; Kola, an artist who is working on a representation of the pantheon of Yoruban (one of Nigeria's dominant ethnic groups) deities; and Bandele, a university lecturer. Each of these young men is stymied by the corruption and pretension that has infected Nigerian society at every level; in addition, each grapples with personal confusion and frustration. Sekoni becomes a particular victim of corruption when his attempt to build an experimental power station that promises to benefit many ordinary people is thwarted by a greedy politician. Devastated by this experience, Sekoni channels his frustration into sculpting and is finally killed in a car accident.

Shaken by Sekoni's death, the surviving friends find a distraction in the mysterious albino Lazarus, who has founded a religious cult. He recruits a young man named Noah whom he saves from an angry crowd convinced he is a thief. Bandele accuses his friends of exploiting the passive Noah for their own ends—for example, Kola is using him as a model for his painting and Sagoe is writing a news story about him. In addition, the homosexual, one-quarter-black American Joe Golder develops an interest in Noah that proves fatal when the latter falls from Joe's apartment window, probably in flight from a sexual advance. The interpreters go on to make their way as best they can within their troubled society.

Characters: Recipient of the Nobel Prize for Literature in 1986, Soyinka is one of the most prominent and celebrated of African writers. His works provide a compelling record of the continent's political turmoil and Africans' struggle to reconcile their traditional heritages with the inevitable encroachment of modern influences. *The Interpreters* expands on many of the themes Soyinka has emphasized in the dramas for which he is best known, providing a sweeping view of post-independence Nigeria. Critics agree that *The Interpreters* is a demanding novel owing to its highly metaphorical prose (which reflects Soyinka's poetic vocation) and loose structure; while some find Soyinka's diction frustratingly convoluted, others appreciate his ability to create a memorable portrait of a troubled time and people.

The novel's title refers to the five young men who return to Nigeria from abroad, eager to participate in the process of developing their newly independent nation. Each attempts to find his niche in a different area—technology, art, media, academia, and government—and each discovers that a corrupt, pretentious black African elite has taken the place of the white colonial elite that once dominated Nigerian society. Soyinka does not, however, portray the interpreters as entirely blameless. Although they are idealistic and sincerely opposed to injustice and hypocrisy, their selfishness, egoism, and aimlessness are also evident. They have retained a sense of their origins and heritage, but their exposure to European and American perspectives has imbued them with a certain detachment; their role seems to focus on interpreting events rather than on instituting change.

The quietly passionate engineer **Sekoni** has been identified as the only interpreter who does not retreat into egotistical fulfillment but, rather, makes an effort to accomplish a material good for his country. He is tragically broken by his confrontation with government corruption, which involves a politician who, determined to hold onto his electricity monopoly, bribes a foreign "expert" to decree Sekoni's project unsafe. Later, Sekoni becomes a gifted sculptor whose tortured work "The Wrestler" depicts his own struggles with society. The sarcastic but dedicated newspaper reporter **Sagoe** channels his frustration with the wrongdoing he witnesses in the journalism field into a theory of "Voidancy," which seems to represent the corruption around him as human waste. Although he would like to produce beneficial, groundbreaking stories on poverty and political misbehavior, Sagoe actually acquiesces in suppressing the truth about a story in order to save his own job. Commentators have identified **Egbo**, a functionary in his country's foreign office, as an autobiographical character. Like Soyinka, he is the son of Western-influenced parents whose grandfather sought to bequeath him a tribal chieftaincy. Egbo takes refuge from the conflicting forces of tradition and modernity in a personal mysticism that involves transforming the people he meets into mythological figures. Egbo also shares with his creator an identification with the Yoruban god Ogun, an explorer, warrior, and creator. Soyinka exposes Egbo's potential for hypocrisy through his seduction of the unnamed female student that he pretentiously calls "the new woman of my generation."

Kola is an artist and academician who uses his friends and acquaintances as models for his painting of the pantheon of Yoruban gods; conversely, the other interpreters also seem to model themselves after these mythical characters as they struggle to understand themselves. Through Kola, Soyinka explores the role of the artist, particularly during periods of social and political turmoil, as well as the concept of art as a dangerous form of self-absorption that blinds the artist to human realities. The serious, considerate professor **Bandele** is perhaps the most clearsighted of the five interpreters, and by the end of the novel he has assumed a dominant role among them as a kind of conscience. To the amazement of the others, Bandele treats the pretentious academics among whom he works with tolerance, and he repeatedly assumes the role of mediator and reconciler. It is Bandele who recognizes and condemns the egoism that has dominated the interpreters' relationship with the hapless Noah.

The novel's many secondary characters help to create a vibrant, panoramic portrait of post-independence Nigerian life. The mysterious albino **Lazarus** demonstrates one method of adapting to social upheaval as he heads a religious cult that practices bizarre rituals. One of his converts is the rescued pickpocket **Noah**, whom Lazarus intends to mold into a successor. A nondescript, vacuous young man, Noah is exploited by several of the interpreters, who find him an interesting subject, and he finally becomes a kind of sacrifice when he falls to his death from **Joe Golder**'s window. Golder is a homosexual who is part African American and who claims to wish he was *more* black; indeed, the neurosis he exhibits seems connected with his being neither black nor white, male nor female.

Members of the academic world in which Bandele circulates include the pretentious, protocol-obsessed **Professor Oguazor**, whose behavior and speech, so closely modeled after the English colonists, compels Sagoe to make at a scene at a party; the professor demonstrates his hypocrisy when he decries the moral turpitude of some of his female students even though he himself has an illegitimate daughter. Similarly, the insensitive **Dr. Lumoye**, publicly ridicules a young girl who had come to him for help and whom he had actually attempted to seduce. Status-seeking radiographer **Ayo Faseyi** disapproves of the his unconventional English wife, **Monica**, who resists conforming to the pretentious protocol valued by her husband. The dynamic, progressive **Mrs. Faseyi**, Ayo's mother, sympathizes with Monica and thinks she should leave Ayo. Corrupt members of the governmental sphere include the venal, now-deceased judge **Sir Derinola**, whom Sagoe encounters in a dream, and the comically grotesque politician **Chief Winsala**; both of these figures are portrayed as simultaneously repellent and pathetic.

Other characters in *The Interpreters* include Sagoe's tolerant girlfriend **Dehinwa**, a sophisticated urbanite who is nevertheless not quite the loose woman her more traditional mother and aunt imagine her; **Mathias**, a messenger at Sagoe's office who is frequently subjected to the latter's lectures on "Voidancy"; and **Simi**, a beautiful, sensual woman with many lovers, who initiates Egbo into sex.

Further Reading

Wright, Derek. *Wole Soyinka Revisited*. New York: Twayne, 1993.

Black Literature Criticism Vol. 2. Detroit: Gale Research.

Contemporary Literary Criticism, Vols. 3, 5, 14, 36, 44. Detroit: Gale Research.

David, Mary T. "The Theme of Regeneration in Selected Works by Wole Soyinka." *Black American Literature Forum* Vol. 22, no. 4 (Winter 1988): 645–61.

Roy, Anjali, and Kirpal, Viney. "Men as Archetypes: Characterization in Soyinka's Novels." *Modern Fiction Studies* Vol. 37, no. 3 (Autumn 1991): 519–27.

Rajeshwar, M. *The Intellectual and Society in the Novels of Wole Soyinka*. New York: Advent Books, 1990.

Jones, Eldred. *The Writings of Wole Soyinka*. London: Heinemann, 1973.

Moore, Gerald. *Wole Soyinka*. London: Evans, 1971.

Muriel Spark
1918–

Scottish-born novelist, short story writer, poet, dramatist, essayist, biographer, editor, scriptwriter, and author of books for children.

The Girls of Slender Means (novel, 1963)

Plot: As the novel begins, London gossip columnist Jane Wright is calling some of her friends to inform them that Nicholas Farringdon, an old acquaintance of theirs who became a missionary priest, has died a martyr's death in Haiti. Farringdon's encounters with Jane and her friends during the final months of World War II are then recounted. Through his friendship with Jane, an overweight publisher's assistant, Nicholas meets the residents of the May of Teck Club, a group of young women who live in a large house in the Kensington area of London. A writer and would-be anarchist who has had difficulty making up his mind about a number of issues in his life, Nicholas develops a fascination for these young women, especially the beautiful, elegant Selina Redwood and Joanna Childe, a rector's daughter with a passion for poetry who gives elocution lessons. Nicholas comes to view the May of Teck Club as an ideal society that illustrates the beauty of poverty, but Selina—who becomes his lover—is impervious to his efforts to fashion her into an embodiment of his ideas. Finally, an unexploded bomb in the garden of the house explodes, starting a fire that traps a number of the women on the top floor. Only the slimmest girls are able to escape through a narrow window, while the rest must wait for the firemen to open a bricked-over skylight. Although the extremely thin Selina is one of the first to exit, she goes back into the house, and Nicholas assumes that she intends to help her friends. But Selina soon emerges, carrying only the elegant evening gown she cherishes. Witnessing this unexpected incidence of "savagery," Nicholas involuntarily makes the sign of the cross. When the building finally collapses, only Joanna is left inside and she perishes. At a VJ celebration some time later, Nicholas witnesses the murder of a woman by a seaman. He decides to give up his writing career and join the priesthood. As Jane later learns, his life ends in 1960 in Haiti, where he is killed after having condemned local superstitions.

Characters: *The Girls of Slender Means* evidences the moral concerns found in all of Spark's novels, as well as her disapproval of romanticism and her commitment to Catholicism. Written with her characteristic clarity and wit, the novel considers the question of how a person may undergo religious conviction and, according to critic Rodney Stenning Edgecombe, the "human deficiencies which are made into channels of grace."

Thirty-three years old when he meets the members of the May of Teck Club, **Nicholas Farringdon** is a shy, good-looking graduate of Cambridge University who is undecided about a number of things, including his sexuality, his religion, and his vocation. A writer of reputed promise, Nicholas records his impressions in a manuscript entitled *The Sabbath Notebooks*. He considers himself a proponent of anarchy, which he views as an inherently natural state, and he finds in the May of Teck Club the embodiment of his ideal of human communities governed not by institutions but by "men's hearts alone." Although he is at least partially aware that he is romanticizing these young women, Nicholas persists in seeing them as brave, lively souls who live impoverished lives with dignity and beauty. He is particularly enthralled by the poetry-declaiming Joanna Childe and by Selina Redmond, whose beauty and calculated poise blind him to her true selfishness. Nicholas hardly seems to notice that his attempts to ignite Selina's interest in his ideas fall on deaf ears. Spark explores the theme of religious conversion through Nicholas, who apparently considered becoming a priest even before the incident that decides his fate. His conversion occurs after he sees Selina returning to the burning house not out of concern for her endangered friends but in order to rescue an evening dress, proving, as he notes in his *Sabbath Notebooks*, that "a vision of evil may be as effective to conversion as a vision of good." The stabbing in the midst of the VJ celebration crowd further confirms for Nicholas the world's evil. A short time later, Nicholas encounters the murderer briefly in the crowd and slips into his pocket a forged letter of praise with which he had planned to promote his literary career, thus denouncing such worldly interests. Although most of the May of Teck Club members barely remember him, the few months Nicholas spends among them change his life: formerly directionless and dilettantish, he acquires purpose and a commitment to help humanity through his work as a missionary priest.

The novel's title refers to the members of the May of Teck Club, a hostel for young women who are in London working during the final months of the war. The term "slender means" denotes not only their economic poverty and the physical slimness of many of them but, as it turns out, their moral deficiencies. Perhaps the most flagrant exemplar of this latter quality is **Selina Redmond**, whose beauty and elegance mask her true self-centeredness and whose poise is calculated to promote her own interests. The other girls listen respectfully whenever Selina recites the creed she garnered from a course in poise: "Poise is perfect balance, an equanimity of body and mind, complete composure whatever the social scene." But Selina's poise is ultimately exposed as complete indifference to others during the fire scene, when her act of savagery confirms for Nicholas the existence of evil and spurs his religious conversion. Nicholas is initially dazzled by Selina's beauty, while she is attracted to his slight eccentricity, which she believes makes a man vulnerable to her control. Although Nicholas wants Selina to personify "an ideal society . . . amongst her bones," her own concerns center on evening gowns and how to acquire some hard-to-find hair-grips. The lovely Schiaparelli dress symbolizes Selina's superficiality, and her asking "Is it safe?" before emerging out of the house with it expresses her concern for herself only.

Many critics identify the naive, unworldly **Joanna Childe** as a foil to Selina, for she practices a self-denial that Selina could neither comprehend nor possess. The daughter of a country rector, Joanna fell in love with her father's curate but the young man did not reciprocate her feelings. Later, Joanna was horrified to find herself attracted to the curate's replacement, for she believes that a person must be constant to only one love in his or her lifetime; therefore she refused to become involved with the young man and came to London. Joanna teaches elocution and is constantly heard reciting poetry, which she loves passionately. As many commentators have noted, her declamations function as a kind of chorus, commenting on the novel's action and themes. Although Spark disapproves of the kind of devotion to romantic ideals that causes Joanna to spurn love, she is otherwise a sympathetic character whose innocent idealism is preferable to the other girls' superficiality. In strong contrast to Selina, Joanna attempts to comfort her endangered friends by reciting poetry as they wait to be rescued, and her subsequent death perhaps anticipates the martyr's demise that Nicholas later meets.

Another notable member of the May of Teck Club is **Jane Wright**, who eventually becomes a London gossip columnist and in that capacity reports Nicholas's death. Although Jane is fat and unattractive (she is constantly sneaking pieces of chocolate she keeps hidden in her room), she has gained status with the other girls through her job with a publisher, the importance of which she inflates by referring to it as "brainwork" in the "world of books." It is Jane who introduces Nicholas (whose worth as a writer her publisher has asked her to investigate) to the May of Teck Club, after Nicholas has pleased her by taking her to several gatherings of poets. Although Jane enjoys her encounters with the Bohemian literary world, she herself harbors a conventional wish for marriage and a family. Despite her mild pretentiousness, Jane is presented as somewhat more intelligent and less superficial than her friends, and Nicholas retains to the end of his life an image of her strength and resilience as she pinned up her disheveled hair as the VJ day crowd surged around her.

Other residents of the May of Teck Club include **Pauline Fox**, a mentally unhinged young woman whose imaginary dinners with a famous actor provide an extreme example of the subjugation of reality to fantasy; and **Collie**, **Jarvie**, and **Greggie**, the three older spinsters who live on the floor below the young women. Throughout the novel, Greggie insists that there is an unexploded bomb in the garden, and her unheeded warning proves well-founded. Jane's employer is the publisher **George Johnson**, who has taken **Huy Throvis-Mew** as his professional name and who considers authors ''temperamental raw material'' over which he must determine how to exert control. Jane's Rumanian friend **Rudi Bittesch** buys the letters she solicits from famous authors in order to attain their signatures; it is Rudi who tells Jane about Nicholas's background. Nicholas's friend **Colonel Felix Dobell** is an American intelligence officer who is also fascinated with the women of the May of Teck Club; he has already slept with Selina, while repeatedly mentioning his wife Gareth, his personal symbol of conscience and respectability.

Loitering with Intent (novel, 1981)

Plot: The novel is narrated by Fleur Talbot, a successful novelist who recounts from a more mature perspective her experiences during a period extending from the autumn of 1949 to the summer of 1950, when she was a struggling, impoverished young writer living in London. Fleur accepts a job with Sir Quentin Oliver, who wants her to type and edit the autobiographical manuscripts written by the ten members of his Autobiographical Association. Sir Quentin explains that the memoirs are not to be published for seventy years, but Fleur soon realizes that they could very easily be used to blackmail the members. In fact, it turns out that Sir Quentin is manipulating the members by goading them into ruthless exposure; he also dominates them by other means, including occasionally giving them Dexedrine. At the same time, Fleur notices that the lives of the association members closely resemble those of characters in the book she is writing, *Warrender Chase*, and that Sir Quentin is very similar to her title character. After learning that Sir Quentin has stolen parts of her novel and incorporated them into the members' autobiographies, she confronts him and demands that he disband the association. Sir Quentin refuses but subsequently dies in a car accident: the same fate met by the fictional Warrender Chase. Although Sir Quentin had destroyed Fleur's manuscript, another copy finds its way to a publisher and the book is finally published, the first in a series of well-received novels Fleur produces over the next several decades.

Characters: Considered Spark's most autobiographical work, *Loitering with Intent* focuses on the novelist's role in manipulating reality and on the relationship between fact and fiction. Praised for the witty, economical prose for which Spark is renowned, the novel reflects her strong, markedly Catholic moral sense as well as the pleasure she takes in practicing her craft.

Fleur Talbot is recognized as one of Spark's most likable, engaging heroines and also the most autobiographical figure to be found in her fiction (Spark too was an impoverished young writer who lived in London during the years following World War II). Lively and self-confident, she addresses the reader in a relaxed, chatty voice that reflects the joy and certainty she feels toward her writing vocation and her interest in and compassion for the people around her. Through Fleur, Spark explores the issue of how the novelist uses reality to create fiction, a process that involves ''loitering with intent''; that is, gathering information and perceptions that are later transformed into literature. In a passage noted by many critics as significant, Fleur describes her awareness of a *demon* inside her who "rejoiced in seeing people as they were, and not only that, but more than ever as they were, and more, and more." The resemblance of Sir Quentin and the members of the Autobiographical Association to the characters in her own novel does not particularly alarm Fleur, for she knows that she created her characters before she met their real counterparts; however, at one point she does wonder if she herself invented the real people. (Interestingly, Spark has invented both the novel's real and its fictional characters!) Fleur's nondogmatic but sincere commitment to Catholicism is evident in her moral perception and in her view of her art as a gift from God that she may use to reveal truth and thus attain grace. Although she admires John Henry Cardinal Newman (the English theologian whose writings influenced Spark's conversion to Catholicism), Fleur aligns herself more with the exuberance and joy she finds in the autobiography of Italian sculptor Benvenuto Cellini, and like him, she says, she is "now going on my way rejoicing."

Whereas Fleur molds reality into fiction in order to reveal truth, **Sir Quentin Oliver** is shown to manipulate fiction in order to gain power over real people. The founder and leader of the Autobiographical Association, Sir Quentin is a wealthy snob to whose face and body "only a high rank or a string of titles could bring an orgiastic quiver." Initially rather charmed by his idea of soliciting memoirs to be published many years later, Fleur soon discovers that her employer is using them to blackmail the writers—not for money, which he doesn't need, but to exert control over them. Recognizing in Sir Quentin the same evil that she has already seen manifested in her character Warrender Chase, Fleur labels him a "sado-puritan" who gathers weak people around him and instills guilt and paranoia in them in order to accomplish his own ends. When Fleur confronts him with the diabolical nature of his deeds, however, Sir Quentin defends himself by claiming that, like Fleur's beloved Cardinal Newman, he has the right to surround himself with a circle of "devoted spiritual followers." In Sir Quentin's case, of course, such a purpose reflects only vanity; indeed, he is one of several characters in Spark's fiction (such as the title character of *The Prime of Miss Jean Brodie*) with an inflated sense of personal entitlement. Sir Quentin is himself both alarmed and fascinated by Fleur's novel, which he initially uses to influence reality and then tries to destroy. The coincident manner of Sir Quentin's and Warrender Chase's deaths seems to strike Fleur as more fitting than strange, for she regards Sir Quentin as an embodiment of evil without whom, like her novel's title character, the world is better off.

One of the more sympathetic characters in *Loitering with Intent* is Sir Quentin's eccentric old mother, **Lady Edwina Oliver**, who differs profoundly from her warped son. Alert, realistic, and honest, Lady Edwina resents her son's superficiality and efforts to control her, and she wreaks her revenge by pretending to be senile. Lady Edwina likes Fleur very much and is admired in return by Fleur, whom she helps by stealing pages from Sir Quentin's diary to help Fleur prove that he has been pilfering from her novel. After Sir Quentin's death, Lady Edwina inherits his fortune and lives happily until her own death at ninety six.

Fleur's friend **Dottie**, whom she derisively calls "the English Rose," provides a strong contrast to Fleur in her shallowness and naivete. Superficially moralistic, she is a representative of false religious values and a practitioner of the kind of bureaucratic Catholicism that both Fleur and Spark detest. The confused nature of Dottie's thinking is evidenced by her views of Lady Edwina as a nuisance and Sir Quentin (for whom she agrees to steal Fleur's manuscript) as a kind, reassuring person. Fleur is remarkably tolerant of Dottie's shortcomings and remains friends with her throughout the next several decades, despite Dottie's repeated accusations that Fleur is always "wriggling out of reality."

Other significant characters in *Loitering with Intent* include the domineering, manipulative **Beryl Tims**, Sir Quentin's housekeeper and Lady Edwina's caretaker, who constantly tries to ingratiate herself with her employer; the pathetically weak **Leslie**, Dottie's husband and Fleur's lover, who finally leaves her to enter a homosexual relationship; and Fleur's dear, devoted friend **Solly**, who saves *Warrender Chase* by (unbeknownst to Fleur) sending a copy of the manuscript to a second publisher. Fleur considers **Maisie Young** the most redeemable of the association members and tries to help her overcome her insecurity about her physical disability by encouraging her to read the autobiography of Cardinal Newman. Unfortunately, Maisie focuses on the concept that there are ''two and two only supreme and self-evident beings, myself and my creator,'' which Fleur feels is neurotic because it denies the reality of everyone and everything else in the world.

Further Reading

Bold, Alan, ed. *Muriel Spark: An Odd Capacity for Vision*. London: Vision Press, 1984.

Contemporary Literary Criticism Vols. 2, 3, 5, 8, 13, 18, 40. Detroit: Gale Research.

Dictionary of Literary Biography Vol. 15. Detroit: Gale Research.

Edgecombe, Rodney Stenning. *Vocation and Identity in the Fiction of Muriel Spark*. Columbia: University of Missouri Press, 1990.

Harrison, Barbara Grizzuti. ''To Be an Artist and a Woman.'' *New York Times Book Review* (May 31, 1981): 11, 48–9.

Hynes, Joseph. *The Art of the Real: Muriel Spark's Novels*. Rutherford, N J: Fairleigh Dickinson University Press, 1988.

Kemp, Peter. ''How Spark Began.'' *Listener* Vol. 105, no. 2713 (May 21, 1981): 684.

Page, Norman. *Muriel Spark*. New York: St. Martin's Press, 1990.

Randisi, Jennifer Lynn. *On Her Way Rejoicing: The Fiction of Muriel Spark*. Washington, D. C.: Catholic University of America Press, 1991.

Richmond, Velma Bourgeois. *Muriel Spark*. New York: Frederick Ungar, 1984.

Rowe, Margaret Moan. ''Muriel Spark and the Angel of the Body.'' *Critique* Vol. 28, no. 3 (Spring 1987): 167–76.

Sproxton, Judy. *The Women of Muriel Spark*. New York: St. Martin's Press, 1992.

Towers, Robert. ''Comic Schemes.'' *New York Review of Books* Vol. 27, no. 11 (June 25, 1981): 45–6.

Walker, Dorothea. *Muriel Spark*. Boston, MA: Twayne, 1988.

Wilson, A. N. ''Cause for Rejoicing.'' *Spectator* Vol. 246, no. 7976 (May 23, 1981): 20–1.

Jean Stafford
1915–1979

American novelist, short story writer, essayist, critic, nonfiction writer, and author of children's books.

The Mountain Lion (novel, 1947)

Plot: The novel begins in Covina, California, where eight-year-old Molly Fawcett and ten-year-old Ralph Fawcett live with their widowed mother and two older sisters, Leah and

Rachel. Molly and Ralph are both sickly due to an earlier bout of scarlet fever, and their health problems as well as their mutual precociousness alienate them from the rest of the family and draw them closer to each other. Mrs. Fawcett and her older daughters revere the memory of Grandfather Bonney, a fastidious button manufacturer and gentile native of Boston whose ashes rest in an urn on the family's mantel. Molly and Ralph, however, prefer crude, wealthy Grandpa Kenyon, their mother's stepfather, who owns four ranches in several western states. Grandpa Kenyon dies during one of his annual visits to the Fawcett home, and his son Claude arrives from Colorado for the funeral. He invites them to spend the next summer at his Colorado ranch, where Ralph gradually enters into the rugged and exaggeratedly masculine life of Claude and his ranchhands, while Molly spends more and more of her time alone, often writing.

Soon after returning to California for the winter, Ralph and Molly slip back into their old closeness, but during the next several summers on the ranch it becomes obvious that they are on divergent paths. Ralph is ready to become a man in the fashion of his much-admired, virile Uncle Claude, while Molly resists the encroachment of adolescence. Molly and Ralph spend an entire year in Colorado, when Mrs. Fawcett decides to take her two older daughters—who are models of beauty, charm, and propriety—on a European tour. During this period, Molly becomes isolated from the people around her, and Ralph grows impatient with his sister's eccentricity. When a magnificent mountain lion, nicknamed Goldilocks, is reported to be in the area, Ralph becomes obsessed with the idea of hunting and killing it. While picnicking with Molly and Uncle Claude, Ralph unexpectedly spots the animal and fires a shot, after which he immediately hears another shot. Ralph soon discovers not only that it was Uncle Claude's shot that has felled the lion but that his own shot has killed his sister.

Characters: Praised for its lucid, economical prose, thematic complexity, and sensitive characterizations, Stafford's fiction often centers on an alienated adolescent's struggle to achieve the transition from childhood to adulthood. Widely acknowledged as one of Stafford's finest works, *The Mountain Lion* has been identified by several critics as a *bildungsroman* (a novel of initiation) that illuminates traditional gender roles and the way they shape identity.

Considered one of Stafford's most memorable and poignant characters, **Molly Fawcett** is clearly modeled after her creator's memories of herself as a young girl. She is a bright, sensitive aspiring writer (one of her poems, "Gravel," was actually written by the young Stafford). Molly idolizes her brother but is physically and emotionally isolated from her mother and sisters. She is described as a thin, homely child with stiff, dark hair and a predilection—shared with Ralph and resulting from their earlier bout with scarlet fever—for nosebleeds. Her precocious intelligence and acerbic tongue are viewed with distaste and even feared by her mother, who obviously prefers her two older daughters to the unfathomable Molly. Struggling with her alienation and the onset of adolescence, she resists the relinquishment of innocence. Molly's denial of her own sexuality are evident in her avoidance of the word "body," the elaborate bath ritual she devises to minimize nudity (she thinks of herself as "a long wooden box with a mind inside"), and her agitated reaction whenever Ralph hints at his own growing awareness of sex. Commentators have interpreted Molly's rejection of sexuality as a manifestation of both self-loathing and distaste for the prescribed roles available to adult women. Limitations circumscribe Molly's life, for she is excluded from both the superficial world of her mother and sisters and the rough, "ride 'em, cowboy," male realm of the ranch. She has no appropriate female role model to demonstrate other alternatives. Molly's dilemma results in a seething hatred that is initially directed at others but finally centers on herself; toward the end of the novel, she adds her own name to her list of unforgivable people and tells Ralph, "I know I'm ugly. I know everybody hates me. I wish I were dead." Although a few commentators fault the novel's conclusion as too violent, most consider Molly's tragic death inevitable since she has been left with no suitable role to play in the world. Molly is closely identified with the image of Goldilocks, the mountain lion, who embodies a natural and distinctly female beauty and freedom that are finally destroyed by the markedly male force of a hostile society. Several critics have viewed Molly's live and death in relation to her brother, for her existence seems to impede his initiation into adulthood. In addition, the fact that Stafford's beloved brother died in young adulthood may be significant; Molly's death could be seen as expressing Stafford's subconscious wish to change places with her brother.

Although Molly is usually identified as the central character in *The Mountain Lion*, her brother **Ralph** shares much of the spotlight with her. Molly and Ralph are initially much alike: both are sickly, prone to nosebleeds, and have poor eyesight; both are physically unattractive; and both are precocious and alienated from the smug, superficial world of their mother and sisters. Over the four years of the novel, however, Ralph accepts the growth and change that his sister refuses, and their former intimacy deteriorates. The events that mark their gradual division include Ralph's abandoning his glasses (Molly tries to give hers up too but cannot see without them); his witnessing the birth of a calf, which awakens in him an awareness of sexuality; and his physical transformation into a reasonably attractive teenager. When Ralph, while traveling by train with Molly to the ranch, asks her to "tell me all the dirty words you know," their relationship is permanently altered. Early in the story, Ralph decides that people can be divided into two categories, the "Kenyon men" and the "Bonney merchants," with the former being far superior in his eyes. Ironically, it is the Kenyon men who ultimately prepare him for his inevitable return to the Bonney merchants, for by the end of the novel he complacently plans to attend Harvard in accordance with his mother's wishes. Ralph's development has been seen as an illustration of how attaining maturity necessitates the acceptance of the loss of innocence. In addition, Stafford suggests that this process is eased for Ralph by the fact of his maleness, which confers privileges that make adulthood much more attractive than for powerless Molly. Even as Molly becomes increasingly isolated, Ralph identifies more thoroughly with the role he is expected to assume, with Uncle Clyde serving as his mentor on his journey to manhood. Ralph does, however, recognize the limitations of Uncle Clyde's otherwise attractive, exaggeratedly male way of life, for he senses his uncle's emotional immaturity and lack of real independence. Critics have viewed Ralph's "accidental" killing of Molly as inevitable, for in refusing to accept her own maturity she threatens his. That her death occurs in the course of his hunt for the mountain lion is also significant, for Goldilocks has been said to embody the female principle that must be overcome if Ralph is to attain manhood. Molly represents the feminine part of Ralph, as well as the innocence that must be sacrificed as a child moves into adulthood. Stafford is thought to have modeled Ralph after her own beloved brother, who was killed during World War II; some critics have even viewed *The Mountain Lion* as Stafford's attempt to come to terms with this loss.

The Fawcett children's two grandfathers represent the two radically different worlds between which Ralph and Molly travel. Although **Grandfather Bonney** is dead when the novel begins, he is still a major figure in the Fawcett family's life, for Mrs. Fawcett worships his memory and maintains a kind of living-room shrine centering on the urn that contains his ashes. Bonney was a plump, bald, fastidious button manufacturer—born in Boston but resident most of his life in St. Louis—whose crowning achievement was meeting Grover Cleveland. A meticulous dresser with a tendency to insert Latin epigrams into his speech, Grandfather Bonney symbolizes everything that Ralph and Molly find smug and stifling about life in Covina. Their crude, rumpled **Grandpa Kenyon**, by contrast, is a teller of tall tales who once entertained Jesse James and who, like them, is unable to conform to their mother's social expectations. Despite his lack of table manners and his near illiteracy, Grandpa Kenyon projects a natural integrity that is obvious to Ralph and Molly; he and her father are the only ones Molly includes on her list of forgivable people. Stafford's fondness for her own paternal grandfather, after whom she modeled Grandpa Kenyon, is evident.

When **Uncle Claude** arrives in California for his father's funeral, the children are delighted to discover that he is a younger version of Grandpa Kenyon. Uncle Claude personifies the manly life of the ranch and serves as Ralph's guide into manhood. His interest and approval in Ralph gradually grow more evident, while at the same time he displays a marked bewilderment and unfriendliness toward Molly that contributes to her rift with her brother. Although Uncle Claude is presented as the epitome of the "Kenyon men," Ralph eventually comes to recognizes Claude's "virile opacity" and essential immaturity.

Critics see in Stafford's portrayal of **Mrs. Fawcett** reflections of her feelings for her own mother, who, like her fictional counterpart, was a native of Missouri. Conventional and vain, Mrs. Fawcett has transferred to her life in California the markedly "Eastern" propriety that characterized her family's habits before her widowed mother married a crude rancher. While she has successfully fashioned her two older daughters in her own image, Mrs. Fawcett does not know what to make of Molly and Ralph, whose precocious intelligence and homeliness repel her. She rejects her younger children by limiting her involvement in their lives and preventing their participation in outdoor activities. Significantly, Mrs. Fawcett treats Ralph less harshly than Molly, particularly as he grows and begins to lose some of his gawky ugliness. Whereas Ralph's maleness seems to be enough to earn him some respect from his mother, Molly exhibits the "brains" that Mrs. Fawcett considers a handicap in a girl. Closely identified with Mrs. Fawcett are her older daughters, **Leah** and **Rachel**, polite, attractive, cheerful girls whose interests revolve around pursuing boys. Whereas Molly is dark and homely, blonde, poised Leah and Rachel conform to conventional standards of female beauty. Like Molly, Stafford had two older sisters, and the Fawcett girls are one of several such negatively portrayed fictional pairs found in her works.

Another significant female character in *The Mountain Lion* is **Winifred Brotherman**, a teenager who works at the ranch during the first summer Molly and Ralph spend there. When they first meet her, Winifred is a tomboyish figure who impresses them with her riding and shooting skill, her independence, and her lack of artificiality. She initially provides an alternative role model for Molly, who views Winifred's dung-covered jeans with admiration. The children return to the ranch one summer, however, to find Winifred physically matured and conforming to conventional expectations of female behavior. She has suddenly become an attractive young woman who is well aware of her sexuality and who eventually leaves college to marry. Bitterly disappointed by the transformation of a potential mentor into version of her older sisters, Molly adds Winifred's name to her list of unforgivable people. Nor is Winifred's mother **Mrs. Brotherman**, the ranch's housekeeper, capable of offering Molly the guidance she needs. Described by critic Melody Graulich as "an absurd island of refinement with no power, no voice, no wit," Mrs. Brotherman is a native of New England who hates the rough western lifestyle and longs to escape.

At the height of her isolation from everyone around her, Molly imagines herself the daughter of **Magdalene**, the ranch's old, ugly, extremely misanthropic black cook, who has been viewed by some commentators as an embodiment of femininity as a threateningly primitive force. The inhabitants of Mrs. Fawcett's Bonney-centered world include the narrow-minded, exaggeratedly gentile **Reverend** and **Mrs. Follansbee**, whose visits Molly and Ralph dread. Reverend Follansbee's hobby, taxidermy, seems a fit metaphor for his deadened existence.

The Catherine Wheel (novel, 1952)

Plot: The novel takes place at Congreve House, the New England summer home of Katharine Congreve, a beautiful, unmarried woman in her late thirties. Katharine has been a close friend of John and Maeve Shipley since the three were teenagers, and the Shipley children—twelve-year-old Andrew and his older twin sisters, Honor and Harriet—are spending the summer at Congreve House while their parents travel in Europe. Andrew feels isolated, resentful, and lonely because his only friend, Victor Smithfield, is neglecting him in favor of his brother Charles, who is on sick leave from the Navy. Andrew becomes obsessed with the unspoken wish that Charles would die, and he suspects that his beloved Aunt Katharine, who has been paying him little attention, is somehow aware of this hidden sin. Unbeknownst to Andrew, however, Katharine is preoccupied with her own secret. Twenty years earlier, Katharine had been in love with John Shipley, but on the night of her seventeenth birthday party she learned that he was in love with her friend (and orphaned cousin) Maeve. Since then, time has stood still for Katharine. She refuses all offers of marriage and maintains a well-ordered, refined existence both in Boston and at Congreve House; meanwhile, her heart continues to smolder with the humiliating memory of her lost love. However, John Shipley begs her to run away with him, and she agrees to the plan if at the end of this summer he decides that he cannot remain married to Maeve. The summer passes with no resolution to the anxieties of either Andrew or Katharine, each of whom remains both ignorant of the other's torment and convinced that the other has knowledge of his or her guilt. Finally, Katharine hosts a party at which are featured six of her favorite fireworks, one of which is the "Catherine wheel" with its spinning, colored flames. When the final wheel is lit, it ignites Victor Smithfield's hair, and in her attempt to save the boy's life, Katharine herself is burned to death.

Characters: *The Catherine Wheel* garnered renewed critical attention in the early 1980s when it was included in Ecco Press's "Neglected Books of the Twentieth Century" series. Although several critics found the novel's symbolism too heavy-handed, most deem it Stafford's finest and most controlled work. Contrasting past and present, youth and maturity, Stafford probes the consequences of hidden envy and guilt. According to Maureen Ryan, the novel represents "the maturation of her fascination with the theme and form of the female novel of development."

Thirty-eight-year-old **Katharine Congreve** has been identified as the only mature female protagonist in Stafford's fiction. She is portrayed as an independent woman who, in her beauty, composure, and apparent satisfaction with her ordered life, defies the stereotype of the aging spinster. Katharine does, however, share several important characteristics with the pre-adolescent Molly Fawcett in *The Mountain Lion*: She refuses to change or compromise, and she meets a tragic end. Twenty years before the action chronicled in the novel, Katharine experienced a loss of love from which she has never recovered. After twenty years of "frugal living upon wreckage," Katharine has remained unhealed—a spiritual death symbolized by her completely white hair. Her life was stalled at the moment she discerned that John loved Maeve, and now for her "[there] is only one time . . . and that is the past time." That she dwells in the past is evidenced by her old-fashioned mode of dress, her maintenance of Congreve House just as it was during her father's lifetime, and her fondness for the town of Hawthorne and its inhabitants with their apparent immunity to change. Despite her serene exterior and carefully maintained stance of ironic detachment, however, Katharine's consciousness is beginning to crack beneath the weight of pain and guilt she bears. She frequently experiences spells of "dislocation," trances that feature the image of the Catherine wheel that is closely related to her memory of the night of her seventeenth birthday party. She even takes the bizarre step of ordering her own tombstone to be engraved with a Catherine wheel, thus foreshadowing (rather too obviously, according to some critics) her own death. Katharine is aware of her own mental unbalance, and her diary-writing is, in fact, an attempt to dispel her demons and thus save herself. Meanwhile, she grows afraid of sullen Andrew, whose adolescent misery she misinterprets as knowledge of her relationship with his father. Katharine enters into that renewed relationship without joy, acknowledging to herself that her feeling of being "in love" with John will cease the moment she achieves her revenge on Maeve. Some critics view Katharine as a disagreeable character whose obsessive hatred, guilt, and self-destructiveness Stafford ultimately condemns. However, others point out that Katharine is sensitive, intelligent, and able to understand the consequences of her refusal to truly engage in life, but she is unable to overcome her inner turmoil.

Undersized, shy **Andrew Shipley** is a dreamy, bookish twelve-year-old who has no friends in Boston, where he spends his winters alienated from his parents and sisters. In his loneliness and frustration, he is typical of other adolescent characters in Stafford's fiction, who are portrayed as struggling to make the transition from childhood to maturity. Andrew's particular isolation is heightened by the rift between him and his beloved Aunt Katharine, who has previously served as a welcome confidante or even second mother to him but who is now preoccupied with her own concerns. Andrew alternates between praying for Charles' recovery and wishing that he would die, either of which solution would return Victor to him. Eventually, however, his hatred for Charles evolves into an obsessive interior chant calling for Charles' death. He becomes convinced that Katharine can somehow hear this chant and that her detached attitude toward him signifies her disapproval. Meanwhile Katharine—who views Andrew with more understanding than he views her—betrays his deep love for her and his need for a supportive friend.

John Shipley, whose loss causes Katharine to freeze her life in place, is portrayed as pointedly unworthy of such a sacrifice. Feckless and bored in his middle age, John begs Katharine to "save him" from his unhappy marriage by running away with him. Katharine's resentment of the "vague, somehow always slightly worried, rather humble, faintly discouraging" **Maeve Shipley**, dates back to when Maeve, as an orphaned cousin raised with Katharine as a sister, briefly enjoyed the preference of Katharine's father. Andrew's sisters **Honor** and **Harriet** are, like other such pairs in Stafford's fiction, silly and shallow, and Andrew feels excluded from the bond they share as twins. The girls adore Katharine and contend that she never married because "no one in the world was good enough for her." Although he is dead by the time the novel takes place, Katharine's father, **Mr. Congreve,** is still present in her veneration of his legacy and efforts to preserve Congreve House as it was when he was alive. Affectionately termed "the Humanist" by his daughter, Congreve bequeathed to her not only the wealth that sustains her physically but the ironic detachment that shields her—as it did him—from full engagement in life. Katharine's father was not only the other person who knew of her heartbreak, but the only man in her life, she finally concludes, who has ever truly loved her.

The town of Hawthorne is populated by a number of odd characters, most of whom idolize Katharine. They include dirty, toothless **Em Bugtown**, epileptic **Jasper**, obese, always-pregnant **Bluebell**, laconic **Peg Duff**, cheerful **Mr. Barker**, and pleasant, wheelchair-bound **Miss Celia Hemingway**. **Beulah Smithwick**, the mother of Andrew's friend **Victor**, is a widow who reads fortunes in cards and tea leaves.

Further Reading

Bawer, Bruce. "Jean Stafford's Triumph." *New Criterion* Vol. 7, no. 3 (November 1988): 61–72.

Contemporary Literary Criticism, Vols. 4, 7, 19, 68. Detroit: Gale Research.

Dictionary of Literary Biography, Vol. 2. Detroit: Gale Research.

Graulich, Melody. "Jean Stafford's Western Childhood: Huck Finn Joins the Camp Fire Girls." *Denver Quarterly* Vol. 18, no. 1 (spring 1983): 39–55.

Hassan, Ihab. "Jean Stafford: The Expense of Style and the Scope of Sensibility." *Western Review* (spring 1955): 185–202.

Hulbert, Ann. *The Interior Castle: The Art and Life of Jean Stafford*. New York: Knopf, 1992.

Mann, Jeanette W. "Toward New Archetypal Forms: Jean Stafford's *The Catherine Wheel*." *Critique: Studies in Modern Fiction* Vol. 17, no. 2 (1975): 77–92.

Ryan, Maureen. *Innocence and Estrangement in the Fiction of Jean Stafford*. Baton Rouge: Louisiana State University Press, 1987.

Walsh, Mary Ellen Williams. *Jean Stafford*. Boston: Twayne, 1985.

White, Barbara. "Initiation, the West, and the Hunt in Jean Stafford's *The Mountain Lion*." *Essays in Literature* Vol. 9, no. 2 (fall 1982): 194–210.

Wallace Stegner

1909–

American novelist, nonfiction writer, short story writer, essayist, editor, and biographer.

Angle of Repose (novel, 1971)

Plot: Narrated by retired history professor Lyman Ward, most of the novel consists of his fictional biography of his grandparents, Oliver and Susan Ward. Confined to a wheelchair because of a debilitating illness, Lyman was earlier abandoned by his wife Ellen. In piecing together (through both the letters Susan Ward wrote to her friend Augusta Drake and his own research and memories) his grandparents' experiences as they struggled to establish themselves in the American West of the 1870s and 1880s, Lyman hopes to make sense of what has happened to him as well.

From its starting point at Zodiac Cottage, Grass Valley, California, in 1970, the novel moves back in time to recount Oliver and Susan's meeting in Brooklyn, New York and their courtship, marriage, and migration to New Almaden, California, where engineer Oliver has secured a job in a mine. Susan is an artist and a writer who contributes to the family's income through the sketches and travelogues she produces during their travels. In New Almaden, the couple's first child, a son named Ollie, is born. They leave New Almaden after Oliver has a dispute with the mine managers over their labor practices, and after an unsuccessful stint with a cement company in Santa Cruz, Susan returns to her parents' home in New York while Oliver works in a mine in Deadwood, South Dakota. One year later, Susan travels to Leadville, Colorado—without Ollie, who is recovering from malaria. Oliver has landed another engineering job, and the couple lives in a ramshackle one-room cabin. Next Oliver receives an assignment to work in Michoacàn, Mexico, but the couple stays there only two months. Susan travels alone again to New York, where she gives birth to a daughter, Elizabeth (called Betsy). She later goes to join Oliver in Idaho, where he is working for a mining and irrigation company that plans to bring water to a large arid region through an innovative canal. The family lives first in Boise, then moves to a rough canyon shack that is eventually replaced by a house. A third child, Agnes, is born there. When the company loses its financial backing, Susan is forced to move to Vancouver with the children while Oliver works in various isolated mines. Some time after the family's return to Idaho, Agnes drowns in the canal when she wanders off during a walk with her mother. This tragedy and other, long-festering tensions cause a rift between Oliver and Susan. Susan takes Ollie and Betsy back to the East Coast, but after depositing Ollie at school she returns to Idaho. She is eventually reconciled with her husband, and the two spend the rest of their lives at Zodiac Cottage, where Lyman (Ollie's son) is raised.

During the course of this reconstruction of his grandparents' lives, Lyman is assisted in his research by young, hippyish Shelly Rasmussen, the daughter of his caretaker, Ada Hawkes, whose aid has allowed him to live alone (over the objections of his son Rodman). As the novel draws to a close, Lyman anticipates Ellen's arrival and wonders if (unlike his grandfather) he can forgive his wife for her wrongdoing and make a new life with her.

Characters: A writer of realistic novels set in the American West, Stegner won the Pulitzer Prize for *Angle of Repose*, which demonstrates his grasp of that region's history, landscape, and culture and his interest in such themes as the connections between art and life, the effect of the past on the present, and relationships between men and women and between parents and children. Another central concern is the quintessentially American conflict between the genteel traditions of the East and the rugged frontier spirit of the West, embodied in the novel by Susan Ward and her husband Oliver.

The novel's narrator, fifty-eight-year-old **Lyman Ward**, is a retired history professor who taught for many years at the Berkeley campus of the University of California, where he won the prestigious Bancroft Award for his research. A degenerative disease necessitated the amputation of one of Lyman's legs just above the knee, and this misfortune was soon followed by the departure of his wife, who left him for the surgeon who had operated on him. Now confined to a wheelchair and living alone in the large old house in which he was raised, Lyman has set himself to the task of sorting through his grandparents' papers with the goal not only of investigating their lives but of understanding his own. Lyman's desire to know "how such unlike particles clung together, and under what strains, rolling downhill into their future until they reached the angle of repose where I knew them" is connected with his need to understand his own wife's betrayal and the complexities of male-female relationships. But he is also interested in the impact of the past on the present (in fact he sees his amputated leg as a metaphor for the modern inclination to be cut off from the past) and in the tension between what he identifies as the female quest for civilization and domesticity and the male hunger for freedom and adventure. Some commentators have found the implacable, pessimistic Lyman too cerebral and self-pitying to be a sympathetic character, and others have suggested that he is, in fact, an unreliable narrator whose views are not necessarily those of his creator. In any case, Lyman's exploration of his grandparents' lives leads him to the conclusion that "wisdom is knowing what you have to accept." At the end of the novel, he has not yet decided whether he can forgive his wife for his betrayal, as his grandfather, he feels, could not.

Stegner based **Susan Burling Ward** on an actual American writer and illustrator, Mary Hallock Foote (1847–1938), whose papers he collected for the Stanford University Library in the 1940s. He has said that his research made him see Foote's husband as the true hero of their story, suggesting that in *Angle of Repose* he sides more with Oliver than with Susan. In any case, critics have praised Stegner for creating in Susan Ward an intriguing, memorable character. The daughter of poor New York Quakers, Susan manages to establish herself as an artist and a friend of such distinguished figures as the poet and editor Thomas Hudson and his wife Augusta. Through Susan's highly descriptive, deeply sentimental letters to Augusta, the reader follows her personal and professional career as she meets and marries Oliver Ward and follows him to various locations across the West. In each place, Susan becomes a popular, indeed revered member of the community and produces an impressive number of sketches, travelogues, and even novels that reproduce for her Eastern audience the places and people she has seen. Wherever she goes, however, Susan continues to train her aspirations and yearnings on the Eastern world of art and upward mobility, never accepting the idea of herself as a Westerner. Described by Lyman as "more lady than woman," Susan brings books, art, and her own personal charm and good manners to the frontier and thus serves as a representative of civilization opposed to the greater freedom her husband embodies. Several critics contend that while Susan's letters make clear her conviction that she is superior to Oliver in refinement and intelligence, they actually reveal him as the better person. At the same time, however, the letters reveal the dilemmas experienced by a nineteenth-century woman with a successful, profitable career outside her home and family. Lyman views his grandparents as opposites who both attracted and resisted each other and who were too much influenced—or even ruined—by their culture's expectations; thus, for example, it could be said that Susan is punished for her relationship with Frank Sargent by the death of her child. Further, some commentators have suggested that Lyman's rather unflattering portrayal of Susan is influenced by his own biases and that the reader must look beneath the surface in order to understand her.

Susan Ward and her husband **Oliver Ward** represent opposite poles: whereas Susan is feminine, romantic, and articulate, Oliver Ward is ruggedly masculine, pragmatic, and taciturn. Terming him "more man than gentleman," Lyman describes his grandfather as a silent but kindly, protective figure whose memory he continues to revere. An ambitious inventor and engineer who is drawn to the West by its myriad of opportunities and openness to anyone willing to try, Oliver is an idealist and a man of integrity who is repeatedly thwarted by the more savvy and ruthless figures around him. Susan repeatedly expresses her frustration with Oliver's mistakes, gullibility, and failure to take advantage of favorable circumstances. Lyman, however, sees his grandfather as a morally superior visionary misunderstood not only by Susan but by a society that would later come to recognize his foresight. Meanwhile, however, the dispirited Oliver takes to drinking binges. After apparently discovering Susan's relationship with Frank and blaming her for the death of their daughter, Oliver becomes estranged from his wife. Although the couple eventually reconciles and seem to maintain their civility and loyalty to each other, Lyman is convinced that Oliver never forgives Susan. However, some critics have offered as contrary evidence the fact that, after methodically pulling up the rose garden that symbolizes the family's happiness in Idaho, he eventually replanted it in Grass Valley. Just as Lyman's portrait of Susan may be shaded by his own biases, it is possible that he does not understand his grandfather as well as he thinks he does.

Stegner also explores relationships between men and women through Lyman and his wife, **Ellen,** who appears only in a dream that occurs near the end of the book. Twenty-six years earlier, Ellen had willingly abandoned her own academic career to marry Lyman and raise their son. Never an enthusiastic participant in activities pursued by other professors' wives, Ellen had been a reader and walker who never complained about her fate. Nevertheless, at what Lyman considers his darkest hour she betrayed him, running off with his own surgeon, who later died in an apparent hiking accident. In Lyman's dream, Ellen arrives at Zodiac Cottage with the intention of reentering his life; in a somewhat comical scene, she and Shelly fight for the right to give him a bath. Lyman knows that eventually Ellen will return and ask for forgiveness, and he wonders how he will respond. Meanwhile, his son **Rodman** also threatens to disrupt his life by forcing him to move to a convalescent home. A confident, good-natured sociologist and Berkeley radical, Rodman contends that Lyman's project is a waste of time—a conclusion due, Lyman feels, to his son's lack of appreciation for the importance of history and its connections to the present.

Lyman's assistant during the writing of his grandparents' biography is **Shelly Rasmussen,** the daughter of his kind, accommodating caretaker **Ada Hawkes,** whose family members have served the Wards for several generations. A college dropout and member of the "hippy" generation of the late 1960s and early 1970s, Shelly is estranged from her freeloading husband (although he eventually entices her to join him in a utopian commune). Shelly gradually grows more intrigued by the story of Susan and Oliver; she contends that since Lyman is "making half of it up" anyway, he should draw the sex scenes more explicitly. In fact, Lyman considers Shelly the voice of the troubling lack of sexual restraint he sees all around him. Braless and ribald, Shelly provides a strong contrast to the well-corseted and modest Susan, thus highlighting what Lyman views as a regrettable decline in standards of behavior.

Characters from the sections of the novel set in the nineteenth century include **Augusta Drake Hudson**, with whom Susan carries on a fifty-year correspondence, and her husband **Thomas Hudson**, a genteel poet and editor whom Susan might herself have married (she actually introduced Augusta to Thomas) and who takes her seriously as an artist, providing her with many assignments and commissions over the course of her career. Born into wealth and constantly surrounded by the most distinguished figures of the day, Augusta leads Susan's ideal life. Lyman muses on the sexual implications of Susan's letters, in which Augusta is addressed quite as a lover might be; he wonders whether this ardent tone is part of the typical Victorian style or implies something more. Another interesting female character is **Mrs. Elliott**, the Wards' friend and neighbor in New Almaden and Santa Cruz and an unconventional feminist who warns Susan that she does not understand her husband and is stifling his aspirations.

The Wards' children include **Ollie**, who at age twelve is sent against his own and his father's wishes to school in the East in order to become a gentlemen and who grows up to be a silent, difficult man, emotionally estranged from his mother; **Elizabeth,** or **Betsy**, a mild, very domestic, and often anxious little girl and adult; and frail **Agnes**, whose sparkling intelligence and artistic bent make her the child who most resembles Susan. Some critics have seen Agnes's drowning death as Susan's punishment for sexual misbehavior; in any case, she, her husband, and their son all seem to blame her for it.

Oliver's assistant and friend **Frank Sargent** makes clear his own sense of responsibility for Agnes' death and general misery when, several days after Agnes's funeral, he kills himself. Susan first meets the handsome, intelligent, and attentive Frank—who is nine years her junior—when she arrives in Leadville, and Frank falls hopelessly in love with her. Frank, deeply troubled by the conflict between his unconquerable feelings for Susan and his loyalty to Oliver, eventually asks Susan to run away with him. Although Lyman never specifies and claims not to know whether Susan and Frank were ever lovers, he surmises that they were saying a private goodbye when Agnes wandered off and fell into the creek. Other characters in the novel include **Pricey**, a sweet-natured, bookish Englishman who works for Oliver until he is savagely beaten and disabled by Oliver's enemies, and Scottish **Nellie**, the Ward children's homely, competent, and devoted governess during their years in Idaho.

Further Reading

Abrahams, William. "The Real Thing." *Atlantic Monthly* Vol. 227, no. 4 (April 1971): 96–7.

Ahearn, Kerry. "Heroes vs. Women: Conflict and Duplicity in Stegner." *Western Humanities Review* (Spring 1977): 125–41.

Burroway, Janet. "Limping Westward." *New Statesman* Vol. 82, no. 2113 (September 17, 1971): 369-70.

Contemporary Literary Criticism Vols. 9, 49. Detroit: Gale Research.

Culligan, Glendy. Review of *Angle of Repose. Saturday Review* (March 20, 1971): 29, 34.

Du Bois, William. "The Last Word: The Well-Made Novel." *New York Times Book Review* (August 29, 1971): 31.

Graulich, Melody. "The Guides to Conduct that a Tradition Offers: Wallace Stegner's *Angle of Repose.*" *South Dakota Review* (Winter 1985): 87–106.

Lewis, Merrill and Lorene. *Wallace Stegner*. Boise, ID: Boise State College, 1972.

Peterson, Audrey C. "Narrative Voice in Stegner's *Angle of Repose.*" *Western American Literature* 10 (Summer 1975): 125–33.

Robinson, Forrest G. and Margaret G. *Wallace Stegner*. Boston: Twayne, 1977.

Amy Tan
1952–
American novelist.

The Joy Luck Club (novel, 1989)

Plot: Set in both pre-World War II China and contemporary San Francisco, the novel comprises sixteen chapters, each narrated by one of four mothers who immigrated to the United States from China or their four American-born daughters. One daughter, Jing-Mei or "June" Woo, opens the book with an account of being invited to take the place of her recently deceased mother, Suyuan Woo, at the weekly meeting of the Joy Luck Club. Suyuan and her three friends have been playing mah-jong together—as well as sharing stories and delicious Chinese food—since 1949. On this evening, the three remaining "aunties" tell June that they have collected enough money to send her to China to meet her two half-sisters. Suyuan was forced to abandon her twin baby daughters during the Japanese invasion of China, when she became extremely ill while trying to flee to find her military officer husband. June agrees to go to China and tell her sisters all about their mother, who died before learning her long-lost babies had survived. Next the story shifts back to China, where An-Mei Hsu lives with her aunt and uncle after her widowed mother disgraced herself by becoming a rich man's "third concubine." Meanwhile, in another part of China, Lindo Jong, betrothed at only two years old, was sent to live with her fiance's family when she was twelve. Married at sixteen, Lindo escapes her unhappy situation by convincing his family that he should divorce her. Ying-Ying St. Clair, the daughter of a wealthy family, tells of an excursion on an opulently appointed barge to see the mysterious Moon Lady perform. The daughters' accounts include those of Waverly Jong, who was a child chess prodigy; half-Caucasian Lena St. Clair, who translated her mother's Chinese for her father; and Rose Hsu Jordan, who remembers the drowning of her youngest brother during a family picnic. June tells of her mother's unsuccessful attempts to fashion her daughter into a prodigy who could compete with the likes of Waverly Jong.

The narrative shifts focus to the daughters' adult lives. Lena describes her marriage to architect Harold, who takes advantage of her passivity and carefully divides all the couple's expenses. Waverly is in love with Rich, an amiable Caucasian man who is, like her, a tax attorney. Although she worries that her mother will not accept Rich as a son-in-law, Lindo surprises her. Rose, in the midst of a divorce from Ted finally summons the courage to thwart his plans for her. June remembers the Chinese New Year's celebration that took place shortly before her mother's death, when she received a jade pendant from Suyuan. Moving further back in time again, An-wei recounts how before her mother's suicide she was brought to live in the house of her mother's wealthy husband, where An-Mei learned of the dismal life and low status of her mother. Ying-Ying describes how she married a brutal man who left her for another woman, then lived for ten years with poor relations, and finally married an American and moved to California. Lindo Jong came to the United States on her own volition, posing as a theology student. She works in a fortune cookie factory until her marriage to a nice Chinese boy. In the final chapter, Jing-Mei travels to China and meets her half-sisters.

Characters: Tan's critically acclaimed and very popular debut novel is a skillful, lyrically written blend of Chinese myths, contemporary situations, humor, and emotional insights. By interweaving stories from the lives of both immigrant Chinese mothers and their American-born daughters, Tan illuminates the nature of generational ties within both cultures and explores the idea that mothers can enrich their daughters' lives by sharing stories about the past. Tan chronicles tensions between the mothers' expectations of obedience and their loving belief in their daughters as well as the struggle of both generations to overcome passivity. Critics praised Tan for successfully capturing both the mothers' fractured English and the daughters' colloquial speech.

Suyuan Woo founded the Joy Luck Club as a refugee in Kweilin while her husband was stationed in Chungking. Deciding it was better to "choose our own happiness" than to worry and despair, she and three friends lifted their spirits by sharing food, stories and laughter at weekly mah jong gatherings. Eventually, however, Suyuan was forced to leave Kweilin and try to reach her husband on foot, carrying all of her possessions and her two babies in a wheelbarrow. Exhausted, sick, and fearful that the Japanese would soon capture her, Suyuan leaves her daughters by the side of the road with a note requesting that they be taken, when it was safe, to her family's home. She never saw the girls again. Her first husband dies in the war and she remarries and moves to San Francisco, where she initiates a new version of the Joy Luck Club. Suyuan secretly continues trying to find her lost twin daughters while living in the United States. A family friend accidentally learns of their existence some time after Suyuan's death.

As a young child, **An-Mei Hsu** endured a painful separation from her mother, who was estranged from her family after becoming a rich man's third concubine (or fourth wife). Her story of seeing her briefly-returned mother attempt to save the life of her dying grandmother by adding a piece of her own flesh to her soup dramatizes the ferocious bond between mothers and daughters of all cultures. An-Mei lives with her mother, where an unpleasant old servant tells her how her mother had been tricked into becoming a concubine. An-Mei's mother eventually dies of an opium overdose, but manages to time her suicide fortuitously, so that her husband would be obligated to provide for his children by her. An-Mei worries about her own daughter's passivity, asserting that while she was "raised the Chinese way: I was taught to desire nothing, to swallow other people's misery, to eat my own bitterness."

Betrothed at two, **Lindo Jong** was forced to leave her own family for the house of her intended husband, whose relatives treated her like a servant and who was himself spoiled and immature. Their marriage is never consummated, and Lindo concocts a clever plan to escape from it: she pretends to have a dream which convinces the family that the marriage is ill-omened and that her husband is destined to marry someone else. Lindo expresses some of the novel's most humorous and poignant sentiments; for example, she laments that "I wanted my children to have the best combination: American circumstances and Chinese character. How could I know these two things do not mix?" and, in response to Waverly's assertion of independence, "How could she be her own person? When did I give her up?" Lindo's narrative passages describe eloquently her relationship with her own mother, her journey to America, and her attempts to instill both obedience and a sense of self-worth.

Ying-Ying St. Clair longs to tell Lena about her own past so that she can somehow pull her troubled daughter "to where she can be saved." Commenting on how both she and Lena seem to be "ghosts" with no will of their own, Ying-Ying says "We are lost, she and I, unseen and not seeing, unheard and not hearing, unknown by others." She attributes her own loss of "chi" or spirit to the abandonment by her first husband, who—after impregnating her with a baby she ultimately aborted—left her for another woman. Brought up in a wealthy family, she lives with poor relatives after this disgrace, brooding on her misfortune for ten years before taking a job in a department store. She meets **Clifford St. Clair**, who finally convinces her to marry him and move to the United States. There she lives in perpetual fear and distrust of her surroundings, and after the stillborn death of her second child she withdraws into a depression that deeply troubles her daughter.

Some commentators have identified **Jing-Mei "June" Woo** as Tan's mouthpiece in the novel, because her circumstances somewhat parallel her creator's (for example, Tan also went to China—albeit in the company of her mother—to meet her two long-lost half-sisters). As a child June always seemed to be overshadowed by her more accomplished friend Waverly, which led to her mother's attempts to make her into prodigy in the realms of beauty, intelligence, and music. These efforts invariably resulted in June's boredom and discontent, however, culminating in a disastrous piano recital. Unlike her mother, June has never believed that she could become whatever she wanted to become, and she has been living a markedly passive existence. Just before her death, however, Suyuan gives her daughter a jade "life's importance" pendant that seems to signify her steadfast belief in June's worth. June's journey to China and touching reunion with her half-sisters ("'Mama, Mama,' we all murmur, as if she is among us") affords her a healing link not only with her dead mother but with her Chinese heritage.

In an apparent attempt to root her in the new land to which her parents had come, **Waverly Jong** was named after the San Francisco street on which the family was living at the time. After a used chess set was given to her brothers at a Christmas party, Waverly discovered within herself a mysterious talent for this game. Playing first with the old men in the park near her home, Waverly won tournament after tournament and eventually became a national chess champion. But her fame and the privileges it brought came to an end when she decided to quit chess in order to spite her mother, whom she accused of trying to take credit for Waverly's accomplishments. When she announced her attention to start playing chess again, Waverly encountered only indifference from her mother, and she soon found that she had lost her old confidence. As an adult, Waverly is a successful tax attorney with a young daughter from an early, failed marriage. She agonizes over her mother's reaction to her Caucasian fiance, **Rich Shields**, but in a confrontation with Lindo learns that she has been imagining problems where none existed.

The childhood of **Lena St. Clair** was marred by her mother's emotional instability and deep fear, which Lena seems to have inherited. Lena was affected by her mother's depression more than her father because she understood the drastic things her mother said in Chinese, which she translated into milder phrases for her father's sake. Lena now lives in a renovated barn with **Harold**, whom she married not so much for love as in gratitude for his attention. He has systematically taken advantage of her passive nature, reaping her sacrificed business benefits of while insisting that they share all expenses "equally."

Rose Hsu Jordan is also struggling with her own passivity as she goes through a divorce from her Caucasian husband **Ted**. She realizes her attraction to Ted as a college student partly because both sets of parents disapproved of the relationship. Rose had always allowed Ted, now a physician, to make all of her choices for her, but he eventually demands that she take responsibility for her own decisions. Indeed, Rose's mother has also told her that she is "without wood"—that she is too liable to bend this way and that to the will of others. Rose changes, however, for she decides not to sign the divorce papers handing her beloved house over to Ted but to fight him for it.

Further Reading

Bestsellers 1989. Vol. 3. Detroit: Gale Research.

Contemporary Literary Criticism. Vol. 59. Detroit: Gale Research.

Dooley, Susan. "Mah-Jongg and the Ladies of the Club." *Book World—Washington Post* (March 5, 1989): 7.

Dorris, Michael. "Mothers and Daughters." *Chicago Tribune—Books* (March 12, 1989): 1, 11.

Koenig, Rhoda. "Heirloom China." *New York Magazine* Vol. 22, no. 12 (March 20, 1989): 82–3.

Miner, Valerie. "The Daughters' Journeys." *Nation* Vol. 248, no. 16 (April 24, 1989): 566–69.

Painter, Charlotte. "In Search of a Voice." *San Francisco Review of Books* (summer 1989): 15–17.

Schell, Orville. "Your Mother Is in Your Bones." *New York Times Book Review* (March 19, 1989): 3, 28.

See, Carolyn. "Drowning in America, Starving for China." *Los Angeles Times Book Review* (March 12, 1989): 1, 11.

Willard, Nancy. "Tiger Spirits." *Women's Review of Books* Vol. 6, nos. 10–11 (July 1989): 12.

Donna Tartt

1964(?)–

American novelist.

The Secret History (novel, 1992)

Plot: The novel's narrator is Richard Papen, a middle-class Californian who wins a scholarship to attend a small, prestigious Vermont college. There he encounters a clique of classics students led by a charismatic professor, Julian Morrow, who allows only a select number of students to study with him. All sophisticated members of the upper class, these students include Henry Winter, who wears old-fashioned round glasses and dark suits; Francis Abernathy, an elegant homosexual, Charles and Camilla Macaulay, extremely attractive twins from the Southern, and Edmund "Bunny" Corcoran, who is just as wealthy but not as cerebral as the others. Initially rejected by Morrow, Richard gains admission into the group through his aptitude for classical Greek. He gradually senses some tension between his new friends and learns that while conducting a session on Dionysian mysticism in the Vermont woods, they killed a farmer who wandered onto the scene. Bunny was not involved in the murder, however, and is now alternately blackmailing the others and threatening to turn them in to the police. Richard's desire to be fully accepted by the group leads him to go along with their subsequent murder of Bunny, whom they push over a cliff. Tensions rise when Charles, who has been incestuously involved with his sister, confronts Henry about his affair with Camilla. Henry shoots Richard, wounding him, then turns the gun on himself. At the end of the novel, Richard reveals that the group's responsibility for the first two murders was never discovered, and that he has since become a college professor.

Characters: Simultaneously a psychological thriller and campus satire, the appearance of *The Secret History* created something of a controversy because of the strenuous promotion conducted by its publisher and the unusually large advance (for a first novel) received by its author. Although some reviewers found the novel pretentious and over-rated, many cited it as proof of Tartt's considerable talent. Marked by elegant, descriptive prose and erudition, *The Secret History* combines suspense and mystery with moral concerns and literary allusions. Through a story that reminded several critics of the 1924 Leopold and Loeb case (in which two wealthy upper-class college students were convicted of murdering a fourteen-year-old boy), Tartt satirizes the self-indulgences of college students while warning of the risks of intellectual arrogance.

The novel's narrator is twenty-year-old **Richard Papen**, a native of Plano, California, who earns a scholarship to tiny, liberal, exclusive Hampden College (reportedly modeled after Tartt's alma mater, Bennington College). Richard's father, like Tartt's, owns a gas station and Richard's mother is a secretary, but in his eagerness to be accepted by a group of students he considers much more sophisticated than himself he suggests that his father is an oil magnate. Although Richard claims to possess only a "mediocre intellect," his aptitude for classical Greek allows him entry into Morrow's exclusive class, to which he has been drawn by his "morbid longing for the picturesque at all costs." Later, his continuing need for acceptance leads to his participation in the murder of Bunny Corcoran and then the coverup of that deed. These events lead to a great deal of mental anguish for Richard, as he ponders whether the murder was "selfish," "evil," or "picturesque" and the extent of his own guilt. At the conclusion of the novel, Richard has reached no positive conclusion, declaring only that "What we did was terrible, but I still don't think any us were bad, exactly." A few critics noted the novel's lack of sexual content and contended that Tartt was not successful in evoking the psyche of a young male. Others compared Richard with Nick Carraway, the narrator in F. Scott Fitzgerald's *The Great Gatsby*, who also serves as the admiring observer and recorder of a more glamorous friend's folly.

While a student at Bennington College, Tartt was a member of a clique of classics students who flocked around an eccentric professor. One of these students was her close friend Paul McGlorin, after whom she reportedly modeled **Henry Winter**. Henry is the leader of a band of bored, scholarly collegians who "shared a certain coolness, a cruel, mannered charm" and devotion to their own erudition and intellectual poses. Brilliant, reserved, and tall, Henry wears dark English suits and carries an umbrella under his arm at all times; he moves with "the self-conscious formality of an old ballerina" and has translated *Paradise Lost* into Latin for his own amusement. Like the modernist poet T. S. Eliot, Henry is a native of St. Louis and even bears the name of Eliot's brother; in fact, critic Amanda Craig describes Henry as a "delicious psychological hybrid of T. S. Eliot and Hannibal Lector." The murder of the farmer during the Dionysian revel in the woods seems to awaken a dark power or depravity in Henry, who observes that he can do anything he wants and that the killing of another human being is after all just a "redistribution of matter." In the end, however, Henry is destroyed by his own arrogant evil, or perhaps he makes a conscious choice to destroy it himself.

Several commentators noted that of the other group members, only **Edmund "Bunny" Corcoran** is a particularly vivid character. His name alludes to the eminent critic Edmund Wilson, whose nickname was also Bunny. Described as a "sloppy blonde boy, rosy-cheeked and gum-chewing, with a relentlessly cheery demeanor," Bunny is a denizen of WASPish, upper-crust Connecticut who often casually sponges off his friends. Vulgar, homophobic, and dyslexic (some critics wondered how, in fact, he could have gained admission to this exclusive group of scholars), Bunny is loud and obnoxious but not really *bad* and certainly not deserving of what happens to him. Thin, elegant, gay **Francis Abernathy,** a native of Boston, lets his friends congregate at the huge house his family owns in the nearby Vermont countryside. A hypochondriac who sports a greatcoat and French cuffs, Francis comments thus on the murder of the farmer: "It's a terrible thing, what we did. I mean, this man was not *Voltaire* we killed. But still. It's a shame. I feel bad about it."

The narrator claims that the blonde, orphaned, Southern twins **Charles** and **Camilla McCauley** are as beautiful as the angels in Flemish paintings. It is eventually revealed that the alcoholic Charles and ethereal, detached Camilla were lovers.

Tartt is said to have based the snobbish, charismatic classics professor **Julian Morrow** on Claude Fredericks, a brilliant, eccentric professor at her own Bennington College and of whose exclusive clique she was herself a member. Morrow was once supposedly an intimate of such literary greats as T. S. Eliot, Ezra Pound, and George Orwell, and he carefully cultivates the image of the suave, worldly aesthete. Described as a "marvelous talker, a magical talker," Morrow is a Svengalian figure who exhorts his students "to sing, to scream, to dance barefoot in the woods in the dead of night," suggesting that it is "terrifying and beautiful . . . to lose control completely." This advice, of course, results in a series of murders and may lead the reader to ponder the extent of Morrow's complicity in what occurs.

Other characters in the novel include the incompetent, foppish, and paranoid French professor **Monsieur Georges Laforgue**, whose name alludes to the French poet Jules Laforgue, who was a major influence on T. S. Eliot; unsophisticated, bulimia-obsessed **Judy Poovey**, who represents the common run of shallow, vulgar college student; and Bunny's parents, **Mr.** and **Mrs. Corcoran**, who exhibit an entertainingly conveyed combination of grief and pretentiousness at their son's funeral.

Further Reading

Allen, Brooke. "Panpipes and Preppies." *New Criterion* Vol. 11, No. 2 (October 1992): 65-8.

Fosburgh, Lacey. "Forbidden and Gothic." *Vogue* 182 (September 1992): 380.

Hajari, Nina. Review of *The Secret History*. *VLS* no. 108 (September 1992): 7.

Kaplan, James. "Smart Tartt." *Vanity Fair* Vol. 55, no. 9 (September 1992): 248, 250–51, 276–78.

Lescaze, Lee. "Groves of Academe Shed Gold and Yawns." *Wall Street Journal* (September 9, 1992): A12.

Star, Alexander. "Less than Hero." *New Republic* Vol. 207, no. 17 (October 19, 1992): 47–9.

Vaill, Amanda. "Beyond Good and Evil." *Book World—Washington Post* (September 13, 1992): 3, 9.

Wood, James. "The Glamour of Glamour." *London Review of Books* Vol. 14, no. 22 (December 19, 1992): 17-18.

Peter Taylor
1917–

American short story writer, novelist, and dramatist.

"The Old Forest" (short story, 1985)

Plot: The story's narrator is Nat Ramsey, a native of Memphis, Tennessee, now in his sixties, who recounts what happened to him in December, 1937. Twenty-three-year-old Nat is engaged to Caroline Braxley, a member, like him, of Memphis' upper class. Despite his engagement, Nat has continued a romantic but innocent friendship with Lee Ann Deehart, a girl from what Nat and his male friends call the "Memphis demimonde." This set comprises a number of fun-loving but respectable, intelligent young women who live independently, work hard, and have no use for the strong links with the past maintained by girls like Caroline. The weekend before his wedding, Nat takes Lee Ann for a ride in his car during which he is involved in a collision. Lee Ann immediately flees from the car and disappears into the nearby forest, thus setting in motion a four-day search by Nat, the police, several newspaper editors, and finally Caroline. It is clear to all that Lee Ann will have to be found and her safety verified if Nat's wedding is to take place. Lee Ann's friends, however, claim no knowledge of her whereabouts, even though Nat receives several telephone calls requesting that he leave Lee Ann alone. After talking to several of Lee Ann's friends, Caroline is ultimately able to locate her at the home of her grandmother, a nightclub owner whose identity Lee Ann had been trying to hide. Lee Ann agrees to notify the police and local newspapers that she is safe. While driving home, Caroline explains to Nat that she had been forced by the binding circumstances of her life to exert what power she had to ensure that their marriage could take place.

Characters: Often identified with the Southern Renaissance or Agrarian Movement initiated during the 1920s and 1930s by such writers as Allen Tate and John Crowe Ransom, Taylor did not gain widespread critical attention until the publication of *The Old Forest and Other Stories* in the mid-1980s. This volume, which received the PEN/Faulkner Award for Fiction, collects stories drawn from Taylor's fifty-year career. "The Old Forest" is cited as a particularly successful example of Taylor's skill in the short story genre. Marked by his characteristic leisurely, ruminative style and his exclusive focus on upper-middle-class residents of the upper South, post-1930, the story explores the extent to which people are bound to and formed by the particular region, class, and family into which they are born.

The story's narrator is **Nat Ramsey**, who muses about an incident from his earlier life from the perspective of advanced age and with a deeper perception than he was able to apply at the age of twenty-three. At the time that the story takes place, Nat has graduated from college and returned to Memphis to live with his parents and take up the position in his father's cotton brokering business that he has always been expected to assume. From the viewpoint of their social set, Nat's fiancee is perfectly suitable for him, and he seems to view Caroline with a great deal of respect and affection. The fact that Nat has nevertheless maintained his ties with the "Memphis demimonde"—the young women whom he and his friends accompany to seedy nightclubs but would not consider marrying—perhaps suggests a subconscious yearning for a different kind of life than that ordained for him, as does his continuing to study Latin even though his parents (and even Caroline) consider it an eccentricity. The older Nat asserts that the strange four days his younger self spent waiting for some indication that Lee Ann was safe were among the most significant in his life, even if at that age he was unequipped to meet the challenge they represented. For the first time in his life, Nat is allowed a glimpse into a world entirely different from his own and people whose existences he cannot possibly fathom, particularly since he is still ignorant of "the binding and molding effect upon people of the circumstances in which they are born." Nat essentially declines this educative glimpse, particularly when he chooses to stay in the car while Caroline goes into Lee Ann's grandmother's home to talk to the girl about her disappearance. Although Nat strongly suggests that he really wanted to—and perhaps should have—married Lee Ann, Caroline proves an ideal partner not only in her efforts to resolve the problem of Lee Ann but in her later support of Nat's decision to change the course of his life and become a college professor. Nat takes this new course when he is thirty-seven and depressed about his shallow, meaningless existence—a depression he knew nothing about at twenty-three but which Lee Ann had known even then.

Memphis debutante **Caroline Braxley** has been called one of Taylor's most memorable characters. Tall, slender, and attractive, Caroline carries herself with a dignified bearing that reflects her awareness of her social role. One of those young women who frequent the Memphis Country Club and marry appropriate young men like Nat Ramsey, Caroline considers herself an "heir to something ... old country manners and old country connections." Thus she contrasts strongly with "city girls" like Lee Ann, who have no particular ties to the past or preordained roles to play. Nat is surprised by the calm reaction of capable, sensible Caroline to the news that he was with another woman when the accident occurred, and he is impressed by her success in finally resolving the mystery of Lee Ann's disappearance. It is only as the couple is returning from the meeting with Lee Ann that Caroline gives Nat an idea of what she has suffered and how she views her own actions. She tells him that she envies Lee Ann and her friends the freedom with which they have shaped their own lives, escaped from the world's censorious eyes, and broken with the past, as well as their mutual enjoyment of life and protection of each other. Caroline understands, however, that her own circumstances require her to take the course that is best for her: marriage to Nat. To that end she exerts the only power she has, for power, she tells Nat, "is what everybody must have some of if he—or she—is to survive in any kind of world. I have to protect and use whatever strength I have." This strength involves employing her considerable psychological skills to locate Lee Ann and convince her to publicly establish her well-being. Later in life, Caroline will again dedicate "her pride of power to the power of freedom [Nat] sought" when she supports his decision to radically change the course of their lives. Critics lauded Taylor for rendering as heroic a character whom readers might otherwise have dismissed as a shallow debutante.

The female character with whom readers might initially be more inclined to sympathize is the lower-class **Lee Ann Deehart**, a representative of the Memphis "city girls" with their good looks, intelligence, independence, and basic decency. Nat has carried on for some time an admittedly romantic, though not sexual, relationship with Lee Ann, whom he speculates may be the girl he should marry. Lee Ann is pretty, petite, and fair-haired, with hazel eyes, a soft, slightly husky voice, and a lively though level-headed personality; Nat describes her as a little more self-possessed than her friends. Supposedly a native of Texas who has never divulged to Nat or his friends anything about her true origins, Lee Ann finally shares the truth with Caroline. Abandoned by her mother—a very successful businesswoman who had no interest in raising a child but who sent money to pay for her daughter's education—Lee Ann was raised by her grandmother, who turns out to be the same physically repellent woman Nat had earlier described as running a nightclub called The Cellar. Lee Ann's panicked escape after the accident was motivated by her fear that her grandmother's identity might be exposed, but after several days of hiding she decided to move back into her old home and stop fleeing her past. Thus Lee Ann's flight into the dark, primeval forest might be said to symbolize her return to her origins in a world that Nat (at least at this point in his life) could not fathom.

Taylor devotes a significant portion of the story to describing the members of what Nat and his friends have snobbishly termed the "Memphis demimonde." These daughters of lower-class or otherwise socially insignificant families have come to the city to live and work independently; they tend to be good-looking and moderately or considerably intelligent and culturally aware, and they are sexually liberated though not promiscuous (they sleep only with men with whom they are in love, and rarely with the younger, wealthy boys they accompany to nightclubs). Although they are viewed with paternalistic indulgence by the older men of Memphis, the "city girls" can protect themselves and each other quite adequately, as they prove when they close ranks to keep Lee Ann's location a secret. Representatives of this set include the frank **Nancy Minnifree**, a secretary at a farm implements warehouse who makes derisive jokes about Nat and his friends; **Lucy Phelan** and **Betsy Morehouse**, who exasperate Caroline by first denying that they ever met her (she distinctly remembers meeting them at a nightclub Nat once took her to) and then that they know where Lee Ann is; and Fern Morris, with whom Nat once had a relationship he describes as "not innocent" and who gives Caroline the clue that helps her find Lee Ann.

A Summons to Memphis (novel, 1986)

Plot: The novel is narrated by Phillip Carver, an editor and rare book collector in his fifties who long ago moved away from his home town of Memphis, Tennessee, to New York City. Structured as a kind of notebook in which Phillip ruminates about both the past and the present, the novel begins with his account of receiving separate phone calls from his sisters, Betsy and Josephine, both unmarried, successful, somewhat eccentric real estate agents who have never left Memphis. The two women want Phillip to come home to help them with their widowed father, eighty-one-year-old George Carver, who has announced his intention to marry again. With much trepidation, Phillip makes the trip to Memphis—a journey that stirs his memories of the past and particularly of the effect of his father's actions on the rest of the family. When his children were teenagers, George was bilked by his business partner and best friend, Lewis Shackleford, and subsequently decided to move his family from old-fashioned Nashville to modern, rather brash Memphis. The move proved traumatic for everyone: Mrs. Carver retreated into invalidism, Betsy and Josephine lost their Nashville beaus and acquired no new ones, older brother Georgie chose escape by signing up to fight (and then die) in World War II, and Phillip suffered from feelings of dislocation and, eventually, resentment after his father thwarted his plan to marry the Chattanooga girl he loved. Although he is aware that his sisters intend to circumvent their father's plan, Phillip experiences a moment of sympathy for him when George picks him up at the airport and asks Philip to serve as his best man at the wedding. Arriving at the church, however, the two men learn that George's intended bride has left town, probably because of some machinations on the part of his daughters. Phillip returns to Manhattan and is reconciled with his companion, Holly Kaplan, a somewhat younger woman from Cleveland, Ohio, with her own family problems, who had previously moved out of their shared apartment. Several years later, Phillip is again summoned by his sisters, this time to help them prevent their father from making an extended visit to Lewis Shackleford, with whom he has recently reconciled. Phillip duly goes to Memphis, this time seemingly in agreement with his sisters, but Shackleford's sudden death makes their interference unnecessary. It is not long after this that George dies, as does Holly's father. Phillip and Holly settle back into their quiet life together, and Phillip speculates that some day this serene pair will simply fade away.

Characters: Long a distinguished writer of short stories, Taylor did not achieve widespread critical acclaim until the mid-1980s. Taylor received the Pulitzer Prize for *A Summons to Memphis*, his first novel, which features his much-admired, ruminative, understated prose style and his exploration of the effects of change on both the society of the upper south and the members of an uprooted family. The novel's themes include the difficulties and ambiguities of familial relations and the coexistent resilience and resistance of the human personality in the face of disorder and change. Although some critics faulted the narrative as repetitive, many admired the closely observed details that create a rich if ultimately inconclusive portrait of the people, places, and situations described.

The novel's narrator is **Phillip Carver**, a forty-nine-year-old editor and rare book collector who records in what he describes as "very irregular notebooks" an account of his relations with his family that shifts from his childhood in the 1930s and 1940s to the present (the 1960s). Phillip's contemplative tone and close attention to detail and nuance reflect not only his intelligence and desire to understand what has happened to him but a certain detachment and an emotional passivity. He admits that he lives a life of limited expectations, sharing a home with the similarly detached Holly Kaplan, far from the city and people who so influenced his early years. Several critics contend that Taylor's portrait of this effete, ruminative bachelor is intentionally ambiguous—that the reader must decide for himself whether Phillip is a sympathetic figure or an unreliable narrator who ultimately exposes his own insecurity and weakness. Although some readers may feel that the grudge Phillip has long harbored against his father is justified, others may conclude that he is himself responsible for what he has made of his life, for he has neither let go of the past nor embraced the future. Phillip is unable to unravel the mysteries of personality and experience—his own and his family's—that he has probed, so the novel ends inconclusively; in an interview, Taylor commented that he intended the novel to ask, "How successful are we ever in understanding what has happened to us?" Just as Taylor's characterization of Phillip may or may not be ironic, the novel's ending may be interpreted either positively or negatively. Some commentators feel that Phillip has gained at least a measure of compassion and a heightened awareness of life's complexity, while others assert that the serene future he contemplates is hopelessly barren and that his delusions about the past remain intact.

Phillip describes his father, **George Carver**, as a formidable figure whose actions irrevocably altered his children's lives. Carver is presented as an embodiment of the traditional southern society into which he was born: handsome, always impeccably dressed, and successful in his legal profession, he radiates integrity and gentility. Phillip's account of what happens after the Carvers move from Nashville to Memphis casts his father, if not as an outright villain, as a self-absorbed, autocratic figure who not only overlooked his family's suffering but blighted their futures through his desire to control them. Yet if Phillip is an unreliable narrator, it follows that the portrait he draws of his father may not be accurate. Indeed, some commentators contend that Carver's children may be blaming him for what actually resulted from their own weaknesses, and that their motives in thwarting his plans to marry and to visit Lewis Shackleford are suspect. Thus Carver may be viewed as either powerful and manipulative or as merely more adaptable than his children; in his old age, he does seem to retain both the hope for the future and the capacity for forgiveness that they lack.

Phillip views his sisters, **Betsy** and **Josephine Carver**, as "frozen forever in their roles as injured adolescents" (a description that, some critics assert, could also be applied to him). Once pretty young girls with plenty of beaus, neither ever married, supposedly because their father destroyed their prospects (either directly or by moving the family to Memphis, where it was impossible for the girls to be presented as debutantes). They reacted to their circumstances first by becoming known as those raucous "Nashville girls," and then by establishing themselves as successful real estate agents with separate, independent households. Several commentators have noted that Phillip's unflattering characterization of his middle-aged sisters, with their highly inappropriate clothing and behavior and their attempts to control and perhaps wreak revenge on their father, may reflect his desire to establish his own superiority. In any case, they seem to share his outlook of limited expectations, whether this is due—as in Phillip's case—to their father's manipulations or to their own inability to adapt to change.

Before the family's move to Memphis, Phillip's mother **Minta Carver** was a lively, witty woman actively engaged with life. Although she wept when she left her old, familiar home, Mrs. Carver initially seemed to enjoy her new life in freer, more casual Memphis. Phillip contends, however, that his father's desire that the family continue to live a Nashville-style existence rather than acquire Memphis ways resulted in his mother's decline into thirty years of invalidism. Her ailments were apparently more imagined than real, a manifestation of the inadaptability that also plagued the rest of the family. Phillip's older brother **Georgie** is only sketchily portrayed; he seems to have reacted to the family's distress by volunteering for combat in World War II, and Phillip suggests that his subsequent death at Normandy on D Day was in part self-willed.

Of the romantic interests Phillip mentions, **Clara Price** is apparently the only one he truly loved. A nice, intelligent girl from Chattanooga, Clara failed to win the approval of Phillip's father, who managed to intervene in the engagement so that Clara was sent away and the young people never saw each other again. Some critics have complained that George Carver's reasons for sabotaging the romance are not adequately explained. Phillip's relationship with **Holly Kaplan** is a much different affair that seems to be based more on mutual comfort than on passion. Fifteen years younger than Phillip, Holly comes from a prosperous, Jewish family that has what she calls "a real life"—the kind of contentious, colorful existence that she does not and never will have. Phillip comments that complaints about and detachment from their families compose the couple's central bond. Like Phillip, Holly is forced to confront the complexities of familial relations when she journeys back to Cleveland for her father's funeral. Near the end of the novel, Holly tells Phillip that they must forgive their parents their selfishness and cruelties because these are what make them "whole human beings and not . . . merely guardian robots of the young," an observation that, according to some commentators, expresses a central theme of *A Summons to Memphis*.

The man who precipitated the Carvers' move to Memphis is **Lewis Shackleford**, a representative of the new business world of the south who nevertheless admires the traditional gentility embodied by his friend George Carver. Shackleford was a trusted legal client of Carver whose shady "manipulation of municipal bonds" nearly ruined him financially. Enraged and humiliated, Carver refused to remain in Nashville, and he did not speak to Shackleford for nearly forty years, after which period the two men—following a chance encounter and much to the shocked dismay of Carver's children—renewed their friendship. Taylor reportedly modeled Shackleford after Rogers Caldwell, a southern investment banker whose financial empire collapsed in 1930 but who managed to regain his stature several decades later. A significant character from the Carver's Memphis life is **Alex Mercer**, Phillip's boyhood friend and a longtime admirer of George Carver whose phone calls alerting Phillip to his sister's intentions to intervene in their father's plans help to convince Phillip to go to Memphis. In his attentions to and concern for George, Alex might be said to act out the role of the devoted son that Phillip long ago rejected. Ironically, Phillip's condescending description of Alex and his wife as being "settled—a little smug and a little disappointed—at their fireside" could well be applied to his own bleak life with Holly.

Other characters in *A Summons to Memphis* include **Mrs. Clara Stockwell**, the "respectable but undistinguished and schoolteacherish woman" George Carver intends to marry, who ultimately leaves him a note informing him that she has decided their marriage would not be happy and that he should consider his children's needs first.

Further Reading

Contemporary Literary Criticism Vols. 1, 4, 18, 37, 44, 50, 71. Detroit: Gale Research.

D'Evelyn, Thomas. "Going Home Again and Again." *Christian Science Monitor* (October 1, 1986): 21–2.

Gray, Paul. "Codes of Honor." *Time* Vol. 125, no. 5 (February 4, 1985): 74.

Griffith, Albert J. *Peter Taylor*, rev. ed. Boston, MA: Twayne, 1990.

Hulbert, Ann. "Back to the Future." *New Republic* Vol. 195, no. 21 (November 24, 1986): 37–40.

Kakutani, Michiko. Review of *A Summons to Memphis*. *New York Times* (September 24, 1986): C23.

Lindsay, Creighton. "Phillip Carver's Ethical Appeal in Peter Taylor's *A Summons to Memphis.*" *Mississippi Quarterly* 167–81.

Miller, Karl. "Memphis Blues." *London Review of Books* Vol. 7, no. 15 (September 5, 1985): 15.

Rae, John. "A Thousand Accidents." *Listener* Vol. 114, no. 2920 (August 1, 1985): 29–30.

Robinson, Marilynne. "The Family Game Was Revenge." *New York Times Book Review* (October 19, 1986): 1, 52–3.

Robison, James Curry, ed. *Peter Taylor: A Study of the Short Fiction.* Boston, MA: Twayne, 1988.

Sullivan, Walter. "The Last Agrarian: Peter Taylor Early and Late." *Sewanee Review* Vol. 95, no. 2 (Spring 1987): 308–17.

Towers, Robert. "Ways Down South." *New York Review of Books* (September 25, 1986): 55–7.

Updike, John. "Summonses, Indictments, Extenuating Circumstances." *New Yorker* Vol. 62, no. 37 (November 3, 1986): 158, 161–65.

Yardley, Jonathan. "Peter Taylor's Novel of Fathers and Sons." *Book World—Washington Post* (September 14, 1986): 3.

Steve Tesich
1943?–
American dramatist, scriptwriter, and novelist.

The Speed of Darkness (play, 1991)

Plot: The play opens on a tranquil domestic scene as Joe, a successful businessman who has just been chosen as South Dakota's "Man of the Year," and his wife Anne wait for their teenaged daughter Mary to return from a date. The play's sometime narrator, a neighborhood boy and future sweetheart of Mary's named Eddie, warns the audience that this idyllic home will soon be the setting for tragedy. The arrival of Lou, with whom Joe fought twenty years earlier during the Vietnam War, sets this prediction in motion. Whereas Joe has achieved success, Lou is now an unkempt, homeless, slightly addled figure who follows a model of the Vietnam Veteran's Memorial as it travels around the country. Lou now reminds Joe of the part the two once played in the disposal—soon after their return from Vietnam, when both were embittered garbage collectors—in pouring toxic waste into some nearby ravines. Joe has recently opposed the development of these sites, ostensibly out of concern for the environment, and has not disclosed his knowledge of the dangerous materials hidden there. At the same time, it is revealed that Mary is not really Joe's daughter, since an encounter with chemical weapons during the war rendered both him and Lou sterile; in fact, Mary is the result of her mother's former promiscuity. The troubled Lou finally commits suicide, prompting Joe to admit to his role in the cover-up. He does so at a community meeting, after which he and his family are banished from the community.

Characters: A native of Yugoslavia who moved to the United States when he was fourteen, Tesich is an accomplished dramatist who works in a variety of styles, often examining the intricacies of personal and societal relationships. With its emphasis on the continuing legacy of the Vietnam War, the environment, and the American family, *The Speed of Darkness* evidences Tesich's customary concern with moral issues. Several critics have noted the influence of nineteenth-century playwright Henrik Ibsen, who also grappled with moral, familial, and societal problems. Tesich was lauded for creating a suspenseful drama that also contains elements of tragedy and particularly asserts the necessity of confronting and overcoming the guilt engendered by America's involvement in the Vietnam War.

As the play begins, wealthy contractor **Joe** is enjoying the distinction of having been voted South Dakota's Man of the Year. He is presented as a hero of the Vietnam War, a self-made businessman, and a devoted husband and father. Soon, however, the audience learns that Joe is harboring several dark secrets. It is fitting that Joe got his start in post-war, civilian life working as a garbage remover, for garbage is used as a metaphor both for the personal misdeeds and the national shame that, Tesich implies, must be squarely faced. Eventually Joe does accept the guilt he must bear for his role in polluting the environment, even if (like Dr. Thomas Stockmann in Ibsen's *An Enemy of the People*) his public admission leads to castigation.

Joe's old friend and war companion **Lou** is a member of America's homeless population whose decline was a result of the physical and emotional harm he suffered due to his involvement in the Vietnam War. Disreputable, at least partially disturbed, and dressed in dirty, shabby clothes, Lou is nevertheless a somewhat appealing character whose street-corner philosophizing can be eloquent and moving. Lou spends his days following a model of the Vietnam Veteran's Memorial—the dramatic black wall inscribed with the names of those killed in the war—around the country. He once tried to carve his own name on the wall and was told it was restricted to those who had died; he feels this is unfair, since he considers himself dead, and he contends that the war's survivors deserve their own memorial as so many of them are MIA (Missing in America). A character whose function is to remind Joe of the evil done in the past in order to try to rectify it, Lou finally commits suicide, thus registering for both Joe and the audience the depth of pain such evil can inflict.

In her patience and frustration, Joe's wife **Anne** has been compared to such Ibsen characters as Mrs. Stockmann in *An Enemy of the People* or Gina Ekdal in *The Wild Duck*. Currently a devoted mother and upstanding member of her community, Anne once lived a much different kind of life, during which she became pregnant with Mary. Raised as if Joe were her real father, **Mary** is an ordinary, confused high school student whose attention to a mock baby has led reviewers to compare her to Ibsen's adolescent Hedvig Werle, who dotes on her pet wild duck. Mary's friend **Eddie** serves as a kind of Greek chorus, informing the audience, for example, that "Love was spilled on the floor of this house" and promising tragedy to come. Some commentators found this character colorless or unconvincingly wise.

Further Reading

Barnes, Clive. "'Darkness' before Dawn for B'way?" *New York Post* (1 March 1991).

Contemporary Literary Criticism, Vols. 40, 69. Detroit: Gale Research.

Kissel, Howard. "Full 'Speed' Ahead for New Tesich Play." *Daily News* (1 March 1991).

Queenan, Joe. "Stage Left." *American Spectator* 24, No. 5 (May 1991): 41-2.

Rich, Frank. "Turning Back the Clock for Nation and a Family." *New York Times* (March 1, 1991): C1, C3.

Simon, John. "Herstories." *New York* 24, No. 10 (March 11, 1991): 90-1, 93.

Weales, Gerald. "Beyond the Mesa." *Commonweal* CXVIII, No. 8 (April 19, 1991): 261.

D. M. Thomas

1935–

British novelist, poet, translator, editor, and critic.

The White Hotel (novel, 1981)

Plot: Composed of a prologue and six sections, *The White Hotel* employs a variety of literary forms. The main characters are the celebrated psychoanalyst and theorist Sigmund Freud and Lisa Erdman, a twenty-nine-year-old, half-Jewish Viennese opera singer who comes to Freud for treatment of hysteria in 1919. In one of the letters that form the prologue, Freud tells a colleague about an erotic poem written by Lisa in which images of sex and death are closely intertwined. The poem seems to reinforce the validity of Freud's theory that the human death instinct may be as strong as the libido. The prologue is followed by the poem itself, which relates in graphic language and imagery Lisa's imagined sexual encounters with a young man (whom she identifies as Freud's son) during a short stay in a white resort hotel. As Lisa repeatedly couples with her lover and a variety of other people, a series of horrifying disasters occur around her, including a fire in the hotel and the collapse of a ski lift. The next section is a prose account of this same fantasy, followed by Freud's analysis of Lisa's case; he concludes that the white hotel represents Lisa's longing to return to the womb. Her symptoms eased, Lisa resumes her career, eventually marrying a widowed, Jewish opera singer with a young son. She moves to Kiev, where, during the Stalinist purges of the late 1930s, her husband disappears. In 1941, Lisa and her stepson are brutally murdered in the Nazi massacre of 250,000 Jews at Babi Yar. The novel's final, dream sequence relates Lisa's journey by train to a paradise that is apparently Palestine, where she is reunited with many of her lost friends and family members.

Characters: To the surprise of many (albeit admiring) critics, this complex, ambitious novel became a bestseller soon after its American publication in 1981. Some commentators faulted the novel as sensationalistic in its representations of sex and violence, and critics differed on whether its ultimate message is one of tragedy or redemption. Most, however, lauded Thomas for his mastery of several literary forms (including letters, poetry, and analytic prose as well as straight narrative), his effective use of symbolism, and his precise, inventive prose. Thomas exhibits in *The White Hotel* the obsession with love and death that is evident in his earlier work. The novel treats such contemporary issues as psychoanalysis, female sexuality, the Holocaust, and the parallels between individual experience and collective history. According to critic Edith Milton, *The White Hotel* offers an ''apocalyptic vision of the eternal destruction and resurrection of the human spirit.''

Thomas's portrayal of **Lisa Erdman**, the novel's central character, is an imaginative reconstruction of two of Freud's actual case studies of patients he called ''Anna O.'' and ''Dora.'' Lisa seeks treatment from Freud for a mysterious malady that her doctors believe may be psychosomatic. A Viennese opera singer of only modest professional distinction, Lisa suffers from pain in her left breast and abdomen, shortness of breath, and anorexia, none of which can be traced to any organic cause. Although she has been unable to enjoy sex with her husband, Lisa is subject to highly erotic fantasies. Her imagined adventure in the white hotel of the novel's title, related in both poetic and narrative forms, features intertwined, vividly described images of sexual ecstasy and violent death: The other hotel residents meet gruesome deaths while Lisa engages in a variety of sexual encounters. The daughter of a Russian-Jewish father and a Polish-Catholic mother, Lisa once had a love affair with a Russian anarchist; her subsequent marriage to an Austrian anti-Semite was a failure. Freud delves even deeper into Lisa's past, however, to uncover the root of her hysteria: as a child she inadvertently witnessed a sexual encounter between her mother, aunt, and uncle, and when her mother and uncle were later killed in a hotel fire, she began to subconsciously connect sex and death. The white hotel, Freud contends, represents Lisa's longing for the security of her mother's womb, where sin does not exist; his further assertion that she has repressed her lesbian nature is rejected by Lisa. Having attained the "common unhappiness" that Freud admits is the most he can help her achieve, Lisa goes on to live a fairly normal life. She takes a sick friend's place in a production of the opera "Eugene Onegin," and after the other singer dies Lisa marries her widower. Given the choice of moving either to the safety of the United States or to Kiev, Lisa chooses Kiev, where she eventually loses her husband to one of Stalin's purges. Tricked by the Nazis into taking her Jewish stepson to the train station at Babi Yar for supposed safe removal to Palestine, Lisa and Kolya are both slaughtered there. Her death is a gruesome fulfillment of her earlier symptoms, for she is kicked in the left breast by one Nazi soldier and raped with a bayonet by another; this circumstance verifies the second sight with which Lisa had previously been credited—even by the highly rational Freud. Although some critics found Lisa too shallow to make her a convincing character, others contended that her ordinariness and unreflecting nature lend her a universality that adds to the novel's impact. Commentators have also differed about the meaning of the novel's final sequence, in which Lisa reaches Palestine safely and is reunited and reconciled with all the most important people in her life. Thomas may be presenting this scene as an impossible though universally longed-for dream or as evidence that redemption is attainable only through love.

Although Thomas's portrayal of **Sigmund Freud** is essentially imagined, most critics praised him for the authenticity with which he renders this character's personality, speech, and writings. Freud is depicted as human and appealing, a kindly, tolerant, insightful figure whose heroism is balanced by vulnerability. The novel begins just after the end of World War I, a time when Freud's brilliance had been universally acknowledged and his private practice was expanding. As he explains in a letter to a colleague, Lisa's case seems to strengthen his suspicion that there is a "death instinct, as powerful in its own way (though more hidden) as the libido." After analyzing both Lisa's elaborate erotic fantasy and her personal history, Freud concludes that her hysteria is rooted both in having seen her mother, aunt, and uncle making love and in repressed homosexuality. In the end, Freud reflects that he can cure Lisa of "everything but life," thus acknowledging that despite his faith in the inherent rationality of psychoanalysis it cannot provide a complete solution. Thomas manages to convey a profound respect for Freud's mastery while suggesting that the deepest mysteries of human nature may still resist penetration.

Further Reading

Ableman, Paul. "Major Talent." *Spectator* (January 17, 1981): 21.

Concise Dictionary of British Literary Biography: 1960 to the Present Vol. 8. Detroit: Gale Research.

Contemporary Literary Criticism Vols. 13, 22, 31. Detroit: Gale Research.

Duchene, Anne. "Feeding the Heart on Freud." *Times Literary Supplement* no. 4059 (January 16, 1981): 50.

Epstein, Leslie. "A Novel of Neurosis and History." *New York Times Book Review* (March 5, 1981): 1, 26–7.

Flanagan, Thomas. "To Babi Yar and Beyond." *Nation* (May 2, 1981): 537–39.

Levine, George. "No Reservations." *New York Review of Books* (May 28, 1981): 20–3.

McPherson, William. "The Pleasure Principle, and Beyond." *Book World—Washington Post* (March 15, 1981): 1–3.

Milton, Edith. "Grand Hotel." *New York* Vol. 14, no. 11 (March 16, 1981): 50.

Press, David P. Review of *The White Hotel*. *North American Review* (September–October 1981): 16.

Sauerberg, Lars Ole. "When the Soul Takes Wing: D. M. Thomas's *The White Hotel*." *Critique* (Fall 1989): 3–10.

Simonds, Peggy Munoz. "*The White Hotel*: A Sexual Satire." *Critique* (Fall 1985): 51–63.

Slung, Michele. "A Freudian Journey." *New Republic* (March 28, 1981): 35–7.

Thompson, Thomas H. "Carnal Innocence, Sinful Indulgence." *North American Review* (December 1981): 67–72.

John Kennedy Toole
1937–1969
American novelist.

A Confederacy of Duncan (novel, 1980)

A Confederacy of Duces (novel, 1980)

Plot: The novel takes place in 1960s New Orleans, where an obese, egocentric thirty-year-old Ignatius J. Reilly lives with his mother. Ignatius has earned a master's degree but (quite accurately) considers himself unfit for conventional employment; instead, he spends his time eating, taking baths, going to the movies, and writing a chronicle of his life that he calls "a lengthy indictment of our century." Despite his propensity for Dr. Nut soda and watching *American Bandstand* on television, Ignatius claims to prefer the medieval period to the modern age, which he finds lacking in "taste and decency." When long-suffering Mrs. Reilly finally demands that Ignatius seek employment, he finds a job as a file clerk at Levy Pants, a clothing manufacturer. The company's innocuous office manager, Mr. Gonzales, gratefully hires Ignatius even though he constantly talks about a capricious "valve" that rules over his digestive system. Ignatius's only co-worker is Miss Trixie, an octogenarian who would have retired long ago except for the owner's wife, Mrs. Levy, an amateur psychologist, insisting such a change would make the old lady feel unwanted. Eager to show up his formal girlfriend, social activist Myrna Minkoff, Ignatius initiates some reforms at Levy Pants. His efforts culminate in the "Crusade for Moorish Dignity," an uprising by the all-black factory staff that ends disastrously. Ignatius is fired, and he eventually finds another job as a hotdog salesman for Paradise Vendors. Dressed in a ludicrous pirate costume, Ignatius eats more hotdogs than he sells. Next Ignatius tries to promote world peace through a "Save the World through Degeneracy" movement (based on infiltrating the military with homosexuals), but this venture is also unsuccessful. Meanwhile, Mrs. Reilly becomes increasingly disgusted with her lazy, tyrannical son. Encouraged by her new fiance, Claude Robichaux, an old man who suspects everyone of being a "communiss," she plans to commit Ignatius to a psychiatric institution. At the last minute, however, Myrna arrives and spirits the grateful Ignatius away from New Orleans.

Characters: Published to resounding critical acclaim in 1981, *A Confederacy of Dunces* was actually written in the early 1960s. Toole's early efforts to get the novel published were unsuccessful, and he committed suicide in 1969 at the age of thirty-two. Due to the efforts of Toole's dedicated mother, who persuaded renowned author Walker Percy to read her dead son's manuscript, the novel finally appeared, and Toole was posthumously awarded the

Pulitzer Prize for Fiction. Called a "gargantuan tumultuous human tragicomedy" by Percy in his foreword to the book, *A Confederacy of Dunces* is considered a comic masterpiece that features one of the most memorable protagonists in literature. Although this satire of Ignatius Reilly and the modern society he detests is so hilarious that many readers laugh aloud while reading it, it also contains an undercurrent of pessimism or even despair that heightens its impact. Toole has been highly lauded for his vivid portrait of 1960s New Orleans—illuminating not only the inhabitants and physical characteristics but some of the social and racial problems of this southern city—and for his cast of very funny, very human characters whose dialects are expertly rendered. The novel takes its title from a quote by eighteenth-century satirist Jonathan Swift: "When a true genius appears in this world, you may know him by this sign, that the dunces are all in confederacy against him." Not surprisingly, Toole's novel has been likened to Swift's work for its deep humor and incisive social commentary.

The central figure in *A Confederacy of Dunces* is **Ignatius J. Reilly,** an obese, flatulent, cantankerous thirty-two-year-old who constantly berates and tyrannizes the devoted mother who supports him. Ignatius speaks in a pretentiously erudite manner, which contrasts strongly with the ordinary speech of those around him. Although he spent eight years in college (thanks to his mother's patronage) and has a master's degree, Ignatius is unemployed when the novel begins. He once held a teaching position, but he treated his students with such lofty disdain that they eventually staged a demonstration against him. Ignatius spends his time eating doughnuts, drinking his favorite soft drink, Dr. Nut, going to movies (during which he shouts insults against the actors), and making only minor progress on his magnum opus, in which he plans to condemn the modern age for its lack of "taste and decency." A devotee of the medieval period, Ignatius particularly reveres Boethius, the author of *Consolation of Philosophy* who was imprisoned for his beliefs; Ignatius identifies with his hero's alienation from society. At the center of his philosophical outlook is a concept of fate, or Fortuna, as a wheel that brings bad or good circumstances into one's life in cycles and which cannot be controlled, only endured. While *A Confederacy of Dunces* satirizes many aspects of contemporary life, it also satirizes its hypocritical protagonist, who lashes out at modernity and popular culture while stuffing himself with junk food and obsessively watching *American Bandstand* and second-rate movies. Attired in baggy tweed pants, a flannel shirt, and a comical green hunting cap with ear flaps that supposedly protect him from catching cold, Ignatius—a virgin despite Myrna's efforts to deflower him—is both sexually repressed and obsessed. His paranoia is expressed in his fear of drafts and his refusal to ride in the front seat of any car, which he believes would be the most dangerous position in the event of a crash. In addition, Ignatius believes that when one leaves New Orleans one enters the "heart of darkness," and he himself has only ventured out once, to that "whirlpool of despair," Baton Rouge. Ignatius is constantly describing his physical condition to everyone he meets—particularly the status of his mysterious gastric "valve," which opens or closes in accordance with his mental state.

Various critics compare Ignatius to such renowned comic figures as Shakespeare's Falstaff, Cervantes's Don Quixote, or the rotund Oliver Hardy from *Laurel and Hardy* films. Others see Ignatius as the kind of picaresque figure found in Henry Fielding's eighteenth-century novels or as a medieval-style pilgrim on a ridiculous "quest." Hoping to best his former girlfriend, Myrna, and make her "seethe with envy," Ignatius sets out to revolutionize the downtrodden, underpaid workers at Levy Pants, but his ill-conceived plans backfire. Similarly, his "Save the World through Degeneracy" program fails miserably. Despite their lunacy, however, Ignatius's social reform efforts are aimed at achieving peace and justice in a world undeniably lacking in both. Despite being repulsed by the physically grotesque, monumentally self-centered Ignatius, we also sense something of his frustration, alienation, and melancholy, and we must admit that much of what he rails against really *is* reprehensible. Several commentators find the novel's ending somewhat ambiguous. Ignatius is saved from confinement in a psychiatric institution, but he must also leave his New Orleans cocoon—a conclusion that may be interpreted as either liberating or ominous.

Many critics speculate on the extent to which Ignatius Reilly's mother, **Mrs. Irene Reilly**, mirrors Toole's own mother, Thelma D. Toole, whose belief in her dead son's manuscript result in its being published—eleven years after his suicide—to critical acclaim. In the novel Ignatius remarks that he will have to keep the chronicle he is writing out of his mother's hands or she may make a fortune on it after his death. Mild-mannered Mrs. Reilly, an apparent alcoholic who stores her wine bottles in the oven, invested great sums of insurance money in Ignatius's eight years of college, and she is disappointed with the result. As the novel begins, she has already endured several years of her son's constant, tyrannical presence in her tiny, dilapidated home. Although Mrs. Reilly defends Ignatius against Patrolman Mancuso's efforts to arrest him for vagrancy, she grows increasingly annoyed with her indolent son. First she insists that he get a job and help her pay for the damage she caused with her car after their drinking binge at the Night of Joy nightclub. Then Mrs. Reilly becomes friends with Mancuso and his elderly aunt, Santa Battaglia, and starts to go out with them at night. Her perspective expanded by these new friends, Mrs. Reilly finally admits that Ignatius has repaid her devotion with nothing but ridicule and aggravation. Lacking education, insight, and taste, Mrs. Reilly still proves wiser than her son when she declares, "You learnt everything Ignatius, except how to be a human being." As the novel ends, she plans to marry the paranoid but attentive Claude Robichaux and to commit Ignatius to a psychiatric hospital.

One of the most successful comic characters in *A Confederacy of Dunces* is **Burma Jones**, an African American who works as a janitor at the Night of Joy nightclub for only twenty dollars a week; the opportunistic proprietress, Lana Lee, threatens to report him to the police for vagrancy if he does not take the job. Jones, whose facial expressions are usually concealed by both his sunglasses and the cloud of cigarette smoke that perpetually hovers in front of him, is a sardonic observer of the sordid goings-on at the Night of Joy. He also serves as a kind of spokesman for the patrons of Mattie's Ramble Inn, a gathering place for poor blacks. While sitting at the bar complaining of the frustrations and hardships black people face, another drinker recommends he engage in small acts of "sabotage" to get his revenge against whites. Thus he secretly writes the nightclub's name on the packages of pornographic photographs Lana is peddling, ultimately leading the police to her door. Most critics find Jones to be the most (or perhaps only) favorably portrayed character in the novel, and Toole was lauded for his authentic rendering of Jones's speech, which not only reveals his insight, sense of humor, and resilience but illuminates some of the very real problems faced by African Americans in the 1960s.

Ignatius's relationship with his former girlfriend from graduate school, **Myrna Minkoff**, is platonic despite Myrna's assertions that what Ignatius needs is a good, "explosive orgasm" and her ever-thwarted attempts to help him achieve one. Described by Ignatious as a "loud, offensive maiden from the Bronx" with wild black hair, Myrna always wears a black leotard. Presenting herself as an outspoken radical activist, she reveals how shallow her convictions are in her letters to Ignatius. It is because he wants to make Myrna "seethe with envy" that Ignatius undertakes his own reform efforts. Despite Ignatius's seeming contempt for Myrna, he is eager to be rescued by her when, at the end of the novel, she sweeps into New Orleans and whisks him away in her tiny car. The novel's last line describes Ignatius taking Myrna's long pigtail "in one of his paws" and pressing it "warmly to his wet mustache," a gesture possibly indicating that he will finally attain carnal knowledge.

The scenes that take place during Ignatius's employment at Levy Pants are some of the funniest in the book. He is warmly welcomed by the company's innocuous, neat, but incompetent office manager, **Mr. Gonzalez**, who hires Ignatius—without interviewing him—as soon as he walks in the door. Mr. Gonzalez approves of Ignatius's bizarre efforts to improve the office's appearance (such as the bean plants that send their tendrils down among the handles of the never-opened file cabinets) and never catches on to Ignatius's filing system, which consists of throwing large stacks of files into the garbage. The factory workers who join Ignatius in his "Crusade for Moorish Dignity" prove unwilling to follow their leader's order to bash in the skull of the kindly Mr. Gonzales. The office's other employee, **Miss Trixie**, an accountant in her eighties, has trouble seeing, hearing, and staying awake and wants nothing more than to retire. She periodically complains about a free Thanksgiving turkey she never received, and she calls Mr. Gonzales "Gomez" and Ignatius Gloria, a reference to a long-gone former co-worker (Ignatius treats Miss Trixie quite kindly, suspecting that she harbors profound insights beneath her semi-demented fog). Miss Trixie has been forced to remain on the staff by the self-serving, manipulative **Mrs. Levy**, who claims to be applying the psychological theories learned in a correspondence course to her husband's company. **Mr. Levy** takes a lackadaisical approach to the firm and spends as little time there as possible; he associates Levy Pants with his deceased father, with whom he often clashed. At the end of the novel, however, Mr. Levy takes a renewed interest in the company, even managing to retire Miss Trixie by attributing to her an insulting letter that Ignatius sent to one of the company's clients.

In addition to Burma Jones, the staff at the Night of Joy nightclub includes **Lana Lee**, the jaded, opportunistic proprietress who treats her janitor in a racist, belittling manner. Lana runs a pornography operation (selling obscene photos to high school students) until she is arrested by Patrolman Mancuso. The pleasant and humane **Darlene** is a "B-girl" (i.e., she persuades male customers to buy expensive, watered-down drinks, earning a small commission for each) who aspires to be an exotic dancer. She convinces Lana to let her perform an act in which she impersonates "Miss Harlett O'Hara," the "Virgin-ny Belle," while her pet bird tears her clothes off. Lana's partner in the pornography operation is teenaged **George**, who sells the obscene photographs at a nearby high school. Already corrupt and jaded, George dresses in cheap, flashy clothes and considers himself quite sophisticated. His suspicions about the dangers of attending school are confirmed by Ignatius, who typifies for him the result of too much education.

The first scene of *A Confederacy of Dunces* features hapless, inept, but basically good-natured **Patrolman Angelo Mancuso**, who is prevented from arresting the suspicious-looking Ignatius by his protective mother and the resentful attitude of the crowd that gathers around. Instead, Mancuso brings a paranoid but innocent grandfather, Claude Robichaux, back to the police station with him. His supervisor considers this show of incompetence disgusting and orders Mancuso back out on the streets, dressed in an assortment of humiliating, ridiculous costumes. Mancuso is also assigned to lurk in a public bathroom to wait for disreputable characters to appear, but he catches only a terrible cold. Mancuso's law enforcement career is saved when he arrests Lana Lee for trafficking in pornography. Mancuso's fun-loving, outrageously tasteless aunt, **Santa Battaglia**, befriends Mrs. Reilly and encourages her to enjoy herself more, pursue a relationship with Claude Robichaux, and commit her obnoxious son to a psychiatric ward. **Claude Robichaux**—the old man who defends Ignatius during his initial encounter with Mancuso and is ultimately arrested himself—thinks that almost everyone (but especially the police) is a "communiss." While courting Mrs. Reilly, he tries to convince her that Ignatius is also a member of this evil, pervasive conspiracy. Informing Ignatius of her plans to marry Mr. Robichaux, Mrs. Reilly admits that he is annoyingly paranoid but that, unlike Ignatius, he treats her kindly.

Other characters in *A Confederacy of Dunces* include **Mr. Clyde**, Ignatius's harried employer at Paradise Vendors, whose desperate need for hotdog sellers leads him to hire the bizarre young man; **Dorian Greene** (an assumed name that refers to Oscar Wilde's nineteenth-century novel *The Picture of Dorian Gray*), a flamboyant homosexual who agrees to invite his fellow "deviants" to a party at which Ignatius plans to promote his "Save the World through Degeneracy" movement—which ends disastrously for Ignatius; and **Betty, Frieda, and Liz**, the combative Lesbians who Dorian says will form the movement's Ladies' Auxiliary.

Further Reading

Beaver, Harold. "Appearance of Genius." *Times Literary Supplement* No. 4080 (June 12, 1981): 672.

Bell, Elizabeth S. "The Clash of World Views in John Kennedy Toole's *A Confederacy of Dunces.*" *Southern Literary Journal* Vol. 21, no. 1 (fall 1988): 15–22.

Brown, Richard. "Tacky Vocations." *Times Literary Supplement* No. 4034 (July 18, 1980): 821.

Contemporary Literary Criticism, Vols. 19, 64. Detroit: Gale Research.

Dictionary of Literary Biography, 1981 Yearbook. Detroit: Gale Research.

Evanier, David. "Behemoth." *National Review* Vol. 33 (June 26, 1981): 729–30.

Friedman, Alan. "A Sad and Funny Story." *New York Times Book Review* (June 22, 1980): 7, 27.

McNeil, David. "*A Confederacy of Dunces* as Reverse Satire: The American Subgenre." *Mississippi Quarterly* Vol. 38, no. 1 (winter 1984–85): 33–47.

Percy, Walker. Foreword to *A Confederacy of Dunces* by John Kennedy Toole. Baton Rouge: Louisiana State University Press, 1980, pp. v–vii.

Simmons, Jonathan. "Ignatius Reilly and the Concept of the Grotesque in John Kennedy Toole's *A Confederacy of Dunces.*" *Mississippi Quarterly* Vol. 43, no. 1 (winter 1989–90): 33–43.

Anne Tyler

1941–

American novelist, short story writer, critic, nonfiction writer, and editor.

Breathing Lessons (novel, 1988)

Plot: The novel's central characters, Maggie and Ira Moran, are middle-class residents of contemporary Baltimore who have been married for twenty-eight years. The action begins on a Saturday morning in early fall as the couple prepares to depart for the funeral of a friend in Deer Park, Pennsylvania. While driving their car back from the garage where it has been undergoing repairs, Maggie hears on a radio talk-show a voice she believes is that of her former daughter-in-law, Fiona Stuckey. Fiona was briefly married to the Moran's fame-seeking but failure-prone son Jessie, by whom she had a daughter she named Leroy. The talk-show voice says that having once married for love and experienced only failure, she now plans to marry for security. Maggie is so startled that she drives her car into a truck, damaging a fender. She and Ira attend the funeral, which the dead man's wife has arranged as a replay of her wedding, complete with home movie and forced singing, by the guests, of songs popular at the time they were married. The reticent Ira refuses to sing "Love Is a

Many-Splendoured Thing" with Maggie. The funeral causes Maggie to reminisce about her own courtship and wedding, and she and Ira make love in an upstairs bedroom until they are discovered and routed by their hostess. During the drive home, Maggie convinces Ira to take a detour to Cartwheel, Pennsylvania, to see Fiona and their granddaughter. Hoping that Jessie and Fiona will reconcile if they can just meet again, Maggie invites Fiona to visit the Morans. Fiona complies, but the reunion with Jessie is a failure and she returns to Cartwheel. As the novel draws to a close, Maggie seems ruefully accepting of things as they are. She and Ira go to bed, planning to deliver their teenaged daughter, Daisy, to college the following day.

Characters: One of America's best known contemporary authors, Tyler writes comic novels that are often underpinned with melancholy and that feature characters who are both eccentric and appealingly ordinary. Despite its understated quality, her prose captures in revealing detail the essence of the lives it depicts. Awarded the Pulitzer Prize for Fiction, *Breathing Lessons* illustrates the shared history and alternating clash and harmony of opposites to be found in a long-term marital relationship, as well as what critic Richard Eder calls "the heroism of enduring" life's tedium as well as its pain. Although some commentators accuse Tyler of sentimentality and of devising unrealistically positive conclusions in her fiction, others laud her emphasis on the primacy of familial relationships and the necessity of accepting and celebrating the given life.

The most prominent character in *Breathing Lessons* is warm, scatterbrained **Maggie Moran**, an emotional, impulsive forty-eight-year-old who exasperates her husband with her meddling and her insistence on telling all her troubles to such perfect strangers as the caller who dialed her telephone number by mistake and the waitress who serves her in a roadside diner. Much of the novel recounts Maggie's struggles to reconcile the past with the present as she reminisces about her own long marriage and tries to bring about a reconciliation between her son and his former wife. Maggie wants those around her to be happy, and in pursuit of this goal, Ira explains, she "believes it's all right to alter people's lives. She thinks the people she loves are better than they really are, and so then she starts changing things around to suit her view of them." In the end, however, Maggie has to accept what she cannot change and focus instead on what has survived intact—particularly her love for her husband. Although their relationship began as the result of a misunderstanding (Maggie heard that Ira had died in a boot camp accident and wrote a letter to his father that expressed more fondness than she actually felt), Maggie concedes that she is now in love with Ira, a circumstance she considers as convenient as "finding right in her pantry all the fixings she needed for a new recipe." Well aware of the difficulties of getting through daily life, Maggie expresses one of the novel's central themes when she muses that people obtain lessons in such pursuits as typing and driving a car, but that these are "nothing, nothing, compared to living day in and day out with a husband and raising up a new human being." Some commentators complained that Maggie's meddling and dizziness are stereotypically female qualities that erode the reader's empathy for her, but others contended that she is redeemed by her resiliency and capacity for love. Carole Angier described Maggie as "wholly attuned to hope and need, deaf and blind to limitations."

Fifty-year-old **Ira Moran** presents a strong contrast to his wife. Compulsively neat, careful, and methodical, Ira is as uncommunicative as Maggie is talkative, and despite his love for her he is constantly frustrated by her impetuosity and impracticality. It is primarily through Ira that Tyler explores the theme of lost opportunity and permanently vanished youth, for Ira once hoped to become a medical researcher but settled instead for managing his ailing father's picture-framing shop. Burdened with supporting a wife, children, father, and two disabled sisters, Ira has reached middle age without realizing any of his youthful dreams. All around him he notices people "squandering their lives," and he ruefully acknowledges that he himself has "never accomplished one single act of consequence."

One of many inarticulate, detached male characters in Tyler's fiction (in which it is usually women who make things happen), Ira indulges in compulsive solitaire playing that may symbolize his isolation, his desire for order, or perhaps even an admirable independent streak. The relationship between Ira and Maggie is characterized by her ability to guage his feelings not through dialogue, in which he rarely indulges, but through the songs he whistles. Owing to Tyler's skill in conveying both the antagonisms and the harmonies of their marriage, we may wonder how these differently constituted people have managed to tolerate each other for so long but we do not doubt that they will continue to do so.

Whereas Maggie views her children through understanding, indulgent eyes, Ira feels both love and resentment for **Jessie**, a high-school dropout whose assertion that he refuses "to believe that I will die unknown" seems to ridicule his father's life of quiet sacrifice and anonymity. Self-indulgent and untalented, Jessie aspires to rock stardom but instead ends up working in a motorcycle shop. His short-lived enthusiasms for various pursuits, such as computers, making baby furniture, and even being a father, leads Ira to call him "Mr. Moment-by-Moment." Jesse's commitment to Fiona proves similarly shallow, and critics have seen their relationship as the most negative of the several views of twentieth-century marriage the novel provides. Jessie's former wife **Fiona Stuckey** was initially attracted to his vaguely dangerous rock-star mystique and failed to see the qualities that would make him a spectacularly unqualified husband and father. During the course of the novel, Maggie reminisces about following Fiona to a clinic to talk her out of having an abortion; some critics have faulted as fence-straddling the scene in which Maggie derides the anti-abortion protesters at the clinic. It was Maggie who, during Fiona's pregnancy, gave her the "breathing lessons" referred to in the novel's title. Maggie is much aggrieved to be separated from her granddaughter, the strangely named **Leroy**, who lives with her repellent grandmother, **Mrs. Stuckey**, and her mother in a tiny Pennsylvania town.

The novel recounts the Morans' journey to the funeral of **Max Gill**, the husband of Maggie's longtime best friend **Serena**. The illegitimate daughter of a flamboyant mother, the always unconventional Serena Palermo had longed for a more ordinary life. When Maggie asked, just before Serena's wedding, how she knew she was marrying the right man, Serena responded, "It's just *time* to marry, that's all. I'm so tired of dating!" This pragmatic approach to marriage seems to have served Serena well, for her relationship with Max—a goodnatured radio-ad salesman who died of a brain tumor before reaching fifty—was quite solid and amicable. At the funeral, the Morans also encounter such old acquaintances as **Durwood Clegg**, whom Maggie rejected during their high school days but who becomes a nearly heroic figure when he salvages her wavering solo by starting to sing with her; and the deceptively glamorous, snobbish **Sugar Tilghman**, who insists on singing not the requested "Born to Be with You" but the much cornier "Que Sera Sera."

Another notable figure in *Breathing Lessons* is **Daniel Otis**, the elderly black man Maggie and Ira encounter during their trip home from the funeral. Annoyed with the man's erratic driving, Maggie signals to him that his car's wheel is about to come off, but when she sees that he is not only black but old, Maggie becomes contrite and insists that Ira pull over and tell him that they were mistaken. Otis continues to worry about the wheel, however, and the Morans accompany him to a garage, where he and Maggie commiserate about the foibles of marriage. While several critics agreed with Robert McPhillips that this character represents the stereotype of "the self-effacing black who defers to the greater wisdom of his white interlocutors," others defended him as an example of Tyler's ability to render any kind of character both foolish and appealing.

Other characters in the novel include Ira's selfish father **Sam Moran**, whose heart condition meant that Ira would have to take over the picture-framing business; and his sisters **Junie** and **Dorrie**, the former incapacitated by agoraphobia and the latter by physical and mental disabilities. The Morans' daughter **Daisy**, who rarely appears in the novel, is a college-age overachiever who started toilet-training herself at thirteen months and taking care of her own wardrobe when she was in the first grade. Rather sullen and humorless, she once asked Maggie if there was "a certain point in your life when you decided to settle for being ordinary?"

Saint Maybe (novel, 1991)

Plot: The novel focuses on the Bedloes, a family that initially seems ideal. Cheerful Bee, its matriarch, is the main promulgator of the Bedloes' sense of its specialness; her husband Doug is an amiable but average high school teacher. The children include Claudia, who has already left home and started her own family, twenty-nine-year-old Danny, who works at the post office, and seventeen-year-old Ian, who is good-looking, likable, and athletic. A slight kink in the family's smooth surface appears in the form of Lucy Dean, a divorced waitress with two children whom Danny suddenly introduces as his intended wife. Only seven months later, Lucy gives birth to another child, who is supposedly born prematurely. Although the rest of the family soon adjusts to the situation, Ian becomes convinced not only that Danny is not baby Daphne's father but that Lucy is carrying on an illicit love affair behind her husband's back. One night, angry because he has had to babysit rather than see his girlfriend, Ian tells Danny of his suspicions. Moments later, Danny drives his car into a brick wall and dies. Aggrieved and apparently overwhelmed by her responsibilities, Lucy also soon dies from an overdose of sleeping pills. Ian begins his first semester of college but cannot escape his sense of responsibility for both deaths. Wandering into the Church of the Second Chance, Ian is moved to ask God for forgiveness. Instead, however, the church's spiritual leader, Reverend Emmet, tells him that he should actively seek atonement by quitting college and returning home to help his parents raise the three orphans who have come under their guardianship. Ian does so, taking a job as a carpenter, retaining his membership in the Church of the Second Chance, and renouncing all relationships outside of his family and church. He spends the next twenty years raising Agatha, Thomas, and Daphne, who love him but eventually come to see him as overly reticent and reclusive. Their attempt to match him with one of Daphne's teachers fails miserably. Finally, however, Ian meets Rita de Campo, a vibrant, sensible woman who recognizes his worth and sets out to win him. By the end of the novel, Ian has not only succeeded in shepherding Lucy's children to adulthood but has achieved his own happiness with Rita.

Characters: Acclaimed for her comic but poignant novels populated by characters who are both quirky and lovable, Tyler often focuses on the rewards and trials of family life and the positive and negative impact family members may exert on each other. In *Saint Maybe*, Tyler explores such themes as whether it is advisable or even possible to atone for one's sins, what constitutes a well-lived life, and whether guilt may be transformed into an act of love.

Many critics and readers find **Ian Bedloe** an appealing character, particularly when he is a handsome, easygoing teenager occupied with such ordinary pursuits as playing baseball and trying to get his girlfriend to have sex with him. The seventeen-year-old Ian is the only member of his family to perceive that its perfection may not be complete, and in his adolescent belief in his own worldliness he decides that he has detected his sister-in-law's infidelity. This conclusion is undoubtedly influenced by the lust Lucy inspired in him as she twirled before him in a new, clingy dress, so it is no surprise when—after both Danny and Lucy have died—Ian's course of redemptive self-denial includes abstention from romance and sex. Ian spends twenty years attempting to atone for his perceived sin, and as a result his personality and aspirations undergo a blunting process. Whereas he had once harbored a sense of himself as potentially heroic, he becomes pious, reticent Brother Ian of the perpetually disheveled hair and limited outlook. Some critics find Ian, whom Brad Leithauser describes as reflecting Tyler's "deeply endearing fondness for boring men," as lacking any charm or interest at all; they conclude that he is simply too passive to retain the reader's sympathy. In addition, commentators have complained that Tyler does not elucidate the inner workings of Ian's faith, which seems to provide him with so much solace and support during the years he is raising his three young charges. It is also possible, however, to interpret Ian's renunciation of his own desires and needs as extraordinary and admirable and thus to approve of the reward he finally receives.

The family matriarch is **Bee Bedloe**, an ever-optimistic homemaker who is responsible for instilling in the Bedloes their sense of specialness: "They believed that every part of their lives was absolutely wonderful." Something like Maggie Moran in Tyler's *Breathing Lessons*, Bee is, according to critic Crystal Gromer, "the family architect, continually striving to make constructions . . . that fit events into her view." What throws Bee off course is the unexpected death of her son, which quickly weakens and ages both her and her husband and changes the family irrevocably. She tells Doug that "Our lives have turned so makeshift and second-class, so second-string, so second-fiddle, and everything's been lost." **Doug Bedloe** is a pleasant but undistinguished high school math teacher whom his wife refers to as an "educator," thus elevating his only modest skills.

The other members of the Bedloe family include **Claudia**, who is usually offstage and whose distinguishing characteristic seems to be her abundant fertility; and the good-looking, amiable **Danny**, who works at the post office after graduating from high school. Danny's death at twenty-nine, which occurs early in the novel, is one of several such events in Tyler's fiction: losses that provoke families into reevaluating and perhaps reconstituting themselves. Danny describes **Lucy Dean**, a beautiful waitress with long black hair and pale skin, as "the woman who changed my life." A divorcee with two young children, Lucy first gained Danny's attention when she asked him for advice on how to mail a bowling ball to her ex-husband in Cheyenne, Wyoming. The vibrant but emotionally fragile Lucy cannot, apparently, face the prospects before her after her husband's death and so takes an overdose of sleeping pills. Significantly for Ian, evidence arrives soon after Lucy's death that she was not having an extramarital affair after all.

Tyler has been much lauded for her complex, sensitive portrayals of children and teenagers, and many critics particularly admired her depiction of the three youngsters in *Saint Maybe*. **Agatha**, who is six when the novel begins, is a rather homely, stolid little girl who worries— both before and after her mother's death—about keeping the family and household together. Along with bright, self-contained **Thomas** (three at the time of his mother's death), she recognizes in Ian a route to safety and security. It is the sassy but lovable **Daphne** who most resembles her mother and who initially shows signs of becoming similarly wild; she never fulfills this destiny, however, and eventually reveals more of her uncle's timidity. It is Daphne who, during her rebellious adolescence, calls the overly cautious Ian "Saint Maybe . . . King Careful."

The leader of the Church of the Second Chance, which proves a major influence on the course of Ian's life, is **Reverend Emmet** (church members are known only by their first names as they feel surnames denote exclusivity), a magisterial but kind figure who insists that a sinner must earn atonement. "God wants to know how far you'll go to undo the harm," he tells Ian. Emmet's church revolves around its members' weekly confessions of sin, mutual aid, and abstention from such evils as coffee, sugar, and premarital sex. Another redemptive character in the novel is **Rita de Campo**, who eventually rescues Ian from dullness and isolation. Tall, forthright, and eminently sensible, Rita is a "Clutter Counselor" who helps her customers divide the detritus of their lives into piles marked "Keep," "Discard," and "Query." Many commentators have compared her with the similarly quirky but life-affirming Muriel Pritchett in Tyler's 1985 novel *The Accidental Tourist*, who also "rescues" a weaker, foundering male character. Some critics have complained that Rita's well-timed arrival provides the novel with a rather too-neat conclusion.

Further Reading

Angier, Carole. "Small City America." *New Statesman & Society* Vol. 2, no. 33 (January 20, 1989): 34.

Cherry, Kelly. "The Meaning of Guilt." *Southern Review* (Winter 1992): 168–73.

Contemporary Literary Criticism Vols. 7, 11, 18, 28, 44. Detroit: Gale Research.

Dictionary of Literary Biography Vol. 6, 1982 Yearbook. Detroit: Gale Research.

Eder, Richard. "Crazy for Sighing and Crazy for Loving You." *Los Angeles Times Book Review* (September 11, 1988): 3.

———. "Quiescence as an Art Form." *Los Angeles Times Book Review* (September 8, 1991): 3, 17.

Flower, Dean. "Barbaric Yawps and Breathing Lessons." *Hudson Review* Vol. 42, no. 1 (Spring 1989): 133–40.

Gromer, Crystal. "Never Far from Home." *Commonweal* (November 8, 1991): 656–57.

Hoagland, Edward. "About Maggie, Who Tried Too Hard." *New York Times Book Review* (September 11, 1988): 1, 43–4.

Leithauser, Brad. "Just Folks." *New York Review of Books* (January 16, 1992): 53–5.

McPhillips, Robert. "The Baltimore Chop." *Nation* Vol. 247, no. 13 (November 7, 1988): 464–66.

Parini, Jay. "The Accidental Convert." *New York Times Book Review* (August 25, 1991): 3, 26.

Petry, Alice Hall. *Critical Essays on Anne Tyler*. New York: G. K. Hall, 1992.

———. *Understanding Anne Tyler*. Columbia: University of South Carolina Press, 1990.

Sage, Lorna. "Compassion in Clans." *Times Literary Supplement* (September 27, 1991): 24.

Stegner, Wallace. "The Meddler's Progress." *Washington Post—Book World* (September 4, 1988): 1, 6.

Stephens, Ralph, ed. *The Fiction of Anne Tyler*. Jackson, MS: University Press of Mississippi, 1990.

Towers, Robert. "Roughing It." *New York Review of Books* Vol. 35, no. 17 (November 10, 1988): 40–1.

Alfred Uhry

1936–

American dramatist and lyricist.

Driving Miss Daisy (drama, 1987)

Plot: Set in Atlanta, Georgia, between 1948 and 1973, the play comprises a series of vignettes that chronicle the developing relationship between a wealthy Jewish woman, Daisy Werthan, and her African American chauffeur, Hoke Coleman. When the play opens, seventy-two-year-old Daisy has just crashed her new car, and her banker son Boolie insists on hiring a driver for her. Resentful of this encroachment on her independence and mistrustful (despite her claim that she is not prejudiced) of blacks, Daisy treats Hoke with caustic peevishness. But during a visit to her husband's grave, Daisy learns that good-natured, dignified Hoke is illiterate, and this discovery awakens her schoolteacher instincts. She teaches Hoke to read, and her attitude toward him begins to soften somewhat. When Daisy's brother dies, Hoke drives her to Mobile, Alabama for the funeral, an experience that allows each more insight into the other's life. Later, Daisy's synagogue is bombed by the Ku Klux Klan, an occurrence that deeply shocks her and that elicits Hoke's memories of similar events in his past. Daisy helps to organize a banquet honoring Martin Luther King, but Boolie declines her invitation to accompany her because he fears the reaction of his racist clients if he expresses good will toward blacks. At the last minute, Daisy invites Hoke to the banquet, but he also declines. As the play draws to a close, Daisy has grown senile and is confined to a nursing home, where Hoke—himself now elderly—visits her. In the final scene, Hoke tenderly feeds Daisy a piece of pumpkin pie.

Characters: Uhry won a Pulitzer Prize for *Driving Miss Daisy*, which depicts the gradual development of understanding and affection between two people who breach their cultural, racial, and religious differences to connect. Praised for its understated approach and lack of sentimentality, the play reflects Uhry's background as a member of a wealthy Jewish family living in the South during a period of social upheaval.

Uhry reportedly based *Driving Miss Daisy* on the relationship between his own grandmother and her chauffeur. Seventy-two years old when the play begins, **Daisy Werthan** is a wealthy Jewish woman with an acidic temperament. Never having forgotten her impoverished childhood and young adulthood as a modestly paid teacher, Daisy is extremely parsimonious, and her objection to Hoke's presence is partly based on her fear that having a chauffeur will alert people to her wealth. Highly independent, stubborn, and fixed in her habits, Daisy initially resists Hoke's attempts to establish a friendly relationship. Although she denies that she is prejudiced against blacks, Daisy is quick to accuse Hoke of having stolen a can of salmon, telling Boolie that this is typical behavior for a black person. Teaching Hoke to read gives Daisy deeper insight into his character and life, as does the trip they take together to Mobile. When Hoke leaves the car to relieve himself, Daisy learns not only that she must treat him with more dignity but that she depends on him for protection and companionship. At the same time, Hoke gains insight into Daisy's life when she poignantly recalls her first visit, as a young girl, to Mobile, when she felt sea spray on her face for the first time. Daisy does seem to lose some of her prejudice, but—perhaps realistically—she and Hoke never reach a complete understanding. For example, Daisy does not accept Hoke's assurance that he knows how she feels when the synagogue is attacked, nor does she want to hear his story about how he saw his friend's father lynched by hostile whites. Nevertheless, in her last years she identifies Hoke as her best friend, and even in her senility she recognizes him as an important part of her life.

Hoke Coleman is a middle-aged, illiterate black man who has met the deprivations and humiliations of his life with pride and dignity. He is both independent and dependable, loyal but not subservient. Initially treated with hostility by Daisy, Hoke succeeds in breaking through her cold exterior with his admission that he cannot read as well as with his general good humor and competence. During the trip to Mobile, Daisy learns not only that Hoke had never been out of Georgia until "25 minutes ago" but that he must be treated like a man. Similarly, Hoke manifests his inherent dignity when he refuses to accompany Daisy to the Martin Luther King testimonial dinner because she has had the invitation for a month before she asks him. When Daisy asserts that blacks have made important gains in recent years, Hoke grumbles, "Things ain't changed that much," thus highlighting the perhaps unbreachable gulf in understanding that remains between him and Daisy despite their affection and loyalty.

It is Daisy's son **Boolie Werthan** who, convinced that his mother's age necessitates her having a driver, hires Hoke and pays him out of his own pocket. Boolie serves primarily as an amiable intermediary between Hoke and Daisy, providing droll or exasperated comments on the action. Significantly, the supposedly liberal Boolie declines to attend the Martin Luther King dinner because he does not want to offend his white, racist clientele. Although Boolie's socially ambitious wife **Florence** never actually appears, she provokes some humorous comments from the acerbic Daisy. For instance, Daisy disapproves of her Jewish daughter-in-law's observance of Christmas, noting that "If I had [her] nose, I wouldn't go around saying Merry Christmas to anyone."

Further Reading

Barnes, Clive. "*Miss Daisy* Blooms." *New York Post* (April 16, 1987).

Brustein, Robert. "Energy for Old Age." *New Republic* Vol. 197, no. 13 (September 28, 1987): 28–30.

Contemporary Literary Criticism Vol. 55. Detroit: Gale Research.

Edwards, Christopher. "Southern Comfort." *Spectator* Vol. 260, no. 8345 (June 18, 1988): 38–9.

Gussow, Mel. Review of *Driving Miss Daisy*. *New York Times* (April 16, 1987): C22.

Kemp, Peter. Review of *Driving Miss Daisy*. *Independent* (June 10, 1988).

Simon, John. "Daisy and Miller." *New York* Vol. 20, no. 18 (May 4, 1987): 122.

John Updike
1932–

American novelist, critic, poet, short story writer, essayist, author of children's books, playwright, and translator.

Rabbit at Rest (novel, 1990)

Plot: Set in 1989, the novel centers on retired car salesman Harry "Rabbit" Angstrom and his wife Janice, who spend their winters in a Florida Gulf-coast retirement community and their summers in the small town of Brewer, Pennsylvania, where their son Nelson runs their successful Toyota dealership. When Nelson, his wife Pru, and their two children visit Harry and Janice in Florida, Nelson behaves strangely. Then Harry has a heart attack while saving his granddaughter Judy after a sailing mishap, and although he recovers, he becomes obsessed with thoughts of death. After the Angstroms return to Pennsylvania, they learn that Nelson has been embezzling money from the dealership to pay not only for his own cocaine habit but for medication for Lyle, his crooked, AIDS-afflicted accountant. The usually indolent Janice springs into action, taking charge of the family business and sending Nelson into a drug rehabilitation program. Meanwhile, Harry flagrantly disregards his doctor's orders to avoid junk food, and he also has a sexual encounter with his daughter-in-law that leads to a rift with Janice. Harry leaves for Florida, and he plays basketball with some black youths and suffers another heart attack. The novel ends with Harry lying close to death, his family around him; he tells his son, "Well, Nelson, all I can tell you is, it isn't so bad."

Characters: Updike is recognized as one of contemporary America's most accomplished and popular writers. The fourth and final work in his "Rabbit" tetralogy—which includes *Rabbit, Run* (1960), *Rabbit Redux* (1971), and *Rabbit Is Rich* (1981)]—*Rabbit at Rest* is considered by many commentators not only the finest novel in this series but Updike's masterpiece. Written in a style that is both realistically detailed and elegiac in tone, the novel was described by critic Jonathan Raban as "an epic, loving inventory of America as Rabbit has known it."

Updike's faithful readers know well his most famous protagonist, **Harry "Rabbit" Angstrom**, through the novels that chronicle his life from the late 1950s through the 1980s. In the first novel, Harry is an irresponsible former high school basketball star in his late twenties who finds life empty and meaningless; in *Rabbit Redux* he grapples with such aspects of the 1960s as drugs, the Vietnam War, and the sexual revolution; and in *Rabbit Is Rich* he is an unexpectedly successful, middle-aged businessman unable to relate to his troubled son. *Rabbit at Rest* finds the title character a sedentary fifty-five-year-old who spends his retirement playing golf in Florida and downing potato chips and candy bars, sensing the diminishment of his role in the world. After his heart attack, Harry becomes obsessed with thoughts of death, which consistently center around such contemporary catastrophes as the 1988 bombing of Pan American Flight 103 over Lockerbie, Scotland. For Harry this tragedy represents the fragility of human life and the instability of any order in events. He feels his own heart ticking inside him like a bomb that could explode at any moment, yet he continues to gorge himself on junk food, and he even indulges in a night of forbidden sex with his daughter-in-law. This disreputable behavior characterizes Harry throughout the Rabbit novels, and readers and critics have found him an unsympathetic figure in his self-indulgence, sexism, and shallowness. Nevertheless, his advocates find Harry appealing despite his flaws, noting his curiosity essential innocence, and empathy as redeeming qualities. Often described as a mirror of American society in general (and comically when he appears dressed as Uncle Sam in a Fourth of July parade), Harry has been compared to such characters as Mr. Pickwick in Charles Dickens's *The Pickwick Papers* and Leopold Bloom in James Joyce's *Ulysses*, who are also said to represent their particular classes, countries, and eras. Critic Thomas M. Disch memorialized Harry as "one of the great originals, a type at once profoundly self-consistent and full of surprises."

Throughout the many personal and societal ups and downs and assorted infidelities on both sides, Harry remains married to the same woman, **Janice Angstrom**, until the end of his life. In *Rabbit at Rest*, Janice undergoes a kind of metamorphosis from a rather indolent life centered around the country club to that of a competent professional woman who manages her family's financial affairs. With both mild resentment and amazement, Harry observes the changes in his wife, grimly noting that she is obviously preparing for life without him. For her part, Janice finds Harry increasingly "drained of spirit," and she seems to gain energy and confidence as he fades.

A small boy when he makes his first appearance in *Rabbit, Run*, **Nelson Angstrom** exhibits though his progress to manhood qualities alarmingly like his father's. In *Rabbit Is Rich* he is portrayed as similarly self-indulgent and irresponsible, yet lacking Harry's essential sweetness. Although Nelson has reached the age of thirty two in *Rabbit at Rest,* he still behaves like a rebellious adolescent and shows little concern for his family members. Critics have noted that Updike is notably harsher in his depiction of the whining, rationalizing Nelson than of Harry, toward whose foibles he extends considerable tolerance.

Other members of Harry's immediate family include his beautiful daughter-in-law **Pru,** After Nelson is committed to a drug rehabilitation program, Harry has sex with her during a visit intended to buoy her spirits. Harry saves his beloved granddaughter **Judy** from drowning but has a heart attack. Judy is closely associated with Harry's long-mourned infant daughter Rebecca, whose tragic drowning death occurs near the end of *Rabbit, Run.*

The large cast of minor characters in *Rabbit at Rest* includes Harry's old girlfriend **Thelma Harrison,** whose unpleasant succumbing to lupus provides one of the novel's most dispiriting portrayals of death, and her husband **Ronnie,** whose hatred of Harry is no doubt capped by the latter's comment, at Thelma's funeral, that she was a "fantastic lay." Another of Harry's old friends is **Charlie Stavros,** who serves as a source of sound advice throughout the Rabbit novels; in *Rabbit at Rest,* he has recently undergone a heart by-pass operation. The most unflattering characters is the greedy, immoral **Lyle,** the AIDS-afflicted accountant at the Angstrom's car dealership who encourages Nelson to embezzle funds from the firm. Many commentators found Updike's depiction of the Japanese businessman **Mr. Shimada,** who announces that Toyota is ending its association with Harry, as tasteless and cartoonishly stereotyped. **Elvira,** a new sales associate is the kind of assured professional woman that Harry views with bewilderment; she humorously misinterprets his comment about American obsolescence in the marketplace ("It's a kind of relief, I guess, not to be the big cheese") as referring to his own diminished role.

Further Reading

Cooper, Rand Richards. "Rabbit Loses the Race." *Commonweal* Vol. 118, no. 10 (May 17, 1991): 315–21.

Contemporary Literary Criticism, Vols. 1–3, 5, 7, 9, 13, 23, 34, 43, 70. Detroit: Gale Research.

Disch, Thomas M. "Rabbit's Run." *Nation* Vol. 251, no. 19 (December 3, 1990): 688, 690, 692, 694.

Eder, Richard. "Rabbit Runs Down." *Los Angeles Times Book Review* (October 7, 1990): 3, 13.

Kakutani, Michiko. "Just 30 Years Later, Updike Has a Quartet." *New York Times* (September 25, 1990): C13, C17.

Lee, Hermione. "The Trouble with Harry." *New Republic* Vol. 203, no. 26 (December 24, 1990): 34–7.

Modern Fiction Studies (John Updike Issue) Vol. 37, no. 1 (spring 1991).

Neary, John. *Something and Nothingness: The Fiction of John Updike and John Fowles.* Carbondale: Southern Illinois Press, 1992.

Oates, Joyce Carol. "So Young!" *New York Times Book Review* (September 30, 1990): 1, 43.

Pearce, Edward. "Rabbit Resartus." *London Review of Books* Vol. 12, no. 21 (November 8, 1990): 19–20.

Raban, Jonathan. "Rabbit's Last Run." *Book World—Washington Post* (September 30, 1990): 1, 15.

Williamson, Chilton, Jr. "Harry's End." *National Review* Vol. XLII, no. 22 (November 19, 1990): 51–3.

Mario Vargas Llosa
1936–

Peruvian novelist, short story writer, critic, essayist, journalist, and dramatist.

Aunt Julia and the Scriptwriter (*La tía Julia y el escribidor*; novel, 1977)

Plot: Set in Lima, Peru in the 1950s, the novel features a central character whose name, like his creator's, is Mario; he is also called Marito or Varguitas. From a vantage point of at least twelve years later, Mario relates his experiences as a young radio journalist and would-be short story writer. Chapters recounting twenty-year-old Mario's life and particularly his love affair with his Aunt Julia alternate with those containing the soap opera scripts of Pedro Camacho, a Bolivian who comes to work for Mario's radio station. At about the same time, the recently divorced, thirty-two-year-old Aunt Julia (who is related to Mario only by marriage) arrives in Lima to live with relatives and perhaps find a new husband. Mario becomes captivated by both Aunt Julia and Camacho, who turns out to be a devoted, even obsessed writer who closely identifies with the characters in his melodramatic, complex serials. Against her own better judgment, Aunt Julia falls in love with Mario and agrees to marry him, despite the ardent disapproval of the rest of their family. Meanwhile, the wildly popular soap operas of Pedro Camacho grow increasingly confusing and bizarre as their author—apparently driven mad by his own obsession—loses his grip on reality. After Camacho has killed off all of his characters in one catastrophe after another, he is committed to an insane asylum. Mario and Aunt Julia marry and leave Lima to live in Europe; a final chapter reveals that the couple divorced after eight years of marriage. Mario became a successful writer and married another, younger woman. On his return to Lima, he learns that Camacho, pathetically diminished, was eventually released from the asylum and works as an errand boy.

Characters: A major Peruvian literary figure, Vargas Llosa has also taken part in his country's political life, running for president in 1989 (he ultimately withdrew from the race). His fiction is often associated with the Latin American "Boom" of the 1960s, when the works of many gifted writers from this region became known to and appreciated by a wider audience. Somewhat less experimental and complex than his previous novels, *Aunt Julia and the Scriptwriter* is nevertheless considered one of his most successful. Vargas Llosa juxtaposes the conventionally narrated story of Mario and Julia with the nearly surreal imaginings of the Bolivian scriptwriter, thus exploring the relationship between reality and fiction, the pleasures and danger of storytelling, and the writer's vocation in general.

The narrator of the novel's conventionally related chapters is **Mario** (also called **Marito** or **Varguitas**), an autobiographical character through whom Vargas Llosa recreates his own coming of age in Lima during the 1950s. Like his fictional counterpart, the young Vargas Llosa worked as a radio journalist while yearning to become a great writer; he also disregarded his family's objections and married his significantly older aunt. Despite the obvious similarities between author and character, Vargas Llosa treats Mario with a detached, if fond, irony. He is portrayed as daring, willful, passionate, and tender but also as naive, pretentious, and eager to make an impression even if it is an inherently false one. Mario spends his days writing news bulletins and his free time writing short stories that always seem to fall short of the greatness to which he aspires. He becomes enamored of both

Pedro Camacho and Aunt Julia at about the same time, attracted by the fierce devotion to writing demonstrated by the former and the beauty, charm, and common sense of the latter. Mario comments that Camacho is the closest to a *real* writer that he has come, and he questions the right of more "literary" writers to deny the same status to someone like Camacho. His admiration for Camacho helps Mario explore his own vocation, just as his love for Aunt Julia helps him mature as a man. Despite his rather puppyish vow that he is willing to "kill a whole bunch of people" to win Julia, Mario takes a relatively levelheaded approach to his unconventional marriage, promising his father (whose opposition initially threatens to take a violent form) that he intends to finish college and support his new wife. In the novel's last chapter, the reader learns that Mario did become the successful writer he envisioned, and that his first marriage lasted even longer than the five years stipulated by Julia. Now thirty years old, he is married to a woman who seems much less charming than Julia, thus underlining the fact that the exciting interlude when Aunt Julia and Pedro Camacho enlivened his world has come to an end.

Described by critic Ben Stoltzfus as an "obsessed Napoleon of the airwaves," the incredibly prolific Bolivian scriptwriter **Pedro Camacho** is a dwarfish figure with long hair, a big nose, and bulging eyes. Attired in a threadbare black suit and a bowtie, he types his scripts with his hands at eye level, so that he seems to be boxing. Between writing the scripts for his many serials and directing the actual productions, Camacho often spends over a hundred hours per week on his work, and his intense involvement extends even to dressing like his characters in order to portray them more accurately. Solemn in manner and entirely humorless, Camacho eschews fame (ignoring the adulation of his listeners) and, fearing undue influence on his own writing, never reads other writers' work; indeed, Mario reports that Camacho is nearly illiterate. His eccentricities include his constant vilification of everything Argentinean (eventually it is revealed that he once had an Argentinean wife who became a prostitute in order to support them) and his characterization of all his soap opera heroes as being fifty years old, his own age. Commentators have asserted that through Camacho, whom Vargas Llosa apparently modeled after Raúl Salmón, a Bolivian with whom he worked in Lima when he was a radio newsman, Vargas Llosa explores the question of what makes a writer and whether someone who lacks literary talent but is devoted to his craft can be considered a real writer. In addition, some critics have interpreted Camacho's outrageous scripts as comments on the arbitrariness of fiction, a concept Vargas Llosa has himself practiced in other novels. As Camacho's mental stability disintegrates, his stories lose their continuity, with characters abruptly changing names and professions and even being brought back from the dead; initially unaware of Camacho's madness, his employer complains about the "modernist gimmicks" the scriptwriter has begun to employ. Camacho's eventual collapse and his later, pathetic appearance in coveralls and tennis shoes tied with string highlight the inherent danger of an obsessive devotion.

Many commentators have found the attractive, winsome **Aunt Julia** a particularly appealing character. Thirty-two years old and newly divorced, Julia has come to Lima to live with her relatives and look for a new husband, although none of the older, stodgy suitors she encounters seem to suit her very well. Independent and sensible, Julia has no intention of falling in love with her young nephew and is quite surprised when it happens. She finally agrees to marry Mario, providing he promises to stay with and love her for at least five years; she will give herself, she decides, the gift of five years of happiness but realizes the marriage is unlikely (given the differences in their ages and temperaments) to last much longer than that. Whereas Mario is naive and brash, Julia is levelheaded and endowed with the ability to appraise people and situations accurately. She tells Mario that this "love affair of a baby and an old lady who's also more or less your aunt" would not be out of place in one of Camacho's soap operas (particularly given Mario's father's threat to kill both of them), thus further highlighting the sometimes blurred lines between fact and fiction.

The colorful characters in Camacho's radio soap operas (many of whose identities shift, dissolve, or are reconfigured during the course of their creator's mental decline) include **Lucho Abril Marroquin**, who develops a vehicle phobia after running over and killing a little girl but is cured by a psychiatrist who convinces him that he hates children; the **Reverend Father Don Seferino Huanco Leyva**, who piously instructs his parishioners in a number of underworld practices; and **Crisanto Maravillas**, a crippled dwarf and poet who falls in love with **Sister Fatima**, who turns out to be the same girl, somehow restored to life, whom Lucho had run over.

Further Reading

Castro-Klarén, Sara. *Understanding Mario Vargas Llosa*. Columbia: University of South Carolina Press, 1990.

Contemporary Literary Criticism Vols. 3, 6, 9, 10, 15, 31. Detroit: Gale Research.

De Feo, Ronald. "Life as Fiction, Fiction as Life." *New Republic* (August 16 & 23, 1982): 38–9.

Goldberg, Gerald Jay. "Ironies of Love and Art." *Nation* (September 25, 1982): 281–83.

Kennedy, William. "Peruvian Soap Opera." *New York Times Book Review* (August 1, 1982): 1, 14.

Rodman, Selden. "Writing on Air." *National Review* (December 10, 1982): 1559–60.

Sheppard, R. Z. "Latins and Literary Lovers." *Time* (August 9, 1982): 70, 72.

Stoltzfus, Ben. Review of *Aunt Julia and the Scriptwriter*. *American Book Review* (July–August 1983): 8–9.

Tittler, Jonathan. "*Aunt Julia and the Scriptwriter*: An Affair with Irony." In *Narrative Irony in the Contemporary Spanish-American Novel*, pp. 129–50. Ithaca, N. Y.: Cornell University Press, 1984.

West, Paul. "Fantasy, Obsession, and Soap Opera." *Washington Post—Book World* (August 1, 1982): 1, 10.

Gore Vidal
1925–

American novelist, essayist, scriptwriter, dramatist, short story writer, and critic.

Hollywood: A Novel of America in the 1920s (novel, 1990)

Plot: Through its two central characters, Caroline Sanford and her half-brother Blaise, the novel recreates the events and atmosphere of two important realms of American life—entertainment and politics—during the years 1917 to 1923. The Sanfords are the wealthy, sophisticated co-publishers of an influential Washington, D.C. newspaper. Bored and restless, forty-year-old Caroline accepts a commission to go to Hollywood to promote the production of propaganda films to support America's role in World War I. To her surprise, Caroline finds herself a successful actress; under the name Emma Traxler, she appears in a series of movies depicting the brutality of America's enemies and the nobility of its own people. Meanwhile, back in Washington, Blaise observes and participates in the nation's political life, hobnobbing with such figures as presidents Woodrow Wilson and Warren G. Harding, William Randolph Hearst, and Alice Roosevelt as they grapple with the formation of the League of Nations, the Teapot Dome scandal, and other issues of the day.

Characters: A respected, sometimes provocative commentator on American society, Vidal is best known for his novels chronicling the history of the United States from the Revolutionary era through the present. *Hollywood* is the sixth work in the series, which comprises *Washington, D. C.* (1967), *Burr* (1973), *1876* (1976), *Lincoln* (1984), and *Empire* (1987). Written in polished, witty, energetic prose and always highly entertaining, Vidal's novels feature a skillful blend of real and imagined events and actual and fictional characters. In *Hollywood*, Vidal focuses on the interrelationship between America's political sphere and its entertainment industry (the ultimate expression of which he has identified in other writings as the presidency of Ronald Reagan). Vidal's abiding concern with America's devotion to empire-building is also evident here as he explores the conflict between isolationism and "making the world safe for democracy."

Caroline Sanford first appeared in *Empire*, the novel that precedes *Hollywood* in Vidal's series. She was introduced as a wealthy, beautiful, twenty-year-old descendant of Aaron Burr who was raised in France and returned to the United States to battle her half-brother Blaise over ownership of the newspaper the two had inherited. Some twenty years later, Caroline and Blaise have resolved their differences and are co-owners of the *Washington Tribune*, which—primarily due to Caroline's drive and intelligence—has become a respected and influential publication. Caroline is now an independent widow who finds herself drifting, in search of some new venture on which to bestow her considerable energy and savvy. She accepts an invitation to go to Hollywood and become a government propagandist, little suspecting that she herself is destined to achieve stardom. Appearing in an anti-German film called *Huns from Hell*, Caroline finds that the camera loves her, as does the audience, and she acquires the name Emma Traxler (supposedly her grandmother's name, but actually that of one of Vidal's relatives). Several critics have cited as implausible that none of Caroline's old friends recognize her in her films and she is thus able to keep her new occupation a secret. Sending Caroline to Hollywood while Blaise remains in Washington allows Vidal not only to cover both arenas but to draw connections between them, and Caroline is employed to voice the concept of cinema's power to reshape the world, to achieve power over people by giving them "the dreams you wanted them to dream." Through her experiences in Hollywood, Caroline discovers that "reality could now be entirely invented and history revised. Suddenly, she knew how God must have felt when he gazed upon chaos, with nothing but himself upon his mind." At the end of the novel, Caroline has decided that after the war she will try to use film to offset any harm that her propagandist work may have wrought to Germans, communists, and blacks.

Like his half-sister, **Blaise Sanford** is portrayed as sophisticated, witty, and impeccably well-mannered, with no strong religious or political bias to serve as a distraction from his observations of the glamorous world he inhabits. Blaise, notably less brilliant than Caroline, has apparently contributed little to the success of their joint publishing venture. He envies Caroline's ability to begin a new adventure in Hollywood, but he is himself too entrenched in the political and social intrigues of Washington to leave. Blaise's main idiosyncracy is his sexual ambivalence: At one point he and Caroline share a lover, and several critics have noted as particularly effective the scene in which he visits a Paris brothel that features male prostitutes and sees there the pathetically aged French novelist, Marcel Proust.

Vidal has often been praised for his ability to bring historical figures to authentic life, and in *Hollywood* he succeeds in this pursuit with his characterization of **President Woodrow Wilson**. Portraying Wilson as a politician of both high ideals and great cunning, Vidal follows him through the negotiations at Versailles to resolve World War I, his efforts to promote America's interests during the formation of the League of Nations, and his saddening decline into illness and old age. Wilson is described as "an odd combination of college professor unused to being contradicted in a world he took to be his classroom and of Presbyterian pastor unable to question that divine truth which inspired him at all times."

Vidal renders **President Warren G. Harding** as softer and less brilliant than his successor; he is an amiable, tobacco-chewing Ohioan whose easygoing nature and tendency toward cronyism create an atmosphere in which the "Teapot Dome" financial scandal, which involved a number of prominent members of the Harding administration, could evolve. Married to the vindictive, domineering **Florence Harding** (known as "the Duchess")— who at one point consults an astrologer about her husband's career—Harding cavorts in the White House with his mistress, **Nan Britton**. Harding's reign is depicted through the eyes of **Jess Smith**, an actual and particularly undistinguished member of the Harding entourage who was ultimately implicated in the scandal that brought it down.

Other historical figures in the novel include the young, ambitious politician **Franklin Delano Roosevelt** and his idealistic wife **Eleanor**; Teddy Roosevelt's acid-tongued daughter **Alice Roosevelt**; the powerful publishing magnate **William Randolph Hearst**; and Vidal's own blind grandfather, **Thomas Gore**, who was a senator from Oklahoma. A fictional character who is prominent in the book's Washington, D. C. sections is **James Burden Day**, a senator and Democratic candidate for president who serves as a detached interpreter of the political scene. Caroline's former lover and the father of her daughter **Emma** (who is now a disagreeable red-baiter), Day made his first appearance in *Empire*. The novel's Hollywood cast includes the fictional **Tim Farrell**, Caroline's left-leaning director and lover, and several actual figures from the world of cinema, including the actress and cocaine addict **Mabel Normand**; alcoholic silent-film star **Mary Pickford**; the narcissistic, irrepressible **Charlie Chaplin**; and the handsome leading man **Douglas Fairbanks**. Reviewers particularly lauded the scene in which Chaplin and Fairbanks sit naked in a steam room discussing some of the scandals currently afloat in Hollywood.

Further Reading

Auchincloss, Louis. "Babylon Revisited." *New York Review of Books* Vol. 37, no. 5 (March 29, 1990): 20–2.

Conarroe, Joel. "Klieg Lights on the Potomac." *New York Times Book Review* (January 21, 1990): 1, 38.

Contemporary Literary Criticism Vols. 2, 4, 8, 10, 22, 33, 72. Detroit: Gale Research.

King, Francis. "A Biography of the United States." *Spectator* Vol. 263, no. 8415 (November 4, 1989): 30.

Leader, Zachary. "Where Everyone Thinks Like a Movie." *Observer* (November 5, 1989): 54.

Parini, Jay, ed. *Gore Vidal: Writer Against the Grain.* New York: Columbia University Press, 1992.

See, Carolyn. "Gore Vidal and the Screening of America." *Washington Vol. 20, Post— Book World* no. 2 (January 14, 1990): 1–2.

Snider, Norman. "Movers and Movies: Gore Vidal Links Washington and Hollywood." *Maclean's* Vol. 103, no. 10 (March 5, 1990): 63.

Tryon, Tom. "Vidal in Tinseltown." *Chicago Tribune Books* (January 28, 1990): 1, 4.

Kurt Vonnegut, Jr.

1922–

American novelist, short story writer, dramatist, scriptwriter, and essayist.

Jailbird (novel, 1979)

Plot: Set primarily in the late 1970s, the novel begins with a prologue delivered by pseudonymous science fiction writer Kilgore Trout, who is confined to the same minimum security prison as the main character, Walter Starbuck. The bulk of the novel is Walter's memoir, relating the events of his past through flashbacks before returning to the present. Walter was born to immigrant parents and sent to Harvard University by their eccentric, wealthy employer, Alexander Hamilton McCone. During his college years, Starbuck was a union sympathizer and the editor of a radical newspaper; he and his girlfriend, Mary Kathleen O'Looney, were idealistic followers of the charismatic labor leader Kenneth Whistler. In the 1940s, however, Walter became a government bureaucrat, and at the end of that decade he testified in a pre-McCarthy congressional hearing during which he named his friend Leland Clewes as a former Communist. Clewes's career was subsequently ruined, and Walter's betrayal also resulted in his own inability to get a job. He was supported by his wife until the presidency of Richard Nixon, who, remembering and respecting Walter's role in the hearings, gave him the position of special advisor on youth affairs. When Walter allowed some money to be hidden in his office, he was implicated in the Watergate scandal and sent to prison. Upon his release, he encounters his old lover Mary Kathleen, who now appears to be a New York bag lady but who is actually Mrs. Jack Graham, the widowed majority stockholder of a huge corporation called RAMJAC. She has never abandoned her youthful ideals and wants to put her company into the hands of the American people, thus revitalizing the economy and improving conditions for everyone. Hearing how several people were kind to Walter during his first two days of freedom, she feels inspired to make these individuals officers of RAMJAC. Mary Kathleen's scheme fails, however, after she is hit by a taxi and dies. Two years later, Walter returns to jail after he is convicted of hiding Mary Kathleen's will.

Characters: One of contemporary America's most acclaimed authors, Vonnegut is lauded for his playfully written, sometimes experimental novels blending social protest, black humor, satire, and elements of science fiction. Some critics who had praised such Vonnegut classics as *Cat's Cradle* (1963) and *Slaughterhouse Five; or, The Children's Crusade* noted a disappointing decline in the quality of his work during the 1970s; *Jailbird*, however, was considered by many to be a return to his earlier mastery. Vonnegut incorporates several notable twentieth-century figures and events (such as the trial and execution of Sacco and Vanzetti, the Holocaust, trade unionism, and Richard Nixon) into a story infused with its author's moral outrage at the rampant greed and social injustice of his society. Although *Jailbird* reflects the same bleak vision of humanity found in Vonnegut's other novels, like them it also hints that humanity's capacity for love and kindness may provide an alternative to the world's evils.

The protagonist and main narrator of *Jailbird* is **Walter Starbuck**, whose name echoes the virtuous but powerless first mate in Herman Melville's 1851 novel, *Moby-Dick; or, The White Whale*. Walter is sixty-six years old when he is released from jail; aging, weary, and guilt-ridden, he feels alone and out of step with contemporary life. Flashbacks relate Walter's idealistic youth as a union sympathizer and editor of a progressive newspaper, who promises to emulate the great labor leader, Kenneth Whistler. However, Walter never musters the courage to behave like his hero. He never takes an active role in anything but is instead propelled along by forces larger than himself, and his ideals are gradually smothered by guilt and fear. Thus he relinquished his youthful liberalism first for a minor government job and ultimately for a position in conservative President Richard Nixon's administration. Released after his imprisonment for a typically accidental role in the Watergate conspiracy, Walter chastises himself for never having been "a serious man," for never risking his own life or comfort for others. This capacity for self-criticism makes Walter a sympathetic character despite his cowardice and bungling. As the dying Mary Kathleen O'Looney asserts, he is redeemed by his concern for what happens in the world, even if he never acts on his ideals.

Walter meets his former girlfriend, **Mary Kathleen O'Looney**, by coincidence on the streets of New York City the day after he is released from prison. Dressed in huge, purple tennis shoes in which there is ample space to store a variety of documents, including her will, Mary Kathleen is posing as a bag lady but is actually the widow of multimillionaire Jack Graham. Convinced that evil individuals have designs on RAMJAC, the huge corporation she inherited from her husband, Mary Kathleen operates her business from hiding (recalling the similarly paranoid behavior of American billionaire Howard Hughes). During the period when Mary Kathleen was a reporter for Walter's college newspaper, the two shared the same liberal ideals, including a belief in socialism that Mary Kathleen has not yet abandoned. In fact, she dreams of fomenting a "peaceful economic revolution" by turning her corporation over to the American people, and hearing about Walter's encounters with several kindhearted citizens inspires her to set her plan in motion. This plan is bound to fail, of course, for as Walter ruefully observes, corporations were "rigged only to make profits, were as indifferent to the needs of the people as, say, thunderstorms." Nevertheless, Mary Kathleen is a representative of faith, hope, and love who, just before her death, assures Walter that "at least you believed what the people with hearts believed—so you were a good man just the same." Several commentators point to Mary Kathleen as one of several positively portrayed female characters in Vonnegut's recent fiction who retain their morality in courage even as the men around them succumb to despair.

Walter claims that he has loved four women in his life, all of whom are portrayed as morally superior to the ruthless, dishonest, or merely ineffectual male characters in the novel. His mother and Mary Kathleen O'Looney are the first two, followed by his Harvard girlfriend **Sarah Wyatt**, who would eventually marry Leland Clewes. Although she lost her fortune (her family had owned a factory in which, coincidentally, Mary Kathleen's mother was killed in a radium-poisoning disaster), Sarah never lost her sense of humor, making her one of several courageous female figures in *Jailbird*. Similarly virtuous is Walter's always-supportive wife **Ruth**, a survivor of the Holocaust whose parents died in a concentration camp but who still approaches life with love and strength.

Walter meets a number of notable characters during his prison term, including **Bob Fender**, a former veterinarian who was mistakenly convicted of treason and given a life sentence. A science fiction writer who uses the pen name **Kilgore Trout**, (a character in several earlier Vonnegut novels, in each of which he takes on different qualities), Fender offers readers some background information in his prologue to Walter's memoir. **Emil Larkin** is a disbarred lawyer and former hatchet man for Richard Nixon who seems closely modeled after Watergate conspirator Charles Colson. Like Colson, Larkin is a former football player who became a born-again Christian while serving a prison sentence. **Clyde Carter**, who is presented as a third cousin of and dead-ringer for President Jimmy Carter, is a prison guard who takes correspondence courses in bartending and locksmithing in the hope of improving his situation.

Characters from Walter's past include **Alexander Hamilton McCone**, the eccentric millionaire and chronic stammerer who was devastated by the sight of his father's factory workers being killed during a strike and who pays for his employee's son to attend Harvard University; and **Leland Clewes**, who was ruined by Walter's testimony that he once belonged to the Communist Party. Modeled after Powers Hapgood, a dynamic labor leader Vonnegut met in 1945, **Kenneth Whistler** is a union organizer from whom Walter and Mary Kathleen hear the story of Sacco and Vanzetti (used throughout the novel as a powerful metaphor for social injustice) and who inspires them with his vision of a Socialist utopia.

Galápagos (novel, 1985)

Plot: The novel begins in the 1980s. American and South American entrepreneurs have arranged the "Nature Cruise of the Century," a tour of the Galápagos Islands aboard the luxury ship *Bahía de Darwin*, which is scheduled to depart from the coast of Ecuador. *Galápagos* is narrated by the ghost of Leon Trotsky Trout, an American veteran of the Vietnam War who was killed in Sweden while working on the construction of the ship. A number of celebrities, including Mick Jagger and Jackie Kennedy Onassis, have signed up for the excursion, but most cancel their reservations when a worldwide economic crisis erupts and the citizens of Ecuador begin staging riots. A few passengers do show up for the cruise, however, including former schoolteacher Mary Hepburn, con-man James Wait (who marries and then abandons wealthy widows), Japanese computer genius Zenji Hiroguchi and his wife Hisako, and a scheming American entrepreneur named Andrew McIntosh who is traveling with his blind daughter Selena. Just as the *Bahía de Darwin* sets sail, war breaks out between Peru and Ecuador, and the ship's confused captain, Adolph von Kleist, runs her aground on one of the Galápagos Islands. Most of the group eventually dies, and the rest of humanity succumbs to a virus that attacks women's ovaries but Mary Hepburn and Captain von Kleist survive and become the progenitors of a new human race. Trout now shifts his story ahead a million years, relating that human beings have evolved into fur-covered, fish-eating creatures endowed with flippers and a much lower level of intelligence that has allowed them to avoid the pitfalls of technology and other twentieth-century dangers. Finding little else on earth to interest him, Trout finally decides to join his father in the Afterlife.

Characters: Vonnegut is an important contemporary novelist who uses satire, irony, iconoclastic humor, and elements of science fiction to explore philosophical questions and comment on social injustice. Often cited as one of Vonnegut's most successful novels, *Galápagos* is narrated in, according to critic Lorrie Moore, his uniquely "grumbly and idiomatic . . . unfakable and childlike" voice. Infused with a sense of human futility and destructiveness, the novel centers on the proposal that intelligence may not be the evolutionary asset it has always been considered. While some commentators claim that the novel's reverse-Darwinian theme reflects Vonnegut's deep pessimism, others claim that it is meant only as a warning and that, as always, beneath his despair lies a considerable measure of compassion and humor.

Leon Trotsky Trout, the novel's narrator, is the son of Vonnegut's recurring character **Kilgore Trout**, a science fiction writer whose personality takes on different traits in different works. As *Galápagos* begins, both Kilgore and Leon are dead; in fact, Kilgore has tried unsuccessfully to persuade his son join him in the Afterlife rather than lingering on earth to witness the misdeeds of humanity. But Leon chooses to haunt the *Bahía de Darwin*, during whose construction he was killed, thus allowing Vonnegut the advantages of a narrative perspective that is both specific and omniscient. Like Billy Pilgrim, the protagonist of Vonnegut's acclaimed 1969 novel *Slaughterhouse Five*, Leon is able to comment on humanity from a great distance (which in Leon's case is a span of a million years). The reader is only gradually given enough information to piece together Leon's identity, so that at first it is not clear who is narrating the story. Eventually, however, it becomes obvious that like many other Vonnegut characters he is, as described by Charles Berryman, a "forlorn and abject plaything of fate,'' a born loser despite his intelligence and sensitivity. After an unhappy childhood during which he felt abandoned by his parents, Leon joined the Marines and went to fight in the Vietnam War, where a steady diet of horrors left him feeling further betrayed. Again, Leon's negative experience with war makes him a quintessential Vonnegut protagonist and also helps to underline the general theme of human destructiveness. Leon finally fled to Sweden, but even this apparent refuge failed him when he was decapitated by a falling sheet of metal. Nevertheless, Leon does not seem to share the cynicism of Kilgore, who tells his son that ''the more you learn about people the more disgusted you'll become.'' Leon's mother, on the other hand, treasured a quote from the diary of Anne Frank, the Jewish girl who ultimately died in the Holocaust: ''In spite of everything, I still believe people are really good at heart.'' Some commentators believe that this resilient optimism lies at the heart of the novel, even though Leon finally does decide to follow the blue tunnel to the Afterlife. He finds nothing to interest him in life on earth among the peaceful but bland creatures that human beings have become, suggesting that this eventuality is not meant to be interpreted as desirable.

Some critics have detected some notable links between **Adolf von Kleist**, the captain of the *Bahía de Darwin*, and his creator, including both his physical appearance and the fact that his name may refer to the nineteenth-century German writer Heinrich von Kleist, whose often ironic works focused, like Vonnegut's, on absurdity and inhumanity. Termed a ''reluctant Adam'' by critic Charles Berryman, Captain von Kleist is a comically confused, inept character who does not realize that his sexual encounters with **Mary Hepburn** result in the artificial insemination of six girls from the Kanka-bono tribe, making him a savior of the human race. The captain is killed while trying to save Mary Hepburn from a shark attack. An aging, recently widowed, retired schoolteacher, she is subject to bouts of nearly suicidal despair as well as doubts about the veracity of biology, the subject she formerly taught. Mary is the only character in the novel who fully understands Darwin's evolutionary theories. Her students nicknamed her ''Mother Nature Personified,'' which becomes an especially apt moniker when, after having sex with Captain von Kleist, she saves the human race by transferring his semen to six young women; thus the narrator calls her ''the most important experimenter in the history of the human race.'' Killed by a great white shark while trying to rescue Hiroguchi's computer, Mary has been seen as a representative and defender of knowledge and learning.

Another significant passenger on the *Bahía de Darwin* is **James Wait**, a con-man who has already married and abandoned seventeen rich, elderly widows and is in search of his eighteenth bride. The product of incest between a father and daughter, Wait was a homosexual prostitute before discovering his particular means to making a fortune. One of several of the novel's characters deemed ''Nature's experiments'' with various traits—in this case, ''purposeless greed''—Wait demonstrates how the human intelligence may be channeled into destructive, hurtful deceit. Vonnegut borrowed Wait's name from the protagonist of Joseph Conrad's 1897 novel *The Nigger of the Narcissus*, but he has also been compared to the title character in Herman Melville's *The Confidence Man* (1857).

Other characters in *Galápagos* include the Japanese computer genius **Zenji Hiroguchi**, the inventor of the fabulous Mandarax computer (which is capable of translating all languages and of calling up famous quotations for all occasions), who perpetually feels that his head is about to explode; and his pregnant, disaffected wife **Hisako**, who is described as ''Nature's experiment with depression'' and who eventually commits suicide by walking into the sea with **Selena**, the daughter of **Andrew McIntosh**. A boisterous American entrepreneur, McIntosh plans to buy up Ecuador at bargain prices and thus take over the country's economy. Egotistical and heartless, McIntosh represents the use of intelligence in dehumanizing ways; thus, by the laws of reverse-Darwinism, he and the similarly endowed Hiroguchi are the first of the passengers to die when they are killed by a maddened soldier.

Bluebeard (novel, 1987)

Plot: The novel is structured as the autobiography of painter and art collector Rabo Karabekian, who relates both the story of his life and the significant events of the summer he has just spent at his Long Island, New York mansion. Rabo's parents were Armenians who barely escaped the Turkish extermination of the late 1920s, only to be bilked out of their fortune by a con-man who sold them a nonexistent home in San Ignacio, California. The young Rabo's gift for drawing led to an apprenticeship with the renowned illustrator Dan Gregory, who banished the young man after discovering his affair with his mistress, Marilee Kemp. Rabo then went off to fight in World War II, becoming a member of a camouflage unit comprised entirely of artists. He was ultimately wounded and captured by the Germans. After the war ended, Rabo returned to New York and became involved with a group of abstract impressionist painters, whose works he bought in order to support their careers. He also attained some acclaim of his own as a painter but lost this standing when the defective paint he had used caused his works to self-destruct. Rabo now lives alone (though he is sometimes joined by his novelist friend Paul Slazinger) in the mansion he inherited from his second wife, where he feels like a "museum guard" to his valuable art collection. His bleak outlook changes, however, when he meets an attractive, energetic widow named Circe Berman, an author of books for teenagers who is currently working on a biography of her husband. She brings a much-needed warmth to Rabo's home but also challenges his preference for nonrepresentational art. At the end of the novel, Rabo shows Circe the masterpiece he has painted and has been hiding from the prying, critical eyes of the world. Entitled "Now It's the Women's Turn," this surprisingly representational work reflects both the sorrowful impact of the Second World War on Rabo and his underlying optimism.

Characters: Marked by the same humor, inventive language, and outrage over societal amnesia and injustice that are found in Vonnegut's other books, *Bluebeard* is one of few with a happy ending. The novel seems to reflect Vonnegut's views of his own, highly autobiographical work and his sense of worth as a writer, his evolving perceptions about sexual roles, and his conviction that it is possible to make sense of past tragedies by transforming them into art and by strengthening one's connections with others.

Rabo Karabekian made his first appearance in Vonnegut's 1973 novel *Breakfast of Champions*, in which he was a minimalist painter whose works sold for outrageously high sums. In *Bluebeard*, Rabo is seventy-one years old and apparently no longer painting (at the end of the novel, of course, the reader learns that he has, in fact, produced a final masterpiece), serving instead as the "museum guard" for the works of his old artist friends. Like many Vonnegut protagonists (and like Vonnegut himself), two factors permanently affect Rabo: the unhappiness of his parents and World War II. His father never recovered from the succeeding traumas he endured—first the Turkish massacre of Armenians, then being swindled of the jewels that might have helped him make a strong new start in America. Thus Rabo grew up in an atmosphere of despair. After his short, abortive apprenticeship with Dan Gregory he went to war, where he lost an eye and spent time in a German prison camp. Emerging alive, if outwardly and inwardly altered, from this experience, Rabo married and moved to New York City, where he joined the circle of painters who would come to be known as the Abstract Expressionists. After the loss of two wives and the collapse of his own artistic career, Rabo still loves abstract paintings, which he says are "about absolutely nothing but themselves." Yet *Bluebeard* in general does not denigrate representational art (which is defended by one of the novel's most sympathetic characters, Circe Berman), and at the end Rabo reveals "Now It's the Women's Turn," the epic and surprisingly realistic work he has been hiding in his potato barn. Blending suggestions of birth and death, pathos and joy, the painting depicts the end of World War II as a large assemblage of people standing in a valley. Although he is a painter and not a writer, Rabo has been interpreted as an autobiographical character in that his career mirrors

Vonnegut's. Whereas Vonnegut began as a journalist, Rabo was an illustrator; and both Vonnegut and Rabo left the realm of representational art, the former for experimental fiction and the latter for abstract painting. Rabo's dismay when his paintings self-destructed and he realized they were not very accomplished to begin with may well reflect Vonnegut's misgivings about his fiction, which some commentators have called shallow and facile. In addition, the creative output of both character and creator becomes more representational late in their careers, with Vonnegut writing novels that are notably more realistic than his early, experimental works and Rabo choosing a representational style for his final masterpiece. Finally, Rabo's painting itself may be seen as an embodiment of the great theme and passion of all of Vonnegut's fiction, World War II.

As a young man with a talent for drawing, Rabo wants nothing more than to serve as an apprentice with the famous illustrator, **Dan Gregory**. With his immense popularity and notably middlebrow sensibility, Gregory is clearly modeled after Norman Rockwell, the American artist whose paintings once appeared regularly on the covers of the *Saturday Evening Post*. Gregory's work is presented as second rate owing to its falsification and sentimentalization of reality, charges often leveled at Rockwell's work as well. A sexist, cruel admirer of Mussolini, Gregory banishes Rabo from his studio when he learns of the liaison between the young man and his mistress. **Merilee Kemp** is a lonely, intelligent woman who plays an important role in Rabo's life by answering his letters to Gregory and arranging for him to serve an apprenticeship with the famous illustrator. Physically and emotionally abused by her lover, Merilee later establishes an all-female community to provide shelter for women who, like herself, have found the male-dominated world a dangerous place. Critics have cited Merilee as evidence of a trend in Vonnegut's fiction toward strong female characters and his evolving sense of their nurturing role in society.

Another positively portrayed female character is **Circe Berman**, a voluptuous, vital widow in her early forties who relieves the dullness of Rabo's existence and stirs his long-deadened emotions. A biographer and author of novels that provide contemporary teenagers with guidance in the form of fiction, Berman is both a purveyor and an advocate of representational art. She believes that the role of art is, above all, to communicate, to create bonds between people, and she finds Rabo's collection of abstract expressionist works cold and meaningless. Despite their ideological differences (which are finally revealed as insignificant in view of Rabo's final painting), Circe transforms Rabo's home into a warm, cozy place where, with her encouragement, he can compose his autobiography.

Other characters in *Bluebeard* include Rabo's friend **Paul Slazinger**, a writer of sophisticated novels who also finds Circe's presence conducive to writing; and **Terry Kitchen**, a famous painter friend of Rabo's (his acquaintances also include such actual abstract artists as Jackson Pollack and Mark Rothko) who commits suicide.

Further Reading

Allen, William Rodney. *Understanding Kurt Vonnegut*. Columbia: University of South Carolina Press, 1991.

Bishop, Michael. "Kurt Vonnegut and the Next Million Years." *Book World–The Washington Post* (September 22, 1985): 1, 10.

Contemporary Literary Criticism Vols. 1–5, 8, 12, 22, 40. Detroit: Gale Research.

Kakutani, Michiko. Review of *Galápagos*. *New York Times* (September 25, 1985): C17.

Moore, Lorrie. "How Humans Got Flippers and Beaks." *New York Times Book Review* (October 6, 1985): 7.

Mustazza, Leonard. *Forever Pursuing Genesis: The Myth of Eden in the Novels of Kurt Vonnegut.* Lewisburg, PA: Bucknell University Press, 1990.

Rackstraw, Loree. "Vonnegut the Diviner and Other Auguries." *North American Review* 264 (Winter 1979): 75–76.

———. "Blue Tunnels to Survival." *North American Review* Vol. 270, no. 4 (December 1985): 78–80.

Reed, Peter J. "God Bless You, Mr. Darwin, for Kurt Vonnegut's Latest." *Minneapolis Star and Tribunal* (October 20, 1985): 10G.

Skenazy, Paul. "Poking Holes in the Social Fabric." *San Francisco Chronicle Review* (October 4, 1987): 1, 10.

Alice Walker
1944–

American novelist, short story writer, essayist, poet, critic, editor, and author of children's books.

Possessing the Secret of Joy (novel, 1992)

Plot: The novel takes place in an unnamed African country (based, perhaps, on Kenya) and in the United States, focusing on the experiences of Tashi, who first appeared in Alice Walker's 1982 novel *The Color Purple.* Born a member of the Olinka people, Tashi was befriended by African Americans Adam and Olivia Johnson when their missionary parents brought them to her village. It was partly through the Johnson family's influence that Tashi was, at that time, spared the traditional ritual of circumcision, which involves the removal (usually in unsanitary conditions and without anesthesia) of a young girl's clitoris and external genitalia and the sewing up—leaving only a small aperture—of the resulting wound. The procedure is intended to ensure a woman's faithfulness to her husband and to enhance his sexual pleasure. As a teenager, Tashi falls in love with Adam and the two plan to marry. While Adam is in America, however, Tashi decides to undergo the circumcision as an act of political solidarity with her people, who are involved in a struggle for independence. The procedure is performed by the same *tsunga*, the old and much-revered M'Lissa, who circumcised Tashi's sister, a hemophiliac who subsequently bled to death. Adam arrives in Tashi's village to find her suffering greatly in the aftermath of the circumcision, the long-term effects of which prove both physically and psychically damaging. Adam and Tashi go to the United States, where Tashi becomes known as Evelyn Johnson. She grows increasingly troubled, for the ordinary processes of urination and menstruation are painful and difficult, she is unable to enjoy sex, and her one son is born mentally disabled due to the difficult birth caused by Tashi's physical mutilation. In addition, she is unable to have any more children. After undergoing therapy with several analysts, including the great Swiss psychiatrist Carl Jung, Tashi's madness and despair turn to anger and she decides to kill the woman she feels has warped her life. She goes to Africa and finds that M'Lissa has become a nationally renowned symbol of traditional values. Tashi does murder M'Lissa and is condemned to death. At her execution, her family members hold up a banner that proclaims, "Resistance is the secret of joy!"

Characters: Walker is acclaimed for her powerful fiction exploring and celebrating the efforts of African American women to achieve personal wholeness and political autonomy.

A self described "womanist," Walker emphasizes the importance of the bonds between women. Although her work is sometimes faulted as polemical and anti-male, she is lauded for the skill and grace with which she renders the experiences of her memorable characters. In *Possessing the Secret of Joy*, Walker looks unflinchingly at the physical and emotional damage wrought by female circumcision, which, she asserts in a note to the reader, has been performed on ninety to one hundred million young women in Africa, the Far East, and the Middle East. Most critics found Walker's detailed descriptions of the procedure horrifying but not sensational, evidencing her belief in the importance of breaking the silence that has shrouded this brutal practice.

Readers of Walker's previous fiction will recognize **Tashi/Evelyn Johnson** from both *The Color Purple* and *The Temple of My Familiar*, in which she played a minor role as an African friend of the missionary Johnson family. Now older and tragically dysfunctional, Tashi takes center stage in *Possessing the Secret of Joy* as she struggles with the effects of circumcision on her life. As a young girl, Tashi is initially spared the ritual that killed her sister, whose death continues to haunt her subconscious. But as a teenager who plans to leave Africa and settle in America and who fears the loss of her own cultural identity, Tashi comes under the influence of her people's new independence leaders, who are urging them to reembrace traditional rituals. She makes a conscious, politically motivated decision to undergo circumcision, convinced that it will make her "completely woman. Completely Africa. Completely Olinka." Its effect, however, is to cripple her both physically and psychologically, robbing her of both her former grace and quickness and her emotional stability. Tashi becomes increasingly bitter and enraged until finally, with the help of two very different but effective analysts, she is able to identify the sources of her distress. She confronts her memories of her sister's death, reaching an important milestone when she can call what happened by its true name: murder. Tashi's resultant anger propels her to Africa, where she achieves literal revenge for her sister's death and the mutilation of hundreds of other girls—as well as symbolic revenge, perhaps, for the damage done to millions of women across the globe—by murdering M'Lissa. Tashi then faces her own death with no apparent remorse or fear, despite her recognition that M'Lissa was herself a victim of culturally sanctioned brutality. The novel's title refers to a passage in the 1982 book *African Saga* by Mirella Ricciardi, an Italian raised in Africa who describes Africans as "natural" beings who possess a "secret of joy" that allows them to endure suffering and humiliation. In an ironic reversal of this concept, the last thing Tashi sees before her death is the banner proclaiming that "Resistance is the secret of joy!"

In her note to the reader, Walker explains that she invented the word *tsunga* as a title for **M'Lissa**, the elderly practitioner of traditional Olinka rituals who has performed hundreds of circumcisions. Through M'Lissa, Walker explores the concept of women's own compliance in a practice that brutalizes them, for mothers whose own lives have been undeniably warped by circumcision send their own daughters to undergo the same torture. In fact, by the time of Tashi's return to Africa the elderly M'Lissa has become a nationally celebrated mother-figure. At the same time, she herself speaks eloquently of her own circumcision, after which she would never again see "that child" that she had once been. And in reference to what she and other circumcisers have done, ostensibly in the service of tradition and of their country, she asks, "But who are we but the torturers of children?"

Tashi's sympathetically portrayed, gentle husband **Adam Johnson** rescues her from the filthy hut in which she is languishing after her circumcision, taking her back to America with him and marrying her. Initially a joyous, loving couple, their relationship is inevitably damaged by Tashi's physical mutilation and resulting madness. Although Adam remains loyal to Tashi and sensitive to her suffering, his need for companionship results in a long-term affair with his French friend **Lisette**, a white woman who grew up in colonial Algeria and who shares both her nostalgia for her idyllic North African childhood and her reflections on the ills of colonialism. Tashi's son **Benny**, whose mental development is stymied owing to his difficult birth, becomes strongly attached to his half-brother **Pierre**, the son of Adam and Lisette. Initially brutally aggressive and resentful toward Pierre, Tashi eventually grows to love him and he lends her a great deal of support. A positively portrayed blend of races, cultures, and even sexualities, Pierre decides to study anthropology in order to understand what happened to his father's wife and how a female sexuality that was originally joyful and affirmative was eventually transformed into something so damaging. Raised with an awareness of feminism and cultural pluralism, Pierre is a uniquely sensitive, intelligent character whom one critic, Yakini Kemp, has identified as one of Walker's "human beings for the new world order." Adam's sister (and Tashi's best friend) **Olivia** is only sketchily drawn.

Walker makes the celebrated Swiss psychiatrist **Carl Jung** a character in the novel, asserting through him that cruelty is a universal evil for which no cultural excuse should be made. In treating Tashi, Jung identifies within his own nature "a self that is horrified at what was done to her, but recognizes it as something that is also done to me. A truly universal self." Tashi's other therapist is the plucky **Raye**, who as an African American woman can relate to Tashi on a level that Jung, despite his deep and universal understanding, cannot. Another significant character in the novel is **Mbati**, the young Olinka woman who is caring for M'Lissa when Tashi returns to Africa and who become Tashi's spiritual daughter. Tashi acknowledges her own deep pain to Mbati, who responds warmly: "I can see you are flawed. You have not hidden it. That is your greatest gift to me."

Further Reading

Ansa, Tina McElroy. "Taboo Territory." *Los Angeles Times Book Review* (July 5, 1992): 4, 8.

Anshaw, Carol. "The Practice of Cruelty." *Chicago Tribune* (June 21, 1992): Sec. 14, p. 3.

Concise Dictionary of American Literary Biography: Broadening Views, 1968–1988. Detroit: Gale Research.

Contemporary Literary Criticism Vols. 5, 6, 9, 19, 27, 46, 58. Detroit: Gale Research.

Dictionary of Literary Biography Vols. 6, 33. Detroit: Gale Research.

Erickson, Peter. "Canon Revision Update: A 1992 Edition." *Kenyon Review* Vol. 15, no. 3 (Summer 1993): 197–207.

Hospital, Janette Turner. "What They Did to Tashi." *New York Times Book Review* (June 28, 1992): 11–12.

Kemp, Yakini. Review of *Possessing the Secret of Joy. Belles Lettres* Vol. 8 (Fall 1992): 57.

Larson, Charles R. "Against the Tyranny of Tradition." *Washington Post—Book World* (July 5, 1992): 1, 14.

Sage, Lorna. "Initiated into Pain." *Times Literary Supplement* (October 9, 1992): 29.

Wilentz, Gay. "Healing the Wounds of Time." *Women's Review of Books* (February, 1993): 15–16.

Winchell, Donna Haisty. *Alice Walker*. New York: Twayne, 1992.

Wendy Wasserstein
1950–
American dramatist.

The Heidi Chronicles (drama, 1988)

Plot: The play comprises thirteen scenes depicting some important moments in the life of central character Heidi Holland, from high school in 1950s Chicago to her current status as a single parent living in New York City. Along the way, Heidi attends a 1968 rally in support of liberal Democrat Eugene McCarthy's presidential campaign, sits in on a women's consciousness-raising session in Ann Arbor, and marches in a 1974 protest against the neglect of women in the arts. In addition, Heidi interacts with several female friends, the opportunistic, womanizing Scoop Rosenbaum—who is occasionally her lover—and the sincere, witty Peter Patrone, a gay pediatrician. Near the end of the play, Heidi delivers a memorable address to a gathering of girls' school alumnae, revealing her sense of abandonment by the women of her generation, who once shared but lost the ideals of the 1960s. As the play draws to a close, Heidi finds contentment through her adoption of a baby girl.

Characters: Wasserstein has been highly lauded for the incisive social observation and humor of *The Heidi Chronicles*, which won a Pulitzer Prize for Drama, a Tony Award, and a New York Critics Circle Award. Wasserstein is recognized as a talented chronicler of her own "Baby Boomer" generation, which she depicts as moving from social activism and idealism in the 1960s to disillusionment in the 1970s to materialism in the 1980s. While many critics interpreted the play as affirming feminism, some complained that its ending was contrived, unmotivated, and even anti-feminist.

The central character in *The Heidi Chronicles* is art historian **Heidi Holland**, an intelligent, witty, attractive woman in her late thirties. Critic Mimi Kramer claims that Wasserstein presents Heidi "not as an advocate of the women's movement but one of its victims—a vessel carrying around the ideals and experiences of her time." Although she has achieved success in her career of promoting the recognition of women artists and seems to have a rich, rewarding life, Heidi feels empty and disillusioned. Independent, strong-willed, and unmarried, part of her discontentment is the absence of a committed, loving man in her life. In scenes that recreate Heidi's experiences from the mid-1960s through the mid-1980s, the audience sees her as a passive but wise-cracking attendee at a 1965 high school dance, a reluctant participant in a women's consciousness-raising session in the 1970s, and a member of a panel discussion on a 1980s television talk-show. Heidi senses keenly the gradual fraying of her generation's idealism and sense of community. In an ad-libbed address on the topic of "Women, Where Are We Going?" to a group of alumnae of her girlhood school, Heidi says she has been abandoned by the women who once shared her values to their personal gain and advancement. Heidi plaintively comments, "I thought the point was we were all in this together." Many critics have identified this monologue as the thematic high point of the play. At the end of *The Heidi Chronicles*, she achieves fulfillment as the single mother of an adopted daughter, without the approval of any man. Although some critics faulted this conclusion as sexist implying women's fulfillment comes only through childbearing, most lauded Wasserstein for imbuing Heidi with the disillusionment and bewilderment, shared by the 1960s generation.

Despite the play's strong feminist content, its second and third most vivid characters are male. Heidi's close friend and soulmate is **Peter Patrone**, a liberal, homosexual pediatrician who is nationally renowned for his work with AIDS-afflicted children (thus allowing

Wasserstein to introduce this highly topical issue into the play). In an especially moving passage, Peter laments the diminishment of his circle of friends in the wake of the AIDS epidemic. Charming, sensitive, and earnest, Peter seems to share all of Heidi's opinions as well as her sharp wit. Peter serves as a strong contrast to **Scoop Rosenbaum**, the arrogant but notably charismatic editor of a slick lifestyle magazine called *Boomer*. Heidi meets Scoop at a 1968 political rally at which he is successfully impersonating a radical; he calls Heidi a ''serious good person'' and predicts that ''You'll be one of those true believers who didn't understand it was just a phase.'' Several commentators have questioned why Heidi holds a longtime affection for this cynical, sexist, manipulative person, who ultimately spurns her for a more conventional marriage prospect.

The most notable of the play's other female figures is probably **Susan Johnston**, a rather flat character serving as a foil to Heidi. She changes her circumstances and personality in accordance with prevailing trends. For example, she starts her career as a Supreme Court clerk, then joins a Montana's women's collective community, and later produces Hollywood television situation comedies. Scoop chooses to marry not smart, spirited Heidi but conventional, affluent **Lisa**, a pampered and decidedly unliberated Southerner whose work as a book illustrator is cast as requiring little intelligence. Also depicted as humorously vacuous is the **talk-show hostess**—with her ever-present mug of coffee and her all-purpose response, ''Boy, I'm impressed''—on whose show Heidi, Peter, and Scoop appear.

Further Reading

Barnes, Clive. ''Hello, I'm the Me Generation.'' *New York Post* (December 12, 1988).

Brustein, Robert. ''Women in Extremis.'' *New Republic* Vol. 200, no. 16 (April 17, 1989): 32–4.

Contemporary Literary Criticism. Vols. 32, 59. Detroit: Gale Research.

Gussow, Mel. ''A Modern-Day Heffalump in Search of Herself.'' *New York Times* (December 12, 1988): C13.

Keyssar, Helene. ''Drama and the Dialogic Imagination: *The Heidi Chronicles* and *Fefu and Her Friends*.'' *Modern Drama* Vol. 34 (March 1991): 88–106.

Kramer, Mimi. ''Portrait of a Lady.'' *New Yorker* Vol. LXIV, no. 45 (December 26, 1988): 81–2.

Robins, Corinne. ''Betrayals.'' *American Book Review* Vol. 11, no. 5 (November–December 1989): 4.

Shapiro, Walter. ''Chronicler of Frayed Feminism.'' *Time* Vol. 133, no. 13 (March 27, 1989): 90–2.

Simon, John. ''Partial Autobiographies.'' *New York Magazine* Vol. 22, no. 1 (January 2, 1989): 48–9.

———.''Jammies Session.'' *New York Magazine* Vol. 22, no. 13 (March 27, 1989): 66, 68.

Weales, Gerald. ''American Theatre Watch: 1988–1989.'' *Georgia Review* Vol. XLIII, no. 3 (fall 1989): 573–85.

Winer, Laurie. ''Christine Lahti as an Angry Heidi in *Chronicles*.'' New York Times (October 9, 1989): C13, C16.

Fay Weldon
1933–

English novelist, short story writer, scriptwriter, and dramatist.

The Life and Loves of a She-Devil (novel, 1984)

Plot: The novel centers on Ruth Patchett, a hulking, profoundly unattractive woman who is married to a handsome accountant named Bobbo and has two ill-behaved children. The insensitive Bobbo married Ruth for convenience and frequently indulges in extramarital affairs that he later describes to his docile, subservient wife. After a particularly unsuccessful dinner party at the Patchett home, Bobbo announces that he is leaving Ruth to move in with his current lover, the beautiful romance novelist Mary Fisher, who lives in a converted lighthouse she calls High Tower. Denouncing his wife's skills as a wife and mother and even her status as a woman, Bobbo calls her a "she-devil." Ruth subsequently decides to become exactly what Bobbo has described. She burns down the Patchett home and, leaving her children at High Tower to be cared for by Mary Fisher, sets about destroying the lives of both Bobbo and his girlfriend. Posing as a nursing home aide, Ruth cleverly maneuvers the institution into sending Mary's vulgar, incontinent mother to live with her. Later Ruth becomes Vesta Rose, proprietor of a temporary agency through which she manages to have Bobbo arrested for embezzlement. Casting herself as domestic servant Polly Patch, Ruth ingratiates herself with the judge who is to sentence Bobbo, so that Bobbo's prison term is greatly increased. Meanwhile, Ruth goes about physically transforming herself—through painful, laborious plastic surgery—into the mirror image of Mary Fisher. Concurrently, Mary's life comes unraveled as her household is overrun by Bobbo's children, her mother, and even her manipulative manservant, Garcia; her imprisoned lover no longer wants her to visit him; and her fiction loses popularity. Mary eventually contracts cancer and dies, while Ruth installs herself at High Tower with Bobbo, who, after his release from prison, is as needy and obsequious as Ruth once was.

Characters: Weldon's fiction focuses on the problems of contemporary women, frequently portraying marriage as oppressive and husbands as insensitive exploiters. Praised for her sardonic humor and polished prose, Weldon often creates outlandish plots in which serious themes are overlaid with comedy. Described as an "exaggerated parable of love and power" by critic Alice Denham, *The Life and Loves of a She-Devil* is a revenge fantasy that takes the concept of retribution to extreme ends.

The novel's narrative voice alternates between a third-person narrator and the central character, the initially unattractive, hulking **Ruth Patchett**. Dark and heavy, Ruth is six feet, two inches tall and has three hair-sprouting moles on her face; her manner, however, is always patient and accommodating. For years she has silently tolerated her husband's philandering, insults, and complete insensitivity, and it is suggested that a childhood spent with a mother who was repulsed by her prepared her for this unhappy existence. But Bobbo's departure and flight to his lover, Mary Fisher, sparks something in Ruth: having been labeled a she-devil, she becomes one. Ruth concludes that it is "better to hate than to grieve. I sing in praise of hate, and all its attendant energy;" that energy is expressed, throughout the rest of the novel, in the red or pink light that glows from Ruth's eyes. Ruth propels herself from docility to self-determination, becoming by turns Vesta Rose, Polly Patch, and, to her admiring but gradually more horrified plastic surgeon, Marlene Hunter. She grows increasingly merciless and domineering, methodically destroying the lives of those who have hurt her. Critics differ in their interpretations of how we are to view Ruth. Some emphasize the novel's porotic quality and thus find Ruth's wickedness and self-alteration entertaining, Whereas others maintain that her transformation is tragically empty.

Indeed, after the excruciating plastic surgery to make her legs shorter, Ruth compares herself to the Little Mermaid, whose "every step . . . was like walking on knives." Her new life is not only physically painful but emotionally and spiritually barren, for she has realized her dream of being loved but not returning love. Several commentators contend that Weldon portrays Ruth as a Frankenstein-like character who fashions herself into a monster, albeit one who wields the same power that was once used against her.

Bobbo Patchett, a handsome accountant whose marriage to Ruth was motivated by a combination of convenience and pity, is typical of the villainous male characters found in much of Weldon's fiction. An insensitive, hypocritical philanderer, he describes all of his extramarital sexual encounters to his wife, whom he expects to remain faithful to him and to uncomplainingly fulfill her domestic duties. Bobbo's excoriation of Ruth, just before he leaves her to move in with Mary, exemplifies his cruelty: "You are a third-rate person. You are a bad mother, a worse wife, and a dreadful cook. In fact I don't think you are a woman at all. I think what you are is a she-devil!" Thus Bobbo unintentionally gives Ruth the impetus for her transformation, at the completion of which she has reversed their roles so that he is, according to Rosalyn Drexler, her "appendage, whipping boy, hanger-on, doormat, [and] love slave."

Ruth cannot initially hope to compete with her husband's lover, the successful, wealthy novelist **Mary Fisher.** A writer of trashy romance novels that Ruth calls "treacherous" because they lull women into a false, passive view of life, Mary is as pretty, petite, and exquisitely dainty as Ruth is ugly, hulking, and clumsy. Owing to Ruth's wickedly ingenious machinations, Mary gradually loses everything she values. Ruth, meanwhile, has fashioned herself in Mary's physical image and eventually establishes herself in Mary's home—the appropriately named High Tower, where she hid herself from the ugliness of lives like Ruth's. Finally, however, in a concession that critics have found effectively ambiguous, Ruth concedes that Mary wins in the end because "she is a woman: she made the landscape better. She-devils can make nothing better, except themselves."

The novel's secondary characters include **Old Carver,** the elderly, unkempt, reportedly brain-damaged caretaker of a nearby sports field whom Ruth seduces as her initiation into life as a she-devil; Mary's venal, calculating manservant **Garcia,** who is ultimately exploited by Ruth in the same way he exploited Mary; the wealthy, arrogant **Judge Henry Bissop,** whose fear of beauty leads him to beat his wife during lovemaking and attracts him to Polly Patch; and Ruth's disreputable but skilled cosmetic surgeon, **Dr. Genghis,** who recognizes as "trivial" Ruth's goal of looking exactly like Mary. Ruth uses Mary's crude, extremely unpleasant mother, **Mrs. Fisher,** to help bring about Mary's downfall; Ruth's bratty, unattractive children, **Andy and Nicola,** also contribute to this process as they torment Mary with their bad behavior and methodically destroy her house.

Further Reading

Contemporary Literary Criticism Vols. 6, 9, 11, 19, 36, 59. Detroit: Gale Research.

Denham, Alice. "Heavy Hands." *Nation* (March 16, 1985): 315–16.

Dictionary of Literary Biography Vol. 14. Detroit: Gale Research.

Drexler, Rosalyn. "Looking for Love After Marriage: *The Life and Loves of a She-Devil.*" *New York Times Book Review* (September 30, 1984): 1, 47.

Glastonbury, Marion. "Days of Judgment." *New Statesman & Society* (January 20, 1984): 24.

Review of *The Life and Loves of a She-Devil. New York Times* (August 21, 1984): C17.

Stewart, J.I.M. "Other Things." *London Review of Books* (February 2–15, 1984): 16.

Wilde, Alan. "'Bold, But Not Too Bold': Fay Weldon and the Limits of Poststructuralist Criticism." *Contemporary Literature* Vol. 29, no. 3 (Fall, 1988): 403–19.

John Edgar Wideman
1941–
American novelist, short story writer, nonfiction writer, and critic.

Sent for You Yesterday (novel, 1983)

Plot: The novel comprises a number of interwoven episodes that shift back and forth in time from 1934 to about 1970. The narrator is Doot Lawson, a young, college-educated African American who lives in Wyoming but returns periodically to Homewood, the Pittsburgh ghetto in which he was raised. There he listens avidly to the older residents' reminiscences, admiring their resilience in the face of racism, material hardship, and various tragedies. Of particular interest and significance is the story of blues singer Albert Wilkes, who fled Homewood after killing the white policeman with whose wife he had been sleeping. Albert returned to Homewood after seven years on the run, but was shot to death by the police as he sat at a friend's piano.

Characters: Winner of the 1984 PEN/Faulkner Award for Fiction, *Sent for You Yesterday* is the most acclaimed work of Wideman's "Homewood Trilogy," which also includes *Damballah* and *Hiding Place* (both published in 1981). Wideman's fiction focuses on the individual's quest for self-knowledge as he grapples both with his own memories and yearnings and the wider experiences of the African American community from which he comes. Wideman's rich language, use of dialect, and meticulous recreation of a setting that he endows with mythic significance have led to comparisons of his work with that of William Faulkner. Written in a dense, demanding, often poetic but controlled prose style, *Sent for You Yesterday* emphasizes the ways in which black Americans have employed storytelling, myth, and creativity to help them transcend the bonds of racism, deprivation, and despair.

The novel's narrator, **Doot Lawson**, is apparently the same character as the John Lawson who appears in Wideman's previous work, *Damballah*. He was first called Doot by Brother Tate, who named him for one of the sounds used in scat singing. Like Wideman himself, Doot is a college-educated, African American writer who was raised in Homewood but now lives in Wyoming. During his occasional vacations in Pittsburgh, he listens to his elders' stories about the past—myths that seem to have lent their tellers a great deal of psychic support over the years. Doot plays a role in his community that is similar to that of Albert Wilkes, the talented blues singer, for he serves as a recorder and a transmitter of his people's history, passions, and sorrows. Critics have identified Doot as a representative of the black intellectual's attempt to secure for himself a place in the nurturing community that he has left behind, a community to which Doot, at the end of *Sent for You Yesterday*, still seems marginal.

Perhaps the most compelling character in the novel is **Albert Wilkes**, a gifted blues pianist and singer who meets a bloody, tragic end. Rootless, daring, and outspoken, Albert not only indulged in an affair with a white woman but killed her policeman husband when the man came after him. After seven years on the run he returns to Homewood, where he is cherished for his music that is "so fine you said Thank Jesus a day early." Commentators have cited

Albert as providing a symbolic link between the novel's characters, plot, and setting. He serves as a source of inspiration for those around him, voicing their passion, suffering, and joy.

One of the patriarchs of the families that inhabit the Homewood Trilogy is **John French**, who plays a minor role in *Sent for You Yesterday* but is more prominent in the previous volumes. Lively, honest, and loyal, John counsels his old friend Albert Wilkes to hide out with Tate family after his return to Homewood. After World War II, John's son **Carl French**, (Doot's uncle) took courses financed by the GI Bill with the intention of becoming a commercial artist, but his ambitions were crushed when a teacher told him that no company would hire a black artist. Carl subsequently became a heroin addict but eventually kicked the habit. Long resigned to the loss of his dreams, Carl has also been in love with **Lucy Tate** since both were thirteen, but she has always refused to marry him. Although she claims that hearing stories about the past makes her weary, Lucy joins in their telling, for, as she tells Doot, "The old Homewood people taught me you don't have to give up."

Lucy's adopted sibling, **Brother Tate**, is one of the most tragic characters in *Sent for You Yesterday*. An albino, he stopped talking after his beloved son **Junebug** (also an albino) was killed in a fire; he now communicates only by making the sounds of scat singing and imitating various instruments. A talented musician and artist, Brother Tate harbors a deepseated despair that eventually leads him to take his own life by jumping in front of a train.

Further Reading

Bennion, John. "The Shape of Memory in John Edgar Wideman's *Sent for You Yesterday*." *Black American Literature Forum* 20, nos. 1–2 (Spring–Summer 1986): 143–50.

Contemporary Literary Criticism Vols. 5, 34, 36. Detroit: Gale Research.

Dictionary of Literary Biography Vol. 33. Detroit: Gale Research.

Kaveney, Roz. "Black Ups and Downs." *Times Literary Supplement* no. 4264 (December 21, 1984): 1484.

King, Francis. "Close Circles." *Spectator* Vol. 253, no. 8162–3 (December 22, 1984): 46.

Review of *Sent for You Yesterday*. *Kirkus Reviews* Vol. 53, No. 8 (April 15, 1985): 350.

August Wilson
1945–
American dramatist.

Ma Rainey's Black Bottom (drama, 1984)

Plot: The play takes place in March 1927, in a Chicago recording studio, where four African American musicians are awaiting the arrival of the celebrated blues singer, Gertrude "Ma" Rainey. Also present are Sturdyvant, the white owner of the studio, and Ma's white manager, Irvin. The musicians include pianist Toledo, a Black Nationalist; group leader and trombonist Cutler, whose frequent role is to defuse tensions among the members; bassist Slow Drag, who masks his problems with humor; and Levee, an energetic and ambitious trumpeter. The men exchange anecdotes about the past that illustrate the difficulties black musicians face as they make their way in racist white America. They speak fondly of Ma, referring to her as the "mother of the blues," and her queenly arrival seems to justify this title. Accompanied by her nephew and a young woman who may be her lover, Ma immediately asserts herself by demanding that someone buy her two bottles of Coca-Cola. Despite her imperiousness, Ma knows that her control does not extend past the limits of this recording session, for which she will be paid scandalously little. A conflict arises when Levee, who derides Ma's music as old-fashioned, wants to record the song "Black Bottom" in the "jazz dance" style he favors, which is gaining popularity over traditional blues. Ma finally fires Levee, whose frustrations are increased when he is unable to negotiate a fair price for the original songs he sells to Sturdyvant. In the play's final scene, Levee's simmering rage is ignited when Toledo accidentally steps on his new shoes, and he stabs the pianist to death.

Characters: Wilson emerged in the 1980s as a prominent new voice in the American Theater. Like his later plays, *Ma Rainey's Black Bottom* was developed at the Eugene O'Neill Theater Center's National Playwrights Conference, debuted at the Yale Repertory Theater, and went on to Broadway. Wilson received the New York Drama Critics Circle Award for *Ma Rainey*, which is praised for its vivid characters and authentic, lively dialogue. The play is the first in Wilson's planned cycle of dramas depicting the experiences of African Americans during each decade of the twentieth century. In highlighting the world of black musicians in the late 1920s, it also lends insight into the struggles of the larger African American population against racism and injustice.

The play's title character is based on an actual blues singer whom some regard as the "mother of the blues." Although the real **Ma Rainey** did record a "Black Bottom" record in Chicago during the same period featured in the play, the episode it depicts is imagined. Ma is a short, heavy woman with a queenly bearing and an imperious, high-handed manner. Her prima donna act could be viewed as either justified or, in view of her true status, foolish, for although she is proud, talented, and a shrewd businesswoman, Ma wields little real power over her own life and profession, and she knows it. She underlines the theme of American culture's exploitation of black people's gift of music when she states that the white record company "don't care nothing about me;" they record her precious voice and then "it's just like I'd be some whore and they roll over and put their pants on." Nevertheless, Ma's struggles, real as they are lack the tragedy that marks those of some of her fellow musicians, and her command of a great African American musical form also lends her genuine grandeur. "You don't sing [the blues] to feel better," she explains at one point in the play. "You sing because that's a way of understanding life."

Wilson employs the brash, ambitious trumpet player **Levee** as an example of how white racism may have the effect of turning blacks against themselves. In his early thirties, the stylish, energetic Levee is the youngest member of the band and the one most eager to modernize its sound. He prefers the new, improvisational jazz style over what he calls the "jugband music" favored by Ma, and he tries unsuccessfully to convince the producers to record his version of "Black Bottom." They refuse, and he is also unable to negotiate a fair deal for the songs he sells Sturdyvant; despite his servility in dealing with the studio owner, he receives only five dollars per song. Levee's long history of pain (he saw his mother gang-raped by white men and his father lynched for killing two of her attackers), anger, and frustration finally erupt in his violent act against Toledo, an ending that some reviewers have called contrived. Interestingly, Ma Rainey's real trumpet player for some of her sessions during the 1920s was Louis Armstrong.

Piano-player **Toledo**, the only band member who regularly reads, is a kind of self-taught philosopher who frequently delivers lectures on African American history and black people's need to work for change. Unlike other blacks of the period, Toledo embraces his African past, claiming that "we done sold ourselves to the white man in order to be like him." The band's leader, **Cutler**, who plays both guitar and trombone, is known for the phrase with which he sets his musicians in motion: "A-one, a-two, y'all know what to do."

Like his friends, Cutler has witnessed much injustice in his life, but he has a fatalistic attitude and simply tries to get by with as little trouble as possible. Sensible and cautious, he focuses on the task at hand and tries to defuse the tensions that arise within the group. Bass player **Slow Drag** has a wide smile, a graceful playing style, and a bored demeanor. He uses humor and the pursuit of pleasure to escape his painful memories.

The play's two white characters embody the racism that was an institutionalized part of American life in the early part of the twentieth century. Their attitudes demonstrate that the struggles of African Americans against oppression were far from over. **Sturdyvant**, the owner of the recording studio in which Ma Rainey and her musicians gather, expresses his contempt for blacks through his statement that he would like to get into a more respectable line of work. Concerned only with the profits he may derive from these people, he peers down at them from a glass-enclosed control room, a particularly apt metaphor for the relationship between whites and blacks in the America of the 1920s. Although he has adopted a more conciliatory manner toward blacks, Ma's tall, heavy manager **Irvin** also considers himself their superior and prides himself on his ability to manipulate them. Other characters in the play include Ma's young, sexy companion **Dussie Mae**, whose ability to cause jealous tension between Levee and Ma suggests that she is Ma's lover; and Ma's nephew **Sylvester**, whom she insists be allowed, despite his stutter, to do the spoken introduction to "Black Bottom," and who she demands receive his own twenty-five dollar fee for this task.

Fences (drama, 1985)

Plot: Set in a Northern industrial city (probably Pittsburgh) in the late 1950s (with the final scene taking place in 1965), *Fences* centers on the conflict between garbage collector Troy Maxson and his son Cory, a talented high school football player. Troy was himself a skilled athlete who learned to play baseball while imprisoned for petty crimes; after his release, however, he was prevented by racial prejudice from playing major league baseball. Now Cory has a chance to attend college on a football scholarship, but out of fear for and envy of his son, Troy refuses to sign the necessary authorization. Tension also arises between Troy and his wife, Rose Lee, when he informs her that he has been involved with a young woman who is about to give birth to his child. The woman dies in childbirth and Troy brings the baby home; Rose Lee agrees to raise the little girl, Raynell, but announces that she will no longer be a true wife to Troy. Troy's life is also complicated by his older son from a previous liaison, Lyons, an irresponsible, would-be musician who regularly asks him for money, and by his brain-damaged brother Gabriel, who believes he is the archangel Gabriel. The resentment between Troy and Cory finally erupts in a physical altercation that is halted by Rose and followed by Cory's departure from home. The final scene takes place in 1965, at Troy's funeral. Although the other family members remember Troy with fondness, Cory— who appears in his Marine uniform—retains ambivalent feelings. The play closes with Gabriel playing his trumpet to tell St. Peter to open the gates of heaven for Troy.

Characters: One of the most respected playwrights of the American theater, Wilson is lauded for his authentic yet often lyrical dialogue and his powerful treatment of the destructive consequences of racism. Winner of the Tony Award, the Pulitzer Prize, and the New York Drama Critics Circle Award, *Fences* is part of Wilson's planned cycle of plays depicting African American life in each decade of the twentieth century. Set in the 1950s (the period of Wilson's own childhood), the play focuses on the universal struggle of father against son and the ways in which people struggle both against real obstacles and those they have invented to protect themselves from harm.

Wilson has said that the character of **Troy Maxson** is based on his stepfather, David Bedford, who was denied a football scholarship because he was black, subsequently went to prison, and then became a Sewer Department worker. Fifty-three-year-old Troy is a big, powerful, ebullient man whose psyche combines both pride in his own hard work and bitterness over lost opportunities. Raised by a stern, overbearing father—whom he has come to resemble in his dealings with his own son—Troy went to jail for a petty crime. Upon his release, he came up square against the immovable wall of racism when he was prevented from playing baseball in the major leagues. He has since become a husband, a father, and a dutiful provider, but his resentment has been smoldering, and it erupts when Cory announces his desire to accept a football scholarship. Although Troy wants to protect Cory from the harm that may be in store for him, a significant element in his negative reaction is pure jealousy. Their physical confrontation drives a permanent wedge between them, for it crushes Troy's ego. Although Troy claims that he has been fenced in by his responsibilities, the truth is that he has himself built the barriers (like the half-built fence in his front yard) that keep his pain locked within and other people without. At the same time, Troy may be considered a positively portrayed African American male character in that he does honor his responsibilities to all three of his children. Critic Michael Feingold describes Troy as "a tragic case, at once hero, victim, and villain, unconsciously perpetuating a fatal cycle in ways that can be blamed partly on racism, partly on his family history, partly on himself." Forty-three-year-old **Rose Lee Maxson** is a quiet, unassertive woman who admires her husband and tolerates his quirks until she learns of his affair with another woman. At that point she says that although she planted herself in Troy's "hard and rocky soil," she never bloomed there, and that their marriage is now effectively over. Nevertheless, her capacity for love and warmth lead her to agree to raise Troy's child by Alberta, and her pragmatic strength aligns her with the archetype of the black woman who holds her family together against all odds. **Cory Maxson** is a talented young football player torn between his desire to please his father and his own ambitions. Cory has to battle Troy's fear, envy, and belief that he is always right, and in the end he apparently loses, for he does not accept the scholarship but instead joins the Marines.

Troy's younger brother **Gabriel** received a head injury while fighting in World War II and consequently believes that he is the archangel Gabriel. Troy has profited from the benefit checks he receives because Gabriel lives with him, but he does truly care for and protect his brother. **Lyons,** Troy's son by a previous liaison, is a dilettante of the jazz world who sports a goatee and appears at Troy's door nearly every Friday to ask for money. Troy feels guilty because he knows he was never a good father to Lyons, who has already served a prison term. Troy shares jokes and philosophical observations with **Jim Bono**, who has been his friend since they were in prison together and who is also a garbage collector. Troy tells Rose Lee that in his relationship with his mistress, **Alberta**, he has sought the passion that was missing in his marriage and that Alberta lets him "be a part of myself that I ain't never been." She dies giving birth to **Raynell**, who is subsequently raised by Rose Lee.

Joe Turner's Come and Gone (drama, 1988)

Plot: The play opens at a Pittsburgh boardinghouse on a Saturday in August, 1911. The proprietors are Seth Holly, a factory worker who makes pots and pans in his spare time, and his warmhearted wife Bertha. The residents include Bynum Walker, an amateur "conjure man" who dispenses advice and charms and claims to have the power to bring people together; Jeremy Furlow, a guitar player and ladies' man who works for a construction company; Mattie Campbell, who is looking for a good man; and cynical Molly Cunningham. The morning's first visitor to the boarding house is a white peddler named Rutherford Selig, who offers a people-finding service for those who have lost track of friends and loved ones. Bynum hires Selig to find the mysterious "Shiny Man" he once encountered in a vision and whose reappearance will signal the success of Bynum's life work. After Selig leaves, a mysterious, black-clad stranger arrives: Accompanied by his young daughter

Zonia, Herald Loomis explains that he is searching for his wife, and he rents a temporary room in the boarding house. In the play's second act the audience learns that ten years earlier, Loomis had been a sharecropper living on a Tennessee farm with his wife Martha and their baby. One day a man named Joe Turner abducted Loomis and forced him into slavery as a cotton picker. Released after seven years, Loomis returned home to find that his wife had departed, leaving Zonia with her grandmother. For the last three years, Loomis has been wandering from city to city, searching for Martha. He waits for Selig's arrival on the following Saturday and hires the peddler to find his wife. That Sunday night, the seething emotions evident beneath Loomis's brooding exterior erupt during the weekly "juba" (an African call-and-response dance) hosted by the Hollys. Loomis goes into a frenzy during the celebration, and consequently Seth wants him to leave the house. He agrees to let Loomis stay, however, until the following Saturday, when Selig returns with Martha. After she explains that she too has been searching for her husband and daughter, Loomis tells her that he wants only to leave Zonia with her and say goodbye. But he is still not free from the pain of the past, and Bynum advises him to locate his own "song" in order to achieve peace. Through a purging ritual involving slashing his chest with a knife, Loomis does seem to discover his identity. He leaves the boarding house, and Bynum identifies Loomis as the second Shiny Man for whom he had been waiting.

Characters: Cited by Wilson as his own favorite among the plays in his cycle chronicling African American experience during several decades of the twentieth century, *Joe Turner* debuted while *Fences* was still running on Broadway—an unprecedented accomplishment for a black American playwright. Lauded for its compelling characters and powerful, lyrical language, the play is more mystical than Wilson's previous works. Like them, however, it focuses on African Americans' need to reconcile the past and present and to connect with their African heritage. Inspired by a W.C. Handy song about an actual figure named Joe Turner (who used his status as the brother of the governor of Tennessee to accomplish a series of misdeeds), the play chronicles the African American struggle for identity and self-esteem in the years following the end of slavery.

The play's title evokes the anger and pain of one of its central characters, **Herald Loomis**, who was Joe Turner's victim and who has not yet reconciled himself to the losses he consequently incurred. Thirty-two-years-old when he arrives at the boarding house, Loomis is a large, disheveled man clothed in black; although he is taciturn, he burns with an intensity that shines through his wild, staring eyes. A decade earlier, Loomis had been a husband and father, a sharecropper, and a deacon in the Abundant Life Church. His existence was shattered when he was forced into labor by Joe Turner, and now he is seeking not only his lost wife but his own identity. In the words of critic Clive Barnes, Loomis is "a man searching for wholeness . . . digging for the roots of his existence . . . reaching into his past to move into his future." At the beginning of the play, Loomis is trapped by his resentment, but by its conclusion he has made some significant steps toward reclaiming his dignity and self-sufficiency. Loomis has been identified as one of several characters in Wilson's plays who defy the stereotype of the irresponsible African American male, for he cares for his daughter and works diligently to reunite her with her mother. Loomis's first name may be seen as significant, in that his attainment of increased self-esteem may herald what Wilson views as an essential quest for African Americans.

Short, round **Bynum Walker**, who is in his early sixties, has been identified as an African American manifestation of the traditional African "conjure man," for he uses the shamanistic skills he inherited from his father to dispense advice, charms, and other forms of consolation to those around him. In addition, he performs a special "binding song" to bring people together, to help them reestablish their ties. Imbued with an aura of wisdom, peace, and insight, Walker encourages his fellow African Americans to seek the strong sense of identity that he has already attained. When he meets Loomis, he senses that the troubled man's "song" of identity is buried deep beneath his painful memories. Walker helps to facilitate Loomis's reconciliation with his past by encouraging him to undergo the purging ritual that does seem to help Loomis. As the play draws to a close, Walker identifies Loomis as the second "Shiny Man" he has long sought, the "One Who Goes Before and Shows the Way."

The boarding house's proprietor, **Seth Holly**, works nights in a factory and days as a skilled craftsman; he hopes one day to establish his own business manufacturing pots and pans. The son of free Northern blacks, Holly is skeptical of Walker's powers and of abstract, mystical quests for redemption. Instead, he believes that African Americans must increase their economic power and achieve equality through the pursuit of the traditional American dream of success. The faith of Holly's sensible, kind wife **Bertha** is centered in the healing power of love and laughter.

The boarding house residents include twenty-six-year-old **Mattie Campbell**, whose husband deserted her after the tragic deaths of their two children and who searches for a man to fulfill her deep need for love and security. A naive romantic, she is first involved with **Jeremy Furlow** but pursues Loomis after the former leaves. Furlow is a confident, carefree native of North Carolina in his mid-twenties. Once a road builder, he lost his job after he refused to pay a white extortionist, and he now travels around trying to earn money from his guitar playing. An irresponsible ladies' man, he lives for sensual gratification. Furlow finally leaves with pragmatic, worldly **Molly Cunningham**, who is also a free spirit.

The play's only white character is **Rutherford Selig**, the son of a man who captured runaway slaves and turned them in for money, who peddles Holly's wares. Known as the People Finder, Selig keeps lists of his customers to help him locate missing people. Loomis's wife, **Martha Loomis Pentecost**, explains that after his capture she lost hope and, leaving her now eleven-year-old daughter **Zonia** with her parents, set out to make her own way. She joins an evangelical church and attempts unsuccessfully to lure Loomis back into religion.

Further Reading

Barnes, Clive. "Fiery *Fences*." *New York Theater Critics Review Vol. 48,* no. 5 (Week of March 30, 1987): 316–17.

———. "O'Neill in Blackface." *New York Post* (March 28, 1988).

Beaufort, John. "New Chapter in Wilson Saga of Black Life." *Christian Science Monitor* (March 30, 1988): 21.

Berman, Paul. Review of *Ma Rainey's Black Bottom. Nation* Vol. 239, no. 19 (December 8, 1984): 626-28.

Black Literature Criticism Vol. 3. Detroit: Gale Research.

Ching, Mei-Ling. "Wrestling Against History." *Theater* Vol. 19, no. 3 (Summer–Fall 1988): 70–1.

Contemporary Literary Criticism. Vols. 39, 50, 63. Detroit: Gale Research.

Feingold, Michael. "The Fall of Troy." *Village Voice* Vol. 32, no. 14 (April 17, 1987): 85.

Freedman, Samuel G. "A Voice from the Streets." *New York Times Magazine* (March 15, 1987): 36, 40, 49, 70.

Kauffmann, Stanley. "Bottoms Up." *Saturday Review* Vol. 11, no. 1 (January–February 1985): 83–90.

Kroll, Jack. "August Wilson's Come to Stay." *Newsweek* Vol. 111, No. 15 (April 11, 1988): 82.

Rich, Frank. "Family Ties in Wilson's *Fences*. *New York Times* (March 27, 1987): C3.

———. "Panoramic History of Blacks in America in Wilson's *Joe Turner*." *New York Times* (March 28, 1988): C15.

———. "Wilson's *Ma Rainey* Opens." *New York Times* (October 12, 1984): C1, C3.

Richards, David. "Look! Ma!: *Rainey* Brings Life to Tired Broadway." *Book World—The Washington Post*. (November 18, 1984): H1, H4.

Weales, Gerald. "Bringing the Light." *Commonweal* Vol. 114, no. 10 (May 22, 1987): 320–21.

Wilson, August. "How to Write a Play Like August Wilson." *New York Times* Section 2 (March 10, 1991): 5, 17.

Jeanette Winterson

1959–

English novelist and editor.

Written on the Body (novel, 1992)

Plot: Set in contemporary London and Yorkshire, England, the novel's unnamed narrator may be either a man or a woman. After a long series of unsuccessful love affairs, he or she falls in love with the beautiful, red-haired Louise, who is married to an oncologist. Louise leaves her husband, Elgin, and moves in with the narrator. The two spend five happy months together before Elgin informs the narrator that Louise is suffering from leukemia. Elgin promises that if the narrator will leave Louise he will get her into an exclusive cancer clinic for treatment that may prolong her life. The narrator decides to make this sacrifice and moves from London to Yorkshire, leaving no forwarding address. He or she takes a job in a trendy wine bar and is pursued by its proprietor, Gail Right. Miserable without Louise, the narrator rhapsodically describes his or her memories and feelings about her and their love for each other. Finally, persuaded by Gail that it was a mistake to leave Louise, the narrator hurries back to London to search for her. But Louise is nowhere to be found (she and Elgin are now apart and Elgin is involved with another woman), so the narrator returns to her Yorkshire cottage. Gail is waiting there, and while the two are talking Louise appears in the kitchen doorway. The novel concludes with the sentence: "I don't know if there is a happy ending here but we are set loose in open fields."

Characters: Acclaimed for her unconventional novels that focus on such concerns as the individual's struggle to achieve a coherent identity and the nature of romantic love and passion, Winterson is considered a fresh, innovative literary voice. Relayed in her characteristically poised, economic style, *Written on the Body* skillfully combines a classic story of love lost and gained again with intense, poetic meditations on love and passion. Some critics view the novel as a continuation of Winterson's autobiographical first work, *Oranges Are Not the Only Fruit*, which chronicles the development of a young woman whose lesbian sexuality and creative faculty lead her out of the world of her Christian missionary parents.

Many critics commented on the fact that Winterson never makes clear whether the novel's unnamed **narrator** is a man or a woman. A few maintained that several clues suggest the narrator is a woman; others contended that this intentional ambiguity heightens the novel's universality. One of the clues pointing to the former conclusion is the narrator's autobiographical quality: Like Winterson, he or she is a translator who specializes in Russian novels. Identified by one reviewer as a Byron-like figure owing to his or her provocative nature, predilection for risk-taking, and strong passions, the narrator has had a long series of love affairs, all of which seem to have ended disappointingly. After meeting Louise, the narrator realizes that these previous relationships were based on lust mistaken for love, and that with Louise he or she does not experience the fear of settling down that previous lovers provoked. The narrator's decision to leave Louise in order to save or prolong her life is indeed reminiscent of Byron, but it turns out to be the wrong decision. Emotionally devastated by the separation from Louise, the narrator composes a poetic meditation on her that is modeled after a medical textbook, with sections on, for example, "The Skin," "The Skeleton," and "The Special Senses." This format serves not only as an outlet for the narrator's emotions but as a way to prepare him or her, through memorization of every part and aspect of Louise, for her possible death. The narrator also begins to volunteer at a cancer ward in order to learn all about the disease and thus to make an indirect connection with Louise. Until the last page of the novel, it appears that the narrator will not be allowed to reverse his or her mistake, but Louise's appearance in the cottage doorway holds the promise of love renewed, even if it is to be short-lived.

The object of the narrator's passion is beautiful, red-haired **Louise Fox Rosenthal**, a native of Australia who, the reader eventually learns, has a Ph.D in art history. Described as maintaining a serene surface under which simmers a "dangerously electrical quality," this character is never endowed with much substance or individuality. Louise's husband, **Elgin Rosenthal**, is a dull, rich, Jewish oncologist who plays medical video games in his spare time. As a distinguished specialist, he can get Louise into a special Swiss cancer clinic where, he tells the narrator, she can receive the most advanced and promising treatment available. Some reviewers faulted Winterson for her uniformly negative portrayal of Elgin, whose blackmail scheme they deemed highly unlikely.

Most of the novel's other characters are the narrator's past or would-be lovers: **Inga,** whose highly romantic nature interfered with her revolutionary ideals; **Bathsheba,** a married dentist with whom the narrator was secretly (owing to her desire not to hurt her husband's feelings) involved for three years; and **Crazy Frank,** the six-foot-tall son of midgets who prefers a combination of sex and friendship to love. The narrator is still involved with nice, rather dull **Jacqueline**, who works as a kind of counselor for troubled zoo animals, when she meets Louise; Jacqueline reacts with unexpected aggression when the narrator leaves her. Fat, middle-aged **Gail Right**, the proprietor of the Yorkshire wine bar in which the narrator works, persistently pursues him or her but finally gives up when she sees that the narrator is still deeply in love with Louise. Gail convinces the narrator that it was a mistake to leave Louise and that he or she should try to find her.

Further Reading

Annan, Gabriele. "Devil in the Flesh." *New York Review of Books* (March 4, 1993): 22–3.

Contemporary Literary Criticism Vol. 64. Detroit: Gale Research.

Petro, Pamela. "A British Original." *Atlantic Monthly* (February 1993): 112–15.

Christa Wolf

1929–

German novelist, essayist, short story writer, and editor.

Cassandra: A Novel and Four Essays (*[Voraussetzungen einer Erzahlung: Kassandra]*; novel, 1983)

Plot: The central character in the novel (which takes place circa 1200 B.C. during the war between Greece and Troy) is the mythical figure of Cassandra, who was made a prophetess by Apollo but doomed by him (after she refused his advances) to be believed by no one. As Wolf's retelling of Cassandra's story begins, she is waiting outside the palace of Agamemnon, king of the Greeks. She knows that Agamemnon is at this moment being killed by his wife Clytemnestra and that she too will soon die at Clytemnestra's hand, and she spends her remaining time recalling her past. Born the favorite daughter of the Trojan king Priam and his queen, Hecuba, Cassandra was a carefree young girl. As she grew older, however, she grew increasingly aware of some unpleasant realities, such as the ways in which women are treated as objects in order to further men's aims and the pointless destructiveness of war. When Cassandra refuses to participate in a plan that involves using her sister Polyxena as bait to entrap the Greek warrior Achilles, Priam has her imprisoned in the palace dungeon. She manages to escape and spends the last two years of the war living in a harmonious community composed primarily of women, where she is visited by her enlightened lover Aeneas and his father Anchises. At the end of the novel, the Greeks conquer Troy and Aeneas prepares to escape with his band of followers. Cassandra refuses to accompany him because she knows that he will eventually have to assume the heroic role that always leads to brutality.

Characters: One of postwar's Germany's most respected and popular writers, Wolf has garnered international acclaim for her novels exploring the problems of individual identity and artistic integrity within repressive societies. *Cassandra* is a recasting of a Greek myth that draws parallels between the ancient and the modern worlds, suggesting the similarities between, on the one hand, the plight of Cassandra and that of modern woman, and on the other, the position of besieged Troy and that of contemporary nations (such as Germany at the time of Hitler's rise) whose blindnesses lead to self-destruction. In the lectures that accompanied the novel's publication, Wolf described her travels in Greece, her close rereading of Aeschylus' *Oresteia*, and the process by which she reinterpreted the story of Cassandra. Wolf rejects the violent heroics that form the base of the male-centered Western literary tradition, promoting instead a "feminine poetics" that elevates subjective consciousness over the rationalism that, Wolf feels, has resulted in so much harm to women and others.

The mythological **Cassandra** was a Trojan princess whom Apollo made his priestess but then punished for refusing his advances. Although Cassandra's dire prophecies were always correct, no one would believe them; thus her name has come to be associated with the unpopularity of doomsayers. Wolf's Cassandra is not so much gifted in prophecy as intelligent and clearsighted enough to see what others either cannot or will not see. By "leading [Cassandra] back out of myth into the (imagined) social and historical coordinates," Wolf explores such themes as the suppression of women's talents, the difficult necessity of resisting conformity, and the importance of developing a separate, subjective voice with which to speak the truth and oppose brutality. Because the novel chronicles Cassandra's development from a merry, lighthearted young girl into a disillusioned outcast who overcomes her reluctance to defy her beloved father and other family members, some critics have called it a kind of *bildungsroman* (novel of initiation into adulthood). The reader witnesses Cassandra's growth as she continues to seek self-knowledge and learn from her experiences. Her journey from early naivete to disillusionment and horror may reflect Wolf's own development, for during World War II she was a member of Hitler's youth organization, and she has since often addressed the question of how so many ordinary Germans were won over by the Nazis. Wolf departs from traditional characterizations of Cassandra—which tend to emphasize the apparent madness manifested in her prophecies— to portray her as an independent thinker and a vibrant, socially committed person who chooses to become a prophetess because she sees it as the only way she can wield power in her society. The refusal of those around her to listen to her is attributed more to her unworthiness as a woman and than to Apollo's curse, which is depicted only in an ambiguous dream.

Several commentators have noted that Wolf's portrayal of the female-centered community in which Cassandra finds refuge and peace is in keeping with the utopian theme that runs through all her work. This harmonious, future-minded community provides an alternative to the war-mongering lifestyle of Troy, just as Wolf proposes "feminine poetics" as an alternative to the male model she sees as contributing to the world's brutalization and self-destruction. Expressing various degrees of either approval or disdain, critics have identified Cassandra as an anachronistic heroine who exhibits the same scorn and awareness as a member of contemporary Germany's liberal "Green" movement, and Wolf's attempt to recast her as a feminist heroine has been seen as both heavy-handed and admirable.

Just as Wolf's Cassandra differs significantly from traditional portrayals, her characterizations of other mythological/historical figures depart from convention. For example, the Greek warrior **Achilles** is consistently referred to as "Achilles the animal"; he is violent, lustful, and even harbors homosexual tendencies that he disguises through his brutality toward women. Achilles seems to embody for Wolf the male barbarity and inhumanity that she considers the most dangerous aspects of mythical heroism. Similarly, the Greek king **Agamemnon** makes up for his sexual impotence with belligerence and cruelty in battle, and Cassandra applauds **Clytemnestra** for killing him (particularly since Agaememnon sacrificed their daughter **Iphigenia** in order to ensure favorable winds for the journey to Troy).

Perhaps the most painful part of the growth process Cassandra undergoes is her estrangement from her beloved father **Priam**, whose power, she recognizes, has been diminished by the corrupt military junta that now rules Troy. Cassandra's mother **Hecuba** has also lost the access to decision-making she once held. Other members of Cassandra's family include her brothers **Helenus** (who, to her dismay, is made a priest before her simply because he is male), **Troilus, Hector** (killed by the Greeks), and **Paris**. Greek myth holds that it was Paris's kidnapping of **Helen**, the beautiful wife of the Greek ruler Menelaus, that initiated the Trojan War, but in the novel this act by a childish, prestige-seeking Paris is unsuccessful, for Helen is snatched away from him by the king of Egypt before he returns to Troy. Thus the cause of the war is cast here as a cruel joke based, significantly, on the objectification of a woman. Also contributing to the novel's feminist theme is Cassandra's sister **Polyxena**, who allows her family to use her as bait in their plan to trap Achilles. Cassandra recognizes her sister's sense of worthlessness and low self-esteem as rooted in her loveless childhood and particularly in their father's preference for Cassandra.

The novel's only positively portrayed male characters are Cassandra's friend and lover **Aeneas** and his father **Anchises**. Cassandra's love for Aeneas begins when he spares her the deflowering that is the cruel fate of every Trojan virgin, while informing her mother that he has performed the deed. Clearly respectful of women's autonomy, Aeneas is later present in the community of women with whom Cassandra finds refuge. Despite her lover's goodness, Cassandra refuses to accompany him when he leads the survivors of Troy's downfall away, for she knows that Aeneas—who is fated to found the city of Rome—will eventually have to assume the heroic mantle that she detests and fears. One of very few Trojans to resist the prevailing corruption, the benevolent, humane Anchises serves as a kind of spiritual father to the female community.

Further Reading

Contemporary Literary Criticism Vols. 14, 29, 58. Detroit: Gale Research.

Crick, Joyce. "The Darkness of Troy." *Times Literary Supplement* no. 4311 (November 15, 1985): 1298.

Lefkowitz, Mary. "Can't Fool Her." *New York Times Book Review* (September 9, 1984): 20.

Lehmann-Haupt, Christopher. Review of *Cassandra: A Novel and Four Essays. New York Times* (July 31, 1984): C17.

Lieskounig, Jurgen. "Christa Wolf's *Kassandra*: Myth or Anti-Myth?" *Theoria* Vol. 70. (October 1987): 67–75.

Naumann, Michael. "A Prophetess and the Pershings." *New Republic* Vol. 191, no. 5 (July 30, 1984): 40–3.

Pawel, Ernst. "Prophecies and Heresies." *Nation* Vol. 239, no. 8 (September 22, 1984): 246–47.

Pickle, Linda Schelbitzki. "Scratching Away the Male Tradition: Christa Wolf's *Kassandra*." *Contemporary Literature* Vol. 27, no. 1 (Spring 1986): 32–47.

Waldstein, Edith. "Prophecy in Search of a Voice: Silence in Christa Wolf's *Kassandra*." *Germanic Review* Vol. 62, no. 4 (Fall 1987): 194–98.

Tom Wolfe

1931–

American novelist, essayist, journalist, critic, and short story writer.

The Bonfire of the Vanities (novel, 1987)

Plot: The novel takes place in contemporary New York City. Its central figure is Sherman McCoy, a successful, wealthy, thirty-eight-year-old bond salesman who claims he is "going broke on a million dollars a year." He and his wife, Judy, and six-year-old daughter, Campbell, live in a sumptuous fourteen-room apartment on Park Avenue. Sherman is having an affair with Maria Ruskin, the rich and beautiful wife of a much older man. While driving Maria home from Kennedy Airport one night, Sherman misses the Manhattan exit and ends up in the South Bronx. Lost, the couple encounters two black youths they think intend to rob them; with Maria at the wheel of Sherman's Mercedes, they flee the scene, but they think they may have hit one of the young men. Fearful that their spouses will discover their affair, Sherman and Maria decide not to report the incident to the police. However, the respectable teenager they seriously injured produced part of Sherman's license plate number before slipping into a coma. The police identify Sherman and arrest, book, and indict him for reckless endangerment and leaving the scene of the accident, during which he spends a short but hair-raising period in jail. Maria's involvement remains unknown. Meanwhile, an aggressive black preacher-activist, who sees the case as an opportunity to expose the racism of the criminal justice system, and a district attorney anxious to win the support of his minority constituents, turn the situation into a media circus. Sherman is reviled in the press and loses the support of his friends, neighbors, and wife as well as his mistress, and he ultimately implicates her in the crime. Although the case gets thrown out of court, Sherman is fired from his job and is unable to pay his massive debts. The novel's epilogue, written as a *New York Times* story dated exactly one year after the main action, relates that the injured boy has died and that Sherman has been indicted for manslaughter.

Characters: Credited with developing the "New Journalism," which combines straight reporting with such novelistic techniques as stream-of-consciousness narration, extensive use of dialogue, and character description, Tom Wolfe is one of America's most acclaimed and original writers. Wolfe modeled his first novel, *The Bonfire of the Vanities,* after the sprawling social novels of nineteenth-century authors William Makepeace Thackeray, Charles Dickens, and Honoré de Balzac, whose works incorporated large casts of characters, meticulous physical detail, profound social themes, and panoramic portraits of the societies on which they centered. Serialized in *Rolling Stone* several years before its publication and subsequently rewritten and expanded, *Bonfire* is a densely detailed portrait of contemporary New York, from the elegant dinner parties of Manhattan to the Bronx courtrooms to the streets of Harlem. It is characterized by Wolfe's virtuoso writing style and features plentiful exclamation points, litanies, and compound adjectives. Wolfe satirizes everyone in the book, especially the self-indulgent wealthy characters and their pretensions, obsession with money, and cowardice. Although a number of critics found Wolfe's characterizations superficial, most praised the novel as a highly engaging, refreshing alternative to the more pared-down prose that dominates contemporary American literature.

Thirty-eight-year-old **Sherman McCoy** is a self-proclaimed "Master of the Universe," a beneficiary of the extravagant financial speculation of the 1980s who earns a million dollars a year as a Wall Street bond salesman. The Yale-educated son of a distinguished lawyer, Sherman lives in a sumptuous fourteen-room Park Avenue apartment (which, despite his high salary, he had to go into debt to obtain). His moral weakness is apparent from the novel's opening pages, when he callously lies to his wife, Judy. Although he claims to love Judy and certainly adores his young daughter, he feels he deserves the luxury of sex with a younger woman; thus he is having an affair with the glamorous Maria Ruskin. The reader also realizes that Sherman is arrogant about his aristocratic breeding, which seems to be symbolized by his prominent chin. While his father followed a strict moral code and was known as an honorable man, Sherman holds to the practice of what Wolfe (in an essay published in the 1970s) called "the Me Generation": he equates money with moral standing; he requires instant gratification; and he leads a shallow, aimless life limited to the pursuit of wealth and social status. Sherman's car accident and the resulting media circus constitute what his tough Irish lawyer calls "an icy dip in the real world." Sherman becomes the "Great White Defendant" who, because he represents a welcome departure from the usual consumer of criminal justice, will be punished not just for his alleged crime but for being white and privileged. During the process, Sherman is stripped of everything that previously defined him—his money, his social standing, his breeding—and abandoned by his employers, friends, neighbors, mistress, and wife. The resulting personality disintegration has been likened to that experienced by many of the characters in the fiction of Edgar Allan Poe. By the end of the novel, however, Sherman begins to fight back: he tells off the people who avoided or exploited him, betrays Maria (who abandoned him to take the rap alone) by taping her incriminating comments about the accident, and even jumps into a brawl in the courtroom when his case is dismissed. The novel's epilogue reports Sherman appearing at his arraignment more modestly dressed than in the days when he wore $2,000 suits, and notably defiant.

Critics consider Sherman a symbol of America's WASP elite, who ceased to believe in their right to power, lost their noblesse oblige, and turned instead to self-gratification. Some commentators question the ending of *Bonfire,* which seems to promote redemption through violence and confirms the paranoia of wealthy, white New Yorkers. Other commentators, however, believe that Wolfe intends neither to sanction nor condemn Sherman but to create an authentic, entertaining portrait of modern life.

Several critics contend that the novel's female characters are disappointingly sketchy, serving not as interesting figures themselves but as foils to the men in the book. Sherman describes his forty-year-old wife, **Judy,** as "starved and Sports Trained to near perfection." The daughter of a midwestern history professor, she lacks her husband's breeding but shares his social ambitions. Like the other rich women of her set, she spends most of her time frantically aerobicizing to stay thin and decorating her swank apartment. The couple has a lovely and adored six-year-old daughter, **Campbell.** Sherman finds it difficult to explain to Campbell exactly what he does for a living, so Judy tells her that her father and his associates deal in a kind of golden cake, the crumbs of which Sherman gathers up. Sherman's mistress, **Maria Ruskin,** is a beautiful, sexy young woman who speaks in a southern drawl; in a review in *America,* Peter A. Quinn noted that she "sounds and acts like an updated Scarlett O'Hara." Some commentators find Maria's accent rather strained and Wolfe's repetitive transliterations of what she says annoying. Unlike Sherman's, Maria's social status is acquired by marrying a wealthy older man. In the end, she reveals her true nature when she betrays her lover by keeping her involvement in the accident a secret and—after Arthur Ruskin dies—by running away with and marrying an Italian artist, **Filippo Chirazzi.**

One of the most notable secondary characters in the novel is Sherman's tough, fast-talking attorney, **Tommy Killian,** whose standard, oft repeated greeting is "Whaddaya whaddaya?" For a $75,000 fee, Killian agrees to defend Sherman and deflect the carnivorous press and politicians who are anxious to vilify him. Aided by another streetwise Irishman, private investigator and former policeman **Ed Quigley,** Killian guides Sherman through the hellish world of criminal justice. Killian embodies an "Irish machismo" to which Wolfe lends a favorable cast; he advises Sherman to emulate the Irish, who "have been living for the last twelve hundred years on dreams of revenge." Although he graduated from Yale University's law school, Killian maintains his ethnic identity and ties with New York City's solid working class. Several commentators contend that Wolfe portrays New York's Irish cops and lawyers as a kind of barrier—and the only one left—between order and chaos.

Leading the crusade against Sherman and, by extension, against the white-run criminal justice system is **the Reverend Bacon,** a black preacher and activist who expertly inflames the anger and resentment of his followers, resembling an actual person known for similar activities, the Reverend Al Sharpton. The dishonest, anti-Semitic, and politically powerful Bacon uses Sherman's case to dramatize how the system neglects crimes against blacks. Two notable white men are also ranged against Sherman: **Abe Weiss** (nicknamed "**Captain Ahab**"), the incumbent district attorney for the Bronx desperately wanting to be reelected, who sees Sherman as an opportunity to win minority votes; and **Larry Kramer,** the ambitious assistant district attorney and liberal middle-class Jew. Kramer is bored with his dumpy wife and new baby and lusts after **Shelly Thomas,** a girl in "brown lipstick" who served as a juror in one of his cases; he hopes to impress her with his prosecutorial fervor against Sherman. Cynical, jaded **Judge Myron Kovitsky,** is a small but powerful character; he finally dismisses Sherman's case after hearing the tape that exposes Maria's role in the accident.

The reporter who initially breaks the story of the injured black boy is **Peter Fallow,** an alcoholic Englishman who works for a tabloid newspaper called *City Lights,* modeled after such sensationalist dailies as the *New York Post.* The seedy, deadbeat, vainglorious Fallow hopes his work on the story will save his precarious job; indeed, the novel's epilogue reveals that he ultimately wins a Pulitzer Prize and marries an English heiress. Gruff, seventy-one-year-old **Arthur Ruskin**, Maria's Jewish husband, dies of a heart attack while eating dinner with Fallow at a trendy restaurant. Before collapsing, Ruskin confides to Fallow that he became wealthy by selling Arabs charter flights to Mecca.

Other characters in *Bonfire* include **Henry Lamb**, the black boy seriously injured when he attempted to help Sherman and Maria. His basic respectability is inflated by the press, which describes him as "the pride of the Edgar Allan Poe Housing Projects." Also featured is Sherman's friend **Rawlie Thorpe**, who tells him that in order to live in New York "you've got to insulate, insulate, insulate," thus highlighting the division between the city's wealthy and poor.

Further Reading

Baumann, Paul. "An Icy Dip in the Real World." *Commonweal* Vol. 115 (February 26, 1988): 120–2.

Bestsellers, Vol. 89, Issue 1. Detroit: Gale Research, 1989.

Black, George. "The Far-Right Stuff." *New Statesman* (February 12, 1988): 31.

Carpenter, Luther. "The Ruling Class." *Dissent* Vol. 35 (summer 1988): 377–9.

Conroy, Frank. "Urban Rats in Fashion's Maze." *New York Times Book Review* (November 1, 1987): 1, 46.

Contemporary Literary Criticism, Vols. 1, 2, 9, 15, 35, 51. Detroit: Gale Research.

Edward, Thomas R. "Low Expectations." *New York Review of Books* vol. 35, no. 1 (February 4, 1988): 8–9.

Lehmann-Haupt, Christopher. Review of *The Bonfire of the Vanities*. *New York Times* (October 22, 1987): C25.

Lemann, Nicholas. "New York in the Eighties." *Atlantic Monthly* Vol. 260, no. 6 (December 1987): 104, 106–7.

Mallon, Thomas. Review of *The Bonfire of the Vanities*. *American Spectator* (January 1988).

Rafferty, Terrence. "The Man Who Knew Too Much." *New Yorker* Vol. 43, no. 50 (February 1, 1988): 88–92.

Salamon, Julie. *The Devil's Candy: The Bonfire of the Vanities Goes to the Hollywood*. Boston: Houghton Mifflin, 1991.

Shomette, Doug, ed. *The Critical Response to Tom Wolfe*. New York: Greenwood Press, 1992.

Yardley, Jonathan. "Tom Wolfe's New York Confidential." *Washington Post Book World* (October 25, 1987): 3.

Marguerite Young

1909–

American novelist, poet, and nonfiction writer.

Miss MacIntosh, My Darling (novel, 1965)

Plot: Written in meandering, stream-of-consciousness prose, the novel loosely recounts the quest of its sometime narrator, Vera Cartwright, to find her childhood nursemaid, Miss MacIntosh, who supposedly drowned when Vera was fourteen. Vera takes a bus ride that, about 900 pages into the novel, ends in a small Indiana town. She recounts experiences from a childhood, spent in a mansion on the Atlantic coast with her opium-addicted mother, Catherine, who inhabited a world of dreams. Catherine was visited only by Mr. Spitzer, a lawyer and would-be composer who confused his own identity with that of his dead brother, Peron. The young Vera considered Miss MacIntosh—who frequently dispensed words of wisdom apparently taken from *Poor Richard's Almanac*—an oasis of common sense in an otherwise disordered world. One day, however, Vera surprised Miss MacIntosh in her room and learned, to her dismay, that the nursemaid was completely bald, her flaming red hair revealed as a wig. A month later, Miss MacIntosh was abandoned by the evangelist who had promised to marry her when he discovered that she was not only bald but had only one breast. Left without her protective illusions, Miss MacIntosh drowned herself, leaving Vera perpetually in search of her or of what she represents. In the novel's last few pages, Vera meets and becomes pregnant by the Stone-Deaf Man, whom she plans to marry.

Characters: Some critics consider this epic-length novel (1198 pages), which took Young eighteen years to write, a little-known classic of American literature. Young's improvisational, repetitive style is controversial; some readers find it infuriatingly obfuscated and unreadable, while others praise its lyricism and descriptiveness. Nearly plotless, *Miss MacIntosh, My Darling* is a complex, hypnotic exploration of dream and illusion. All of its characters harbor obsessions that they pursue relentlessly if misguidedly, in keeping with Young's description of her central theme as "the human desire or obsession for utopia." Among this work's admirers is novelist Anne Tyler, whose character Macon Leary in *The Accidental Tourist* finds it an "invariably interesting" book to read while traveling on airplanes.

Most of *Miss MacIntosh, My Darling* is narrated by **Vera Cartwright**, who is perpetually haunted by her memories of her childhood nursemaid and sets off on a kind of quest to "find" her. Although she never actually locates the long-dead Miss MacIntosh, Vera's meandering thoughts probe the interplay of reality versus illusion; she concludes that "Whatever one found was real was real . . . and even the unreal things were real, even those who were ignored, rejected, despised, abandoned, unloved." This description certainly encompasses Miss MacIntosh, who hid her baldness with a red wig and tried to maintain the supremacy of common sense but finally succumbed to the loss of these illusions. Vera credits Miss MacIntosh with teaching her about the "sorrows of the human heart . . . enlarged beyond nature" and the essential loneliness of each person, which can be alleviated through the realization that "every heart is the other heart." This realization seems to prepare Vera to align herself with the bizarre, flawed, Stone Deaf Man, with whose child she is contentedly pregnant at the end of the novel.

In an interview, Young described **Miss MacIntosh** as the novel's central character, from which its other characters radiate out like the spokes of a wheel. Vera remembers her as an oasis of reason in her otherwise bewildering childhood home, "fusty, busty . . . the salt of common sense, her red hair gleaming to show that quick temper she always had," dispensing advice gleaned from *Poor Richard's Almanac*. But Miss MacIntosh was transformed into a "monstrous stranger" when Vera saw her without her wig, which the nursemaid had used to disguise her baldness—a flaw that several critics have identified as a symbol of reality. Miss MacIntosh's suicide may be attributed to her defenselessness when her illusions (including not only physical wholeness but also the prospect of love and marriage with Mr. Bonebreaker) are shattered. According to critic Marianne Hauser, Miss MacIntosh represents "the phantom of love, pursued by all of us and never captured." Through her memories of and grief over Miss MacIntosh, Vera recognizes her alliance with the suffering, yearning, dreams, and lost dreams of others.

Young very likely modeled Vera's mother after the wealthy, opium-addicted woman who employed her while she was a graduate student at the University of Chicago. Described by her daughter as "more beautiful than the angels of light," **Catherine Cartwright** lives a secluded existence in her East Coast mansion, entertaining imaginary visitors and pretending "that the real was the dream, that the dream was the real." Because she saw herself as "everybody and everything," Vera explains, her mother could not distinguish "what was her personal identity among so many trans-shifting objects and flickering shadows." Catherine's loyal friend and lawyer **Mr. Joaquin Spitzer,** who harbors a secret, unrequited love for her, is also a befuddled character. He confuses his own identity with that of his dead twin brother, **Peron Spitzer,** a gambler with whom Catherine was in love. Named executor to the estate of the famous suffragette Cousin Hannah, the methodical Mr. Spitzer expects to "establish her identity" but is confounded by his discovery of her forty wedding dresses.

Marianne Hauser called **Cousin Hannah,** a Boston suffragist, lesbian, famous explorer, and intrepid mountain climber, "one of the most fiercely individual women in literature." Despite her accomplishments and independence, however, Cousin Hannah was a secret collector of wedding gowns, suggesting that she was no more immune from illusion than anyone else. Explaining that she created Cousin Hannah after hearing the story of an unmarried suffragist who was discovered to have kept fifty wedding dresses in trunks that were opened after her death, Young called her "the alter ego of the opium lady if she'd been set loose in the world." Another compelling character in the novel is **Esther Longtree,** a waitress in a cafe in the small Indiana town in which Vera finally arrives. Esther's tragicomic fate is to suffer from perpetual false pregnancies that are connected, she claims (perhaps falsely), with her having murdered her own baby.

Other characters in the novel include the elderly, dreaming **Dr. Justice O'Leary,** who delivers imaginary babies; loud, aggressive **Mr. Titus Bonebreaker,** the sidewalk preacher and Bible salesman who promises to marry Miss MacIntosh (despite what he calls her abundant sinfulness) but flees when he discovers her physical flaws; and the bizarrely talkative **Stone Deaf Man,** whom Vera vows to marry not in spite of but because of his flawed nature, which she recognizes as the common link between all human beings.

Further Reading

Bergonzi, Bernard. "Queen for a Day." *New York Review of Books* Vol. 5, no. 8 (November 25, 1965): 34–5.

Contemporary Literary Criticism Vol. 82. Detroit: Gale Research.

Feeley, Gregory. "Concerning the Divine Miss M." *Washington Post—Book World* Vol. 24, no. 33 (August 14, 1994): 4.

Friedman, Ellen G., and Fuchs, Miriam. Interview with Marguerite Young. *Review of Contemporary Fiction* Vol. 9, no. 3 (Fall 1989): 147–54.

Fuchs, Miriam. "Marguerite Young's Utopias: 'The Most Beautiful Music They Never Heard.'" *Review of Contemporary Fiction* Vol. 9, no. 3 (Fall 1989): 166-76.

Goyen, William. "A Fable of Illusion and Reality." *New York Times Book Review* (September 12, 1965): 5.

Hauser, Marianne. "The Crucial Flower." *Sewanee Review* Vol. 75, no. 4 (Autumn 1967): 731–34.

Hicks, Granville. "Adrift on a Sea of Dreams." *Saturday Review* Vol. 48,, no. 37 (September 11, 1965): 35–6.

Shaviro, Steven. "Lost Chords and Interrupted Births: Marguerite Young's Exorbitant Vision." *Critique* Vol. 31, no. 3 (Spring 1990): 213–22.

Strehle, Susan. "Telling Women's Time: *Miss MacIntosh, My Darling*." *Review of Contemporary Fiction* Vol. 9, no. 3 (Fall 1989): 177–82.

Character and Title Index

497